POETRY

for Students

Advisors

Susan Allison: Head Librarian, Lewiston High School, Lewiston, Maine. Standards Committee Chairperson for Maine School Library (MASL) Programs. Board member, Julia Adams Morse Memorial Library, Greene, Maine. Advisor to Lewiston Public Library Planning Process.

Jennifer Hood: Young Adult/Reference Librarian, Cumberland Public Library, Cumberland, Rhode Island. Certified teacher, Rhode Island. Member of the New England Library Association, Rhode Island Library Association, and the Rhode Island Educational Media Association.

Ann Kearney: Head Librarian and Media Specialist, Christopher Columbus High School, Miami, Florida, 1982–2002. Thirty-two years as Librarian in various educational institutions ranging from grade schools through graduate programs. Library positions at Miami-Dade Community College, the University of Miami's Medical School Library, and Carrollton School in Coconut Grove, Florida. B.A. from University of Detroit, 1967 (magna cum laude); M.L.S., University of Missouri–Columbia, 1974. Volunteer Project Leader for a school in rural Jamaica; volunteer with Adult Literacy programs.

Laurie St. Laurent: Head of Adult and Children's Services, East Lansing Public Library, East Lansing, Michigan, 1994–. M.L.S. from Western Michigan University. Chair of Michigan Library Association's 1998 Michigan Summer Reading Program; Chair of the Children's Services Division in 2000–2001; and Vice-President of the Association in 2002–2003. Board member of several regional early childhood literacy organizations and member of the Library of Michigan Youth Services Advisory Committee.

Heidi Stohs: Instructor in Language Arts, grades 10–12, Solomon High School, Solomon, Kansas. Received B.S. from Kansas State University; M.A. from Fort Hays State University.

POETRY
for Students

Presenting Analysis, Context, and Criticism on
Commonly Studied Poetry

VOLUME 27

THOMSON

GALE

Detroit • New York • San Francisco • New Haven, Conn. • Waterville, Maine • London

GALE

Poetry for Students, Volume 27

Project Editor
Ira Mark Milne

Editorial
Jennifer Greve

Rights Acquisition and Management
Beth Beaufore, Aja Perales, Kelly Quin, Robyn Young

Manufacturing
Drew Kalasky

Imaging and Multimedia
Lezlie Light

Product Design
Pamela A. E. Galbreath, Jennifer Wahi

Vendor Administration
Civie Green

Product Manager
Meggin Condino

ISBN-13: 978-0-7876-8717-5
ISBN-10: 0-7876-8717-0
eISBN-13: 978-1-4144-2935-9
eISBN-10: 1-4144-2935-5
ISSN 1094-7019

Printed in the United States of America

10 9 8 7 6 5 4 3 2 1

Table of Contents

Just a Few Lines on a Page

I have often thought that poets have the easiest job in the world. A poem, after all, is just a few lines on a page, usually not even extending margin to margin—how long would that take to write, about five minutes? Maybe ten at the most, if you wanted it to rhyme or have a repeating meter. Why, I could start in the morning and produce a book of poetry by dinnertime. But we all know that it isn't that easy. Anyone can come up with enough words, but the poet's job is about writing the *right* ones. The right words will change lives, making people see the world somewhat differently than they saw it just a few minutes earlier. The right words can make a reader who relies on the dictionary for meanings take a greater responsibility for his or her own personal understanding. A poem that is put on the page correctly can bear any amount of analysis, probing, defining, explaining, and interrogating, and something about it will still feel new the next time you read it.

It would be fine with me if I could talk about poetry without using the word "magical," because that word is overused these days to imply "a really good time," often with a certain sweetness about it, and a lot of poetry is neither of these. But if you stop and think about magic—whether it brings to mind sorcery, witchcraft, or bunnies pulled from top hats—it always seems to involve stretching reality to produce a result greater than the sum of its parts and pulling unexpected results out of thin air. This book provides ample cases where a few simple words conjure up whole worlds. We do not actually travel to different times and different cultures, but the poems get into our minds, they find what little we know about the places they are talking about, and then they make that little bit blossom into a bouquet of someone else's life. Poets make us think we are following simple, specific events, but then they leave ideas in our heads that cannot be found on the printed page. Abracadabra.

Sometimes when you finish a poem it doesn't feel as if it has left any supernatural effect on you, like it did not have any more to say beyond the actual words that it used. This happens to everybody, but most often to inexperienced readers: regardless of what is often said about young people's infinite capacity to be amazed, you have to understand what usually does happen, and what could have happened instead, if you are going to be moved by what someone has accomplished. In those cases in which you finish a poem with a "So what?" attitude, the information provided in *Poetry for Students* comes in handy. Readers can feel assured that the poems included here actually are potent magic, not just because a few (or a hundred or ten thousand) professors of literature say they are: they're significant because they can withstand close inspection and still amaze the very same people who have just finished taking them apart and seeing how they work. Turn them inside out, and they will still be able to come alive, again and again. *Poetry for Students* gives readers of any age good practice in feeling the ways poems relate to both the reality of the time and place the poet lived in and the reality of our emotions. Practice is just another word for being a student. The information given here helps you understand the way to read poetry; what to look for, what to expect.

With all of this in mind, I really don't think I would actually like to have a poet's job at all. There are too many skills involved, including precision, honesty, taste, courage, linguistics, passion, compassion, and the ability to keep all sorts of people entertained at once. And that is just what they do with one hand, while the other hand pulls some sort of trick that most of us will never fully understand. I can't even pack all that I need for a weekend into one suitcase, so what would be my chances of stuffing so much life into a few lines? With all that *Poetry for Students* tells us about each poem, I am impressed that any poet can finish three or four poems a year. Read the inside stories of these poems, and you won't be able to approach any poem in the same way you did before.

David J. Kelly
College of Lake County

Introduction

Purpose of the Book

The purpose of *Poetry for Students* (*PfS*) is to provide readers with a guide to understanding, enjoying, and studying poems by giving them easy access to information about the work. Part of Gale's "For Students" Literature line, *PfS* is specifically designed to meet the curricular needs of high school and undergraduate college students and their teachers, as well as the interests of general readers and researchers considering specific poems. While each volume contains entries on "classic" poems frequently studied in classrooms, there are also entries containing hard-to-find information on contemporary poems, including works by multicultural, international, and women poets.

The information covered in each entry includes an introduction to the poem and the poem's author; the actual poem text (if possible); a poem summary, to help readers unravel and understand the meaning of the poem; analysis of important themes in the poem; and an explanation of important literary techniques and movements as they are demonstrated in the poem.

In addition to this material, which helps the readers analyze the poem itself, students are also provided with important information on the literary and historical background informing each work. This includes a historical context essay, a box comparing the time or place the poem was written to modern Western culture, a critical overview essay, and excerpts from critical essays on the poem. A unique feature of *PfS* is a specially commissioned critical essay on each poem, targeted toward the student reader.

To further aid the student in studying and enjoying each poem, information on media adaptations is provided (if available), as well as reading suggestions for works of fiction and nonfiction on similar themes and topics. Classroom aids include ideas for research papers and lists of critical sources that provide additional material on the poem.

Selection Criteria

The titles for each volume of *PfS* were selected by surveying numerous sources on teaching literature and analyzing course curricula for various school districts. Some of the sources surveyed included: literature anthologies; *Reading Lists for College-Bound Students: The Books Most Recommended by America's Top Colleges*; textbooks on teaching the poem; a College Board survey of poems commonly studied in high schools; and a National Council of Teachers of English (NCTE) survey of poems commonly studied in high schools.

Input was also solicited from our advisory board, as well as educators from various areas. From these discussions, it was determined that each volume should have a mix of "classic" poems (those works commonly taught in literature classes) and contemporary poems for which information is often hard to find. Because of the interest in expanding the canon of literature, an emphasis was also placed on including works by international, multicultural, and women poets. Our advisory board members—educational professionals—helped pare down the list for each volume. If a work was not selected for the present volume, it was often noted as a possibility for a future volume. As always, the editor welcomes suggestions for titles to be included in future volumes.

How Each Entry Is Organized

Each entry, or chapter, in *PfS* focuses on one poem. Each entry heading lists the full name of the poem, the author's name, and the date of the poem's publication. The following elements are contained in each entry:

Introduction: a brief overview of the poem which provides information about its first appearance, its literary standing, any controversies surrounding the work, and major conflicts or themes within the work.

Author Biography: this section includes basic facts about the poet's life, and focuses on events and times in the author's life that inspired the poem in question.

Poem Text: when permission has been granted, the poem is reprinted, allowing for quick reference when reading the explication of the following section.

Poem Summary: a description of the major events in the poem. Summaries are broken down with subheads that indicate the lines being discussed.

Themes: a thorough overview of how the major topics, themes, and issues are addressed within the poem. Each theme discussed appears in a separate subhead and is easily accessed through the boldface entries in the Subject/Theme Index.

Style: this section addresses important style elements of the poem, such as form, meter, and rhyme scheme; important literary devices used, such as imagery, foreshadowing, and symbolism; and, if applicable, genres to which the work might have belonged, such as Gothicism or Romanticism. Literary terms are explained within the entry, but can also be found in the Glossary.

Historical Context: this section outlines the social, political, and cultural climate *in which the author lived and the poem was created.* This section may include descriptions of related historical events, pertinent aspects of daily life in the culture, and the artistic and literary sensibilities of the time in which the work was written. If the poem is a historical work, information regarding the time in which the poem is set is also included. Each section is broken down with helpful subheads.

Critical Overview: this section provides background on the critical reputation of the poem, including bannings or any other public controversies surrounding the work. For older works, this section includes a history of how the poem was first received and how perceptions of it may have changed over the years; for more recent poems, direct quotes from early reviews may also be included.

Criticism: an essay commissioned by *PfS* which specifically deals with the poem and is written specifically for the student audience, as well as excerpts from previously published criticism on the work (if available).

Sources: an alphabetical list of critical material quoted in the entry, with full bibliographical information.

Further Reading: an alphabetical list of other critical sources which may prove useful for the student. Includes full bibliographical information and a brief annotation.

In addition, each entry contains the following highlighted sections, set apart from the main text as sidebars:

Media Adaptations: if available, a list of audio recordings as well as any film or television adaptations of the poem, including source information.

Topics for Further Study: a list of potential study questions or research topics dealing with the poem. This section includes questions related to other disciplines the student may be studying, such as American history, world history, science, math, government, business, geography, economics, psychology, etc.

Compare & Contrast: an "at-a-glance" comparison of the cultural and historical differences between the author's time and culture and late twentieth century or early twenty-first century Western culture. This box includes pertinent parallels between the major scientific, political, and cultural movements of the time or place the poem was written, the time or place the poem was set (if a historical work), and modern Western culture. Works written after 1990 may not have this box.

What Do I Read Next?: a list of works that might complement the featured poem or serve as a contrast to it. This includes works by the same author and others, works of fiction and nonfiction, and works from various genres, cultures, and eras.

Other Features

PfS includes "Just a Few Lines on a Page," a foreword by David J. Kelly, an adjunct professor of English, College of Lake County, Illinois. This essay provides a straightforward, unpretentious explanation of why poetry should be marveled at and how *Poetry for Students* can help teachers show students how to enrich their own reading experiences.

A Cumulative Author/Title Index lists the authors and titles covered in each volume of the *PfS* series.

A Cumulative Nationality/Ethnicity Index breaks down the authors and titles covered in each volume of the *PfS* series by nationality and ethnicity.

A Subject/Theme Index, specific to each volume, provides easy reference for users who may be studying a particular subject or theme rather than a single work. Significant subjects from events to broad themes are included, and the entries pointing to the specific theme discussions in each entry are indicated in **boldface**.

A Cumulative Index of First Lines (beginning in Vol. 10) provides easy reference for users who may be familiar with the first line of a poem but may not remember the actual title.

A Cumulative Index of Last Lines (beginning in Vol. 10) provides easy reference for users who may be familiar with the last line of a poem but may not remember the actual title.

Each entry may include illustrations, including photo of the author and other graphics related to the poem.

Citing Poetry for Students

When writing papers, students who quote directly from any volume of *Poetry for Students* may use the following general forms. These examples are

based on MLA style; teachers may request that students adhere to a different style, so the following examples may be adapted as needed.

When citing text from *PfS* that is not attributed to a particular author (i.e., the Themes, Style, Historical Context sections, etc.), the following format should be used in the bibliography section:

"Angle of Geese." *Poetry for Students*. Eds. Marie Napierkowski and Mary Ruby. Vol. 2. Detroit: Gale, 1998. 8–9.

When quoting the specially commissioned essay from *PfS* (usually the first piece under the "Criticism" subhead), the following format should be used:

Velie, Alan. Critical Essay on "Angle of Geese." *Poetry for Students*. Eds. Marie Napierkowski and Mary Ruby. Vol. 2. Detroit: Gale, 1998. 7–10.

When quoting a journal or newspaper essay that is reprinted in a volume of *PfS*, the following form may be used:

Luscher, Robert M. "An Emersonian Context of Dickinson's 'The Soul Selects Her Own Society.'" *ESQ: A Journal of American Renaissance* Vol. 30, No. 2 (Second Quarter, 1984), 111–16; excerpted and reprinted in *Poetry for Students*, Vol. 1, eds. Marie Napierkowski and Mary Ruby (Detroit: Gale, 1998), pp. 266–69.

When quoting material reprinted from a book that appears in a volume of *PfS*, the following form may be used:

Mootry, Maria K. "'Tell It Slant': Disguise and Discovery as Revisionist Poetic Discourse in 'The Bean Eaters,'" in *A Life Distilled: Gwendolyn Brroks, Her Poetry and Fiction*. Edited by Maria K. Mootry and Gary Smith. University of Illinois Press, 1987. 177–80, 191; excerpted and reprinted in *Poetry for Students*, Vol. 2, eds. Marie Napierkowski and Mary Ruby (Detroit: Gale, 1998), pp. 22–24.

We Welcome Your Suggestions

The editorial staff of *Poetry for Students* welcomes your comments and ideas. Readers who wish to suggest poems to appear in future volumes, or who have other suggestions, are cordially invited to contact the editor. You may contact the editor via E-mail at: ***ForStudentsEditors@gale. com.*** Or write to the editor at:

Editor, *Poetry for Students*
Gale
27500 Drake Road
Farmington Hills, MI 48331-3535

Literary Chronology

1667: Jonathan Swift is born on November 30 in Dublin, Ireland.

1722: Jonathan Swift's "A Satirical Elegy on the Death of a Late Famous General" is published.

1745: Jonathan Swift dies after a stroke on October 19 in Dublin, Ireland.

1792: Percy Bysshe Shelley is born on August 4 in Sussex, England.

1817: Percy Bysshe Shelley's "Ozymandias" is published.

1822: Percy Bysshe Shelley dies of drowning on July 8 in the Gulf of Spezia, off the coast of Lerici, Italy.

1830: Christina Georgina Rossetti is born on December 5 in London, England.

1862: Christina Rossetti's "Goblin Market" is published.

1875: Rainer Maria Rilke is born René Karl Wilhelm Johann Joseph Maria Rilke on December 4 in Prague, Bohemia, now the Czech Republic.

1889: Anna Akhmatova is born Anna Gorenko on June 23 in Tsarsko Selo, Russia.

1894: Christina Rossetti dies of cancer on December 29 in London, England.

1899: Jorge Luis Borges is born on August 24 in Buenos Aires, Argentina.

1907: W. H. Auden is born Wystan Hugh Auden on February 21 in York, England.

1908: Rainer Maria Rilke's "Archaic Torso of Apollo" is published.

1911: Elizabeth Bishop is born on February 8 in Worcester, Massachusetts.

1914: John Berryman is born John Allyn Smith on October 25, in McAlester, Oklahoma.

1920: Amy Clampitt is born on June 15 in New Providence, Iowa.

1923: Wislawa Szymborska is born July 2 in Bnin, Poland.

1926: Rainer Maria Rilke dies of leukemia on December 29 in Switzerland.

1929: A. K. Ramanujan is born Attipat Krishnaswami Ramanujan on March 16 in Mysore, India.

1934: Wole Soyinka is born Akinwande Oluwole Soyinka on July 13 in Isara, Nigeria.

1939: W. H. Auden's "September 1, 1939" is published.

1941: Lyn Hejinian is born on May 17 in San Francisco, California.

1946: Elizabeth Bishop's "The Man-Moth" is published.

1948: W. H. Auden is awarded the Pulitzer Prize for Poetry for *The Age of Anxiety*.

1956: Elizabeth Bishop is awarded the Pulitzer Prize for Poetry for *A Cold Spring*.

1957: Jorge Luis Borges's "Borges and I" is published.

1957: Claudia Emerson is born on January 13 in Chatham, Virginia.

1962: Wislawa Szymborska's "Conversation with a Stone" is published.

1963: Anna Akhmatova's "Requiem" is published.

1963: Wole Soyinka's "Telephone Conversation" is published.

1964: John Berryman's "Dream Song 29" is published.

1965: John Berryman is awarded the Pulitzer Prize for Poetry for *77 Dream Songs*.

1966: Anna Akhmatova dies on March 5 in Leningrad (St. Petersburg), Russia.

1972: John Berryman commits suicide on January 7 by jumping off a bridge in Minneapolis, Minnesota.

1973: W. H. Auden dies of heart failure on September 28 in Vienna, Austria.

1979: Elizabeth Bishop dies of cerebral hemorrhage on October 6 in Boston, Massachusetts.

1980: Lyn Hejinian's "Yet we insist that life is full of happy chance" is first published.

1986: A. K. Ramanujan's "Waterfalls in a Bank" is published.

1986: Wole Soyinka is awarded the Nobel Prize for Literature.

1986: Jorge Luis Borges dies of cancer on June 14 in Geneva, Switzerland.

1993: A. K. Ramanujan dies of a heart attack on July 13 in Chicago, Illinois.

1994: Amy Clampitt dies of cancer on September 19 in Lenox, Massachusetts.

1996: Wislawa Szymborska is awarded the Nobel Prize for Literature.

1997: Amy Clampitt's "Iola, Kansas" is published.

2005: Claudia Emerson's "My Grandmother's Plot in the Family Cemetery" is published.

2006: Claudia Emerson is awarded the Pulitzer Prize for Poetry for *Late Wife*.

Acknowledgments

The editors wish to thank the copyright holders of the excerpted criticism included in this volume and the permissions managers of many book and magazine publishing companies for assisting us in securing reproduction rights. We are also grateful to the staffs of the Detroit Public Library, the Library of Congress, the University of Detroit Mercy Library, Wayne State University Purdy/Kresge Library Complex, and the University of Michigan Libraries for making their resources available to us. Following is a list of the copyright holders who have granted us permission to reproduce material in this volume of *PFS*. Every effort has been made to trace copyright, but if omissions have been made, please let us know.

COPYRIGHTED EXCERPTS IN *PFS*, VOLUME 27, WERE REPRODUCED FROM THE FOLLOWING PERIODICALS:

American Literature, v. 65, March, 1993. Copyright, 1993 Duke University Press. All rights reserved. Both used by permission of the publisher.—*Blackbird*, v. 1, fall, 2002. Reproduced by permission of the publisher, http://www.blackbird.vcu.edu.—*Comparative Literature*, v. 46, summer, 1994 for "Poetic Speech and the Silence of Art," by Shimon Sandbank. Copyright © 1994 by University of Oregon. Reproduced by permission of *Comparative Literature* and the author.—*Contemporary Literature*, v. 39, spring, 1998. Copyright © 1998 by

the Board of Regents of the University of Wisconsin System. Reproduced by permission.—*Eighteenth-Century Studies*, v. 5, summer, 1972. Copyright © 1972 The Johns Hopkins University Press. Reproduced by permission.—*ELH*, v. 72, fall, 2005. Copyright © 2005 The Johns Hopkins University Press. Reproduced by permission.—*The Explicator*, v. 36, winter, 1978; v. 47, spring, 1989; v. 51, fall, 1992; v. 62, winter, 2004. Copyright © 1978, 1989, 1992, 2004 by Helen Dwight Reid Educational Foundation. All reproduced with permission of the Helen Dwight Reid Educational Foundation, published by Heldref Publications, 1319 18th Street, NW, Washington, DC 20036-1802.—*Extrapolation*, v. 45, spring, 2004. Copyright © 2004 by The Kent State University Press. Reproduced by permission.—*Fence*, v.3, 2000 for "Some Notes toward a Poetics," by Lyn Hejinian. Reproduced by permission of the author.—*The Kenyon Review*, v. 21, winter, 1999 for "What to Make of an Augmented Thing," by Willard Spiegelman. Copyright © 1998. All rights reserved. Reproduced by permission of the author.—*The New Criterion*, v. 18, November, 1999 for "Jorge Luis Borges & the Plural I," by Eric Ormsby. © 1999 The New Criterion. Reproduced by permission of the author.—*New Literary History*, v. 22, spring, 1991. Copyright © 1991 The Johns Hopkins University Press. Reproduced by permission.—*The New Republic*, v. 203, 1990. Copyright ©

COPYRIGHTED EXCERPTS IN *PFS*, VOLUME 27, WERE REPRODUCED FROM THE FOLLOWING BOOKS:

COPYRIGHTED EXCERPTS IN *PFS*, VOLUME 27, WERE REPRODUCED FROM THE FOLLOWING WEBSITES OR OTHER SOURCES:

From *Contemporary Authors Online*. "Wole Soyinka," www.gale.com, Gale, 2006. Reproduced by permission of Gale.

Contributors

Bryan Aubrey: Aubrey holds a Ph.D. in English. Entries on *Dream Song 29* and *Waterfalls in a Bank*. Original essays on *Dream Song 29* and *Waterfalls in a Bank*.

Jennifer Bussey: Bussey holds a Master's degree in Interdisciplinary Studies and a Bachelor's degree in English Literature. She is an independent writer specializing in literature. Entry on *Ozymandias*. Original essay on *Ozymandias*.

Klay Dyer: Dyer holds a Ph.D. in English literature and has published extensively on fiction, poetry, film, and television. He is also a freelance university teacher, writer, and educational consultant. Entries on *Telephone Conversation* and *Yet we insist that life is full of happy chance*. Original essays on *Telephone Conversation* and *Yet we insist that life is full of happy chance*.

Joyce M. Hart: Hart has degrees in English and creative writing and is a freelance writer and published author. Entries on *The Man-Moth* and *Requiem*. Original essays on *The Man-Moth* and *Requiem*.

Neil Heims: Heims is a writer and teacher living in Paris. Entries on *Archaic Torso of Apollo* and *A Satirical Elegy on the Death of a Late Famous General*. Original essays on *Archaic Torso of Apollo* and *A Satirical Elegy on the Death of a Late Famous General*.

Diane Andrews Henningfeld: Henningfeld is a professor of English who writes widely on literary issues. Entry on *Borges and I*. Original essay on *Borges and I*.

Sheri Metzger Karmiol: Karmiol has a doctorate in English Renaissance literature. She teaches literature and drama at the University of New Mexico, where she is a lecturer in the university honors program. Karmiol is also a professional writer and the author of several reference texts on poetry and drama. Entry on *My Grandmother's Plot in the Family Cemetery*. Original essay on *My Grandmother's Plot in the Family Cemetery*.

David Kelly: Kelly is an instructor of literature and creative writing in Illinois. Entries on *Iola, Kansas* and *September 1, 1939*. Original essays on *Iola, Kansas* and *September 1, 1939*.

Emily Reardon: Reardon holds an M.F.A. in poetry. She writes poetry, fiction, and criticism. Entry on *Conversation with a Stone*. Original essay on *Conversation with a Stone*.

Claire Robinson: Robinson has an M.A. in English. She is currently a freelance writer and editor and a former teacher of English literature and creative writing. Entry on *Goblin Market*. Original essay on *Goblin Market*.

Archaic Torso of Apollo

RAINER MARIA RILKE

1908

Rainer Maria Rilke's "Archaic Torso of Apollo" was published, in German, in 1908, in a volume of his poems called *New Poems*. Not only are these *new* poems in the sense of being (at the time) poems recently written, but they are poems in which Rilke intended to bring something new to poetry, to in fact make a new kind of poem.

Rilke attempted in *New Poems* to write poems about objects, like statues or animals, which stood before the reader like concrete things in their own right, realities that were independent of the observer. "Archaic Torso of Apollo," a poem written about an encounter with a sculpture, ought to exist itself for its reader like a piece of sculpture or a painting. Both the sculpture and the poem serve as models for the reader, defining how the reader might be or, in fact, ought to be. That is the creative agenda behind the poem "Archaic Torso of Apollo." The observer does not define the object. The object defines the observer.

It is clear from works like "Archaic Torso of Apollo" that some of the strongest influences on Rilke came from other arts, particularly sculpture and painting. The sculptor Rilke most admired was Auguste Rodin, for whom Rilke worked as secretary from 1905 until 1906. From Rodin, Rilke learned the importance of things, that inert matter transformed by art can become spiritually alive. The painter Rilke most admired

Rainer Maria Rilke *(© Bettman | Corbis. Reproduced by permission)*

was Paul Cézanne. Following Cézanne's influence, the art Rilke favored tended to present objects to the beholder in such a way that the beholder experiences the object (a poem, a sculpture, a painting) anew, as if it had never been seen or understood before.

"Archaic Torso of Apollo," in a translation by Stephen Mitchell, alongside the original German, can be found in the 1989 edition of *The Selected Poetry of Rainer Maria Rilke*, edited and translated by Stephen Mitchell, and published by Vintage International.

AUTHOR BIOGRAPHY

René Karl Wilhelm Johann Joseph Maria Rilke was born on December 4, 1875, in Prague. His father, Joseph Rilke, was a minor railroad official. His mother, Sophia Entz, was thirteen years younger than her husband, and separated from him when Rilke was nine years old.

Born prematurely, Rilke was a sickly child. His delicate health was cause for concern to his mother, especially because a daughter, born a year before Rilke, died a week after her birth.

To compensate for the loss of that child, Rilke's mother dressed Rilke in long dresses, despite her husband's objections. Joseph Rilke, however, gave his son dumbbells for exercise and toy soldiers to play with. Rilke's mother, again in opposition to her husband's wishes, encouraged Rilke, beginning when he was seven, to write poetry. Joseph nevertheless supported Rilke as a young man. Rilke's biographer, Ralph Freedman, reports that Rilke wrote that his mother was "a pleasure-loving, miserable being." Of his father, Rilke wrote: "Only my papa bestowed upon me love combined with care and solicitude."

After his parents' separation, Rilke was sent, at the age of ten, to a military boarding school, where he spent the next four years. When he left St. Pölten's in 1890, Rilke had two ambitions, to be a soldier and to be a poet. He had a notebook full of poems; many of them were about soldiering, but he was hardly successful or happy as a practicing soldier in the gymnasium (or high school) and on the drilling field. He enrolled in the Mahrisch-Weisskirchenn Military Academy but left in 1891 before obtaining his commission. Rilke then attended the Handelsakademie, a business school in Linz, Austria, but he left in 1892 without completing a degree. From 1895 to 1896, Rilke attended the University of Prague. In 1897, Rilke changed his name to Rainer Maria Rilke.

In 1901, Rilke married Clara Westhoff, a sculptor who had been a pupil of Rodin. Rilke and Westhoff had a daughter, but separated after a year, leaving Ruth in the care of Westhoff's mother, as they each pursued their respective careers. Rilke had by this time published many lyrics, lyrical stories, and essays. He was particularly interested in painting and sculpture, and as part of a project to write about Rodin, he became Rodin's secretary in 1905. Working with Rodin taught Rilke to think of his own poetry as an attempt to represent spiritual and psychological conditions through the re-creation of concrete things in his lyrics. "Archaic Torso of Apollo" is one of the poems that emerged from his period of apprenticeship to Rodin, as it appeared only a few years later in *New Poems* in 1908.

In 1910, Rilke published *The Notebooks of Malte Laurids Brigge*, his most important work of prose fiction. That year, too, Rilke began the *Duino Elegies*, verse meditations on beauty, solitude, and terror, written at a castle called Duino, in Switzerland. The onset of World War I interrupted the work, and Rilke returned to Germany to serve in the War Department in 1916. Afterwards, he spent most of his time in Switzerland, tending his rose garden. In 1923, he finished the ten *Duino Elegies*, which are considered to be his masterwork. That same year, he composed the *Sonnets to Orpheus*. Rilke died of leukemia in 1926. It is said that in his last weeks he told friends that the specific cause of his dying was an infection he got pricking his finger on a rose's stem. Since his death, Rilke has come to be regarded as one of the greatest German lyric poets. Rilke also garnered a reputation for existential wisdom after the publication of *Letters to A Young Poet*, a series of letters written throughout the first decade of the twentieth century.

POEM TEXT

We cannot know his legendary head
with eyes like ripening fruit. And yet his torso
is still suffused with brilliance from inside,
like a lamp, in which his gaze, now turned to
    low,

gleams in all its power. Otherwise   5
the curved breast could not dazzle you so, nor
    could
a smile run through the placid hips and thighs
to that dark center where procreation flared.

Otherwise this stone would seem defaced
beneath the translucent cascade of the
    shoulders   10
and would not glisten like a wild beast's fur:

would not, from all the borders of itself,
burst like a star: for here there is no place
that does not see you. You must change your life.

POEM SUMMARY

Stanza 1

"Archaic Torso of Apollo" begins with a statement of fact: since the head of the statue is missing, "we" do not know what it looked like. The rest of the poem explores the torso, which is what remains of the ruined statue. The poet finds that the trunk, which ought to be a mute and meaningless piece of stone, contains the life force and the meaning that might have been found in the head. Thus, the absence of the head does not diminish the expressive power of the statue. The qualities that existed in the incomprehensible head—incomprehensible because it is absent as

well as because it is a rendering of an unseen divinity—may still be found in the body itself. The absence of the head signifies a hole in "our" knowledge, not a defect or deficit in the statue. This is the thing "we cannot know," but it is something "we" can imagine. The speaker imagines the eyes as "ripening fruit," in Mitchell's translation, or "apple-eyes" (the German *augenäpfel*) in the original. In either case, the image suggests the eyes are growing into ripeness and are glowing with that ripeness, full with roundness and rich with light and life. The poem's transition from the imagined head to the actual body, which still exists, comes with the abrupt "and yet" towards the end of the second line. It is a transition that is even sharper in the original German.

In the original, the word "but" (*aber* in German) stands alone as the last word on the second line. "But," the speaker says, even if "we cannot know" his head, the body of the statue remains and is, in Mitchell's translation, "suffused with brilliance from inside, / like a lamp, in which his gaze, now turned to low, / gleams in all its power." This can be confusing. The headless body can gaze, and that gaze is "like a lamp." And, though the sculpture's gaze is dimmed ("turned to low"), it still shines brightly ("gleams in all its power"). If the lamp is dim, how can it "gleam"? In the original German, however, the lines roughly translate as "his Torso yet glows like a candelabra, / in which his gaze, only turned back / shines and gleams." William H. Gass, in his book *Reading Rilke: Reflections on the Problems of Translation*, quotes J.B. Leishman, an early translator of Rilke's verse, in order to explain that "in Germany and Austria the word *Kandelaber* 'was the usual word for a streetlamp: not for the comparatively short post with a single square lantern, but for the much taller and more elegant sort with two globes, each suspended from either end of a wide semicircular crosspiece.'" In Gass's translation, then, the image that Rilke created becomes clear and can be pictured: "his Torso glows as if his look were set above it in suspended globes that shed a street's light down." The missing eyes are now not like apples, but like two street lamps suspended on each end of a curved crosspiece atop a pole, hanging above the street. The way they cast light back down onto the pavement is the way the invisible, no longer present eyes they represent cast light down onto and into the torso. In this way, the torso is illuminated and is also illuminating.

Stanza 2

Although there is a new stanza, there is not a new sentence. Line 4 in stanza 1 flows into line 5, the first line of stanza 2. This blurring of boundaries provides an indication of Rilke's belief in the unity of perception that exists despite the formal separations art makes (i.e. the separate stanzas) in conveying perception. The speaker, then, concludes that the source of light, the eyes, although apparently missing, must be illuminating the torso because, "otherwise / the curved breast could not dazzle you so, nor could / a smile run through the placid hips and thighs / to that dark center where procreation flared." The poet is describing not only the unity of vitality that the trunk reveals, but also the effect of viewing that vitality; he is, in a word, "dazzle[d]." He also attributes this impression to several things about the art work: the way the curve of the breast has been sculpted, the gentle fashioning of the hips and thighs that move the eyes of the viewer to the center of the body, to the genitals. The pleasure the poet experiences because the sculpture guides his eyes in a graceful movement becomes an attribute of the torso. In the original German, there is no corresponding adjective for the "dark center." There is only a suggestion of awe at the delicately carved masculinity in the stone; awe at the artistry that transforms the torso from inexpressive rock to the repository and source of the essential spirit of a primary life force. The poet does not interpret the trunk; he beholds it. In doing so, the speaker realizes that the force of life, with which the god he perceives in the torso is imbued, is his as well as the torso's. The speaker sees, and the poem shows, that the torso is a commentary on him (and on "us") showing him what he (and "we') might be.

Stanza 3

The third stanza continues by repeating the word "otherwise," to explain that the light of the staue's gaze is actually a property of the ruined torso and not only of its missing eyes. "Otherwise this stone would seem defaced / beneath the translucent cascade of the shoulders," the speaker explains. "Defaced" in Mitchell's translation, signifying mutilated or deformed, by a play of language, also suggests the part of the statue that is missing—the face. This word play does not exist in the original. The words *enstellt* and *kurz* signify "deformed" and "shortened," as indeed the statue ought to look, being a trunk without the upward sweep of a neck meeting a face. But something

about the craftsmanship of the body prevents it from appearing stunted. There is a "translucent cascade of the shoulders" that gives length to the torso, and the body "glisten[s] like a wild beast's fur." With the strange image comparing marble to an animal's pelt, the poem does not compare visible surfaces but rather compares the qualities suggested by visible surfaces. This work of art, an ancient representation of the trunk of a god, confined in a museum, has in it the same element of vital energy that radiates from a living wild animal because of the artist's skill.

Stanza 4

If the life of the eyes were not somehow glowing in the trunk, the trunk would not have the power to fascinate the observer. It would not seem like the representation of something vital. Nevertheless, the vitality of the trunk is so intense that it "burst[s] like a star" beyond the "borders of itself." The effect that the torso has on the poet/observer of the torso makes it seem to him that he is the observed, that "there is no place / that does not see you." The speaker is indeed in the presence of a god. He is watched, seen, by the thing he is looking at. Then, the tone of the poem changes abruptly. The lyrical description of the torso gives way to a realization and an exhortation: "You must change your life."

How does looking at a marble torso, no matter how artfully crafted, lead to such a conclusion? One wonders to whom the word "you" actually refers. Does it refer to the poet or to the reader, and who is speaking, the poet or the statue? Is the poet, speaking to himself, being overheard by the reader? Or is the poet addressing the reader just as the torso addresses the poet? If so, then the poem has become the torso—a work of art that demands change of its viewer (i.e. the reader).

What about the torso or the poem leads to such an exhortation? The torso contains a life power, it is something that "burst[s] like a star" beyond the "borders of itself." The torso in its vibrancy is a critique of the observer and a revelation of a primal human force, a force that the viewer senses is lacking in his own being. Seeing the torso, the speaker is overwhelmed by this insight. If "we,"—the "we" that opens the poem (meaning all humanity, including the poet)—see the torso through the poet's eyes, then we are obliged to realize that we are not who we ought to be. That is to say, we are not our true selves;

we are instead the selves constructed, and thus curtailed, by our society. The trunk is authentic. "We" are not. Although the Apollo is decapitated, it is still whole. Thus, the presence of the headless, yet vibrant, torso reveals that "we," who seem to be whole, are far more "defaced" than the faceless statue.

THEMES

The Ability of Matter to Represent Spirit

The speaker is clear in "Archaic Torso of Apollo" that the object looked upon is stone, something that exists entirely in the realm of matter. Yet, at the same time, the speaker is looking at something immaterial that is revealed by the stone. The poem is not about the material object that he stands before in contemplation. The poem is about the spirit invested in that stone and its intangible effect on the beholder. That spirit is represented in the stone through the sculptor's art. Through the poet's contemplation of the physical object, that spirit breaks out of the stone ("from all the borders of itself, / burst[s] like a star") and is reconstituted as an idea in the poet: "You must change your life."

Authenticity

Implicit in "Archaic Torso of Apollo" is a critique of a life led without authenticity. This critique is the result of a revelation achieved through artistry, which the torso imparts. The physical beauty of the statue is a metaphor for an authentic aspect of humanity that the poet senses is lacking in both his body and his spirit. The poem does not reveal what authenticity is. Finding or defining that is another pursuit. The poem, rather, only forces awareness on the poet, the understanding that he is missing something that the statue, fragmented as it is, still possesses.

Change

"Archaic Torso of Apollo" begins with the poet's awareness that the statue he is observing has been changed by time. It is now a decapitated ruin. The poem ends by returning to the idea of change, but this time as a deliberate act that "must" be undertaken. The speaker's awareness of change comes from an understanding that the torso possesses a force of life within it that negates the change that ruin has wrought upon it.

TOPICS FOR FURTHER STUDY

- Using a German-English dictionary and other translations of the "Archaic Torso of Apollo," make a translation of your own and write a set of notes, at least two notes per line, explaining the choices you made in composing your translation.

- Visit a museum near you and select one particular work of art—a painting, a sculpture, or an installation—that interests you. Do not be judgmental about your response, as you may choose a work that you either like or dislike. In a poem, describe the work and its effect upon you. During the process, see if you can or cannot discover why the work intrigues you.

- Ask the following set of questions of six people that you know, and try to interview people in varying age groups: Have you ever had a life-changing experience or an experience that made you realize "you must change your life"? If so, what was it? Describe in detail the cause of the experience, the nature of the experience, and the nature of your response to the experience. Next, write up the individual responses. Discuss, as well, what differences and similarities you find when you compare and contrast responses.

- After researching the works and the aesthetic ideas of Rodin and Cézanne, imagine a conversation between them in which they discuss Rilke's "Archaic Torso of Apollo."

- "Archaic Torso of Apollo" touches upon philosophical ideas that can be attributed to Modernism and Phenomenology. Prepare a short lesson to present to your class in which you define and explain these two schools of thought. Note any similarities you perceive between Modernism and Phenomenology, and the ways in which they do or do not relate to the poem.

The change that "must" be made by the poet, and by the reader, is the kind that will restore the unchanging power the torso embodies.

Knowledge

"Archaic Torso of Apollo" speaks first of what "we" do *not* know. The idea of knowledge is thus introduced into the poem as an absence. The lines that follow constitute an attempt at knowing, at discovering a way through ignorance to knowledge, past what is missing towards what is present. First presented as intuition (the poet intuits what the eyes of the statue were like), knowledge then becomes a matter of deductive reasoning, as the repeated word "otherwise," indicates. The light from the eyes is still in the trunk, "otherwise" the torso would be rubble rather than art, a ruin rather than an icon. The accumulation of details, revealed by the images they suggest, whether a street lamp, a missing set of genitals, or a beast's pelt, coalesce into a sudden configuration, into the conclusive insight of the poem, the poet's realization that "You must change your life."

Mind-Body Connection and Opposition

Implicitly, Rilke confronts the idea of the connection and opposition between the mind and the body. The head of Apollo no longer exists. There is only the body. Yet, in the torso, there seems to be nothing lacking. The power of the head, which is supposedly achieved in the intensity of its gaze, feels somehow present in the remaining trunk. The mind-body split, however, results from the conflict of two forces or tendencies—intellectual apprehension of the world in conjunction with repression of deep rooted currents of being, which together seem essential for civilized society. This physical, emotional, or intuitive aspect of human beings results in a connection to the world that is immediate and that overrides the intellect. Perhaps it is this mode of being that the speaker becomes aware of, and wishes to emulate, as he contemplates the ruined statue.

The Relationship between a Work of Art and the Observer of the Work of Art

Rilke breaks down the subject-object, observer-observed duality. Instead he postulates a reciprocal unity of perception between the observer and the thing perceived. Each becomes a part of the other; each, the object of the other's gaze. The poet himself becomes aware of being the statue's object of contemplation and as such is vulnerable to the statue's critique of him, which is inherent in its formal perfection—a perfection that, although it is his birthright, the poet realizes he lacks.

STYLE

Conversational Tone

"Archaic Torso of Apollo" is a difficult poem. In complex images and telescoped metaphors (apple eyes; street lamp; beast's fur) it expresses a strong critique of how people construct themselves in civilized society. In the original German it is, also, a formally well-constructed sonnet. It is a fourteen-line poem with an exemplary rhyme scheme (*abba, cddc, eef, gfg*), which Mitchell does not try to reproduce in the English. Nevertheless, the tone of the poem is conversational in both languages. The poet seems to be talking to someone or to a group, as if he were a guide leading a group through a museum and stopping to explain the exhibits. He begins the poem with the word "We" and continues as if lecturing with a pointer, exploring the surface and the notable aspects of the torso of Apollo.

Polysyndeton

Technically, polysyndeton refers to the repetition of a conjunction, usually "and," for the creation of an overwhelming effect: tables and chairs and sofas and mirrors and beds and desks and lamps and bookcases. In "Archaic Torso of Apollo," Rilke does not repeat the word "and" in this manner. He does, however, strategically repeat the word "otherwise," as the introduction to a counter statement. Moreover, "otherwise" follows the use of the word "but" in order to serve the same function of contradicting what might be expected. The effect of this kind of repetition is to endow the poem with the feeling that it is a logical argument, that it is a kind of discourse with premises and a conclusion that follows from those premises. In actuality, the poem is not an intellectual diagram but the diagram of an insight the poet experiences following intellectual contemplation.

Sensuous Imagery

The curved breast of the statue, the turn of the hips, the absent genitals, the fur of an animal, a starburst—these are all sensuous images. Because there are several such images over the course of fourteen lines, they combine to present the object the poet observes as a tangible thing

COMPARE
&
CONTRAST

- **1900s:** Rilke lives in a time when great cultural transitions in Europe are occurring, ways of seeing, understanding, and representing the world are changing, and even governments and national empires are changing or crumbling.

  Today: Geopolitical arrangements are undergoing significant change, as the European and North American domination of culture, thought, and politics is being challenged by Islamic cultures, and American technological supremacy is being superseded by advances made in Japan, China, and Korea. Additionally, recent theories put forth by physicists, such as String Theory, have again changed the way people view their experience of the world.

- **1900s:** For Rilke and those of his generation, Paris is the center of the artist's universe, where poetry, sculpture, and painting are being reinvented.

  Today: Artists find Paris to be a museum of past achievement, and they view New York City and Berlin as centers for innovative art.

- **1900s:** Philosophers, psychologists, and artists challenge accepted notions of perception, asserting the inadequacy of objectivity and arguing that reality is a creation of individual perception.

  Today: Cultural conservatives challenge the idea that reality has a basis in subjective experience determined by individual perceptions. Cultural progressives defend a multi-dimensional idea of reality that acknowledges the interplay of individual experience with external events as forces that work in combination to define reality.

and to suggest the climactic response the poet has to the object. Thus, the poem seems to indicate that sensuous experience is what teaches, not intellectual activity. The torso, by means of what it can only suggest because of its mutilation, as well as by what still remains of it, exists as the distillation of these images.

HISTORICAL CONTEXT

Apollo

A god of the ancient Greeks, Apollo represented many functions. Primarily, he was the god of medicine and the healing arts. As such he also represented light (the sun) and truth, and, by extension, Apollo was the god of poetry and music. He was always represented as a handsome young man. In Rilke's poem, all the identities or functions of the god coalesce. The ruined, but still handsome, statue of Apollo

inspires Rilke's lyric through the higher implications of physical or artistic beauty.

Modernism and Phenomenology

Modernism was a movement in the arts that arose during the last years of the nineteenth century and the first years of the twentieth century as a reaction to what its practitioners considered the excesses of the nineteenth century, particularly in the way nineteenth-century artists proposed a strictly objective experience of reality. Modernism destroyed such objectivity and instead favored the subjectivity of perception as the defining element of reality. In her essay, "Modern Fiction," the English novelist, Virginia Woolf, 1878–1941, succinctly set forth the aim of Modernism. "Let us," she wrote, "record the atoms as they fall upon the mind in the order in which they fall, let us trace the pattern, however disconnected and incoherent in appearance, which each sight or incident scores upon consciousness."

The Temple of Apollo at Corinth, Greece *(Hulton Archive / Getty Images)*

Phenomenology is a philosophical system developed by Edmund Husserl over the same period of time. It is an attempt to study the observation of things as they are, which means as they are perceived, ignoring pre-existing ideas about them. Phenomenology argues that the natures of the thing perceived and of the person perceiving are interdependent, and thus concludes that subjective perception is the only true perception. Things do not have objective existence independent of any perception of them, so the thing that is perceived takes its identity from the perceiver, and the one perceiving takes identity from the thing perceived. In "Archaic Torso of Apollo," the poet and the torso derive their identities from each other.

Rodin and Cézanne

A sculptor and a painter, not another poet, exerted the greatest influence on Rilke. The French sculptor, Auguste Rodin, 1840–1917,

changed the course of sculptural representation, presenting the art of sculpture at a level of heightened realism that had previously been lacking. Sculpture had been a formal and decorative art, often taking ancient and monumental figures for its models. Rodin celebrated the actual human body (as opposed to the ideal) in complex yet common positions, often showing the embrace of lovers, in an attempt to evoke a more spiritual effect. This sensitivity is at the heart of Rilke's "Archaic Torso of Apollo."

French, Post-impressionist painter Paul Cézanne, 1839–1906, drew on the work of the Impressionists like Claude Monet, 1840–1926, building even further upon their ideas. Like them, he used the visual subject of his paintings to explore the art of painting itself, the underlying spirit of the visual subject, and the psychology of perception. This approach reinforces the idea that the visual subject exists not in itself but as the object of perception.

CRITICAL OVERVIEW

Acknowledged in Jeffrey Hart's *National Review* article as "one of the most important poets of the European modernist movement," Rilke has come to represent the archetypal poet as an inward-looking lyricist. In his poetry, Rilke defines himself by his relation to the world about him. His is a poetry that gathers images from the world, absorbs and reflects them, and extracts their spiritual meanings through verse. "Rilke's most immediate and obvious influence has been upon diction and imagery," and he was able "to express abstract ideas in concrete terms," the poet W.H. Auden argues in a *New Republic* article. "With a romantic naivete for which we may feel some nostalgia now, and out of a precocity for personality as well as verse, Rilke struggled his entire life to be a poet— not a pure poet, but purely a poet," William H. Gass asserts in his *Nation* review of Rilke's *Uncollected Poems.* Lee Siegel, writing in the *Atlantic Monthly*, comments that "Rilke was one of the most gifted and conscientious artists who ever lived. ... His poetry, fiction, and prose embody a search for a way to be good without God." Rilke was a poet, according to Mark Rudman in the *Nation*, who "raid[ed] the knowable through the visual." Judith Ryan observes, in *Rilke, Modernism, and Poetic Tradition*, that "the radiance that emanates from the sculpture is not an effect of wholeness, but rather of its fragmentary nature." Rudman argues, that, influenced by Cézanne, "Rilke insists that we should learn to look at things as if no one had ever looked at them before." Rudman notes, too, that Rilke said of Cézanne's paintings: "It's as if every place were aware of all the other places." Rudman adds that "one hears this insight amplified, transformed, in the poem 'Archaic Torso of Apollo.'" Jeffrey Meyers, writing in the *National Review*, objects to the general admiration surrounding Rilke. Meyers also objects to the assessment that Rilke is a poet who exemplifies profound human sensitivity. He argues that Rilke missed a "meaningful connection with the outside world and [was incapable of] either friendship or love." These alleged failings, Meyers concludes, "led to an exquisite and ethereal poetry that lacked human emotion." But Rudman, discussing Rilke's inward quest, sees the poet differently: "His work tells us that we are solitary by nature but that absence is not loss, that in forever taking leave, we encounter being." Gass calls Rilke "a priest of the poet's art," and asserted that Rilke "takes the European lyric to new levels of achievement."

CRITICISM

Neil Heims

Heims is a writer and teacher living in Paris. In the following essay, Heims discusses Rilke's belief in the reciprocal, linked relation between an object and the person who beholds it. Heims asserts that this belief is not only defined in "Archaic Torso of Apollo," but that the poem itself is an invitation to the reader to experience this reciprocity.

Rilke is a difficult poet, especially for readers who must approach him in translation. Often, in translation, the lyricism of his German turns into slightly awkward, intellectualized, and out-of-focus English. His subject, moreover, is, in large part, the sudden perception of philosophical realities. Indeed, although these realities shape and define our responses to the material world, and although they arise as the result of our encounters with the material world, they are not material in and of themselves. They are something like unseen electrical or spiritual currents running through us and connecting us to the objects and events of the surrounding material world that confront us and that we confront. These currents give matter its vitality. They are available to be perceived when we see beyond matter, when we look with an inward gaze and attempt to perceive the world with the sensitivity of a poet; i.e., when we experience the world through our spirituality. For Rilke, a poet is defined less as the practitioner of a craft than as the possessor of an exceptional sensibility that informs the craft.

"Most events are inexpressible, taking place in a realm which no word has ever entered," Rilke wrote on February 17, 1903, in a letter to Mr. Kappus, a young poet who had written to him for criticism and guidance. In their correspondence, written over a period of five years, Rilke suggested that there is a depth of silence within each person and that a fundamental, personal truth resides in that silence. Rilke also indicated that the closer a person approaches to that silence, the closer he or she comes to approaching their own particular and fundamental nature and, consequently, their own truth. Thus, there is not one truth that is universally applicable. There are innumerable personal truths and it is the existential burden of each person to discover the truth by which he or she is formed. Because of the multiplicity of human beings, multiple perspectives and points of view determine truth. Truth is embodied and embedded in each individual. An object of

WHAT DO I READ NEXT?

- Sigmund Freud's *The Interpretation of Dreams* was published in 1900. In this revolutionary study, Freud postulates the idea of an unconscious, a hidden part of ourselves that, despite being hidden from us, or because it is hidden from us, exerts strong power over us without our knowledge. According to Freud, the unconscious can be revealed through the study of dreams.

- John Keats's poem "Ode on A Grecian Urn" was first published in 1820. The poem contemplates the scene of an ancient celebration engraved on an ancient urn and considers the art's ability to reveal truth.

- Rilke's *Duino Elegies* were written from 1912 to 1922. In this series of ten poems, Rilke grapples with the problems of describing the human experience from the point of view of an inner-directed, subjective consciousness as it encounters the pleasures and terrors of being alive in the world as an isolated individual.

- Percy Bysshe Shelley's poem "Ozymandias" was published in 1818. Shelley's sonnet tells of an encounter with a traveler who speaks of the ruined statue of an ancient king, and of the lesson that is derived from that encounter.

- Wallace Stevens's "Anecdote of the Jar" was published in 1923. In this puzzle of a poem, Stevens meditates on the function of art in bridging the distance between wild and cultivated nature.

- *Spring's Awakening* was published in 1891 by Frank Wedekind. *Spring's Awakening* is a play that concerns the sexual awakening and sexual torment of teenagers. It is set at the end of the nineteenth century, a time when the forces of repression and the forces of desire were about to come into cultural conflict.

- Virginia Woolf's *To the Lighthouse* was published in 1927. Woolf's tale of a family in conflict with itself, told from subjective points of view, is a principal work of Modernism, as is Rilke's "Archaic Torso of Apollo."

---

art, like a poem or a sculpture, for Rilke, is a particular expression of a particular truth.

A work of art, rather than being an object, is an encounter that produces a revelation. It is the product of an encounter between two silences, the silence of the person in quest of truth or authenticity and the silence of the inner, underlying self. This revelation is illustrated in "Archaic Torso of Apollo." According to Rilke, an artist is a person who can emerge from such an encounter between two silences with something new, an object of art—a poem or a sculpture or a musical composition. A reader of a poem, or the viewer of a sculpture, provides a third silence contemplating the silence of the art work, of the poem or the sculpture, as if it were his or her own silence. Thus, "Archaic Torso of Apollo" is not only an

illustration and product of this phenomena, it also perpetuates the phenomena each time it is read.

An encounter with art is complex not just because it is an encounter with another silence but because it is an encounter with one's own silence as that silence is represented within a given work of art. According to Rilke, art is a thing outside oneself that startles one into realizing his or her essential inwardness represented in an apparently external thing. An external thing, according to the principles of Phenomenology (of which Rilke was an adherent), is not really external at all. The archaic torso of Apollo (the thing, not the poem) is nothing other than the poet or person who is looking at it. In the poem, the torso represents the hidden body of the poet that the poet discovers in the sculpted marble form—which is itself really

THE TORSO IN 'ARCHAIC TORSO OF APOLLO' STANDS FOR BOTH THE HUMAN IDEAL AND THE DECAY OF THAT IDEAL, BUT EVEN THE DECAY ITSELF IS VIEWED AS AUTHENTIC."

nothing more than a piece of ruined stone—but that is also dazzlingly alive with a revelation of the truth of life because of the poet's gaze upon it. The poet's discovery of the silent part of himself in the silent part of the statue embodies the narrative of "Archaic Torso of Apollo."

The ideas of mutuality and interdependence (the linked relationship between the viewer and the object) are primary for Rilke's understanding of the experience of art. The artist, in Rilke's understanding of art, embodies a sensitivity that can enter into the silence of another sensitivity, and then merge with it. By doing so, the artist discovers something essential about himself, and if he is a very great artist, presents those who encounter his work with something essential about themselves. This is why "Archaic Torso of Apollo" ends with a revelation. The "You must change your life" is a statement that is not meant as a command or entreaty. It simply expresses the poet's epiphany, and perhaps it invites the reader to experience this epiphany as well.

What is there in the Greek statue that speaks to the poet? In a short essay called "Concerning Landscape," which Rilke wrote in 1902, he addresses the difference between the way the Greeks saw people and the way people were viewed after the introduction of Christianity.

> It is safe to assume that [Antiquity] saw people as later painters have seen landscape. In the scenes of their vases ... the surroundings ... are only mentioned ... but the naked human beings are everything, they are like trees bearing fruit ... and like springs in which the birds are singing. In that age the body, which was cultivated like a piece of land, tended carefully like a harvest ... was the thing looked upon, was beauty, was the image through which all meanings passed in rhythmic movements, gods and animals, and all life's senses. ... Christian art lost this connexion with the body.

The Greek representation of the body in art shows the way the Greeks saw and thought about the body. When the poet looks at the torso of Apollo he sees and understands the Greek point of view. Additionally, the poet is made aware that his own persona has been shaped by the societal concepts and beliefs of his day, and that this is what he must change or transcend. In other words, the formative Christian culture must be changed. Seeing the statue reveals to the poet that the culture has devitalized the body and consequently robbed it of the spirit that turns matter into vitality. This realization is brought about by viewing art, and by creating art, Rilke attempts to represent this. The torso in "Archaic Torso of Apollo" stands for both the human ideal and the decay of that ideal, but even the decay itself is viewed as authentic. What is required of the artist, or even of the life that "must" be changed, is a sensitivity that can probe the artifact and discover its undisturbed essence, a sensitivity that can allow the observer/poet to fuse his consciousness with the consciousness discovered within the artifact.

Source: Neil Heims, Critical Essay on "Archaic Torso of Apollo," in *Poetry for Students*, Gale, 2008.

William Waters

In the following excerpt, Waters explores the similarities of the theme in "Archaic Torso of Apollo" and the theme in Rilke's Sonnet 2.12 from Sonnets to Orpheus. *Both poems exhort the reader to change or transform, and both, Waters posits, are successful because they do not indicate how to effect that change. The poems thus become ethically ambiguous and this, Waters concludes, is where their resonance lies.*

If there is a theme pervading the *Sonnets to Orpheus* as a whole, it is that of transformation. One poem in which this theme is explicit (2.12) moves from stanza to stanza as a progress through the four elements of fire, earth or rock, water, and air:

> Wolle die Wandlung. O sei für die Flamme begeistert,
> drin sich ein Ding dir entzieht, das mit Verwandlungen prunkt;
> jener entwerfende Geist, welcher das Irdische meistert,
> liebt in dem Schwung der Figur nichts wie den wendenden Punkt.
>
> Was sich ins Bleiben verschließt, schon *ists* das Erstarrte;

HOW YOU MUST CHANGE YOUR LIFE IS NOT
SPECIFIED, SINCE THE POEM IS NOT, AND EVEN YOU
YOURSELF ARE NOT, IN A POSITION TO SPECIFY WHAT
YOUR LIFE IS, STILL LESS TO NAME THE RESPECTS IN
WHICH YOU DO NOT SEE IT WHOLE."

wähnt es sich sicher im Schutz des unschein-
baren Grau's?
Warte, ein Härtestes warnt aus der Ferne
das Harte.
Wehe—: abwesender Hammer holt aus!

Wer sich als Quelle ergießt, den erkennt die
Erkennung;
und sie führt ihn entzückt durch das heiter
Geschaffne,
das mit Anfang oft schließt und mit Ende
beginnt.

Jeder glückliche Raum ist Kind oder Enkel
von Trennung,
den sie staunend durchgehn. Und die ver-
wandelte Daphne
will, seit sie lorbeern fühlt, dass du dich
wandelst in Wind.
(Rilke 1997:92)

[Want transformation. Oh be inspired for
the flame
in which a thing eludes you that bursts into
something else;
the spirit of re-creation that masters this
earthly form
loves most the pivoting point where you are
no longer yourself.

What tightens into survival is already rigid;
how safe is it really in its inconspicuous
grey?
From far off a far greater hardness warns
what is hard,
and the absent hammer is lifted high!

He who pours himself out like a stream is
acknowledged by Knowledge;
and she leads him enchanted through the
cheerful creation
that finishes often with starting, and with
ending begins.

Every fortunate space that the two of them
pass through, astonished,
is a child or grandchild of parting. And the
transfigured Daphne,
as her feeling turns laurel, wants you to
change into wind.
(Rilke 1985: 95; modified)]

The "pivoting points" in this poem are many, as from the "swing of the figure" we turn to the hardness of rock; when the rock is shattered by the "absent" hammer (Mörchen 1958: 289 pro- poses that this hammer is Time), water breaks forth from it; and as the water passes, riverlike, through "fortunate space," the poem returns to the *you* of its opening lines: it is you who are asked to become the airy element. Beginning with the moth-and-flame metaphor, which had concluded Goethe's famous poem "Blessed Longing" with the injunction "Die and become," Rilke's sonnet likewise turns to the imperative form as a way of expressing the relentless urgency of the task it names: transformation is work that never stops, work that takes the place of the agent who under- takes it. The one who pours herself out like a spring (recalling Ovid's nymph Byblis in *Metamorphoses* 9:454–665) is recognized, known as herself, when she has acquiesced to having no fixed identity that could be known. "The way of life is wonderful," writes Ralph Waldo Emerson (1983: 414); "it is by abandonment"; and Rilke's poem serves this same wisdom, as what you pur- sue withdraws from you (lines 2, 13–14) like your own solid identity and as parting (line 13) governs also your relation to yourself.

The command "Want transformation" is par- adoxical. Philosophers of ethics have noted "the importance of our capacity to have second-order desires—desires to have certain desires" (Williams 1985: 11) if we are to act or reflect ethically. But Rilke's command may mean even "want to make yourself open to having other wants that you may not specify." Furthermore, in the imperative form, the verb "wolle" urges a desire, though a desire is not something acquired at urging; and the next command repeats these contradictions with "oh be inspired for the flame" (where *sei begeistert* should be as absurd a command as *wolle*). The absurdity begins to resolve as the mention of being loved (in line 4) anticipates a revealing transformation at the end of the poem: the same desire (*wollen*) for your transformation is there said not to come from you but to come back at you from the fleeing object of your desire. The poem urges you (in the first line) to want to become not-you, and then, as if restating the same thing, it says (in the last line) that the thing you already do want (but cannot have) is what wants you to become not-you. The apparently impossible urging that opened the poem turns out, in other words, to be the urging of the voice of love, and what seemed to be your impossibly bootstrapping act of will is, instead, a response (and therefore completely possible). The laurel feeling of Daphne asks you to become its invisible complement, passing through it in a possession-less caress on the way to somewhere else. This is, in turn, a figure for what it is like to be the reader of a poem.

The sonnet also recalls, in two ways, a point that Bernard Williams makes about the nature of a first-person ethical disposition (how a virtu-ous person thinks about what to do) as opposed to a third-person description of a virtue (how others might describe the way the virtuous per-son thinks about his or her actions, for example with words like *brave* or *modest*): "The deliber-ations of people who are generous or brave, and also the deliberations of those who are trying to be more generous or braver, are different from the deliberations of those who are not like that, but the difference does not mainly lie in their thinking about themselves in terms of generosity or courage" (Williams 1985: 11). The trait of doing without these self-conscious thoughts brings to mind the cheerful (*heiter*, line 10) accommodation to not-having that sums up Rilke's sonnet. In addition, I would develop Williams's point by saying that the impulse to do a generous or brave act is first of all a response to something outside oneself rather than the enactment or demonstration of a first-person characteristic that one owns. This quality of responsiveness is the leading principle of Rilke's sonnet, as each stanza's images emerge from and answer to what has preceded, and as the evasiveness and disappearance of the object of desire turn out to be not just enticement but the beckoning of love.

Rilke's poem knows nothing of the futile coerciveness of any simple injunction to virtue. The command "Want transformation" recalls, instead, that most celebrated exhortation in Rilke's verse, the closing half line of the 1908 poem "Archaic Torso of Apollo": "You must change your life." *How* you must change your life is not specified, since the poem is not, and

even you yourself are not, in a position to specify what your life is, still less to name the respects in which you do not see it whole. In "Archaic Torso of Apollo," as in our sonnet 2.12, the ethical content of the exhortation is left blank for each recipient to fill in with her own life circumstances and feeling as they are evoked by her own read-erly reception of the poem. This blank would become empty in a different, pointless way were the command taken to be something detachable from the poem that voices it. Instead, the content of the imperative belongs to the total experience of trying to be the reader on whom nothing of the poem is lost. This atten-tiveness, if one could attain it, would be like being the wind that feels, and is felt by, each leaf of the laurel at the same time. To read, to be played upon, to give up what we are holding back and to be carried somewhere we did not design to go, is one way we can be transformed in the hands of another. The aesthetic effect of the poem *is* its ethical force, but to know what that means, we must surrender ourselves and become, instead, the poem's reader.

Source: William Waters, "Rilke's Imperatives," in *Poetics Today*, Vol. 25, No. 4, Winter 2004, pp. 711–30.

Shimon Sandbank

In the following excerpt, Sandbank compares "Archaic Torso of Apollo" to Italo Calvino's poem "The Birds of Uccello." Both poems are inspired by an external work of art and both, according to Sandbank, focus predominantly on what is physically missing from the artwork at hand. Thus, Sandbank concludes: "Rather than engaging exclusively in carrying the forms of art over to poetry, they concentrate on the absences of art to the advantage of poetry."

A salient case in point is Rilke. His *Dingdich-tung*, inspired by Cézanne and Rodin, is often seen as a heroic attempt—perhaps *the* heroic attempt beside Gerard Manley Hopkins's—to subject poetic language to the physical "inscape" of things (Hartman 95). His famous sonnet on the "Archaic Torso of Apollo," with all its seeming glorification of a purely physical presence, insistently dismisses the physical . . .

This poem throughout focuses on absence, on what the torso lacks: its lack of head, of genitals, of arms. Rilke attributes the statue's impact to these gaps in the visual, to what is invisible and non-physical—the mysterious inte-riorization of the gaze. The poem's end, with its famous moral call to a change of life, is altogether beyond the physical.

Formally, this sonnet is miles apart from Calvino's "The Birds of Uccello." Nevertheless, they share a certain deep structure. Rilke's starting point, like Calvino's, is absence. Though the two absences are different in kind—Calvino's absence of birds derives from an inherent limitation of the visual medium, its inability to present time-sequentiality, while Rilke's absence of head, arms, and genitals is contingent, a result of the ravages of time—both serve as springboards to a destruction of the physical presence of the work of art concerned. Both Rilke's defaced stone and Calvino's painted soldiers are destroyed by the imaginative extensions of absence: the eyes that owing to the head's absence have been interiorized into the body; the birds that, having been scattered and absent, now swoop down in counteroffensive. Both writers have deleted their visual objects so as to clear imaginative space for themselves, as Harold Bloom would put it.

In addition, they have reaffirmed the traditional topos of the resilience of poetry, in contrast to art. "You shall shine more bright in these contents," Shakespeare assures the beloved, referring to his sonnets, "than unswept stone besmeared with sluttish time." Rilke shows how the statue's physical deterioration results in an enduring spiritual resilience, like poetry; it has become a eunuch, but, as Hopkins puts it in a letter to Bridges, "it is for the kingdom of heaven's sake." Now as immaterial as a poem, the statue has overcome art's inability to deal with spiritual matters and actually become a poem.

One is reminded of Gertrude Stein's frivolous but profound "pictures," described in a lecture she delivered during her 1934 American tour. "I always ... liked," she says, "looking out of windows in museums. It is more complete, looking out of windows in museums, than looking out of windows anywhere else." But then, during a long hot summer in Italy, she "began to sleep and dream in front of oil paintings." She still looked out of the windows of the museums, but it was no longer necessary. "There were very few people in the galleries in Italy in the summers in those days and there were long benches and they were red and they were comfortable at least they were to me and the guardians were indifferent or amiable and I would really lie down and

sleep in front of the pictures. You can see that it was not necessary to look out of the windows."

Is that not what Calvino and Rilke are doing? They look out of windows or sleep and dream, but they must do it in a museum in front of paintings. Uccello and the torso must be there for Calvino and Rilke to turn their backs on and dream. Even in a time of "physical poetry," ekphrastic poets thus half turn their back to the physical painting. Rather than engaging exclusively in carrying the forms of art over to poetry, they concentrate on the absences of art to the advantage of poetry. An ekphrastic poem therefore remains what M.J. Kurrik, in an entirely different context, calls "a presence based on absences." It is "from the perspective of what it excludes" that the ekphrastic poet reads his visual object, and "the perception of absence" is what "institutes [his] creative act" (1,x,5).

Source: Shimon Sandbank, "Poetic Speech and the Silence of Art," in *Comparative Literature*, Vol. 46, No. 3, Summer 1994, pp. 225–39.

SOURCES

Auden, W.H., "Rilke in English," in the *New Republic*, Vol. 100, No. 1292, September 6, 1939, pp. 135–36.

Freedman, Ralph, *Life of a Poet: Rainer Maria Rilke*, Farrar, Straus and Giroux, 1996, p. 11.

Gass, William H., *Reading Rilke: Reflections on the Problems of Translation*, Alfred A. Knopf, 2000, pp. 90–1.

——, Review of *Uncollected Poems*, in the *Nation*, April 1, 1996, pp. 27–32.

Hart, Jeffrey, "The Best of Rilke," in *National Review*, November 10, 1989, p. 67.

Meyers, Jeffrey, "A Ringing Glass: The Life of Rainer Maria Rilke," in *National Review*, August 29, 1986, p. 46.

Rilke, Rainer Maria, "Archaic Torso of Apollo," in *The Selected Poetry of Rainer Maria Rilke*, translated and edited by Stephen Mitchell, Vintage International, 1982, p. 61.

——, *Letters to a Young Poet*, translated by M.D. Herter Norton, W.W. Norton & Company, Inc., 1963, pp. 17, 20.

——, *Selected Works: Volume I, Prose*, translated by G. Craig Houston, Hogarth Press, 1954, pp. 1, 3.

Rudman, Mark, "New Poems: The Other Part—1908," in the *Nation*, September 26, 1987, pp. 6–9.

Ryan, Judith, *Rilke, Modernism, and Poetic Tradition*, Cambridge University Press, 1999, p. 80.

Siegel, Lee, "Life of a Poet: Rainer Maria Rilke," in the *Atlantic Monthly*, Vol. 277, No. 4, April 1996, pp. 112–16, 118.

Woolf, Virginia, "Modern Fiction," quoted in, "Recomposing Reality: An Introduction to the Work of Virginia Woolf," by Neil Heims, in *Bloom's BioCritiques: Virginia Woolf*, edited by Harold Bloom and Neil Heims, Chelsea House Publishers, 2005, p. 67.

FURTHER READING

Buber, Martin, *I and Thou*, Charles Scribner's Sons, 1958.
    In *I and Thou*, originally published in German in 1923, Buber presents a religious and philosophical meditation on the varieties of relationships that are possible between people, and between people and things.

Flores, Angel, ed., *An Anthology of French Poetry from Nerval to Valery in English Translation*, Doubleday Anchor Books, 1958.
    This excellent anthology is predominantly a collection of nineteenth-century French poetry, one of the significant literary influences on Rilke.

———, *An Anthology of German Poetry from Hölderlin to Rilke*, Anchor Books, 1960.
    This companion volume to the anthology of French verse offers a clear indication of the poetic context and tradition from which Rilke's verse emerged.

Freud, Sigmund, *Civilization and Its Discontents*, translated from the German by James Strachey, W.W. Norton & Company, Inc., 1961.
    In *Civilization and Its Discontents*, Freud examines the opposition between the fundamental human instincts, which crave expression, and the forces of civilization, which seem to depend on curbing or repressing those instincts.

Malinowski, Bronislaw, *Sex and Repression in Savage Society*, Meridian Books, 1959.
    Malinowski was an anthropologist whose fieldwork among the Trobriand Islanders of New Guinea involved him in the study of a culture unlike that of Europe and other civilizations. The force of repression of bodily instincts, he observed, was not a primary, defining force in the formation of that culture.

Mann, Thomas, "Death in Venice," in *Death in Venice and Seven Other Stories*, translated from the German by H.T. Lowe-Porter, Vintage Books, 1989.
    In "Death in Venice," Mann presents the story of an artist who encounters such beauty that all the values of his past are challenged and undermined.

Rilke, Rainer Maria, *The Notebooks of Malte Laurids Brigge*, translated by M. D. Herter Norton, W. W. Norton & Company, Inc., 1992.
    Published in 1910, *The Notebooks of Malte Laurids Brigge*, Rilke's only novel, is a semi-autobiographical account of Rilke's life as an artist in search of his calling in an age of religious doubt, including themes about personal anxiety and the deterioration of industry.

Tolstoy, Leo, *Great Short Works of Leo Tolstoy*, translated by Louise and Aylmer Maude, edited by John Bayley, Harper & Row, Perennial Library, 1967.
    Tolstoy was one of Rilke's heroes. In stories like "Farther Sergius," "Master and Man," "The Death of Ivan Ilych," "The Devil," and "The Kreutzer Sonata," Tolstoy's particular genius for expressing ideas in concrete images and in the narration of actual events is clearly evident.

Borges and I

JORGE LUIS BORGES

1957

In "Borges and I," the great Argentine writer Jorge Luis Borges meditates on the relationship between his private and public selves. The poem is quintessentially Borges: puzzling, ambiguous, and even shocking. First published in 1957 in Spanish as "Borges y yo" in the journal *Biblioteca*, the poem was included in Borges's 1960 collection, *El Hacedor* (*The Maker*). This volume was translated into English and released in 1964 as *Dreamtigers*. It was here that "Borges and I" was first made available in English.

"Borges and I" is very short, barely three hundred words long. However, while the vocabulary and the words of the poem are simple, the ideas contained in the poem are very complex. Indeed, even the genre of the work is hard to determine. Is "Borges and I" even a poem at all?

During his early career, Borges published many poems. After about 1938, however, he began writing short stories, including some of his most famous, "The Garden of Forking Paths," "Death and the Compass," and "The Library of Babel." By 1955, however, Borges had grown nearly blind, and his work became increasingly enigmatic and brief.

During this period, he began producing short meditations he called parables. Without rhyme or meter, and without special lining, the works resemble very short fiction; nevertheless, these small pieces of writing are poetic in their images, their themes, and their allusive, metaphoric

Jorge Luis Borges (The Library of Congress)

Borges was born on August 24, 1899, in Buenos Aires, Argentina. He grew up living with his parents in the home of his paternal grandmother. Because Borges's grandmother was an Englishwoman, he learned to speak English at the same time he learned to speak Spanish, as had his father. In addition, his father's library, the source of much of Borges's education, was almost exclusively comprised of English language books. He early on demonstrated fascination with the workings of language; in addition to his native fluency in both English and Spanish, he later learned French, German, Latin, and Old English.

As a young man, Borges traveled to Europe with his family. While they were there, World War I broke out, and the family was forced to remain in Geneva, Switzerland, for the duration of the war. Borges attended college in Geneva, graduating in 1918. Rather than returning home at that time, the family continued their tour of Europe, living in Spain for the next three years. It was while he was in Spain that Borges began to write poetry under the influence of a group of Spanish poets known as the Ultraístas.

After returning to Argentina in 1921, Borges published his first book of poetry, *Fervor de Buenos Aires* (*Passion for Buenos Aires*) in 1923. Over the next several years, he published two more books of poetry and three books of essays. As a result, he became increasingly well known in the Argentine literary community.

In 1937, beset with financial difficulties, Borges accepted a post as a librarian in the municipal library. There was little work for him to do, and he spent much of his time reading, particularly work by Franz Kafka. During his time at the library, Borges began to formulate some of the ideas that eventually found their way into some of his most important work, such as the short story, "The Library of Babel."

The late 1930s were difficult years for Borges. His father's death in 1938 was a tremendous loss for him. Borges credited his father with introducing him to language and poetry. In addition, Borges suffered an accident in the same year, just months after his father's death, gashing his head on an open casement window. The wound became infected, and Borges nearly died. When he recovered, he no longer wrote the poetry of his youth, but turned instead to a

language. "Borges and I," then, is best considered a prose poem, an intensely focused and sharply tuned exploration into the heart of public and private identity. When asked about his writing in several interviews, Borges always responded that he thought of himself as a poet, first and foremost.

"Borges and I" is perhaps Borges's most frequently anthologized and best known poem, and remains available in several editions of Borges's writing, including *Labyrinths* (1964), edited and translated by Donald A. Yates and James E. Irby. While this anthology was published over forty years ago, it has been through thirty-two printings and remains the standard source for the English translation (by Irby) of "Borges and I." Indeed "Borges and I" has become Borges's most emblematic poem, translated by various writers and appearing in many anthologies. The poem title even serves as the title of a documentary detailing the writer's life.

"Borges and I" continues to fascinate popular readers and scholars alike. Through the poem, readers walk with Borges through the streets of Buenos Aires and find themselves confronted with the ultimate question: who is writing the tale?

completely new genre, something that he called *ficciones*. He published a book of these short stories in 1941, titled *El jardín de senderos que se bifurcan* (*The Garden of Forking Paths*).

During the 1940s and 1950s, Borges grew increasingly blind; while his production of new writing decreased, his international fame increased. "Borges y yo" was published during this period in the journal *Biblioteca* in 1957. The poem was next included in Borges's 1960 collection, *El Hacedor* (*The Maker*). This volume was translated into English and released in 1964 as *Dreamtigers*. It was in this volume that "Borges and I" was first available in English.

By the time of the publication of "Borges and I," the author was known throughout the world. In 1961, he shared with Samuel Beckett the prestigious Formentor International Publishers Prize. From this point on, he began traveling around the world, giving lectures and teaching classes at universities. In 1985, Borges left Argentina for the last time, traveling to Europe. It was there that he died on June 14, 1986, in Geneva, Switzerland.

POEM SUMMARY

Lines 1–6
Because the poem is written in more of prose-like form, the thoughts and ideas that are expressed often run together and are not as clearly divided as they would be if they were split up into more formal poetic stanzas and lines. Thus, the poem as is it discussed here is broken up into sections that also overlap.

Indeed, "Borges and I" has no plot. Rather, it is a poem that explores the relationship between private and public selves, as well as the ways that text multiplies and refracts further identities. The poem opens with an unnamed narrator referring to "the other one, the one called Borges" as someone who experiences life; he "is the one things happen to." The implication, then, is that things do not happen to the narrator, but that he is somehow connected to Borges, since he calls Borges "the other one." This reference suggests that the narrator is also Borges, perhaps the private human being behind the public persona known as "Borges."

The narrator is capable of action, rather than being someone acted upon; he walks the streets of Buenos Aires, he looks at architectural features,

MEDIA ADAPTATIONS

- A recording of Borges reading some of his best known works in Spanish was released in 1999 by the Argentine government. Samples from this compact disk, including "Borges y yo," are available in RealAudio at www.terra.com.ar/especiales/borges/bor_audios.shtml.

- *Selected Fictions* was released as an audiotape by Penguin Audio Books in 1998. The stories were translated by Andrew Hurley and read by George Guidall. "Borges and I" is also included on this audiotape.

- A documentary based on interviews with Borges titled *Borges and I* was produced by Gilles Couture in 1983, and is available on tape through Home Vision. Phrases from "Borges and I," are used throughout, though the film is predominantly a look at Borges's life.

he reads the mail. The narrator knows about Borges from text he sees included in the mail, in biographical dictionaries, and "on a list of professors." In other words, he seems to know Borges in the same way he knows the architecture of Buenos Aires, from the outside. Furthermore, it is through text itself that he knows something about Borges. This implies that the narrator has no real knowledge of the inner Borges, perhaps because the narrator *is* the inner Borges.

Lines 6–13
The narrator next lists a series of things that he likes, ranging from hourglasses to "the prose of Stevenson." Readers familiar with Borges's life know that the work of Robert Louis Stevenson was influential for Borges, and that he had a fascination with time and timepieces. Likewise, the narrator tells the reader that he and Borges share the same list of preferences. However, the narrator also says that Borges's appreciation of these items is somehow false, in the same way that an actor is false. The narrator, it seems, distinguishes between preferring something for itself and preferring something for the impression it gives.

In the next few lines, the narrator makes the connection between himself and Borges through the literature that Borges writes. Although the narrator says that the "literature justifies" him, he also reports that the "pages cannot save" him. This is because literature does not belong to one person or any person; rather, good writing is the product of language and tradition. This statement, the notion that individual authors do not matter, but what *does* matter is tradition, is at the core of many of Borges's writings.

Lines 13–19

At the midpoint of the poem, the tone shifts. The narrator recognizes that he is mortal, and "destined to perish." Although there will be something left of him in the literature that Borges writes, the narrator understands that he, the person who he understands himself to be, will ultimately disappear. Indeed, even in his present life, he is being taken over by Borges, who may, or may not, represent him accurately, since Borges has the "custom of falsifying and magnifying things." The poem seems to be making a case that the public persona of a writer can overtake, subsume, and ultimately destroy the private life of the individual person who is the writer. In addition, the poem makes the point that the living, breathing human being who is Borges will cease to exist in time and space. All that will be left are texts created by Borges the writer that will somehow point to the living human being who once walked the streets of Buenos Aires.

Lines 19–24

In the next line, the narrator alludes to Spinoza, a seventeenth-century Dutch philosopher of Jewish origin. Spinoza believed, as the narrator relates, that beings want to continue being at an essential level. That is, all human beings want to continue being that which is essentially human. The narrator finds, however, that as Borges writes about him, he loses his own recognizable essence. In fact, he becomes more and more a text of Borges's creation and less and less of a human being. In effect, the narrator realizes that he has become another character in Borges's writing.

Lines 24–29

In the end, the narrator knows that he will either be obliterated, or he will become totally subsumed by Borges. In either case, the narrator's essence will have been erased. In the last line, the identity of the narrator and that of Borges have become so entwined that neither reader nor the writer, the narrator nor Borges, knows who has written the page.

THEMES

Identity

In "Borges and I," Borges demonstrates how problematic the concept of identity can be. In this short poem, the narrator, who can be identified variously as Borges the narrator, Borges the writer, or an unnamed narrator, speaks about his own identity. He establishes his personhood by listing the things that he likes: "hourglasses, maps, eighteenth-century typography, the taste of coffee, and the prose of Stevenson." To enjoy such things implies a physical being; abstract ideas, for example, cannot sip coffee. Thus, by listing his preferences, the narrator establishes that he is an individual with specific likes and dislikes. Such a list creates an identity for the narrator. In addition, he attempts to distinguish his own identity from that of the "other" Borges (the public persona) by telling the reader that Borges, too, enjoys these same things.

He further attempts to distinguish himself from Borges (and thus solidify his own identity) by stating that "It would be an exaggeration to say that ours is a hostile relationship." The word "relationship" necessarily implies a second, distinct individual with a second identity, as does the narrator's insistence that there is a Borges who is other than himself. However, while the first section of the poem works hard to develop an identity for the narrator as distinct from Borges, by the middle of the poem, the boundaries between the two begin to blur as the narrator comes to understand that "little by little, I am giving over everything to him." The identity that the narrator has attempted to forge for himself in the first half of the poem crumbles as he confronts his own mortality and the realization that he is no longer even recognizable, except perhaps "in the laborious strumming of a guitar." Nevertheless, although the movement of the poem is away from a discrete narrative identity toward a melding of the narrator and Borges, the last line of the poem still comes as a shock: "I do not know which of us has written this page." In this final line, set off

TOPICS FOR FURTHER STUDY

- In 1994, the writer Daniel Halpern invited many writers to produce short parables in the style of "Borges and I." The resulting book, *Who's Writing This?*, is a collection of those efforts. Read this book and then compose your own parable, using "Borges and I" as your starting point. Ask some of your classmates to join the project and collect their work into a class anthology of Borges-like parables.

- Read Borges's short story "Death and the Compass," Edgar Allan Poe's" The Purloined Letter," and Luis Fernando Verissimo's novel *Borges and the Eternal Orangutans*. What details from Borges's life and stories does Verissimo use to structure his novel? How does an understanding of Poe help in understanding the novel? What connections can you find between Verissimo's novel and "Borges and I"? Write a book review of Verissimo's novel in which you demonstrate why having a knowledge of both Borges and Poe is helpful in understanding the novel.

- Research the ideas of Baruch Spinoza. Why do you think that Borges alludes to Spinoza in this poem? Prepare a poster presenting Spinoza's ideas and how they intersect with Borges's ideas, as revealed in "Borges and I."

- One of the most important metaphors in Borges's work is that of the labyrinth. Read the Greek myth of the labyrinth before reading several additional short stories by Borges, including "The Garden of Forking Paths." Why do you think that the labyrinth symbol is so important to Borges? How is the poem "Borges and I" like a labyrinth? Create a visual representation of a labyrinth to share with your classmates, and demonstrate how Borges uses the metaphor in several of his stories.

- In "Borges and I," Borges creates himself as a literary character. Likewise, other writers such as Umberto Eco and Luis Fernando Verissimo have used Borges as a character in their stories. After researching Borges's life and work, write a short story or poem that alludes to Borges and uses him as a character.

---

as a new paragraph, the distinction between the identity of the narrator and the identity of Borges is fully erased.

Metafiction

Although Borges wrote "Borges and I" and the rest of his work before the time commonly associated with the postmodernism movement, most critics would agree that in Borges, postmodernists find a precursor to their own ideas. (This is ironic, of course, since it was Borges who argued that all writers invent their own precursors.) One of the most important literary concepts of postmodernism that Borges exploits in his own work is that of "metafiction." Metafiction, at its most fundamental level, is simply writing about writing.

However, the idea can be both complicated and complex in its execution.

Throughout the nineteenth century, many writers increasingly attempted to capture reality in their stories. That is, through the faithful recounting of the details of life, they attempted to give life to their characters and stories, even when these details were ugly or difficult to bear. Over time, readers began to expect that stories would be realistic, or somehow true to life. Indeed, in realistic fiction, both reader and writer enter into a sort of covenant: the writer agrees to follow certain conventions in the creation of his or her story, and the reader agrees to suspend disbelief and enter the fictional world. Together, the writer and the reader create a world that functions according to the rules of fiction, but that nonetheless seems to point to a real world beyond the fiction.

Metafiction, however, demonstrates that stories are not real life, but rather are always necessarily fictions. By calling attention to themselves as pieces of writing, rather than life, metafictional stories remind the reader that, in the final analysis, a piece of writing is no more than black ink on white pages. Ironically, one of the ways that metafiction accomplishes this task is by blurring the lines between so-called fact and fiction. By interspersing a story with events or characters or truths from the world outside of the story, the writer blurs the distinction between fiction and nonfiction, a favorite Borgesian ploy.

"Borges and I" functions as a metafictional poem by using the name of its writer as a character, thus blurring the distinction between fact and fiction. By doing so, the poem encourages the reader to believe that it is saying something important and autobiographical about the Argentine writer, Borges. In some ways, the struggle of the poem's narrator to maintain the distinction between himself and Borges reflects the reader's struggle to learn something factual about the writer Borges from the words on the page. The poem, while seeming to reveal some important melancholy truth about the relationship between a writer and his work, ultimately serves to conceal the writer behind the work.

"Borges and I" plays a game with the reader by forcing the reader to question the identity of the narrator of the poem. As Kane X. Faucher writes in his article "The Decompression of Meta-Borges in 'Borges and I'," "'Borges and I' presents its readers with a perplexing riddle: who is the author?" Faucher then delineates all possible answers to that question. However, it is only through the recognition that "Borges and I" is metafictional that the reader comes to understand that neither the narrator nor the Borges of the poem are *really* Borges, the writer of the poem. The living and breathing Borges no longer exists, and all he has left behind is ink on paper. When Borges concludes his poem, "I no longer know which one of us has written this page," he is being ironic. Neither of the characters of the poem, the narrator nor Borges, has written the page, since they are fictional characters, incapable

of independent action apart from the pages that create them.

STYLE

Imagery

Imagery, or the use of words and phrases that figuratively connect to the senses, is one of Borges's characteristic devices in "Borges and I." The poem begins as a walk through the streets of Buenos Aires while the narrator recounts what he sees: "the arch of an entrance hall and the grillwork on the gate." The attention to architectural detail engages the reader's sense of sight. The narrator next lists a number of items that both he and Borges like, including "the taste of coffee." Again, Borges appeals to the senses. In so doing, he begins to create a reality for the narrator and for the "other" Borges, a reality in which there are concrete, physical objects that can be sensed. Later, the narrator says that he recognizes himself "less in his books than … in the laborious strumming of a guitar," an appeal to the sense of hearing. It is as if the narrator tries to place himself outside of language by suggesting that he himself is more like music than typography. Throughout the poem, then, sensory detail serves to both create, then destroy, the character of the narrator, and to build the "other" Borges.

Narrative and Identity

A narrator is, quite simply, the "I" of a story or poem. Often, the narrator is no more than a presence, or a voice. However in "Borges and I," the narrator is a full character. On first reading, it is easy to assume that the "I" is Borges himself. However, on subsequent readings, it becomes difficult to determine whose voice it really is: Borges the narrator; or Borges the writer; or perhaps some other unnamed voice; or, quite possibly, another voice named "Borges." Through his complication of the notion of the narrator, Borges creates a labyrinth of possible meanings for his poem. Rather than offering a simple distinction between the public and private persona of Borges the writer and Borges the man, the poem, through the multiplicity of the narrative voice, becomes not two voices, but an infinite chorus.

COMPARE
&
CONTRAST

- **1950s:** In Argentina, Juan Perón continues his presidency through 1955, when he is ousted by a military coup.

   Today: A civilian government is in power in Argentina and is attempting to redress the wrongs committed in previous decades against intellectuals, writers, and journalists, many of whom were kidnapped and killed by the government then in power.

- **1950s:** Adolfo Prieto's book *Borges y la nueva generación* (*Borges and the New Generation*) appears in 1954. This is the first volume of literary criticism devoted solely to Borges's work.

   Today: New critical articles and books about Borges regularly appear worldwide in many languages.

- **1950s:** Across the world, the Cold War pits Communist and Democratic nations against each other. In Latin America, there is a rapid growth of communist groups, leading to the Cuban Revolution in Cuba. Likewise, in

many other countries including Argentina, left-wing political groups agitate for change.

   Today: Communist and socialist groups in several Latin American countries continue to press for power, but left-wing political parties in Argentina have not been overly successful. Cuba remains a communist country.

- **1950s:** Existentialist philosophers such as Jean-Paul Sartre write about the importance of human existence and moral choices, in spite of their belief that life is devoid of ultimate meaning. For the existentialists, God is dead. Borges's interest in language, rather than in human existence, placed him out of step with prevailing philosophical trends of his day.

   Today: Philosophers such as Michel Foucault and Jacques Derrida focus on the function of language as a tool for the construction (and deconstruction) of reality. For the postmodernists, the Author is dead. Most contemporary critics see Borges as the precursor of Foucault and Derrida.

HISTORICAL CONTEXT

During his lifetime, Borges saw his home country of Argentina go through repeated political upheavals. As a member of an Anglophile, patrician family, Borges saw his own fortunes wax and wane as various political factions rose, then fell from power.

For Borges, the historical and cultural contexts that informed his work were not limited to Argentina, however. Borges grew up speaking both English and Spanish. In addition, he received much of his education in Geneva, during World War I. There he became acquainted with the work of writers such as Franz Kafka, Friedrich Nietzsche, and Arthur Schopenhauer. After World War I,

Borges remained in Europe and discovered the leading voices of a new way of thinking called modernism: James Joyce, T.S. Eliot, and Luigi Pirandello, to name just a few. When he returned to Argentina, Borges brought this influence with him.

However, by the 1930s, Argentina began an economic slide, pushing many Argentines to question European ideas and influence. The outbreak of World War II served to isolate Argentina somewhat from Europe. The country maintained its neutrality throughout the war, only declaring war on the Axis powers near the end of hostilities in 1945. Borges and his family openly aligned themselves with the Allies, largely due to their English heritage and their distaste for nationalism and fascism.

Buenos Aires (AP Images)

Argentina, however, became increasingly nationalistic after World War II. Old patrician families such as the Borges found themselves in the minority in the new order. In 1946, Juan Perón, a military general, came to power. This was significant for Borges who, although fairly apolitical, had signed a petition denouncing fascism in all forms. As a result, Perón removed Borges from his post at the municipal library and appointed him as a poultry inspector, a position that Borges refused. Some critics argue that the fantastic stories that Borges wrote during the 1940s and the 1950s were his escape from the difficulties of World War II and the Perón years; however, there are others who see in Borges a rejection of contemporary history and politics.

Perón and his wife Eva were popular with the common people in the years immediately after his election. However, he grew increasingly despotic, although he was reelected as president in 1951. Perón began interfering with universities and took control of the newspapers. In addition, he began making moves against the Catholic Church.

By 1955, however, Perón's regime was toppled by a coup. Borges, and other members of the middle class were overjoyed to see him go. Perón went into exile. Back in favor, Borges was appointed the Director of the National Library in 1955. The year, however, was bittersweet for Borges, as it was in 1955 that his blindness became total and irreversible.

After the departure of the Peróns, Argentina moved through periods of military dictatorships followed by periods of constitutional democracy. The country repeatedly moved from times of greater restriction and repression to times of a more open society. By the late 1950s, young people were once again looking to Perónism as a potential answer to their country's woes. As a result, through the early 1960s, Borges was regarded with suspicion as a member of the old guard.

In 1961, six international publishing houses decided to join together to create a prestigious literary award. This prize, called the Formentor Prize, was awarded to Samuel Beckett of Ireland and to Borges. As a result, Borges was able to leave the political tribulations of his homeland, and begin the journeys that marked the remainder of his life. Just as Borges had been deeply influenced by European values and aesthetics as a young man, he was able to establish himself as a citizen of the world during the turbulent 1960s.

CRITICAL OVERVIEW

Borges's work has been in the public and critical eye for nearly seventy years, and interest in both the writer and his literary productions shows no sign of slowing. Indeed, his fame seems to grow with each passing year. As early as 1973, J. M. Cohen recognized in his book *Borges* that Borges was ahead of his time and that "prophetically he understood the situation of a generation then unthought of, which has come to doubt the metaphysical assumptions of its fathers and grandfathers."

"Borges and I," first published in Argentina as "Borges y yo," in the January 1957 issue of the journal *Biblioteca*, was later collected in Borges's 1960 volume, *El Hacedor* (*The Maker*). This collection was later translated by Mildred Boyer and Harold Moreland as *Dreamtigers*; the book appeared in the United States in 1964. In a still later translation, Andrew Hurley returned the title of the book to the direct translation of the Spanish title, *The Maker*.

The Maker is an odd collection of prose, poetry, fiction, and essay, comprised of various pieces of previously unpublished writing Borges kept around his house. When his publisher asked him to produce a new book, Borges, by then completely blind, gathered this work, and also created some additional new pieces. Of all the individual works collected in this volume, "Borges and I" stands out as the one most frequently cited. Donald A. Yates in *Modern Fiction Studies* argues that "Its significance as a key of sorts to the interpretation of Borges's work has ... been widely acknowledged."

For Emir Rodriguez Monegal, author of *Jorge Luis Borges: A Literary Biography*, the unifying characteristic of the poems and stories in *The Maker* is that they seem to be autobiographical. He calls "Borges and I" "explicitly autobiographical" and argues that it became Borges's "final statement on his literary persona."

More recently, Thomas H. Ogden, in an article in *Psychoanalytic Dialogues*, approaches "Borges and I" from a psychological perspective, also linking the poem to events in Borges's life. He theorizes that Borges wrote both this work and "Pierre Menard, Author of the *Quixote*" as a result of "enormous emotional losses." He further suggests that "successful mourning centrally involves a demand that we make on ourselves to create something—whether it be a memory, a dream, a story, a poem, a response to a poem—that begins to meet, to be equal to, the full complexity of our relationship to what has been lost and to the experience of loss itself."

On the other hand, Edwin Williamson in his 2004 biography, *Borges: A Life*, argues that both "Borges and I" and "The Maker" grow out of the historical context; Williamson writes that they are texts "written out of a growing sense of dread, for in the course of 1957, Borges must have realized that the prospects of creating a democratic Argentina ... depended critically on the outcome of the presidential elections that were scheduled to take place in July 1958."

Still other critics find in Borges's work connections to writers who came before him, as well as to writers who came after. For example, in an article titled "Eliot, Borges, Tradition, and Irony," José Luis Venegas looks at the connection between the English poet T.S. Eliot's famous essay, "Tradition and the Individual Talent," and Borges's work. Venegas argues "that Borges's views on tradition and the individual talent, although superficially in accordance with Eliot's, can in fact be read as their ironic reversal." Further, critic James Gardner, writing an obituary for Borges in the *New Criterion*, compares Borges to the Italian writer Italo Calvino, suggesting that while both writers demonstrate postmodern concerns in their writing, Calvino will be most remembered by future literary critics and philosophers. Gardner's analysis has proven wrong; while Calvino is still an important name in literature today, his works are not nearly as popularly or critically acclaimed.

Regardless of the interpretation, however, "Borges and I" has become an emblematic work for Borges scholars, one that points to Borges's understanding of both the role of the author, and the role of the subject. Indeed, one can nearly trace the last fifty years of literary theory by looking at the critical interpretations of this poem, ranging from psychological analysis, to deconstruction and to new historical criticism. It is indicative of the power that Borges holds for literary scholars that this small parable continues to shed light on the relationship among writers and readers.

CRITICISM

Diane Andrews Henningfeld

Henningfeld is a professor of English who writes widely on literary issues. In this essay, she examines Borges's growing stature as a cultural icon, a development anticipated by Borges himself in poems such as "Borges and I."

There are few writers better known worldwide than Borges. Scholars credit him with influencing such diverse writers as Gabriel García Márquez, Italo Calvino, Manuel Puig, and Umberto Eco. Borges's influence on postmodern literature and thought is all the more remarkable when one realizes that his entire literary output is only about five hundred pages, and that his stories rarely run more than ten or twelve pages. Indeed, as he aged, and his blindness increased, Borges's individual works shrank, with many pieces, such as "Borges and I" running three hundred words or less. Perhaps even more astonishing, however, is the way that Borges has crossed the cultural divide and is on his way to becoming not only a highly regarded writer and philosopher among scholars, but also an icon within Western popular culture.

The word "icon" comes out of a religious context, and originally meant an image or symbol of sacred significance. Icons historically held a special place of importance in the Greek Orthodox church. Over time, the meaning shifted to include people, places, or items of cultural importance. Individuals who might qualify as cultural icons are more than just famous. To be an icon, a person must be recognized by a wide number of people across the culture, and noted for his or her widespread influence. Icons, whether people, places, events, or objects, lend themselves to reproduction. They are copied, parodied, emulated, and disseminated widely across the culture. In the case of an individual person, this reproduction can include the visual image of the person; his or her ideas; his or her words; and/or events where the person was present. For example, Albert Einstein is a cultural icon. With his wild hair and quirky personality, he is instantly recognizable to most Americans. His image is readily available and his ideas color even daily life. In one extremely well-known picture, Einstein sticks out his tongue at the photographer taking the picture. The humor of the photo, coupled with the knowledge that Einstein's genius led to the creation of the

WHAT DO I READ NEXT?

- Luis Fernando Verissimo's *Borges and the Eternal Orangutans* (2004) is novel about a man called Vogelstein who admires Borges. When he goes to an Edgar Allan Poe conference in Buenos Aires and encounters a locked-room mystery, he teams up with Borges to solve the mystery. The book is both an homage to Borges and a parody at the same time.

- *The Aleph* (1949) is a collection of some of Borges's best short fictions and serves to introduce the reader to some of the writer's most enduring images and themes, including the labyrinth, mirrors, and time. The collection is still in print.

- *Labyrinths* (1962), also by Borges, is a widely available collection of Borges's stories, poems, and essays. This collection is essential for any student who wants to learn more about Borges and his writing.

- *The Name of the Rose* (1984), by Umberto Eco, is a medieval murder mystery that features a blind librarian obsessed with mirrors and labyrinths and named Jorge of Burgos. Eco's encyclopedic knowledge rivals Borges's own. Anyone interested in how Borges has been used as a literary character will enjoy this novel.

- *The Martian Chronicles* (1950) by Ray Bradbury is a collection of short and fantastic stories. Borges is reported to have asked his mother to read him stories from Bradbury after his near fatal accident, and he maintained a lifelong admiration for the American writer.

atomic bomb creates the multi-layered and complex response to the image necessary for its classification as iconic. Thus, when Americans see Einstein, they see more than just a person: they see a symbol of genius, a symbol of the great (and sometimes terrible) power of the human mind. Likewise, Shakespeare has become iconic in Western culture. His image is recognizable across

> THAT BORGES SAW HIS FUTURE SEEMS EVIDENT IN HIS WORK, AND THE IRONY OF THIS MOVEMENT— FROM BLIND LIBRARIAN TO CULTURAL ICON—WAS NOT LOST ON HIM."

national, socioeconomic, and ethnic boundaries. Moreover, his words have entered common parlance to such an extent that most people are not even aware that they are quoting Shakespeare as the words come out of their mouths.

Something similar has happened to the figure of Borges in the late twentieth- and early twenty-first centuries. Borges himself seemed to predict this in "Borges and I." However, few, if any critics, would have assigned the role of cultural icon to Borges while he was alive. In 1986, for example, in an obituary for Borges in the *New Criterion*, critic James Gardner, while comparing Borges to Italian writer Italo Calvino, wrote,

> While the recently deceased Calvino remains very much a writer of the moment, Borges, one is sad to report, has probably had his day. This is not to say that he is no longer read, nor no longer admired, since the spate of laudatory articles that his death occasioned handsomely confirmed the esteem in which he had been held internationally for a generation. And yet, he no longer means to the general literary public as much as he did only ten years ago.

It is not surprising that Gardner held this view. Who could have predicted in 1986 that an elderly blind librarian from Argentina who wrote only short poems, stories, and essays would enter the collective consciousness of Western culture to such an extent?

In retrospect, it seems very clear that Gardner was wrong. Borges's fame has continued to spread, and he means a great deal *more* to the general literary public today than he did at the time of his death. In an article in *World Literature Today*, published in 2006, critic Pablo Brescia argues that "on the twentieth anniversary of his death, the competing chorus of scholarship on Jorge Luis Borges ... seems to be never ending."

Oddly, Borges seems to have anticipated this turn in "Borges and I," as he does in several other of his short fictions. Borges implies that there are two distinct stages in the establishment of an icon. In the first place, the object or person must first be stripped of any inherent meaning in and of itself. In order for the symbolic significance of the figure to become universal across the culture, the individual personality or the characteristic individuality of the object must be erased. What remains is a recognizable shell. In the second stage, stories, events, and traits, some having their source in the facts of the individual's life and others manufactured to increase symbolic significance, begin to adhere to the shell. These stories, events, and traits serve to support the symbolic significance of the figure rather than the human being who once inhabited the shell. Whether the stories, events or traits are true or not is immaterial; they become true in their support of the icon.

For example, George Washington, another American icon, was a Virginia planter who became the commander in chief of the colonial army at the time of the American Revolution and who ultimately became the president of the United States. Did he drink tea? What time did he typically get up? What was his favorite food? None of these things matter. What existed of the physical human being who was called George Washington has long since vanished. At this point, the first step of the iconic process is complete: the erasure of the individual who was Washington and the creation of a shell to which stories, events, and objects can adhere. Thus, the story of Washington and the cherry tree, while not factual, is symbolically significant for the iconic Washington in that it emphasizes Washington's truthfulness.

Likewise, in "Borges and I," Borges begins (or continues) his ongoing maneuver of demonstrating the ways that a writer's work erases the writer himself or herself. "Borges and I" demonstrates this maneuver clearly. The poem has many autobiographical details, the specific details that make up an individual personality. For example, the narrator tells the reader that he likes "hourglasses, maps, eighteenth century typography, the taste of coffee and the prose of Stevenson." These details, however, are erased in the next sentence when the narrator reports that Borges "shares these preferences, but in a vain way that turns them into the attributes of an actor." The movement of the specific details from the internally held preferences of the narrator to the externally visible attributes of an actor demonstrates the process of erasure of the private individual and creation of the public iconic persona. Those attributes formerly associated with the individual now adhere to the shell.

As further illustration of the process, the narrator reports, "Little by little, I am giving over everything to him, though I am quite aware of his perverse custom of falsifying and magnifying things." Borges, of course, did just what his narrator accuses him of. There are countless instances of Borges changing the details of his life in various interviews and autobiographies. By doing so, he effectively nullifies himself as a human being, and begins the creation and recreation of himself as icon, an ongoing project picked up by others once Borges the person ceased to exist.

In an article for *World Literature Today*, Pablo Brescia describes an "intertextual phenomena" that he calls "literaturization." In this process, a writer other than Borges appropriates Borges's topics, images, style, ideas, and even the personhood of Borges himself by using him as a character in a story, play, or novel. Brescia examines several such usages, including two anthologies of Borges-like writing published in 1999: *Borges multiple* (*Multiple Borges*) and *Escrito sobre Borges* (*Writing about Borges*). Brescia could also have included in his discussion *Borges and the Eternal Orangutans*, a 2004 novel by Luis Fernando Verissimo that features Borges as a main character. In one of the earliest examples of Borges-as-character, Umberto Eco created the character Jorge of Burgos as the primary villain of his popular 1984 novel, *The Name of the Rose*.

Further, in 1995, Dan Halpern invited multiple writers to produce short work that used "Borges and I" as their starting point. Published as *Who's Writing This?*, the volume demonstrates how widely the iconic Borges has filtered into Western culture. In addition, literary journals regularly publish poems in the style of Borges or that allude to Borges, such as "The Blue Borges" by Terrance Hayes, appearing in the *Antioch Review*. Hayes concludes his poem thusly: "I long as Spinoza said all things long in their being to persist." In its length, style, images, allusions, and themes, "Blue Borges" pays homage to, and helps create, the iconic Borges, while it also continues to erase the man who was Borges.

There is more. Borges is not only being "literaturized," to use Brescia's coinage. His iconic stature continues to grow through the Internet. *YouTube* is a wildly popular Internet site where videos and multi-media clips are available for free access to whomever wishes to view them. The site, then, disseminates images, text, and sound quickly and freely. Not surprisingly, Borges has a home on *YouTube*. Indeed, one popular short video clip is called "Borges y yo a Go Go." In this clip, photo and films of Borges, along with manuscript pages of "Borges y yo," move across the screen while the audio track includes a recording of Borges reading "Borges y yo" with a guitar playing a tango in the background. In addition, in March of 2007, there were some eighty-six different clips of Borges present for downloading and viewing on *YouTube*. Perhaps even more astounding is that a search for the phrase "Jorge Luis Borges" on *Google* in March of 2007 produced 1,450,000 hits. Clearly, Borges holds significance for the postmodern generation of Western culture.

Near the end of "Borges and I," Borges writes, "Thus my life is a flight and I lose everything and everything belongs to oblivion, or to him." In this line, Borges captures the entire process, from person to icon. The final line, "I do not know which one of us has written this page," set off as a new paragraph, signals that the process is complete. What once was Borges is gone; what now remains is Borges. That Borges saw his future seems evident in his work, and the irony of this movement—from blind librarian to cultural icon—was not lost on him. He closes his 1964 poem, "Elegy" with these words: "Oh destiny of Borges, / perhaps no stranger than your own."

Source: Diane Andrews Henningfeld, Critical Essay on "Borges and I," in *Poetry for Students*, Gale, 2008.

Pablo Brescia

In the following essay, Brescia claims that Borges's political views and various writings about Borges have contributed to the phenomenon in which Borges's persona became something of an independent object that existed, and still exists, independently of Borges himself. Brescia then goes on to note that "Borges and I" not only acknowledges and plays with this concept but simultaneously adds to it as well.

> AS USUAL, HE WAS THE FIRST ... TO CALL FOR
> THE DEATH OF THE AUTHOR, TO UNDERSTAND THE
> AUTHOR-FUNCTION, TO BECOME A CHARACTER IN HIS
> OWN STORIES, AND TO BE IRREVERENT WITH HIM. HE
> [BORGES] BEGAN TO 'DIS-AUTHORIZE' HIMSELF AND
> BECAME, IN THE PROCESS, A LITERARY OBJECT."

Borges and I, and I, and I ...

Seven years after the centennial of his birth, and on the twentieth anniversary of his death, the competing chorus of scholarship on Jorge Luis Borges (1899–1986) seems to be never ending: new editions of his work, worldwide academic conferences, and a Center for Studies and Documentation located, until moving recently to Iowa, in a very Borgesian-sounding place, the University of Arhus in Denmark. In that chorus, the critical readings by John Updike, John Barth, Susan Sontag, Angela Carter, Julian Barnes, Italo Calvino, Antonio Tabucchi, Octavio Paz, Carlos Fuentes, and Mario Vargas Llosa, among others, are testimonials to the Argentine writer's impact on reading and writing for many contemporary authors.

However, there is an echo in those voices that goes beyond what might be written about Borges's fictions or essays on literature. I am referring to writers "writing Borges." What happens when Borges is written? Two books published in 1999, *Borges multiple: Cuentos y ensayos de cuentistas* and *Escrito sobre Borges: Catorce autores le rinden homenaje*, provide some answers. In the first section of *Borges multiple*, short stories either play with Borgesian topics—labyrinths, apocryphal texts, doubles—or introduce him or one of his characters into the story. In the second volume, well-established Argentine writers—Mempo Giardinelli, Angelica Gorodischer, and Luisa Valenzuela, among others—rewrite a Borges story of their liking to their liking, thus the *Escrito sobre Borges* title, writing not about Borges but literally over Borges, in palimpsest-like fashion.

To begin approaching this intertextual phenomenon, which we might call the "literaturization" of writers, let us look at "La entrevista"

(1979; The interview), by Argentine writer Mempo Giardinelli, and "Borges el comunista" (1977; Borges the communist), by Mexican writer Rene Aviles Fabila. Both stories engage Borges as a literary object: Giardinelli fictionalizes him to debate Borgesian poetics; Aviles Fabila subverts the political persona created by Borges's public comments. My main intent is thus to address the effects produced by texts that appropriate Borgesian poetics and politics.

Interview with the Vampire

At the beginning of "The Interview," the narrator, who is a writer and a journalist, summarizes his relationship with that "unusual old man whom I have admired, and, of course, I still hate" (Borges multiple). He had seen Borges twice before: in a restaurant and near a bank. The interview, however, happens in a nightmare that ends with vertigo and a scream. The narrator-protagonist wakes up, figures it was a bad dream, and comes to a reassuring yet disappointing conclusion: "The simple fact is nobody is ever going to ask me to interview Borges." Some of the story's narrative elements are in clear dialogue with Borgesian poetics, especially the play with time, the story-within-a-story frame, and the foreshadowing technique.

The story takes place in 2028; the narrator is eighty-one years old, and Borges is one hundred and thirty. This allusion to Borges's "eternity" elicits a smile and underlines the writer's ubiquitous figure. The timeline has another curious effect, though, since the distant future (although not so distant at the time of our reading, it is forty-nine years from the time of the writing of the story) establishes a distance for readers, perhaps making it easier to accept this Borges as a pervasive character. On the other hand, the first "real" meeting between the protagonist and Borges occurs at the restaurant around 1970–71, and the second encounter, at the bank, can be dated to 1974–75. The 1970s, a period of extreme social and political upheaval in Argentina, are the most prominent time in the story. In the real world, the real Borges turned more conservative, the military junta took over the government in 1976, and Giardinelli's story was published. In the story, this second meeting takes place, the narrator explains, "before I had left Buenos Aires when the long night began in 1976." Besides bringing to the surface the collective political situation at the time, the date makes readers equate the narrator with the real Giardi-nelli, who left the country that year, lived in Mexico until 1986, and is now back in his country. The third meeting, meanwhile, happens in the dream and corresponds to the time of the interview and the story.

These juxtapositions of times hint at another recognizable Borgesian device, the mise-en-abime structure, exemplified in "The Interview" with two stories told by the character of Borges. In one of them, he follows a writer and erases everything he writes without his victim knowing it; in the end, Borges discovers that the writer is himself.

Like the stories-within-stories frame, inlaid details figure prominently in "The Interview." In the dream, the blue suit that Borges wears when he goes out with Giardinelli is the same suit he had on when his interviewer "really" saw Borges in 1974–75; the 1970–71 tablecloth with red-and-white squares reappears in the dream when Borges and Giardinelli go into a restaurant; and, when both are at the bank, the impatient young man who is lined up behind them in the dream is the twenty-five-year-old Giardinelli. These repetitions foreshadow the inevitable yet surprising revelation: "Borges had entangled me in his spider's web, in a horrible paradox where reality was fantastic and fantasy real," the narrator realizes. Readers may wonder if it isn't the architecture of Borges's stories that causes Giardinelli's agitation at the end of the tale.

For all the protagonist's animosity and angered tone throughout, "The Interview" cannot evade a few elements of the Borgesian universe. Some are a parody in its most elementary sense of mockery (e.g., the list of critics, a mix of real people and imaginary characters who, like parasites, live off Borges); others become a parody, given that they refer to a prior literary discourse: Borges's literature. In the end, the dream becomes a nightmare and the narrator encounters his own sel[f] there are two possible endings, and the interviewer is "a capricious old man who suffers from gastritis and is determined to imagine the impossible."

El "Che" Borges

Between 1940 and 1960, the mature years of his writing, Borges made three important decisions as a citizen: he repudiated Juan Domingo Peron's rise to power; he praised the military-led "Revolucion Libertadora" that overthrew Peron in 1955; and he aligned himself with the Allies during and after World War II. From the 1960s on, the time of his international acclaim, Borges was deemed a political reactionary, a reputation fueled by countless interviews wherein he seemingly lashed out at almost anything or anybody, even though nobody bothered to find out if he was kidding or, well, being Borges.

Perhaps no other Latin American writer has been more confronted for his political views than Borges. Is there any other writer who holds the dubious distinction of having two books, Contra Borges (1978) and Anti-Borges (1999), critical of his political views? This apparent animosity could be explained in part by the fact that he went against the grain and did not sympathize with socialism like many of his contemporaries (e.g., Pablo Neruda and Julio Cortazar). In this sense, Borges might have been a revolutionary of a different sort, a "Che" of letters, fighting for the autonomy of his craft in times that called for "committed" literature. However naive this revolution may be, the books mentioned not only signal the body of criticism on Borges's political thought—although Borges himself would deny partaking of such a thing—but also make evident his importance for the relationship between politics and literature in Latin America.

Unlike the character created by Giardinelli, Borges was never a communist. That is the reason why "Borges the Communist," Aviles Fabi-la's story, creates such an oxymoronic effect. The genealogy of the tale reinforces an ironic context of reception. It first appeared in *El Machete*, a publication of the Mexican Communist Party, and was later included in Aviles Fabi-la's 1988 book, *El diccionario de los homenajes* (A dictionary of tributes). What might be considered a private joke in one context may be viewed as a curious yet careful selection of one aspect of Borges's larger-than-life legacy for Latin American writers in another. Written as a newspaper article, the story's objective style acts as a counterpoint to the amusing repercussions that a communist Borges would have had. Starting from an "as if" Borgesian framework, the results of such a contrary-to-fact situation produce the subversive outcome.

On the one hand, we find the reactions of those involved in this affair. The Argentine Communist Party supports Borges's conversion, which confirms that "historical reason" is on his side. However, he will have to follow the road that leads from the Communist Youth to the party: "The Argentine comrades are very severe on this: many years of experience and maturity are required to achieve change. For this reason, Borges, although eighty years old, shall remain in the Communist Youth ranks so as to obtain, through his study of Marxism, the necessary knowledge to be a member of the Party." The repercussions of Borges's imaginary membership in the Communist Party emphasizes the double-edged sword of irony, making the readers see through the veil of language and reinforcing the idea that politics is not the art of the possible but the art of the convenient. The Trotskyites, holders of "the Holy Grail of revolutionary purity," are still critical of Borges and accuse him of being a Stalinist, but the military junta believes that this conversion is a clear example of the freedom that reigns in Argentina, where only "extremists" are persecuted. Of course, the logical conclusion would be that "Borges will now receive the Nobel Prize in Literature, like other communist writers before him such as Neruda."

To characterize this political persona, Aviles Fabila mixes real data with imaginary actions or comments by this "born again" Borges. Throughout the story, we find references to the criticism Borges received because of his political positions, to his infamous handshake with Pinochet and equally infamous support for the Vietnam War, to his breakfast with the junta. But all this comes under a different light in the story since, in it, Borges understands that, to his customary themes (the self, time, mirrors), he will need to add dialectical materialism and class struggle. He will also need to read the classics: Marx, Engels, and Lenin.

On the surface, Aviles Fabila's story is a witty exercise about a most ironic writer. But the critical dimension of this narrative warns readers both about the dangers of blind praise and the idea of a Borges "for export" as well as the ineffectiveness of a critique that confines Borges to a ready-made ideological cast.

The Influence of Anxiety

In a time (1949) when Borges was barely beginning to be "Borges," or recognized as such, Augusto Monterroso, an early reader of his, said: "When we meet Borges, we become, in a way, ill. We are not prepared for this illness, and the restlessness that overtakes us is aggravated by not knowing if this illness will be over one day or if it will end up killing us. I suppose no greater compliment can be given to a writer. We all know similar diseases: they are called Proust, Joyce, Kafka."

The stories discussed here are examples of that "illness" that keeps leaving its mark on readers and writers. Both Giardinelli and Aviles Fabila dialogue with a canonical literary figure, but they also try to create their own space within the Latin American literary horizon. They could be experiencing Harold Bloom's "anxiety of influence." In this case, however, we might be better off speaking about the "influence of anxiety." Why? Because Latin American writers are eager to move out from the shadows of the masters. "Post-Boom" writers such as Giardinelli and Aviles Fabila did not define an agenda to achieve this distancing, but the younger generations, admirers of Borges, are confronting another major legacy of Latin America's fiction in the twentieth century: exporting magical realism. Speaking of writers, the interviewer in Giardinelli's story says: "The little fish is the one who fears the big fish; the shark never worries about the sardine."

In the case of Borges, one of the ways this process takes place is through the objectification of his figure as a writer. The modus operandi appears to be "if we cannot beat him, let's make him literature." What are the effects of this process? Giardinelli, for all his attempts at humor, attacks both what Borges represents and his veneration of the critics. Result? The narrator ends up a pawn in Borges's plot, and Giardinelli has written—what else?—a Borgesian story. Thus, we could speak of a contamination effect, derived from the strong pull of Borgesian poetics. As for Aviles Fabila's story, the invention of a contrary-to-Borges real political persona generates complexity in meaning, and we could thus refer to an ironic distancing. The sharpness of this ironic distancing seems to fade when applied to Borges, due to the open-ended quality of his works and words. But when applied to some of his supporters as well as some of his critics, that distancing makes evident the ridiculousness and rigidity of certain political and cultural institutions. There is an old joke that one of Borges's first biographers (presumably Emir Rodriguez Monegal) believed that when Borges wrote his classic "Borges and I," the "I" referred to the late Uruguayan critic.

The option exercised by Giardinelli and Aviles Fabila, to make Borges a literary fetish, makes manifest, among other things, the tension between tradition and rupture, the effects of a writer's life and works on other writers, and the shortcomings and hopes of sardines.

In the 1954 preface to the second edition of his Universal History of Iniquity, Borges declares: "I would define the Baroque as that style that deliberately exhausts (or tries to exhaust) its own possibilities, and that borders on self-caricature" (1998). Perhaps this is the Borgesian phase we are in. Borges is being used. It should come as no surprise that he anticipated this in "Borges and I," "The Other," "August 25th, 1983," and other texts. As usual, he was the first, before Roland Barthes, Michel Foucault, Giardinelli, and Aviles Fabila, to call for the death of the author, to understand the author-function, to become a character in his own stories, and to be irreverent with him. He [Borges] began to "disauthorize" himself and became, in the process, a literary object.

Legend has it that when Witold Gombrowicz left Argentina, he shouted from the rail of the ship: "Boys, you better kill Borges." Obeying that order looks more and more unlikely, since the stories discussed here are only a sample of the ever-increasing phenomenon of Borges's literaturization. I wonder if this points to one of the directions post (but not past) Borgesian fiction might take: a writing that proposes both dialogue and play, not of characters in search of an author, but of writers in a struggle with the legacy of their precursors. Borges once defined the essential condition for the survival of a book or a page: it had to be "everything for everyone" (1996). Little did he know—or, perhaps, he did suspect?—that he would continue to be "everything to everyone," and I imagine he might accept happily the idea that one of his destinies is, still, the literary page.

Source: Pablo Brescia, "Post or Past Borges? The Writer as Literary Object," in *World Literature Today*, Vol. 80, No. 5, September–October 2006, pp. 48–52.

Kane X. Faucher

In the following essay, Faucher presents a detailed textual analysis of "Borges and I." In his examination, Faucher tries to determine if the narrator is or is not Borges, and he also proposes the existence of a "meta-Borges," the "real author ... who sets the semi-fictional characters of Borges

> IF ANYTHING ELSE, BORGES' WRITING 'HAPPENS' TO THE NARRATOR AND, IF WE ARE TO BELIEVE THAT THE NARRATOR'S EXISTENCE IS DEPENDENT UPON BORGES' WRITING, THEN IT WOULD APPEAR THAT BORGES—NOT THE NARRATOR—IS THE AGENTIVE FORCE, AND THAT BORGES IS NARRATING THE NARRATOR IN NARRATING BORGES (!)."

and the narrator into motion." Faucher also looks at the many philosophical and metaphysical theories of identity that are revealed by a close reading of "Borges and I."

The Text

"Borges and I" presents its readers with a perplexing riddle: who is the author? The narrative, set in Buenos Aires, proceeds by detailing a first-person account of the narrator's feelings of detachment and resignation that the other part of him, the dominant ego or subject of the exposition, is eclipsing his own unique and honest life as a scribe of the people. The narrator speaks of a Borges as someone who is only interested in the acclaim of being a recognized author rather than having any true investment in the craft itself. It is a somewhat sorrowful account of the narrator who tells of his slow and inevitable surrender to the demands of the ego. Apart from the salient significance this story has for psychoanalytic study, we will here limit ourselves to a few overarching philosophical themes and linguistic nuances. ...

Within the fundamental question of authorship in this story, we are confronted with the implicit understanding that, yes, Borges wrote this story as is evidenced by the fact that his name appears upon the cover of the book in which the story appears. But what is curious is the first-person account of the narrator who refers to Borges as someone other, but as an other that shares a great deal of similar traits to the narrator. ... Already, the reader is called upon to incorporate two separate input spaces (narrator and Borges) and perform a blend of identity. As we will postulate, there are three possible solutions or interpretations that we will here subsume categorically. . . .

Solution 1: The Narrator Is Not Borges

In the opening lines, the framework is established that the reader is possibly dealing with two entities: a narrator and Borges. The separation of the two (id)entities by a principle of difference is textually supported by the opening disjunction of being acted upon versus not being acted upon: "The other one, the one called Borges, is the one things happens to." . . .

Is Borges as subject the progenitor of the narrator? How is one's existence dependent upon a piece of text? In colloquial speech, we could say that a writer's existence, understood as financial livelihood and acclaim, is dependent upon textual production and publication. But this cannot be the case in this instance, for the presupposition fails when we keep in mind that the narrator and Borges are (in this reading) separate entities, and it seems inconsistent to assert that someone else's writing could sustain the narrator. . . .

Moreover, in a mapping, the entire story is based on the narrator's account, and so a matter of his belief or interpretation of the event. The paradox becomes quite clear when we consider that in order for the narrator to have a belief or an interpretation, that he is acted upon, which is already contradicted in the first line of the story. If anything else, Borges' writing "happens" to the narrator and, if we are to believe that the narrator's existence is dependent upon Borges' writing, then it would appear that Borges—not the narrator—is the agentive force, and that Borges is narrating the narrator in narrating Borges (!). . . .

If we are not to commit too heavily to the idea that there is an empirical separation between this narrator and Borges, then there is cause to believe on this rather short account that an advocacy is being tendered toward a separation of being and thinking . . .

Lastly, there is a troubling line that highlights this perplexing text, a one line flourish dropped at the end of the text which we are left to ponder: "I do not know which of us has written this page." The operating words of "which" and "us" reifies the division between two separate entities, both capable of writing. The question of authorship is left to the reader

to determine—or to leave as an aporia, an open-ended text. But what we do discover is that there are too many epistemic lacunas and doubts that do not fully satisfy our demands to prove that, indeed, two separate entities exist in this story.

Solution 2: The Narrator Is Borges

This formulation would strike the reader as more sensible, for even when considering fictional texts that utilize fictional characters, they are being "narrated" into existence by an author who wrote the book. It is only by our suspense of disbelief that we attribute any degree of reality to the characters as independent speakers. . . .

In a brief list of textual clues given throughout this text, we learn that if Borges is the narrator, Borges has a relationship with himself that is not hostile, Borges justifies his own life by writing, Borges gives everything to Borges (or oblivion), Borges falsifies and magnifies himself, Borges once attempted an escape from Borges, and one day Borges will perish in Borges. These are troubling propositions, but they follow from a declaration that the narrator is Borges. We may not wish to remain committed to this reading either on this basis.

More troubling still is the notion that Borges not only resides in himself, but that he is not himself (where the narrator claims that he is not in Borges, but will one day perish in him). This sets up a logical contradiction where Borges both is and is not. Temporally speaking, we could assert this as in "I am now, and I will one day (in death) no longer be." However, the added clause problematizes even this explanation, for it is implied that the narrator (who is Borges) will perish in Borges, and will survive as a kind of residual presence in Borges. This is to say that Borges, if he is also the narrator, will be both alive and dead at the same time. The reader must now settle the disjunction of Borges or not-Borges, and the riddle of authorship. . . .

Are we to infer that in some bizarre postulation that Borges somehow represents the narrator who represents Borges (who, in turn, represents the narrator in a vicious circle)? This would, indeed, set up a circular paradox, one that is linked to the idea of naming and identity. On this point, we could perhaps just hang up the entire operation and withdraw, claiming that the text is an irresolvable paradox and nothing more, but speculation drives us on to quest further for some sort of reasonable explanation. In order to do this, we may require taking our leave of reasonable explanation and going forth into uncharted terrain. We have yet to consider the Borges behind the curtain, the progenitor of this discourse. This will unduly complicate matters, but it is necessary if we are to be thorough in our mapping. Our next possible solution will perhaps be as equally bizarre as the text that inspired it.

Solution 3: Meta-Borges

... [T]he meta-Borges is the real author that lurks behind the text, who sets the semi-fictional characters of Borges and narrator into motion. These are meant to be extensions or projections of the real Borges and how he reflects upon himself. As a self-reflexive critique, artfully done through figural representation, he utilizes the innovative strategy of textually abstracting these properties of himself as if they were two distinct entities rather than two attributes of himself. ... Using the narrator as the mouth-piece, meta-Borges comments on the more repugnant features of his being, shedding light upon his occasional inauthenticity, but also salvaging himself with the use of the narrator to whom we feel a kind of pity. The narrator is constrained, and there is a direct pathos that is evoked, that this "false Borges" is some kind of tyrannical force that keeps the narrator in bondage, as evidenced by the narrator's lack of free will in having to surrender everything to Borges the ego. And no doubt, in the real writer's life, such constraints exist in the mind: control of subject matter, use of hyperbole (as a means of distorting, magnifying and falsifying real events), editing of content, etc. The narrator is set up as a journalist and martyr, for he both reports back to Borges all that he sees and experiences, and sacrifices his whole "being" to an enterprise that will most likely not justify or save him. The narrator is aware of his own mortality, destined that his utility will one day be at an end. And though the narrator has made attempts to flee the constraints of being in Borges, these have all come to naught, and he still holds out the vague hope that he will be justified through Borges writing. ...

Essentially, this story boils down to an issue of time and the ego. Through an enumeration of pronoun references, we learn very little aside from the fact that the references to the narrator and Borges are roughly equal in number, and that there are two special instances when they are united by "ours" and "us" to denote a shared situation....

The narrator is uncertain whether he has an I to speak of, and whether this notion of an I is inherently pernicious seeing how Borges' strong sense of I has led to so many distortions and a disconnection from the people. The ego drives the work, not honesty. Not to say that all the pages are invalid, as the narrator charitably offers, but that they become increasingly tainted by an encroaching egotist view that desires popularity, honours, and acclaim. How do we deal with the death of the narrator? What will become of this attribute of meta-Borges? When the narrator perishes in Borges, leaving only an "instant" of himself behind as a kind of surviving residue, what remains will simply be the narrating function (empty and devoid of true authentic substance). ...

Authorship

Who is writing the story? This question may in the final analysis appear moot, for the "moral" of this parable is that there is no "I" in the written word; the author does not own the work, for the intellectual property is transferred to the ages. To assert the "I, author" is futile, as the narrator on occasion alludes. But are we getting the whole account? The narrator's confession is mediated through Borges the writer's writing, and so could prove to be a distortion—and we already know that the narrator is not free to express himself, that he is in thralldom to Borges who owns all of the narrator's thoughts.

Meta-Borges is thoroughly dissatisfied with what he has become. In parable form he has related his self-dissatisfaction that is in the spirit of irony: we would expect that the accomplished and recognized writer has succeeded in his tasks and can now experience the joy of his acclaim. But for meta-Borges, this prospect is the source of a great melancholy, and hence this parable. ...

Source: Kane X. Faucher, "The Decompression of Meta-Borges in 'Borges and I,'" in *Variaciones Borges*, Vol. 17, January 2004, pp. 159–86.

Eric Ormsby

In the following excerpted passages, Ormsby remarks that the "nullification of personal identity" found throughout Borges's writing appears "side by side with a sort of wonder at the profusion of selves even the most ordinary life entails." This, of course, is particularly evident in "Borges and I."

Throughout the essay, Ormsby attempts to interpret this theme by placing it within the context of biographical facts and anecdotes about the author, discussing several of Borges's other works along the way.

It was ironic of fate, though perhaps predictable, to allow Jorge Luis Borges to develop over a long life into his own Doppelgänger. In a 1922 essay entitled "The Nothingness of Personality," Borges asserted that "the self does not exist." Half-a-century later, an international personality laden with acclaim, he had to depend on wry, self-deprecating quips to safeguard his precious inner nullity. "*Yo no soy yo*" ("I am not I"), wrote Juan Ramón Jiménez; this was a proposition that Borges not only endorsed but also made a fundamental axiom of his oeuvre. In his story "The Zahir," written in the 1940s, he could state, "I am still, albeit only partially, Borges," and in "Limits," a poem from the 1964 collection aptly entitled *The Self and the Other*, he ended with the line (as translated by Alastair Reid), "Space, time, and Borges now are leaving me." By 1980, however, to an interviewer who said, "Everyone sitting in this audience wants to know Jorge Luis Borges," he would reply, "I wish I did. I am sick and tired of him." On the lecture circuit, Borges, playing Sancho Panza to his own Quixote, perfected the sardonic stratagems that would keep his huge prestige at bay. Not fortuitously perhaps, his renown grew as, after 1955, his final blindness deepened: fragile and vaguely Chaplinesque in his rumpled linen suit, he emanated a prophetic aura, a shy Tiresias enamored of the tango.

It had not always been thus. The prim and diffident mama's boy whose idea of a date, well into middle age, was to bring a girl home to sit dumbfounded before his overpowering dowager of a mother while she rehearsed the martial glories of "Georgie's" military forebears; the indolent librarian for whom a day of work at the Miguel Cané Municipal Library meant slipping off into some secluded nook to study works by Léon Bloy, Paul Claudel, or Edward Gibbon (a combustible ménage à trois!); the awkward intellectual so self-conscious that he could appear in public only by hunching down behind the lectern while a friend read his words to the audience— all these tentative and inchoate identities (along with many others) coalesced to fabricate "Borges," that self-shaped golem of audacious erudition who accompanied, and often eclipsed, Borges

> IN UNEXPECTED MOMENTS ON A COLLEGE STAGE OR ON SOME TALK SHOW, THE BORGESIAN ORACLE WOULD FALL SILENT, AND A PERSONAGE OF SLY, CALM, MISCHIEVOUS, AND YET GENTLE DEMEANOR WOULD PEER FORTH FROM HIS SIGHTLESS EYES."

himself on the triumphal peregrinations of his last three decades.

If the nullification of personal identity exists in his work side by side with a sort of wonder at the profusion of selves even the most ordinary life entails, this must be viewed in the context of Borges's larger obsessions. For he was haunted by infinitude. A horrified fascination with the limitless in space and in time animates all his finest works. The horror arises not because of immeasurable magnitude as such, but because of the fact that the unbounded is infinitely divisible. This is why Borges returns so frequently in essays and fictions to the ancient paradox of Achilles and the tortoise. For Borges, infinity is always serial; it demands replication *ad infinitum*. One of his favorite figures for infinitude is the mirror image, that vertiginous repetition of the same mute yet glimmering reflection. Hence, too, his related horror of mirrors: "I have been horrified before all mirrors," he wrote in the poem "The Mirrors": "I look on them as infinite, elemental / fulfillers of a very ancient pact / to multiply the world."

In "Averroës' Search" the narrator speaks of the "dread of the grossly infinite," by which he means "mere space, mere matter." The Borgesian infinite, by contrast, is filled, and its images are all ultimately double. Every identity, like the commonplace but magical coin in "The Zahir," possesses its obverse: each side both negates and reaffirms the other.

The library, whether the Library of Babel in his great "fiction" of the same name or the National Library of Argentina where Borges served as director for some eighteen years, is a fitting metaphor for infinitude. The fact that Borges was almost completely blind during his tenure as national librarian must have strengthened his sense of boundlessness. Anyone who has wandered in a large library at night when all the lights are out will appreciate the eerie sensation of limitlessness; the books on serried shelves, each foreshadowing its neighbor, appear to extend into endlessness, and to perceive this purely by touch must be doubly persuasive. In his magnificent "Poem of the Gifts," Borges wrote, "Aimlessly, endlessly, I trace the confines,/ high and profound, of this blind library."

Borges's two predecessors as national librarian had both been blind as well; this weird coincidence led him to identify with the more distinguished of them, Paul Groussac, and to muse on whether their identities were not after all interchangeable. The sharpened sense of recurrence, the fixed conviction that nothing is truly new, the awareness of fate as a player on a field of infinite yet starkly delimited possibilities, give a claustrophobic cast to Borges's most powerful fantasies. Small wonder that one of his favorite lines from Shakespeare is Hamlet's "I could be bounded in a nutshell, and count myself a king of infinite space, were it not that I have bad dreams!" And it is this pinched infinitude, if I may so put it, that ultimately makes of Borges, for all his fabled brevity, an epic writer. . . .

Borges wrote in the prologue to his 1975 collection of poems, *The Unending Rose*, that "verse should have two obligations: to communicate a precise instance and to touch us physically, as the presence of the sea does." Lovers of Borges's prose, especially of the incomparable stories in *Fictions* (1944) and *The Aleph* (1949), tend to dismiss his poetry; and yet, Borges saw himself, and with justice, first and foremost as a poet. An oddity about Borges, one of several, lies in the fact that his stories are many-layered and densely allusive while his verse by and large is plain and univocal. The demonic Borges penned the prose but in the poetry, Borges— not "Borges" in all his sly, Protean guises, but quotidian, all-too-human Jorge Luis—spoke in his soft but unmistakable individual voice.

Borges was probably too intelligent to become a great poet, most of whom seem to have a certain saving stupidity in abundant supply. He approvingly quotes a line by his compatriot, the often marvelous poet Leopoldo Lugones: "*Iba el silencio andando como un largo lebrel*" ("Silence was moving like a long greyhound"). The simile is slightly comical, and yet, as Borges recognized,

the verse has a curious magic that arises not only from its intrinsic music, but also from its very strangeness. Despite the profound strangeness of his own imagination, Borges rarely captured such effects in verse. He usually does "communicate a precise instance," but he almost never manages to "touch us physically."

In the Viking *Selected Poems*, beautifully assembled by Alexander Coleman, we can, however, appreciate Borges's true strengths as a poet. Though he set out to become the "poet of Buenos Aires," Borges mainly succeeded as a poet, it seems to me, in the quite honorable but currently unfashionable tradition exemplified in English by such authors as Kipling, Stevenson, Belloc, and Chesterton; this is the tradition which T. S. Eliot, somewhat sniffily, referred to as "verse" as opposed to "poetry." If one thinks of Borges as a poet in this tradition—as, that is, an English poet who happened to write in Spanish—it is easier to appreciate his poetic achievement. Borges the poet suffers when set beside Lorca (whom he detested as a "professional Andalusian") or Neruda, or such brilliant compatriots as Lugones or Enrique Banchs, not because he necessarily possessed lesser gifts, but because he chose to write within an alien, and sharply circumscribed, tradition.

Borges excelled particularly in such forms as the ballad. The best of these is probably "The Golem." The version in the new edition, by Alan S. Trueblood, captures its playful mood (though not its mystery) rather well:

> That cabbalist who played at being God
> gave his spacey offspring the nickname Golem.
> (In a learned passage of his volume,
> these truths have been conveyed to us by
>   Scholem.)

In a 1968 recording of Borges reading his poems, he comments that he and his one-time collaborator Adolfo Bioy Casares consider this the best poem he has ever "perpetrated," and when he reads "The Golem," one understands why. What Borges was attempting in this and other such poems was not to create radical imagery or startling phrases but rather, with a maximum of craft and self-effacement, to tap into the age-old and immemorial sources of balladry. In Borges's soft yet distinct articulation of the poem, the listener senses his awareness of the old Scots Border ballads, of the German ballad tradition, of the medieval Spanish *coplas.*

Despite his rather childish glee in the rhyme *Golem/Scholem* (he uses it twice), Borges demonstrates that one side of him—one Borges, as it were—would have liked nothing better than to meld into some primordial and anonymous tradition within which he would be indistinguishable from his fellows. Indeed, in his celebrated "Borges and I," he notes that "good writing belongs to no one in particular, not even to my other, but rather to language and tradition." . . .

There was after all something of the *exemplum*, if not exactly the saint, in Borges. In unexpected moments on a college stage or on some talk show, the Borgesian oracle would fall silent, and a personage of sly, calm, mischievous, and yet gentle demeanor would peer forth from his sightless eyes. Anecdotes abound; I give only one example from the large (and growing) literature. On his first visit to the desert in North Africa, Borges is seen sifting sand grains through his fingers and, when asked what he is doing, replies, "I am rearranging the Sahara." Such tales, whimsical, a bit sardonic, cryptic even, resemble the tales of the ancient philosophers as much as the tales of the Hasidim (a sect Borges identified with). Except for Kafka, no other modern writer has become as emblematic of himself and his own curious world as Borges has.

How extraordinary that so many-selved, so ultimately vaporous, a personage as Borges, or "Borges," should come to play this role. What other modern author was routinely quizzed for his views on time and memory, the enigma of personality, the possibility of an afterlife and personal immortality, among other ponderous topics, as was Borges? He cheerfully declared that he held no belief in an afterlife and that he personally welcomed the inevitable oblivion that would engulf his own name, as if extinction alone offered an escape from the claustrophobia of infinitude. "No one is someone," he wrote in "The Immortal," "a single immortal man is all men. Like Cornelius Agrippa, I am god, hero, philosopher, demon, and world—which is a long-winded way of saying that *I am not*." Dignified despite his dishevelment, his crumpled fedora in one hand, his inquisitive white cane in the other, Señor Borges, our improbable psychopomp, shows us the way into unanimous night.

Source: Eric Ormsby, "Jorge Luis Borges & the Plural I," in *New Criterion*, Vol. 18, No. 3, November 1999, 13 pp.

SOURCES

Bell-Villada, Gene H., *Borges and His Fiction: A Guide to his Mind and Art*, revised edition, University of Austin Press, 1999, pp. 247–54.

Borges, Jorge Luis, "Borges and I," in *Labyrinths*, edited by Donald A. Yates and James E. Irby, translated by James E. Irby, New Directions Publishing, 1964, pp. 246–47.

———, "Elegy," in *Labyrinths*, edited by Donald A. Yates and James E. Irby, translated by James E. Irby, New Directions Publishing, 1964, p. 251.

Brescia, Pablo, "Post or Past Borges? The Writer as Literary Object," in *World Literature Today*, Vol. 80, No. 5, September-October 2006, pp. 48–52.

Cohen, J. M., *Borges*, Oliver & Boyd, 1973, p. 1.

Faucher, Kane X., "The Decompression of Meta-Borges in 'Borges and I,'" in *Variaciones Borges*, Vol. 17, January 2004, p. 159.

Gardner, James, "Jorge Luis Borges, 1899–1986," in the *New Criterion*, Vol. 10, No. 2, October 1986, pp. 16–24.

Hayes, Terrance, "The Blue Borges," in the *Antioch Review*, Vol. 62, No. 1, Winter 2004, pp. 96–7.

Monegal, Emir Rodríguez, *Jorge Luis Borges: A Literary Biography*, E.P. Dutton, 1978, p. 439.

Ogden, Thomas H., "Borges and the Art of Mourning," in *Psychoanalytic Dialogues*, Vol. 10, No.1, 2000, pp. 65–88.

Ormsby, Eric, "Jorge Luis Borges & the Plural I," in the *New Criterion*, Vol. 18, No. 3, November 1999.

Venegas, José Luis, "Eliot, Borges, Tradition, and Irony," in *Symposium*, Vol. 59, No. 4, Winter 2006, p. 237.

Williamson, Edwin, *Borges: A Life*, Viking, 2004, p. 338.

Yates, Donald A., "Behind 'Borges and I,'" in *Modern Fiction Studies*, Vol. 19, No. 3, Autumn 1973, p. 318.

FURTHER READING

Borges, Jorge Luis, *Ficciones*, Grove Press, 1969.
  A collection of some of Borges's most famous stories including "Pierre Menard, Author of the *Quixote*," "Three Versions of Judas," and "Death and the Compass."

———, *Selected Poems*, edited by Alexander Coleman, Penguin, 2000.
  This collection contains some of Borges's best-known works, including the full text of "Borges and I" in a translation that is not as

well known as the Irby translation quoted in this entry. What is most interesting in this book is the diversity of translators. Indeed, students interested in Borges can profitably compare the work of several different translators here.

Halpern, Dan, *Who's Writing This?*, Ecco Press, 1995.
In 1995, Dan Halpern asked assorted writers to create a piece of writing in response to "Borges and I." He asked that individual pieces be of the same length as "Borges and I," and that the writers use Borges as their starting point. This book is a collection of those responses.

Strathern, Paul, *Borges in 90 Minutes*, Ivan R. Dee, 2006.
Strathern's introduction to Borges is an ideal place for a student to begin learning about the great writer. The book is accessible, and includes a good annotated bibliography.

Conversation with a Stone

WISŁAWA SZYMBORSKA

1962

"Conversation with a Stone" is one of the most widely read poems by 1996 Nobel Prize winner Wisława Szymborska. Published in 1962 in a collection called *Salt*, the poem is one of her earlier works. But it is often seen as a strong example of Szymborska's resistance to political and social ideologies, her accessible language, questioning poetic style and her detached lyric voice. Szymborska enjoys wild popularity in her native Poland.

The idea of the self confronting the external world is played out in "Conversation with a Stone" by means of an imaginary dialogue between the speaker of the poem and a stone. The speaker knocks on the stone's door and asks the stone to see inside of it, and the stone refuses. Essentially, the speaker represents the human desire to know each detail of the world around us, and the stone represents the impossibility of knowing. For the stone, we find, has no door.

"Conversation with a Stone" appears in Stanizław Barańczak and Clare Cavanagh's 1995 award-winning translation of Szymborska, *View with a Grain of Sand*, published by Harcourt Brace & Company.

AUTHOR BIOGRAPHY

Szymborska was born on July 2, 1923 in a town in western Poland called Bnin (now Kornick.) Her family moved to Kracόw in 1931, and

Wisława Szymborska (*Photograph by Filip Miller. AP Images. Reproduced by permission*)

Szymborska has remained there since—throughout the occupation of Poland during World War II and under the Soviet Communist state that controlled Poland until the mid-1980's. Much of her poetry reflects on the pain and political oppression of those years.

Szymborska studied literature and sociology at the Jagiellonian University from 1945 to 1948. She made her literary debut in 1945 with her poem "Szukam Slowa" ("Searching for a Word"), published in the daily *Dziennik Polski*.

Dlatego żyjemy ("That's What We Live For"), Szymborska's first collection of poems, appeared in 1952. It consisted of a highly revised version of a manuscript she had submitted four years earlier that had been rejected on the basis of being insufficiently socialist. Her second collection, *Pytania zadawane sobie* ("Questions Put to Myself"), was published in 1954. These earliest two books are often dismissed as mediocre attempts to conform to socialist realism, the officially approved literary style of Poland's Communist regime, and Szymborska herself has since rejected these collections. In fact, poems from neither of these collections are included in the most widely read English translation of her

selected poems, *A View with a Grain of Sand* (1995), translated by Stanisław Barańczak and Clare Cavanagh.

Szymborska joined the Communist Party in 1952 out of genuine ideological commitment. In a 1996 interview with the *Los Angeles Times*, she said: "I really wanted to save humanity, but I chose the worst possible way. I did it out of love for mankind. Then I came to understand that you should not love mankind, but rather like [individual] people." Szymborska remained in the party much longer than most of her fellow writers, who left in the mid-1950's, finally defecting in 1966 as a gesture of protest against reprisals raised against the prominent philosopher Leszek Kotakowska.

In 1957, when censorship had loosened its stronghold in Poland, Szymborska released her third collection of poems, *Wolanie do Yeti* ("Calling out to Yeti"). This collection is considered the beginning mark of Szymborska's true poetic intentions. Underlying its poems is a running critique of Stalinism, and by extension, any collective ideologies.

"Conversation with a Stone" appeared in the author's fourth volume, called *Sól* ("Salt," 1962). The poem is her most widely anthologized, perhaps because it embodies her method of questioning the world around her.

Szymborska has since published eleven volumes of poetry. Her poems have been translated (and published in book form) in English, German, Swedish, Italian, Danish, Hebrew, Hungarian, Czech, Slovakian, Serbo-Croatian, Romanian, Bulgarian and other languages. They have also been published in many foreign anthologies of Polish poetry.

In 1996, Szymborska was awarded the Nobel Prize in Literature. She is also the Goethe Prize winner (1991) and Herder Prize winner (1995). She has a degree of Honorary Doctor of Letters from Poznan University (1995). In 1996, she received the Polish PEN Club prize.

POEM SUMMARY

Stanza 1

In one sense, the title, "Conversation with a Stone," neatly describes the plot of the poem itself. However, it is also somewhat ironic in that, while there are two voices in the poem, the poem's speaker seems to remain deaf to the meaning of the stone's words throughout much of the poem.

In the first stanza, the speaker of "Conversation with a Stone" repeatedly knocks at the front door of a stone. This speaker seems to see herself as innocent or insignificant, which is implied by the repeated phrase: "It's only me." She seems to feel justified in her desire to enter the stone. Indeed, the phrase "have a look around" seems innocent enough. But the speaker's strong desire to possess a complete knowledge of the stone is indicated by the phrase "breathe my fill," which indicates the wish to procure something from the stone for her own gratification.

Stanza 2

The voice of the stone replies in the second stanza. This signals that the poem is not merely a speaker's meditation on an inanimate stone, but that an actual dialogue will take place. The stone denies the speaker entrance, noting the physical impossibilities of the request. This denial serves to dampen the lightheartedness of the first stanza.

Stanza 3

In the third stanza, after the first two lines of the poem are repeated, the speaker continues her part of the dialogue. Again, the speaker paints her mission as innocent, using the word "pure" to signify her lack of ulterior motives. However, she not only insults the stone's dignity by ignoring his resistance to her entry, but she then hurries him, citing her mortality in relation to the stone's immortality. The use of the word "should" in the last line is significant in that it implies that, if the stone were just, it would comply with her wishes (out of pity for her mortal state) and that the speaker is under the presumption that she and the stone exist on the same planes of meaning.

Stanza 4

The stone however, is not shaken by the speaker's insinuations. Its rebuttal of the speaker is harsher here than in the second stanza, as though it is tiring of her persistence. To the stone, the speaker's assumption that it "should" be touched is laughable.

Stanza 5

After the refrain of "I knock at the stone's front door. / 'It's only me, let me come in,'" the speaker again attempts to offer persuasive reasons as to why she should be allowed to enter. The speaker's suggestion that the stone's beauty is "in vain" because it does not share it with the rest of the world is undeniably self-centered. She seems to see herself as speaking from a place higher in the natural hierarchy when she taunts the stone, urging it to "admit" what she supposes it does not know.

Stanza 6

In the sixth stanza, the stone delivers the first of several of its seeming contradictions. For in terms of human logic, something that is "great and empty" would necessarily have room. However, the stone reasserts that the speaker will "never know" it. The stone seems to be implying that there is no use arguing with it.

Stanza 7

Nevertheless, the speaker continues to argue that she ought to be allowed entrance. Because of her refusal to simply listen to the fact that the stone does not want her to enter, it seems that the speaker has come up with reasons in human terms of why it might not want her to visit. She denies that she will set up camp inside the stone; she will not be one of those guests who seem to stay forever. Also, she essentially declares that she is not a thief, as if the stone is afraid that she will steal from it. However, in presenting the stone with this mundane reasoning, she reveals her deafness to the stone's voice more than ever.

Stanza 8

Continuing with this line of thought, the speaker assures the stone that, by leaving "empty-handed," she will not be able to prove that she has entered the stone. Furthermore, "no one will believe" she has done so because all she will have to show for it is her "words."

Stanza 9

The ninth stanza contains what is perhaps the stone's most poignant reply of the poem. The stone has essentially leveled the notion of natural hierarchy by positing that it possesses a sense that a human cannot. The stone makes clear that its existence is so vastly different from the speaker's that its way of being cannot even be imagined. The stone also calls into question the power of imagination, which humans tend to hold in high regard. For even with the "all-seeing" eyes of a god, the stone's sense of being will still be unreachably remote from human existence.

Stanza 10

In the following stanza, the speaker remains unmoved by the stone's words. She persists in asking to be let in, often using phrases identical to, or almost identical to, those she has used before.

Stanza 11

As in stanza four, laughter strikes the stone as the appropriate response to the speaker's ignorance in stanza eleven. Again, the difference between the stone's existence and that of the speaker is highlighted by the stone's contradiction. It is untroubled by the fact that it laughs without knowing how. In fact, it is this very confidence in and acceptance of contradiction that makes the stone's voice resonate so powerfully.

Stanza 12

The speaker responds by once again knocking at the stone's door and repeating: "It's only me, let me come in." It is as if she has run out of excuses. Rather than engaging in fair argument, she falls back, in a childlike manner, to merely restating her desire, almost as if she were begging.

Stanza 13

In the last line of the poem (the only one-line stanza throughout), the stone simply replies: "I don't have a door." Both the speaker and the stone seem to have worn themselves out by their inability to communicate. The poem ends at an impasse, nothing has actually changed or happened.

THEMES

The Other

As Szymborska's speaker in "Conversation with a Stone" tries to persuade the stone to allow her to enter it, she is confronted with its complete foreignness. Not only does the stone cite the impossibility of allowing her to physically enter ("Even if you break me to pieces, / we'll all still be closed"), it seems to work on a whole different plain of logic and existence ("'Great and empty [are my insides], true enough,' says the stone, / 'but there isn't any room.'" Within the human

TOPICS FOR FURTHER STUDY

- Pick an inanimate object that interests you and write down an imagined conversation with it. What "naive questions" would you ask of it? What would its answers signify? Consider what the implications of that dialogue are in more abstract political terms. Then, using the same themes of the conversation in your first dialogue, write another between two political or religious figures.

- Research various totalitarian states of the twentieth century. How has the world changed or not changed in reaction to these states in the past twenty years? In an essay, connect your ideas with Szymborska's idea that "not knowing" is the responsibility of any political, cultural, scientific or literary thinker.

- Consider various debates of Postmodernist theory, some of which lament the loss of an age of truth and some of which embrace the inclusiveness and plurality of voices in postmodern culture. Comment on how one group's objective truth might become another group's source of oppression. Do you feel that objective truth is real and attainable? Break your class into two sides for a debate on this question.

- Poland has had a tumultuous history involving invasions, revolutions, and significant bloodshed. Research Poland's history and consider the fact that Poland has one of the most vibrant literary cultures and one of the highest rates of poetry readership in the world today. Then, think of a time when you were treated unfairly by a force or authority larger or more powerful than yourself. Write a lyric poem about that time or incident.

system of reasoning, if something can be said to have an inside, then it should be possible to enter that inside. If something has great and empty insides it can be said to be roomy. The speaker lacks a certain "sense of taking part" that the stone presumably has. The tendency to view humans as the top of the natural hierarchy is upset here by the fact that a stone possesses a quality that the human speaker cannot comprehend. This makes the stone, the other (i.e., any person or thing outside our normal realm that we cannot understand), even more mysterious. The stone serves as a metaphor for all that is incomprehensible to us that we might wish to learn about.

In historical and literary theory, the concept of "the other" has most often been used to designate how a dominant, particularly an imperialist, culture views other cultures. Dominant cultures tend to see others both as inferior and as exotic simply because the former do not understand the latter. Dominant cultures have often invaded other cultures in order to study (often in ways causing suffering for those being studied) and exploit under the guise of seeking knowledge and truth. Echoes of the rhetoric of the imperialist view of "the other" reverberate throughout "Conversation with a Stone."

Szymborska seems to be confronting here how humans are to deal with the other. It is natural to be curious about the other, as the speaker in the poem is about the stone. But Szymborska submits that our curiosity does not justify invasion. The borders and wishes of "the other" may be sought, but they must be respected.

The Naive Question

It is often presumed that the quest for knowledge and truth are inherently noble. It is also often presumed that, while humans certainly don't know everything, there are some authoritative facts out there. Szymborska would disagree with both of these presumptions. Wary of totalitarian ideologies, Szymborska submits that knowledge is never set, and must constantly be questioned and revised. However, one must go about seeking knowledge cautiously, as so often in human history, knowledge has been gained only at the expense of vast human suffering.

In her writing, her method of conducting these discoveries of new knowledge has come to be known as naive questioning. In her poem, "The Century's Decline," she writes:

> 'How should we live?' someone asked me in
>   a letter.
> I had meant to ask him
> the same question.
>
> Again, and as ever,
> as may be seen above,

the most pressing questions
are naive ones.

The method involves confronting each object, person, or idea one encounters without assumptions of prior knowledge. Or, as Szymborska has done in many of her poems, the naive question is put to some culturally dogmatic opinion, exposing, through her interrogation, either its insufficiency or its error.

In "Conversation with a Stone," Szymborska confronts the very idea of the human desire to gain knowledge. The subtext of the poem seems to ask, How does one recognize the other's border? When is curiosity about another innocent, and when does it offend? How does one deal with the incomprehensibility of the other? Humans face these questions everyday and unfortunately, as history shows, the human tendency is to view what it cannot understand as inferior. Szymborska, dissatisfied with this tendency, sets out to examine the ways in which knowledge is acquired through human-to-nature and human-to-human interactions through looking at something as seemingly simple as a stone.

Totalitarianism

Modern regimes in which the state regulates nearly every aspect of public and private behavior are known as totalitarian. These regimes maintain their political power by means of a secret police force, propaganda disseminated through the state controlled mass media, and the regulation and restriction of free discussion and criticism.

Szymborska came of age as a writer under a totalitarian state and even participated in it as a party member. It would take her some years before she realized the immense dangers of limiting free speech and enforcing ideologies on groups of people. However, when this realization did come it had a profound affect on Szymborska's views and writing. Her mistrust of political ideologies and suspicion of all generalities has led her to question any and all accepted cultural, social, or political dogma. She now strives to examine each individual person, object, or idea on its own merits rather than resorting to preconceived notions of political or ideological correctness.

For Szymborska, there can be no generalizations of meaning. A naive question must be put to each and every idea. It is this resistance to generalizations that necessitates a conversation with a stone.

STYLE

Lyric Poetry

Lyric poems are short poems with a single speaker who speaks directly to the reader (as opposed to the more public forms of epic and dramatic poetry). The subject of the poem is not usually a story that is told but rather an expression of the evolution of complex thoughts or feeling. Put simply, lyric poems involve a single voice working out an idea through language.

As Clare Cavanagh notes, in her essay "Poetry and Ideology: The Example of Szymborska," in the last decades lyric poetry has come under attack because "It [supposedly] privileges personal voice over postmodern textuality; it seeks to circumvent history through attention to aesthetic form; it turns its back on the public realm in its quest for private truths." It is difficult to imagine that Szymborska would view any of these criticisms, especially the last, as particularly bad things. The individual viewpoint takes precedence in all of her poems as a direct result of her suspicion of and resistance to public ideologies. The form therefore suits her task.

Szymborska's form of the lyric poem differs only from the traditional form in that her poems do not strike the reader as autobiographical. They involve an individual speaker addressing a reader, but it seems in most of Szymborska's poems that a created persona is speaking. By creating a persona, she is establishes an ironic distance between herself and the speaker who supposedly represents herself. It's as if she wants to show that she does not hold even herself beyond questioning. Certainly this is the case in "Conversation with a Stone." Szymborska would seem to be ambivalent toward her speaker. On one hand the speaker's curiosity, her "mortality," draws sympathy, but the speaker obviously pushes the stone too far in her quest for knowledge. It is almost as if, for Szymborska, there is a voice behind the lyric speaker of the poem saying "Look at yourself! Look how you offend. Even while you try to learn, you are full of presumption." Her lyric speakers act as vehicles for self-meditation, both for Szymborska and for readers.

Common Diction

As noted above, Szymborska's poems are lyrical. Like many modern Polish poets, she employs a common, everyday diction in her poetry. This is fitting, given that most often her subject is the common, everyday person/object/idea. In "Conversation with a Stone," the speaker and the stone use the type of language that two friends might use at a cafe; there is nothing lofty or obscure in their words. In fact, the phrase "it's only me, let me come in," which is repeated throughout the poem, resonates with readers as something they might say at the door of any ordinary acquaintance. By way of this technique, the reader is brought into the poem because she can identify with its tone and language. It is therefore easier to place herself in the shoes of either the speaker or the stone which in turn allows her to more fully grasp the meaning of the conversation.

There is more to this common diction, however, than matching one's tone to one's subject matter or drawing the reader in. Edward Hirsh notes in his essay "After End of the World," "The radical accessibility of contemporary Polish poetry has sometimes bewildered advanced American readers who often miss the point that for these poets stylistic clarity is a form of ethics. One might say that the very clarity of this poetry is a response to ideological obfuscations, political double-talk." For Szymborska, a lack of clarity signals deception. That is partly why she chooses to make questions in her poems naive—she fears that any obscure language might confuse and thus deceive the reader.

Repetition

Szymborska repeats the first two lines of "Conversation with a Stone" ("I knock at the stone's front door. / 'It's only me, let me come in'") five times following their initial appearance. It is likely that she uses this device of repetition (also known as anaphora) to invoke the feeling of incantation. Incantation is a form of repetitious chanting deemed to have magical or moving power and is often associated with strong spiritual feeling. Perhaps the incantatory repetition is used by the speaker to persuade the stone of her primal desire to enter, as well as to cast a spell over the stone which might cause it to change its mind and allow her to enter.

Free Verse

Szymborska's poems in both the original Polish and English translations are in the form of unrhymed free verse. Free verse is a term for the style of poems that do not use formal meter or rhyme. The use of repetition, symmetry, alliterative sounds, near or half rhyme and varying line lengths are just a few of the devices used in free verse poems which make them recognizable as poems.

Free verse is suitable to the tone and task of "Conversation with a Stone." The imposition of formal poetic structure might serve to undermine the naturalness of the dialogue between the speaker and the stone. For, one's every day conversational tone does not come out fully crafted and metered. Formal meter and rhymed verse tends to lend the feeling of a crafted song to the reader. Szymborska is not, however, setting forth what she has already established; she is not singing what she knows for certain. Rather, she is depicting a struggle for understanding between two entities. She shows this struggle through the use of repetition, as discussed above. Also, the varying lengths of the lines serve to show changes in the moods of the speaker and the stone, as well as shifts between efforts at engagement in the conversation and attempts to pull away from it.

HISTORICAL CONTEXT

Pre-World War II Romanticism

Before World War II, much of Polish poetry could be classified as Romantic, meaning that it stressed emotion as a source of aesthetic experience and placed much emphasis on the awe experienced before the sublimity of nature and the world. Romanticism also legitimized the individual imagination in literature, giving credence to the lyric voice as a critical authority. However the inevitability of natural and historical progress was also stressed. Poets such as Julian Tuwim and Julian Przybos advocated a formal poetry and shared an aesthetic of sonorous, elaborate diction. Pre-war Polish poets also tended to hold strong nationalistic beliefs and shared optimism about the imminent progress of the twentieth century.

World War II

Poland was invaded by Germany and the Soviet Union in the fall of 1939, early in the second World War. Although the Polish government in exile never formally surrendered, the Nazi regime occupied the country throughout the war. The Auschwitz concentration camp was established late in 1939, only about thirty-five miles from Kraców where Szymborska lived. Six million Polish citizens died during the war; this was nearly a fifth of the country's population at the time.

The Soviet occupation of Poland during World War II created a state of terror. The Soviets, who claimed about fifty percent of Polish territory, imprisoned 1.5 million Poles, most of whom died of famine or exhaustion. Polish military officers, who had been called to service at the beginning of the war, and numbered around 15,000 people, were systematically murdered.

The German side of the occupation of Poland was arguably worse. Any Polish civilian who resisted the occupation or who was thought capable of resisting, as determined by social status, was killed or sent to a concentration camp. Tens of thousands of government officials, former army officers, landowners, and members of the intelligentsia were killed in mass murders. Operation Tannenberg, the name of one of Hitlers' extermination plans for Poland, identified 61,000 Polish activists and intelligentsia who were to be killed. During September and October of 1939, over 20,000 of those on the list were murdered.

Also part of Hitler's plan to destroy Polish culture was to create a generation of completely uneducated Poles. This plan aimed to foster a Polish race of serfs for German use. The Germans closed or destroyed all schools, universities, museums and libraries in Poland. However, almost immediately so-called "secret universities" sprang up all throughout Poland. Hundreds of lecturers met secretly with groups of students in apartments throughout the country at the risk of deportation or death. Indeed, Szymborska attended an underground university during the war.

Survivors as Writers

World War II had a profound affect on the writers of Poland. They had lived through what, to many, seemed like the Apocalypse and had witnessed the mass genocide. Romantic optimism was rejected in the face of collective guilt. Czesław Milosz, a Polish poet who was awarded the Nobel Prize in 1980, poignantly notes in an essay called "On Szymborska": "Szymborska, like Tadeusz Rozewicz and Zbigniew Herbert [two other major post-war Polish poets] writes *in the place* of the generation of poets who made their debut during the war and did not survive." The burden of loss, and of speaking

COMPARE
&
CONTRAST

- **1940s:** Socialist Realism is introduced as the mandated style of all literature in Poland. Szymborska will publish her first collection of poetry, *This is What We Live For* in this style, based on her faith in, and optimism about, the possibility of Socialist ideology creating a utopian reality.

  1990s: Szymborska makes the claim in her Nobel Prize acceptance speech that "Poets, if they're genuine, must ... keep repeating 'I don't know.'" This indicates her rejection of her earlier adherence to Socialist Realism.

  Today: Socialist Realism can still be found in the literature of North Korea.

- **1940s:** Literary Modernism, which celebrated metanarratives (narratives that attempt to encompass all human experience) of ultimate truth, reason, and possible redemption, all while emphasizing the importance of weaving literary tradition into one's work, reaches its peak.

  1990s: Postmodernism is one of the major literary discourses of the decade, emphasizing society's incredulity toward metanarratives

  and denouncing metanarratives as inherently false and useless. Szymborska, in her poem "We're Extremely Fortunate," writes: "We're extremely fortunate / not to know precisely / the kind of world we live in." This signifies her opinion that all ideologies that promise ultimate understanding or knowledge must be treated as suspect.

  Today: Postmodernism continues to exercise considerable influence, though a reaction to its scepticism and relativism has given rise to what some critics have called post-postmodernism.

- **1940s:** Poland is under the power of both the Soviets and Nazi Germany. Poland is ultimately abandoned by the West to Soviet control.

  1990s: Poland emerges from the Cold War as an independent democratic state, peacefully transitioning from being a Soviet Satellite State to become the Third Polish Republic.

  Today: Poland has been a member of the European Union since 2004.

for those who could not, resulted in Polish writers feeling a resistance to any lack of linguistic clarity, especially that of flowery elevated dictions and false sentiments. Edward Hirsh notes in his essay "After the End of the World" that "It was as if poetry had to be reinvented again from the ground up." Polish poets were acutely aware of their responsibility to the reality, historical and political, around them.

Post-War Poland and Social Realism

After the war, the Soviet Union forced Germany out of Poland. At the Yalta Conference in 1945, the People's Republic of Poland, a Soviet satellite state, was formed. No Polish representation was allowed at the conference, and the handing

over of Polish territory by the Allied forces to Soviet control was, and is still today, seen by many as a betrayal of Poland for the benefit of Britain and France in appeasing the Soviet leader, Josef Stalin.

The Stalinist regime imposed many harsh oppressions on Polish cultural, educational and religious institutions. One of these oppressions mandated that all art and literature adhere to the rules of Socialist Realism. Socialist realism is a style of realistic art that had its roots in pre-Soviet Russia, in which all art and literature was subject to censorship. Its main requirement is that all art and literature further communist and socialist ideologies. Szymborska published

Judean Desert, the Caves of Qumran (© *Shai Ginott /*
Corbis)

her first volume of poetry, *That's What We Live
For* in the Socialist Realism style. She later
rejected this work.

Following Stalin's death in 1953, restrictions became less severe in Poland, and a period
of comparatively liberal government arrived,
known as "the thaw." This thaw marked the
end of Socialist Realism. Periods of harsh
oppression recurred intermittently throughout
the following decades. But restrictions on literature progressively fell away. Most Polish writers were left with a strong distaste for collective
thought; they felt resistance toward any public
or ideological pressure to speak for anyone but
themselves.

Remembrance and Forgetting

In her 1993 collection, *The End and the Beginning*,
Szymborska begins her poem "Reality Demands"
with the lines: "Reality demands / we also state
the following: / life goes on." After World War II,

survival guilt and the ethical responsibility to
reality were the pressing, almost crushing, issues
in Polish poetry. Many poets, including Milosz,
considered elegy their most important duty.
Even then, however, Szymborska recognized the
need to move forward. She, perhaps even more
than her contemporaries, saw an additional responsibility to continue to grow as a poet and as an
individual. Stephen Tapscott and Mariusz Pryzbytek in their essay "Sky, the Sky, a Sky, Heaven,
the Heavens, a Heaven, Heavens: Reading Szymborska Whole," note: "Szymborska argues that
progress [as opposed to constant remembrance]
might also consist in 'not knowing'—in strategic
forgetting in order to make room for continuity,
for new growth, even for liberated daydream-
ing." For Szymborska, this growth involves the
continual push to rediscover meaning from an
individual perspective. In doing this, she honors
those lost to the atrocities committed in the
name of collected ideologies in her own important way.

CRITICAL OVERVIEW

Critical interpretation of Szymborska's work in
English is sparse. This is due partly to the fact
that her work has been translated into English
for less than twenty years. It is also due to the
fact that she has a relatively small oeuvre (less
than three hundred published poems), especially
considering her lengthy career of over fifty-five
years of writing. And finally, the paucity of critical work may also have to do with Szymborska's own reticence on the subject of poetry, her
own or others'. She rarely gives interviews, and
although she does review popular books, she
does not engage in academic critical writing.
Therefore the critics have only her small body
of poems to work with.

Critics who have written about her work generally agree that her first two collections of poetry
differ widely from the rest of her body of work
given Szymborska's efforts in them to conform to
the style of Socialist Realism, the main requirement of which is to further the goals of socialism
and communism. Critic Edward Hirsh, in regard
to Szymborska's first two volumes, noted in the
American Poetry Review: "Those poems make
discouraging reading today." Most critics agree
that her third volume, *Calling Out to Yeti*, marks

WHAT DO I READ NEXT?

- *Poems New and Collected* by Wisława Szymborska was published by Harvest Books in November 2000. This volume includes all poems from the 1995 award-winning collection *View with a Grain of Sand* as well as a selection of Szymborska's most recent work.

- *New and Collected Poems* by Czesław Milosz was published by Ecco Press in 2003. In this hefty volume of works by Szymborska's contemporary and fellow Nobel Prize winner, Milosz, one can gain a sense of the literary world in which Szymborska emerged and has flourished. Milosz is widely considered one of the best poets of our age.

- *The Burning Forest: Modern Polish Poetry*, which was edited and translated by Adam Czerniawski, was published by Bloodaxe Books in 1988. This anthology presents an important selection of the work of Szymborska's contemporaries.

- *Breathing under Water and Other East European Essays* by Stanizław Barańczak was published by Harvard University Press in 1992. This book of essays by Barańczak, Szymborska's main English translator and a contemporary poet himself, depicts the political and cultural scene of Eastern Europe.

a clear departure from her earlier works and heralds the emergence of the questioning lyric style that she still employs today.

Stanizław Barańczak, a contemporary of Szymborska's and one of her English translators, has written more widely about her and perhaps with the greatest importance. Barańczak was the first critic to make the important observation of the concept of the naive question as the driving force behind the majority of Szymborska's poems. In an article titled "The Reluctant Poet," he writes: "The typical lyrical situation on which a Szymborska poem is founded is the confrontation between the directly stated or implied opinion on an issue and the question that raises doubt about its validity." In an earlier essay, "Eastern Europe: The Szymborska Phenomenon," Barańczak notes that Szmborska's success "stems from the fact that these [naive questions] are 'questions' she actually asks." Barańczak separates Szymborska from poets who might use a question simply as a poetic device or frame for their poem in which they might then expand upon an answer of which they already feel sure.

Most critics agree on Szymborska's fairminded ambivalence toward her poems' subjects. Discussing "Conversation with a Stone" in her essay "'My Poet's Junk': Wisława Szymborska in Retrospect," Eva Badowska notes that "The poem distinguishes between intellectual and sensory knowledge, clearly favoring the latter, which remains outside the human supplicant's reach (after all the stone is 'made of stone')." Others might argue that Szymborska favors neither intellectual nor sensory knowledge, but rather merely has shown the reader the uncrossable border between the two separate but equal beings. It seems most critics would concur with Edyta M. Bojanowska, who writes in her essay "Wisława Szymborska: Naturalist and Humanist" that "Szymborska denounces the hierarchical order we impose on the world as our own ridiculous construct." The critical consensus is that Szymborska does not submit authoritative opinions for the readers' consideration but rather asks her naive questions and explores possible answers through the framework of her poems.

CRITICISM

Emily Reardon

Reardon holds an M.F.A. in poetry. She writes poetry, fiction, and criticism. In the following essay, Reardon considers how the lyric form of "Conversation with a Stone" functions within the context of postmodern discourse.

Postmodernism is a literary and cultural discourse that describes contemporary society as a fragmented pastiche of voices, opinions, and information. The modernist movement it succeeded holds that both society and the individual were alienated from an established "Truth" or "Knowledge" by the isolating effects of industrial society. Modernist theory posits that abstract

> HOWEVER, IT SEEMS THAT, FOR SZYMBORSKA, IT IS NOT THE *ACTUAL* KNOWLEDGE OF THE OTHER THAT IS IMPORTANT, BUT RATHER GAINING AN UNDERSTANDING OF THE NATURE OF THE BORDER BETWEEN THE SELF AND THE OTHER."

truths or systems of knowledge do exist; society is unable to grasp them only because it has become so remote from them. In postmodernist theory, which takes into account the age of information overload, the disintegration of notions of family and community, and the difficulty of grasping a unified reality, there is no single or established truth. For some critics, the postmodern represents an age of surface, of depthless, dehistoricized bits of information that have no authentic basis of meaning. Others see it as a kind of ethical utopia involving a plurality of voices endowed with equal validity, in which one group's "truth" can not stamp out another's.

In either case, the search for individual meaning and knowledge is problematic because both notions assert that there are no authoritative facts to be trusted and nothing can be taken for granted. Humans, however, tend to crave some sort of order and fixed knowledge as a means of coping with the chaotic nature of life. This essay examines the ways in which Szymborska uses the inherent ordering function of lyric poetry as a means of grappling with the problem of the human desire for meaning and the ethics of realizing a plurality of truths in her poem "Conversation with a Stone."

In the acceptance speech for her 1996 Nobel prize, Szymborska said:

> Any knowledge that doesn't lead to new questions quickly dies out: it fails to maintain the temperature required for sustaining life. In the most extreme cases, cases well known from ancient and modern history, it even poses a lethal threat to society. That is why I value the phrase, 'I don't know' so highly."

This stance that a collective fixed truth or knowledge is an impossibility fits decidedly well within postmodern cultural thought. It seems that Szymborska would admit that the external world, (i.e. nature, politics, any thing "other"), is per se unknowable. However, she is not willing to give up her hunt for individual meaning. For, while postmodernist theory would submit a lack of any over-arching truths to impose on others, it offers no valuable alternative, thus leaving the individual without a path to meaningful existence.

"Conversation with a Stone" depicts this scenario of an individual, represented by the poem's speaker, confronting the otherness of the external world, which is represented by the stone. In one sense the speaker, who repeatedly knocks at the stone's door, is a sympathetic figure, in that she seems to see herself as innocent. In the third stanza, she says "I've come out of pure curiosity. / Only life can quench it. / I mean to stroll through your palace, / then go calling on a leaf, a drop of water." It is difficult to blame someone for being curious. However, the speaker's inquiry seems to lack depth. Clearly she desires an ordering of knowledge for herself. But it is as if that is all she desires, as if she yearns to discover whatever truth the stone might hold only so that she may put a stamp on it and check it off her list of truths to learn, before moving on to the next thing and doing the same. The desire for a quick fix of truth contributes to postmodern superficiality in that it discounts the complexity of the other. It is tantamount to one person meeting another for the first time for five minutes and walking away with the feeling that she knows who the other person is, what that person is like.

Despite the stone's protests that it is impossible for the speaker to enter it, either physically or metaphysically, the speaker persists in asking to be let in for a quick peek. But the stone will not hear of being reduced to being used like an empty hall that may simply be entered, observed and left. The ninth stanza begins: "'You shall not enter,' says the stone. / 'You lack the sense of taking part. / No other sense can make up for your missing sense of taking part.'" And two lines later, the stone continues: "You shall not enter, you have only a sense of what that sense should be, / only its seed, imagination." The speaker (the individual self) and the stone (the other) are on two different planes of logic. Although they may have a dialogue, the idea of them knowing each other as each knows itself is impossible. The stone finally makes this undeniably clear to the speaker in the last line of the poem when, after the speaker has yet again asked to be let in, the stone says "I don't have a door."

In an interview and commentary titled "Wisława Szymborska: The Enchantment of Everyday Objects," Joanna Trzeciak quotes Szymborska as commenting that "All the best [writers] have something in common ... a regard for reality, an agreement to its primacy over the imagination. ... Even the richest, most surprising and wild imagination is not as rich, wild and surprising as reality." In "Conversation with a Stone" the speaker is so fixated with her preconceptions of the stone that she does not even take the time to listen to what the stone is trying to say about their differences. The speaker says "'I hear you have great empty halls inside you / unseen, their beauty in vain.'" The stone's enigmatic replies (e.g., "'Great and empty, true enough,' says the stone, / 'but there isn't any room'") are fascinating to the reader, especially because they are spoken with such confidence. But the speaker is interested in little besides accomplishing her goal of entering. She seems to want the ease of having what she has already heard or imagined about a stone's insides to *be* the stone's reality. For not only is reality more rich, wild and surprising than imagination; it is infinitely more complex and therefore takes much more patience and effort to understand.

Drawing away from the text of the poem a bit, it is notable that Szymborska, as the writer, could have imagined an entrance into the stone. However, it seems that, for Szymborska, it is not the *actual* knowledge of the other that is important, but rather gaining an understanding of the nature of the border between the self and the other. For if, as the stone implies, it is not possible to fully understand the other, then any imagining on the part of the self that she does understand the other is necessarily false. Eva Badowska, in her essay "'My Poet's Junk': Wisława Szymborska in Retrospect," writes:

> [Szymborska] highlights moments and fragments from the earliest volumes, underlining the distance between "us" and [the other], for such barriers can only be "describe[d]—they cannot be traversed by any effort of the imagination or bridged by any act of empathy. Paradoxically, what poetry can do is only protect "them" against facile and spendthrift sympathies.

In a postmodern context in which objective truth is nonexistent and any source of knowledge is suspect, the self cannot even trust her own empirical experience of the other. And so, instead of adding falsehoods based on her impressions to the postmodern debris of baseless knowledge, she can only learn *how* to relate to the external other, where the borders lie and what they signify—not *what* the other is.

The question arises, then, of how one goes about writing a poem that has no didactic aim and only aids the self in learning about her relation to the world. In a 1996 interview with Dean E. Murphy in the *Los Angeles Times*, Szymborska commented: "There are some poets who write for people assembled in big rooms so they can live through something collectively. I prefer my reader to take my poem and have a one-on-one relationship with it." Given that Szymborska realizes the danger in accepting neatly packaged external knowledge, she knows that the search for meaning must take place through a private process of questioning and observation. In "Conversation with a Stone," she creates a circumstance in which the reader may observe the interaction between the speaker and the stone as though it is taking place between two external entities, or she may place herself in the shoes of one or the other of the "characters" in the poem. For in order to understand how one may go about confronting the foreignness of the other, one must consider both how it feels to be the other and also how one's seemingly innocent curious imaginings can risk trivializing reality and creating false knowledge. That, anyway, is what Szymborska has worked out for herself in the poem. The reader is free to participate in the poem as much or as little as she wishes.

Lyric poetry is generally characterized by a single speaker directly addressing the reader. In an essay simply titled "Poetry," Gregory Orr calls the lyric poem "an expression of [one's] experience of disorder and [one's] need for order. It will be in the form of a poem, an unfolding interplay [of] disorder and order." In order to avoid being caught up in or overwhelmed by a postmodern flood of unreliable facts, one must first acknowledge the disorder and choose a place to define order for oneself. Orr goes on to write:

> In the personal lyric, the self encounters its existential crises in symbolic form, and the poem that results is a *model of this encounter*. By making such a dramatized, expressive model of its crisis, the self is able to acknowledge the

existence, nature and power of what is destabilizing it, while at the same time asserting its ultimate mastery over disorder by the power of its linguistic and imaginative orderings.

Szymborska chooses the area in which to define order and dramatizes this area in "Conversation with a Stone" by way of creating a confrontational dialogue between the self and the other. Therefore, although she does not know anything more about the other per se, she has worked out a system of what this confrontation means to her.

The lyric is suitable to Szymborska's suggestion that the phrase "I don't know" is the most important phrase for a writer or thinker because, as Orr notes, it places the origin of meaning within the self. In doing so, the lyric subtly undermines the significance of societal ideologies or any fixed systems of knowledge that may be imposed on the self. However, the voice of lyric poetry is usually at least ostensibly autobiographical. In "Conversation with a Stone," this is not the case. The speaker is a bit narrow-minded, when clearly, Szymborska, who crafted the poem, is not. And one gets the sense that the confident voice of the stone is not necessarily the poet's voice either. Clare Cavanagh, in her essay "Poetry and Ideology: The Example of Wisława Szymborska," views Szymborska's lyrical poetry as "philosophical meditation on what it means to have an individual viewpoint, and what is lost or gained each time we take up this or that angle of vision." Szymborska must engage postmodern plurality on some level, by virtue of the simple fact that she is part of postmodernist culture. She does this not by holding a lens to the "true" facts or details of her own life, but by finding how the unstable self relates to the world around it. And in doing so, she shows the reader how to find meaning of her own.

Source: Emily Reardon, Critical Essay on "Conversation with a Stone," in *Poetry for Students*, Gale, 2008.

Mary Ann Furno

In the following essay, Furno presents a straightforward nearly line-by-line explication of "Conversation with a Stone." The essay also delves into the etymology of the diction, or the history of the changing meanings of the words used throughout the poem. This method invites a deeper interpretation of "Conversation with a Stone," and Furno ultimately characterizes the theme as an attempt to achieve wisdom through folly.

> WHAT WAS OVERLOOKED (THE STONE IN ITS VERY APPEARANCE) AND WHAT WAS MARGINALLY IMAGINED (PALACES AND GREAT HALLS) COLLAPSE INTO EACH OTHER, GIVING US AN EXPERIENCE OF STONE AS STONE."

"Throughout the Middle Ages ... the stone remained the main symbol of folly-hard, impenetrable, stolid. ... It was above all a metaphor which demonstrated well-nigh mythologically the intrinsically foolish nature of human beings." References are found to the surgical removal of stones as a method of curing someone of his folly.

In "Conversation With A Stone," Wislawa Szymborska gives "her" stone a voice; further, she allows a dialogue with an unidentified speaker who remains quite insistent throughout that this stone should allow entrance to its "insides" so as to "have a look around." Quite a bit of folly takes place here as the ensuing exchange develops. But then, Szymborska is a poet, and she considers it her business to rekindle Memory with its original Understanding that reality is not what it appears to be. Let us also remember that until the sixteenth century, Folly was often the voice of Wisdom.

We come in on this "conversation" not knowing what led up to it. It does seem that a familiarity between speaker and the stone has already been established, immediately placing us in this novel situation and relationship:

I knock at the stone's front door
"It's only me, let me come in"

Szymborska lets us know that the speaker has somehow come to "know" about—imagines—this "other side" of the stone, its "insides." This poem will function as metaphor insofar as metaphor is understood as a radical—at its roots—*mode* of conceiving and experiencing reality. The ongoing conversation between stone and speaker captures this fundamental alteration of consciousness with irony as its driving force. Szymborska's "Conversation With A Stone" becomes a "pleasurable corrective to the ordinary single-visioned world."

A radical transformation of the stone's reality is forcefully presented to the speaker, as we can infer from the speaker's wish to "breathe my fill of you." The stone is "more" than what is ordinarily seen or presented in reality, as the speaker has already sensed, albeit "out of pure curiosity": "I mean to stroll through your palace."

Momentum builds with the speaker's growing insistence to be allowed inside the stone, which offers only resistance:

"Even if you break me to pieces,
we'll all still be closed.
You can grind us to sand,
we still won't let you in."

It is not about "great empty halls" or a beautiful palace—at least, not as far as the stone is concerned. A stone that speaks. The dialogue has begun, and Szymborska immediately thrusts us into a "world that loses its footing," and where irony takes hold. And herein, the significance of this "conversation" is brought to bear on our senses. The speaker urges that "only life can quench" this curiosity, further appealing that

"I don't have much time
My mortality should touch you."

Life is only possible in a voice which, in this "conversation," is the voice of folly; a stone that in response, reaffirms that it is

"made of stone ...
and must therefore keep a straight face."

The irony of this reply reflects the speaker's impenetrability. The speaker's concern with mortality—a search for certainty about reality—is entirely misplaced. The speaker will, in any event,

"then go calling on a leaf, a drop of water."

missing the stone's point, as reflected in the speaker's inexorable refrain of

I knock at the stone's front door,
"It's only me, let me come in."

Only senses predominate for the speaker, whose deluded thinking the stone confronts:

"great and empty halls ...
beautiful perhaps, but
not to the taste of your poor senses."

The conversation takes a turn with potential for the speaker's self-understanding through conversation with a stone—another ironic twist wrought by Szymborska. The stone observes:

"You may get to know me, but you'll never know me through
My whole surface is turned toward you,
all my insides turned away."

The speaker maintains a division in its relationship to the stone—as though the stone, as stone, did not exist:

"You'll never know me
through" [italics mine, MAF]

Thoughtless insistence rooted in misunderstanding continues as the speaker retreats into self-doubt, perhaps despair, in the search for self understanding, reassuring the stone instead that

"I'm not unhappy.
I'm not homeless
My world is worth returning to.
I'll enter and exit empty-handed,
And my proof I was there
will be only words,
which no one will believe."

The stone responds with its most poignant volley:

"You shall not enter ...
You lack the sense of taking part.
No other sense can make up for your missing sense of taking part.
Even sight heightened to become all-seeing
will do you no good without a sense of taking part.
You shall not enter, you have only a sense of what that sense should be,
only its seed, imagination."

"It's only me, let me come in" still stands as what has become the speaker's contrived reply. The reality of "I haven't got two thousand centuries" reveals the speaker's growing *angst* about "mortality" uttered at the outset of this conversation; while hyperbole, that intends its opposite, hints that a denouement with understanding is possibly drawing near. The stone now mentions believing:

"If you don't believe me ...
just ask the leaf, it will tell you the same.
Ask a drop of water, it will say what the leaf has said.
And, finally, ask a hair from your own head."

These words hit close to home. Laughter is even closer:

"I am bursting with laughter, yes laughter, vast laughter,
although I don't know how to laugh."

This stone is in a state of ecstasy that only irony can produce, an ecstasy that is recaptured in its original meaning: "to put out of place," "to drive a person out of his wits" (*Oxford English Dictionary*). The stone's "insides" are truly not about "great empty halls" or a "palace," but about its "inner life"—the place where folly inheres, along with laughter—in each and every bit and piece, and grain of sand. The speaker's response:

"I knock at the stone's front door.
It's only me, let me come in."

The stone's conclusive reply:

"I don't have a door."

Szymborska leaves us to ponder "[a]bsurdity brought to a halt." One can almost hear the "door" slam, leaving the speaker shaken, hopefully.

That the speaker continues relating "over and against" the stone is unsustainable. That the stone is otherwise bursting with laughter, at this point, suggests an unendurableness which will confound the speaker. Having "only the *seed* of imagination" inhibits understanding the stone's true nature, Szymborska seems to suggest. It is the "sense of taking part" that is critical to any understanding and *through* which the stone's "interior" is recognized. The stone's "I don't have a door" undermines the speaker's presumption throughout the conversation that the stone has a door—and with that, the speaker "is thrown back upon [him/her]self and the problem of [his/her] own reality and truth." Szymborska quite aptly chooses laughter as the "stuff" through which the stone shakes itself "out of place," which we will believe has similarly shaken the speaker "out of place." Szymborska's laughter "bursts"—"breaks forth into a sudden manifestation of inner force... Chiefly said of things possessing considerable capacity for resistance" (*Oxford English Dictionary*)—from conceptions founded in the "seed of imagination," leading us instead to ponder a "sense of taking part." We could leave it at that, but Szymborska's choice of "burst" truly leads us to ponder further. In its more "obscure origin burst is associated to umbilicus," (*Oxfoxd English Dictionary*) as in "to burst the navel" (Shipley's *Dictionary of Word Origins*).

Life becomes the predominating association with respect to this stone's image, once the "front door" disappears. But Szymborska's choosing a stone in and of itself suggests the natural force of

irony which she humanizes with a voice—a sign of life. The images of the stone as having inner/outer (demarcated by the "front door") now "burst" one into the other: what is inner, is now outer; what is outer, is now inner. The speaker's perception of reality is shaken.

What was overlooked (the stone in its very appearance) and what was marginally imagined (palaces and great halls) collapse into each other, giving us an experience of stone as stone. "The great joke, Hegel wrote in a personal note, is that things are what they are." The world we call reality becomes "inverted" once "I'm made of stone and must therefore keep a straight face" voices "I am bursting with laughter, yes laughter, vast laughter, although I don't know how to laugh." Szymborska's "voice" acts as a metaphor that captures the irony of inverted reality: understanding "interior difference", its necessity of stone remaining a stone. Hence, "conversation": two voices participating in life force whenever the speaker "must needs" enter into a "sense of taking part" with the stone's "insides," "know[ing]" them "through" as his/her very self and "exit[ing]" "quenched" in a mutual self-recognition that reaps self-understanding. Szymborska gives us a "double vision that is only learned by the art of inversion ... [and] folly is the example of this art." In her poem, we discover inner life through a conversation. Folly is not a stranger to poets who keep close company with the Muses. In "Conversation With A Stone" Szymborska, a contemporary poet, acts as interlocutor for the Muses. Her perhaps unwitting "choice" of a stone, an object sometimes identified with the beginning of time and which, in its mythological heyday, was "associated with eternal, immutable, divine powers... often understood as an expression of concentrated force ... and generally ... as life giving" seems to make it so. The "conversation" one almost hears, along with the "burst" of laughter and the closing of the "door," "dispelling self-delusion"—all "point ironically to a different order of meaning" that Szymborska simply but dramatically speaks from.

Poets, along with philosophers, who were once in their close company, understand the significance of memory that only the language of poets now points to. Szymborska reminds us of the folly of language in its capacity for irony. With that, she is right in line with the Muses, whose eloquence is voiced through poets' "double vision" of reality. Irony foils ignorance. If

"

TEMPERAMENTALLY AND IDEOLOGICALLY,
SZYMBORSKA IS A POET OF MODERATION AND
SKEPTICISM. SHE PREFERS UNDERSTATEMENT TO
CONFIDENT ASSERTION, AMBIVALENCE TO RESOLVE,
DOUBT TO DOGMATISM, CONCRETENESS TO
ABSTRACTION, PARTICULARITY TO TYPICALITY, AND
EXCEPTIONS TO RULES."

there is a need or wish to draw some "conclusion," one might be inclined to say that in "Conversation With A Stone" Szymborska reminds us that stones of folly lie deep within us, "the link to our primordial heritage," and they are at risk in a world growing increasingly "single-visioned." The Muses also impart Wisdom. Wisława Szymborska will need to continue to give us many more "conversations" of folly and illusion, lest we forget.

Source: Mary Ann Furno, "'Conversation with a Stone': An Interpretation," in *Sarmatian Review*, Vol. 26, No. 1, January 2006, pp. 1192–96.

Edyta M. Bojanowska

In the following excerpt, Bojanowska investigates Szymborska's poetical treatment of consciousness— that which appears in mankind, and that which appears to be lacking in inanimate objects. Although Bojanowska solely refers to the poems "View with a Grain of Sand" and "The Apple Tree" here, given the topic, her findings are certainly relevant. For instance, Bojanowska remarks upon what Szymborska's critics have defined as the "'naive question' strategy"; a device that can certainly be seen in "Conversation with a Stone."

Consciousness

> Man is only a reed, the weakest in nature, but he is a thinking reed. ... [E]ven if the universe were to crush him, man would still be nobler than his slayer, because he knows that he is dying and the advantage the universe has over him. The universe knows none of this. Thus all our dignity consists in thought.
>
> (Pascal 66)

Pascal's famous notion of man as a "thinking reed" resounds throughout Szymborska's poetry. She shares Pascal's notion of consciousness as man's defining characteristic and plays with it in her "View with a Grain of Sand". (*PB*; [*Ludzie na moscie*; *People on a Bridge*]). The poem ponders the idea that whatever names, values, states, or actions we ascribe to nature, they are all but outgrowths of our consciousness, human imputations, rather than nature's inherent characteristics. Nature remains unaware, as it were, of its own nature.

> We call it a grain of sand,
> but it calls itself neither grain nor sand.
> It does just fine without a name,
> whether general, particular,
> permanent, passing,
> incorrect, or apt.
>
> Our glance, our touch mean nothing to it.
> It doesn't feel itself seen or touched.
> And that it fell on the windowsill
> is only our experience, not its.
> (137)

Although the poet does not doubt the real, material existence of the world, its aesthetic and sensual values exist, according to her, only in our perceptions of them:

> The window has a wonderful view of a lake,
> but the view doesn't view itself.
> It exists in this world
> colorless, shapeless,
> soundless, odorless, and painless.
> (135)

The poem describes the pace of time as also a human invention, since the three seconds that have passed in viewing the landscape are "three seconds only for us."

"View with a Grain of Sand" may be seen as an elaboration of Ruskin's notion of pathetic fallacy, the poetic convention of endowing nature with human feelings, the overuse of which he criticized. Szymborska broadens the bounds of this "fallacy" to include the very *act of perceiving* nature. The poem underscores the idea that any observation is first and foremost an experience of the perceiving subject, and that the sole indisputable truth it conveys is the blueprint of the viewer's perspective, his *ways* of seeing. The insistent focus on the human-specific lens foregrounds Szymborska's exploration of the epistemological value of individual perception *vis-à-vis* objective reality.

Indeed, the poem questions the ability of human perception to accurately comprehend the world. Our perception yields refractions rather than reflections, cognitive skepticism being Szymborska's and Pascal's common trait. At the same time, our human viewpoint so thoroughly pervades and determines how we think about nature and verbalize our thoughts that occasional falsification is inevitable. The poem paints an image of human speech as a fossil that bears the imprints of our past cognitive blunders:

> And all of this beneath a sky by nature
>   skyless
> in which the sun sets without setting at all
> and hides without hiding behind an unmind-
>   ing cloud.
> The wind ruffles it, its only reason being
> that it blows.
> (136)

Scientific facts constitute an important underpinning of the poem. Science has demystified some of our cherished assumptions about nature. There really is no "sky," there is only air. A "sunset" is only an illusion created by the earth's rotation. Clouds cannot possibly "hide" the sun: they can merely intrude on our line of vision. Yet while deconstructing this non-referential idiom, the poet demonstrates its indispensability in describing the world. The impasse is not merely linguistic. The poem paints an image of man's complete alienation from nature: on the one hand—the inscrutable *Ding an sich*, on the other—man's persistent, if quixotic, quest to comprehend it.

Szymborska differs from Pascal with respect to the *value* of human consciousness. The French philosopher considers it a sign of greatness that man realizes his wretchedness, while a tree—though just as wretched—lacks this awareness (Pascal 29). In contrast, Szymborska's position as evident in "View with a Grain of Sand" is essentially ambivalent. She carefully avoids asserting that consciousness *elevates* us over "consciousless" nature and merely notes it as a point of *difference*, which is in keeping with her anti-anthropocentric views. Szymborska does not concern herself in this poem with the question of whether a grain of sand is any worse off by virtue of not knowing its name or realizing where it fell.

She does take up this question in another poem, "The Apple Tree" (*LN* [*Wielka liczba*; *A Large Number*]). Szymborska's choice of a tree in the context of the theme of consciousness is reminiscent of Pascal's "wretched tree" metaphor, which might suggest that Szymborska's polemic with Pascal is indeed intended, The apple tree's lack of consciousness is conveyed, as in the previous poem, by a series of negatives. This lack, however, hardly implies a deficiency. The apple tree's "conscious-*less*-ness" allows it to maintain freedom, peace, and a harmonious union with nature (incidentally, the diminutive in the poem's title, "*Jablonka*," unlike its neutral equivalent "*jabloń*," has a homey, peaceful ring to it). By contrast, the poem's human protagonist—encumbered by consciousness—feels "imprisoned" and restless. She revels in the soothing conscious-lessness of the apple tree that

> ... brims with flowers, as with laughter;
> that is unaware of good and evil,
> shrugs its branches about it;
> that is no one's, whoever may say mine
>   about it;
> burdened with the foreboding of fruit only;
> that is uninterested about which year it is,
>   which country,
> which planet, and whereto it circles;
> [...] carefree about whatever happens,
> shivering with patience with each of its
>   leaves ...

The comparison of the tree with a human being hinges on a clever transformation of common idioms that usually refer to human emotions. For example, the tree shrugs its branches just as people shrug their shoulders. Yet this nonchalant gesture is juxtaposed with moral categories ("good and evil"), which for humans usually represent a cause for grave concern. The state of "shivering," usually associated with fear, excitement, or anticipation, is combined here with a quite incongruous patience. Furthermore, the natural semantic pull of the word "foreboding" anticipates an object that will signify something bad or harmful. Instead, the tree has a foreboding of fruit, of life. Thus the word "burdened," which at first seems to denote psychological distress, returns to its original meaning of "encumbered with physical weight" when it becomes related to the expectation of heavy fruit. The context of fruit and expectation, in turn, draws attention to the root "-ciaz-," which the word "burdened" (*obciazona*) shares with the word "pregnancy" (*ciaza*). Thus within one line the initially negative ring of the word "burdened" becomes returned twice: into a neutral and then positive tone. In sum, the tree's lack of consciousness actually betokens a benefit. Even more—it recalls prelapsarian bliss: the apple tree is unaware of good and evil and inhabits "may paradise." Grammatically speaking, the poem consists of one sentence without a predicate. Its main clause, interrupted by an extended description of the tree, expresses the speaker's wish to remain in its shadow instead of returning home, since "only prisoners wish to return home." As Wojciech Ligeza rightly notes, consciousness in Szymborska's poetry appears as both a curse and a blessing (1993, 5). In "The Apple Tree" it appears as the former.

Interestingly, a poem that presents the opposite view, *"In Praise of Feeling Bad about Yourself"* directly follows "The Apple Tree" in the volume (*LN*). This proximity of the negative and positive views of consciousness may imply that the poet considers them inseparable and equally valid. "In Praise" contains an encomium to conscience, itself a corollary of consciousness, characteristic of humans but unknown in the animal world:

> The buzzard never says it is to blame.
> The panther wouldn't know what scruples
>   mean.
> When the piranha strikes, it feels no shame.
> If snakes had hands, they'd claim their
>   hands were clean.
>
> ... Though hearts of killer whales may
>   weigh a ton,
> in every other way they're light.
>
> On this third planet of the sun
> among the signs of bestiality
> a clear conscience is Number One.

Pascal believed man to be great because he knows himself to be wretched. Szymborska's poem gives Pascal's idea a significant twist: man is great because he realizes that his actions cause *others* to be wretched, while piranhas and killer whales do not. Although the poem clearly applauds the human experience of pangs of conscience, as even the title suggests, Szymborska's criticism of remorselessness sounds a muted tone, so characteristic of her poetry in general. To call a clear conscience "bestial" may imply fierce condemnation, but in the context of the poem it may also suggest a mere statement of fact: a clear conscience is characteristic of beasts, that is, animals (the Polish word *"zwierzece"* functions more freely on both these levels than its English counterpart). This tension between the idiomatic and literal meanings of words and phrases greatly contributes to Szymborska's "muted" quality.

Temperamentally and ideologically, Szymborska is a poet of moderation and skepticism. She prefers understatement to confident assertion, ambivalence to resolve, doubt to dogmatism, concreteness to abstraction, particularity to typicality, and exceptions to rules. Moderation and skepticism also characterize her portrayal of nature and man, which maintains her typical dynamic of "on the one hand" / "on the other hand." Her affinity with Pascal emerges here again, since he believed each thing partly true and partly false, and considered contradiction no more a sign of falsehood than lack thereof an indication of truth (54). Szymborska's penchant for dwelling on contradictions to generally accepted truths and her refusal to commit herself entirely to one side of an issue inspires her extensive use of a "naive question" strategy, as Stanislaw Baranczak has brilliantly observed. This technique "always brings the 'dogmatic opinion' down to the level of an individual exception that contradicts the general rule and by the same token renders it, if not invalid, then at least suspect" (1994: 264). I would add that Szymborska does not presume to propose new truths or to entirely deconstruct the ones she "naively questions." Rather, she attempts to reconstruct a full picture, which for her—as for Pascal—includes at once the truth and falsity about each thing. Szymborska does not create her own version of the world, she merely "adds glosses 'on the margin' of the established version of reality" (Ligeza 1983, 89).

Source: Edyta M. Bojanowska, "Wislawa Szymborska: Naturalist and Humanist," in *Slavic and East European Journal*, Vol. 41, No. 2, Summer 1997, pp. 199–223.

Bogdana Carpenter

In the following essay, Carpenter presents a comprehensive overview of Szymborska's body of work, including a brief discussion of "Conversation with a Stone." The essay also provides readers with a more profound understanding of the poem's 'meaning in light of the recurring symbols and themes that appear throughout Szymborska' oeuvre. Ultimately, Carpenter finds that Szymborska is a poet who favors the use of the ordinary as a means of exploring the extraordinary.

> I am no longer certain that what is important
>   is more important than the unimportant.
>
> —"No Title Required"

For the second time in sixteen years, a Polish poet has been awarded the Nobel Prize in

" ONE OF THE MOST STRIKING FEATURES OF

SZYMBORSKA'S POETRY IS THAT REFLECTIONS ARE

PROMPTED NOT BY ABSTRACT IDEAS BUT BY CONCRETE

AND ORDINARY EXPERIENCES: THE SIGHT OF THE SKY,

SITTING ON THE SHORE OF A RIVER, LOOKING AT A

PAINTING, A VISIT TO THE DOCTOR."

Literature. This is not a coincidence: the decision of the Swedish Academy to bestow the world's most prestigious literary award on Czeslaw Milosz in 1980 and on Wislawa Szymborska in 1996 is tribute to the exceptional vitality and prominence of contemporary Polish poetry. More than anyone else, it is Czeslaw Milosz who gave Polish poetry its international visibility, both as a poet and translator and its enthusiastic promoter in America. It is Milosz's seminal anthology Postwar Polish Poetry, first published in 1965, that contained—together with twenty other poets —the first English translations of Szymborska's verse. But Milosz's significance is even deeper, and lies in the impact he has had on the shape of postwar Polish poetry. More than any other twentieth-century poet, Milosz has created a model and a yardstick against which younger poets have to measure themselves. Wislawa Szymborska is the one who has done so with the greatest success.

To most readers outside Poland, Szymborska's Nobel Prize came as a surprise. Long recognized in her native country as a leading voice in contemporary poetry, Szymborska has not achieved the same popularity in the English-speaking world enjoyed by other poets of her generation such as Zbigniew Herbert, Tadeusz Rozewicz, and Miron Bialoszewski. Not a political poet (though some of her early poems were written according to the precepts of socialist realism), Szymborska drew little attention at a time when Western interest in Eastern Europe had a largely political motivation. She defied the "mold" used to describe literature "behind the iron curtain." However, a number of English translations of her poetry had appeared: Milosz's anthology was followed in 1981 by the

translations of Magnus Krynski and Robert Maguire, published as *Sounds, Feelings, Thoughts: Seventy Poems*; Adam Czerniawski brought out *People on a Bridge* in England in 1990; and in 1995 there appeared the comprehensive collection *View with a Grain of Sand*, a set of award-winning translations by Stanislaw Baranczak and Clare Cavanagh. It is only with this most recent publication that Szymborska's poetry came fully into the view of the English-speaking audience.

In contrast, Szymborska's reputation in Poland has been steadily growing ever since her third volume, *Wolanie do Yeti* (Calling Out to Yeti), appeared in 1957. The publication of each successive volume—*Sol* (Salt; 1962), *Sto pociech* (No End of Fun; 1967), *Wszelki wypadek* (Could Have; 1972), *Wielka liczba* (A Large Number; 1976), *Ludzie na moscie* (1986; Eng. *People on a Bridge*), and *Koniec i poczatek* (The End and the Beginning; 1993)—has been an important poetic event, winning the author an ever-widening audience. Szymborska's ability to speak in simple language has made her poetry accessible and attractive to an unusually broad spectrum of readers.

Paradoxically, Szymborska's very simplicity and directness present the greatest challenge to a critic, and probably also account for a relative dearth of studies about her poetry. The analytic language of literary criticism often seems powerless and inadequate when dealing with these deceptively transparent poems; it is heavy-handed and clumsy in comparison with the lightness and agility of the poetic lines. Attempts at description and analysis frequently end in a frustrating realization of failure and the necessity to go back to the poems themselves, to let the poet speak with her own voice and defend herself against the awkward approximations of the critic. An important and integral part of her poetics, Szymborska's apparent ease conceals a conscious and determined effort. Her simplicity is careful, a result of struggle, and is hard to trace since the poet covers her tracks: "I borrow weighty words, / then labor heavily so that they may seem light."

Szymborska is a poet of philosophical reflection. Like most Polish poets of her generation, she avoids personal effusions and an emotional tone. Absent as a person, she is nevertheless strongly present as a voice—a voice which is unmistakably her own and impossible to confuse with that of any other poet. It is a voice of a Cartesian consciousness and of a cognitive subject, a voice that narrates and at the same time reflects upon the meaning and implications of its own narrative. Often the very structure of Szymborska's poems reproduces the cognitive process, and the poems become a direct and unrhetorical form of "thinking aloud."

> It has come to this: I'm sitting under a tree beside a river on a sunny morning.

> And since I'm here I must have come from somewhere, and before that I must have turned up in many other places.

They may search memory, as in "May 16, 1973": "One of those many dates / that no longer ring a bell. // Where I was going that day, / what I was doing,—I don't know." Most often, they pose a question: "Maybe all this / is happening in some lab? / Under one lamp by day / and billions by night?"

Szymborska's reflection rarely takes the form of categorical statements, and this is especially true of her later poetry. Reluctant to provide definitive answers, the poet prefers a margin of uncertainty. It is the initial premise of Descartes's formula, the "dubito" that describes best her philosophical attitude. But unlike the French philosopher, the Polish poet is unwilling to cross the threshold of uncertainty and step into the bright light of certitude: "certainty is beautiful, / but uncertainty is more beautiful still," she admits. Szymborska's reluctance is not the result of a lack of moral determination, but rather an expression of openness. It is an awareness that truth is complex and ambiguous, that reality is thick and consists of a myriad details, all of which need to be taken into account. In Szymborska's version of the well-known biblical story, Lot's wife looks back not only out of curiosity but with a number of different motives: regret, fear, anger, shame, the desire to go back. The poet shuns the didactic clarity of the biblical account in favor of a more tentative conclusion, but one closer to the complexity of psychological truth: "It's not inconceivable that my eyes were open. / It's possible I fell facing the city."

In another poem Szymborska praises ignorance: "We're extremely fortunate / not to know precisely / the kind of world we live in." What appears to be an ironic, tongue-in-cheek statement has in fact a deeper meaning, for the choice of ignorance is tantamount to an acceptance of the human condition, together with all its temporal,

spatial, and cognitive limitations. It is a choice of the human over the inhuman, the concrete over the abstract, the particular over the universal. Szymborska's island of Utopia, where "all is elucidated" and dominated by "Unshaken Confidence," is uninhabited. Footprints point toward the sea, "As if all you can do here is leave / and plunge, never to return, into the depths." Written in the 1970s, the poem can be read as an allusion to communist ideology and a depiction of the totalitarian state. It functions beyond its political context, however, and expresses the author's dislike of easy solutions and categorical assertions. Avoiding anything that might smack of dogmaticism or didacticism, Szymborska prefers to conclude her poems with an admission of ignorance or doubt: "I am," she says, "a question answering a question."

This philosophical option explains also her predilection for paradox, a stylistic figure that undermines accepted truths and leaves questions open. For example, "To change so that nothing changes," reads a line from the poem "A Feminine Portrait." Elsewhere we find: "You expected a hermit to live in the wilderness, / but he has a little house and a garden, / surrounded by cheerful birch groves, / ten minutes off the highway. / Just follow the signs." In "Elegiac Calculations," a metaphysical poem about death, each statement is followed by a parenthetic clause in the conditional mode.

> How many of those I knew (if I really knew them), men, women (if the distinction still holds) have crossed that threshold (if it is a threshold) passed over that bridge (if you can call it a bridge)—

The poem concludes on a note of uncertainty: "I've been given no assurance / as concerns their future fate."

One of the most striking features of Szymborska's poetry is that reflections are prompted not by abstract ideas but by concrete and ordinary experiences: the sight of the sky, sitting on the shore of a river, looking at a painting, a visit to the doctor. Like Bialoszewski, although in a different idiom, Szymborska extols the everyday and the ordinary: her "miracle fair" is made up of barking dogs, trees reflected in a pond, gentle breezes, and gusty storms—the world "everpresent." At the theater she is moved by a glimpse of actors caught beneath the curtain more than by tragic tirades. The very triviality of these experiences betrays a philosophical parti pris on the part of the poet, who questions and at the same time reverses the accepted opinion of what is important and what is unimportant. The usual hierarchies are stood on their head. Is the death of an insect less important than our own? Only if seen from "high above," that is from a human perspective, according to which "important matters are reserved for us." Metaphysics are not above everyday reality, and need not be sought in the "starry night" of the philosophers; they pervade every aspect of our existence. In a series of paradoxes, Szymborska questions the division into the high and the low, the meta- and the physical, the earth and the sky.

Even the highest mountains are no closer to the sky than the deepest valleys. There is no more of it in one place than another. The sky weighs on a cloud as much as on a grave. A mole is no less in seventh heaven than the owl spreading her wings. The object that falls in an abyss falls from sky to sky.

In Szymborska's poetry, reality is "democratized," and "anniversaries of revolutions" are much less prominent than "ants stitching in the grass" and "the pattern of a wave." Szymborska pitches ontology against history and politics, the private and the individual against the public and the collective, and here she reveals a deep affinity with Czeslaw Milosz. Common and humble reality is put forward at the expense of history and politics: "Even a passing moment has its fertile past, / its Friday before Saturday, / its May before June. / Its horizons are no less real / than those that a marshal's field glasses might scan."

For Szymborska, man's life is short and marked by suffering and death. No historical event can alter or has altered this basic existential condition: "Nothing has changed. / The body still trembles as it trembled / before Rome was founded and after, / in the twentieth century before and after Christ." On the contrary, history has only added to human suffering through wars and oppression. In her early and well-known poem "Breughel's Two Monkeys" she wrote:

This is what I see in my dreams about final exams:
two monkeys, chained to the floor, sit on the windowsill,
the sky behind them flutters,
the sea is taking its bath.

The exam is History of Mankind.
I stammer and hedge.

One monkey stares and listens with mocking disdain,
the other seems to be dreaming away—
but when it's clear I don't know what to say he prompts me
with a gentle clinking of his chain.

History is not a manifestation of the human spirit, or an extension of the individual and man's projection into time, but a force inimical to man. A deeply humanistic poet, Szymborska sees history as the principal source of evil. Disrespectful of human life, it fails to account for the number of its victims, as it "rounds out skeletons to the nearest zero" ("A Hunger Camp at Jaslo"). It provides fertile ground for hatred, as in the poem "Hatred": "Gifted, diligent, hard-working. / Need we mention all the songs it has composed? / All the pages it has added to our history books? / All the human carpets it has spread / over countless city squares and football fields?"

The sharpest edge of Szymborska's irony is reserved for politics. In an age which she ironically describes as "political," everything becomes "food" for politics.

To acquire a political meaning
you don't even have to be human.
Raw material will do,
or protein feed, or crude oil,

or a conference table whose shape
was quarreled over for months:
Should we arbitrate life and death
at a round table or a square one.

A pacifist, Szymborska sides with ordinary people against history: "I prefer the earth in civilian clothes. / I prefer conquered rather than conquering countries. / . . . / I prefer Grimm's fairy tales to the first pages of newspapers" ("Possibilities").

Szymborska has a deep respect for reality and a sense of wonder at its diversity and inexhaustible richness. This once again brings her close to Milosz: "So much world all at once— how it rustles and bustles!" This is accompanied by a realization that there is a disparity between the unlimited vastness of reality and the limitations of the poetic imagination: "Four billion people on this earth, / but my imagination is still the same."

The mathematical value of [Pi] comes closer to expressing the infinite richness of the universe than does the poetic imagination: "It can't be comprehended six five three five at a glance, / eight nine by calculation, / seven nine or imagination, / not even three two three eight by wit, that is, by comparison." Art can seize only individual facts and existences, a fraction of reality.

> On the hill where Troy used to be seven cities have been discovered. Seven cities. Six too many for a single epic poem. What can be done with them? What can be done? The hexameters are bursting.

("Population Census")

The poet describes her own imagination as one that is moved not by "large numbers" but by what is particular, by that which can be described only in the singular. Even her dreams, she concedes, are not populous and "hold more solitude than noisy crowds." With a touch of irony, she speaks of herself as "a mouse at the foot of the maternal mountain," as a "jester" who prefers "Thursday over infinity." Poetry, marked by insufficiency and imperfection, is a selection, a renunciation, a passing over in silence, and a "sigh" rather than a "full breath." Like anyone else, the poet is unable to step outside her own "I," her own particular existence. Being herself, she cannot be what she is not: "My apologies to everything that I can't be everywhere at once. / My apologies to everyone that I can't be each woman and each man. / I know I won't be justified as long as I live, / since I myself stand in my own way."

Faced with a task that is impossible, Szymborska makes a choice—to describe what is immediate and accessible, the ordinary and the small: "Inexhaustible, unembraceable, / but particular to the smallest fiber, / grain of sand, / drop of water— / landscapes." After all, every particle reflects the whole, every drop of water contains the entire universe: "A drop of water fell on my hand, / drawn from the Ganges and the Nile, // from hoarfrost ascended to heaven off a seal's whiskers, / from jugs broken in the cities of Ys and Tyre."

In the opposition between reality and art, life and intellect, the poet declares herself on the side of reality and life. Ideas are most often pretexts to kill, a deadly weapon whether under the guise of an artistic experiment ("Experiment"), a political Utopia ("Utopia"), or ideological fanaticism ("The Terrorist, He Watches"). Even poetry is "a revenge of a mortal hand" ("The Joy of Writing"). Szymborska sides with reality against

art and ideology, and this choice situates her in the mainstream of postwar Polish poetry alongside Milosz, Herbert, and Bialoszewski.

Despite its familiarity and ordinariness, Szymborska's poetry is neither relaxing nor comforting. It is permeated by a consciousness of death, temporariness, and human vulnerability.

> Nothing's a gift, it's all on loan.
> I'm drowning in debt up to my ears.
> I'll have to pay for myself
> with my self,
> give up my life for my life . . .
>
> Every tissue in us lies
> on the debit side.
> Not a tentacle or tendril
> is for keeps.
>
> The inventory, infinitely detailed,
> implies we'll be left
> not just empty-handed
> but handless, too.

Not only do we live on credit, but life is a constant improvisation, a rehearsal in an unfamiliar setting, a play without a script. What is more, the rehearsal is also the only performance we are granted, and all our actions —regardless how tentative—acquire the permanence of a perfective tense: "And whatever I'll do, / will turn for ever into what I've done" ("Instant Living").

In Szymborska's world, man is alone and distinct from the world of nature and objects; the division between the human and nonhuman world is unbridgeable, as in "Conversation with a Stone."

> I knock at the stone's front door.
> "It's only me, let me come in.
> I want to enter your insides,
> have a look round,
> breathe my fill of you."
>
> "Go away," says the stone.
> "I'm shut tight.
> Even if you break me to pieces,
> we'll all still be closed.
> You can grind us to sand,
> we still won't let you in."

The ontology of objects is beyond man's reach, and giving them anthropomorphic features is a misunderstanding. Consciousness is a human attribute; nature is unaware of itself. The sense of time, place, and purpose, colors, shapes, sounds, and names are products of human consciousness alone.

We call it a grain of sand,
but it calls itself neither grain nor sand.
It does just fine without a name,
whether general, particular,
permanent, passing,
incorrect, or apt.

Our glance, our touch mean nothing to it.
It doesn't feel itself seen and touched.
And that it fell on the windowsill
is only our experience, not its.

There is a contrast between nature's pure externality and its lack of self-awareness, on the one hand, and man's tortured consciousness on the other: "Our skin is just a coverup / for the land where none dare go, / an internal inferno, / ... / In an onion there's only onion / from its top to its toe." Because it lacks consciousness, nature is spared existential despair and metaphysical anxiety, and seems to us to be edenic. The communication between man and the external world is one-way, from human consciousness toward external reality, from man to objects. But the two realms remain distinct and strange to each other.

Szymborska's poetry is one of existential terror, but what makes it even more terrifying is that it avoids spectacular decorations and a tragic tone. Szymborska's tone is matter-of-fact, constantly kept in check: "if joy, then with a touch of fear; / if despair, then not without some quiet hope." The tragic content is attenuated by humor, wit, and an abundance of verbal games and puns: "Life, however long, will always be short. / Too short for anything to be added." The situations are trivial, and the effect is often a result of contrast between the triviality of the scene and the metaphysical dimension of the event.

A dead beetle lies on the path through the
field.
Three pairs of legs folded neatly on its belly.
Instead of death's confusion, tidiness and
order.
The horror of this sight is moderate,
its scope is strictly local, from the wheat
grass to the mint.
The grief is quarantined
The sky is blue.

Death is banal and inscrutable in its mystery. The room of a suicide gives no clues to the man's tragedy.

I'll bet you think the room was empty.
Wrong. There were three chairs with sturdy
backs.

A lamp, good for fighting the dark.
A desk, and on the desk a wallet, some
newspapers.
A carefree Buddha and a worried Christ.
Seven lucky elephants, a notebook in a
drawer.
You think our addresses weren't in it?

In one of her most popular and finest poems, "Cat in an Empty Apartment," the poet describes grief—and the sense of emptiness after the death of someone close—from the perspective of a cat.

Die—you can't do that to a cat.
Since what can a cat do
in an empty apartment?
Climb the walls?
Rub up against furniture?
Nothing seems different here,
but nothing is the same.
Nothing has been moved,
but there's more space.
And at nighttime no lamps are lit.

Wislawa Szymborska is not a prolific writer, and her poetic oeuvre consists of only some two hundred poems. Each poem, however, is a masterpiece. In crystalline and carefully wrought language, with a tone that is unpretentious, this poetry speaks to everyone and is about everyone. The ostensibly "unimportant" questions it poses prove to be the only questions that truly matter.

Source: Bogdana Carpenter, "Wislawa Szymborska and the Importance of the Unimportant," in *World Literature Today*, Vol. 71, No. 1, Winter 1997, pp. 8–13.

SOURCES

Badowska, Eva, "'My Poet's Junk': Wisława Szymborska in Retrospect," in *Parnassus: Poetry in Review*, Vol. 28, No. 1/2, 2005, pp. 151–68, 454.

Barańczak, Stanisław, "Eastern Europe: The Szymborska Phenomenon," in *Salmagundi*, Summer 1994, pp. 252–65.

———, "The Reluctant Poet," in the *New York Times Book Review*, October 27, 1996, p. 51.

Bojanowska, Edyta M., "Wisława Szymborska: Naturalist and Humanist," in *Slavic and East European Journal*, Vol. 41, No. 2, Summer 1997, pp. 199–223.

Cavanagh, Clare, "Poetry and Ideology: The Example of Wisława Szymborska," in *Literary Imagination: The Review of the Association of Literary Scholars and Critics*, Vol. 1, No. 2, Fall 1999, pp. 174–90.

Eliot, T. S., "Tradition and the Individual Talent," in *Selected Prose of T.S. Eliot*, edited by Frank Kermode, Harvest Books, 1975.

Epstein, Mikhail, "The Place of Postmodernism in Postmodernity," translated from the Russian by Slobodanka Vladiv-Glover, edited by Thomas Epstein, http://www.focusing.org/apm_papers/epstein.html (accessed August 1, 2007).

Hirsh, Edward, "After the End of the World," in *American Poetry Review*, Vol. 26, No. 2, March-April 1997, pp. 9–12.

Milosz, Czesław, "On Szymborska," in the *New York Review of Books*, Vol. 43, No. 18, November, 1996, p. 17.

Murphy, Dean E., "Creating a Universal Poetry Amid Political Chaos," in the *Los Angeles Times*, October 13, 1996.

Orr, Gregory, "Poetry," in the *Writer's Chronicle*, Vol. 35, No. 1, September 2002, pp. 12–20.

"Poland National Anthem," http://www.national-anthems.net/countries/index.php?id = PL (accessed August 1, 2007).

Portal, Jane, "Art under Control in North Korea," http://www.opendemocracy.net/arts-commons/art_northkorea_3690.jsp (accessed August 1, 2007).

Szybmborska, Wisława, "The Century's Decline," in *View with a Grain of Sand*, translated by Stanizław Barańczak and Clare Cavanagh, Harcourt Brace & Company, 1995, p. 148.

———, "Conversation with a Stone," in *View with a Grain of Sand*, translated by Stanizław Barańczak and Clare Cavanagh, Harcourt Brace & Company, 1995, pp. 30–2, 148.

———, "Nobel Address," http://nobelprize.org/nobel_prizes/literature/laureates/1996 (accessed May 14, 2007).

———, "Reality Demands," translated by Joanna Maria Trzeciak, http://www.pan.net/trzeciak/ (accessed May 14, 2007).

———, "We're Extremely Fortunate," http://neptune.esc.k12.in.us/socratic/resources/FORTUNE.html (accessed May 14, 2007).

Tapscott, Stephen, and Mariusz Pryzbytek, "Sky, the Sky, a Sky, Heaven, the Heavens, a Heaven, Heavens: Reading Szymborska Whole," in *American Poetry Review*, Vol. 29, No. 4, July-August 2000, pp. 41–6.

Trzeciak, Joanna, "Wisława Szymborska: The Enchantment of Everyday Objects," in *Publishers Weekly*, Vol. 244, No. 14, April 1997, pp. 68–9.

FURTHER READING

Anders, Jaroslaw, "The Revenge of the Mortal Hand," in the *New York Review of Books*, Vol. 29, No. 16, October 1982, pp. 47–9.

Anders examines the subject of remembrance in Szymborska's work, and also her emphasis on being able to move on from the burden of history.

Baudrillard, Jean, *Simulacra and Simulation (The Body, In Theory: Histories of Cultural Materialism)*, University of Michigan Press, 1981.

This is Baudrillard's philosophical treatise on postmodern culture in which he describes all reality as a simulation and the world as a place where meaning has been replaced by symbols and signs.

Czerwinski, E. J., Review of *Poems New and Collected 1957–1997*, in *World Literature Today*, Vol. 74, No. 2, pp. 440–41.

Czerwinski discusses Szymborska's wide use of metaphor and irony as a means of reaching philosophical summation.

Eagleton, Terry, "Capitalism, Modernism and Postmodernism," in *Modern Criticism and Theory*, edited by David Lodge, Longman Singapore Publishers, Ltd., 1988, pp. 384–98.

Eagleton weighs whether postmodernist theory works as a significant critique of contemporary culture.

Jameson, Fredric, "The Politics of Theory: Ideological Positions in the Postmodernism Debate," in *Modern Criticism and Theory*, edited by David Lodge, Longman Singapore Publishers, Ltd., 1988, pp. 373–83.

Jameson examines how postmodern discourse inspires both passionate advocacy and seething opposition from both political reactionaries and progressives in every possible permutation.

Orr, Gregory, *Poetry as Survival*, University of Georgia Press, 2002.

Orr examines how a variety of subjects ranging from the Holocaust to medicine relate to the evolution of the personal lyric.

Osherow, Jacqueline, "'So These Are the Himalayas': The Poetry of Wisława Szymborska," in the *Antioch Review*, Volume 55, No. 2, pp. 222–28.

Osherow comments on the ways in which the translation of Szymborska's poems to English have affected readings of her work.

Vendler, Helen, "Unfathomable Life," in the *New Republic*, Vol. 214, No. 1, January 1996, pp. 36–9.

Vendler discusses Szymborska's evolution as a poet. She marks the universality of suffering as Szymborska's major theme.

Worozbyt, Theodore, Review of *View with a Grain of Sand: Selected Poems*, in *Prairie Schooner*, Vol. 73, No. 2, Summer 1999, pp. 197–202.

Worozbyt explores how the self-effacing nature of Szymborska's tone achieves an intimacy with her audience.

Dream Song 29

JOHN BERRYMAN

1964

"Dream Song 29," by American poet John Berryman, was first published in *77 Dream Songs* in 1964. The collection was awarded the Pulitzer Prize. Several years later, Berryman published more dream songs in *His Toy, His Dream, His Rest* (1968). Taken together, the two volumes contain 385 dream songs and can be read as one long poem. The central character in the dream songs is named Henry. He is a semi-autobiographical figure. Berryman denied that Henry was a version of himself, but critics have taken his denials with a pinch of salt. In his note on the dream songs that appeared in *The Dream Songs*, a one-volume edition of all the dream songs that was first published in 1969, Berryman commented on the songs as a whole: "The poem . . . is essentially about an imaginary character (not the poet, not me) named Henry, a white American in early middle age sometimes in blackface, who has suffered an irreversible loss." This loss endured by Henry, which many critics assume to be the suicide of Berryman's father, forms a background to "Dream Song 29," in which Henry confesses to a constant feeling of sorrow and guilt and falsely imagines that he has committed a murder. It is one of the most accessible of the dream songs, some of which are obscure, their meaning difficult to puzzle out. Taken as a whole, Berryman's dream songs are his most enduring work and represent a significant contribution to American poetry in the second part of the twentieth century.

John Berryman *(Terrence Spencer / Time Life Pictures / Getty Images)*

AUTHOR BIOGRAPHY

Berryman was born John Allyn Smith, Jr., in McAlester, Oklahoma, on October 25, 1914. His father, also named John Allyn Smith, was a banker; his mother, Martha, a schoolteacher. In 1926, the family moved to Tampa, Florida, but in that same year, Smith, depressed over marital and business difficulties, shot himself. Berryman was only eleven years old, and his father's suicide affected him for the rest of his life. After Smith's death, the family moved to New York City, and Martha Smith remarried, to a man named John Berryman, who adopted her two sons. The future poet's name then became John Berryman.

As a boy, Berryman excelled at academics, graduating one year early from South Kent School in Connecticut. In 1932, he enrolled at Columbia College (now University), where he studied literature and philosophy. When he was an undergraduate, he decided he wanted to become a poet, and in 1935 he began publishing poems in the Columbia literary magazine, and had one poem published in the *Nation*. After graduating Phi Beta Kappa in 1936 with a degree in English, Berryman was awarded a fellowship to Clare College, Cambridge, England. During this period he met some of the great poets of the age, including William Butler Yeats, W.H. Auden, and Dylan Thomas. He also traveled in France and Germany and was awarded the Oldham Shakespeare Prize. He was awarded a Bachelor of Arts degree by Cambridge in 1938.

Returning to New York City in 1938, Berryman began a lengthy job search, which ended with the start of his teaching career at Wayne University (now Wayne State) in Detroit in 1939. Then he worked as an instructor in English composition at Harvard University from 1940 to 1943. After this, until 1951, excluding a two-year break for some independent research on Shakespeare, he taught creative writing at Princeton University.

Berryman's first collection of poetry, "Twenty Poems," was included in *Five Young American Poets* (1940); a second collection, *Poems*, was published in 1942, and a third, *The Dispossessed*, appeared in 1948. Up to this point Berryman's poetry was conventional, rooted in the poetry of the day, but his next publication, the long poem *Homage to Mistress Bradstreet* (1953), represented a leap into a more original form of writing. From then on, Berryman forged a reputation as an innovative poet with a highly distinctive voice. In 1955, he joined the faculty of the University of Minnesota in Minneapolis, where he taught until his death.

Berryman had begun drinking heavily in the 1940s, and in 1947 he had undergone psychoanalysis. He had a restless, brooding nature, given to fits of despair. In the mid-1950s, after a period of intensive dream analysis, he began to write the dream songs with which his name is most frequently associated. In 1964, *77 Dream Songs* was published and was awarded the Pulitzer Prize. In 1967, a collection of sonnets that he had written twenty years earlier was published as *Berryman's Sonnets*. In 1968, another volume of dream songs, *His Toy, His Dream, His Rest* was published; the following year, it won the National Book Award. In 1970, his poetry collection *Love & Fame* was published.

Berryman was married three times. In 1943, he married Eileen Patricia Mulligan; they separated in 1953 and were divorced in 1956. Very shortly thereafter, Berryman married Elizabeth Ann Levine. They had a son in 1957 and were divorced in 1959. In 1961, he married Kathleen Donahue. They had two children.

On January 7, 1972, Berryman committed suicide by jumping off a bridge in Minneapolis. Two of his works, *Delusions, Etc.* (1972) and *Recovery* (1973), a novel, were published posthumously.

POEM SUMMARY

Stanza 1

"Dream Song 29" begins by describing an unspecified "thing" that has, apparently for a long time, been afflicting a man named Henry. Henry feels a great weight on his heart and also appears to feel hopeless about it. The poem states that even if a hundred years were to pass, and Henry was to weep and remain sleepless for all that time, he "could not make good." In other words, he would still be suffering from this grief—the cause of which remains as yet unstated—and unable to recover. Commentators have often believed that Henry represents Berryman the poet, and the grief from which he suffers is the suicide of his father, which occurred when the poet was eleven years old. However, such an explanation is not essential for understanding the poem, and stanza 3 will provide another clue to the reason for Henry's state of mind.

The last two lines of the first stanza suggest that Henry is always reliving the memory of some aspect of whatever it was that caused his grief. He keeps hearing, again and again it would seem, "the little cough somewhere, an odour, a chime." Some commentators suggest that this may be a recollection of the funeral of Berryman's father—perhaps someone coughed and broke the silence at the service or burial; a certain odour was present that always brings back the memory of the event (it is unclear how an odour could "start" in Henry's ears); the chime may be of a church bell somewhere. Once again, this is speculation; the lines are too cryptic to permit definitive interpretation.

Stanza 2

The first line, "And there is another thing he has in mind," introduces a new idea. It appears that there is another aspect to Henry's grief and distress, another event that is contributing to it. What that might be is not stated explicitly in

MEDIA ADAPTATIONS

- There is a recording available on compact disk of the first public reading by Berryman of his dream songs, including "Dream Song 29." The recording was made on Halloween night in 1963 and was sponsored by the Academy of American Poets. Berryman reads more than a dozen dream songs and gives introductions to many of them. Robert Lowell also reads. The recording is on two disks and is available from http://www.poets.org/viewmedia.php/prmMID/17047, which is the website of the Academy of American Poets.

this stanza, but it is something so serious that because of it, Henry feels that for more than a thousand years (which is ten times more than the hundred years mentioned in the first stanza) he would face the reproach of "a grave Sienese face" in profile. This reference cannot be explicitly identified. It suggests perhaps a painting in which Henry somehow sees a reproach for whatever it is he feels guilty about (which so far has not been explained). Siena is a city in Italy that Berryman visited, and he may have seen there the religious portraits created by painters from that city in the thirteenth and fourteenth centuries.

The next sentence, "Ghastly, / with open eyes, he attends, blind," suggests that Henry, perhaps with a ghastly look on his face, is contemplating some as yet unknown (to the reader) horror, but even as he tries to look directly at it and concentrate on it, he cannot see it. Perhaps it is too awful for him to contemplate.

The next line suggests that in Henry's mind, he can do nothing about whatever is distressing him so much. It is "too late" to change anything, and this message is conveyed by "all the bells," another obscure reference, perhaps referring to church bells, the tolling of which remind him of his sins without giving him the means to redeem himself from them. "This is not for tears; /

thinking" is another cryptic line, perhaps suggesting that since it is too late for Henry to take any corrective action, it is too late for tears as well; the word "tears" harks back to the "weeping" mentioned in stanza 1.

Stanza 3

This stanza sheds some small light on Henry's situation. It transpires that he feels guilty and has attached that feeling of guilt to the belief that he has murdered someone. However, he is mistaken. He never did "end anyone" or cut her body up and hide it, even though he imagines he has done this and has hidden the pieces of the dismembered body where they would be found. It appears that Henry is obsessed by this act that he believes he committed, even though he knows, at a rational level, that he did not murder anyone. He knows this because he "went over everyone, & nobody's missing," which suggests a rather deranged or disturbed mind frantically going through a mental inventory of his friends and acquaintances and finding that they are all still alive and therefore concluding that he could not have killed anyone. This thought is then repeated in two successive lines, which suggest the obsessive nature of his mental processes: "Often he reckons, in the dawn, them up. / Nobody is ever missing." The phrase "in the dawn" suggests that Henry is remembering a recurring nightmare; the poem is, after all, a dream song.

THEMES

Guilt

The main theme of the poem is guilt. Henry's sense of his own guilt is so all-enveloping that nothing he can do can remove or alleviate it. The irony is that the act he feels so guilty about is clearly an imaginary one. Henry did not commit a murder; he only imagines that he did. At one level of his mind, Henry is aware of this fact. ("He knows.") He has an obsessive habit, apparently when he wakes up in the morning, of making sure that no one he knows is missing (which suggests he believes that his dark fantasy is about someone he knows). But this does not assuage his feelings of guilt, since at another level of his disordered, disintegrated mind he continues to think that he has committed such a deed. Henry appears to be in the grip of an irrational obsession, perpetually experiencing intense feelings of guilt and spontaneously inventing a justification

TOPICS FOR FURTHER STUDY

- Write a confessional poem in the style of "Dream Song 29," or of another confessional poet whose work you admire. The poem could deal with difficult emotions regarding your relationship with a family member, or with some other aspect of your life that is problematic for you.

- Pick two more of Berryman's dream songs that you like. Write an essay in which you explicate both poems and describe why you respond to them. How do these poems compare to "Dream Song 29?"

- What is the relationship between suffering and creativity? Does suffering enhance creativity? If Berryman had been happier, would he ever have written the dream songs? Was his personal turmoil the engine of his best work? You may consider the work of other poets or artists, such as Sylvia Plath or Vincent van Gogh, and any others you discover in your research. Make a class presentation on this topic.

- Research the topic of suicide, especially the effect of the suicide of a close relative on other family members. If a mother or father commits suicide, does that increase the risk that their son or daughter will also commit suicide? What are the warning signs of suicide? If a friend of yours seemed suicidal, what would you do? Make a class presentation in which you present your findings.

for them, even though that justification has no basis in objective reality. The lurid nature of the crime he believes he has committed suggests that violence lurks somewhere in his mind, even though he has not, it seems, acted on it. The fact that he can think himself capable of killing someone, and hacking the body to pieces and hiding them, suggests the habitual violence of his thoughts, presumably about women, since the victim he believes he has killed is female. His imaginary hiding of the body parts "where they may be found" suggests that he wants to be found out; he desperately wants someone to catch him and stop him from performing such deeds, even though all this is going on only in his imagination. What he really wants is for the feelings of guilt to stop. He is desperate for help, even though he believes no help is possible; as the bells say, it is "too late." Henry, it seems, is in a kind of hell of his own making, and there is no way out of it.

Perhaps, if the autobiographical interpretation of stanza 1 is accepted, the grief that crushes Henry's heart resulted from the suicide of Berryman's father. This would equate Henry with the poet himself. Even though Berryman repeatedly denied this was the case, many critics have read the poem in this way. According to this view, the suicide left the boy feeling guilty as well as grief-stricken, perhaps assuming that he was in some way to blame for the death of his father, perhaps feeling that he was not worthy of his father's love. This left a wound that runs so deep in Henry it can never be healed, and through the mysterious alchemy of the unconscious mind, the guilt he feels over this tragic event translates itself into incessant guilt for a crime he never in fact committed.

Sin

Henry's guilt acquires a faint tint of sin also, for which he seems to be reproached by a vague sense of religious feeling. "All the bells say: too late," suggests the tolling of church bells, perhaps calling the worshippers to a service, but for Henry it is too late to be a part of a church. He cannot join the community of believers; his sin, his guilt, permanently excludes him. So does the "grave Sienese face." This could be a portrait of the Madonna, or of a saint whose calm, holy countenance can only be felt by Henry as a reproach. The serenity of this unnamed face is thus a counterpoint to the restless turmoil and distress in Henry's mind. He knows he can never attain this serenity; he is cut off from it forever, and it therefore appears to him only as a look of censure and judgment.

STYLE

Sestet, Rhyme, and Meter

A sestet is a stanza of six lines. (Sestet is from the Latin word for six.) Usually the term refers to the last six lines of a sonnet, but it can also be used, as in this case, to refer to a stanza comprising six lines.

The general stanzaic pattern in the nearly four hundred dream songs is for each sestet to have four lines with five strong stresses, and two lines, usually the third and sixth, with only three strong stresses. Lines 3 and 6 are therefore usually shorter. (A strong stress indicates a syllable which is pronounced louder, and sometimes held for a longer duration, than another syllable that has a "weak" stress.) However, this pattern is varied constantly in the dream songs sequence. In "Dream Song 29," the lines vary in length but none of the three sestets follows the standard form or any other regular pattern. The metrical pattern is extremely flexible, varying between as many as six stresses ("would fail to blur the still profiled reproach of. Ghastly,") and as few as one stress (the one-word line at the end of stanza 2).

There is an occasional inversion of the iambic foot to create a spondee (two approximately equal stresses in one foot), as in the first two syllables of "só heavy" (the poet himself has marked the word "so," which would normally not be stressed, for emphasis), and the first two syllables of "grave Sienese."

The poet makes use of end rhyme but the rhyme scheme is not consistent from stanza to stanza. In stanza 1, line 2 ("years") rhymes with line 5 ("ears"), and line 3 ("time") with line 6 ("chime"). In stanza 2, however, lines 1 and 4 ("mind" and "blind") rhyme, as do lines 2 and 6 ("years" and "tears"). In stanza 3, the rhymes consist of repeated words identical in spelling and meaning: "up" in lines 2 and 5, and "missing" in lines 4 and 6. This is sometimes called identical rhyme. (Thematically, this type of rhyme helps to convey the obsessive, repetitive nature of Henry's thoughts.)

Language and Grammar

The poet uses some colloquial language as well as ungrammatical expressions. In stanza 1, "in all them time," should be, to be grammatically correct, "in all that time." In line 4, "Henry could not make good" is a colloquial, perhaps even childlike way of saying that Henry could not recover from, or remove, his feelings of grief, distress, and guilt. In the final stanza, "end anyone" is a colloquial way of describing murder, and the lines "But never did Henry, as he thought he did, / end anyone and hacks her body up / and hide the pieces" is ungrammatical, since the phrase "hacks her body up" is in the present tense but the sentence of which it forms a part is in the past tense. The discrepancy suggests the logic of dream and obsession; even though the imagined murder is in the past, Henry seems to keep reliving it, as if it is in the present, still going on.

HISTORICAL CONTEXT

Confessional Poetry

Confessional Poetry is a type of autobiographical poetry, written in the first person, in which the poet candidly reveals some of the most intimate details of his or her own life experiences. These may be shocking, sometimes even shameful details of sexuality, illness, depression or other emotional states, and difficult family relationships; the poet willingly confides in the reader the raw (although still artfully presented) truth about themselves.

Confessional poetry became a force in American poetry in the late 1950s, when Robert Lowell, one of the leading poets of the day, published *Life Studies* (1959), which had a more directly personal and emotional focus than any of his previous poems, some of which were difficult, veiling rather than revealing any emotion that lay behind them. In *Life Studies*, Lowell wrote about the mental illness he experienced in the 1950s, as well as his relations with his parents and grandparents, and his marital problems. The collection won the National Book Award, and in his acceptance speech Lowell explained that he was seeking a kind of poetry that was more personal than the restrained, objective approach approved by what was known as the New Criticism, which held sway in American poetry criticism from the late 1930s until the 1960s.

Lowell's new approach was stimulated by the self-confessional style of Allen Ginsberg and the other Beat poets in San Francisco who had made a name for themselves on the West Coast in the mid-1950s. Ginsberg's most famous early poem, "Howl" (published in *Howl and Other Poems* in 1956) contains the following passage, which well expresses the new confessional mode: "[To] . . . stand before you speechless and intelligent and shaking with shame, rejected yet confessing out the soul to conform to the rhythm of thought in his naked and endless head."

In 1959, the same year that Lowell published *Life Studies*, W.D. Snodgrass, a former student of Lowell's, published *Heart's Needle*, a collection in similar confessional mode, which won the Pulitzer Prize. It included poems about Snodgrass's divorce and his difficult relationship with his young daughter.

During the 1960s, confessional poetry continued to gain in popularity. Anne Sexton, a student of Lowell's, published her first book of poems, *To Bedlam and Part Way Back* (1960); her subject matter included guilt, madness and suicide; she wrote about the time she spent in a mental hospital, and how she tried to reconcile with her daughter and husband when she returned. Sexton's later work often dealt with suicide, and she took her own life in 1975. Another confessional poet who committed suicide was Sylvia Plath. Plath, who like Snodgrass and Sexton was a student of Lowell's, is chiefly known for her collection, published posthumously, titled *Ariel* (1965). It was a year after Plath's death in 1963 that Berryman published *77 Dream Songs*. The path that led to Berryman's semi-autobiographical confessional work had therefore been laid out in the five years that preceded its publication.

The Interpretation of Dreams

In the mid 1950s, Berryman began analyzing his dreams. By the summer of 1955, he had catalogued 120 dreams, and he wrote that doing so had proved to be a painful process. However, he also reported that he was gradually gaining insight and discovering that some of his simplest dreams were in fact more complex than any poem he had read. He considered publishing the analyses themselves but instead decided to use the insights he had gained in a new kind of poem.

Berryman's interest in dream analysis was not uncommon during the period. Indeed, interpreting dreams aroused significant interest amongst psychologists and educated lay people ever since the publication of Sigmund Freud's *The Interpretation of Dreams* in 1900. Freud believed that the unconscious mind expressed its desires in dreams. However, Freud stipulated that such desires were subject to censorship by what he would later call the "superego." According to Freud, the wish that the unconscious wants to express is therefore disguised or transformed by several processes, including *representation*, in which a thought is translated into a visual image, and *symbolism*, in which a symbol replaces an action or idea. Freudian dream

COMPARE
&
CONTRAST

- **1960s:** The confessional movement expands the subject matter of American poetry; poets reveal the intimate details of their personal lives.

  Today: The tradition of confessional poetry continues; in the United States, Marie Howe and Sharon Olds are two poets whose work often deals with aspects of their personal experiences.

- **1960s:** The sixties are a decade of social upheaval, marked by the continuing success of the civil rights movement and the rise of feminism and the gay rights movement. Many thousands of young people adopt a countercultural lifestyle, emphasizing sexual freedom and recreational use of drugs such as marijuana and LSD, as well as political and social activism on the left of the political spectrum. The decade is also marked by student unrest on college campuses, and protests against the Vietnam War. This rebellion against tradition is echoed in the work of the confessional poets of this period.

  Today: The United States is in a more conservative period. Many conservatives blame current social problems on the liberal ethos that prevailed in the 1960s. Although the United States is engaged in a war in Iraq that some argue resembles the Vietnam War, there are few demonstrations on college campuses against the Iraq war. This conservatism may be reflected in contemporary poetry as many critics note that the genre has become stagnant.

- **1960s:** With the publication of *77 Dream Songs*, Berryman's literary reputation rises; during the 1960s he is considered among the front rank of contemporary American poets and acquires an international reputation.

  Today: Berryman's critical reputation has been in decline for nearly two decades and shows no signs of being revived. He is now represented less fully in contemporary poetry anthologies than his near contemporary Adrienne Rich, even though during the 1960s his reputation exceeded hers. In this decline, Berryman is joined by another confessional poet, Anne Sexton, and other poets admired in the 1960s, friends of Berryman such as Delmore Schwartz and Randall Jarrell. Meanwhile, the work of poet Weldon Kees, virtually ignored during the period of Berryman's success, is now undergoing renewed interest.

---

analysis is thus meant to reveal hidden wishes for the purpose of resolving psychic conflict.

During the 1950s, Freud's theories about dream interpretation were losing some ground to newer ideas propagated by Carl Jung and other psychologists. At the same time, the first researchers also began to investigate the brain during sleep, discovering that dreams were most likely to occur during sleep stages known as rapid eye movement or REM. Since REM is controlled by the part of the brain responsible for such functions as breathing and reflexes, the researchers concluded that the parts of the brain responsible for emotions and memories were inactive during dreams. Dreams were therefore only random images, without the meanings Freud ascribed to them, or any meaning at all. However, such research did not dissuade psychologists and their followers from continuing to research and interpret the meaning of dreams.

CRITICAL OVERVIEW

Berryman's dream songs have attracted much critical attention, and a number of critics have singled out "Dream Song 29" for particular comment. Berryman's fellow-poet Robert Lowell reviewed *77 Dream Songs* in the *New York Review of Books* (and reprinted in *Robert Lowell: Collected Prose*), and quoted "Dream Song 29" in its entirety. He regarded it as one of the best of the songs and commented on it as follows:

> The voice of the man becomes one with the voice of the child here, as their combined rhythm sobs through remorse, wonder, and nightmare. It's as if two widely separated parts of a man's life had somehow fused. It goes through the slow words of *"Henry could not make good,"* to the accusing solemnity of the Sienese face, to the frozen, automatic counting of the limbs, the counting of the bodies, to the terrible charm and widening meaning of the final line.

Edward Mendelson, in his essay "How to Read Berryman's 'Dream Songs,'" sees a pattern in "Dream Song 29" that is present in many of the other dream songs, too. The first sestet describes a private experience, in Henry's own heart; in the second sestet, Henry "notices or remembers the world outside," and in the final sestet he "acknowledges almost in defeat the social world of others, all those who persist in surviving despite his dreams of violence . . . who remind him that the thing on his heart is only private." Mendelson sees this threefold pattern ("awareness of self, things, others") as reflective of the epistemology of the German philosopher Edmund Husserl (1859–1938).

For Joel Connarroe, writing in *John Berryman: An Introduction to the Poetry*, the last sestet of the poem describes "morning horrors of an alcoholic who has no memory at all of what he may have done during a blacked-out period the night before, and who automatically fears the worst." Connarroe argues that Henry's knowledge that he is capable of murder helps to explain his sympathetic identification in another dream song (number 135) with Richard Speck, the notorious murderer who killed several nurses in Chicago in 1966, and the Texas sniper Charles Whitman, who killed thirteen people, also in 1966.

Like Connarroe, Lewis Hyde interprets the poem in light of the alcoholism from which Berryman suffered, taking a similar view of the meaning of the final sestet. Hyde argues in *Alcohol and Poetry: John Berryman and the Booze Talking* that the poem is about anxiety, which is a major symptom of alcoholism and also of withdrawal from alcohol addiction. He differentiates anxiety from fear, because anxiety has no object. This means that there is no action a person (such as Henry in the poem) can take to relieve it. "The sufferer who does not realize this will search his world for problems to attend in hopes of relieving his anxiety, only to find that nothing will fill its empty stomach."

Paul Mariani explains in his *Kenyon Review* article that Henry's terror in biographical terms, referring to Berryman's "overwhelming sense of being unloved. As his father had shown him by blowing his heart out with a single .32 caliber shot." Mariani also mentions the rejection of Berryman by Eileen, his first wife, and believes that the "grave Sienese face" in "Dream Song 29" is in part the reproachful image Berryman retained of Eileen.

Thomas Travisano suggests that the poem "may be an elegy for childhood losses." He argues that:

> a child's consciousness is suggested not through the direct evocation of a child's experiences . . . [but] through the preservation or stylized recreation of childlike forms of speech . . . [which] convey Henry's feeling of his own incomplete maturity, the struggles caused by the fact that a part of himself remains locked in childishness, emotionally uncompleted.

Travisano also notes that the dream songs were written soon after Berryman had engaged in a period of intensive dream analysis, and the poem's "sudden shifts and surprising juxtapositions," which are especially notable in the second sestet, "reflect his extensive exploration of and immersion in unconscious experience."

CRITICISM

Bryan Aubrey

Aubrey holds a Ph.D. in English. In this essay, he considers the themes of "Dream Song 29" in light of similar themes that appear in many of the other dream songs.

The mind of Henry, the semi-autobiographical figure presented in "Dream Song 29" and throughout the 384 dream songs, is an uncomfortable place to inhabit. Henry is a tormented individual, constantly afflicted by irrational feelings of anxiety and guilt that nothing can assuage. He is also aware of the violent impulses that lurk within him and even believes, in spite of the evidence he carefully, even obsessively, assembles to the contrary, that he has committed

WHAT DO I READ NEXT?

- *John Berryman: Poems Selected by Michael Hofmann* (2004) contains selections from the whole range of Berryman's poetry, including, in addition to *The Dream Songs*, selections from his books, *Berryman's Sonnets, Homage to Mistress Bradstreet, Love & Fame,* and *Delusions, Etc.* Hofmann contributes an appreciative introduction.

- Robert Lowell was Berryman's contemporary and is considered to be one of the finest American poets of the twentieth century. His *Selected Poems: Expanded Edition, including selections from Day by Day* (2007), offers generous selections from the entire range of Lowell's work, including his seminal book, *Life Studies,* in its entirety.

- Before her suicide in 1975, Anne Sexton had established herself as one of the more prominent confessional poets. Her poetry has so far stood the test of time, and her voice remains a distinctive one in twentieth century American poetry. *The Complete Poems: Anne Sexton* (1999) contains her work.

- The poet Randall Jarrell was a friend of Berryman; the two men respected each other's work. Jarrell is the subject of "Dream Song 127," which alludes to Jarrell's death in 1965 being ruled a suicide. Jarrell is considered to be one of the best American poets from the period immediately following World War II. His *Collected Poems* (1981) preserves the entirety of his poetry.

> IT APPEARS FROM OTHER SONGS THAT HENRY IS A MAN OF SOME RELIGIOUS SENSIBILITY WHO MOURNS THE APPARENT LOSS OF GOD IN HIS OWN LIFE."

"thing" that sat down on Henry's heart, crushing his spirits and perpetually disturbing him, was the suicide of Berryman's father, when Berryman was eleven years old. John Allyn Smith was apparently depressed because his wife had fallen in love with another man and wanted a divorce. During his final days he took to walking up and down the beach on Clearwater Isle, across the bay from Tampa, with a gun in his hand. Around dawn on the morning of June 26, 1926, he shot himself behind the apartment building where the family lived. His wife, awakened by the shot, found his body. According to John Haffenden, Berryman's biographer, Berryman wrote as an adult that after his father's death he felt "desolation and rage," although for many years he had believed that his primary emotion was grief. Haffenden continues, "Later in life Berryman believed that he had been stunned by his loss, and took it as the *point d'appui* of his psychological problems."

Given this belief on the part of the poet, it is perhaps not surprising that the dream songs contain many references to his father's suicide. The second sestet of "Dream Song 1," for example, looks back to a time when Henry appears to have been happy, and all the world was on his side; but "Then came a departure. / Thereafter nothing fell out as it might or ought." The last two lines of this sestet explain that Henry does not know how he managed to survive, following this sudden departure, which is clearly of his father. In "Dream Song 15," the cryptic reference to one who "hides in the land" is often taken to be a reference to his dead father. "Dream Song 34" is about the suicide of Ernest Hemingway in 1961, who, like Berryman's father, shot himself. Sestet 2 in this song, which contains the phrase "the dove light after dawn at the island" refers to Berryman's father. Berryman was aware of the fact that Hemingway's father had also committed suicide; referring to the writer he says, "whose sire as mine

a murder. "Dream Song 29" can stand alone as a disturbing poem about the mind of a suffering individual, but further insight can be gained by a knowledge of how similar themes appear in many of the other dream songs.

Suicide, one of the elements that makes up "Dream Song 29" is a recurring theme in the dream songs. Critics are widely agreed that the one same way." (Tragically, Berryman, when he took his own life in 1972, completed the symmetry in the fate of the two sons whose fathers took their own lives.) "Dream Song 76" contains an explicit, no doubt painful to write, description of the scene that early morning in 1926:

> A bullet on a concrete stoop
> close by a smothering southern sea
> spreadeagled on an island, by my knee.

From the evidence of the dream songs, Berryman's own feelings about his father were ambivalent. "Dream Song 143," which is entirely about Henry's father, makes a reference to his threat to swim out to sea, taking Henry or his brother Robert Jefferson with him, and drown both himself and the boy. In this song, the poet insists that he loves his father, and he repeats this sentiment even more powerfully in "Dream Song 145," which is also devoted entirely to his father: "Also I love him: me he's done no wrong / for going on forty years—forgiveness time—." He takes solace in the fact that his father did not carry out his apparent threat to drown himself and one of his sons, but only took his own life. He also admits that he does not know what was going on in his father's mind, "so strong / & so undone," at the time of his suicide. In "Dream Song 384," however, the poet expresses a different view. He records a visit he made to his father's grave (which according to his biographer he never in fact made) and writes "I spit upon this dreadful banker's grave / who shot his heart out in a Florida dawn." He remains angry about what his father did and longs for some peace from the unrest it is still causing him. He expresses a desire to hack the casket open with an ax and then bring the ax down on the remains of his father. He believes, it would appear, that only through this violent act, in which the father is symbolically killed again, can he be free of the tragic event that took place when he was a boy.

Another theme in "Dream Song 29" is a feeling of guilt so pervasive that it dominates Henry's thoughts, allowing him no respite. A feeling of personal guilt is apparent in many of the other dream songs. "Dream Song 20" presents a long list of what Henry regards as serious personal failings. He has failed to write to a friend; he has not listened when, presumably, he feels he should have done; he has told lies; he has hurt others and wonders whether he has ever done any good for anyone. In "Dream Song 43," he imagines himself standing trial as "The Man Who Did

Not Deliver" and being deservedly convicted. In other songs, he seems to feel that he deserves punishment. In the fantasy that makes up "Dream Song 8," he imagines being subjected to some kind of physical torture in which an unidentified "they" removed his teeth, weakened his eyes, put burning thumbs in his ears, and finally, "They took away his crotch." In "Dream Song 81," he imagines being mutilated after death; in "Dream Song 236," he imagines himself being hanged, apparently for killing a woman with a knife, and he admits to his guilt, referring to himself in the third person: "It's true he did it." This is a clear parallel to Henry's guilty thoughts in "Dream Song 29" about the murder he thinks he has committed.

In several other songs, Henry considers suicide. "Got a little poison, got a little gun" he says in "Dream Song 40"; in "Dream Song 159," he says, "Maybe it's time / to throw in my own hand," but he decides against it because he thinks he may yet learn to understand some secrets hidden in history, theology and poetry; in other words, Berryman's work—he was a scholar and teacher as well as a poet—offers him some small hope, at least in this song, to counteract the tedium and distress apparent in such lines as "We suffer on, a day, a day, a day" ("Dream Song 153") or the "panic dread" that afflicts him each morning when he wakes ("Dream Song 268") and which recalls the Henry of "Dream Song 29," frantically counting in the dawn to see if anyone is missing.

In "Dream Song 29," Henry's psychic turmoil is set against the comfort offered by religion, hinted at in the tolling of the bells, from which he is excluded. The "grave Sienese face" in the second sestet, suggestive of equanimity and perhaps the product of an austere religious life, Henry can experience only as a reproach. It appears from other songs that Henry is a man of some religious sensibility who mourns the apparent loss of God in his own life. For example, "Dream Song 17," which Berryman described as a conversation between Henry and the devil, ends with Henry seeking solace in a variety of religious figures from different religious traditions: a Catholic saint, a saint of the Eastern Orthodox Church, and distinguished representatives of the Buddhist and Jewish faiths. In "Dream Song 20," discussed earlier in terms of Henry's guilty feelings, Henry appeals to God to "Hurl... /... down / something," and ends by noting something that he has heard: the more sin increases, the more grace abounds. He has chosen his words carefully here; he has *heard* this, but certainly has not experienced it for himself. In "Dream Song 47," about the feast-day of St. Mary of Egypt, Henry states in the last lines, "We celebrate her feast . . . / whom God has not visited." In "Dream Song 48," he refers to the crucifixion of Christ and mourns "the death of love"; he is more distressed by the death than comforted by the gospel account of the resurrection, a notion which he regards as "troublesome."

Thus do the dream songs as a whole elaborate on the troubled, perpetually restless mind of the Henry of "Dream Song 29." They present a picture of a man torn by guilt and self-reproach, struggling to find a way of making his life worth living, aware that he could find no answers in religion, but occasionally managing to rise above his own gloom by means of a wry, self-deprecating wit: "Henry bores me, with his plights & gripes" ("Dream Song 14"). Perhaps it was this ironic humor which helped the poet Berryman, afflicted by alcoholism and desperate states of mind, to carry on as long as he did, until that tragic Friday morning in January, 1972, when he jumped to his death from a bridge in Minneapolis.

Source: Bryan Aubrey, Critical Essay on "Dream Song 29," in *Poetry for Students*, Gale, 2008.

John Haffenden

In the following essay, Haffenden gives a critical analysis of Berryman's work.

John Berryman is associated with a group of poets who have become known as the "Middle Generation," a group that includes Delmore Schwartz, Randall Jarrell, Theodore Roethke, and Robert Lowell. It is a critical convenience to label much of the work of Berryman and Lowell, along with that of Sylvia Plath, as "confessional," but the tag is certainly belittling. It suggests a poetry which indulges in vulgar self-exposure, and neglects to note, for example, that Berryman's poems—even in *The Dream Songs* (1969) and *Love & Fame* (1970), which are supposedly his most confessional volumes—are in fact the products of sustained imagination and craft. Berryman and his contemporaries certainly had highly disturbed lives, with elements of self-victimization, but the poems should not be mistaken for the lives. Literary historians must eventually evaluate those lives from the

> IT [*THE DREAM SONGS*] IS NEITHER A NARRATIVE NOR A PHILOSOPHICAL POEM, BUT A POEM TO WHICH BERRYMAN OPENED HIS ENTIRE MIND AND BEING, ACTS AND EVENTUALITIES, HIGH THOUGHTS AND DARK OBSESSIONS."

perspectives both of individual psychology and of cultural context. Robert Lowell worried the question in an 18 March 1963 letter to Berryman "What queer lives we've had even for poets! There seems something generic about it, and determined beyond anything we could do." In view of the fact that this generation reached adulthood just before World War II, they had also to wonder, as Lowell later put it, "Were we uncomfortable epigoni of Frost, Pound, Eliot, Marianne Moore, etc? This bitter possibility came to us at the moment of our *arrival*."

Faced with such great antecedents, Berryman had to serve a long apprenticeship as a poet, burdened by influence, which lasted until the late 1940s. "Berryman's earlier work," Kenneth Connelly has observed, "is often that of a very self-conscious, sometimes too respectful scholar sweating in the poet's academy, with results, as Dudley Fitts noted long ago, which were marred by 'an aura of contrivance'" (*Yale Review*, Spring 1969). But the apprenticeship paid off, for his major works, *Homage to Mistress Bradstreet* (1956) and *The Dream Songs*, are sui generis, unprecedented long poems of humane interest and high literary art, not of unmeditated expressiveness or merely confessional interest. As Denis Donoghue observed of *The Dream Songs*, "the poem is all perception, surrounded by feeling. The feeling is not on show, on parade; it comes into the lines only because it attends upon perceptions which could not appear without that favour." Berryman's life is at the center of his best poetry, and his poetry is a function of his obsessions. He in fact experienced the whole gamut of obsessions—emotional, psychological, philosophical, religious—which a modern man might endure, but he managed to stand outside himself in his poems by means of personae. "His poems are so close to a sense of life, an imparting of truth complete with the bias of technique and personality, that they have the true flavour of fiction," Douglas Dunn has written. "An enormously comprehensive and unsentimental pathos slips out of his work, complicated and perplexing. We realize that although it may all be about ordinary Berryman, it generalizes itself, it has compass."

Berryman suffered from mismatched parents. His father, John Allyn Smith, had migrated from the family home in Minnesota and worked in the banking business in Oklahoma, where he met and married a young schoolmistress, Martha Little. It is evident that honor came before passion in their marriage, for Martha soon realized her incompatibility with her husband; she was snobbish, capable and ambitious, while Smith seems to have been a decent but unstriving character. After ten years in Oklahoma, Smith resigned from the bank, and the family, including a second son, Robert Jefferson (born in 1917), moved to Florida to try their business prospects. But the Florida boom collapsed in the mid-1920s; Smith's professional hopes foundered and he became depressed and withdrawn. In addition, perhaps because he had come to feel emotionally dispossessed by his wife's strong, exclusive love for the children, Smith showed every sign of being dangerously unstable and fickle in his behavior. He committed suicide by shooting himself on 26 June 1926.

Berryman often regarded that event, which took place in his twelfth year, as the trauma of his life, and in later years he was obsessed with grief, self-identity, and psychological dislocation, as well as with questions of temporal and religious destiny, all of which infused his major poetry. His cast of mind construed affliction as a creative stimulant. Burdened by his mother's influence and dominance, he continually worried the neurotic conflict he believed his father's suicide had triggered. From time to time, in an effort to rationalize the tribulations which fed his poetry, he quizzed his mother for the truth about his father, but most of what she told him characterized Smith as a man deeply alienated, at a point of existential crisis, and irremediably selfish. Although Berryman often reckoned with the fact that his mother must have contributed to the sense of rejection Smith experienced, he mostly suppressed his own feeling of disaffection for her and so perpetuated the self-divisions which charged his best poetry. While self-dramatization galvanized his mature creative output—as late as 1970, he claimed that he retained "enough feelings" about his father to "dominate" *The Dream Songs*—he struggled through his personal life in a state of continual disequilibrium, rage and remorse, relieved only by periods of exultation.

In Florida the Smiths had been befriended by a man named John Angus McAlpin Berryman. Late in 1926 he married Martha Smith, and the family presently moved to New York City. Young John, who duly adopted his stepfather's surname, attended the newly founded "jock" school, South Kent School in Connecticut, where he boarded for four years from 1928. At that time the school set the highest value on excellence in competitive sports, much more than on academic accomplishments, and it is clear that Berryman, who had all too little aptitude for the playing field, was grievously misplaced. He was subjected to an emotionally confusing existence which forced him to separate his natural abilities from his pretended ambitions and interests. Although he attained high academic success he had to do so while affecting self-disparagement and in the face of what amounted to the school's depreciation. He suffered from a certain amount of bullying, which provoked him to one suicide attempt on 7 March 1931, but his studiousness and cleverness, much encouraged by his mother, at last worked to his good: he was the first boy in the history of the school to bypass the sixth form and to go straight from the fifth into college.

At Columbia College of Columbia University in New York, he spent two years compensating to himself by becoming a great social success and a lion among the coeds, but his failure in one examination shocked him so much that he soon made steadier academic progress. His mother played an enormously influential part in fostering his intellectual and creative talents, but it was the example and guidance of Mark Van Doren, who became a fatherly mentor, which finally fixed his ambitions. Berryman credited Van Doren as being "the presiding genius of all my work until my second year, when I fell under the influence of W.B. Yeats," and characterized his teaching as "strongly structured, lit with wit, leaving ample play for grace and charm .... It stuck steadily to its subject and was highly disciplined .... If during my stay at Columbia I had met only Mark Van Doren and his work, it would have been worth the trouble. It was the force of his example, for instance, that made me a poet." For his part, Van Doren remembered Berryman as "first and last a literary youth: all of his thought sank into poetry, which he studied and wrote as if there were no other exercise for the human brain. Slender, abstracted, courteous, he lived one life alone, and walked with verse as in a trance." Berryman published several poems and reviews in the *Columbia Review*, and studied so hard that the dean of Columbia College eventually considered him "conspicuously qualified ... for academic distinction."

He finally won the distinction of becoming Kellett Fellow, which enabled him to study for two years (1936-1938) at Clare College, Cambridge, where he worked under George Rylands and won the prestigious Oldham Shakespeare Scholarship in his second year. He met W.H. Auden in England, befriended Dylan Thomas[...] and received an audience with his hero W.B. Yeats, who left him, as he recorded at the time, with "an impression of tremendous but querulous force, a wandering intensely personal mind which resists natural bent (formal metaphysics by intuition, responsible vision) to its own exhaustion." Also in England, he became engaged to a young woman, who visited him in New York when he returned there for the academic year 1938-1939, but the relationship could not last when she decided to stay in England for the duration of World War II.

While in England Berryman had determined to become a teacher, but he failed to gain a job on returning to New York and spent one year in a state of considerable nervous stress, writing poems (some of them were published in *Southern Review*), abortive plays, and book reviews for *New York Herald Tribune Books*. In 1939 he became for one year part-time poetry editor of the *Nation*, and took up an appointment as instructor in English at Wayne University in Detroit (now Wayne State University), where he lived and worked with a charismatic young friend, Bhain Campbell. A poet and Marxist, Campbell strove to inject some social and political consciousness into Berryman's apprentice poetry, but Berryman's early work manifests a concern with the craft of poetry—the dynamics of style, form, metrics—to the extent of neglecting content. The strain of his year at Wayne caused Berryman to suffer from exhaustion and from attacks which were diagnosed as petit mal epilepsy. Furthermore, Bhain Campbell contracted cancer and died late in 1940, an event which caused Berryman a profound grief which he associated with the death of his father. In 1940 he

began work as an instructor in English at Harvard University, and in 1942 he married his first wife, Eileen Patricia Mulligan, whose love and moral support for his work and whose sufferance of his increasingly bizarre neurotic drives kept them together for a period of more than ten years.

Berryman's earliest poems were first brought together, along with poems by Mary Barnard, Randall Jarrell, W.R. Moses, and George Marion O'Donnell, in *Five Young American Poets* (1940), and then in a slim volume of his own, *Poems* (1942). Most of the items in those first collections were written in 1939, and have been well characterized by Joel Conarroe as "ominous, flat, social, indistinctly allusive, exhausted ... an echo chamber." Well schooled and crafted, infused with a sense of loss and unlocated portentousness, they mostly fail to synthesize personal feeling and reflection, and have pretensions to the meditative poise Berryman valued in the poetry of Yeats's middle period. Too much in them is labored and realized only through rhetoric, so that even poems which figure socio-political subjects (prompted by Berryman's association with Bhain Campbell) bury the contemporary ills and evils they treat in specious gestures and solemn style. Conrad Aiken, R.P. Blackmur, Allen Tate, Oscar Williams, and John Crowe Ransom spotted the promise of Berryman and of Randall Jarrell in the group volume of 1940, and indeed certain poems, such as Berryman's "Winter Landscape," deserve their reward as anthology pieces. However, Berryman recognized at an early stage that he had been beguiled by literary influences, Yeats, Auden, and Delmore Schwartz being chief among them, and that both the forms and attitudes of his first published poems derived as much from works of literature as from subjects of real personal concern. "Desires of Men and Women," for example, might have been entitled "Variation on a Theme by Delmore Schwartz"; [....] (Likewise, what really interested Berryman about "The Animal Trainer," a poem in two parts completed by March 1940 but published four years later, was that its form derived from poems by Conrad Aiken and Bhain Campbell.) Berryman struggled to find his own voice throughout the 1940s, trying all the while to break away from the dominant influence of Yeats on what he called "the compositional base" of his poems. Since he protractedly worried the claims of literature over life [...]—it is ironic that his greatest achievements as a poet finally came from fashioning the literature of life.

In 1943 he started teaching as an instructor in English at Princeton University, where he worked under another of his heroes, Richard Blackmur, and numbered among his talented students W.S. Merwin, Frederick Buechner, and William Arrowsmith. Berryman showed great respect and affection for Blackmur, Frederick Buechner recalls: "Blackmur seemed an old gull drying his wise wings in the sun, Berryman a sandpiper skittering along the edge of the tide." Princeton was Berryman's home for the next decade, and his circle of friends expanded markedly during that time. After his initial period of teaching, in 1944 he undertook a two-and-a-half-year stretch of independent research in Shakespearean textual criticism (supported by a Rockefeller Foundation research fellowship, he virtually completed an edition of *King Lear* which has never been published) before he was again appointed to the teaching faculty in 1946. He was successively associate in creative writing, resident fellow in creative writing, and Alfred Hodder Fellow and became a conspicuously successful teacher with a charisma that awed his students. Those students and other friends who were closest to him nonetheless discerned the psychological pressure and pain under which he labored, a restlessness of the spirit coupled with a deep despair of himself. At Harvard University from 1940 to 1943 he had suffered a more oppressive intellectual climate, from much of which (unlike his colleague Delmore Schwartz) he had shielded himself, only to indulge in increasingly morbid and paralyzing self-appraisal. At Princeton long hours of isolated study caused him to brood more and more. His tolerance for personal and professional setbacks became lower than ever, and by the late 1940s he assumed a sort of a second nature, a guise in which to face what he believed to be the overwhelming demands of his work and society. Many of his acquaintances saw his public role as that of an eccentric, a combination of braggart, womanizer, unpredictable drinker, and formidable—sometimes savagely assertive or dismissive—intellectual. In fact, whether intimidating or endearing, his behavior was often just the superficial aspect of a temperament that was all too often tormented by acute insecurity, self-recrimination, and self-exaction. To a degree, after 1947, Berryman came to hide his fears in drink. His diaries from the 1940s give the impression of a man stricken by neurosis and self-analysis, paradoxically sustaining himself by greater demands on the self, and

too little evidence of the many happy times he enjoyed with his wife.

In 1948 William Sloane Associates published *The Dispossessed*, a volume of rhymed stanzaic poems burdened by feelings of hopelessness and confusion, wielding abstruse images and torturing syntax in an unrewarding fashion. It was characteristic of Berryman's desolated attitude during the early and mid-1940s that he should have followed in some verses the example and tone of Louis Aragon, especially as in *Le Crève-Coeur* (1941; Berryman later complained that he had been "conned" by Aragon), where a bitter sentimentality and sense of personal defeatism vis-a-vis World War II harmonized with Berryman's sense of affairs. He tended to see his own inner conflicts mirrored in the European holocaust. Some of the poems of *The Dispossessed*, milling with inflated sentiment and opaque image, are virtually incomprehensible in whole or in part. The title poem, for instance, begins with a quotation from Luigi Pirandello and leads into a surrealistic assemblage of images; it is easy to miss the point that the poem actually concerns the dropping of the atomic bomb on Hiroshima[....] Joel Conarroe properly comments: "The humorless, abstract, often bloodless quality of much of the early work, inhibited even in an age of arid art, gives evidence of the price Berryman paid for rejecting the validity of his own sensory experience .... Berryman succeeds less well with the social-ironic speculative poem, by way of Auden, than with the personal lyric ... that has its source in his own feelings." Contemporary reviewers understandably felt they could find little to praise in the collection, though a number of them expressed hopes for Berryman's future. While Randall Jarrell reasonably discovered "raw or overdone lines side by side with imaginative and satisfying ones" (*Nation*, 17 July 1948), Yvor Winters taxed Berryman's "disinclination to understand and discipline his emotions. Most of his poems appear to deal with a single all-inclusive topic: the desperate chaos, social, religious, philosophical, and psychological, of modern life, and the corresponding chaos and desperation of John Berryman" (*Hudson Review*, Fall 1948). However, one group of nine dramatic monologues, "The Nervous Songs" (which are to some extent influenced by Rainer Maria Rilke), stand out as psychologically vibrant dramas which prefigure Berryman's mature work. As Conarroe has written, "In its form, the three six-line stanzas with flexible rhyme schemes, and in its mood of intense auto-revelation, the sequence is an important forerunner of *The Dream Songs.*"

The year 1947, however, had finally brought contingent reality directly into the center of Berryman's creative life. He had an illicit affair with a woman to whom he gave the pseudonym Lise and wrote a running commentary on its progress in the form of a sequence of sonnets which were published only twenty years later as *Berryman's Sonnets* (1967). The sonnets use a Petrarchan rhyme scheme, much archaic or antic diction, and dislocated syntax (which at best reflects the turbulence of the poet's moods and at worst draws attention to itself as factitious and gauche). The sequence in some ways corresponds to a traditional and perhaps artificial scheme—moving from hope and anxiety through dangerous and guilty fulfillment to withdrawal and reproach—but that paradigmatic design was in fact fortuitous, for the sequence at all stages logs the actuality of the affair. *Berryman's Sonnets* provides an inventory of the poet's being, mind, and moods, at stages on a blind road. Berryman quickly assumed the role of a spectator of his own drama, and the sonnets served appetite as much as satisfaction. He became at once obsessively "in love" with his mistress and self-consciously withdrawn, exercising a double consciousness which left a discrete gap between the man who experienced and suffered and the writer who evaluated and composed emotion into a literary artifact.

Since circumstances kept Berryman and Lise apart for much of the summer, he was often compelled to fashion an image of her, a myth, drawing on imaginative invention and on literary analogues. Accordingly, the sonnets sometimes fall short of what Roy Pascal has called a "correlative in the outer world" (*Design and Truth in Autobiography*, 1960). Berryman leaned toward literature to find models of his love, sometimes with a consequent excess of self-regard. In sonnet 75, he compares himself to Petrarch, in 29 to Honoré de Balzac, in 21 to David in relation with Bathsheba; sonnet 16 was suggested by Philip Sidney's second sonnet to Stella. In other words, by comparing himself to well-known precursors in the role of adulterer or sonneteer, he was drawn to behold himself in the role of poet and to diminish attention to the lady. His literary self-consciousness is marked even in the first sonnet of the sequence [...] which alludes to Stéphane Mallarmé's poem "M' introduire

dans ton histoire"; the first four lines of sonnet 102 (a poem, Berryman recorded in his journal, written on "15 August in the morning after my worst nightmare for months: a killer, mad") are a loose imitation of the first four lines of Tristan Corbière's poem "Heures"; sonnet 105 is a virtuoso performance prompted by a reading of the Grimms' tale "The Duration of Life." Likewise, the final line of sonnet 52 includes a slightly mistranscribed quotation from the last line [...] of Wilhelm Müller's "Wasserflut" ("The Water's Flow"), set to music, as part of *Winterreise*, by Franz Schubert: it is one of many private references in the sequence, for Berryman and Lise loved playing recordings of Schubert's song cycle together. A good deal of the obscurity and inscrutability of the sonnets may be attributed, not only to the necessity of subterfuge and secrecy, but to the fact that much of their content and thematic linkage was the product of the poet's isolation from his love, compelling him to be self-conscious and literary. Many of the sonnets, he knew, were authentic in impulse but made insincere by artistic devices.

On the other hand, perhaps just as many were written in direct response to the lover, and they include the best of all the sonnets, which are fully charged with personal emotion, anguish, and poignancy, and communicate it to the reader. They served, like Jonathan Swift's *Journal to Stella* or Laurence Sterne's *Journal to Eliza* , as a way of imparting his feelings to Lise. In that sense the most accomplished sonnets were a form of homage, poems about as well as to his love. Berryman's journal entry for 16 July 1947, for instance, includes the sincere comments: "(... she is my *conscience* as well as my inspiration); four new sonnets, and even better (what I couldn't get peace for earlier) four old ones perfected—still I die of longing: if I hadn't faith in her I don't know what I would do." Milton Gilman points to the cold surface texture of many of the allusive sonnets, and perceptively argues that Lise "is, in a sense, the creative agent of every poem, the source of tone, rhythm, image, and theme." She is "a provisional deity .... The real center of interest is the increasingly complex psychological state of the speaker .... the *illicit* nature of the affair is so important in the Sonnets, providing an opportunity to release all kinds of feeling: lust, longing, scorn, guilt, pity, fatigue, despair, fear, impatience, joy."

Reviewers of *Berryman's Sonnets*, when they at last appeared in 1967, highlighted the importance of their style as laying the ground for Berryman's use of disrupted syntax in his major works, *Homage to Mistress Bradstreet* and *The Dream Songs*, where style—what Anthony Thwaite called in a review for the *New Statesman* (17 May 1968) the "awful spasmodics" of *Berryman's Sonnets*—is integrated with subject, functional and not gratuitous. But what is perhaps equally important about the achievement of *Berryman's Sonnets* is that they showed him the way to marry his creative gift to his life. The essence of Berryman's art and his literary success lay in his ability to tap and impart the deepest reaches of the human personality and consciousness.

Berryman's desire and guilt over the affair of 1947, and over other illicit affairs in the late 1940s, immediately charged the theme and form of his first major work, *Homage to Mistress Bradstreet*, which he began in 1948 and finished in 1953. A long poem of fifty-seven stanzas, with a complex metric and sophisticated rhyme scheme, it succeeds both as lyric and as drama, and has been called by Edmund Wilson "the most distinguished long poem by an American since *The Waste Land*." Berryman himself declared that he "set up the *Bradstreet* poem as an attack on *The Waste Land:* personality, and plot—no anthropology, no Tarot pack, no Wagner." He deplored Eliot's notion of the impersonality of the poet, and rather professed the "passionate sense of identification" he found in Walt Whitman.

Homage to Mistress Bradstreet employs an apparently objective scheme of two voices—the voice of Anne Bradstreet, the first poet of New England, and that of the "poet" who both conjures up the heroine and appears to be conjured up by her (since the poem largely follows the putative experiences of her life). Berryman's Bradstreet is rendered as an alienated, creative woman, rebellious against husband, father, and God. She registers a sense of spiritual and domestic displacement, bears a child, momentarily succumbs to the seductive blandishments of the "poet" who figures as a sort of demon lover, but then withdraws from him and moves forward into her declining years and death. The poem ends with a sense of historical quietus and fatalism. Much of the poem draws on the facts of the life of the real Anne Bradstreet, some of which are distorted, even perverted, for imaginative purposes which

justifiably serve the work's major themes—religious apostasy, adulterous inclination, creative stultification, guilt, retribution, remorse—all of which match Berryman's personal obsessions. Berryman's own marriage and adulteries are sublimated in the poem, so that its fictive form actually speaks directly for the poet's passionate concerns. In depicting a relationship beyond space and time, Berryman deploys a conceptual device which transcends and encompasses subjective utterance and accordingly succeeds on a multiplicity of structural and thematic levels. In a sense *Homage to Mistress Bradstreet* does offer a personal confession and an exploration of its subject, but in a form which transfigures self-exhibition through art.

It may be fair, as John Frederick Nims wrote in a 1958 review, to judge that the poem stresses "a sort of depressing propaganda for the view that the flesh is evil," but it needs to be said that the poem is stylistically far more flexible (moving swiftly, for example, between moments of tenderness, triumph, hysteria, and pathos) than the limits Nims sets: "In Berryman's stanza everything is tense, numb, shivering, painful .... Throughout the poem I find this alternation of strength, gravity, even nobility with a shrill hectic fury, a whipped-up excitement, a maudlin violence of *mal protesi nervi*." (Berryman himself reasonably explained, "I was taking chances at the time of my poem. I had to get a language that was not hers, but not mine, but would *not be pastiche*, like Ben Jonson's projection of Spenser.") Nims's comments are as just as those by any other adverse critic of the poem (compare, for instance, the severely critical long essay "The Life of the Modern Poet," in the 23 February 1973 issue of the *Times Literary Supplement*), where the anonymous reviewer perceptively argues that "purportedly concerned with Anne Bradstreet, [Berryman's] poem is really about 'the poet' himself, his romantic and exacerbated personality, his sense of loneliness, his need for a mistress, confidante, confessor"; but his conclusion that Berryman "has too little human reality to sustain his myth" may be disputed by emphasizing the transcendent imaginative richness of the achievement.

Homage to Mistress Bradstreet , as one or two critics have pointed out, has some likeness to Robert Lowell's poem *Lord Weary's Castle* (1946), but any comparison necessarily fails in essentials: Berryman's poem is peculiar to himself in both style and concerns. He was undoubtedly correct when he observed, "In the Bradstreet poem, as I seized inspiration from [Saul Bellow's novel *The Adventures of Augie March*, [1953], I sort of seized inspiration, I think, from Lowell, rather than imitated him." Berryman had befriended Lowell as early as 1944, and enthusiastically reviewed *Lord Weary's Castle* in 1947.

Lowell himself recalled that Berryman "was humorous, thrustingly vehement in liking ... more adolescent than boyish.... Hyperenthusiasms made him a hot friend, and could also make him wearing to friends—one of his dearest, Delmore Schwartz, used to say that no one had John's loyalty, but you liked him to live in another city .... John could quote with vibrance to all lengths, even prose, even late Shakespeare, to show me what could be done with disrupted and mended syntax. This was the start of his real style."

There is no doubt that Berryman managed to be both fiercely loving and very competitive toward Lowell and other poets, but he invariably gave his love and kept the rivalry to himself. On the whole, he felt that his own achievements as a poet came second to Lowell's, as he wrote in an undated, not necessarily disingenuous letter to his mother shortly after Robert Frost's death in 1963: "Frost's going puts—as you wouldn't think it would—a problem to me. I have never wanted to be king .... I've been comfortable since 1946 with the feeling that Lowell is far my superior .... "

Berryman's obsessional self-inquisition and his growing dependence on alcohol (he first began to drink heavily in 1947) put undue strains on his private life, but it enabled him to develop a strong sense of identification with what he discovered to be (in a sometimes willful and not always strictly scholarly way) the psychological problems of Stephen Crane. Reviewers received *Stephen Crane* (1950), his critical biography, respectfully but on the whole skeptically, for a number shared Graham Greene's criticism of the book's "tortured prose" and of Berryman's dubious use of depth psychology as a mode of literary criticism. Morgan Blum, on the other hand, considered it a "flawed but distinguished book"—distinguished in its treatment of the intersections between Crane's life and work.

Berryman's bravura teaching continued to flourish: he taught at the University of Washington in early 1950, and spent a most successful semester as Elliston Professor of Poetry at the University of Cincinnati in Spring 1952. His endeavors as a Shakespearean scholar (which at many stages of his life he valued as highly as his work in poetry) and his poetry writing were equally rewarded with a Guggenheim Fellowship for critical study and for creative writing, which enabled him to complete *Homage to Mistress Bradstreet*. But his psychological disturbances compelled him to seek the help of a psychiatrist, whom he consulted at length in the late 1940s and early 1950s, and he also spent some time in group therapy. Moreover, the stresses of his drinking, his anguished disposition, and his increasingly wayward conduct caused his first wife to leave him at the end of a hectic summer in Europe in 1953. Eileen Berryman Simpson has recently published two books of her own, a worthy novel, *The Maze* (1975), which is, according to one reviewer, "quite transparently the story of the marriage's breakup .... less satisfying as fiction than as biography," and a memoir, *Poets in Their Youth* (1982).

Berryman then taught in the Writers' Workshop at the University of Iowa in spring 1954 and at Harvard University during that summer. ("He taught by exemplitude," Edward Hoagland, who studied under him at Harvard, has recalled. "He taught mostly about books he had loved with a fever that amounted to a kind of courage"). He returned to the University of Iowa that fall, but he was obliged to resign after a drunken altercation with his landlord which resulted in a night's imprisonment. (His students in the Writers' Workshop included W. D. Snodgrass, Donald Justice, William Dickey, and Jane Cooper.) Allen Tate, whom he had regarded as a master since they first met at Columbia in 1935, saved the situation by inviting him to Minneapolis [...], where he started teaching courses in humanities in 1955. It was in Minneapolis that Berryman became fast friends with Saul Bellow, whom he always looked to as a model of literary style and energy. In 1956 he married Elizabeth Ann Levine, who bore him a son, Paul, the following year, but the relationship fared badly and ended in divorce in 1959.

Berryman's sense of personal dereliction led him to undertake a long period of dream analysis on his arrival in Minneapolis, and to embark upon the greatest work of his career, *The Dream Songs*, first published in two parts, *77 Dream Songs* (1964) and *His Toy, His Dream, His Rest* (1968).

"I set up *The Dream Songs* as hostile to every visible tendency in both American and English poetry," Berryman later declared. "The aim was ... the reproduction or invention of the motions of a human personality, free and determined ...." *The Dream Songs* is a long poem of 385 sections, each (with small exceptions) being composed of three six-line stanzas, which deal with the multitudinous preoccupations and adventures, notions, and emotions, of a persona named Henry (alias Henry Pussycat, Henry House, Mr. Bones). Henry is now and then challenged and ineffectually corrected by an unidentified friend, his interlocutor. It is neither a narrative nor a philosophical poem, but a poem to which Berryman opened his entire mind and being, acts and eventualities, high thoughts and dark obsessions. [...] The shifting pronominal identification of Henry (who *is* obviously, to all intents and purposes, Berryman himself) became a function of Berryman's self-exploration, an ironic device which throws character and attitude free of solipsism or egotism. Berryman told Jane Howard that "the various parts of [Henry's] identity are fluid. They slide, and the reader is made to guess who is talking to whom. Out of this ambiguity arises richness. The reader becomes more aware, is forced to enter into himself."

The device of splitting facets of himself into dramatis personae owed much to Freud's analysis of ego and id, and to the classical opposition of alazon and eiron (the egoistic and pretentious man confronted by an ironic man who staggers self-possession), but also to an insight which Berryman independently perceived but later found rehearsed by W.H. Auden in "Balaam and His Ass" (*The Dyer's Hand*, 1963)[...].

In an interview dating from 1963, Berryman said, "I have an anti-hero in [*The Dream Songs*] who's a character the world gives a hard time to." The poem is often obscure and abstruse, especially in *77 Dream Songs*, with private references and arcane allusions; it also uses daring and lively syntax, and a mixed diction including what the poet himself called "coon talk." Such a motley style owes much to a tradition which reaches back through the ethos, rhythms, and attitudes of the blues to the minstrel tradition. Berryman himself pinpointed one source of his inspiration in the figure of Thomas Dartmouth Rice, a white actor of the early-nineteenth century who mimicked a black—"Jim Crow"—so finely that he managed to transform painful dispossession into art. Berryman identified with the social and spiritual underdog, and his Henry in a black mask expresses his own pain and pathos in a mode which extends beyond egotism and embraces other outcasts. Minstrelsy, as William Wasserstrom has written, "represents the climactic and synoptic solution to the poet's 'long, often back-breaking search for an inclusive style, a style that could use his erudition,' Robert Lowell says, and 'catch the high, even frenetic, intensity of his experience, disgusts and enthusiasm.'"

The Dream Songs, which Berryman called an epic, is a poem as ambitious as Walt Whitman's *Song of Myself*, William Carlos Williams's *Paterson*, or Hart Crane's *The Bridge*, but unlike *Song of Myself*, for instance, it proposes no system. It contains and bodies forth a personality, and philosophical and theological notions, but it is above all a pragmatic poem, essaying ideas and emotions, love, lust, lament, grief. Several of the finest poems are elegies for fellow poets—Delmore Schwartz, Randall Jarrell, Theodore Roethke, Sylvia Plath—and certain key songs compass Berryman's ambivalent feelings for his dead father. "Always," Kenneth Connelly has written, "Henry stands above his 'father's grave with rage,' resentful, compassionate, jealous, accusing, finally gaining the courage to spit upon it. (The mystery of a careless earthly father modulates inevitably into Henry's analogous broodings over the Heavenly Father and his family, provoking some of the most brilliant religious poems of our time.)" Through the persona of Henry, Berryman, as Wasserstrom expresses it, "synthesizes all fragments of the self [and] helps the self to mediate, accommodate, comply and in this way avoid all menace of extinction."

Berryman believed that feelings might be imaginatively controlled in the order of art, and hoped that *The Dream Songs* might be as useful to the reader as to himself. [...] He felt that Whitman's *Song of Myself* was a poem that "will do good to us," and the same may be true of *The Dream Songs*, which is by turns highly comic and savagely painful. It also has inevitable weaknesses and faults, one of which is perhaps not unlike the fault Berryman found in *Song of Myself* when he described it as "too idiosyncratic[...]" A number of critics have objected to Berryman's "abuse" of syntax, the whirligig of his demotic and literary diction (Robert Lowell found himself "rattled" by "mannerisms"), and what Denis Donoghue has called his "hotspur materials." However, a larger area of unrest, which Berryman always shared, concerns the shape and structure of *The Dream Songs,* epic or otherwise. Berryman continually attempted to model his poem on traditional epic structures, including Dante's *Divine Comedy,* the liturgy of the Bible, and the *Iliad,* and included a group of poems in which the hero dies and visits the underworld (book 4, the opus posthumous sequence which occupies the middle section of the poem, many critics consider to be among the finest of the songs; Robert Lowell told Berryman he considered book 4 "the crown of your wonderful work, witty, heartbreaking, all of a piece .... one of the lovely things in our literature"), but the nature of the songs entirely depended on the plotless fortunes of Berryman's own life during the thirteen years of writing. The "individual human soul under stress" to which he referred in a 1970 conversation with Richard Kostelanetz is that of Berryman as Henry; Berryman could no more map the poem to a prefigured narrative or philosophical conclusion than he could forecast the luck of his own life, as he virtually acknowledged in an interview for the *Paris Review:* "I was what you might call open-ended. That is to say, Henry to some extent was in the situation that we are all in in actual life—namely, he didn't know and I didn't know what the bloody f——ing hell was going to happen next. Whatever it was he had to confront it and get through."...

The dissociated "pieces," as Denis Donoghue has explained, go to make up the whole of the man and his work: "This is not Whitman's way. Whitman's aesthetic implies that the self is the sum of its experiences, not the sum of its dissociated fragments ...." In a 29 April 1962 letter to Robert Lowell, Berryman worried that the songs "are partly independent but only if ... the reader is familiar with Henry's tone, personality, friend, activities; otherwise, in small numbers, they seem simply crazy ...," but many good critics have demonstrated not only the folly of accusing the poem of confessional self-indulgence and disorder but also that what Berryman thought a weakness is actually a strength. Adrienne Rich, for instance (in a review Berryman called "the most serious study any large area of my work's ever had"), observed "first of all, the presence through the book of an effective unifying identity, and second, the power of that identity to define its surroundings so accurately .... a truly original work, in the sense in which Berryman has

made one, is superior in inner necessity and by the force of a unique human character."

Berryman fought hard to finish *The Dream Songs,* and incorporated into it all the adventures, observations, and vicissitudes of his life. In 1957, for instance, he undertook a successful but exhausting lecture tour of India, which gave him acute insights into a foreign culture. At home in Minneapolis the disestablishment of the department of inderdisciplinary studies in 1958 sustained his sense that his professional life would always be hapless and harrowing. He nonetheless fully committed himself (for the rest of his life, as it turned out) to teaching in the humanities program at the University of Minnesota, and developed a spectacular pedagogical style, ardent and terrified, and accentuated by the problems of alcoholism. The *Minneapolis Star* reported after his death: "In the classroom, Berryman was electrifying .... When he was wrapped up in a lecture—and he usually was, whatever the specific topic—he would stalk from one side of the room to the other, now whispering, now bellowing, invariably trembling with emotion and perspiring freely." His academic career reached a peak in 1969, when he was appointed Regents' Professor of Humanities, a distinction which left him far more humbled than conceited, and Drake University conferred on him an honorary doctorate. He also became a formidably successful performer in the role of public bard, and in his last decade he gave many campus readings at which his voice was by turns thick with drink, engagingly bombastic, and even menacing. His audiences found him thrilling, alarming, exhilarating, ripe with quips and asides. Jane Howard's profile of the poet (*Life,* 21 July 1967) served as much as any other report of the 1960s to sell Berryman in an image reminiscent of Dylan Thomas; she perfectly reflected the eccentric style—sensational, temperamental, learned—he had encouraged in his conduct. William Heyen, Berryman's host at a visit to the Brockport Writers Forum in 1970, likewise described him as "Charming, disputatious, dominating, brilliant." Like Samuel Johnson, however, Berryman always felt the anxieties of fame, and sustained himself with equal parts of arrogance, self-irony, and terror.

He gained much happiness and a focus for his personal life when he married his third and last wife, Kathleen (Kate) Donahue, in 1961. Three years later they managed to buy a modest house, the first and last home Berryman ever owned, on Arthur Avenue in Minneapolis. The couple had two children, Martha in 1962 and Sarah Rebecca in 1971. In 1966-1967 the family lived on a Guggenheim Fellowship in Dublin, where Berryman passed long hours drinking but finally assembled *The Dream Songs*. The conclusion of that poem after thirteen years of work could not but be a great loss to him, for reasons he might have known when he recalled (in "A Tribute," *Agenda*, 4, 1965) how he had once pressed T.S. Eliot to urge Ezra Pound to finish *The Cantos:* "'Oh no,' Eliot said gravely, 'I could never do that. That would be the end of him. He would have nothing to do.' I did not then like this attitude but it was right and I was wrong."

The consensus of critical opinion on Berryman's next volume of poetry, *Love & Fame* (1970), is that it marks a falling off in inspiration and technique, an unfortunate return to the lyric form. Wistful for the ambition and scope of his major works, even Berryman registered the inevitable limits of his latest venture[...]. Half of *Love & Fame* consists of autobiographical poems, which Robert Lowell considered "profane and often in bad taste, the license of John's old college dates recollected at fifty." Quite apart from the question of "bad taste" (which several reviewers impugned), the lyrics are in fact compellingly accessible, witty, and often ironic. The volume acquired a fortuitously ironic structure when Berryman ended it with "Eleven Addresses to the Lord," a group of lyrics which reaffirm a querulous and ambiguous religious faith [...] and require the reader to measure the secular and lubricious poems which precede them only in the context of the book as a whole. One reviewer, Walter Clemons, gave this perceptive and generous construction of *Love & Fame:* "Some of those poems are very hard to take. Behind a coarse jocularity, a desperate man was trying to cheer himself up, I thought when I first read and disliked them. I now think he was deliberately caricaturing, in bold poster colors, the bumptious, lost eagerness of his youth." However, no reader can afford to overlook the cautionary irony of Robert Lowell's comment that Berryman may have found his autobiographical excursions "too inspiring and less a breaking of new ground than he knew."

As with all Berryman's major works, the writing of *Love & Fame* ran in tandem with the experience of his life. He recovered his faith in Christ while undergoing treatment for alcoholism in 1970. He had suffered from alcoholism for more than twenty years, and first took steps to recover in 1969. The lessons he learned during two courses of treatment at St. Mary's Hospital, Minneapolis, in 1970, which included his conviction that a "God of rescue" had interceded in his life, established him as a recovering alcoholic but also left him feeling perilously self-exposed. He tried hard to take a stable view of his anguished sensibility and of his disturbed career (which he too often insisted on dating back to his father's suicide), but years of sickness and waste of spirit had taken their toll. Berryman's "late conversion," Douglas Dunn has saliently written, "proves the honesty of his anguish at the cruelty of the world, the competition without kindness. Yet it derives from fatigue."

Berryman drafted an autobiographical novel about the process of becoming a recovering alcoholic, but most critics have judged that the unfinished *Recovery* (1973) stands as an extraordinary and readable document about Berryman himself rather than as a fully realized work of literary art. He also completed a last book of poems, *Delusions, Etc.* (1972), but it fails on the whole to embody the passionate intensity of his best work, despite the undoubted success of certain poems—the idiosyncratic relish, for example, of "Beethoven Triumphant" and "Scholars at the Orchid Pavilion," the fierce identification of "Drugs Alcohol Little Sister" and "Tampa Stomp," and the poignant lament of "He Resigns." As the anonymous author of "The Life of the Modern Poet" (*Times Literary Supplement*, 23 February 1973) has written, "The last books have an intense but narrowly documentary appeal," and represent "the brave valediction of a man who chose his own way to die." In 1971 Berryman won a Senior Fellowship from the National Endowment for the Humanities in order to complete a critical biography, Shakespeare but he would not live to do so. He found that he no longer had the patience or energy for persevering with his writing, and ultimately that his capacity had failed; he committed suicide by jumping from the Washington Avenue Bridge in Minneapolis on 7 January 1972.

Berryman spent himself in his dedication to the work of poetry, as Daniel Hughes, who witnessed him at his desk in the early 1960s, observes: "I have never seen before or since such concentration .... I felt the presences of his terrible cost and commitment, and I loved him." When an interviewer asked him in 1965 to state the most important elements of good poetry, he replied, "Imagination, love, intellect—and pain. Yes, you've got to know pain." In at least one other interview Berryman seemed to find self-gratification in his "overdevelopment of sensibility"—"It's the price we pay," he announced. But whatever strain of misplaced and painfully ironic complacency that observation contains need not condition our reading of his best creative work, in which he found a dynamic form and style to make art of his life and obsessions. *Homage to Mistress Bradstreet* offers a remarkably imagined and densely achieved drama, with conceptual vigor and intricate execution, and deserves the praise it received from Edmund Wilson, Conrad Aiken, and Robert Lowell. That poem and *The Dream Songs* survive as the supreme achievements of a poet[...]. Despite its vaunted difficulty and occasional weakness—local incoherence, word thickness, stylistic obscurity—*The Dream Songs* is a richly imagined and moving work. Berryman also merits attention as one of the most notable religious poets of recent years.[...]

It is worth emphasizing the word *heroic* in Robert Lowell's claim that *The Dream Songs* is "the single most heroic work in English poetry since the War, since Ezra Pound's *Pisan Cantos*." Any discussion of literary history since World War II will also need to take account of the fact that *The Dream Songs* manifestly inspired Lowell to emulate Berryman's achievement with his own *Notebook* (1969), a work he subsequently refashioned and (according to some critics) weakened by imposing on it an overtly chronological and possibly lame form in its revised version, *History* (1973).

Source: John Haffenden, "John Berryman," in *Dictionary of Literary Biography*, Vol. 48, *American Poets, 1880–1945, Second Series*, edited by Peter Quartermain, Gale Research, 1986, pp. 20–37.

Muffy E. A. Siegel

In the following excerpt, Siegel examines the grammatical elements of "Dream Song 29," showing how Berryman's guilt about a murder that he did not commit is actually related to the artistic creation of the poem itself. Siegel compares the language patterns of the poem to those of the larger body of The Dream Songs *to illustrate that the protagonist's "crime is really art, not murder."*

> IN 'DREAM SONG 29,' HENRY, IN PARALLEL FASHION, ATTEMPTS TO TRANSFORM HIS INTERNAL STATES, WHICH SEEM TO BE DEPRESSION, HOSTILITY, AND SELF-LOATHING, INTO ANOTHER KIND OF EXTERNAL EVENT THAT INVOLVES OTHERS, A MURDER."

On an ordinary reading, Berryman's "Dream Song 29" conveys to the reader its hero's feeling of amorphous and paradoxical guilt, but the details and sources of the effects remain mysterious. Apparently a main character by the name of Henry has at some time in the past committed some sort of crime against someone, for which he is reproached by a "thing." Yet we feel that Henry is greatly mistaken about the crime he thinks he committed. We find out in stanza three that Henry's supposed murder has no victim. The poet repeats with perplexing emphasis that "nobody's missing." From this we can only conclude that Henry's crime, or at least the particular crime of murder, is just a horrible fantasy. But the question remains as to why anyone would continue inventing and living with something as frustrating and guilt-inducing as a non-existent murder. The poem seems to offer only the answer that Henry believes in his story and, in some way, needs it.

"Dream Song 29," however, is meant to be understood as part of a "large work, which will appear, / and baffle everybody" (D.S. 308), that is, the 385 *Dream Songs* as a whole. When we have read the rest of the *Dream Songs*, we know a good deal more about Henry than is stated explicitly in "Dream Song 29." Henry hasn't in fact murdered anyone, but he feels just as guilty as if he had, because of other events in his past. For one, Henry's father committed suicide when Henry was a child, after threatening to kill his son as well: "He was going to swim out, with me, forevers, / [...] but he decided on lead" (D.S. 143). The suicide seems to have made Henry feel guiltily murderous for the first time. Henry feels so angry with his father for leaving him (D.S. 145) that he would like to be able to re-kill him. Although Henry says, "while all the same on forty years I love him" (D.S. 143), he wants to get "right down / away down under the grass / and ax the casket open ha to see / just how he's taking it, [...] & then Henry will heft the ax once more [...]" (D.S. 384). Later in his life, Henry has turned out to be an alcoholic ("Madness & booze, madness and booze. / Which'll can tell who preceded whose?" [D.S. 225]) and an unfaithful husband ("He was always in love with the wrong woman" [D.S. 213]). Both of these problems make him feel murderous and guilty. In a *Dream Song* about admittance to a hospital for the treatment of alcoholism, he sees himself as a destructive ally of the alcohol attempting to murder "the brains": "I saw the point of Loeb / at last, to give oneself over to crime wholly, / baffle, torment [...] / until with trembling hands hoist I my true / & legal ax, to get at the brains. I never liked brains—" (D.S. 95). Naturally, he feels guilty about the attempted murder: "Why drink so, two days running? / two months, O seasons, years, two decades running?" (D.S. 96). He also considers his promiscuity to be a serious crime against his lovers (D.S. 222), his wife (D.S. 187), and society in general:

> for years Henry has been getting away with
> *murder*
> the Sheriff mused. There'll have to be an
> order
> specifically to stop climbing trees.
>
> & other people's wives:
> (D.S. 350)

In fact, throughout the *Dream Songs*, Henry constantly identifies with criminals, especially with murderers of multiple victims (Conarroe, 1977:99). He has fantasies of patricide (D.S. 384), rape-murders (D.S. 222), and even infanticide (D.S. 271).

Henry is not, however, a professional murderer. It becomes clear quite early in the *Dream Songs* that he is an artist of some sort. We read "The glories of the world struck me, made me aria, once" (D.S. 26), and "Tides of dreadful creation rocked lonely Henry" (D.S. 260). As the songs progress, we learn that Henry is a writer: "Turning it over, considering, like a madman / Henry put forth a book" (D.S. 75). In fact, it turns out that Henry is the poet who is writing the *Dream Songs*. We receive early hints of this in "Dream Song 47," in which a friend of Henry's asks him about the title of the poem, as if Henry were responsible for it. A bit later, in "Dream Song 168," Henry excuses himself, saying, "I pass

on to the next song." The later Dream Songs, though, actually contain comments about other people's reactions to the earlier songs (D.S. 267, 333) and complaints about the difficulty of finishing the later ones:

> he couldn't say whether to sing
> further or seal his lonely throat, give himself
> up.
> . . .
> There was a time he marched from dream to
> dream
> but he seems to out of ink,
>
> he seems to be out of everything again
> save whiskey & cigarettes, both bad for him.
> (D.S. 356)

If Henry is the writer of the *Dream Songs*, then Henry is John Berryman. The facts fit; Berryman's father also committed suicide, and Berryman was also alcoholic and promiscuous. However, in a well-known note to *His Toy, His Dream, His Rest*, Berryman denied being Henry, writing that the *Dream Songs* are "essentially about an imaginary character (not the poet, no me) named Henry, a white American in early middle age, sometimes in blackface, who has suffered an irreversible loss and talks about himself sometimes in the first person, sometimes in the third, sometimes even in the second." On the other hand, in his own criticism, he reminds us that "poetry is composed by actual human beings, and tracts of it are very closely about them" (1976:316). In a discussion of his peculiar use of pronouns (partially described in the note by Berryman presents a reconciliation of his two apparently contradictory positions on how autobiographical his work is. He says, "The poet is both left out and put in [...] we are confronted with a process which is at once a process of life and a process of art" (1966:98). Most critics have concluded that at least the content of the *Dream Songs* can be considered largely autobiographical: "Henry is an imaginary character simply in the sense of serving as an alter ego, a device whereby the poet may look at himself, talk about himsef, talk to himself, and be a multifarious personality" (Martz, 1969:39).

The fact that Henry is very close to being Berryman suggests another possible source for Henry's feelings, expressed in "Dream Song 29" and elsewhere, that he is a guilty murderer. Berryman, it seems, felt at least as guilty about his *art*, as about his drinking and womanizing. In Sonnet 115 (lines 5–8) a flirtation with a woman in fact wards off the more serious crime of poetry:

> my head was frantic with a following rime:
> it was a good evening, an evening to please,
> I kissed her in the kitchen. ecstasies—
> among so much good we tamped down the
>   crime

But by the middle of the Dream Songs, it becomes clear that Henry-Berryman is incorrigible as an artist:

> Restless, as once in love, he put pen to
>   paper—
> a stub point with real ink, he hates
>   ballpoints—
> and on a thick pad, on lap—
> how many thousand times has this been the
>   caper,
> in fear & love, with interest, whom None
>   anoints,
> taking instead the fourth rap—
>
> habitual—life sentence—will he see it
>   through?
> (D.S. 261)

The crime of poetry outlasts his criminal "lust-quest" (D.S. 163). It even outlasts his drinking. In a hospital, alcohol-free, he reports that he is still driven to write: "They are shooting me full of sings. / I give no rules. Write as short as you can, / in order, of what matters" (D.S. 54). Poetry is the crime which he cannot stop himself from committing.

Charles Molesworth has written (1975:21) that we must "give over any attempt to name his [Henry's] guilt, or ours, in explicit terms." However, even in "Dream Song 29," where there is little explicit reference to art, there is some indication that a good deal of Henry's guilt stems from activities which are actually artistic, and not homicidal in the least. The small indications in the content of the poem that Henry has his crime all wrong, that he has actually created the murder, are matched, elaborated, and reinforced by iconic syntax and other language patterns. These patterns, against the background of the rest of the *Dream Songs*, help to bring out the more specific interpretation that Henry is wrong about his crime in that the crime is really art, not murder, and that Henry's invention of the murder is just another instance of his criminal, that is, artistic tendencies.

The crucial language patterns, those that help maintain the artist-as-criminal theme in "Dream Song 29", fall into two groups: patterns which suggest either directly or through an iconic correlative experience that Henry's crime is more like art than like murder, and patterns which identify Henry more directly as an artist. The first group contains three patterns of systematic stylistic choice which support art, more than murder, as an underlying theme. First, the grammatical aspect is marked contradictorily in the poem. Aspect, which can be *perfective* or *imperfective*, is an indication in the grammar of how long an activity continues and what kind of activity it is, a complete event (perfective aspect) or an ongoing process (imperfective aspect). Berryman writes lines which seem to be in both aspects at once, and of course such lines often sound peculiar: "end anyone and hacks her body up." The contradiction in aspect forms part of a cross-level pattern with the contradiction in the account of Henry's crime: Was there a murder or wasn't there? Through the correlative experience induced by the pattern, the contradictions in aspect marking take on meanings from the contradiction described in the poem, the non-murder. Henry is presenting as a discrete event, a murder, what is actually an ongoing process, more like the experience of art. Second, several transformations are applied to the sentences of "Dream Song 29" that have the effect of removing or de-emphasizing as subjects of main clauses the noun phrases that refer to Henry or the vengeful thing that is tormenting him. Since the subject position is most commonly occupied by a noun phrase expressing the agent of an action (Chomsky, 1970), such syntactic choices would pattern iconically with any theme that involved the failure of someone or something to act, In "Dream Song 29," they correlate with the revelation in stanza three that Henry has not been the agent of any murder, and so there is probably no real avenging thing that is actively oppressing him. Finally, as Berryman wrote, "a commitment of identify can be 'reserved' so to speak, with an ambiguous pronoun" (1966:98). In "Dream Song 29," vague and missing anaphoric pronouns very nearly obliterate the distinction between Henry and the "thing," thus suggesting that they are part of the same person. Henry the artist may have created the "thing."

The second group of syntactic patterns that I will discuss indicates more directly that Henry is an artist, and that his art is somehow wrong. "Dream Song 29" contains repetitions of syntactic constructions which are typical of traditional fairytales. Consequently, it suggests that Henry is to be associated with traditional creators of fiction in the same way that other syntactic constructions can indicate that the speaker or writer is to be associated with certain sociolinguistic groups or literary schools. There is in addition a repeated logical pattern that can mean only that Henry's story about a murder is an infelicitous attempt at a tall tale. From the rest of the *Dream Songs* we know that Henry is not just any teller of tales; he is a poet. The murder story, then, is a kind of metaphor for a poem. Berryman uses this metaphor more explicitly in "Dream Song 355," where Henry says to a woman, "You would have made a terrific victim in one of Henry's thrillers." By this point in the *Dream Songs*, Henry has been identified clearly as the writer of the *Dream Songs*, so the "thrillers" must be the Songs. The analogy is appropriate. Conarroe has written that "the songs represent, as much as anything else, Berryman's attempts to get his dreams, memories, and fears out in the open [...]" (1977:95). The poet, then, transforms feelings and experience into a discrete public event or object, the poem. In "Dream Song 29," Henry, in parallel fashion, attempts to transform his internal states, which seem to be depression, hostility, and self-loathing, into another kind of external event that involves others, a murder. Henry's real crime can be seen as this essentially artistic one of creation, rather than murder.

Let us consider how the first group of language patterns, those which, when correlated with the meaning of the whole *Dream Song* and of the longer work of which it is a part, indicate iconically that the crime involved is not murder, but more like art itself. In themselves, of course, the language patterns can have only very abstract significance. The use of aspect shows that there is some confusion of an ongoing process with a discrete event. The syntactic operations that demote subjects show that there is some failure of agentive action, and the manipulation of pronouns shows that there is some question about the status of the characters as individual independent entities. In the context of the poem, however, all these pattern with various aspects of the theme of the non-existent murder.

Let us consider first the use of aspect in the poem. As I have said, the common aspectual distinction, one important in the verb systems of French, Russian, and many other languages, is between habitual or continuous action (imperfective aspect) and complete or discrete action (perfective aspect). Aspect is not always unambiguously marked in the English verbal system, but the progressive is usually imperfective:

(5)a. Carol is eating the carrot. (imperfective)
b. Carol ate the carrot. (perfective)

We can use adverbs or other locutions to make the distinction clearer:

(6)a. Carol is always eating carrots. (imperfective)
b. Carol ate carrots for the first time on Thursday. (perfective)

The devices for marking aspect in English are used frequently in "Dream Song 29." However, something peculiar happens with them in the first stanza:

1 There sat down, once, a thing on Henry's heart
2 so heavy, if he had a hundred years
3 & more, & weeping, sleepless, in all them time
4 Henry could not make good.
5 Starts always again in Henry's ears
6 the little cough somewhere, an odour, a chime.

First, we encounter *sat down*, which is marked as perfective by the appearance of *once*, then a weakly imperfective verb or two—*had, weeping*—and finally two verbs, *made good* and *starts*, which are contradictorily marked for both aspects. In the non-standard dialect that Berryman uses from time to time in the *Dream Songs*, "in all them time," the adverbial that modifies "could not make good," should have read either, "in all them times," where both *them* and *times* are plural, or "in all that time," where both the determiner and the noun are singular. The plural version would have indicated that Henry's unsuccessful efforts to make good were repeated discrete events, or perfective in nature, while the singular version would have indicated that the effort continued over a long period of time continuously, or that it was imperfective. Berryman has used a little of each version, indicating that there is some confusion. Which is correct? Since the noun in "them time" is the head, or more important word (Chomsky, 1970), and it is singular, and since the plural "them" is in the right case only for a non-standard dialect, it would seem that the singular, imperfective version is the more correct one. The "mistake" is the introduction of the plural which acts here as an indicator of perfective aspect.

Similarly, in line 5, *always* indicates that the *starts* are habitual or continuous, that is, imperfective, while *again* seems to indicate that they are discrete events, or perfective. Since the overall aspect of the stanza is imperfective, the imperfective interpretation seems, once again, to be the more correct grammatically. The stanza sounds a good deal more peculiar read with *again*, but not *always* in line 5, than it does with only *always* left in it. The conflict on the grammatical level between perfective and imperfective aspect, then, if it forms a cross-level pattern with the conflict on the semantic level, will reinforce the theme that the murder is a deviant delusion. When perfective aspect markings conflict with imperfective ones, the imperfective item is the more grammatically appropriate one. In parallel fashion, when Henry's story that he has perpetrated a real, discrete murder conflicts with the evidence that he has done nothing but create poetry, the latter crime, the continuous making of poetry, is seen as the more accurate charge.

There is a short suspension of the aspect conflict during stanza two. The grammatical tense is mostly present—one conditional *would*, to which I return in section VII, the progressive *thinking*, and five simple present verbs. The semantic time, though, jumps wildly from the present to one thousand years into the future, back a bit to the indeterminate past (*reproach*, *too late*), and back again to the present. Yet there are no discrepancies in aspect marking and no ungrammatical markings of such discrepancies. Actually, aspect is not really marked on the verbs in this stanza at all. However, the consistent use of the grammatical present to represent widely divergent semantic times produces an idea of the kind of continuum usually expressed in the imperfective aspect. The grammatical aspect of stanza two, then, is consistent with the idea that Henry's problems are due to an ongoing condition, not to any discrete event.

The imagery in stanza two carries on, more strongly than the grammar, the theme that the discrete events of Henry's guilty past are of his own creation, a fiction. In fact, this imagery provides the only indication at the level of lexical content within "Dream Song 29" that Henry is an artist. The stanza begins by telling us that another thing that Henry has in mind is "like a

grave Sienese face." Henry's first "thing," the one in stanza one, oppresses Henry's heart like an emotion; this second "thing" is in his mind like an idea. "A grave Sienese face" sounds as if it is an idea of a portrait or statue. Like other artists, Henry has recreated a thing of the heart as "another thing" of the mind. Henry imagines either that the reproach that the face expresses is "still profiled" even now, or that it is in a still, that is, unmoving, profile. Either way, Henry sees that the thing his mind has created is perpetual (or imperfective), and he finds its permanence awful, perhaps because human beings in general are mortal (perfective), and it is "too late" for him in particular. The artist is not only out-lived, but also intimidated and accused by his art. Henry might wish to retreat to his murder fantasy, a source of guilt more self-contained, more explicable, than art. However, after he has been "thinking" about his art, he realizes that "this is not for tears." He has not, after all, murdered anyone.

Stanza three presents Henry's grudging realization that the murder could not really have taken place. Once again, the manipulation of grammatical aspect helps set the fondly imagined murder against the true source of guilt, which is imperfective. The stanza is divided into two contrasting sections. Each section is built around an interrupted sentence:

13 But never did Henry, as he thought he did,

17 Often he reckons, in the dawn, them up.

The first section, the one built around line 13, is a description in the negative. The negative element *never* is moved by transformation from its usual place before the verb toward the beginning of the sentence. Compare line 13 with the same words in ordinary word order in line 13'.

13 But never did Henry, as he thought he did,
14 end anyone and hacks her body up
15 and hide the pieces, where they may be found.

13' But Henry never did, as he thought he did,
14 end anyone and hacks her body up
15 and hide the pieces where they may be found.

This preposing has the effect of emphasizing the *never* and, since it makes the word order of the first half of the line different from that of the second, it also has the effect of pointing up the discrepancy between what Henry did and what he thought he did. The description, so clearly negated, in lines 13 through 15 is of the perfective crime that Henry never committed. "But never did Henry [. . .] end anyone [. . .]" means 'It is NOT TRUE that Henry killed someone at some time.' The sentence which is negated, *Henry killed someone at some time*, is very strongly perfective. So line 13 denies the perfective fantasy, insisting that Henry never performed the single, contained act of killing a person. But the guilt is real; there must be some crime. In line 14, the crime begins once more to show itself as a process, not an event. The unexpected inflection of *hacks* in line 14 and *may* in line 15 is not a change in time or tense, but a threat of an imperfective aspect. It is an example of the continuous present, also found in a sentence like *Carol eats carrots* (generally). That the crime is, in fact, a continuous state is indicated more strongly in the second section of stanza three. The opening of the section contrasts sharply with the first section. It is both strongly positive and strongly imperfective: "He knows." The last two lines of the poem describe the clearest bit of reality that Henry glimpses. These lines are marked imperfective by *often* and *ever*.

> 16 He knows: he went over everyone, & nobody's missing.
> 17 Often he reckons, in the dawn, them up.
> 18 Nobody is ever missing.

Henry has been so taken in by his fictional murder that he is baffled by the dull continuous reality of everybody's being there. The simple present of "nobody's missing," because its aspect is ambiguous, is not strong enough to make the point that whatever crime exists is ongoing. Simple present tense can conceivably refer to perfective point-action in a present tense narrative. The line is repeated, this time clearly marked for imperfective aspect: "Nobody is ever missing." . . .

"Dream Song 29" presents the paradox of Henry's debilitating, yet groundless guilt in language that is notably old and mannered. From a critical perspective that includes a theory of iconic syntax, I have tried to show that Berryman's manipulations of elements of morphology, syntax, and logic constitute stylistic choices that contribute to the significance of the poem. They form patterns that reflect important semantic elements not only of "Dream Song 29" itself, but also of a theme that is central to the 385 Dream Songs as a whole and to other modern confessional poetry, the theme of the guilty artist . . .

In "Dream Song 29", Berryman develops and articulates this theme as he examines what he calls, in "Dream Song 29", "the original crime: art, rime." Largely through iconic user of idiosyncratic grammar, Berryman presents a frightening metaphorical vision: The artist who is the subject of his own art is the victim of his own murder.

Source: Muffy E. A. Siegel, "'The Original Crime': John Berryman's Iconic Grammar," in *Poetics Today*, Vol. 2, No. 1, Autumn 1980, pp. 163–88.

Jack Vincent Barbera

In the following excerpt, Barbera explores the patterns found throughout Berryman's Dream Songs, *noting that the poet does not create a structured narrative that is brought to an end with the last song. Rather, the critic asserts, Berryman offers only "local" patterning. Occasionally, he groups a few songs together into a somewhat cohesive whole, but overall Berryman refuses to imbue his songs with any larger sense of order or meaning.*

It may or may not be true that, as Nietzsche's Zarathustra says, unless a man is full of chaos he cannot create a dancing star. But John Berryman was and he did. The patterned movement of *The Dream Songs* is its dancing; its fiery mass Berryman's life of chaotic circumstance and his powerful imagining. Ultimately one cannot divorce dance from dancer, the overall flow of *The Dream Songs* from John Berryman. I mean more than just the impossibility of *wholly* distinguishing Berryman from the singer of the Songs, Henry—though that too. *The Dream Songs* is open-ended: open to Berryman's life and ended by an act of his will and, irrevocably, by his death. One could say the poem stops rather than ends: this in contrast to long poems which complete some narrative or logical design. Although patterning is everywhere in the poem, it is everywhere local. There is the structured movement within Songs and the grouping of Songs; but there is no actual or implied overall pattern by which all the groups are ordered, the whole finished and sealed. Thus the poem combines shape and flow, patterning and openness.

Pattern is tightest in the individual Songs with their surface arrangement of triple sestets (there are about twenty exceptions, most of which consist of an added line), the sestets following only casually a stress order of 5-5-3-5-5-3. Just as important is Berryman's shaping of Song content. Before leaving for Ireland to assemble the last four Books of *The Dream Songs* he told Jonathan Sisson that, besides unpublished Songs whose fate he would decide, he was taking with him "a large body of manuscript which is fragmentary, dealing with beginnings and ends and some middles." Remarkably the Songs—with their beginnings, middles, and ends—are not formally monotonous.

Consider a few examples. "Song 56" opens with the vision of an empty Hell, in accord with Origen's belief that at the end of time God will have mercy on all. Lines 10–11 indicate that the second sestet account of a terrified deer encircled and clubbed by hunters is emblematic of a ruthless fate for all. In the last sestet Henry weighs these contrasting visions and alludes to Daniel's vision of the fiery judgment throne of the Ancient of Days (Dn 7.9–14). "What sigh borrowed His mercy?"—Henry asks—thinking of the Son of Man. The Song's structure, then—its beginning, middle, and end—is along the lines of a Hegelian triad: a vision, its antithesis, and an allusion suggesting a possible reconciliation between Absolute ruthlessness and universal mercy.

By way of contrast the beginning, middle, and end of "Song 33" define a narrative action, Henry relating the anecdote of Alexander's slaying of Kleitos. The Song moves from the king's rage in the first sestet; to the hustling out, return, and killing of Kleitos in the second; culminating, finally, in Alexander's grief. Turning to "Song 171," which echoes Waller and Pound, one finds a purely lyrical movement: Henry tells his book to go to his beloved; he lists all the qualities for which she should be praised; and he concludes that he and his beloved are permanently and beautifully linked. Many other Songs are in the mode of self-conscious monologue or dialogue, much of *The Dream Songs'* dramatic context resulting from its minstrel machinery banter between Henry and the unnamed friend who calls him "Bones." Berryman's experimentation sometimes leaves one at a loss for a descriptive label. For example, consider the arrangement of "Song 66." The powerful and clear spiritual stance of a fourth-century Desert Father, humorously conveyed "over the telephone," ironically contrasts with the lunatic medley of the world and Henry circa early June 1963, the Father's

words woven through the whole Song yet, appropriately, parenthetically isolated from it. The weaving keeps the form from being a simply juxtaposed presentation of one thing, then another; the isolation keeps it from being an interaction. Perhaps such structuring should be called "thematic counterpoint." Whatever the label, both strands have their identifiable beginning, middle, and end. Despite the consistency of such structuring, the Songs' several modes—logical, narrative, lyric, dramatic, and other—give them a greater formal variety than, say, the lyric meditations in a sonnet sequence—be it Shakespeare's or Berryman's own.

Besides creating patterned movement within the Songs, Berryman arranged many of them into clusters of varying cohesion: for example, the elegiac *Three around the Old Gentlemen* for Frost ("Songs 37–39", preceded by two which mention that Frost is "dying" but "still around") and the twelve for Delmore Schwartz ("Songs 146–57"). In Book 6, the longest, there are three titled clusters, but other groups can be recognized, such as the sequence from 163–66 touching on Henry's various infirmities. "Song 56"—which, as I have noted, presents contrasting views of God's final judgment—is preceded by a Song in which Henry imagines himself before St. Peter, and is followed by a Song in which Henry says he doesn't believe in Hell, "save sullen here." These three Songs are preceded by three set in a hospital, Henry recovering from perhaps a mental breakdown. In his *Harvard Advocate* interview Berryman observed that "Some of the Songs are in alphabetical order; but, mostly, they just belong to areas of hope and fear that Henry is going through at a given time." In fact, alphabetical order is not very extensive in the poem; what little of it there is could be accounted for by chance, so it does not seem an ordering principle at all. But Berryman's mention of alphabetical order suggests that for some Songs a search for immediate thematic context will prove fruitless. Immediate context is worth checking, however, for as Berryman also maintained, it clarifies certain Songs: "you don't need to follow the specific details if you hear the tone of the Song in relation to the Songs around it" (Sisson, p. 34).

Source: Jack Vincent Barbera, "Shape and Flow in *The Dream Songs*," in *Twentieth Century Literature*, Vol. 22, No. 2, May 1976, pp. 146–62.

SOURCES

Berryman, John, "Dream Song 29," in *77 Dream Songs*, Farrar, Straus, 1964, p. 33.

————, *The Dream Songs*, Farrar, Straus and Giroux, 1969, pp. vi, 3, 10, 16–17, 22, 33, 38, 44, 47, 51–52, 83, 96, 160, 162, 172, 178, 255, 287, 406.

Conarroe, Joel, *John Berryman: An Introduction to the Poetry*, Columbia University Press, 1977, p. 101.

Ginsberg, Alan, "Howl," in *The Norton Anthology of American Literature*, 2nd edition, Vol. 2, W.W. Norton & Company, pp. 2415–16.

Haffenden, John, *The Life of John Berryman*, Routledge & Kegan Paul, 1982, p. 29.

Hyde, Lewis, *Alcohol and Poetry: John Berryman and the Booze Talking*, Dallas Institute Publications, 1986, p. 12.

Lowell, Robert, "John Berryman," in *Robert Lowell: Collected Prose*, edited by Robert Giroux, Farrar, Straus and Giroux, 1987, pp. 110–11.

Mariani, Paul, "'My Heavy Daughter': John Berryman and the Making of *The Dream Songs*," in the *Kenyon Review*, Vol. 10, No. 3, Summer 1988, p. 19.

Mendelson, Edward, "How to Read Berryman's 'Dream Songs,'" in *American Poetry Since 1960: Some Critical Perspectives*, edited by Robert B. Shaw, Carcanet Press Limited, 1974, p. 41.

Travisano, Thomas, *Midcentury Quartet: Bishop, Lowell, Jarrell, Berryman and the Making of a Postmodern Aesthetic*, University Press of Virginia, 1999, p. 246.

FURTHER READING

Gustavvson, Bo, *The Soul Under Stress: A Study of the Poetics of John Berryman's Dream Songs*, Uppsala, 1984.

Gustavvson explores Berryman's debt to Walt Whitman. He also discusses Berryman's desire to record how the soul under stress determines both the craft and the content of the poem. Gustavvson sees Book 2 of *77 Dream Songs* (numbers 27–51) as being concerned with the sense of being rejected and abandoned by both earthly father and heavenly father.

Kirsch, Adam, *The Wounded Surgeon: Confession and Transformation in Six American Poets (Robert Lowell, Elizabeth Bishop, John Berryman, Randall Jarrell, Delmore Schwartz and Sylvia Plath)*, Norton, 2005.

Kirsch approaches the work of these confessional poets in terms not of how shocking their personal revelations were, but of the ways in which they were able to translate their difficult experiences into art.

Mariani, Paul, *Dream Song: The Life of John Berryman*, University of Massachusetts Press, reprint edition, 1996.

In this biography Mariani examines Berryman's brilliant but self-destructive life, using accounts given by his family, friends, students and other associates, Berryman's letters and journals, and of course his poetry. The biography provides insight into both the man and his work.

Vendler, Helen, *The Given and the Made: Strategies of Poetic Redefinition: The T.S. Eliot Memorial Lectures at the University of Kent*, Harvard University Press, 1995, pp. 49–50.

Vendler points out that there are similarities between "Dream Song 29" and the religious lyrics of grief and guilt by earlier poets such as George Herbert and Gerard Manley Hopkins. In an unusual twist to Freudian analysis, she argues that Henry's guilt is caused by his repression of chastity and asceticism, this being conveyed by the reproach he feels from the Sienese face in the second sestet.

Goblin Market

CHRISTINA ROSSETTI

1862

The English Victorian poet Christina Rossetti's allegorical poem "Goblin Market" initially appeared in *Goblin Market and Other Poems* (1862), the first volume of her poetry to be commercially published. The poem is also available in *The Complete Poems of Christina Rossetti* (1979) and the 2001 issue of the same edition, simply titled *The Complete Poems*.

"Goblin Market" is the most discussed of Rossetti's poems and is widely considered to be her greatest work. Though Rossetti always maintained that "Goblin Market" is a children's poem, the strongly erotic elements underlying what is superficially a moral lesson make it a multi-layered and complex work. It can be read as a study of female sexuality, an allegory (or symbolic story) about divine and earthly love, a celebration of female heroism, or as a metaphor for Christ's sacrifice on the cross, among many other possibilities. Most of the potential interpretations are not mutually exclusive.

"Goblin Market" and the collection in which it was first published led to Rossetti's standing as a writer of allegorical and lyric poetry. With the rise of feminist criticism in the 1980s, the poem's standing grew in tandem with an awareness of Rossetti as a notable female poet. As of the early twenty-first century, Rossetti's appeal has expanded and she is widely considered one of the greatest Victorian poets of any gender.

Christina Rossetti *(Time Life Pictures | Mansell | Time Life Pictures | Getty Images)*

AUTHOR BIOGRAPHY

Christina Georgina Rossetti was born on December 5, 1830, in London, England, the fourth child of an Italian immigrant family with strong literary and artistic leanings. Her father, Gabrielle Rossetti, was an Italian poet and political exile whose support for revolutionary nationalism drove him to seek refuge in England. One of Rossetti's brothers was the painter and poet Dante Gabriel Rossetti. His work is also discussed and studied today. Her other brother, William Michael Rossetti, was a writer and critic who later acted as her editor. Both brothers were members of the Pre-Raphaelite Brotherhood art movement. Rossetti's sister, Maria Francesca Rossetti, was an author who later in life became an Anglican nun. Indeed, Rossetti dedicated "Goblin Market" to Maria. Rossetti's mother, Frances Polidori (later Rossetti), was the daughter of another Italian exile and the sister of John Polidori, the physician of the famous poet Lord Byron.

As a child, Rossetti was close to her maternal grandfather, Gaetano Polidori. She often stayed at his house in the Buckinghamshire countryside. She was educated at home by her mother, who periodically worked as a governess to help support the family. In the 1840s the family suffered financial difficulties due to the poor health of Rossetti's father. During this period Frances, Christina, and Maria Rossetti became deeply committed to Anglicanism (the Church of England). Rossetti's religious faith played a major role in her life. In her late teens she became engaged to the painter James Collinson but ended the engagement when he converted to Roman Catholicism. Later she became involved with the linguist Charles Cayley but did not marry him, also for religious reasons.

The young Rossetti was of a passionate and volatile nature. Her father (cited by Mary Arseneau in the *Dictionary of Literary Biography*) called her and Dante Gabriel the "two storms" of the family. She later learned to control her temperament, and was an adult of unusual, perhaps excessive, self-restraint.

Rossetti's first book, *Verses* (1847), was published by her maternal grandfather on his own press when she was only sixteen. This collection dealt with themes that are characteristic of her later work: death, rejection by a loved one, spiritual and earthly love, the transience of love and beauty, and the importance of acceptance. Beginning in 1848, Rossetti had poems published in periodicals, sometimes using the pseudonym Ellen Alleyn. She continued to write and publish her poetry throughout her life. "Goblin Market" appeared in 1862 in *Goblin Market and Other Poems*, establishing her reputation as a major poet. Other notable editions of her work include *The Prince's Progress and Other Poems* (1866), and *Poems* (1890). She also wrote a series of poems for children that was published in 1872 as *Sing-Song: A Nursery Rhyme Book*. She published religious prose and poetry with the Society for Promoting Christian Knowledge. In the last year of her life, she broke with the Society over its refusal to make a stand against vivisection, which she strongly opposed.

In 1853, Frances, Christina, and Gabriele moved to Frome in Somerset, England, where they attempted to run a school to improve the family finances. The school failed, and in 1854 they returned to London, where they were supported by William and Maria. During the 1860s, Rossetti did charity work at the Highgate Penitentiary, aiding fallen women (prostitutes) who wanted to change their lives. She taught them reading, writing, and sewing. Some critics and biographers believe that Rossetti's experience at the penitentiary inspired her to write "Goblin Market."

Rossetti had struggled with ill health since her teens, when a doctor (probably inadequately) diagnosed her condition as "religious mania." In 1871, she became seriously ill with Graves' disease. The illness affected her heart and permanently altered her appearance, causing her eyes to protrude. In May, 1892, Rossetti was diagnosed with breast cancer. A mastectomy performed in her home proved ineffectual, and she died in London two years later on December 29, 1894. Her brother William continued to edit and publish her poetry after her death.

POEM TEXT

Morning and evening
Maids heard the goblins cry:
"Come buy our orchard fruits,
Come buy, come buy:
Apples and quinces,   5
Lemons and oranges,
Plump unpecked cherries,
Melons and raspberries,
Bloom-down-cheeked peaches,
Swart-headed mulberries,   10
Wild free-born cranberries,
Crab-apples, dewberries,
Pine-apples, blackberries,
Apricots, strawberries;—
All ripe together   15
In summer weather,—
Morns that pass by,
Fair eves that fly;
Come buy, come buy:
Our grapes fresh from the vine,   20
Pomegranates full and fine,
Dates and sharp bullaces,
Rare pears and greengages,
Damsons and bilberries,
Taste them and try: 25
Currants and gooseberries,
Bright-fire-like barberries,
Figs to fill your mouth,
Citrons from the South,
Sweet to tongue and sound to eye;   30
Come buy, come buy."

Evening by evening
Among the brookside rushes,
Laura bowed her head to hear,
Lizzie veiled her blushes: 35

Crouching close together
In the cooling weather,
With clasping arms and cautioning lips,
With tingling cheeks and finger tips.
"Lie close," Laura said,   40
Pricking up her golden head:
"We must not look at goblin men,
We must not buy their fruits:
Who knows upon what soil they fed
Their hungry thirsty roots?"   45
"Come buy," call the goblins
Hobbling down the glen.
"Oh," cried Lizzie, "Laura, Laura,
You should not peep at goblin men."
Lizzie covered up her eyes,   50
Covered close lest they should look;
Laura reared her glossy head,
And whispered like the restless brook:
"Look, Lizzie, look, Lizzie,
Down the glen tramp little men.   55
One hauls a basket,
One bears a plate,
One lugs a golden dish
Of many pounds weight.
How fair the vine must grow   60
Whose grapes are so luscious;
How warm the wind must blow
Thro' those fruit bushes."
"No," said Lizzie: "No, no, no;
Their offers should not charm us,   65
Their evil gifts would harm us."
She thrust a dimpled finger
In each ear, shut eyes and ran:
Curious Laura chose to linger
Wondering at each merchant man.   70
One had a cat's face,
One whisked a tail,
One tramped at a rat's pace,
One crawled like a snail,
One like a wombat prowled obtuse and furry,   75
One like a ratel tumbled hurry skurry.
She heard a voice like voice of doves
Cooing all together:
They sounded kind and full of loves
In the pleasant weather.   80

Laura stretched her gleaming neck
Like a rush-imbedded swan,
Like a lily from the beck,
Like a moonlit poplar branch,
Like a vessel at the launch   85
When its last restraint is gone.

Backwards up the mossy glen
Turned and trooped the goblin men,
With their shrill repeated cry,
"Come buy, come buy."   90
When they reached where Laura was
They stood stock still upon the moss,
Leering at each other,
Brother with queer brother;
Signalling each other,   95
Brother with sly brother.

One set his basket down,
One reared his plate;
One began to weave a crown
Of tendrils, leaves and rough nuts brown   100
(Men sell not such in any town);
One heaved the golden weight
Of dish and fruit to offer her:
"Come buy, come buy," was still their cry.

Laura stared but did not stir,   105
Longed but had no money:
The whisk-tailed merchant bade her taste
In tones as smooth as honey,
The cat-faced purr'd,
The rat-paced spoke a word   110
Of welcome, and the snail-paced even was
    heard;
One parrot-voiced and jolly
Cried "Pretty Goblin" still for "Pretty Polly;"—
One whistled like a bird.

But sweet-tooth Laura spoke in haste: 115
"Good folk, I have no coin;
To take were to purloin:
I have no copper in my purse,
I have no silver either,
And all my gold is on the furze   120
That shakes in windy weather
Above the rusty heather."
"You have much gold upon your head,"
They answered all together:
"Buy from us with a golden curl."   125
She clipped a precious golden lock,
She dropped a tear more rare than pearl,
Then sucked their fruit globes fair or red:
Sweeter than honey from the rock,
Stronger than man-rejoicing wine,   130
Clearer than water flowed that juice;
She never tasted such before,
How should it cloy with length of use?
She sucked and sucked and sucked the more
Fruits which that unknown orchard bore;   135
She sucked until her lips were sore;
Then flung the emptied rinds away
But gathered up one kernel-stone,
And knew not was it night or day
As she turned home alone.   140

Lizzie met her at the gate
Full of wise upbraidings:
"Dear, you should not stay so late,
Twilight is not good for maidens;
Should not loiter in the glen   145
In the haunts of goblin men.
Do you not remember Jeanie,
How she met them in the moonlight,
Took their gifts both choice and many,
Ate their fruits and wore their flowers   150
Plucked from bowers
Where summer ripens at all hours?
But ever in the noonlight
She pined and pined away;
Sought them by night and day,   155

Found them no more but dwindled and grew
    grey;
Then fell with the first snow,
While to this day no grass will grow
Where she lies low:
I planted daisies there a year ago   160
That never blow.
You should not loiter so."
"Nay, hush," said Laura:
"Nay, hush, my sister:
I ate and ate my fill,   165
Yet my mouth waters still;
Tomorrow night I will
Buy more:" and kissed her:
"Have done with sorrow;
I'll bring you plums tomorrow   170
Fresh on their mother twigs,
Cherries worth getting;
You cannot think what figs
My teeth have met in,
What melons icy-cold   175
Piled on a dish of gold
Too huge for me to hold,
What peaches with a velvet nap,
Pellucid grapes without one seed:
Odorous indeed must be the mead   180
Whereon they grow, and pure the wave they
    drink
With lilies at the brink,
And sugar-sweet their sap."

Golden head by golden head,
Like two pigeons in one nest   185
Folded in each other's wings,
They lay down in their curtained bed:
Like two blossoms on one stem,
Like two flakes of new-fall'n snow,
Like two wands of ivory   190
Tipped with gold for awful kings.
Moon and stars gazed in at them,
Wind sang to them lullaby,
Lumbering owls forbore to fly,
Not a bat flapped to and fro   195
Round their rest:
Cheek to cheek and breast to breast
Locked together in one nest.

Early in the morning
When the first cock crowed his warning,   200
Neat like bees, as sweet and busy,
Laura rose with Lizzie:
Fetched in honey, milked the cows,
Aired and set to rights the house,
Kneaded cakes of whitest wheat,   205
Cakes for dainty mouths to eat,
Next churned butter, whipped up cream,
Fed their poultry, sat and sewed;
Talked as modest maidens should:
Lizzie with an open heart,   210
Laura in an absent dream,
One content, one sick in part;
One warbling for the mere bright day's delight,
One longing for the night.

At length slow evening came: 215
They went with pitchers to the reedy brook;
Lizzie most placid in her look,
Laura most like a leaping flame.
They drew the gurgling water from its deep;
Lizzie plucked purple and rich golden flags,   220
Then turning homewards said: "The sunset
    flushes
Those furthest loftiest crags;
Come, Laura, not another maiden lags,
No wilful squirrel wags,
The beasts and birds are fast asleep."   225
But Laura loitered still among the rushes
And said the bank was steep.

And said the hour was early still,
The dew not fall'n, the wind not chill:
Listening ever, but not catching   230
The customary cry,
"Come buy, come buy,"
With its iterated jingle
Of sugar-baited words:
Not for all her watching   235
Once discerning even one goblin
Racing, whisking, tumbling, hobbling;
Let alone the herds
That used to tramp along the glen,
In groups or single,   240
Of brisk fruit-merchant men.
Till Lizzie urged, "O Laura, come;
I hear the fruit-call but I dare not look:
You should not loiter longer at this brook:
Come with me home.   245
The stars rise, the moon bends her arc,
Each glowworm winks her spark,
Let us get home before the night grows dark:
For clouds may gather
Tho' this is summer weather,   250
Put out the lights and drench us thro';
Then if we lost our way what should we do?"

Laura turned cold as stone
To find her sister heard that cry alone,
That goblin cry,   255
"Come buy our fruits, come buy."
Must she then buy no more such dainty fruit?
Must she no more such succous pasture find,
Gone deaf and blind?
Her tree of life drooped from the root: 260
She said not one word in her heart's sore ache;
But peering thro' the dimness, nought
    discerning,
Trudged home, her pitcher dripping all the
    way;
So crept to bed, and lay
Silent till Lizzie slept;   265
Then sat up in a passionate yearning,
And gnashed her teeth for baulked desire, and
    wept
As if her heart would break.

Day after day, night after night,
Laura kept watch in vain   270

In sullen silence of exceeding pain.
She never caught again the goblin cry:
"Come buy, come buy;"—
She never spied the goblin men
Hawking their fruits along the glen: 275
But when the noon waxed bright
Her hair grew thin and gray;
She dwindled, as the fair full moon doth turn
To swift decay and burn
Her fire away.   280

One day remembering her kernel-stone
She set it by a wall that faced the south;
Dewed it with tears, hoped for a root,
Watched for a waxing shoot,
But there came none;   285
It never saw the sun,
It never felt the trickling moisture run:
While with sunk eyes and faded mouth
She dreamed of melons, as a traveller sees
False waves in desert drouth   290
With shade of leaf-crowned trees,
And burns the thirstier in the sandful breeze.

She no more swept the house,
Tended the fowls or cows,
Fetched honey, kneaded cakes of wheat,   295
Brought water from the brook:
But sat down listless in the chimney-nook
And would not eat.

Tender Lizzie could not bear
To watch her sister's cankerous care   300
Yet not to share.
She night and morning
Caught the goblins' cry:
"Come buy our orchard fruits,
Come buy, come buy:"—   305
Beside the brook, along the glen,
She heard the tramp of goblin men,
The voice and stir
Poor Laura could not hear;
Longed to buy fruit to comfort her,   310
But feared to pay too dear.
She thought of Jeanie in her grave,
Who should have been a bride;
But who for joys brides hope to have
Fell sick and died   315
In her gay prime,
In earliest Winter time,
With the first glazing rime,
With the first snow-fall of crisp Winter time.

Till Laura dwindling   320
Seemed knocking at Death's door:
Then Lizzie weighed no more
Better and worse;
But put a silver penny in her purse,
Kissed Laura, crossed the heath with clumps of
    furze   325
At twilight, halted by the brook:
And for the first time in her life
Began to listen and look.

Laughed every goblin

When they spied her peeping: 330
Came towards her hobbling,
Flying, running, leaping,
Puffing and blowing,
Chuckling, clapping, crowing,
Clucking and gobbling, 335
Mopping and mowing,
Full of airs and graces,
Pulling wry faces,
Demure grimaces,
Cat-like and rat-like, 340
Ratel- and wombat-like,
Snail-paced in a hurry,
Parrot-voiced and whistler,
Helter skelter, hurry skurry,
Chattering like magpies, 345
Fluttering like pigeons,
Gliding like fishes,—
Hugged her and kissed her,
Squeezed and caressed her:
Stretched up their dishes, 350
Panniers, and plates:
"Look at our apples
Russet and dun,
Bob at our cherries,
Bite at our peaches, 355
Citrons and dates,
Grapes for the asking,
Pears red with basking
Out in the sun,
Plums on their twigs; 360
Pluck them and suck them,
Pomegranates, figs."—

"Good folk," said Lizzie,
Mindful of Jeanie:
"Give me much and many:"— 365
Held out her apron,
Tossed them her penny.
"Nay, take a seat with us,
Honour and eat with us,"
They answered grinning: 370
"Our feast is but beginning.
Night yet is early,
Warm and dew-pearly,
Wakeful and starry:
Such fruits as these 375
No man can carry;
Half their bloom would fly,
Half their dew would dry,
Half their flavour would pass by.
Sit down and feast with us, 380
Be welcome guest with us,
Cheer you and rest with us."—
"Thank you," said Lizzie: "But one waits
At home alone for me:
So without further parleying, 385
If you will not sell me any
Of your fruits tho' much and many,
Give me back my silver penny
I tossed you for a fee."—
They began to scratch their pates, 390

No longer wagging, purring,
But visibly demurring,
Grunting and snarling.
One called her proud,
Cross-grained, uncivil; 395
Their tones waxed loud,
Their looks were evil.
Lashing their tails
They trod and hustled her,
Elbowed and jostled her, 400
Clawed with their nails,
Barking, mewing, hissing, mocking,
Tore her gown and soiled her stocking,
Twitched her hair out by the roots,
Stamped upon her tender feet, 405
Held her hands and squeezed their fruits
Against her mouth to make her eat.

White and golden Lizzie stood,
Like a lily in a flood,—
Like a rock of blue-veined stone 410
Lashed by tides obstreperously,—
Like a beacon left alone
In a hoary roaring sea,
Sending up a golden fire,—
Like a fruit-crowned orange-tree 415
White with blossoms honey-sweet
Sore beset by wasp and bee, —
Like a royal virgin town
Topped with gilded dome and spire
Close beleaguered by a fleet 420
Mad to tug her standard down.

One may lead a horse to water,
Twenty cannot make him drink.
Tho' the goblins cuffed and caught her,
Coaxed and fought her, 425
Bullied and besought her,
Scratched her, pinched her black as ink,
Kicked and knocked her,
Mauled and mocked her,
Lizzie uttered not a word; 430
Would not open lip from lip
Lest they should cram a mouthful in:
But laughed in heart to feel the drip
Of juice that syrupped all her face,
And lodged in dimples of her chin, 435
And streaked her neck which quaked like curd.
At last the evil people
Worn out by her resistance
Flung back her penny, kicked their fruit
Along whichever road they took, 440
Not leaving root or stone or shoot;
Some writhed into the ground,
Some dived into the brook
With ring and ripple,
Some scudded on the gale without a sound, 445
Some vanished in the distance.

In a smart, ache, tingle,
Lizzie went her way;
Knew not was it night or day;
Sprang up the bank, tore thro' the furze, 450
Threaded copse and dingle,

And heard her penny jingle
Bouncing in her purse,
Its bounce was music to her ear.
She ran and ran   455
As if she feared some goblin man
Dogged her with gibe or curse
Or something worse:
But not one goblin skurried after,
Nor was she pricked by fear;   460
The kind heart made her windy-paced
That urged her home quite out of breath with
    haste.
And inward laughter.

She cried "Laura," up the garden,
"Did you miss me?   465
Come and kiss me.
Never mind my bruises,
Hug me, kiss me, suck my juices
Squeezed from goblin fruits for you,
Goblin pulp and goblin dew.   470
Eat me, drink me, love me;
Laura, make much of me:
For your sake I have braved the glen
And had to do with goblin merchant men."

Laura started from her chair,   475
Flung her arms up in the air,
Clutched her hair:
"Lizzie, Lizzie, have you tasted
For my sake the fruit forbidden?
Must your light like mine be hidden,   480
Your young life like mine be wasted,
Undone in mine undoing
And ruined in my ruin,
Thirsty, cankered, goblin-ridden?"—
She clung about her sister,   485
Kissed and kissed and kissed her:
Tears once again
Refreshed her shrunken eyes,
Dropping like rain
After long sultry drouth;   490
Shaking with aguish fear, and pain,
She kissed and kissed her with a hungry mouth.

Her lips began to scorch,
That juice was wormwood to her tongue,
She loathed the feast: 495
Writhing as one possessed she leaped and sung,
Rent all her robe, and wrung
Her hands in lamentable haste,
And beat her breast.
Her locks streamed like the torch   500
Borne by a racer at full speed,
Or like the mane of horses in their flight,
Or like an eagle when she stems the light
Straight toward the sun,
Or like a caged thing freed,   505
Or like a flying flag when armies run.

Swift fire spread thro' her veins, knocked at her
    heart,
Met the fire smouldering there
And overbore its lesser flame;

She gorged on bitterness without a name: 510
Ah! fool, to choose such part
Of soul-consuming care!
Sense failed in the mortal strife:
Like the watch-tower of a town
Which an earthquake shatters down,   515
Like a lightning-stricken mast,
Like a wind-uprooted tree
Spun about,
Like a foam-topped waterspout
Cast down headlong in the sea,   520
She fell at last;
Pleasure past and anguish past,
Is it death or is it life?

Life out of death.
That night long Lizzie watched by her,   525
Counted her pulse's flagging stir,
Felt for her breath,
Held water to her lips, and cooled her face
With tears and fanning leaves:
But when the first birds chirped about their
    eaves,   530
And early reapers plodded to the place
Of golden sheaves,
And dew-wet grass
Bowed in the morning winds so brisk to pass,
And new buds with new day   535
Opened of cup-like lilies on the stream,
Laura awoke as from a dream,
Laughed in the innocent old way,
Hugged Lizzie but not twice or thrice;
Her gleaming locks showed not one thread of
    grey,   540
Her breath was sweet as May
And light danced in her eyes.

Days, weeks, months, years
Afterwards, when both were wives
With children of their own;   545
Their mother-hearts beset with fears,
Their lives bound up in tender lives;
Laura would call the little ones
And tell them of her early prime,
Those pleasant days long gone   550
Of not-returning time:
Would talk about the haunted glen,
The wicked, quaint fruit-merchant men,
Their fruits like honey to the throat
But poison in the blood;   555
(Men sell not such in any town:)
Would tell them how her sister stood
In deadly peril to do her good,
And win the fiery antidote:
Then joining hands to little hands   560
Would bid them cling together,
"For there is no friend like a sister
In calm or stormy weather;
To cheer one on the tedious way,
To fetch one if one goes astray,   565
To lift one if one totters down,
To strengthen whilst one stands."

POEM SUMMARY

Lines 1–31

"Goblin Market" opens with a description of how every morning and evening, "maids," that is, unmarried and virgin women, hear goblin men advertising the fruits they have grown, with the cry, "Come buy, come buy." The goblins call out a long list of the many sorts of fruits they have brought to market, emphasizing their delicious taste and freshness, and inviting the passers-by to try them.

Lines 32–63

This section introduces the "maids" mentioned in the previous lines. They are two sisters, Laura and Lizzie. As they lie beside a stream in a loving embrace, Laura listens intently to the goblin men's cries while Lizzie blushes with embarrassment. Laura cautions Lizzie that they must not look at the goblin men or buy their fruits, as the fruits are grown in unfamiliar and unknown soil. In spite of her own words, Laura is apparently unable to resist taking a peep at the goblin men, as Lizzie, covering her own eyes, rebukes Laura for looking at them. Laura sees the goblin men walking into the valley bearing baskets of fruit and thinks that the vines and bushes that bear such crops must be exceptionally beautiful.

Lines 64–80

Lizzie sternly warns Laura that they should not be charmed by the goblins' fruit, which would harm them if they were to taste it. Lizzie puts her fingers in her ears, shuts her eyes, and runs away from the goblin market. But Laura, overcome with curiosity, lingers to watch the goblins. They have animal characteristics: one has a cat's face, another a tail, and so on. Their voices are described as kind and loving, like doves cooing.

Lines 81–104

Laura's self-restraint breaks down. She attempts to get a closer look at the goblin men. Seeing her curiosity, they carry their baskets of fruit back along the valley to where Laura is standing. They put their baskets down and offer her dishes of fruit. One begins to weave a crown for her of leaves, tendrils, and nuts. They continue their cry, "Come buy, come buy."

Lines 105–140

Laura gazes longingly at the fruit. A goblin with a tail suggests that she taste it. The goblins speak smoothly and welcomingly to her. Laura says that she has no money, so if she were to take their fruit, she would be stealing. She says that the only gold she has is the yellow flowers of the bushes that grow on the heath. In unison, the goblin men reply that she has gold on her head, meaning her blonde hair, and they will accept a lock of hair as payment for their fruit. Laura sheds a tear and hungrily sucks at the fruits' juices. She sucks until her lips are sore and throws the rinds away. She picks up a stone (pit) from one of the fruits she has eaten and returns home in such a state of intoxication that she does not know if it is night or day.

Lines 141–162

Lizzie meets Laura at the gate and rebukes her for staying out so late. Twilight, she says, and loitering in places frequented by goblin men, "is not good for maidens." Lizzie reminds Laura of a girl named Jeanie, who met the goblin men in the moonlight, ate their fruit, and wore their flower garlands. Afterwards, Jeanie unsuccessfully looked for the goblins at every opportunity, trying to purchase more fruit. Jeanie ultimately pined away and died. No grass will grow on her grave, and the daisies that Lizzie has planted there do not flower.

Lines 163–198

Laura tries to calm her sister. She says that she wants more fruit and will attempt to find the goblin men again tomorrow night. She describes the wonderful fruits she has eaten, and offers to bring Lizzie some tomorrow.

Lines 199–252

The next day, the sisters rise at dawn. They gather honey from their beehives, milk the cows, bake cakes, make butter and cream, and feed the poultry. Then they sit and sew, and talk together. Lizzie is her usual contented self, but Laura seems distant and somewhat sick. Laura longs for nightfall.

Twilight comes, and the sisters go to the stream to collect water. As soon as they're done, Lizzie tries to bring her sister home with her, but Laura complains that the riverbank is steep and loiters there. Laura intently listens for the goblins' cry of "Come buy, come buy," but she cannot hear or see a single goblin. Lizzie, on the other hand, can hear and see the goblins. She refuses to look in their direction and begs Laura to come home with her before it gets too dark, when they could become lost.

Lines 253–298

Laura becomes cold when she realizes that her sister can hear and see the goblins and that she herself cannot. She trudges home with her sister in silence, the water dripping from her jug. After Lizzie is asleep, Laura sits in bed and weeps bitterly.

As the days pass, Laura keeps looking for the goblin men, but she never sees them or hears them. Her hair turns gray and she becomes weaker. One day, she remembers the fruit stone that she kept. She puts it next to a south-facing wall and waters it with her tears, hoping that it will sprout, but it does not. Desperate for another taste of the goblins' fruit, she dreams of it, which only increases her hunger. She neglects her domestic duties, becomes listless, and will not eat.

Lines 299–328

Lizzie is upset by her sister's suffering. As she hears the goblins' call every night and morning, she longs to buy fruit to comfort her sister, but fears the consequences in light of Jeanie's fate. Jeanie should have married but instead fell sick and died "for joys brides hope to have." The "joys" refer to the goblins' fruit. Thus, the fruit is presented as acceptable for married women, but not for unmarried ones.

When Laura is almost dying, Lizzie decides that she must act. She puts a silver penny in her purse and goes to the goblin market. For the first time in her life, she actively seeks the goblins.

Lines 329–407

The goblins greet Lizzie warmly with hugs and kisses, making strange faces and grimacing. They offer their fruits to her, inviting her to taste them. Lizzie, remembering Jeanie, is careful not to do so. Instead she throws them her silver penny, and asks to buy a large number of fruits. They refuse to take the penny, asking her to sit and eat with them as their honored guest. Lizzie refuses politely, saying that she must go home. If they will not sell her any fruit, she says, she would like her penny back.

The goblins grow angry and accuse Lizzie of being too proud and ill-mannered to sit with them. They begin to attack her physically, stamping on her feet, pulling out her hair, and tearing her dress. They try to force their fruits into her mouth.

Lines 408–474

As the goblins try to kick, pinch, and cajole Lizzie into submission, she simply stands still in silence and does not respond to the attack. She refuses to open her mouth and allow them to force in the fruit, but in the struggle, the fruits' juices are smeared all over her face and neck. At last, the goblins give up, worn out by Lizzie's resistance. They throw her silver penny back at her and retreat, kicking their fruit along the path before them. Lizzie runs home, laughing inwardly.

As Lizzie approaches her house, she shouts for Laura to come out and kiss her. In her passionate cry, "Eat me, drink me, love me," Lizzie asks her sister to suck the goblin fruit juices from her face. She explains that she has braved evil for Laura's sake.

Lines 475–542

Laura reacts to Lizzie's news with horror because she believes that Lizzie has eaten the goblin fruit. Laura fears that her sister's life will be ruined just as her own has been. But, unable to resist a taste of the goblin fruit, Laura kisses Lizzie hungrily. The juices begin to burn her mouth, and she goes into a mania, leaping, singing, and tearing her dress until she faints.

Lizzie sits awake by her sister's side all night long. The next morning, Laura awakes, laughs in her old innocent way, and hugs Lizzie. Her unhealthy desire for the goblin fruit has disappeared.

Lines 543–567

The last lines of the poem function as an epilogue, or a concluding section that rounds out the narrative. The poem jumps ahead in time by many years, when both sisters are married and have children. Laura tells her children the story of her encounter with the goblin men, of how their fruit poisoned her, and of how her sister risked her own life to save her. Laura joins the hands of her children together as she teaches them the moral of the story: that in order to stay virtuous "there is no friend like a sister."

THEMES

Earthly and Divine Love

"Goblin Market" draws a contrast between earthly and divine love. Earthly love (physical or sexual) can be a distraction from divine (spiritual or nonphysical) love. Earthly love, embodied by Laura, is portrayed as selfish. Divine love,

TOPICS FOR FURTHER STUDY

- Rossetti's "Goblin Market" has been illustrated by (among others) three famous artists: Dante Gabriel Rossetti, Laurence Housman, and Arthur Rackham. Study some of these illustrations. (They are available on the Internet and also in older print editions of the poem.) Write an essay explaining what each illustration contributes to your understanding of the poem. Note the incidents or characters that the artists choose to illustrate and how their choices shift the emphasis to different aspects of the poem. Note whether each illustration reflects or enhances the dramatic power of Rossetti's narrative, and why.

- Create your own set of at least three illustrations of "Goblin Market" and give a class presentation on what you were trying to convey about the poem in your work.

- Research the Pre-Raphaelite artistic movement. Based on your findings, write an essay explaining any Pre-Raphaelite influence you detect in "Goblin Market." Include a section on the ways in which you feel Rossetti departs from the conventions of the Pre-Raphaelite movement in her poem.

- Research the role of women in Victorian England with relation to either sexual attitudes and politics, art and literature, or commerce. Identify women who were pioneers, activists, writers, or thinkers in these fields. What was their view of women's role or status? How did they want to change things? Did anything finally change, and if so, why and how? Create a video on your findings and present your video to the class.

- Write a poem in which you describe a temptation that you have faced, and in which you express the outcome of your giving in to, or resisting, that temptation.

their ensuing attack. She withstands both, maintaining her virtue. This selfless act is rewarded, as Lizzie is now able to save her sister's life with the fruit juices smeared upon her face.

As an application of this theme, it is possible to interpret the two sisters as aspects of the same psyche: the selfish, materialistic side (Laura), and the selfless, spiritual side (Lizzie). Winston Weathers presents this interpretation in his essay "Christina Rossetti: The Sisterhood of Self." As all humans have these aspects, the combined sisters thus become a kind of everywoman. In this interpretation, the poem becomes a story of conflict within the psyche between the materialistic and spiritual aspects of humankind, and the epilogue showing the two sisters as married with children represents the psyche's return to unity. This interpretation is visually supported by the indistinguishable appearance of the two sisters (both are golden-haired beauties), and by their habit of sleeping and resting in a close embrace.

Female Sexuality

Many critics point to the homoerotic tone of the poem, commenting that Laura and Lizzie are more like lovers than sisters. They lie in close embrace, "With clasping arms and cautioning lips, / With tingling cheeks and finger tips." The poem abounds with torrid lines such as "She kissed and kissed her with a hungry mouth." Yet the love between the sisters is portrayed as pure and divine. The heterosexual relationships, in contrast, between the sisters and the male goblins, are portrayed as an evil seduction (when Laura eats the goblins' fruit) and as an attempted rape (when the goblins try to force Lizzie to eat their fruit). The homoerotic theme is underlined by the lack of a male hero and by Lizzie's assumption of this classical role.

Female Heroism and Solidarity

Though female protagonists were common in literature in and before the Victorian age, female heroes (people distinguished by extraordinary courage or ability) were extremely rare. Convention demanded that any heroic action in defense of purity, such as the act that Lizzie performs in the poem, was made by men. Lizzie is therefore unusual in her single-handed rescue of her fallen sister. It is true that her heroic action is of a passive nature: she does not fight the goblins, but merely stands still and keeps her mouth firmly shut against the fruit until they give up. But it could be argued that passive resistance, as

in contrast, embodied by Lizzie, is selfless and self-sacrificial. Motivated by a selfless (divine) love for her sister, Lizzie sacrifices herself by exposing herself to the goblins' temptations and in Mahatma Gandhi's campaign to drive the British occupiers out of India, can be effective. It is also, crucially, the tactic that Christ used when dealing with his persecutors. His death on the cross was marked by passive suffering. As Lizzie shares some Christ-like qualities, her passive demeanor fits Rossetti's purpose.

Lizzie's saving of Laura gives rise to the last lines of the poem in praise of sisters as the best possible supporters and friends. While these lines are so trite and moralistic that they appear to be from a different poem altogether, the poem's predominantly sensual and passionate treatment of the deep bond between the sisters clearly shows Rossetti's promotion of female heroism and solidarity.

Societal Anxieties and the Supernatural

The Victorians were extremely interested in fairies and the land in which they were supposed to live, which was termed *Faerie*. Fairies both frightened and fascinated Victorians in equal measure, becoming a repository of many qualities and activities that were considered alien or threatening to respectable society. These included sexual power and appetite (particularly of the female variety), physical deformity, human difference or strangeness, and everything deemed irrational and unscientific. Some of these anxieties are evident in "Goblin Market." The goblins are male, and they tempt maidens with their illicit fruit. In essence, they are agents of male sexual passion, and the appetite they awaken in Laura for their fruit is clearly symbolic of feminine sexual desire. The goblins' sexual nature is underlined by their animal characteristics, as animals were often used to symbolize base appetites. Base appetites, such as sexual desire, were viewed by Victorians as the cause of most sin. This is also why the devil is often portrayed as being half animal and half human in form.

Furthermore, it was traditionally believed that silver offered protection against the mischief of fairies. This is why Lizzie insists on paying for the goblins' fruit with a silver penny.

STYLE

Allegory

An allegory is a representation of an abstract or spiritual meaning through concrete or material forms. Although Rossetti reportedly denied that "Goblin Market" had any deeper meanings, it seems clear that, whatever her conscious intention, deeper meanings are indeed present. Certainly, critics have always dismissed her claim, and have discussed the poem as an allegory of a variety of possible themes. These include temptation, the biblical Fall of Adam and Eve, and redemption; the contrast between earthly and divine love; the triumph of selfless love over selfish lust; the importance of female solidarity in a world dominated by hostile males; and the superiority of society over the individual. Some critics propose that the poem represents the affirmation of the domestic role for women in preference to activity in the masculine world of commerce (as represented by the consequences of going to the goblin market), while others suggest that the poem represents female heroism in a male-dominated world. But in fact, none of these interpretations excludes another. Rosetti's poem has remained under discussion for over 100 years for this very reason; it is successful because it is an open-ended allegory with many feasible, non-exclusive symbolic meanings.

Symbolism

The major symbol of the poem is the goblin fruit. The fact that eating the goblin fruit or even looking at the goblin men is out-of-bounds for "maids" suggests that it is symbolic of illicit sexual passion that tempts women away from chastity and virtue. This is underlined by Rossetti's portrayal of the fruit as juicy, and full of apparent vitality. The image of Laura sucking hungrily on the fruit "until her lips were sore" is loaded with sexuality.

As an extension of this symbolism, the goblin fruit can be seen as representing the biblical forbidden fruit that tempts Eve into sin. It is noteworthy that after Adam and Eve taste the forbidden fruit, for the first time they feel sexual shame and cover their genitals with fig leaves. After this so-called Fall, they lose their innocence (they are ejected from the Garden of Eden) and their lives are filled with suffering. This turn of events is similar to Laura's experiences after she has eaten the goblins' fruit.

Laura's suffering is such that she can never fully satisfy her hunger for more goblin fruit. This is emblematic of the inability of mankind (all of whom are fallen as they are the descendants of Adam and Eve) to gain true happiness from the pleasures of the material world. The poem shows that these pleasures only serve as distractions from the true and fulfilling love of God (symbolized by Lizzie's contentment, and her subsequent self-sacrifice for her sister).

Jeanie is not saved by the intervention of a loving sister, and though she "should have been a bride," she can never marry because she has been defiled. The implication is that the defilement is sexual, as previously unmarried women in Victorian society were considered unmarriageable if they were not virgins, even if they had been raped. Thus, the only way forward for Jeanie is death because societal views at the time considered a defiled woman useless and subsequently better off dead (this belief is still held by some cultures today). Rossetti here reflects the strong expectation of her time that women should be virgins when they married and that the only place for sexuality was within marriage. Sexual passion outside marriage was viewed as sinful, but the sacrament of marriage was a way of legitimizing such passion as a tool solely for the purpose of procreation. The last lines of the poem, which show the previously fallen Laura as a happily married woman teaching her children moral lessons about the value of a sister, support this interpretation.

Rhyme Scheme and Meter

The poem uses an irregular rhyme scheme. There are many couplets (where two consecutive lines rhyme with each other) resulting in *aabb* rhyme patterns. Sometimes rhymes are repeated over three consecutive lines. At other points, several lines go by before a rhyme is completed. Internal rhymes, where the syllable that completes a rhyme appears in the middle rather than at the end of the line, are also used, as in "Her hair grew thin and gray; / She dwindled, as the fair full moon doth turn / To swift decay and burn / Her fire away," where the rhymes fall on the words *gray, decay* (the internal rhyme), and *away*. In addition, the ending syllables of the last two lines rhyme with their ending words *turn* and *burn*.

The meter is irregular, though generally there are four or five stresses in each line.

Recurring Imagery

Images of fire are used to describe Laura's hunger for the goblin fruit. During the sisters' walk to the stream, shortly after Laura has eaten the fruit, she is described as being "like a leaping flame" in her eager anticipation of meeting the goblins again. During her illness, she is compared to a waning moon that "doth turn / To swift decay and burn / Her fire away." The fire imagery is used to emphasize the destructive nature of Laura's actions and also connotes the flames of hell.

Imagery of night and day, or darkness and light, is used to symbolically illustrate the events of the poem. The goblins, as sinister creatures of darkness, appear during the evening twilight. Lizzie warns her sister, "Twilight is not good for maidens." After Laura's first taste of the goblin fruit, she "knew not was it night or day," which symbolically points to her loss of moral sensibility. The line indicates that Laura can no longer recognize right from wrong. Before Laura's illness takes hold, she gets up at dawn with her sister to perform her duties. But already, she is "longing for the night." As expected, Laura loiters by the stream in the evening, attempting to obtain fruit from the goblins, ignoring her sister's plea to return home "before the night grows dark." Now, darkness is Laura's element, and she seems to grow more and more ill as "the noon waxed bright." After Laura is redeemed by her sister, in contrast, the darkness retreats and the "light danced in her eyes."

Images of life and death also recur, often with relation to natural phenomena and seasons, and they convey spiritual qualities. The fruit's glowing vitality is an illusion. It has deathly qualities, as surrounding imagery tells the reader: it is offered in the twilight, and it is unnatural, as it is grown in a place "Where summer ripens at all hours." When Laura tries to sprout the fruit pit that she saves from her feast, it will not grow because "It never saw the sun." Lizzie, seeing Laura's decline, thinks of Jeanie, whose grave is barren, as the flowers planted on her grave refuse to bloom. Jeanie died at the first snowfall of winter, traditionally viewed as a season of death. Laura's return to health is marked by the birds and plants coming back to life at the onset of spring, traditionally viewed as a season of birth. Indeed, her breath is described as being as "sweet as May." The life-affirming imagery reaches its peak in the final picture of Laura with her children.

HISTORICAL CONTEXT

The Pre-Raphaelite Brotherhood

Both of Rossetti's brothers, Dante Gabriel and William Michael, were members of the Pre-Raphaelite Brotherhood art movement, founded

COMPARE
&
CONTRAST

- **1860s:** Women in the United Kingdom are not allowed to vote; in fact, the 1832 Reform Act specifically disenfranchised women.

  Today: Women in the United Kingdom may vote and there are many female members of Parliament. From 1979 to 1990, the country had its first female prime minister, Margaret Thatcher.

- **1860s:** The Contagious Diseases Acts are passed by the United Kingdom Parliament in 1864, 1866, and 1869. The Acts allow plain-clothed police to examine prostitutes for signs of venereal disease and require them to undergo mandatory medical examination and treatment in locked hospitals. The prostitute's male clients are not affected by the Act.

  Today: In the United Kingdom, sexually transmitted diseases are treated under the government-subsidized National Health Service in specialized clinics. Attendance is voluntary and the clinics trace all the sexual partners (male and female) of infected individuals in order to offer them treatment. The confidentiality of infected people is preserved.

- **1860s:** Female sexuality is seldom openly discussed or expressed in art, literature, or society in general. Artistic and literary expressions of female sexuality are often symbolically coded or appear to emerge against the artist's conscious intention.

  Today: Female sexuality is openly discussed in a wide variety of media. Many bookshops and adult stores have sections devoted to female-oriented erotica.

- **1860s:** Belief in fairies is widespread across a broad section of society, and fairies abound in the literature and visual art of the period. Psychologists observe that they act as a repository for a number of social anxieties prevalent in Victorian England, such as female sexual power, physical deformity, and class and racial difference.

  Today: Belief in fairies has largely been replaced by belief in extraterrestrial beings, or aliens. Psychologists observe that they act as a repository for a number of social anxieties prevalent in contemporary Western society, such as the dehumanizing effects of modern science, the invasiveness of modern medical procedures, and the destructive potential of certain technologies such as nuclear missiles.

---

in 1848. The Pre-Raphaelites focused on the detailed study of nature and their subject matter was drawn from morally uplifting stories and legends, often from the Bible, or from medieval tales of honor and chivalry. The movement was strongly Christian. The Pre-Raphaelite movement was a rebellion against Victorian materialism and artistic neoclassicism, a movement that promoted order and symmetry. Members believed that the Italian artist Raphael (1483–1520) was responsible for introducing a mechanic tendency into art, and hence they adopted the name *Pre-Raphaelite*. They looked to the Italian and Flemish art of the 1400s for their models,

emulating the intense colors, complex compositions, and fine detail.

Although Rossetti herself sometimes modeled for Pre-Raphaelite artists, she was never officially a member of the movement. However, many critics, including Dorothy Mermin ("Heroic Sisterhood in 'Goblin Market'"), see Pre-Raphaelite influences in Rossetti's poetry in general and in "Goblin Market" in particular. Mermin suggests that Rossetti uses elements of the Pre-Raphaelite artistic movement in the poem, particularly the visual images, the heroic theme, and "the erotic and imaginative intensity" that the movement favored. But, according to Mermin, she subtracts them from the overwhelmingly male viewpoint expressed in the Pre-Raphaelite works.

Female Sexuality in Victorian England

Victorian England has become a byword for sexual repression, particularly in relation to women. Women were expected to be virgins when they married for the first time, though the same standard was not applied to men; doctors removed women's sexual and reproductive organs because they were thought to be a cause of mental illness (the words *hysterical* and *hysteria* are derived from the Greek word for the uterus); and respectable women were not supposed to enjoy sex or to seek it.

Hypocrisy abounded, as can be seen from the social problems of the time. Prostitution was common, and the children that were idealized as innocence personified were sent to hard labor in factories and sent as sweeps up chimneys.

On the other hand, many progressive ideas and movements emerged in Victorian times, and modern historians see it as an age of contradictions rather than solid repression. Some doctors and psychologists of the day actually promoted sexual expression for women, and the social and political reform organizations acting, for example, on behalf of prostitutes or working women, proliferated. Notably, the stereotypical image of Queen Victoria and her husband Prince Albert as sexually naive and repressed has been shown by biographers to be inaccurate. The Queen of England was simply careful about her public image because she knew that loose morals among the monarchy and aristocracy had historically led to public hostility towards those institutions.

In matters of both sexual repression and sexual license, women were held to a double standard. While sexually active women were seen as guilty and in need of punishment, men were not condemned or punished for sexual license. Indeed, men may have even been encouraged to make sexual conquests.

An example of these double standards was a set of laws called the Contagious Diseases Acts, the first of which was passed in the United Kingdom in 1864. These laws forced prostitutes to undergo inspections for venereal diseases. If signs of the disease were found, the woman could be locked up in a prison hospital for up to three months, where she was subjected to the brutal treatments of the time. Though it was claimed that the purpose of the law was to prevent the spread of venereal disease, the male clients of the prostitutes were never inspected. It was assumed that inspecting men was an unacceptable intrusion into privacy, whereas the women were so far degraded that further humiliation was of no consequence.

At first glance, "Goblin Market" seems to conform to conventional notions of female sexual transgression, and Laura's wasting sickness after eating the goblin fruit my be seen as a deserved punishment. Her illness also undoubtedly reflects contemporary concerns about venereal diseases such as syphilis. But Rossetti subverts contemporary attitudes about fallen women in her redemption of Laura, who, unusually in literature, goes on to marry happily and have children.

Women and Economic Power in Victorian England

Married women in Western societies were not allowed to personally own property until the late nineteenth century. If a property-owning woman married, her property automatically became her husband's. Most single women also had no money of their own, going immediately from their father's care to their husband's when they married. Laura, in common with many women in Victorian England, has no money of her own ("I have no coin," she says) so she must pay for the fruit with part of herself, a lock of hair. This may be a comment on the commodification of women in the marriage market, in that the only commodity that women could use to bargain with was their bodies, as that was the only thing they truly owned. Lizzie is careful to take a silver penny with her when she goes to the goblin market, insisting on paying with money rather than giving the goblins a piece of herself. The goblins' fury at this can be interpreted as male resistance to Victorian women's attempts to gain economic freedom and equality.

The Industrial Revolution and Society

The Industrial Revolution began in England in the late eighteenth century and reached its peak in the mid-nineteenth century, around the time that Rossetti wrote "Goblin Market." Writers such as the poet William Blake (1757–1827), the novelist Elizabeth Gaskell (1810–65), and the critic (and friend of the Rossettis) John Ruskin (1819–1900) wrote at length about the social problems and anxieties caused by the Industrial Revolution. In particular, there was concern that relationships and interactions previously based on human values were becoming tainted by financial transactions. In parallel with these concerns, there arose a heightened appreciation and idealization of the rural activities and trades that were rapidly being abandoned as thousands flocked to the cities in order to work in factories. The rural trades, it was believed, tied man to nature and resulted in innocent and happy lives. The factories, on the other hand, were seen as hellish, filthy, unhealthy places that enslaved, degraded, and separated people from sustaining nature.

Rossetti introduces such concerns and idealizations into her poem. The goblins are men and they are merchants, so they can be seen as symbolizing agents of the almost exclusively male-controlled Industrial Revolution. The two sisters, in contrast, are engaged in purely rural activities such as milking cows, keeping bees, and making cakes. Their troubles begin when they venture into the commercial world of the goblins. The goblins' attempts to seduce Laura and Lizzie with their fruit could be seen as parallel to commercial advertising. The gain for the goblins if the women buy, however, is not money, but the women's bodies and souls. This may be a comment on the degrading nature of a society based on commerce.

CRITICAL OVERVIEW

In 1861, Dante Gabriel Rossetti sent "Goblin Market" to the influential critic John Ruskin in the hope that he would recommend it to William Makepeace Thackeray, the editor of *Cornhill* magazine. But Ruskin (cited by Mary Arseneau in the *Dictionary of Literary Biography*) was largely unimpressed. He praised the poem's "beauty and power" but claimed that nobody would publish it because of its many "quaintnesses and offences." About the irregular meter that has been so praised by more recent critics, Ruskin commented, "Irregular measure ... is the chief calamity of modern poetry ... your sister should exercise herself in the severest commonplace of metre until she can write

as the public like." Fortunately, Alexander Macmillan of the Macmillan publishing company disagreed, and the following year he brought out Rossetti's first commercially published volume of poetry, *Goblin Market and Other Poems* in 1862.

The collection was an immediate critical success and received many favorable reviews in the year of publication, including in the *London Review*, the *Spectator* and the *Saturday Review* (all cited by Mary Arseneau in the *Dictionary of Literary Biography*). A reviewer for the *Athenaeum* (April 26, 1862) describes "Goblin Market" as "suggestive and symbolical without the stiffness of set allegory." In a comment on the entire collection that could apply to "Goblin Market," the reviewer compares the experience of reading Rossetti's poems after other contemporary poetry to "passing from a picture gallery, with its well-feigned semblance of nature, to the real nature out-of-doors which greets us with the waving grass and the pleasant shock of the breeze." The reviewer notes that "Goblin Market" can be read as a simple legend, or with attention to "an inner meaning for all who can discern it."

Caroline Norton, reviewing the collection for *Macmillan's Magazine* (September 1863), remarked on the ambiguity of "Goblin Market": "Is it a fable?—or a mere fairy story—or an allegory against the pleasures of sinful love—or what is it? Let us not too rigorously inquire, but accept it in all its quaint and pleasant mystery." Norton, in common with the reviewer for the *Athenaeum*, notes that the poem can be read on different levels: on the level of a simple ballad for children, or as a work that "riper minds may ponder over."

The poem continued to attract critical interest throughout the twentieth century. In the Autumn 1956 issue of the *Victorian Newsletter*, the critic Marian Shalkhauser examines "Goblin Market" as a "Christian fairy tale") in which Lizzie symbolizes Christ and Laura represents "Adam-Eve and consequently all of sinful mankind." In his book *Wonder and Whimsy: The Fantastic World of Christina Rossetti*, Thomas Burnett Swann emphasizes the alien, imaginative, and fantastic elements of the poem. He calls "Goblin Market" "a masterpiece, because, like a child's daydream, it is both terrifying and unspeakably beautiful."

From the 1980s, the poem attracted much attention from feminist critics, among them

Dorothy Mermin. Mermin argues that the cheerfulness and energy of the poem and its serene ending make it "not a poem of bitter repression but rather a fantasy of feminine freedom, heroism, and self-sufficiency and a celebration of sisterly and maternal love." As of the early twenty-first century, partly as a result of the feminist critics' work and partly because of a growing fascination with biographies of Rossetti, the poem's appeal has widened. It continues to be read and studied, and its complexities continue to be analyzed.

CRITICISM

Claire Robinson

Robinson has an M.A. in English. She is a former teacher of English literature and creative writing, and is currently a freelance writer and editor. In the following essay, Robinson examines Rossetti's "Goblin Market" as a spiritual allegory on temptation, fall, and redemption.

In line with Rossetti's strong religious beliefs, "Goblin Market" can be read as a spiritual allegory on the temptation, fall, and redemption of humankind as represented in the Bible. Laura's succumbing to the temptation of the goblin fruit is symbolic of the Biblical Eve's temptation by the forbidden fruit in the Garden of Eden. God tells Eve not to eat the fruit of the tree of the knowledge of good and evil: "For when you eat of it you will surely die" (Genesis 2:17). Tempted by Satan in the form of a serpent, Eve disobeys God, eats the fruit, and brings God's curse and much suffering upon herself and Adam (and all mankind from that point forward). Similarly, Laura is tempted by the goblins, whose animal-like characteristics, such as tails and the faces of beasts are reminiscent of traditional portrayals of Satan and his fellow devils.

After Laura has tasted the goblin fruit, she suffers an insatiable hunger for more fruit, becomes self-absorbed, loses interest in life, and develops an illness that we know—from the story about Jeanie—will end in death. This can be seen as a state of sin, which embroils the sinner in a never-to-be-satisfied desire to feed a given vice. It is also a state of addiction, whether the fruit is taken to stand for illicit sexual passion or a drug, or both. Opium addiction was common in Rossetti's time, the so-called fruit of the poppy being the drug of choice for writers and

WHAT DO I READ NEXT?

- "Goblin Market" ends with a tribute to sisters. Rossetti's poems "Sister Maude" and "Noble Sisters" (both first published in *Goblin Market and Other Poems* in 1862) present very different relationships between pairs of sisters. In each poem, one sister suffers treachery at the hands of another.

- Samuel Taylor Coleridge's poem "The Rime of the Ancient Mariner" (first published in *Lyrical Ballads* in 1798), like "Goblin Market," has as its theme temptation, sin, and redemption through suffering. It shares with Rossetti's poem supernatural elements and the use of symbolism.

- *Forbidden Journeys: Fairy Tales and Fantasies by Victorian Women Writers* (1993), edited by Nina Auerbach and U. C. Knoepflmacher, is a collection of fairy tales written by women in the 1860s and 1870s. Each story's plot features a girl's journey to forbidden or strange places and thus explores unexpected emotional areas. Aside from stories by Rossetti, the book includes stories by Jean Ingelow, Anne Thackeray Ritchie, Maria Molesworth, Juliana Horatia Ewing, and Frances Burnett.

- *The Making of Victorian Sexuality* (1995), by Michael Mason, argues that Victorian attitudes toward sexuality were more progressive than are commonly thought. He neither endorses the stereotypical perception of Victorian prudery nor implies that the age was characterized by extreme sexual license. Instead, he provides evidence of evolving practices and beliefs about sexuality that in some cases seem surprisingly modern.

- In *Suffer and Be Still: Women in the Victorian Age* (1973), editor Martha Vicinus brings together a collection of essays about different aspects of the life of Victorian women. The essay topics include prostitution, working class women, economic status and power, and marriage.

UNLIKE THE STEREOTYPICAL FALLEN WOMAN OF VICTORIAN LITERATURE, WHO, AS SOILED GOODS, COULD NOT MARRY AND WAS DOOMED EITHER TO AN EARLY DEATH OR TO BACK-BREAKING PENITENTIAL WORK, LAURA IS REBORN TO LEAD A RIGHTEOUS AND FULFILLING LIFE."

artists. In drug addiction, the addict becomes deadened to the stimulant effect and requires stronger and stronger doses of the drug to regain the original experience. However much Laura hungers for the fruit, she can never be satisfied and will always seek more. Surely these are symptoms of addiction. The common ingredients of sin and addiction are a selfish attachment to the material world, a state that the poem portrays as being at odds with spiritual purity.

Lizzie's response to Laura's fall is selfless and self-sacrificial love. She courageously refuses to give in to temptation and withstands the goblins' attack, maintaining her maidenly chastity and virtue. As a symbol of her triumph, she carries home the juices smeared on her face. Her invitation to Laura to kiss and "make much of" her thus becomes an invitation to share in this pure love, which both nourishes Laura and saves her from death. On the psychological level, Lizzie ends Laura's morbid self-absorption and obsession. Lizzie's gift of herself and her love inspires Laura to respond in kind. As a result of Lizzie's heroic action, she brings "Life out of death."

Thus the poem unfolds the Biblical dictum, "For the wages of sin is death; but the gift of God is eternal life through Jesus Christ our Lord" (Romans 6:23). The sin is Laura's decision to eat the goblin fruit; the wages are her subsequent sickness; and the bringer of life is Lizzie, the Christ-like figure. Indeed, Laura's redemption is accomplished by sucking the fruit juices from Lizzie's body. This act is reminiscent of the Christian rite of the Eucharist, or Holy Communion, in which members of the congregation eat the consecrated bread and wine in the belief that they embody or represent the body and blood of Christ. The rite stems from an incident recounted in the Bible in which Christ gave thanks to God for the bread, broke it, and then offered it with wine to his disciples, with these words:

Take, eat: this is my body, which is broken for you: this do in remembrance of me.

After the same manner also he took the cup, when he had supped, saying, This cup is the new testament in my blood: this do ye, as oft as ye drink it, in remembrance of me.

(1 Corinthians 11:24–25)

Lizzie's words to Laura, "Eat me, drink me, love me" are extremely close to those of Christ.

Furthermore, according to Christian belief, Christ sacrificed himself to wash away the sins of humankind and to ensure eternal life; he "bare our sins in his own body on the tree, that we, being dead to sins, should live unto righteousness: by whose stripes ye were healed" (1 Peter 2:24). Similarly, Lizzie stands still and patient, her "White and golden" figure demonstrating her Christ-like purity, while the goblins torture her flesh and tempt her soul. As a result of Lizzie's self-sacrifice, Laura is healed and regains her old innocence.

Unlike the stereotypical fallen woman of Victorian literature, who, as soiled goods, could not marry and was doomed either to an early death or to back-breaking penitential work, Laura is reborn to lead a righteous and fulfilling life. The epilogue shows her married with children. In terms of Victorian conventional religious values, she has sublimated her sexual passion within the sacrament of holy matrimony. Laura's redemption from her fallen state is one of the elements that has given rise to a feminist interpretation of the poem, in that it shows that illicit sexual passion need not end a woman's claim to an honorable and dignified family life. However, Laura's latter happiness also follows the Christian view of redemption.

Some critics have questioned why the fruit juices that poisoned Laura should, on the second taste, cure her. At first glance it would seem that the allegory of the Eucharist breaks down at this point, since bread and wine, consecrated or not, are not poisons (nor are they akin to the fruit of the tree of the knowledge of good and evil). However, the idea that something can be both a poison and therapeutic would not have been strange to Rossetti. The statements *like cures like* or *cure by similars* is an accepted principle of homeopathic medicine, a system widely practiced in the London of Rossetti's time and by people in her family's circle. Homeopathy is based on curing a symptom by administering minuscule doses of a substance that in larger doses would cause the same symptom, somewhat like the principle that underlies vaccination or substance abuse withdrawal (take cigarette smokers and nicotine patches, for instance). Thus it is conceivable that Laura could be cured of her goblin fruit-induced disease by a second taste of the fruit.

Nevertheless, it seems unlikely that Rossetti would abandon her Eucharistic allegory for a homeopathic one so late in her poem. The answer to the conundrum lies in the same Biblical passage in which Christ establishes the rite of the Eucharist. Christ gives his disciples a vital warning of which Rossetti, who was devoted to her religion, will have been aware, and which, it can be argued, she built into her allegory.

In the passage, Christ emphasizes that the act of consuming the blessed bread and wine must be done in remembrance of him. He says that whoever consumes the bread and wine "unworthily, shall be guilty of the body and blood of the Lord" (1 Corinthians 11:27). He therefore advises that before people eat the consecrated bread and drink the wine, they should examine themselves to confirm that they are worthy. This is why in the Catholic Church, adherents are supposed to confess their sins to a priest and do penance for them before they take communion. The Protestant Church encourages the same process, but without the priest: it takes place between the adherent, his conscience, and God. Christ explains that he who eats and drinks "unworthily, eateth and drinketh damnation to himself, not discerning the Lord's body. For this cause many are weak and sickly among you, and many sleep" (1 Corinthians 11:29–30). In other words, the same food that sustains and heals when taken in remembrance of Christ, poisons and damns the eater when taken in disregard of him.

This principle can be seen in Laura's two experiences of the goblin fruit. Laura takes her first taste unworthily, in order to gratify a selfish appetite. She disregards her love and duty to her sister, and all other moral and spiritual considerations. Accordingly, the fruit weakens and sickens her. Her second taste of the goblin fruit is taken at a point when she has repented her "wasted" time and is fully aware of her sister's loving sacrifice. She consumes the juice by kissing Lizzie, both out of hunger for the fruit juices and out of love and gratitude for her sister. While Laura's first taste of the goblin fruit seemed sweet, now it tastes bitter with repentance. She undergoes a violent cure, writhing like a person in the throes of an exorcism as the second, therapeutic dose of the fruit overpowers the first, poisonous dose.

The goblin fruit, while it can and does represent sexual passion, is also more generally symbolic of the material world. It is a truism of many religions that attachment to the things of this world leads to suffering and is a sin. The so-called three fires or three poisons of Buddhism are ignorance (of the divine essence of the soul and of the divine source of material creation), greed or desire, and hatred. Due to ignorance of the divine unity of all things, the soul becomes enslaved and bound to the things of the world by desire and hatred, which are insatiable and therefore lead to potentially endless suffering or damnation. The way out of this cycle of suffering, say religious teachers of many faiths, is to recognize that the things of this world cannot be owned, but belong to God (or some form of divinity).

Material things can therefore be binding or liberating; they can addict and enslave a person, or they can act as symbols and reminders of God's love and benevolence. As the ancient Indian religious text *Srimad Bhagavata Mahapurana* notes, "the same substance which contributes to a particular malady cannot ordinarily counteract the disease; but, when taken in a properly medicated form, it does cure the ailment." This is a perfect description of what happens with Laura's cure by a second taste of the fruit juices. Her second taste is, in a symbolic sense, properly medicated, mediated as it is by the loving self-sacrifice of her sister. *Srimad Bhagavata Mahapurana* continues by saying that while all worldly activities are of a binding nature in that they attach people to the material world, "the same, when offered to the Lord, lose their binding character." Moreover, the text says that duties performed in the world "for the pleasure of the Lord" lead to "the attainment of wisdom combined with Devotion."

Lizzie exposes herself to temptation and overcomes it in Christ-like self-sacrifice for Laura;

> **HOWEVER, THE TWO ARE NOT IDENTICAL; RATHER, THEY ARE LIKE THE ID AND THE SUPEREGO, WITH LIZZIE BEING THE MORE LOGICAL, AND LAURA THE MORE IMPULSIVE."**

Laura purifies her selfish desire and hunger in her love and gratitude to Lizzie. The fruit juices that previously enslaved Laura, transformed by the divine love embodied in Lizzie, now liberate her.

Source: Claire Robinson, Critical Essay on "Goblin Market," in *Poetry for Students*, Gale, 2008.

Helen Pilinovsky

In the following excerpt, Pilinovsky examines "Goblin Market" in light of Victorian culture, paying special attention to the role of the Victorian marketplace. Pilinovsky draws on the work of several other critics to make her points, concluding that the poem reinforces the Victorian practice of valuing society above the individual.

... Fundamentally, the market represents both economic and a social transgression—or, rather, the amalgamation of the two by a society that came to see money as being equivalent to honor and power. Social transgression came to be expressed through economic means. Thus, all of those instances of mortals buying goods unintended for their hands, as in Rossetti's "Goblin Market," or of stealing them, cheating others, and breaking contracts, to set only a few examples, become newly significant of their transgression against the norms of society, and doubly significant because of their occurrence in the liminal state of the market—a place where the norms must be *more* strictly observed, rather than less, so as to maintain the borders between the permissible and the forbidden.

The impression that Rossetti creates in her presentation of the two girls are both similar and dissimilar. The two girls are comparable in many ways, as can be seen in the following description:

> Golden head by golden head, / Like two pigeons in one nest / Folded in each other's wings, / They lay down in their curtain'd bed: / Like two blossoms on one stem, / Like two flakes of new-fall'n snow, / Like two wands of ivory / Tipp'd with gold for awful kings. / Moon and stars gaz'd in at them, / Wind sang to them lullaby, / Lumbering owls forbore to fly, / Not a bat flapp'd to and fro / Round their rest: / Cheek to cheek and breast to breast / Lock'd together in one nest.

The symbolism here implies the beauties of homogeneity, and the love and recognition of the familiar—this seems representative of Victorian society. However, the two are not identical; rather, they are like the id and the superego, with Lizzie being the more logical, and Laura the more impulsive. Lizzie is shown to be the more cautious of the two; potential danger does not engage her curiosity, but simply warns her off, as we can see in the lines where she reacts to her sister's curious reaction to the goblin men; we read, "'No,' said Lizzie, 'No, no, no; / Their offers should not charm us, / Their evil gifts would harm us." Lizzie heeds example of other girls' fates, and behaves carefully, in the prescribed manner; later, she will act as storyteller, as the experienced voice of reason. Laura, in marked contrast, is also aware of the dangers, but she is more rash; despite her knowledge of the likely consequences, we read how she disregards her sister's reiteration of the warning that she herself initially makes; she throws caution to the winds, and begins the process that will temporarily part the two when she ignores her own good sense and her sister's actions. We read,

> Laura rear'd her glossy head, / And whisper'd like the restless brook: / "Look, Lizzie, look, Lizzie, / Down the glen tramp little men. / One hauls a basket, / One bears a plate, / One lugs a golden dish / Of many pounds weight. / How fair the vine must grow / Whose grapes are so luscious; / How warm the wind must blow / Through those fruit bushes."

The nature of Laura's transgression is very telling. Laura knows that to buy the fruits is forbidden to her. As Terrence Holt notes that "the ostensible function of [the] discourse of the marketplace is to stress the difference between maidens and goblins. Exchange, 'Goblin Market' claims, is the province of goblins, not little girls. The market is dangerous to maids, who belong safely at home," a fact of which both girls appear to be aware. Laura, in particular, is aware of their dangers and their unfamiliar source. She says so herself, when she first warns Lizzie: "We must not look at goblin men, / We must not buy their fruits: / Who knows upon what soil they fed / Their hungry thirsty roots?" Yet she herself, referred to as "curious Laura," and "sweet-toothed Laura," is vulnerable;

she commits her actions while being aware of their consequences, if not of their full extent. Nevertheless, Laura yields to temptation. She resists it at first; we read, "Laura stared but did not stir, / Long'd but had no money" She attempts to explain her situation, saying, "Good folk, I have no coin; / To take were to purloin: / I have no copper in my purse, / I have no silver either, / And all my gold is on the furze / That shakes in windy weather / Above the rusty heather," and then, finally, accepts the goblin bargain to trade a lock of her golden hair when they offer to barter. Rossetti writes, "'You have much gold upon your head,' / They answer'd all together: / 'Buy from us with a golden curl." According to the magical Law of Contagnation, which states that any part of a thing is equivalent to the entirety, Laura has given them herself; in exchange, she has taken their corruption into herself. It appears, as well, that she knows what she has done; after clipping off a lock of her hair, we read how she "dropped a tear more rare than pearl," signaling her knowledge of her doom.

The description of Laura sampling the fruit is very sensual. We read,

> She dropp'd a tear more rare than pearl, / Then suck'd their fruit globes fair or red; / Sweeter than honey from the rock, / Stronger than man-rejoicing wine, / Clearer than water flow'd that juice; / She never tasted such before, / How should it cloy with length of use? / She suck'd and suck'd and suck'd the more / Fruits which that unknown orchard bore; / She suck'd until her lips were sore; / Then flung the emptied rinds away / But gather'd up one kernel stone, / And knew not was it night or day / As she turn'd home alone.

This brings us to the concrete nature of the market goods. The fruits of the poem have been thought to represent the desires of the flesh—the sensual nature of the poem is quite evident. This can also be seen in the references to the earlier goblin victim, Jeanie, who pines for the goblins as for lost lovers, described by Lizzie thus:

> Do you not remember Jeanie, / How she met them in the moonlight, / Took their gifts both choice and many, / Ate their fruits and wore their flowers / Pluck'd from bowers / Where summer ripens at all hours? / But ever in the noonlight / She pined and pined away; / Sought them by night and day, / Found them no more, but dwindled and grew grey; / Then fell with the first snow, / While to this day no grass will grow / Where she lies low: / I planted daisies there a year ago / That never blow.

That implication is strengthened later on in the poem, when we read how Lizzie "thought of Jeanie in her grave, / Who should have been a bride; / But who for joys brides hope to have / Fell sick and died / In her gay prime." As Carole G. Silver sees it, the goblins "have ... ravished and destroyed Jeanie ..." her choice of verb is particularly interesting, and apt, in that it implies transports of delight, abduction, and violation, all of which Jeanie has suffered, in one way or another. This reading foreshadows all that is to befall the two sisters, from Laura's initial pleasure in the fruit, to the way that it takes her away from Lizzie, and finally, to the abuses committed upon Laura in her attempt to save her sister. The fruits have been thought to represent narcotics as well as sensuality, as the Victorian period was rife with drug abuse, particularly that of opium, which is also known as the fruit of the poopy. Laura's inability to hear the goplin men thereafter seems similar to the tolerance that a drug user builds up; as can be seen in her reaction to the realization that the fruits will no longer affect her as they had is certainly reminiscent of withdrawal. We read,

> Laura turn'd cold as stone / To find her sister heard that cry alone, / That goblin cry, / "Come buy our fruits, come buy." / Must she then buy no more such dainty fruit? / Must she no more such succous pasture find, / Gone deaf and blind? / Her tree of life droop'd from the root: / She said not one word in her heart's sore ache; / But peering thro' the dimness, nought discerning, / Trudg'd home, her pitcher dripping all the way; / So crept to bed, and lay / Silent till Lizzie slept; / Then sat up in a passionate yearning, / And gnash'd her teeth for baulk'd desire, and wept / As if her heart would break.

The use of fruit as a symbol of temptation has both Biblical and Classical roots, in the apple of Eden, and the pomegranate of Hades. Both are well represented in the goblin's wares, referred to, respectively, simply as "apples," and as "[p]omegranates full and fine." In "Goblin Market," as in both of the former cases, knowledge of the forbidden is equivalent to death.

The manner of Laura's rescue from the goblin's by Lizzie is particularly interesting. She goes to buy fruit for her sister, but offers no more than mortal coin; the goblins receive it, not of their own volition, but when she tosses it at them. Rossetti writes, "'Good folk,' said Lizzie, / Mindful of Jeanie: / 'Give me much and many':—/ Held out her apron, / Toss'd them her penny." This is not their preferred payment; they wish to gain her company, and herself, and they demur, attempting to put her off with half-truths. In the typical way of fairies, they avoid outright lies, as these would invalidate any resulting bargains. They say,

> "Nay, take a seat with us, / Honour and eat with us," / They answer'd grinning: / "Our feast is but beginning. / Night yet is early, / Warm and dew-pearly, / Wakeful and starry: / Such fruits as these / No man can carry: / Half their bloom would fly, / Half their dew would dry, Half their flavour would pass by. / Sit down and feast with us, / Be welcome guest with us, / Cheer you and rest with us."

They speak the truth concerning the effects of consumption of their fruits absent of their presen[ce], but they avoid informing potential customers of the effects of their wares; truly, a case of "Buyer, Beware," as Lizzie does. She is interested in partaking of their custom only on her own terms, a fact which obviously displeases them. Nevertheless, they have accepted payment, which they do not return when she says "If you will not sell me any / Of your fruits though much and many / Give me back my silver penny / I tossed you for a fee." The deal has been struck, and sealed with silver; by ancient rules of fairy, with which Rossetti appears aware, and which still operate in full force even in the confines of the market, they must attempt to fulfill their bargain; they "give" her the fruit by attacking her with it. We read,

> They began to scratch their pates, / No longer wagging, purring, / But visibly demurring, / Grunting and snarling. / One call'd her proud, / Cross-grain'd, uncivil; / Their tones wax'd loud, / Their look were evil. / Lashing their tails / They trod and hustled her, / Elbow'd and jostled her, / Claw'd with their nails, / Barking, mewing, hissing, mocking, / Tore her gown and soil'd her stocking, / Twitch'd her hair out by the roots, / Stamp'd upon her tender feet, / Held her hands and squeez'd their fruits / Against her mouth to make her eat ...

As Silver asserts, "What marks ... Rossetti's goblin men as particularly threatening ... is their grotesque materiality, their physical ludicrousness combined with their 'primitive' sexuality ... Their elbowing, jostling, pinching, and clawing, amount to near rape, or at least sexual assault." They attempt to have their will of her physically, when they cannot coerce her through other means, to force the metaphorical properties of the fruit—carnality—when it will not be taken through manipulation. However, for Rossetti, free will is paramount, not only on the basis of religious principle, though those are invoked, as we shall soon see, but also on the principles of the market. Rossetti writes,

> One may lead a horse to water, / Twenty cannot make him drink. / Though the goblins cuff'd and caught her, / Coax'd and fought her, / Bullied and besought her, / Scratch'd her, pinch'd her black as ink, / Kick'd and knock'd her, / Maul'd and mock'd her, / Lizzie utter'd not a word; / Would not open lip from lip / Lest they should cram a mouthful in: / But laugh'd in heart to feel the drip / Of juice that syrupp'd all her face, / And lodg'd in dimples of her chin, / And streak'd her neck which quaked like curd.

Regardless of what they resort to, Lizzie will not accept. They literally cannot force her to acquiesce under conditions that she had not agreed to, and finally, we read how

> At last the evil people, / Worn out by her resistance, / Flung back her penny, kick'd their fruit / Along whichever road they took, / Not leaving root or stone or shoot; / Some writh'd into the ground, / Some div'd into the brook / With ring and ripple, / Some scudded on the gale without a sound, / Some vanish'd in the distance.

They return her penny, and storm off, unable to gain any advantage over her. They have attempted to fulfill the bargain on their terms, by forcing the goods that she had inquired about and paid for in advance upon her, which she will not allow; they refuse to fulfill the bargain on her terms, by simply giving her the fruit to carry off, knowing that they will not gain her "spirit" in that way, and perhaps that they will lose the benefits of a former "customer." Thus, matters have concluded with a draw; except, by breaking the rules of the marketplace by using physical force, they have granted her what she wanted all along, the means to rescue her sister from their coils. Lizzie has triumphed, simply by knowing the rules of the marketplace.

Lizzie's actions are heroic, but they are put forth in a singularly passive manner; martyr like, Lizzie allows herself to be brutally attacked so that she may bring the fruits of her labor back home to heal her sister. She is described thus;

> White and golden Lizzie stood, / Like a lily in a flood,—/ Like a rock of blue-vein'd stone / Lash'd by tides obstreperously,—/ Like a beacon left alone / In a hoary roaring sea, / Sending up a golden fire,—/ Like a fruit-crown'd orange-tree / White with blossoms honey-sweet / Sore beset by wasp and bee,— / Like a royal virgin town / Topp'd with gilded

dome and spire / Close beleaguer'd by a fleet / Mad to tug her standard down.

Rossetti alludes to the Virgin Mary, clothing Lizzie in her colors, and using the adjective "virgin" to describe her. The original, destructive, nature of the fruit is transmogrified by Lizzie's sacrifices on behalf and love for her sister. Upon returning home, she offers herself and her sacrifice to her sister; we read how

> She cried, "Laura," up the garden, / "Did you miss me? / Come and kiss me. / Never mind my bruises, / Hug me, kiss me, suck my juices / Squeez'd from goblin fruits for you, / Goblin pulp and goblin dew. / Eat me, drink me, love me; / Laura, make much of me; / For your sake I have braved the glen / And had to do with goblin merchant men.

Here, finally, we see Laura begin to break free of the goblin spell, more out of concern for her sister than through any magical properties. Breaking free of her artificial lethargy,

> Laura started from her chair, / Flung her arms up in the air, / Clutch'd her hair: / "Lizzie, Lizzie, have you tasted / For my sake the fruit forbidden? / Must your light like mine be hidden, / Your young life like mine be wasted, / Undone in mine undoing, / And ruin'd in my ruin, / Thirsty, canker'd, goblin-ridden?

Laura begins to kiss her from concern, rather than selfishness, and continues when she feels the restorative power of the medicine that her sister has fetched for her. Rossetti writes,

> She clung about her sister, / Kiss'd and kiss'd and kiss'd her: / Tears once again / Refresh'd her shrunken eyes, / Dropping like rain / After long sultry drouth; / Shaking with aguish fear, and pain, / She kiss'd and kiss'd her with a hungry mouth ...

Rossetti implies that Laura is still operating under the influence of the fruit when she performs these actions, saying, "Ah! fool, to choose such part / Of soul-consuming care!" Her concern for her sister is overtaken by her need for succor, with little sense of the depth of the support behind it. When Laura sucks the juices of the fruit from her sister's flesh, she is nurtured, like a babe by her mother. One has the sense that it is her sacrifice and love that heals Laura, as much as any goblin fruit. However, when she wakes, healed, she realizes the full extent of Lizzie's concern. We read how, recovered, "Laura awoke as from a dream, / Laugh'd in the innocent old way, / Hugg'd Lizzie but not twice or thrice."

The last lines of the poem reiterate the Victorian value of society over individualism. Laura and Lizzie lead lives of virtue, mirroring one another as they had in the past, implying their reintegration into a homogenous, harmonious union. It is Laura who appends a moral to the tale of their experiences; she tells their collective brood that

> ... there is no friend like a sister / In calm or stormy weather; / To cheer one on the tedious way, / To fetch one if one goes astray, / To lift one if one totters down, / To strengthen whilst one stands.

Source: Helen Pilinovsky, "Conventionalism and Utopianism in the Commodification of Rossetti's 'Goblin Market,'" in *Extrapolation*, Vol. 45, No. 1, Spring 2004, pp. 52–64.

David B. Drake

In the following essay, Drake contends that "Goblin Market" displays numerous characteristics of an epyllion, a small epic poem. Among these qualities, notes Drake, are that the poem features "an epic heroine who engages in quintessentially epical exploits."

Christina Rossetti's "Goblin Market" exhibits several of the characteristics and conventions of epic poetry and should be studied as a somewhat modified version of the epyllion—a poem that emulates the classical epic in subject matter and technique, but is decidedly shorter (typically depicting just a single heroic episode) and narrower in scope—modified because the epyllion is ideally composed using dactylic hexameter, and "Goblin Market" is, of course, written in free verse.

A substantial number of critics have noted that Rossetti's heroine, Lizzie, resembles a transfigured Christ who redeems her peccant sister by sacrificing herself to the malevolent goblins. Feminist critics, meanwhile, have designated Lizzie a pioneering member of their own movement who is earnestly determined to protect the sanctity of sisterhood against any form of patriarchal corruption (i.e. the goblin men). Inherent in both these persuasive exegeses is the understanding that Lizzie is an individual of historic, or even cosmic, consequence. Moreover, one need not examine her victorious encounter with the goblins (lines 363–446) too scrupulously to recognize that Lizzie's actions are not only valorous, but utterly herculean in magnitude (keep in mind that she is but a child and is greatly outnumbered). In short, Lizzie, while ostensibly not an imposing personage, is truly an epic heroine.

Thematically, "Goblin Market" incorporates a pair of archetypal motifs that frequently appear in epic poetry. To begin with, Lizzie's journey into the glen to combat the demonic, preternatural goblins—the poem's epic machinery—is analogous to a descent into the underworld. And accordingly, her subsequent reemergence from this underworld clearly signifies a resurrection, not so much for herself, but more precisely for the moribund Laura (again, Lizzie the Christlike healer), as well as for all maidens, since Lizzie (the seminal feminist) has emphatically demonstrated that they indeed possess more resourcefulness and tenaciousness than the goblins, and consequently need no longer be the victims of their misogynistic tyranny.

Besides featuring an epic heroine who engages in quintessentially epical exploits, Rossetti's poem also features some of the unifying stylistic devices commonly employed by epic poets, such as the refrain (exemplified here by the goblins' exhortation, "Come buy, come buy") and anaphoristic repetition. In fact, the anaphora in "Goblin Market" repeatedly involves the clustering of similes, with each cluster devoted to describing a lone primary object and thus functioning much like an aggregate epic simile. In other words, when making a comparison, Rossetti does not offer merely one secondary vehicle developed well beyond its patent correspondence with a primary object (as occurs in the epic simile), but rather a consecutive string of secondary vehicles, of similes. Granted, none of these secondary vehicles; is intricately developed; still the immediate effect is exactly the same as in the epic simile: the primary object is deemphasized. Perhaps this is best explained through illustration:

> Laura stretched her gleaming neck
> Like a rush-imbedded swan,
> Like a lily from the beck,
> Like a moonlit poplar branch,
> Like a vessel at the launch
> When its last restraint is gone.
> (81–86)

These simile clusters appear throughout the poem, most notably to depict a somnolent embrace between Laura and Lizzie (184–91), a steadfast Lizzie as she prepares to face the goblins (408–21), and Laura's frenzied reaction after ingesting the vivifying fruit juice that her sister has so courageously procured for her (510–20).

"Goblin Market" additionally includes two epic catalogues, albeit these martial catalogues, like those found in Pope's mock-heroic "Rape of the Lock," are metaphoric. The first comes at the start of the poem (5–29), listing the goblins' poisonous produce, their armaments, while another, itemizing the goblins or warriors themselves, occurs approximately between lines 55 and 76.

In his essay "Simple Surfaces: Christina Rossetti's Work for Children," Roderick McGillis briefly mentions that Laura's miraculous reanimation near the close of "Goblin Market" recalls the passage in Homer's *Odyssey* when "Odysseus' sailors return to human form after Odysseus has overpowered Circe" (211). They, like Laura, actually seem to have been favorably transformed by virtue of surviving their mystical ordeal. Unfortunately, however, McGillis neglects to develop this evocative thesis further and comment explicitly upon the striking number of parallels between "Goblin Market" and epic poetry in general. Because Rossetti's poem manifests not simply one or two, but a number of epic attributes, it seems thoroughly unlikely that their presence is entirely coincidental. And seeing that a poem need not be written in dactylic hexameter to be considered an epyllion (e.g. Arnold's "Sohrab and Rustum"; Tennyson's "Idylls of the King"), it is only appropriate that "Goblin Market" be likewise regarded as an epyllion or small epic.

Source: David B. Drake, "Rossetti's 'Goblin Market,'" in *Explicator*, Vol. 51, No. 1, Fall 1992, pp. 22–24.

Saturday Review

In the following review of Goblin Market and Other Poems *dated shortly after the publication of the volume, the critic praises the volume as a whole while lamenting that the title poem is not able to bear the weight of the imagery with which Rossetti infuses it. The critic remarks on the "pleasant flow of sound and stream of imagery" in the poem but contends that a "deeper meaning" remains hidden.*

Miss Rossetti's poetical power is most undeniable. She is gifted with a very good musical ear, great strength and clearness of language, and a vivid imagination, which only now and then wants to be restrained. Some of the shorter pieces in [*Goblin Market and Other Poems*] are as faultless in expression, as picturesque in effect, and as high in purity of tone as any modern poem that can be named. It is a pleasure to meet an authoress who has obviously given such conscientious labour to the tasks she has set herself to accomplish, and who has succeeded so frequently in saying the right thing to be said in the best and shortest way.

Yet there is one ground upon which we are inclined to quarrel with Miss Rossetti; and that ground is the poem which is placed in the front of her volume and of its title. "*Goblin Market*" is a story of too flimsy and unsubstantial a character to justify or to bear the elaborate detail with which it is worked out. As it deduces a moral at the close in favour of sisterly affection, it may be presumed to be in some sense or other an allegory. But what the allegory is, or how far it runs upon all-fours with that of which it is the shadow, we cannot undertake to say ... Where the moral inculcated is so excellent and proper, it may seem ungracious to complain of the unreal texture of the fable through which it is conveyed. The language of the story is very graceful and musical, and the picture of the sisters in their daily labour and rest is drawn with a pretty simplicity which gives a momentary substantiality to the dreamland in which they live ...

An artist of Miss Rossetti's power ought to know by instinct a theme which will bear filling out with shape and colour, from one of which the inconsecutiveness and unreality show only the more strongly in proportion to the labour used in its embodiment and ornament. A picture of which half is a photographically accurate representation of nature, and the other half a purely symbolical imagination worked out with equal distinctness and detail, can never be really harmonious or satisfactory; and the same may be said of a story. The eye and the ear equally like to know to what extent they are bound to believe what they see and hear, and what is the result of it all. The reader of "*Goblin Market*" may be carried on by the pleasant flow of sound and stream of imagery; but the real thought of the poem is a mere rope of sand, carrying no deeper consistency or meaning than the revelations from the unseen world interpreted now-a-days by a professional spirit-medium.

Miss Rossetti's genius appears to tend very naturally towards symbolical expression. One of the most perfect little pieces in the volume is the statement of a very serious enigma called "*Up-hill*". It is remarkable for saying not more than is needed on a text which tempts many sermonizers to be prolix ...

There is a subdued and grave simplicity about ... [the poem] which very clearly marks Miss Rossetti's power of accommodating her style to the subject. Equal simplicity, combined with a more detailed picturesqueness and a more plaintive tone, is to be found in "*An Apple-Gathering*" ...

[In this poem, the] idea of the composition is rather pictorial than poetical; and it is so graceful when regarded in this light that we can afford to overlook the slight artifices of the verbal interpretation which Miss Rossetti has given to her own painter's imaginings. The foundation of the whole picture is a genuine and human sentiment, quite different from the sheer unreality which underlies the conception of the "*Goblin Market*"; and for the strength and success with which this sentiment has been caught and impressed upon the sense of the reader, it is prudent to forgive some of the questionable truth of detail.

The devotional poems which fill a large portion of this volume are excellent in tone, and generally very clear and good in expression. Every reader of one of these called "From House to Home," will be forcibly reminded of the manner of Mr. Tennyson's "Palace of Art and Dream of Fair Women;" but the poem is not wanting in originality of thought. The highest specimens of Miss Rossetti's power, however, will be found in the secular division of her works ...

It would be easy to point out various instances of a slight affectation in language and in rhythm, and an unnecessary preference for the use of unfamiliar in lieu of familiar terms. Such faults are, perhaps, theoretically, less excusable in an authoress who shows her thorough command of metre, and of a very sufficient vocabulary of good sterling English. Yet in such a case these errors are practically the more venial, as they may be expected to correct themselves in the course of study. Miss Rossetti displays the talent of conscientious hard work in her verses, as Mr. [Dante Gabriel] Rossetti does in his very remarkable and original paintings. Sooner or later they will both, as we trust, work out for themselves in their respective arts the desirable conviction that quaintness is not strength, and that it generally interferes with beauty.

Source: Saturday Review, Review of "Goblin Market," in *Saturday Review*, Vol. 13, No. 343, May 24, 1862, pp. 595–96.

SOURCES

Arseneau, Mary, "Christina Rossetti," in *Dictionary of Literary Biography*, Vol. 240, *Late Nineteenth- and Early Twentieth-Century British Women Poets*, edited by William B. Thesing, The Gale Group, 2001, pp. 210–31.

King James Bible, http://www.hti.umich.edu/k/kjv/ (accessed February 28, 2007).

Mermin, Dorothy, "Heroic Sisterhood in 'Goblin Market,'" in *Victorian Poetry*, Vol. 21, No. 2, Summer 1983, pp. 107–18.

Norton, Caroline, "'The Angel in the House' and 'The Goblin Market,'" in *Macmillan's Magazine*, Vol. 8, No. 47, September 1863, pp. 398–404.

Review of *Goblin Market and Other Poems*, in the *Athenaeum*, No. 1800, April 26, 1862, pp. 557–58.

Rossetti, Christina, "Goblin Market," in *The Complete Poems of Christina Rossetti*, edited by R.W. Crump, Louisiana State University Press, 1979, pp. 11–26.

Shalkhauser, Marian, "The Feminine Christ," in the *Victorian Newsletter*, No. 10, Autumn 1956, pp. 19–20.

Srimad Bhagavata Mahapurana, Part 1, translated by C.L. Goswami and M.A. Sastri, Gita Press, 1971, p. 20.

Swann, Thomas Burnett, "'Goblin Market': Fantastic Masterpiece," in *Wonder and Whimsy: The Fantastic World of Christina Rossetti*, Marshall Jones Company, 1960, pp. 92–106.

Weathers, Winston, "Christina Rossetti: The Sisterhood of Self," in *Victorian Poetry*, No. 3, Spring 1965, pp. 81–9.

FURTHER READING

Bell, Mackenzie, *Christina Rossetti: A Biographical And Critical Study*, Kessinger, 2006.

Bell's biography of Rossetti, first published in 1898, provides a fascinating insight into Rossetti and her family, the pre-Raphaelite circles in which they moved, and the literary life of the period.

Bowra, Cecil M., *The Romantic Imagination*, Harvard University Press, 1957.

Bowra discusses the literary reputation of Christina Rossetti, ultimately defining her as a Romantic poet.

Bristow, Joseph, ed., *Victorian Women Poets: Emily Bronte, Elizabeth Barrett Browning, Christina Rossetti*, St. Martin's Press, 1995.

This book contains a selection of essays by various critics on different poets, including one on Rossetti's religious poetry. The other essays are highly relevant to a study of Rossetti's work and the social and literary context in which she worked; the essays cover such topics as sexual power and politics, fallen women, and consumerism.

Marsh, Jan, *Christina Rossetti*, Viking, 1994.

In this biography, Marsh makes use of letters and diaries to show how Rossetti's verse was a response to the people and events that shaped her life. Marsh quotes extensively from Rossetti's poetry and throws considerable light on her preoccupation with grief and death.

Rossetti, Christina, *Goblin Market*, illustrated by Arthur Rackham, Beaufort Books, 1985.

This edition features illustrations by one of the greatest illustrators of children's literature, Arthur Rackham (1867–1939). As of 2007, it is out of print, but second-hand versions are available for purchase on the Internet.

Silver, Carole G., *Strange and Secret Peoples: Fairies and Victorian Consciousness*, Oxford University Press, 1999.

Silver explores the widespread belief in, and fascination with, fairies in the Victorian period, further discussing the social anxieties that fueled this belief.

Iola, Kansas

AMY CLAMPITT
1997

Amy Clampitt's poem "Iola, Kansas" is typical of her poetry, using her much-lauded command of the language to show that a small, almost unnoticed moment in life can be much more significant than it might at first seem.

The poem concerns a cross-country bus ride that passes from Oklahoma into Kansas, driving through miles and miles of seemingly empty country before coming to a stop at a diner in a small speck of a rural town. The poem's speaker is moved by the honesty and simplicity of the woman at the diner in Iola and realizes that, though she would never have expected it, she has found happiness at the end of her trip. Clampitt presents the plainness of the bus trip, the town, and the diner with complex language and imagery that might, at first, seem contrary to her subjects, but that end up showing off the depth and significance of things too often taken for granted.

Clampitt's career as a poet is notable for the quality of her work, but also for the fact that, at age 63, she seemed to suddenly appear out of nowhere, publishing her first collection of poetry to great critical acclaim. She published four more collections in the next decade, with a meteoric rise to the highest echelons of American poetry. "Iola, Kansas" was published in *The Collected Poems of Amy Clampitt* which appeared in print in 1997, four years after her death.

Amy Clampitt (AP Images. Reproduced by permission)

AUTHOR BIOGRAPHY

Clampitt was born on June 15, 1920, in New Providence, Iowa, a town of 200 people. She was the first of five children. Her father, Roy Justin Clampitt, was a farmer, and the family lived on the 3000 acre farm that was owned by the poet's grandfather until Amy was ten. They then moved to an uncultivated patch of land a few miles away; this was the first of many moves throughout Clampitt's life.

Growing up, Clampitt was encouraged to be a writer by her paternal grandfather, who, in addition to being a farmer, was a fan of literature—he had written and self-published his own autobiography. She began writing poetry at the age of nine, almost fifty years before her first publication. After graduating from New Providence Consolidated School, she attended Grinnell College in Grinnell, Iowa, earning a Bachelor of Arts with Honors in 1941. She then received a scholarship to Columbia University, and went to New York for graduate school. She left school within a year,

however. Throughout the 1940s, she worked for Oxford University Press, eventually rising to the position of promotions director for college textbooks. When she left that job in 1951, Clampitt took a long, five-month tour of Europe before returning to New York. From 1952 to 1959 she was a reference librarian for the National Audubon Society. In 1960, she began working as a freelance editor and writer, and she continued to do so for the rest of her life. In addition, from 1977 to 1982 she worked for the E.P. Dutton publishing house as an editor.

While working in various jobs associated with literature, Clampitt continued to write. At first, she thought of herself as a novelist, and wrote three novels during the 1950s that were never published. She turned to poetry in the 1960s, publishing a small edition of her first collection in 1974. Her first commercial publication came in 1978 when, after attending poetry writing classes, her work was read by the poetry editor of the *New Yorker*, one of the most respected magazines in the country. For years, her works were published in that magazine.

With the publication of her book *The Kingfisher* in 1983, Clampitt became a literary sensation at the age of 63. Over the next ten years, she published five more collections of poetry, as well as collections of her critical essays. She received some of the highest honors available to poets, including a Guggenheim Fellowship in 1992, a fellowship from the Academy of American Poets in 1984, and a MacArthur Foundation Fellowship in 1992. In the final decade of her life, Clampitt taught at William and Mary College, Amherst College, and Washington University. She died of ovarian cancer on September 19, 1994. In 1998, "Iola, Kansas" was published posthumously in *The Collected Poems of Amy Clampitt*.

POEM SUMMARY

Stanza 1

The first line of "Iola, Kansas" establishes the poem's basic situation: the speaker is riding a bus through the middle of the country, referred to here as "the interior."

Lines 2 through 4 concern the flatness along the route of the interstate highway the bus is taking through Oklahoma. Although the state is known for having the most diverse terrain of any state, away from the major urban areas, the state has areas that are flat and empty, with miles of nothing more notable along the interstate than oil refineries, referred to in line 2 as "cities" because they often, from a distance, look as big and bright as actual towns rising on the horizon. Even before it became a state in 1907, Oklahoma was famous for oil production: though its yield of oil has diminished as the wells have dried, it is still an important spot for drilling, and for refining the oil culled from off-shore drilling sites. The first stanza refers to the wastefulness of off-shore drilling as "crass" and yet "indispensable." It mentions the drilling rigs that tower above the flat Oklahoma landscape as "homunculi."

A "homunculus" (the singular form of "homunculi") is a legendary figure that comes from early scientific theory. It originally referred to a small deformed humanoid figure that could be created by a scientist, and the word was later adapted in reproductive theory to indicate that sperm were actually tiny men, or homunculi. An artistic rendering of a human being with exaggerated features, showing the relative sensitivity of certain nerve paths, is called a "sensory homunculus." Such portrayals, with large hands, lips, and genitals, look somewhat similar to oil drilling rigs.

Stanza 2

The poem's second stanza contains a litany of the things that the speaker observes outside of the bus, along the side of the highway, in small towns, and in the yards of houses adjacent to the road. In line 7, after describing the bright color of the bumper-stickers that talk about Jesus, the speaker expresses bewilderment in an aside to the reader: "who knows / what it means." The implication is that religious conviction is not only different than, but contradictory to, the showiness of bright fluorescent coloring, which should properly be more subdued.

Line 8 refers to a "Barbie-doll barbecue": the poem is indicating that the people who bought the barbecue in the backyard of a house on the highway are trying to emulate the aesthetically sterile make-believe world of Barbie dolls, buying products that are more suited for an image of perfection than for real life. Unlike the graffiti that might be observed in an urban setting, written on a stationery wall, this scene of self-expression and chaos passes by the bus's window like a motion picture, which the poem refers to as "graffiti in video."

Stanza 3

Line 9 has lyrics from popular songs, which the poem refers to, disparagingly, as "dirges." The phrase "*heart like a rock*," which appears in the poem in italics, is an inexact meshing of two songs. Bob Seeger's "Like a Rock," which talks about being young and powerful, never includes the word *heart*. Seeger's song, adapted to well-known commercials for pickup trucks, has led to an association with rural America, the area described in the song. A closer connection can be made to Paul Simon's song "Love Me Like a Rock." This song does not use the word *heart* as the poem does, either, but its meaning is similar. The second song lyric, "*I said Kathy I'm lost*," which also appears in the poem in italics, comes directly from Simon's song "America," which chronicles a couple in love on a bus ride, laughing together and commenting on the other passengers, with a refrain that reflects the point of "Iola, Kansas": "All come to look for America."

In line 10 the poem announces the transition from Oklahoma to Kansas, which, it observes, is less orderly, lacking the same "scheme."

"Sere groves," mentioned in line 11, are groves that have withered and dried. The "horizonless belch and glare," an image that begins on that line and continues on to the next, indicates the fires that refineries emit into the sky, to burn off gasses released in the refining process. "Alluvium," mentioned in line 12, is usually used to indicate sediment that is deposited by a flowing river: here, Clampitt uses the word to indicate that the flow of time and life has dropped old automobiles off in junkyards in the same way that a flowing river might naturally drop silt.

Stanza 4

The setting established in the first three stanzas changes at the start of stanza 4, as the speaker explains that the bus has crossed over from Oklahoma to Kansas. The scenery, which was ugly and commercial, turns to that of a more peaceful rural landscape as the bus turns off of the large freeway and travels down smaller country roads. In place of the oil derricks of Oklahoma are the symbols of community in small Kansas towns: churches and bandstands represent places where individuals come together, partaking with each other in religion and music.

The water towers that are likely to be the tallest structures in the towns have the names of the towns painted on them, and the towns are named for girls, which makes them seem friendly and sweet.

Stanza 5

The first two lines of stanza 5 are concerned with describing the churches in the small towns, and with drawing connections between the churches and the colorful bumper stickers previously referred to in line 6. Although the stained glass windows are meant to be beautiful and inspiring, the poem calls them "banalities," pointing out the disparity between their intention to worship Jesus and the lack of imagination that they inspire: the question "who is this Jesus?" indicates that the speaker receives no religious uplift from viewing them.

The last half of stanza 5 is about the way that life in a small Kansas town baffles the poem's speaker, who not only fails to recognize Jesus from the churches' tributes to Him but also feels a growing sense of "strangeness." The sights described in the first stanzas were worth noting, but the speaker could at least make some sense of them, unlike the experiences in Kansas.

Stanza 6

The town of "Iola" is first identified. For a bus traveler, accustomed to food from vending machines and rest stops that feature attention-grabbing videos, the homines of the rest stop is remarkably unusual. In line 24, the claim that the boysenberry pie was just made that very day is characterized as having been said "believably." The fact that the poem's speaker would include this word indicates, first, that one would assume that the pie would not be fresh, and also that one would expect that a person would lie about its freshness. The word indicates surprise on both counts.

At the end of stanza 6, the speaker of the poem uses "I" for the first time. All previous personal pronouns have been "we," referring to the people on the bus collectively. The experience of receiving the pie from an honest person (who also refers to herself as "I") has made the poem's speaker more reflective, more self-aware.

Stanza 7

The poet does not say that she reveres the pie, but that she feels "something akin" to reverence,

thereby identifying the specific emotion with a general term, much as she earlier is only able to come up the idea of "strangeness" to describe the town of Iola.

In line 26, using the name "Silex" for the coffee pot marks it as an old device that was manufactured before Proctor Electric and Silex Corporation merged in 1960. The Silex coffee maker was a glass vacuum device, heated on a stove burner, that was first patented in 1915.

The air brakes mentioned in line 27 are common on buses used for interstate transit, and, when engaged, are loud enough to wake any people who may have stayed on the bus to sleep while it was at the rest stop.

The use of the word "agency" in line 28 indicates something acting according to the will of God. While the word is more commonly used to refer to branches of a bureaucracy such as the government, there is a long-standing tradition of using the word to identify an "agent" that God uses to carry out His plans. In the same line, the word "assembly" refers to the passengers on the bus, but it does so in a way that likens them to a church congregation.

Stanza 8

The poem's reverence for the simple country life is felt by all of the bus passengers in line 29, bringing them together as a community, a feeling that they did not have before. The speaker refers to herself as a "rock" in line 30: her heart, or emotions, are only able to narrowly escape from her body through "some duct" when she is moved by what she has seen in Iola. The poem ends with the same recognition of the inability to impose order that was mentioned in line 10, but, after having absorbed the "mess" and lived with it, not just experienced it intellectually but emotionally, the speaker finds that the uncertainty that people in the country accept as being the way of life makes her happy.

THEMES

Small Town Life

After establishing a sense of disconnect that dominates the speaker's feelings about America during the bus trip, this poem focuses in on a sense of community that comes from life in a small town. Small town collective thinking is characterized in several ways.

TOPICS FOR FURTHER STUDY

- Write a short play for four to eight actors playing characters riding on the bus described in the poem, giving each character dialog that is related to the stop at the diner.

- "Iola, Kansas" describes a road trip, and road trips are an inherent part of American culture. Why might that be? Research road trips and how diners and buses fit into this topic. Also research other famous works of art that feature a road trip. How do their themes differ from those in this poem? Present your findings to your class.

- The speaker of this poem seems to think that the slogans about Jesus she sees on bumper stickers are in bad taste. Find some bumper stickers that you think sound awkward or crude, and rewrite them to more clearly express the sentiments that you think they are trying to convey.

- Make a playlist of songs that you would listen to on a bus trip across any five states. Write a paragraph about each explaining which songs should be listened to in which particular places, and why.

One characteristic of the ways that people are said to think in the towns of Kansas, the "interior" of the country, is represented by the names of the towns in this poem. They are identified as girls' names, which the poem presents as a sign of closeness, of intimacy, of friendship. This aspect of the town names is briefly foreshadowed in the song lyric quoted in line 9, which refers to "Kathy" as if one is overhearing a snippet of conversation between friends. Later, when the specific town in Kansas is identified as "Iola," the same sense of personal closeness has already been established.

The poem mentions monuments, seen through the bus window, that are associated with life in a small town: a bandstand in a park, water towers, and churches all reflect a rural mentality that seems alien to the observer.

The most potent symbol of small-town life giver here, though, is the food one finds in this culture. For one thing, it is fresh food, not to be gotten from a vending machine but prepared by hand. It is not fresh in the sense of healthy or nutritional—the specific items mentioned are processed white bread, coffee, and pie—but it has a personal connection with the person serving it. The fact that the pie is "believably" fresh-baked implies much about the speaker's assumptions and findings about small-town life. In a world where pies are routinely churned out of machines and then presented as being fresh, this one, though not described in a very appetizing way, is something that someone has taken the time and inclination to create. In this one image, the poem captures a sense of honesty and industry that represent the values of small-town life.

Quest

This poem presents a quest for happiness, even though the poem's speaker does not seem to even be aware of being on a quest. It is focused on forward motion, as the bus carrying the observer moves through the Oklahoma landscape that is filled with "illusory cities," yards full of objects that betray their owners' pretense, and claims of religious fidelity that are too showy, with their day-glo neon backgrounds, to take seriously. Clampitt never openly expresses any particular resentment toward this life, but the choices of objects make it clear enough that there is no satisfaction for the reader in them.

The bus's arrival at Iola, Kansas, does not at first seem to bring any particular comfort to the poem's speaker. The elements of the small town are viewed coldly from the bus window, with a tone that is slightly judgmental, looking at the town's water towers and churches as clichés of small-town life. It is only after a meal at a restaurant, when a particular inhabitant of Iola has been introduced, that the speaker of the poem feels her "heart go out." By the last line, she has found the satisfaction that she never specifically said she was lacking. The journey that was characterized with discontent ends with happiness, implying, though not directly saying, that the speaker of the poem has, in the end, found what she was searching for all along.

Order and Disorder

This poem uses the phrase "the scheme is a mess" twice, in line 10 and in line 31, with the second time bracketed in parentheses to indicate that it is an echo of the first. The expression is, of course, self-contradictory: a "scheme" cannot imply anything but a sense of order, but it is at the same time a "mess," which can mean nothing but disorder. This contradiction points to a greater sense of ambiguity felt by the poem's speaker. The area of the country that the poem takes place in is open rural country: though there are few signs of civilization, they are imposing, like highways and oil refineries. Orderly civilization is spread out, though, strewn across the expanse of land in a mess.

The first half of the poem is dominated by the oil refineries, which are complex and orderly structures, similar to cities. They are not placed in order along the highway, though, but are interspersed with junkyards and backyards and the comings and goings of other vehicles along the road.

The second half of the poem is about the town of Iola, where order and disorder blend together in harmony. Life in Iola is not mechanical, as indicated by the absence of video and vending machines. Instead of imposed order, a natural order has been established: one where people, without being told to, respond to their environment in unison. The people in the bus form a "community" from their experience of stopping at a small-town diner, while before the experience of Iola they were just disconnected travelers.

STYLE

Quatrain

Although "Iola, Kansas" does not follow a regular rhythm or rhyme scheme, Clampitt does stay with a rigid organizational scheme by dividing the poem into four-line stanzas. The four-line stanza, called a "quatrain," is the most common stanza used in English poetry. One reason that this form is so often used is that it lends itself to a balanced symmetry: rhyming poems can end the second and fourth lines with rhymes (the *abcb* pattern), they can rhyme the first and third lines in addition to the second and fourth (*abab*), or they can rhyme the first and second, then third and fourth lines (*aabb*). Using such a

well-known, traditional form as the quatrain, even in the absence of a rhyme scheme, imposes a sense of order on "Iola, Kansas." Readers who might otherwise be inclined to think that the author is simply recording her experiences are constantly reminded of the controlling hand of the poet, who has imposed such a strict, regular order on the ideas presented.

Diction

Clampitt is known as a writer who uses a wide range of language to engage readers' curiosity. This poem uses some common, everyday expressions that sound like a person might use in an average conversation. It also uses the sort of colloquialisms that one might find in rural Kansas, such as "swigging" or "innards" or "mess." Clampitt is even willing to include a new word of her own making, "purply," to describe a pasty substance that is not exactly purple. But the most conspicuous use of diction is her freeness with complex words that common readers might need to look up in a dictionary, such as "illusory," "banalities," "homonuculi," or "alluvium" By challenging her readers with her poem's diction, the poet forces them to become active participants in reading; they have put some work into understanding her message. Using simpler language might make the poem easier to understand, but easy reading would not necessarily be an accurate reflection of Clampitt's vision.

HISTORICAL CONTEXT

Oklahoma and Kansas

Clampitt wrote most of her poetry, including this poem, while living in New York, nearly 1300 miles away from where the poem takes place. The poem therefore reflects some truths about the places that it talks about and some stereotypes that would be common to someone viewing it from a distance. For instance, one would naturally be more likely to come across more bumper stickers announcing the car owner's love of Jesus in Oklahoma and Kansas than in New York; the area is at the center of the section of the country that is referred to as the "Bible Belt," which is a term coined by journalist H.L. Mencken in the 1920s to describe the swath from the Carolinas to Texas where evangelical Protestants are vocal about their Christian faith. New York, by contrast, like many urban areas

COMPARE
&
CONTRAST

- **1990s:** Bus travel in rural areas continues to decline steadily ("the bus [is] half empty"), as stable gas prices and a booming economy make car ownership affordable for most Americans.

  Today: Rising gas prices and concerns about the environmental effects of driving have encouraged a significant amount of the population to reconsider using public transportation, though automobiles are still the most common means of transport for most Americans.

- **1990s:** A bus traveler from an urban part of the country to a rural part of the country can expect to find distinct ideas and attitudes that reflect the traditions of each individual region.

  Today: Regional cultures, while still distinct, may be less so than ever before. The prevalence of the internet and cable television, and the powerful influence of the media provide news and cultural information to all regions instantaneously, exposing all places to the same cultural influences.

- **1990s:** Rural areas are sparsely populated. The landscape is dominated by farms and "auto junkyards."

  Today: While the landscape remains the same, populations in rural areas continue to decrease, as individual farmers have been mostly forced out of business by large, industrialized farms and by a burgeoning global trade that provides low-cost produce from abroad.

---

across the globe, has a much higher mix of Jews, Muslims, Buddhists, and other non-Christian religions than any of the places described in the poem, which would make the sorts of proclamations about Jesus one might find in the Bible Belt conspicuous when seen by a New Yorker like Clampitt.

Another aspect of the region that Clampitt identifies correctly is the dominance of oil production on life in Oklahoma. This area, which had and still has one of the densest populations of Native Americans in the country, was flooded with Americans of European descent in the last decade of the eighteenth century, when oil was found there. Ever since then, Oklahoma, like neighboring Texas, has been associated with the fortunes to be made in the oil industry. Though Clampitt's association of Oklahoma with oil might seem a little cliché, the poem does show a fine distinction between the past and present when it recognizes that the rigs that pump the oil out of the ground have moved to offshore drilling as the easily-accessed deposits

have dried up, but that the area still has retained the refineries to process the oil.

The poem's views of small-town life in Kansas reflect a city-dweller's view of country life, even if it is based in Clampitt's small-town Iowa upbringing. The fact that she is either mis-remembering a trip through Kansas or exercising poetic license with what she found there can be seen in the way she characterizes the towns as being named after girls. In the general area of Iola, there are in fact towns named Mildred, Florence, Rose and Selma, but the same area has a fair share of towns with boys' names, too, such as Benedict, Neal, Dennis, and Vernon.

Perhaps her broadest generalization that reflects an urban bias in discussing the mid-southwest is the poem's use of Wonder Bread as a symbol of American rural homogeneity. Wonder Bread is a brand of white bread, which is a mass-produced, bland form of bread that is most popular in areas lacking in culinary input from other cultures. In many parts of the world, bread making is an art, and living in New York, a city that draws off of international diversity, Clampitt would be much more aware of white bread as a symbol of the monoculturalism that thrives in the American heartland than the people that eat that bread themselves would know. The term "white bread" has even come to be symbolic of American provincialism, indicating the sense that commercialism, a lack of nutrition, and predominantly pale northern European ancestry preside at the center of American culture.

CRITICAL OVERVIEW

Clampitt was over sixty when her first commercial book of poetry, *The Kingfisher*, was published in 1983, and she immediately became an important figure in the literary world. *The Kingfisher* was reviewed in papers and magazines of national and international prominence. The year after its release, Clampitt was given the Award in Literature by the American Academy and Institute of Arts and Letters, and she received a fellowship award for distinguished poetic achievement from the Academy of American Poets. In the following decade, Clampitt went on to publish four more full volumes of poetry and a few limited edition books. Though they were all praised by critics, *The Kingfisher* is still recognized as her greatest achievement.

"Iola, Kansas" comes from *The Collected Poems of Amy Clampitt*, published in 1997. With this volume, critics were able to look at Clampitt's brief career in one place, at one time. Mickey MacAdam, reviewing the collection in the publication *Hurricane Alice* in 2000, focused on the poet's reputation for being a difficult read, with words and literary allusions that only readers with extensive backgrounds would understand. "Regardless of the reader's previous knowledge of or desire to research her allusions," MacAdam concluded, "the rich and intensely woven musicality of Clampitt's language more than compensates for whatever particular facts the reader is unable to immediately negotiate." A reviewer for the *Economist* described the book as "a rare and enduring achievement," explaining Clampitt's genius as coming from the combination of her poetic skill with the experiences of her lifetime: "She has done time on the Greyhound bus, and was, in her time, both in the world and out of it."

On the rare occasions when there have been any negative criticisms about Clampitt, they usually pale when put in perspective. Willard Spiegelman, for instance, quoted the poet Mary Karr as having noted that Clampitt's writing can sometimes seem a little too rich, quoting Karr's essay "Against Decoration," in which she compares one passage of Clampitt's poetry to "Swinburne on acid or Tennyson gone mad with his thesaurus." Still, Spiegelman dismisses Karr's concerns, asking for, if anything, more. "All of her intellectual and cultural appetite is easy to miss amid the sheer gorgeousness of Clampitt's sounds," he said in the *Kenyon Review*, "streaming, even gushing from the page as though released after years of captivity."

CRITICISM

David Kelly

Kelly is an instructor of literature and creative writing in Illinois. In this essay, Kelly looks at the way the poem's structure is slightly forced, which serves to make it more alive and engaging.

Clampitt is a poet known for the complexity of her works. The most obvious characteristic of her poetry is that she does not hold back her extensive, fluent vocabulary: an intelligent reader can expect the need to refer to the dictionary at least once or twice in the course of reading the average Clampitt poem. There is no question that she makes her works challenging on purpose. When things are not handed over to them easily, readers can become engaged in the act of seeking understanding. The relationship between the poet and the reader becomes one of partnership, with both sides seeking the truth, instead of feeling one-sided, like a lecture, with all of the ideas flowing toward a passive receiver who may or may not have a stake in what is being said.

Clampitt's use of difficult language is as obvious as it is legendary. And her imagery is no more accessible than the words themselves, leaving it to future generations of literary analysts to parse the many possible implications of the details that she has given. Added to this is the way that Clampitt manipulates the structure of the poem, playing with the arrangement of the words while making it seem as if she is doing anything but that. Her poems take readers away from the page to look up allusions, references,

WHAT DO I READ NEXT?

- Readers can gain insight into Clampitt's ideas about life and art by reading *Love, Amy*, a collection of her letters to family members and friends written over the course of forty years. It was edited by Willard Spiegelman and published by Columbia University Press in 2005.

- Clampitt came to the attention of the literary world in 1983 with the publication of her first mass-market collection, *The Kingfisher*. It is still considered by many to be her most moving and forceful work.

- Critics frequently link Clampitt's poetry with the works of Elizabeth Bishop, who was only nine years older than Clampitt, though she published her works a generation before Clampitt did. In particular, Bishop's 1946 poem "A Miracle for Breakfast" shows similarities to "Iola, Kansas" in its phrasing, sensibilities, and in its use of language. It can currently be found in Bishop's *Complete Poems*, published by Chatto and Windus in 2004.

- Another contemporary poet often linked to Clampitt is Jorie Graham, whose complex word choices resemble Clampitt's own word usage. Her collection *Dream of a Unified Field* (1995) is a selection of twenty years of her poetry, which spans 1974 to 1994 and has been referred to as being as continuous in the story it tells, start to finish, as a novel.

- Mary Jo Salter wrote the introduction to *The Collected Poems of Amy Clampitt*. Salter's poem "Tromp L'oeil," included in her collection *Open Shutters* (2003), reflects the kind of complexity and linguistic playfulness that one finds in Clampitt's poetry.

and definitions, certainly, but they also draw readers into the work, to try to follow what is going on and why. What might, for example,

> THE REPEATED USE OF COLONS THROUGHOUT THE POEM IS SUSPICIOUS, AND THE USE OF A COLON HERE, WHERE THE RUNNING SUCCESSION OF IDEAS REALLY RUNS OUT AND A NEW THOUGHT CLEARLY BEGINS, REPRESENTS THE AUTHOR FLAUNTING THE RULES OF GRAMMAR."

seem to be a poem that lends itself to an easy, casual reading often turns out to have been built over a maze, a complex design that one might not even notice without looking. Then, just when the reader is feeling intimidated by Clampitt's depth of knowing, it becomes apparent that she is really writing about the familiar world after all. She achieves some of her effects by knowing much more than the reader, but she is not above bending the rules to achieve other effects: not with the intent of cheating, but with a sense of fun.

Take, for example, the poem "Iola, Kansas." The poem's message is fairly obvious and can be restated in simple terms. It tells the story of a person who takes a long, interstate bus trip, passing by symbols of excessive consumption and superficial religious devotion, eventually ending up in a small town—Iola—where emotions are true. As a result of an encounter with one particularly sincere woman running a diner, the people on the bus find camaraderie, leaving the poem's speaker ultimately happy. Of course, it is an oversimplification to phrase the events of the poem in these terms, and could give the false impression that the poem is using unnecessarily complex language to hide the fact that the story it tells is an old and familiar one. What matters is the details that she uses to convey these events—the line from Paul Simon's *America*; the look and texture of a slice of boysenberry pie; the desolation of clusters of pecan trees along the side of an empty highway. These and countless others are things that no summary could capture, which is precisely why, even if its core message is nothing too new, the poem itself still has something important to say.

Structurally, this poem does something interesting. At first glance, it appears to be just as commonplace as the story that it tells of finding happiness in small-town honesty. Clampitt has cut the poem into lines that have a consistent, uniform width, and arranged them into quatrains, four lines per stanza. Augmenting this is that most of the lines, 19 out of 32, end with some sort of punctuation. Although the poem does not follow a formal structure in terms of a repeating rhythm or rhyme scheme, it certainly gives readers the feel of formal poetry by following these consistent patterns from beginning to end. Readers take from this the feeling, whether consciously realized or not, that the poet is not merely stating emotions, not just following her whims or her inspiration, but that Clampitt has a very careful, deliberate intention in mind. This sense of the poem's shape and her measured, complex choices of language build on each other, leading to the greater overall impression that there is more to the events here than meets the eye. It could be argued that this feeling, forcing readers to look more and more closely, is what all poetry is about.

But what seems to be the structure of this poem is something of an illusion. A tightly structured poem would cover one and only one idea per stanza, building on the sum of them. But this idea is difficult to follow very strictly in the case of a narrative poem like this one, because the details of the story that the poet is trying to tell don't often fit into the poem's shape. The four-line stanza helps a poet simplify complex points, but the story has a shape of its own. There ends up being a struggle between the material and the form that the author is trying to impose upon it. Clampitt amplifies this natural contradiction by choosing to tell the whole poem, start to finish, with one continuous sentence.

The most obvious reason for this continuity would be that doing so keeps the action moving, fluid, to the end: in spite of the constant punctuation and the seven stanza breaks, some readers might praise the poem by noting that it "flows." But if the need for continuity were in itself an excuse for stretching one sentence out further and further, there would be short stories and novels that try to follow the same principle, rambling on and on for pages without a period. The desire to keep a work bouncing along without ever coming to a stop is always offset by the basic principles of English grammar: there are only so many twists and turns a piece of writing can take before it comes to an end of its logical sense.

"Iola, Kansas" does an admirable job of using its punctuation to fold its ideas neatly into each other, and of keeping readers in touch with what is happening in the poem, even as their minds come close to the point of fatigue. Clampitt uses commas freely, often coinciding with the ends of lines. If she phrased things differently, with the commas and the line breaks each creating separate pauses in the poem, it would lose its luxurious texture and end up choppy. The poem even uses the dash, Emily Dickenson's preferred method of redirecting the reader's train of thought down one sidetrack after another, but, while Dickenson might use five or six in a sentence, Clampitt uses just one. She does not alter the poem's direction with her one dash, but instead uses it to bring the whole poem to a halt, three lines from the end. In this way, her dash works like the final line break of a traditional sonnet, announcing the coming of a summary. Readers pause with that one dash in "Iola, Kansas" and then go on to find a direct statement of what had previously only been implied.

In two cases, the poem directly steps outside of the narrative progression to make comments on the side, in parentheses. The first instance of this asks "who is this Jesus?"—a philosophical question that theologians have grappled with for ages. It comes at a time when the poem is thick with physical description that has been superimposed over the bleakness of the Oklahoma/ Kansas landscape. In the second case, the poem has almost settled on what it is going to accept as meaning when it parenthetically interjects, "the scheme is a mess." To some extent, this echo of line 10 can be read as a reminder of the former confusion that has finally been settled. It can also, though, be taken as a reminder that any sense of resolution this poem offers should be recognized as illusory, that the underlying problem of "mess" still exists where apparent order exists, haunting the poem like a ghost.

The thing that really enables Clampitt to push the poem through to the end in just one sentence is her use of colons. She uses a total of six colons in "Iola, Kansas." Independently, each colon might be significant, but together they take on a cumulative mass that builds almost to the point of ridiculousness. For instance, the colon at the end of the first stanza brings the sentence to a stop to introduce a list, as colons most often do. The one in line seven also introduces a list, as does the one in line nine (introducing a short list of songs heard) and line 21 (things not found at the rest stop). In line 22, there is a colon to introduce a direct quote from the woman at the lunch counter.

These are each legitimate uses for colons, in separate sentences, but the fact that they show up one after another indicates an infringement of the rules of grammar and logic. Most grammar books will shy away from pronouncing a hard and fast law that prohibits multiple colons in one sentence, though they are clear about why one would not want to use the device in that way. The colons mentioned are supposed to introduce lists and phrases, which would in each case imply that the end of the sentence is coming up, but Clampitt goes on past the introduced list or phrase, bringing the sentence back to life after it should have died a natural death. What she does is unusual, but poetry is built on writers taking just such thought-provoking turns.

There is one more colon, however, that does not fit the rules. The colon that Clampitt uses in line 25 is probably a true infraction of the rules of logic. What follows it is not a list, and it is not a phrase that is introduced by "with something akin to reverence," any more than anything in any other case is an introduction to the words that follow it. The logical connection between "reverence" and "free refills" might be ironic in that they do not compliment each other but have a contrasting effect: there is a difference, though, between compliment and contrast, which makes this the most questionable bit of punctuation in the whole poem. The repeated use of colons throughout the poem is suspicious, and the use of a colon here, where the running succession of ideas really runs out and a new thought clearly begins, represents the author flaunting the rules of grammar.

It is proper that poets should flaunt the rules of grammar: it keeps things interesting. When we use the phrase "poetic license" to identify places where poets are allowed to bend the rules of grammar in order to attain an artistic effect, the implication is that poets and only poets are licensed to take such liberties. In the case of this poem, the multiple colons work, along with the other punctuation marks, to keep this long, inclusive sentence going, and the long sentence serves, like the complex grammar, to keep readers involved in what they are reading. Clampitt's control of words and grammar allow her to achieve effects that writers with less skillful hands might have trouble sustaining. She keeps every element of the poem in motion, always pushing forward toward her meaning.

Source: David Kelly, Critical Essay on "Iola, Kansas," in *Poetry for Students*, Gale, 2008.

Willard Spiegelman

In the following excerpt from a review of Clampitt's Collected Poems, *Spiegelman analyzes the subjects and characteristics of the poet's work. Of "Iola, Kansas," which Spiegelman calls a "one-sentence tour de force," the critic notes how the poem's themes of community and wariness are similar to those found in some of the poems of the twentieth-century American poet Elizabeth Bishop.*

... For all of the richness in her poetry, Clampitt is, like James Merrill, equally an elegiac poet of loss and dislocation. "Losing Track of Language" examines one kind of loss and compensatory gain; "Midsummer in the Blueberry Barrens" begins with a nod in the direction of Wordsworth and Frost ("Tintern Abbey" and "Directive," respectively) by conveying a pattern of disappearance within a landscape: "Away from the shore, the roads dwindle and lose themselves / among the blueberry barrens" (266). Clampitt is sensitive to natural erosion and encroachment for more than merely ecological or aesthetic reasons. All evidence of change echoes personal instability. As early as "On the Disadvantages of Central Heating," she remarks, "the farmhouse long sold, old friends / dead or lost track of" (17). Later in that volume, *The Kingfisher*, in her first great long poem, "A Procession at Candlemas," Clampitt alludes to Native Americans as merely one of many migratory tribes:

... The westward-trekking
transhumance, once only, of a people who,
in losing everything they had, lost even
the names they went by, stumbling past
like caribou, perhaps camped here.

Such renderings of loss, forgetting, unwrapping, returning, and unpeeling are the essential cause of all those accumulations—in imagery, metaphor, rhythm, and syntax—that annoy or fatigue Clampitt's thoughtless critics. She always put the weight of her style at the service of diminishments. She is, in fact, as likely to dismiss as to welcome ornament for its own sake; she disdains the merely cute, once referring condescendingly to "Guido Reni, master / of those who prettify." Her true Americanness comes out in those moments when she adheres to a Yankee's, or a farmer's, sense of value: she loves "all that / utilitarian muck down underfoot" ("The Local Genius" [62]), or *objets trouvés* that are dear for their fragility *and* their usefulness, like the straw racks in "Stacking the Straw" that exemplify the biblical ephemerality of all flesh. Yet these "beveled loaves" also amount to "the nearest thing the region had / to monumental sculpture" (63). Like Whitman ("This Compost"), Stevens ("The Man on the Dump") and A. R. Ammons (*Garbage*), she bears witness to the beauty of accumulated masses of compost, of "the pleasures of the ruined," as in "Salvage":

> I find esthetic
> satisfaction in these
> ceremonial removals
> from the category of
> received ideas
> to regions where pigeons'
> svelte smoke-velvet
> limousine, taxiing
>
> in whirligigs, reclaim
> a parking lot . . . (36)

She abhors wastefulness, admiring the Darwinian elegance of destruction on the Serengeti Plain where first lions, then "down-ruffed vultures," then "feasting maggots / hone the flayed wildebeest's ribcage / clean as a crucifix" ("Good Friday" 68). Of such natural selection does Clampitt build her own theology.

One typical misunderstanding of ornament resents it for manufacturing false, unwarranted *Sturm und Drang* and for confusing mere excess with depth. In fact, Clampitt proves everywhere that "depth is not everything," as she aphoristically announces in "The Spruce Has No Taproot." We can take this arboreal example as one of Clampitt's own talismans: like all the weeds, seedlings, easily displaced persons, tribes, and species with which she identifies, it roots itself shallowly in order to adapt and to form a subtle community:

> . . . the spruce
> has no taproot, but to hold on
> spreads its underpinnings thin—
>
> a gathering in one continuous,
> meshing intimacy, the interlace
> of unrelated fibers
> joining hands like last survivors
> who, though not even neighbors
>
> hitherto, know in their predicament
> security at best is shallow. (117)

Such shallowness makes freedom the reward for truancy. Thus, the "pokeweed, sprung from seed / dropped by some vagrant" ("Vacant Lot with Pokeweed" 329), which seizes a temporary foothold; or, in the same group, some bamboo curtains, "going up where / the waterstained old ones had been, and where the seedlings— / O gray veils, gray veils—had risen and gone down," in the apartment of a Greenwich Village eccentric ("A Hedge of Rubber Trees" 335). "Nothing stays put," she announces in a poem of that title in this series that celebrates as well as laments eternal impermanence: "All that we know, that we're / made of, is motion" (340).

Motion has political—as well as psychological—causes and effects. She cites the words of an Omaha Indian in her signature piece "The Prairie":

> *The white man does not understand America,*
> a red man wrote: *the roots of the tree of his life*
> *have yet to grasp it.* (346)

Above all, the essence of such motion has, as it must for a poet who seeks the proper form for her vision, syntactic consequences. The "interlace" of her spruce tree is also the right word for the meshings by which Clampitt—here and elsewhere—duplicates and represents those other familial, cultural, and historical reticulations, the elaborately constructed networks that enable our individual lives to flourish. Where uprooting and exile—even when temporarily denied or held at bay—pose a constant threat, the only home a poet may finally claim is a strongly built, involved, poetic structure. (A bit less compulsively than Merrill and the younger contemporary poet Mark Doty, Clampitt has a fondness for little stanzaic "rooms" that offer one kind of refuge.) The early poem "Black Buttercups" (*What the Light Was Like*) makes the best case for the wariness Clampitt learned as a child in the face of unhousing and exile. Although she never suffered, as Merrill did, from a "broken home," from divorce, she lost her Edenic farmstead in the Depression when she was ten and her family was forced to move. Exile and menace were the lot of her ancestors, always on the go, but even the original farmstead gave onto a symbol of final menace:

> . . . the terrain began to drop (the creek
> down there had for a while powered a sawmill,
> but now ran free, unencumbered, useless)—

that not-to-be-avoided plot whose honed
    stones'
fixed stare, fanned in the night
by passing headlights, struck back
the rueful semaphore:
There is no safety. (125)

Like Hopkins, Frost, and Heaney, other
masters of rural pleasure and rural coldness,
Clampitt knows how to brace her Latinate syntax and vocabulary with a harsh, grim monosyllabic string ("plot whose honed stones' . . . ") for
a maximally chilling effect.

The sense of dispossession allies her as well
with Elizabeth Bishop, our most famous poet-
orphan, who was always deeply skeptical of happiness and wisdom in equal measure. "Iola, Kansas"
is an implicit homage to the Bishop of such poems
as "Arrival at Santos," "Cape Breton," and especially "The Moose," which square the fear of the
unknown with the thrill of (even touristic) adventure, and which ask us to measure the satisfactions
of a seldom achieved community of feeling against
the relative unlikeliness that we should ever experience—let alone deserve—happiness, pleasure,
and personal identity even for an instant.

This one-sentence tour de force, reporting an
all-night bus ride through the heart of the country, actually begins by echoing "Arrival at
Santos," which ends with an ominous flat statement ("we are driving to the interior") after thirty-
seven lines of wittily observed details. Clampitt's
journey is more industrialized, more noun-heavy:

> Riding all night, the bus half empty, toward
>   the interior,
> among refineries, trellised and turreted illu-
>   sory cities,
> the crass, the indispensable wastefulness of
>   oil rigs
> offshore, of homunculi swigging at the gut
>   of a continent . . .

As the bus proceeds from Texas, through
Oklahoma and into Kansas, it pauses at a rest
stop in the godforsaken town of the title, where
the narrator "with something akin to reverence"
eats a piece of simple home-baked boysenberry
pie, before piling back onto the bus with her
fellow travelers:

> . . . then back to our seats,
> the loud suction of air brakes like a thing
>   alive, and
> the voices, the sleeping assembly raised, as
>   by an agency

> out of the mystery of the interior, to a
>   community—
> and through some duct in the rock I feel my
>   heart go out,
> out here in the middle of nowhere (the
>   scheme is a mess)
> to the waste, to the not knowing who or
>   why, and am happy. (291)

Like the bus riders in Bishop's "The
Moose," stopped by a giant creature in the middle of the road, and then united by a "sweet /
sensation of joy" before resuming their journey,
Clampitt and her companions join together in
one of those rare moments of what we can only
call grace. Spiritual longing and an awareness of
"the strangeness of all there is" inspire her, in
spite of her spiritual, political, and emotional
wariness, to be ready to relish such moments
when they do come.

Rejoicing often takes place within a context
of sharing—within a community of other people
whose very presence assures greater pleasure—
and it takes place as well within the syntactic
equivalent of community: a long sentence (Clampitt writes longer sentences than practically anyone else, and more one-sentence poems as well)
with deeply subordinated clauses. The so-called
"literariness" of her writing serves, therefore, a
political as well as an aesthetic purpose: it proves
that words and phrases, like human beings, are
intricately enmeshed in greater units.

Source: Willard Spiegelman, "What to Make of an
Augmented Thing," in *Kenyon Review*, Vol. 21, No. 1,
Winter 1999, pp. 172–81.

Blake Morrison

In the following review of Clampitt's Westward,
*Morrison places the volume in the larger context
of the poet's overall work. In comparing the volume to "Iola, Kansas," Morrison notes how a key
grammatical characteristic of that poem—its use
of a single long sentence, with no periods, over the
course of the poem's eight stanzas—is used to even
greater effect in* Westward.

Amy Clampitt's new book opens with a bold
piece of imaginative transportation, "John Donne
in California," setting down a poet who alluded to
America but never visited it among the giant redwoods and "New World lizards" of the West:

> Is the Pacific Sea my home? Or is
> Jerusalem? pondered John Donne,
> who never stood among these strenuous,
> huge, wind-curried hills, their green

"

SHE IS DRAWN TO, AND LIKES TO DRAW OUR
ATTENTION TO, THE NEGLECTED, THE REMOTE, THE
OUT OF THE WAY; AND THERE IS NOWHERE LIKE ONE'S
OWN DOORSTEP FOR FINDING THEM."

gobleted just now with native poppies'
opulent red-gold . . .

Donne is far from being the only figure, or indeed the only literary figure, to be uprooted in the course of Clampitt's collection. The central theme of the book, as dominant in the last poem as in the first, is of men and women driving westward—pioneers, settlers, immigrants, dreamers, poets. But Donne is the right person for Clampitt to start with, for the poem of his that she cites and expects us to turn to (though uncharacteristically she gives no source in the endnotes) is a "Hymne to God my God, in my sicknesse," in which Donne imagines his prostrate body as a map (and his doctors as cartographers) and celebrates a heavenly union of East and West. "Is the Pacifique Sea my home? Or are / The Eastern riches? Is Jerusalem?" asks Donne (and Clampitt after him), implying an answer he had already reached in one of his sermons: "In a flat Map, there goes no more, to make West East, though they be distant in an extremity, but to paste that flat Map upon a round body, and then West and East are all one."

Nearly four centuries after Donne, the idea of West and East being united, "all one," remains as frail a conceit as it has always been, but in the euphoria of the present moment, with the bad old empires on their sickbeds all around the globe, it is proper that Clampitt, if ever so obliquely, should catch something of that utopian dream. She is not a political poet, but nor is she so unworldly as she sometimes sounds, and her collection, susceptible to historical changes, offers its own special version of late twentieth-century glasnost. It is no coincidence that "The Prairie," which closes her collection, should offer us another fusion of East and West, comparing the experiences of Anton Chekhov in the

Russian steppes with those of her own grandfather in the American prairies.

So *Westward*, despite its title, is as much about the East as the West, the Atlantic as the Pacific, Europe as North America. Clampitt calls the opening section of it "Crossings," and it is a word she has earned the right to use, for she is a great poet of crossings over, mediation, cultural exchange. In Europe, or at any rate in Britain, we are very conscious of this: Clampitt, it seems, is the first American poet since Robert Lowell to explore the continuities between her country and ours.

Until Clampitt's arrival, it had become a critical commonplace to assert that American poetry and British poetry were no longer on speaking terms. Since that brief, glorious moment in the late 1950s when the British and American poetic traditions took a parallel course, with the marriage of Ted Hughes and Sylvia Plath an initially beneficent but finally tragic symbol of the union, the two traditions have been all but severed. Indeed, the suspicion had begun to arise that they have always been implacably opposed, and that separatists like Poe, Whitman, and Williams, for whom being in the American grain meant kicking against the old colonialist British heritage, had it right.

Part of Clampitt's attraction (to us at least) is that she offers a more hopeful version of the relationship between Old World and New. She finds it, for example, in the image of her grandfather, a late nineteenth-century pioneer, whom she describes composing a sonnet in the middle of the prairies. "We have listened too long to the courtly muses," wrote Emerson, and sought instead American "self-trust." Clampitt's grandfather, terrified of the infinite spaces, lacking self-trust and clinging to the reassurances of the Mayflower legacy, cannot oblige him:

There crowd my mind (he wrote) vague
    fancies
of Aeolian harpings, twined with weird
    oaks'
murmurings . . .

Aeolian harpings in Dakota: it is an image that admits dislocation, opposition, even a faint sense of the ridiculous. But for Clampitt's grandfather, a prey to terrible anxieties and crying "Lost, Lost," those Aeolian harpings are a way of finding himself, or at least of comforting a troubled mind. So Clampitt does not judge it reprehensible that the Old World should continue to penetrate the New. She goes on to ask whether it still does so a century later:

> Can the courtly muses
> of Europe, those bedizened crones, survive
> the manholes, the vaunt and skitter of
>   Manhattan, or
> consort with the dug-in, the hunkering
>   guardians
> of the Dakotas?

The answer, for her, is that they can and they do. *Westward*, like her three earlier books, is forever turning up connections and continuities: between the European skylark and the North American meadowlark; between a New England violet and a field pansy in Holland; between Scottish heather and blueberries in Maine; between the history of Virginia and the mockingbirds and warblers who move through the state's colonial habitats unheedingly, "ignorant of royal grants, crests / charters, sea power, mercantile / expansion, the imperative to / find an opening, explore, exploit ... "

For Old World readers, touchy these days about seeming marginal, it is reassuring to find themselves reinstated on the map in this way. The welcome the British gave to *The Kingfisher*, Clampitt's first book, must have had a lot to do with such feelings of gratitude, though perhaps we didn't recognize it at the time: at last an American poet who made us feel we mattered; at last an American poet we could appreciate without having to feel defensive about our own achievements; at last, after futile endeavors to get a grip on Ashbery and Ammons, an American poet we could understand. This may be simply another way of saying that Clampitt is an Anglophile, and it is true that, though the guiding spirits of *The Kingfisher* were Elizabeth Bishop and Marianne Moore, the book also displayed a rich appreciation of such components of English life as damp bed sheets, Peak Frean biscuits, hassocks, toasting forks, sheepdogs, windowboxes, and rain.

That same Anglophilia has since manifested itself in more literary appreciations—of Coleridge, the Wordsworths, Hopkins, George Eliot, Virginia Woolf, and above all of Keats, to whom Clampitt dedicated one of the sequences in her second book, *What the Light Was Like*. In *Archaic Figure*, her last collection, Clampitt's imagination moved outward and backward to Greece, leading her into a reclamation of female deities and toward her most feminist collection

to date. But even here, a reverence for English figures like Dorothy Wordsworth and George Eliot were central to the pattern. And in the new book it is impossible to read beyond the first page without feeling that the British (or the Irish) are at the back of it—whether Hopkins, whose compounding technique is imitated in Clampitt's image of "lofted strong-arm / redwoods' fogfondled silhouette," or Seamus Heaney, whom one glimpses in "the frail wick of metaphor I've brought to see by."

Yet Anglophilia will not quite serve as an explanation for why it is that Clampitt should have been taken up so enthusiastically on our side of the Atlantic as on her own. One might as easily explain her appeal in terms of what, for the British reader, is its exotica: in birds, beasts, and flowers (porcupines, turtles, sundews, the sea mouse, the beach pea, the grosbeak) familiar to us only from books. It is true that such natural phenomena must look exotic to readers in New York, too, but they are hardly likely to feel the vertiginous thrill that British readers do on reading a Clampitt poem about, for example, a whippoorwill. A whippoorwill! My *Columbia Encyclopedia*, referring me to "Goatsucker," gives me a fuller description than Clampitt can offer, but she has the better explanation of why it is that rare birds like the whippoorwill should exert such fascination:

> The webbiness,
> the gregariousness of the many are what
> we can't abide.
> We single out for notice
> above all what's disjunct, the way birds are,
> with their unhooked-up, cheekily anarchic
> dartings and flashings, their uncalled-for
>   color ...

A taste for the exotic is not one that Clampitt would necessarily like to see attributed to her, though, and not only because it might raise questions about her centrality. In "Nothing Stays Put," she wonders whether the exotic can really be said to exist in a world where distance has collapsed, where nowhere is more than a plane-hop away, and where supermarket shelves blaze with the "largesse" of the tropics. Clampitt, who grew up a Puritan and can still sound like one, recoils from this unmerited glut ("we are not entitled"), much as an earlier poem of hers recoiled from central heating.

But this isn't so much a recoil from the contemporary world as a desire to suggest that "the strange and wonderful" can be indigenous, too. She is drawn to, and likes to draw our attention to, the neglected, the remote, the out of the way; and there is nowhere like one's own doorstep for finding them. This holds for people as well. The human beings Clampitt likes to celebrate, women mostly, are also neglected and out of the way, and often come associated with a particular piece of indigenous yet exotic fauna: one with a "potted hedge of rubber trees," another with *Rosa rugosa*, a third with the "ubiquitous, unaspiring" beach pea.

The sympathy that Clampitt brings to her descriptions of people and plants does indeed make us feel that they are "strange and wonderful," but this is not because she likes to wow us with their oddities. On the contrary, she has a humdrum care to represent them accurately. Even the whippoorwill sounds pretty familiar by the time Clampitt has finished with it:

> Night after night, it was very nearly enough, they said, to drive you crazy: a whippoorwill
> in the woods repeating itself like the stuck groove
> of an LP with a defect, and no way possible
> of turning the thing off.
>
> And night after night, they said, in the insomniac
> small hours the whipsawing voice of obsession
> would have come in closer, the way a sick thing does when it's done for— . . .

An evocation like this might serve better than the *Columbia Encyclopedia* in helping you to recognize the whippoorwill's call. . . .

> the oats grow tall,
> their pendent helmetfuls
> of mica-drift, examined stem
> by stem, disclose
>
> alloys so various, enamelings
> of a vermeil so
> craftless, I all but despair of
> ever reining in a
>
> metaphor for . . .

But rein in her metaphors she does, of course: the "liquid millennium" of the dawn chorus, the "charred and single coal" of an oriole, the "yearning seedling choir" of canary droppings in a cage. The rush of physical impressions can threaten to overwhelm not only the reader but the poet, too, who describes herself a couple of times as "fazed," and who in her most intense moments comes across as the sort of woman you

might meet at dusk on the shoreline with an armful of shells, driftwood and fishing net—wideeyed, pantheistic, half-cracked. But she is prepared to risk a reputation for genteel craziness so long as that also allows her a place in posterity as (to adapt Hardy) a woman who used to notice such things.

The contradictions of such a persona—the poet whose genius for noticing is also held to be an eccentricity, whose careful attention to the look of things is held to be, socially, a carelessness—are ones she writes well about in "The Field Pansy," which uncovers a connection between three different kinds of flowers, and speaks of

> this gushing insouciance that appears at the same
> time capable
> of an all but infinite particularity: sedulous,
> patient, though
> in the end (so far as anyone can see) without consequence.
> What is consequence? What difference do the minutiae
> of that seeming inconsequence that's called beauty
>
> add up to? . . .

Phrased as a question though this is, it offers an implicit defense of Clampitt's art, which will put up with being called "inconsequential" so long as it has the consequence of capturing and creating beauty.

It is a difficult double-act to perform—insouciance on the one hand, sedulousness on the other—and Clampitt does not always bring it off. At times her thoroughness becomes a self-defeating pedanticism, as if she has thought out and read up on her subject to the point where there is nothing left to discover in the act of writing the poem, and where a scholarly paper (or indeed one of her ample source notes) might serve equally well. At this point her poetry can sound academic, prone to an Eng. Lit. piety (all *hommages* to the giants) and to a fussy, ornate, affected vocabulary—"the zenith's frescoed-by- / Tiepolo cerulean."

But if at its worst her poetry smells of the lamp, at its best it works like a flashlight, purposeful in its glare but always likely to chance on bright objects in the dark. Her casual-seeming line breaks help this effect of spontaneity: resistant to rhymes and end stops, it is a verse that stays alert to lucky breaks, sudden insights, the brief epiphanies of a life lived on the move. Her poetry is full of lists, accumulating and itemizing in verbless sentences the riches of things read or observed ("spring mud and summer dust, / burdocks, beatings, piety," "Collectives. Tractor lugs. / Names: brunizem and chernozem; culm / rhizome and stolon"). More usually, though out of the same restlessly notating spirit, she prefers long sentences. "Iola, Kansas," for example, is one long sentence running over eight stanzas and bringing us the Midwest as seen from a Greyhound:

> we're in Kansas now, we've turned off the
> freeway,
> we're meandering, as again night falls,
> among farmsteads,
> the little towns with the name of a girl on the
> watertower,
> the bandstand in the park at the center, the
> churches
>
> alight from within, perpendicular banalities
> of glass
> candy-streaked purple-green-yellow (who is
> this Jesus?),
> the strangeness of all there is, whatever it is,
> growing
> stranger, we've come to a rest stop, the name
> of the girl
> on the watertower is Iola: no video, no vend-
> ing machines,
> but Wonder Bread sandwiches, a pie: "It's
> boysenberry,
> I just baked it today," the woman behind the
> counter
> believably says, the innards a purply glue . . .

Whether this stands up, grammatically, as a sentence is doubtful (". . . growing stranger, we've come to a rest stop" surely requires stronger punctuation than a comma), but there can be no doubt that it is the *mode juste*, the commas and the colons acting like rest stops on a long journey, the full stop delayed for the end.

The long sentence, often broken up by one or several sets of parentheses, has become an increasing feature of Clampitt's work and has never seemed more appropriate than in *Westward*. It expresses the rootlessness and the restlessness that is her subject here, the feeling of drawnout journeys and great movements and migrations, of destinations finally arrived at but even then perhaps only provisionally, and certainly only after several detours so elaborate that the direction in which we are moving looks to have been forgotten. The most spectacular

example of this comes in the title poem itself, which is an account of a journey Clampitt took to Iona, in the Western Isles of Scotland, home of St. Columba and Christianity.

Beginning in London, among the "reverse" migrants of a spent commonwealth, those from the fringe returning to the old imperial heart, Clampitt heads northward and westward, her journey becoming a symbol for all the "embarkations, landings, dooms, conquests" of people in search of God, or of the promised land. It takes two interminable sentences toward the end before Clampitt brings us to "the brim of an illumination" about

> a zeal ignited somewhere to the east,
> concealed in hovels, quarreled over,
>
> portaged westward: a basket weave, a
> fishing net, a weir to catch, to salvage
> some tenet, some common intimation for
>
> all flesh, to hold on somehow till
> the last millennium: as though the routes,
> the ribbonings and redoublings, the
>
> attenuations, spent supply lines, frayed-out
> gradual of the retreat from empire, all
> its castaways, might still bear witness.

This is Clampitt's most high-flown and religious version of what the westward impulse means. As the title poem, it acquires a certain definitiveness. But other meanings multiply throughout the course of the book. "Westward" is the search for gold, money, jobs, opportunity, a home; it is a flight from the fear of infinite spaces; it is the urge to civilize, colonize, tame, subdue, settle; it is an existential quest, the search for a freedom to "throw one's life away" as one chooses:

> This being what all the rush
> of westward-the-course-of-empire
> finally comes down to:
>
> to be free, as Isabel Archer pigheadedly
> put it, to meet one's fate,
> to take one's chances, try on
> disguises . . .

Above all, "westward" is Clampitt's own search for roots, the return she makes from points east to the "evangelhaunted prairie hinterland" of her upbringing, a "farmhouse childhood, kerosene-lit, tatting and mahogany-genteel," which she left as an "intemperate" teenager to head for the "glittering shambles / of enthrallments and futilities" that goes by the name of Manhattan. As that image shows, Clampitt now shrinks from the vacuity of urban "monoculture": the color and generosity of what she finds in nature are a reproach to the gray human alternative in Manhattan, "every pittance under lock and key / a party to the general malfeasance." But this is not to say that there was anything especially wholesome about her ancestor-settlers, "far from hot baths," who, social outcasts of a kind, fled to discover new worlds but soon enough were imposing a "neat and fearful grid of settlement" that would enable them in turn to find someone else more vagrant "to look down on." Clampitt, in other words, is not sentimental about her roots.

Hovering over her book is a play on the word "settled": conscious (from reading his privately printed pamphlet) of her grandfather's unsettled mind, she tries to settle something in her own mind. Is not settlement primarily an attempt to ward off spiritual unsettlement? Is it not therefore doomed to failure, however often roots are put down and civilization spreads? And isn't man's natural state, however much he may seek to be at rest somewhere, to be mobile? Some such suggestion underlies "The Prairie" and allows its ending, which might otherwise be a sad record of Clampitt's failed homecoming, to have an air of exhilaration about it:

> No one
>
> I know or ever heard of lives there now.
> On Summit, from some long-obliterated
> snapshot, I thought I recognized the house
>
> a great-aunt lived in once: the number
> not quite right, the tenant an old
> deaf Mexican who did not understand.

Not being able to return to where you came from leaves you freer to be what you are: that would seem to be the almost joyous consolation Clampitt takes from her frustrated journey. It is the same exultant note that one hears at the end of "Iola, Kansas":

> and through some duct in the rock I feel my
>   heart
> go out,
>   out here in the middle of nowhere (the
>   scheme is a mess)
>   to the waste, to the not knowing who or
>   why, and
> am happy.

It is this surrender that makes Clampitt a more truly modern poet than her occasional snappishness at contemporary urban culture would lead you to think. In the brightness and the diversity

and the "unhooked-up" independence of the bird world she finds a model ("free as a bird") to live by; and in the migrations of her ancestors she confirms her own migrating spirit, which, unlike theirs, will never seek to find *the* place to settle. *Westward* is not her most accessible book, but it is her most self-aware one. Failing to come home at the end of it, she can now be said to have truly arrived.

Source: Blake Morrison, "The Cross-Country Poet," in *New Republic*, Vol. 203, No. 1, July 2, 1990, pp. 29–32.

SOURCES

Clampitt, Amy, "Iola, Kansas," in *The Collected Poems of Amy Clampitt*, Alfred A. Knopf, 1997, p. 291.

MacAdam, Mickey, Review of *The Collected Poems of Amy Clampitt*, in *Hurricane Alice*, Vol. 14, No. 2, Spring 2000, p. 11.

Spiegelman, Willard, "What to Make of an Augmented Thing," in the *Kenyon Review*, New Series, Vol. 21, No. 1, Winter, 1999, p. 172–73.

"War of Words," in the *Economist*, Vol. 348, No. 8081, August 15, 1998, p. 72.

FURTHER READING

Costello, Bonnie, "Amy Clampitt: Nomad Exquisite," in *Shifting Grounds: Reinventing Landscape in American Poetry*, Harvard University Press, 2003.
> Costello's book looks at the ways that poets have changed their styles of imaging the wide open land, devoting a chapter to Clampitt and her intimate sense of the Great Plains.

Morgan, Grady Hall, *Memoirs of a Greyhound Bus Driver*, Infinity Publishing, 2005.
> The experience of interstate travel is becoming lost to history. Morgan's book is not at all academic, but the stories that he tells offer insight into a way of life covered in "Iola, Kansas."

Shortridge, James R., *Cities on the Plains: The Evolution of Urban Kansas*, University of Kansas Press, 2004.
> This book looks at the recent history of the area of the country where the poem is set, charting the growth of towns that were, like Iola, small and isolated just a few years ago.

———, *The Middle West: Its Meaning in American Culture*, University of Kansas Press, 1989.
> James R. Shortridge's examination of the ways that middle western values and culture have looked to Americans in general gives the kind of insight that only someone who is both an intellectual and an insider can offer.

The Man-Moth

ELIZABETH BISHOP

1946

Elizabeth Bishop's poem "The Man-Moth" was written very early in the poet's life, just as she had graduated from college. It is a poem unlike the rest of Bishop's work in that it leans toward the surreal. The abstract images in this poem leave "The Man-Moth" open to a diverse range of interpretations. Indeed, the poem may be read as a meditation on the interplay between light and dark. It has also been suggested that the poet's destructive bouts with alcoholism might have influenced the poem, as the image of the Man-Moth going backward on a too fast train is an experience that the poem associates with poison. Another interpretation, based on the significance of the Man-Moth's attempts to reach the moon, suggests that the poet is attempting to express her spirituality.

Furthermore, it is this quality of open interpretation that has helped the poem endure over the decades, appealing to readers in much the same way today as it did when it was first published. Many literary critics refer to "The Man-Moth" as one of the best poems Bishop ever wrote. Notably, the poem was inspired by a typo in a news article in the *New York Times*, in which the word *manmoth* was used instead of the correct term: *mammoth*.

Bishop wrote "The Man-Moth" in 1935, when she was twenty-four years old. The poem was first published in 1946 in Bishop's first collection, *North and South*. More recently, the

Elizabeth Bishop *(Photograph by J. L. Castel. The Library of Congress)*

poem was published in *The Complete Poems, 1927–1979*, by Farrar, Straus and Giroux in 1999.

AUTHOR BIOGRAPHY

Bishop was born on February 8, 1911, in Worcester, Massachusetts. Her father, William Thomas Bishop, who was a building contractor, oversaw the construction of the Boston Museum of Fine Arts and the Boston Public Library. He died, however, when Bishop was only eight months old. His sudden and early death caused Bishop's mother, Gertrude Bulmer, to suffer severe depression. Gertrude was institutionalized several times, and when Bishop was five years old, her mother was permanently committed to a mental hospital. Bishop never saw her again.

For the next two years Bishop lived with either her maternal grandparents in Nova Scotia, Canada, or with her paternal grandparents in Massachusetts. When she was seven, Bishop suffered from a list of ailments, which included asthma. Bishop's maternal aunt, Maud Bulmer Shepherdson, lived near Boston, and

was given the young girl to raise. Bishop credits her aunt for inspiring her to write poetry. Bishop, because of her childhood illnesses, was mostly home schooled. But when she was old enough to enter college in 1930, she attended Vassar College. While there, she met the poet Marianne Moore, who would become a close friend and would greatly influence Bishop's early work.

While Bishop's poetry appeared steadily in magazines, success did not come easily for Bishop. She endured a whole array of rejections from publishers before 1946, when her first collection of poems, *North and South*, which includes "The Man-Moth," was finally published. By then, Bishop was already thirty-five years old. At this time in her life, she had lived in many different locations, a pattern that would continue throughout her life. She lived in New York City and Europe, and then in Key West, Florida, for short periods of time. In 1951, after having served as U.S. Poet Laureate (from 1949 to 1950), Bishop decided to take a boat tour around South America. When she reached Brazil she suffered from food poisoning, which delayed her departure. The incident gave her an opportunity to explore the country, and Bishop eventually decided to live there. While living in Brazil, she met and fell in love with Lota de Macedo Soares. The couple stayed together until de Macedo Soares's death, more than a decade later.

In 1955, Bishop's second collection, *North & South—A Cold Spring* (which was republished in 1956 as *A Cold Spring* and is commonly referred to under that tile) was published and went on to win the Pulitzer Prize the next year. Ten years later, her third collection, *Questions of Travel*, was printed. In this volume, Bishop explores her childhood as well as her experiences in Brazil. The following year, in 1966, Bishop tired of Brazil and decided to move back to the United States. De Macedo Soares joined her in New York City, but died of an overdose the day after her arrival. The tragedy did not stop Bishop from writing and publishing, and in 1969, Bishop published *Complete Poems*, which won the National Book Award the following year. It was this same year that Bishop accepted a teaching position at Harvard, where she met Alice Mathfessel, with whom she maintained a relationship until her death.

In 1976, Bishop was awarded the *Books Abroad*/Neustadt International Prize for literature, the first woman to receive the honor. That same year, she also published *Geography III*, the last collection released during her lifetime. It won the Book Critics' Circle Award the following year. Roughly three years later, on October 6, 1979, Bishop died of a cerebral hemorrhage at her apartment in Lewis Wharf, Boston. She is buried in Worcester, Massachusetts.

Bishop's work has remained popular to this day. In 2007, the *New Yorker* poetry editor Alice Quinn put together a collection of otherwise unpublished poem fragments and entries from Bishop's journals in the publication *Edgar Allan Poe & the Jukebox: Uncollected Poems, Drafts, and Fragments*. Some critics have stated that Bishop, who was so meticulous about her work, sometimes taking a year or more to refine a single poem, may not have wanted this material published in its unfinished state. However, critics also have made it known that this material, especially the insight it provides into Bishop's writing process, is invaluable.

POEM TEXT

Here, above,
cracks in the buildings are filled with battered
    moonlight.
The whole shadow of Man is only as big as his
    hat.
It lies at his feet like a circle for a doll to stand
    on,
and he makes an inverted pin, the point mag-
    netized to the moon.   5
He does not see the moon; he observes only her
    vast properties,
feeling the queer light on his hands, neither
    warm nor cold,
of a temperature impossible to record in
    thermometers.

But when the Man-Moth
pays his rare, although occasional, visits to the
    surface,   10
the moon looks rather different to him. He
    emerges
from an opening under the edge of one of the
    sidewalks
and nervously begins to scale the faces of the
    buildings.
He thinks the moon is a small hole at the top of
    the sky,
proving the sky quite useless for protection.   15

He trembles, but must investigate as high as he
    can climb.

Up the façades,
his shadow dragging like a photographer's
    cloth behind him,
he climbs fearfully, thinking that this time he
    will manage
to push his small head through that round
    clean opening   20
and be forced through, as from a tube, in black
    scrolls on the light.
(Man, standing below him, has no such
    illusions.)
But what the Man-Moth fears most he must
    do, although
he fails, of course, and falls back scared but
    quite unhurt.

Then he returns   25
to the pale subways of cement he calls his
    home. He flits,
he flutters, and cannot get aboard the silent
    trains
fast enough to suit him. The doors close swiftly.
The Man-Moth always seats himself facing the
    wrong way
and the train starts at once at its full, terrible
    speed,   30
without a shift in gears or a gradation of any
    sort.
He cannot tell the rate at which he travels
    backwards.

Each night he must
be carried through artificial tunnels and dream
    recurrent dreams.
Just as the ties recur beneath his train, these
    underlie   35
his rushing brain. He does not dare look out the
    window,
for the third rail, the unbroken draught of
    poison,
runs there beside him. He regards it as a disease
he has inherited the susceptibility to. He has to
    keep
his hands in his pockets, as others must wear
    mufflers.   40

If you catch him,
hold up a flashlight to his eye. It's all dark
    pupil,
an entire night itself, whose haired horizon
    tightens
as he stares back, and closes up the eye. Then
    from the lids
one tear, his only possession, like the bee's
    sting, slips.   45
Slyly he palms it, and if you're not paying
    attention
he'll swallow it. However, if you watch, he'll
    hand it over,
cool as from underground springs and pure
    enough to drink.

MEDIA ADAPTATIONS

- Bishop reads some of her poems on the audio tape *Elizabeth Bishop*, from the series *Voices and Visions* produced by Unapix Inner Dimensions (1997). The tape also offers commentary on Bishop's works and life by poets such as Octavio Paz and James Merrill, among others. Bishop also reads "The Man-Moth" on this tape.

POEM SUMMARY

Stanza 1

Bishop's poem "The Man-Moth" is a third-person narrative about the strange creature described in the poem's title. The poem begins with a caesura, or a pause, as does each verse. This puts the opening phrases in the spotlight, emphasizing them. For example, in the first stanza, in the first line, the speaker signifies a specific position: "Here, above." At this point, the reader does not know where the "above" is or what it is higher than, or even where "Here" might be. However, with this phrase, the reader is not only made aware of some place above but also senses that there may well be a 'somewhere below' that will soon follow. This turns out to be the case, as the second stanza indicates that the Man-Moth lives underground.

The second line begins as the speaker describes all that exists "above," none of which is necessarily pleasant. There are "cracks in the building," which could suggest instability. And the moonlight that falls into these cracks is "battered." There is also "Man," (as opposed to the Man-Moth) whose whole shadow "is only as big as his hat." In the next sentence, either the Man-Moth's hat "lies at his feet," or "the shadow of Man" does (the wording is ambiguous). This ambiguity allows for several different interpretations, one of which emphasizes man's smallness. This smallness is doubly enforced by a simile, or comparison, as the hat (or man's shadow, which

also is portrayed as equal to the size of the hat) is likened to a "circle for a doll to stand on." In stating that "the whole shadow of Man" is the same size as the Man-Moth's hat and then referring to the hat or the shadow as a place "for a doll to stand on," the speaker minimizes the figure of man. Thus man (and in this poem the word might actually be a reference to the rational side of humanity) is completely diminished. Speaking symbolically, it is, essentially, no bigger than a doll.

In line 5 the speaker refers again to the moon. But in the next line, the speaker informs readers that the Man-Moth "does not see the moon"; he senses it as a "queer light on his hands, neither warm nor cold." This light has an otherworldly feel to the Man-Moth, it is "of a temperature impossible to record in thermometers."

Stanza 2

In the second stanza, the Man-Moth emerges from underground, a "rare, although occasional" occurrence. Above ground, "the moon looks rather different to him." His world, as well as his vision, the narrator suggests, has been transformed. The Man-Moth emerges from a crack in the sidewalk ("an opening under the edge of one of the sidewalks"), which is reminiscent of the cracks in the building that the narrator mentioned at the beginning of the poem). The Man-Moth is not as confident above ground as he supposedly is underground, because he is away from his usual element. He "nervously begins to scale the faces of the buildings." This act is reminiscent of the superheroes and comic book characters popular when the poem was written. The Man-Moth feels compelled to climb in order to "investigate" the moon, which he now perceives as "a small hole at the top of the sky." This hole frightens him, as if he believes he will fall into and out of the sky by way of it. Indeed, the sky is now described as "quite useless for protection."

Stanza 3

The third stanza begins with the phrase "Up the façades," as the Man-Moth continues to climb the buildings. The word "façade" has several meanings. It can refer to the front of a building or to a false presentation (i.e., what is presented on the surface deceives one as to what is beneath the surface). The narrator then describes the Man-Moth's shadow as "dragging like a photographer's cloth behind him."

In line 3 of the third stanza, the narrator reminds readers that this venture, on the part of the Man-Moth, is not an easy one. The Man-Moth is climbing "fearfully." Nevertheless, the narrator states that this is not the first time that the Man-Moth has attempted to "investigate" the moon. This is indicated by his belief that "this time" he will be successful. He will "push his small head through that round clean opening" and will "be forced through, as from a tube, in black scrolls on the light." Some literary critics suggest that this is a reference to birth or rebirth, while others have theorized that this may refer to addiction. Still others have interpreted this image as symbolic of the creative process; i.e., by creating art one seeks to not only reach an impossible height (the moon), but also to exceed it and look beyond it. The narrator further refines this image in the next three lines of the stanza: whereas man "has no such illusions" of climbing so high, the Man-Moth does not, and "he fails, of course." Even though the Man-Moth dreams of reaching the moon, he cannot do so. His dreams are bigger than his abilities.

Again, as in the second stanza, there is a reference to compulsion: "what the Man-Moth fears most he must do." This statement may reinforce the interpretation of the Man-Moth's striving as an indirect comparison with a hidden meaning, a metaphor for the creative process. In order to create, the artist must attempt to achieve and surpass what they fear most. If this understanding is accurate, the Man-Moth thus represents the artist.

Stanza 4

So the Man-Moth returns home, underground, to the subway. He is not comfortable there. The trains that pass through the tunnels make him nervous, again, as "He flits / he flutters" and he cannot board the train in a way that "suit[s] him." When he finally sits down, he sits backward, the "wrong way," and the forward movement of the train is consequently disorienting. Everything moves too fast, keeping a steady speed from beginning to end. The speed is monotonous and without variation, yet it is also described as "terrible." One could perhaps interpret this to mean that monotony itself is "terrible."

Stanza 5

In the fifth stanza, the tension increases, as does the discomfort of the Man-Moth: "he must / be carried" through the tunnels and through his recurring dreams as if against his will. The Man-Moth's actions are more passive than in the opening stanzas, in which he shows a determination and passion to reach the moon. His will is limited as is his vision, for he is afraid to look outside of the train. If he does, he might see the "third rail, the unbroken draught of poison." Marilyn May Lombardi, in her book *The Body and the Song: Elizabeth Bishop's Poetics*, has suggested that Bishop's reference to the third rail is an allusion (reference) to her own propensity toward alcoholism, as Bishop herself indicates this in her personal notes on the poem. Furthermore, the Man-Moth sees the third rail "as a disease / he has inherited the susceptibility to." Notably, alcoholism is believed to be hereditary or genetic; it is something that is "inherited."

The narrator next tells readers that the Man-Moth buries his hands in his pockets "as others must wear mufflers," suggesting that the Man-Moth is attempting to keep his hands warm. However, readers might interpret this on a deeper level. Is the Man-Moth really attempting to keep his hands warm, or is he hiding or confining his hands so he does not reach out toward the third rail?

Stanza 6

In the sixth and final stanza, the narrator directly addresses the reader by using the pronoun "you." The stanza begins, "If you catch him," and goes on to instruct the reader on what to do should they "catch" the Man-Moth. Strangely, though man is initially shown to be metaphorically diminutive (small), it seems as if this interpretation is turned on its head here, as the Man-Moth suddenly becomes a creature that is able to be caught, presumably by man—it would seem to go without saying that the reader being addressed is presumably human. First, the reader is to closely observe or examine the Man-Moth. Here, as in the beginning of the poem, there is the interplay of light in darkness. In the first stanza, the source of light is the moon, which is naturally occurring. But in the final stanza, the light is artificial, derived from a flashlight. There is also another notable comparison between the beginning of the poem and its ending: Whereas in the first stanzas, the dark is represented by large things like the night sky, in the last stanza, the dark is compressed, appearing only in the pupil of the Man-Moth's eye. However, the narrator goes on to describe the pupil as equal to "an entire night itself."

There is a reward, the narrator suggests, if the reader takes the time to examine the Man-Moth. The reader will receive "one tear, his only possession." The narrator warns the reader that if they are not paying attention, the Man-Moth will consume the tear, swallowing the gift back into himself (presumably so that it can be shed again). But if the reader does pay attention, the Man-Moth will present them with his tear, which is "cool as from underground springs and pure enough to drink." Returning again to the idea that much of the poem is a metaphor for the creative process, the "pure" gift of the tear, received for paying attention, might represent artistic creation or inspiration, both of which the artist seeks to achieve by same method; i.e., by paying close attention to the world around them.

THEMES

Darkness and Light

Throughout Bishop's poem there are images of darkness and light. Darkness is spoken of in the mention of the "shadow of Man" and later in the shadow of the Man-Moth, "dragging like a photographer's cloth behind him." In contrast to the darkness, there is the light of the moon, which the Man-Moth does not directly see but instead feels. There is also the light of the flashlight that the narrator suggests should be shone into the Man-Moth's eye. The eye, the reader will find, is "all dark pupil, / an entire night itself."

This contrast between darkness and light can be interpreted in many different ways. If the poem is read as an explanation of the subconscious and how it works to create art, then the darkness could conceivably represent the unknown. The light, then, might refer to the rational mind, just as man may refer to the rational. The Man-Moth, being a creature (and a supernatural one at that) who dwells in the dark, would then represent the irrational. Following this, and reading the poem in a slightly different manner, the light could represent an ordinary existence, like the everyday habits of a person (man); whereas the dark could represent the extraordinary, as the Man-Moth himself is indeed extraordinary. In a third interpretation, the light might stand for discipline or even artistic inspiration. The dark, in contrast, might then be seen as the corrupting influence that fear (or insecurity) has on the achievement of inspiration.

TOPICS FOR FURTHER STUDY

- "The Man-Moth" is often referred to as being surreal. Look up the definition and the attributes of surrealism. Create a presentation on the key figures of the surrealist movement, including all the arts: painting, sculpture, literature, and any other examples you can find. Make sure that you understand this form of art well enough to answer questions at the end of your presentation.

- Aside from a description of the Man-Moth's eye, Bishop's poem does not discuss what he might look like. Create a painting or drawing of the Man-Moth as you imagine him. Working with a classmate, compare both of your drawings. Take notes on how your classmate's image differs from yours. Note how it is similar.

- Bishop suffered from alcoholism, and some critics have found allusions to this affliction in "The Man-Moth." Since Bishop wrote this poem in 1935 upon graduating from college, research alcoholism in the United States with a particular emphasis on college-aged students. Provide statistics for your class, either in a report or through a graph, comparing alcoholism in the 1930s with alcoholism today.

- Bishop had at least three long-term relationships with females during her lifetime. Research how societal reactions to homosexuality, or more specifically to lesbianism, has changed in the United States since the 1930s. Have laws governing sexuality changed over time as a result of changing attitudes? Write an essay about your findings.

Fear and Perseverance in the Face of Fear

The Man-Moth, even though he is much larger than ordinary man (at least metaphorically), possesses a spirit that exhibits both strength and weakness. The Man-Moth emerges from his dark hiding space to climb the tall buildings that surround him. As he climbs, he reaches for the moon, an act that he is not sure of, but he climbs nonetheless. He fears that the moon is a hole in the sky that renders the sky a useless protection. Although he shakes with fear, he continues to climb. As a matter of fact, he is driven to face his fears. However, in the end, he is unsuccessful, and he "falls back scared."

Then, back in the subway, although he is able to overcome his fear and gain a seat on the train, the Man-Moth remains too afraid to look out of the window. He is afraid to see the "third rail," which is likened to a poison. Furthermore, the third rail in a subway system provides the electricity which powers the trains; it is essentially a large, live electrical wire that runs beside every set of tracks. As moths are drawn to flame, perhaps the Man-Moth is drawn to the electricity contained by the third rail, despite the danger inherent in it. The Man-Moth appears constantly torn between his fears and his desire to overcome his fears, as if he were walking a tight rope, balanced between the two. Despite his fears, he attempts to proceed even though he senses he will fail.

Confinement

Although the Man-Moth is capable of leaving his subterranean home, he rarely does so, and a sense of confinement is present throughout. The Man-Moth seems trapped in the subway train, and he also seems to be confined by a possible addiction. The Man-Moth thinks of the third rail (the item symbolic of addiction) as a disease that "he has inherited the susceptibility to." This confines his vision, which he must control and must focus in a narrow line so he does not look directly at the third rail. If he does not confine his vision, he fears he might die. Throughout the poem, something (usually fear) is always holding the Man-Moth back from reaching his goals.

Loneliness

The setting of the poem is urban, filled with large concrete buildings and subway trains; yet amidst what should reasonably be a populated urban landscape, the Man-Moth consistently appears to be alone. There is mention of the generalized "Man," the doll, and, of course, the Man-Moth—all of which are singular figures. There is also one moon, one pin, one flashlight, one eye, and one tear drop. This singularity brings with it a sense of loneliness. The one tear drop, "his only [single] possession," at the end of the poem emphasizes this loneliness. Even the great attempt, on the part of the Man-Moth, to climb to the moon, is a lonely endeavor. The Man-Moth climbs and fails, and no one takes notice either way. There is no one to console him or to encourage him to try again.

The only time this poem comes close to suggesting a relationship is at the end of the poem, when the narrator addresses a "you" who should catch the Man-Moth and shine a bright light into his eye, taking his only possession as a gift. This image does not conjure up any sense of a friendship, though. Rather, in many ways it seems rather cruel. It is as if the bright light causes the tear, and then the "you" person takes the tear away before the Man-Moth can swallow it.

The loneliness in this poem is filled with sadness. It is not the solitude a monk might enjoy or that an artist might be inspired by. It is a heart-wrenching and gut-wrenching loneliness that compels the Man-Moth to do things he does not quite understand or even enjoy, like climbing buildings, riding trains, sitting backward, and experiencing the unwilled dreaming of his own recurring dreams.

STYLE

Monosyllables

Monosyllables are words that are made up of only one syllable, such as each of these words in this phrase from Bishop's poem: "It lies at his feet." Using monosyllabic words in a poem was one of the traits of George Herbert's writing style, which Bishop often emulated (Herbert was an early seventeenth-century poet). Monosyllabic words offer a transition in the rhythm of a poem. Their beat can be staccato (abrupt and distinct) on one hand, but can also become monotonous and therefore easily overlooked. Polysyllabic words, or words with more than one syllable, have an inborn accent that poets can use to adjust the rhythm of each line. For instance, the word *mother* has a natural accent on the first syllable. This means that in natural conversation one would stress the "mo-" and almost swallow the second syllable, "-ther."

When monosyllabic words are alternated with polysyllabic words in an individual line, the effect of the monosyllabic words goes almost unnoticed. However, when monosyllabic words are strung together, they become more obvious.

Notice, for instance, in the fourth line of the first stanza: "It lies at his feet like a circle for a doll to stand on." In this line, every word except "circle" is monosyllabic. Also notice that the word "circle" appears almost perfectly in the middle of this line. This draws attention and emphasis to the word "circle," almost as effectively as if a spotlight were shining on the word. Notice also how the strong beat of monosyllabic words works in line 6 of the first stanza. "He does not see the moon," this line begins, all in monosyllabic words, alerting readers to the significance of the statement. However, following this is a softer mix of monosyllabic and polysyllabic words that explain more fully what the narrator is attempting to say. The strong message of the Man-Moth not seeing the moon is tempered by the explanation that he, nonetheless, is not entirely oblivious to it.

Caesura

A caesura causes the reader to pause briefly at a certain point in the poem. In many poems, this is used in the middle of a line. However, in this poem, Bishop uses a caesura at the beginning of each stanza. In doing so, the shorter phrases at the beginning are given more emphasis. In "The Man-Moth," the caesura also brings an element of suspense or mystery. For example, the opening phrase, "Here, above" momentarily makes the reader ask several questions: Where is here? Above what?

In the second stanza, the first phrase introduces the name of the mysterious "he" who is mentioned in the first stanza: the Man-Moth. This is done in such as way that readers know that the Man-Moth is different from ordinary Man. Not only is this opening phrase a caesura, the wording of the phrase, "But when the Man-Moth," also connotes a contradiction to what has been previously stated.

Enjambment

Enjambment is another form of manipulating the rhythm, and thus the meaning or interpretation, of a poem. With enjambment, the sense or meaning of a line is distorted slightly by the pause, or break, between each individual line. For example, in the fourth stanza, third line, the narrator states: "he flutters, and cannot get aboard the silent trains." This sounds as if the Man-Moth cannot board a train, but this is not true. As readers continue to the next line, they discover that the Man-Moth successfully catches

the train. He just does not do so "fast enough to suit him," as line 4 conveys. Using enjambment adds an element of surprise to a poem. The reader mistakenly expects one meaning, only to discover another, different meaning.

Another example of enjambment occurs in the fifth stanza, line 4. "Just as the ties recur beneath his train, these underlie," the line reads. It is surprising, once again, when the narrator quickly switches, in the next line, from the image of the train to "his rushing brain." Few readers would have expected this transition, and it is made even more startling because of the unexpected rhyme between "train" and "brain."

One more example is found in the last stanza. Line 3 reads in part: "whose haired horizon tightens." This is a reference to the eyelid of the Man-Moth. The image presented is that of the Man-Moth with closed eyes (the tightened horizon). However, in the next line, the narrator announces that the Man-Moth is still seeing: "as he stares back." This creates a somewhat upsetting image. Just when the reader believes that the Man-Moth's eyes are closed, the reader discovers that the he is still looking, still observing. The description of the Man-Moth's eyelashes as a "haired horizon" is also interesting because his eye is described as "an entire night itself." Thus, his eye is a night sky, and his eyelashes are a horizon.

Extended Metaphor

A metaphor is used to indirectly compare two seemingly different things. The figure of the Man-Moth is clearly metaphorical, but the meaning of that metaphor is unclear. Literary critics have been trying to interpret the metaphor of the Man-Moth for a long time, and various theories abound. Nevertheless, because the metaphor continues from the beginning of the poem to the end of the poem, it is referred to as an extended metaphor.

Simile

A simile is similar to a metaphor. One of the differences is that a simile uses one of the following words to create a comparison: like, as, or than. In Bishop's poem, readers can find several similes. In the first stanza, line 4, the phrase, "like a circle," is a simile. It compares "the whole shadow of Man" to being "like a circle." In the third stanza, the Man-Moth scales the face of the building. Behind him is his shadow, which

COMPARE & CONTRAST

- **1930s:** Just as there is an overall sense of fear in the poem, there is a similar sense of fear in the world at-large. International tensions are high as Adolph Hitler advances his troops throughout Europe. While the United States considers sending troops overseas, citizens still suffering from the effects of the Great Depression live in an ever-present state of fear.

  Today: Following the September, 2001, destruction of the World Trade Center, U.S. cities practice emergency drills to be better prepared against the threat of future terrorist attacks. Citizens are asked to be on the lookout for suspicious characters, and many fear the possibility of chemical, biological, or nuclear attacks.

- **1930s:** The stories of fantasy and science fiction focus on fantasy adventures or the possibilities of new technologies. The surreal quality found in many such stories can also be found in "The Man-Moth."

  Today: Science fiction takes a new turn with stories about the drawbacks of relying on machines, specifically computers, which are shown as dominating the lives of the story's characters.

- **1930s:** The first production of the movie *King Kong* horrifies audiences as a giant gorilla is portrayed climbing the Empire State building in New York City.

  Today: The 2005 version of *King Kong* does not instill fear in its audiences. Rather, much like "The Man-Moth," it evokes sympathy for a misunderstood creature.

---

is "like a photographer's cloth." Similes are used to provide readers with an image that might better explain what the narrator is saying. Similes are like pictures used to illustrate a story. The preceding sentence not only describes similes, but it is also a simile itself.

HISTORICAL CONTEXT

George Herbert (1593–1633)

Bishop was influenced by the work of the poet and minister George Herbert. Her poems often explore spirituality (directly and indirectly), an approach that was inspired by Herbert's poetry. Herbert's poems are often characterized by his love of God, which he once explained should be stronger than man's love of a woman. His collection of poems *A Priest to The Temple* was published in 1652, nineteen years after his death, and proved to be quite popular. This collection was originally written by Herbert as a gift to his parishioners and contains poems that explain Herbert's own spiritual path,

which he hoped would help to guide the members of his church. Herbert's writing is often praised for its clarity, humbleness, and imagery, characteristics that Bishop aspired to achieve in her own work. Bishop also made a point of keeping her poetic language simple, often using monosyllabic words, a technique that she admired in Herbert's writing. Many of Herbert's influences are apparent in "The Man-Moth."

Marianne Moore (1887–1972)

One of Bishop's mentors, Marianne Moore had many personal similarities to Bishop. Moore lost her father early in her life, traveled a lot throughout her life, and was a lesbian. Moore's poems are noted for their witty, ironic, and inventive style. Moore's poems, like Bishop's, often include animals and nature (Moore earned her degree in biology) and are characterized by their precision of detail, condensed language, and unusual verse patterns and rhyme schemes. Scholars have tried to define or note more precise indications of Moore's influence on Bishop's work and life,

New York City with almost all lights off *(© Bettman / Corbis)*

but much is open to speculation. It has been proposed by several scholars that Moore might have been a mother-figure to Bishop on a personal level. In 1951, Moore won the Pulitzer Prize for her *Collected Poems* which was published earlier that year. Bishop won the Pulitzer Prize five years later, in 1956, for her second collection, *North & South—A Cold Spring*, which was published in 1955.

Robert Lowell (1917–1977)

Robert Lowell was another poet who greatly influenced Bishop, and the influence was actually mutual. Lowell was a contemporary of Bishop, and the two poets inspired one another, although their styles differed. Lowell's Pulitzer Prize–winning collection *Lord Weary's Castle* was published in 1946, and Lowell gained recognition as one of the leading poets of his time. But in spite of this, Lowell suffered through a long depression, which required medical intervention during the 1950s. As part of his journey back to mental health, he began writing more personalized material with a less rigid form. Lowell later wrote his poem "Skunk Hour," in response to Bishop's poem "The Armadillo." Both poets dedicated their respective poem to the other, and the poems may be read as a conversation about poetry or poetic style.

Post–World War II American Life

Bishop was at the peak of her career following the end of World War II. She published her first collection of poetry, *North and South*, completed her tenure as U.S. Poet Laureate, and won a Pulitzer Prize, establishing her as a serious professional poet. Her voice as a poet was one of the first to emerge as being different from her predecessors, the so-called modernist poets, and she inspired the next group of poets, who would be called the postmodernists.

American poetry, as well as American society, was in a state of transition after the war. This was an era, especially in the 1950s and 1960s, when many members of the younger generation began to question the traditional, or accepted, values of their parents, and they also sought new and different ways to express themselves artistically. Bishop's poetry, with its references, though subtle, to the self, helped to lay the groundwork for a major shift in American poetry; the art form moved away from discussion of the broader concepts of life to a deeper exploration of personal and individual experience. Indeed, Bishop is credited as having influenced the Beat movement, including literary figures such as Jack Kerouac, Lawrence Ferlinghetti, and Allen Ginsberg.

CRITICAL OVERVIEW

"The Man-Moth" is both one of Bishop's earliest poems and one of her most unusual. The poem, according to some critics, is very hard to interpret, and that may be why it has remained one of her most popular poems throughout the years. The meaning of the poem is obscure, allowing for varied interpretations. Some critics have stated that this poem is one of Bishop's best. The voice and tone of this work is also unlike any other of her poems.

For the critic Helen Vendler, writing in *Critical Inquiry*, "The Man-Moth" is, at least in part, about Bishop's reflections on her "self and her art." Vendler continues: "Many of Bishop's poems take a sinister view of what a poem is." She then adds that even in "The Man-Moth," one of Bishop's "more sympathetic poem[s] . . . the radical solitude of the poet is emphasized." Vendler believes that it is through the metaphors in "The Man-Moth," which "insist that poetry is a natural secretion but insist as well that it must be processed in a painful way before it is valuable," that Bishop makes clear how difficult the creation of poetry can be, at least for herself.

Furthermore, this poem, Vendler states, points out the poet's sense of not belonging. The Man-Moth "is the prototype of Bishop's socially unacceptable beasts." Vendler adds that the allegory of the poem is that "the Psyche-moth-butterfly is in tatters; the artist works on the edge of the unregarded." Vendler sums up the characteristics that are the mainstay and defining attitudes in Bishop's work, such as "her sense of

deformity, her cold capacity for detachment, her foreignness in human society, her suspicion that truth has something annihilating about it, her self-representation as observer of meaninglessly additive experience, her repugnance for social or political or religious association." Certainly, some of these traits may be seen in the figure of the Man-Moth. Vendler also finds that Bishop's admiration of Herbert's writing, which employed "very common means for very subtle effects" is what helped Bishop create her successful poetic style: "The combination of somber matter with a manner net-like, mesh-like, airy, reticulated to let in light, results in the effect we now call by her name—the Bishop style."

S. R. Murthy, writing for the *Explicator*, points out that "The Man-Moth" is "often praised for daintiness if not preciosity." However, Murthy states that if one completes a closer reading of Bishop's poem, one would find that it is about "man's subconscious impulses—swinging between the heights of aspiration and depths of despair." In a critical analysis of Bishop's poetry for *American Literature*, Margaret Dickie quotes the poet Sylvia Plath (a slightly younger poet than Bishop) who describes Bishop's writing as having "fine originality, always surprising, never rigid, flowing, juicier than Marianne Moore, who is her godmother." Dickie also quotes literary critic David Kalstone in this same article. Kalstone finds that poems such as "The Man-Moth" "allow her [Bishop] simultaneously to be a keen observer . . . and yet to identify with figures absent, withdrawn, practically lifeless." Like other critics, Dickie interprets this poem as a reflection on the process of writing. The image of the tear being handed over, Dickie writes, "is a surrealistic tear that exists only in writing, and in this image the speaker inscribes both herself and the man-moth as writers, possessed by the other, the darkness." Dickie continues: "For these writers, creation is a deadly and painful experience which requires the relinquishment of the man-moth's 'only possession, like the bee's sting,' and which is, like the bee's sting, life-exacting."

In her article, "Conceal/Reveal: Passion and Restraint in the Work of Elizabeth Bishop or Why We Care about Elizabeth Bishop's Poetry," written for the *Massachusetts Review*, Kathleen Spivack discusses what makes Bishop's writing unique. The critic describes Bishop's poetry as historically falling "between the 'impersonality' so admired in the poetry of T. S. Eliot, Wallace

Stevens, Marianne Moore, and others of her early education; and the 'confessional' movement of her contemporary Robert Lowell and his group, who wrote directly about their personal lives." According to Spivack, "Bishop chose the 'middle way.'" She then adds: "Elizabeth Bishop, like Emily Dickinson, wrote delicately and elliptically. Much was unsaid, left out, alluded to. What is most important is what is *not* said." And finally, fully admitting that she is a "fanatic" when it comes to Bishop's poetry, Angela Garbes, writing in the *Stranger*, a Seattle-based alternative newspaper, states: "in the second half of the 20th century, no American artist in any medium was greater than Bishop." Garbes then describes the poet's style as "ferociously detailed, restrained and subtle, undeniably intimate."

CRITICISM

Joyce M. Hart

Hart has degrees in English and creative writing and is a freelance writer and published author. In the following essay, Hart interprets the poem as an extended metaphor about the rational and emotional, or the conscious and subconscious.

Many critics have described Bishop's poem "The Man-Moth" as being surreal. When they do so, they are alluding to the dreamlike images that are contained in the poem; from the narrative of the poem that is only vaguely rational; to the underlying emotions of the poem that feel somehow universal. Dreams, some psychologists and psychiatrists believe, are messages for the dreamer, sent by the subconscious in an attempt to reveal emotions and desires that are suppressed by the conscious mind. Because these desires are suppressed, dreams speak to the dreamer in symbolic images just like those that appear in "The Man-Moth." This theory is based on the idea that the conscious and subconscious are constantly in conflict with one another, as the rational constantly attempts to repress the irrational. Yet the irrational nevertheless constantly attempts to send messages (by way of dreams) to the rational. If Bishop's poem is based on dreamlike images, what might the poem be saying? It seems appropriate that if we interpret the Man-Moth as a symbol of the emotional or irrational, then his adventures, or misadventures, are the result of repression and his attempts to break free of that repression, or at

> JUST AS THE MOON AFFECTS THE TIDES, IT IS POPULARLY BELIEVED THAT IT AFFECTS MAN'S EMOTIONS. THUS, IT AFFECTS THE MAN-MOTH (THE EMOTIONS), ENCOURAGING HIM TO VENTURE OUT OF HIS SUBTERRANEAN HOME."

least to attempt to communicate some sort of message. Certainly the poem's dualities (sets of two opposites), such as dark and light, above and below, and Man (rational) and the Man-Moth (irrational), all reinforce this idea.

The poem begins above ground, a place where daily routines keep one in a rational mode, busy with life's details, a place or state of mind where emotions are temporarily shoved aside. After stating this phrase, the narrator indicates that all is not well "Here, above." There are cracks in the buildings and cracks in the sidewalks. The façades of the buildings that the poem refers to also indicate a sort of disconnect between the surface of things and the things behind, beneath, or below that surface.

The image of the "whole shadow of Man," mentioned in the first stanza of this poem could well be intended to represent the rational part of Man. The poem portrays this aspect of Man as being very small in comparison to the subconscious as it is represented by the Man-Moth. The Man-Moth is the emotional part of Man that looms over the rational, making the rational aspect appear insignificant in comparison to the emotional power of the subconscious, or psyche. An allusion in the poem that reinforces this concept of the Man-Moth as the psyche, or as the symbol of suppressed emotions, is the image of the "inverted pin, the point magnetized to the moon." This statement symbolizes a compass, directing the Man-Moth to the moon. Just as the moon affects the tides, it is popularly believed that it affects Man's emotions. Thus, it affects the Man-Moth (the emotions), encouraging him to venture out of his subterranean home. So, at this point in the poem, the Man-Moth rises through the cracks in the sidewalk and appears in the upper world of the rational mind. This symbolizes the emotions or subconscious seeping into the rational or conscious.

WHAT DO I READ NEXT?

- Bishop's prose and fiction were collected and published after her death. In this collection, *The Collected Prose* (1984), fragments of short stories as well as observations Bishop made about her first job and her life-long friend and mentor, fellow poet Marianne Moore, are included.

- *One Art: Letters* (1991) is a collection that includes letters by Bishop that are about her life, and, as of 2007, it is the most autobiographical book about Bishop that is available. Letters Bishop wrote to her peers, such as poets Marianne Moore and Robert Lowell, and letters that expose some of Bishop's rawest emotions provide the reader with a very personal insight into her poems.

- More than twenty years older than Bishop, Marianne Moore was friend and mentor for Bishop throughout her life. Although their poetic styles differed, Moore inspired Bishop. To gain an understanding of Moore's writing, read *The Poems of Marianne Moore* (2004). Both poets are often praised for their unique manner of seeing the world and for bringing even the smallest details into a new and more interesting light. Both Bishop and Moore at one time considered becoming painters, and to read their poems is to see the world through an artist's eye.

- The poet Robert Lowell was also one of Bishop's friends, and his work influenced her as well. Their poetry differed greatly, as Lowell's writing is more confessional (personal), a form that Bishop did not favor. Lowell, like Moore, belonged to the generation preceding Bishop's, and like Moore, Lowell appreciated Bishop's potential as a poet and encouraged her to write. Lowell's *Collected Poems* (2007) encompasses much of his writing style, which, like Moore's and Bishop's, also contains a great deal of visual imagery.

- Covering a span of twenty-five years, *Conversations with Elizabeth Bishop* (1996) provides insights into the poet's evolving personality as she matures. In this collection of actual interviews, Bishop talks about her childhood, her jobs, her poetry, and some of the challenges that she faced as a woman and poet. Also included is a short piece from one of Bishop's students, which talks about the student's experiences in Bishop's poetry classes.

- Adam Roberts has written one of the most comprehensive critical analyses of modern fantasy. His *History of Science Fiction* (2005) begins with Greek literature and follows the genre through the ages, ending with a critical look at modern science fiction as developed in books, films, and comic books. This book will aid students who wish to place the fantastical aspects of "The Man-Moth" within the larger context of the genre's development.

When the emotions are suppressed (or when the Man-Moth is underground), the moon causes a different reaction than when the emotions are expressed. Underground, the Man-Moth cannot see the moon. He can only feel its light. But on the surface, as the Man-Moth climbs up the sides of buildings, he notices that the moon looks quite different. The moon is no longer felt, but is instead seen as a hole in the sky.

This hole, like the cracks, presents a feeling of insecurity, and also of fragility. The sky, it is assumed, was once seen by the Man-Moth as a protective dome, and this dawning belief that the sky has a hole in it makes the Man-Moth tremble. The Man-Moth, in the meantime, continues to climb "as high as he can climb." He is relentless despite his fear. He is the epitome of passion and is driven by it. In contrast, the rational side of Man "has no such illusions." The rational side of Man, this poem might be suggesting, is fearful of passion and does not strive to accomplish the impractical or the seemingly impossible. Man does not strive for anything emotional, but rather he hides from such immeasurable feelings. Instead of climbing and pushing through the hole that the moon leaves in the sky, he pushes down his emotions. Because of this, (and because the subconscious is largely subordinate to the conscious) the Man-Moth "falls back scared but quite unhurt."

Unsuccessful, the Man-Moth climbs back down "to the pale subways of cement he calls his home." Man has suppressed his emotions once again. It is in this state of suppression that the Man-Moth flits around until he finally succeeds in getting on one of the subway trains, and perhaps the subways here represent a rational invention. Once aboard, the Man-Moth is uncomfortable, he feels awkward as he sits backward, his chest facing the direction that is opposite of where he wants to go. The speed at which he retreats (or proceeds?) is "terrible" and also monotonous. As a passenger on the train, the Man-Moth is caught in a recurring dream of long nights spent in "artificial tunnels," tunnels that are directly opposed to the one through which he had hoped to enter in order to reach the other side of the moon. The Man-Moth's passion is gone. His drive is suppressed. He is confined in a manmade machine with little hope of escape. Not only is he forced to endure this long-lasting and monotonous ride, he also cannot even look out the window.

On the other side of the window there is something beyond the train that frightens the Man-Moth. This image could well be the clue that explains why Man suppresses the Man-Moth. The so-called "third rail" is a poison to which Man, through the Man-Moth (or, perhaps, vice-versa) has a deathly propensity. Is this a weakness for alcohol, as some critics suggest? Or is this the fear of emotion? Notably, Bishop's mother spent most of her adult life in a mental institution, and it is reasonable to say that a common view of the insane is that they are overly emotional or entirely irrational. Could this then explain the "disease / he has inherited the susceptibility to"? Or could it at least clarify why the Man-Moth (and, by extension, Man) is so frightened? Is this why the Man-Moth must push his hands into his pockets and keep them

there? He cannot reach out for fear of touching or arousing his feelings.

The poem ends by directly addressing the reader, almost in a confiding tone as if a secret is being shared. The last stanza seems to indicate that there is a way to deal with one's emotions. It is as if the narrator of the poem is saying that people should not be afraid of their emotions, or maybe, that they should not be afraid of their dreams, as dreams are irrational, and they are also symbolic messages that stem from the irrational. Both (emotions and dreams) can, in fact, be nourishing (the gift given by the Man-Moth is described, after all, as "pure enough to drink"). The advice in the poem is that one should shine a light on emotion ("If you catch him, / hold up a flashlight to his [the Man-Moth's] eye"). There the reader will find a gift, the Man-Moth's only possession. However, there is also a warning. If the reader does not pay attention to their dreams and emotions, the gift will be lost.

Source: Joyce M. Hart, Critical Essay on "The Man-Moth," in *Poetry for Students*, Gale, 2008.

Jeffrey Powers-Beck

In the following excerpt, Powers-Beck examines the influence that the poetry of George Herbert had on Bishop's work. Herbert was an early seventeenth-century Welsh poet. In particular, Powers-Beck discusses the imagery of tears in the work of both poets, including in Bishop's poem "The Man-Moth."

The Stuart poet-divine George Herbert was one of Elizabeth Bishop's favorite poets and greatest influences: she read Herbert from age fourteen to the end of her life; she kept his poetry by her writing desk, and usually travelled with it; she maintained a long friendship with the Herbert scholar Joseph Summers; she mentioned the poet frequently in her letters and interviews; early in her poetic career, she consciously imitated several of his verses; and at twenty-four, she dreamed of discussing prosody with Herbert and Marianne Moore, and recorded the dream in her notebook. The dream ended auspiciously with Herbert's promise to prove "useful" to Bishop, to which assurance of influence and patronage she rejoined wryly: "Praise God!" (Merrin 39).

Bishop's biographer Brett Millier attributes the poet's love of Herbert to his technical virtuosity and his "distinctly modest voice," a voice that served for Bishop as an antidote to the self-absorption and self-celebration of contemporary confessional poetry ("Modesty" 49). Similarly, in *An Enabling Humanity*, Jeredith Merrin claims that Herbert's example of "humility," a "complex and subtly combative attitude," was crucial for Bishop, allowing her to create her own secular poetics of spiritual struggle (7). In both Bishop and Herbert, says Merrin, one finds the "persistent depiction of spiritual striving and strife, in their painstaking investigation of ... 'inner weather' (48)." A ubiquitous element in this "inner weather" is the imagery of tears, which pervades the lyrics of both Herbert and Bishop, especially her early poems. Indeed, the weeping poems of Herbert's *The Temple* served as seminal examples to Bishop of how painful emotions could be controlled and sublimated by poetic art, and so encouraged her to cultivate her own poetics of expressive restraint.

Several critics have recognized the wellsprings of tears in Bishop's poetry. Among them, Lorrie Goldensohn says: "Salt water flows freely in many of Bishop's metaphors—the pond of tears in 'Chemin de fer,' the crying of the sea that streaks the boardinghouse of 'A Summer's Dream,' the tearstains of the waterfall in 'Questions of Travel,' the teakettle's tears that dance on the Little Marvel Stove in 'Sestina,' even the bitumen tears ... [of] 'Night City'—all of these tears have their source in a pervasive sadness, struggling to put its sorrow into acceptable speech (44)." Goldensohn's catalog rightly stresses Bishop's lifelong struggle to find expression for her childhood sufferings, although the tears are especially predominant in her early poetry and notebooks. The tears of early poems such as "The Reprimand," "Three Sonnets for the Eyes," "Chemin de fer," "The Man-Moth," "The Weed," "Roosters," and "Three Songs for a Colored Singer (IV)" distinguished Bishop as a lachrymose observer, but never a weepy poet. . . .

Closely related to the fable of "The Weed" is the tear of "The Man-Moth." Bishop published "The Man-Moth" in March 1936, almost a year before she published "The Weed" in February 1937. It too is a parable of an alienated artist, especially of a modern urban artist. Lost among the skyscrapers and subway trains, ever dreaming, and attempting to fly to the moon, the fantastic Man-Moth is, as Williamson puts it, "*Pierrot lunaire*, the lover of the moon, of unattainable ideals and romantic strangeness" (106). What most distinguishes the Man-Moth, however, is not his isolation or exotic dreams, but his

"one tear, his only possession." Bishop introduces this "one tear" in the final stanza of the poem:

> If you catch him,
>   hold up a flashlight to his eye. It's all dark
>   pupil,
>   an entire night itself, whose haired horizon
>   tightens
>   as he stares back, and closes up the eye.
>   Then from the lids
>   one tear, his only possession, like the bee's
>   sting, slips.
> Slyly he palms it, and if you're not paying
>   attention
> he'll swallow it. However, if you watch him,
>   he'll hand it over,
> cool as from underground springs and pure
>   enough to drink.

Catching and observing the Man-Moth requires the care of an entomologist, but it is an artistic act. Within the dark void of the "eye" (again the Herbertian pun on "I") is the lambent Arethusan drop: the distilled essence of his dreams and his art. The drop "cool as from underground springs and pure enough to drink" recalls the Romantic glorification of poetic inspiration: "O, for a draught of vintage! That hath been / Cool'd a long age in the deep-delved earth" (Keats, "Ode to a Nightingale"). Yet, the Man-Moth does not effuse his feelings—he holds back his "one tear" cautiously, or palms it, avoiding the dangers of fervent confession. When he does hand over his tear, it is as a kind of ritual offering of emotion refined and transformed into art.

The Man-Moth's offering of "one tear" emblematizes well Herbert's poetic of "silent tears"—the amplification of emotion through expressive restraint. Moreover, that "one tear" may belong specifically to Herbert's poetry. In several poems of *The Temple*, Herbert offers "a vial full of tears" to God (for example, "Hope"). In "Praise (3)," Herbert compares his own "glass" of tears to one teardrop of his Lord:

> I have not lost one single tear:
> But when mine eyes
> Did weep to heav'n, they found a bottle
>   there ...
> Ready to take them in; yet of a size
> That would contain much more.
> But after thou hadst slipped a drop
> From thy right eye ...
> The glass was full and more.

Christ's tear resembles the Man-Moth's, both in the phrasing ("thou hadst slipped a drop" and "one tear ... slips"), and in the depth and purity of the emotion. In 1967, Joseph Summers noted this possible source for "The Man-Moth," and Bishop responded agreeably in a letter: "Of course I'm amazed at the obvious reflection of Herbert in the 'one tear' stanza [in "The Man-Moth"]. I'm sure you're quite right, but it had never occurred to me at all. I'm always delighted when people discover these things" (*Letters* 477). As Bishop humorously pointed out, influence is seldom entirely a deliberate matter.

Elizabeth Bishop's letters and interviews continued to testify that her affinity to Herbert was lasting and profound. Indeed, she turned to Herbert's poetry in some of the roughest patches of her life. In July 1954, when she was admitted to the Hospital Estrangeiros for treatment of alcoholism and asthma, she wrote to Joseph Summers that she had taken his book *George Herbert: His Religion and Art* with her. And in 1967, in the same letter in which she told the Summerses about the suicide attempt of her longtime companion Lota de Macedo Soares, she noted poignantly: "I've been reading some of the poems [of Herbert] again—some even help a bit, I think" (469). Then, soon after Lota's death, she wrote again: "Well, I still read ... Herbert—he's the only poet I can bear these days" (477). As a teacher at Harvard, she asked her students to read Herbert, and she amused Lloyd Frankenberg with an anecdote about one student's mishap (554). Sometime after her death in 1979, her friend Frank Bidart reflected: "Her favorite poet, I think, was Herbert; like Herbert her own poems have an astonishingly unvarnished force, the intimacy of a unique self speaking" (Schwartz and Estess 215). By the end of her career, Elizabeth Bishop was indebted to Herbert, not only for poetic effects, but also for poetic consolation—her closest approach to religious faith.

Source: Jeffrey Powers-Beck, "'Time to Plant Tears': Elizabeth Bishop's Seminary of Tears," in *South Atlantic Review*, Vol. 60, No. 4, November 1995, pp. 69–87.

Margaret Dickie

In the following excerpt, Dickie explores the man-moth as a "borderline creature" between man and moth. The critic also examines the imagery of tears and of hair in "The Man-Moth."

The detail that I want to examine is at the end of "The Man-Moth," where, at the climax of

> THE IMAGE IN THE POEM POINTS AWAY FROM THE EYE'S VISION TOWARD A KIND OF LACK OF VISION, AN INSISTENCE ON THE INEXTRICABLE INTERCONNECTION BETWEEN DARKNESS AND PURITY."

a haunting poem about the mysterious activity of the surrealistic man-moth, the speaker turns the man-moth into what looks like a kind of Charlie Chaplin figure, pitiful, self-pitying, but insistently reminding us of *lacrimae rerum* or "a disease / he has inherited the susceptibility to." The speaker says:

> If you catch him,
> hold up a flashlight to his eye. It's all dark pupil,
> an entire night itself, whose haired horizon tightens
> as he stares back, and closes up the eye. Then from the lids
> one tear, his only possession, like the bee's sting, slips.
> Slyly he palms it, and if you're not paying attention
> he'll swallow it. However, if you watch, he'll hand it over,
> cool as from underground springs and pure enough to drink.

David Kalstone has linked this image to a notebook observation of a deadened woman in the New York subway whom Bishop transforms here into a "glimpse of purity and spirit." As in a similar image in "The Weed," Bishop connects vision and tears. Kalstone comments that such poems as "The Man-Moth" "allow her simultaneously to be a keen observer—the figure who 'tells' the poems scrutinizes every detail to extract her meaning—and yet to identify with figures absent, withdrawn, practically lifeless" (20) ...

The man-moth himself is a borderline creature between man and moth, and he manifests some of the symptoms of borderline patients as Julia Kristeva describes them: first, "'borderline' discourse gives the analyst the impression of something alogical, unstitched, and chaotic—despite its occasionally obsessive appearances—which is almost impossible to memorize"; and second, borderline discourse is an effect or out-break of abjection ("what disturbs identity, system, order"). In treating borderline patients, Kristeva argues, the analyst often encounters a "language that gives up."

The analyst may respond to this language by either construction or condensation. Shuli Barzilai claims that Kristeva's idea of construction resembles a more or less conventional but essentially "thematic" criticism; "the analyst is a kind of contractor who builds meanings out of disparate, 'empty' elements" (301). Condensation, by contrast, seems analogous to deconstructive criticism: it calls for a free play of signifiers, an imitation by the analyst of "the patient's rhetoric, rhythms, and intonations, thereby invoking heterogeneous dispositions (the semiotic), in addition to trying to reassemble linguistic signs (the symbolic)." This kind of treatment is often effective because it activates a "maternal transference" and prompts the emergence of a pre-symbolic, infantile organization (302).

The speaker in Bishop's "The Man-Moth" appears to approach this borderline creature by means of what Kristeva terms condensation. Bishop records the obsessional action of the man-moth's "rushing brain," as he "nervously begins to scale the faces of the buildings," "proving the sky quite useless for protection," as "He flits, / he flutters," "always seats himself facing the wrong way," must "dream recurrent dreams," "does not dare look out the window," "has to keep / his hands in his pockets." She reports these nonsensical or compulsive movements and habits without comment and as if they were consequential.

She records experience that does not quite make sense, as, for example, "He does not see the moon; he observes only her vast properties." She concludes illogically, "He trembles, but must investigate as high as he can climb" or "what the Man-Moth fears most he must do, although / he fails, of course, and falls back scared but quite unhurt." The speaker details the man-moth's fear and his compulsion to act on what he fears most as if these emotions were "of course" related when actually they are normally dissociated. Her language here seems to share some of the qualities of the borderline patient: "Beneath the seemingly well-constructed grammatical aspects of these patients' discourse we find a futility, an emptying of all affect from meaning—indeed, even an empty signifier" (41). The

speaker as analyst here does not "take up the bits of discursive chaos in order to indicate their relations" (45), as in Kristeva's constructive interpretation; rather, she "activates all of the sign's components, but with no logico-constructive protection" (46), as in condensation. Thus, she encourages a maternal transference, enabling the man-moth to experience a fusion with her and thus a second birth.

By practicing condensation, the speaker here dramatizes the way in which the borderline patient shares with the poet what Kristeva calls the heterogeneity of language. It is within this heterogeneity and on the borders of the symbolic that art exists, Kristeva argues, claiming that "all literature is probably a version of the apocalypse that seems to me rooted, no matter what its socio-historical conditions might be, on the fragile border (borderline cases) where identities (subject/object, etc.) do not exist or only barely so—double, fuzzy, heterogeneous, animal, metamorphosed, altered, abject" (*Powers*, 207). If Bishop's speaker and the man-moth she describes exist on this fragile border, the eye—"all dark pupil, / an entire night itself"—is where their identities blur and merge; it neither sees nor reveals anything. From this border, the pupil "whose haired horizon tightens / as he stares back," the tear slips. Although the tear belongs to the borders of the body, it has none of the polluting powers of the body. The setting of the eye in the body with its "haired horizons" is the site of defilement, the obverse of the pure tear. In this slippage of purity from the dark and hairy body, the speaker acknowledges abjection, recognizes the other in the self in what Kristeva calls a "maternal transference." She explains: "If 'something maternal' happens to bear upon the uncertainty that I call abjection, it illuminates the literary scription of the essential struggle that a writer (man or woman) has to engage in with what he calls demonic only to call attention to it as the inseparable obverse of his very being, of the other (sex) that torments and possesses him" (*Powers*, 208). What fascinates the speaker of this poem is the horror of the night in the eye's dark pupil. That the pure tear slips from it only adds to its fascination. The intertwining here of the pure and the dark or demonic is a culmination of such connections in the poem from the "battered moonlight" of the first line to the man-moth's desire to "push his small head through that round clean opening" and be forced through in "black scrolls on the light."

This final image of the man-moth's eye appears far from Kalstone's linkage of vision and tears (20). It belongs more to the notebook observation of a deadened woman in the subway with "an empty interior expression" (19). The image in the poem points away from the eye's vision toward a kind of lack of vision, an insistence on the inextricable interconnection between darkness and purity. In the "dark pupil" with its "haired horizon," the speaker sees confirmed the "whole shadow of Man," "the pale subways of cement he calls home," "the unbroken draught of poison," "disease." Yet she also sees the pure, cool tear that emerges from this darkness.

This strange combination of vaguely repulsive hair and purity has a long history in Bishop's imagination. As far back as her high school days, in the short story "The Thumb," she describes the narrator's attraction to a beautiful young woman at whom he stares and finds, to his horror, that she has a man's thumb; he "looked—and saw on the back of the thumb, where it lay in the sunlight, there was a growth of coarse, black hairs." Despite himself, he is attracted to her, only to be finally repelled and overcome with disgust. He leaves her without a word, and, trying to explain his actions later, he claims, "Perhaps it was because I suddenly felt tired, sick to death of the whole affair." Even here, at this early age, Bishop's speaker seems to give up, to fail to explain, in the manner of the borderline patient.

In the later poem "O Breath," Bishop again evokes the image of hair to convey an emotional experience that she cannot comprehend. She writes, "Beneath that loved and celebrated breast... I cannot fathom even a ripple," and then goes on:

(See the thin flying of nine black hairs
four around one five the other nipple,
flying almost intolerably on your own
    breath.)
Equivocal, but what we have in common's
    bound to be there,
whatever we must own equivalents for,

The nipple, the thumb, the eye, each with its "haired horizon," are all boundaries of the body itself, where images of nurturance and intolerance, of beauty and monstrosity, of darkness and deeply troubling vision, combine and blur. Although as a woman in the position of subject Bishop appears to be always attracted to these images, it was only as she matured that she invested them with more and more significance. Writing as a high school student, Bishop speaks as a male suitor more horrified than fascinated by what appears corrupt in the beautiful woman. In "The Man-Moth," transposing sexual identification, she appears less repulsed by the "haired horizon." And finally, in "O Breath," without ascribing sexual identity, the speaker affirms the common bond between the lovers as she focuses without comment on the black hair around the nipple of the breast. In this way Bishop gradually takes on the full power of the woman as subject in the one role in which she is always subject, that of the mother. The mother, as Kristeva claims, lives "on the border" as a "crossroads" being and experiences "a continuous separation, a division of the very flesh. And consequently a division of language." Kristeva elaborates: "For a mother, on the other hand, strangely so, the other as arbitrary (the child) is taken for granted. As far as she is concerned—impossible, that is just the way it is: it is reduced to the implacable. The other is inevitable, she seems to say, turn it into a God if you wish, it is nevertheless natural, for such an other has come out of myself, which is yet not myself but a flow of unending germinations, an eternal cosmos."

In "O Breath," Bishop accepts the divided nature of the body's unfathomable purity and intolerable corruption, acknowledging the other in herself. Far from judging and dismissing the coarseness of her own flesh, as she had in "The Thumb," Bishop in this later poem accedes to "whatever we must own equivalents for, / something that maybe I could bargain with" (79).

In "The Man-Moth," the speaker is not quite so eager to bargain. Yet she connects the slippage of the tear from the dark pupil to the division of creation and the way that language, like the child, comes out of the self. The tear that can be "palmed" or "handed" over is a surrealistic tear that exists only in writing, and in this image the speaker inscribes both herself and the man-moth as writers, possessed by the other, the darkness, that Kristeva calls the powers of horror. For these writers, creation is a deadly and painful experience which requires the relinquishment of the man-moth's "only possession, like the bee's sting," and which is, like the bee's sting, life-exacting.

The man-moth, who possesses only one tear and (again like the bee's sting) can shed it only once, may be the writer who "hands over" or writes a life and who may, if s/he is not watched carefully, take back what s/he has let slip, swallow rather than "palm" it. The speaker advises her readers to "hold up a flashlight to his eye" if they catch the man-moth, because only such an eye can see and, it appears, reflect darkness.

Source: Margaret Dickie, "Seeing Is Re-Seeing: Sylvia Plath and Elizabeth Bishop," in *American Literature*, Vol. 65, No. 1, March 1993, pp. 131–46.

S. R. Murthy

In the following essay, Murthy examines the poem's language as a way to uncover its meaning. The critic focuses on the Man-Moth as a vessel through which Bishop explores "man's inner being."

Elizabeth Bishop's poem "The Man-Moth," often praised for daintiness if not preciosity, unravels a much deeper ontological connotation on closer reading.

A newspaper misprint for the word "mammoth" provided the occasion for the poem. Bishop wrote thus on the genesis of the poem: "An oracle spoke from the page of *The New York Times*, kindly explaining New York City to me, at the least for the moment." The poem's meaning, therefore, has to be read in this context.

Man's subconscious impulses—swinging between the heights of aspiration and depths of despair—surface momentarily only to be caught again in the relentless current of day-to-day urban living that tempts with an illusion of progress.

Man, with the unrealized urges of his inner being controlled by the visible natural order, maintains a contact of inverted equilibrium with the environment, for "he makes an inverted pin / the point magnetized to the moon." He stands rooted on the "fact" of his existence. He has no use for perceptions. "He does not see the moon." Because his view of the outer, natural world is marked by scientific precision, he becomes "blind to the moon," but is quite alive to her "vast properties" and registers her temperature, which seems to defy even the scientifically calibrated thermometer. For the man in New York, nothing is exciting and nothing could be depressing.

But the subconscious impulses that surface gain another view of life: "the moon looks rather different to him." Implying an analogy between the "moth" and man's inner being, Elizabeth Bishop delicately suggests its insubstantiality and apparent vulnerability. Like the moth, the Man-Moth rises timorously—unable to resist the glare of the moon even if it were to spell disaster. It is in character for the moth to emerge from an unseen habitat and move toward certain destruction. Though he is filled with fear, the curiosity that impels him onward is irresistible. "He trembles, but must investigate as high as he can climb."

Imagining the moon as a small hole, he doubts the efficacy of the sky to offer protection against earth's tyrannies. In a moment of intensely exalted idealism, he wishes to proceed beyond the moon, questing for eternal security. He has attempted it many times, and this time he hopes to succeed. Man has no such illusions. Once again the attempted ascent ends in fiasco for the Man-Moth. He falls down afraid, but not hurt. The tug of the cloak of Reality that hangs about him, "his shadow dragging like a photographer's cloth behind him," impedes his movement, and he falls deeply into the "subways" of consciousness. The subconscious that momentarily buoyed up is rudely pulled back; "he returns to the pale subways." But accommodation is not easily gained. He "flits" and "flutters," for he has lost pace with the world of reality that runs on with relentless speed. He is involuntarily pushed in and the "doors close swiftly" like the doors of a prison.

The nocturnal adventure has incapacitated him for moving with the current of life. But willy-nilly he is swept on. Of one thing he is certain—that he is moving only backward. The recurrence of these experiences—"the dreams"—sustain man in this interminable movement. Yet there is a haunting fear of the noxious whiff of reality: "the third rail, the unbroken draught of poison" that may affect his healthy inwardness. He adopts his unique defense against this inevitable disease—"one tear," which he is ready to hand over, "cool as from underground springs and pure enough to drink."

The quality of man's life ultimately has to be measured in terms of the epiphanic realization, however momentary, of the hidden springs of being, of the essence that supersedes existence.

Source: S. R. Murthy, "Bishop's 'The Man-Moth,'" in *Explicator*, Vol. 47, No. 3, Spring 1989, pp. 52–53.

SOURCES

Bishop, Elizabeth, "The Man-Moth," in *The Complete Poems, 1927–1979*, Farrar, Straus and Giroux, 1999, pp. 14–5.

Dickie, Margaret, "Seeing Is Re-Seeing: Sylvia Plath and Elizabeth Bishop," in *American Literature*, Vol. 65, No. 1, March 1993, pp. 131–46.

Garbes, Angela, "The Guilt Rubs Off," in the *Stranger*, Vol. 15, No. 33, April 27–May 3, 2006, p. 35.

Jung, Carl, *Memories, Dreams, Reflections*, Vintage Books, 1973.

Lombardi, Marilyn May, *The Body and the Song: Elizabeth Bishop's Poetics*, Southern Illinois University Press, 1995.

Murthy, S. R., "Bishop's 'The Man-Moth,'" in *Explicator*, Vol. 47, No. 3, Spring 1989, pp. 52–3.

Spivack, Kathleen, "Conceal/Reveal: Passion and Restraint in the Work of Elizabeth Bishop, or: Why We Care about Elizabeth Bishop's Poetry," in the *Massachusetts Review*, Vol. 46, No. 3, Fall 2005, pp. 496–527.

Vendler, Helen, "The Poems of Elizabeth Bishop," in *Critical Inquiry*, Vol. 13, No. 4, Summer 1987, pp. 825–38.

FURTHER READING

Bishop, Elizabeth, *Exchanging Hats: Paintings*, edited by William Benton, Farrar, Straus, Giroux, 1996.

> Bishop did not only write poetry, she also painted, and this could explain why her poems are often full of visual imagery. Although Bishop claimed that her paintings could not be considered art, this collection may prove otherwise. Her landscapes and portraits of friends demonstrate Bishop's ability to capture images that reflect the very emotions often found in her poems. The book also juxtaposes various paintings with lines from some of Bishop's poems.

Goldensohn, Lorrie, *Elizabeth Bishop: The Biography of a Poetry*, Columbia University Press, 1993.

> Goldensohn studies Bishop's poetry and links it to experiences in the poet's life, showing how specific events influenced her writing. Much of the material that Goldensohn uses came from previously unpublished poems and fragments, so this book offers not only Goldensohn's reflections on how Bishop's life affected her poetry, but also a glimpse into some of the incomplete works of this great poet.

Millier, Brett C., *Elizabeth Bishop: Life and the Memory of It*, University of California Press, 1995.

> This is the first ever full-length biography of Bishop, covering the many tragedies that befell the poet. Millier, a university professor, does not shy away from sensitive topics such as Bishop's homosexuality or her addiction to alcohol. Based on her research, Millier also provides some of her own speculative conclusions about the poet.

Oliveira, Carmen L., *Rare and Commonplace Flowers: The Story of Elizabeth Bishop and Lota de Macedo Soares*, Rutgers University Press, 2002.

> Oliveira, herself a Brazilian, took an interest in the romantic relationship between Bishop and her Brazilian lover, de Macedo Soares. Using a combination of fact and fiction, Oliveira conceptualizes the sixteen-year long relationship between these two women, a relationship that Bishop claimed was the first in which she experienced happiness.

Travisano, Thomas J., *Elizabeth Bishop: Her Artistic Development*, University of Virginia Press, 1989.

> Travisano not only discusses Bishop's development as a poet but also provides his own understanding and interpretation of some of Bishop's poems. His commentary is based on Bishop's remarks that she became more personally available in her later works, as opposed to the more objective stance of her early poems.

My Grandmother's Plot in the Family Cemetery

CLAUDIA EMERSON

2005

"My Grandmother's Plot in the Family Cemetery" was first published in 2005 by Claudia Emerson in her poetry collection *Late Wife*. Emerson's poem is part of a semi-autobiographical sequence of poems that explore her first marriage—which ended in divorce after nineteen years—the time after her divorce when she lived in solitude, and her subsequent marriage to a widower. The poems in this Pulitzer prize-winning collection began as letters written, though never mailed, in which the author explores the grief she felt when her first marriage ended and the happiness that she feels in her second marriage; both events are tinged with loss, which is explored through a poetic sequence of emotions and memories. Emerson's new happiness is derived from grief, since this second marriage occurs only after the death of her husband's first wife. This complexity of emotion is revealed in "My Grandmother's Plot in the Family Cemetery," in which the second wife in the poem receives only the barest recognition compared to the first wife. Emerson's own life is mirrored in the life of her grandmother, in that both the poet and her grandmother married men who have lost beloved first wives.

Late Wife is Emerson's third book of poetry, and the initial press run of about 700 copies sold out quickly after Emerson was awarded the 2006 Pulitzer Prize in Poetry. A second printing of 14,000 copies makes this book Emerson's best selling collection.

Claudia Emerson *(Photograph by Barry Fitzgerald. Courtesy of H. Kent Ippolito)*

AUTHOR BIOGRAPHY

Emerson was born January 13, 1957 in Chatham, Virginia, where her parents, Claude and Molly Emerson, ran the small town's furniture store. Emerson graduated from Chatham Hall, an all-girls boarding school, in 1975, and then attended the University of Virginia, where she earned a bachelor's degree in English in 1979. She married Jesse Andrews soon after graduation and returned to Chatham, where for the next ten years she worked in a variety of jobs, including work as a substitute teacher, librarian, meter reader, and part-time letter carrier. She also ran a used book store in Danville, Virginia. The used book store allowed Emerson some of the free time necessary to write poetry and short stories. Eventually, Emerson decided that if she wanted to be serious about writing, she needed to return to school. In 1991, she earned an M.F.A. in Creative Writing from the University of North Carolina. That same year, she was awarded the

Academy of American Poets Prize. After completing her degree, Emerson began teaching poetry as an adjunct professor at Washington and Lee University and at Randolph-Macon Women's College. Even though she was often busy teaching four or five poetry classes, Emerson continued to write poetry. In 1994, Emerson was awarded a National Endowment for the Arts Fellowship and the following year received the Virginia Commission for the Arts Individual Artist Fellowship. Her first collection of poetry, *Pharaoh, Pharaoh* was published in 1997. The following year she became an associate professor at the University of Mary Washington in Fredericksburg, Virginia. Shortly after taking the position, Emerson's first marriage ended in divorce. In 2000, Emerson married Kent Ippolito, whose wife had died of lung cancer three years earlier. In 2002, the year that Emerson's second collection of poetry, *Pinion, An Elegy*, was published, she received a second Virginia Commission for the Arts Individual Artist Fellowship. She was honored in 2003 with the University of Mary Washington Alumni Association Young Faculty Award. Emerson published her third collection of poetry, *Late Wife*, which includes "My Grandmother's Plot in the Family Cemetery," in 2005, the same year that she received the Witter Bynner Fellowship in poetry from the Library of Congress. In addition to the 2006 Pulitzer Prize in Poetry, Emerson also received the 2006 Mary Pinschmidt Award, an award given by graduating seniors to the professor they consider to have had the greatest impact on their lives.

POEM TEXT

> She was my grandfather's second wife. Coming late
> to him, she was the same age his first wife
> had been when he married her. He made
> my grandmother a young widow to no one's surprise,
> and she buried him close beside the one whose sons   5
> clung to her at the funeral tighter than her own
> children. But little of that story is told
> by this place. The two of them lie beneath one stone,
>
> *Mother* and *Father* in cursive carved at the foot
> of the grave. My grandmother, as though by her own design   10
> removed, is buried in the corner, outermost plot,
> with no one near, her married name the only sign

she belongs. And at that, she could be *Daughter*
   or pitied
Sister, one of those who never married.

POEM SUMMARY

Lines 1–4

"My Grandmother's Plot in the Family Cemetery" is a fourteen-line sonnet that begins with a simple declarative sentence telling readers that "She was my grandfather's second wife." Emerson writes in a clear narrative voice that explains her grandmother's position in this marriage. Emerson is herself a second wife. In both cases the first wife has died, leaving a grieving widower. Readers also learn that the grandmother was young when she married. In fact, she was "the same age" that the first wife had been on her wedding day. While the poet does not provide either the grandmother's age or the age of her husband, the words "Coming late to him" imply that there was a significant difference in their ages. The young wife is "coming late" into his life. This disparity in age is confirmed in line 4, when readers learn that the grandmother was left a young widow "to no one's surprise." The acknowledgement of "to no one's surprise" confirms there was a significant difference in the couple's ages. These first four lines establish a history in common between the grandmother and the grandchild, and the poet's use of "my" in the first line suggests that she is speaking of her own grandmother. Since the collection of poems from which "My Grandmother's Plot in the Family Cemetery" is taken explores events in Emerson's own life, it is reasonable to make the connection between her grandmother's experience and her own. Furthermore, these first lines of the poem are straightforward prose, as if they were part of a letter, in which the author recalls events from her family history.

Lines 5–8

The first four lines of the poem establish the background information for the events that are related in the next four lines. The sonnet's octave, an eight-line stanza, continues in line 5, when readers learn that when her husband died the young widow buried him next to his first wife. Emerson's words relate how the young widow stands at the grave with her stepsons, clinging to her "tighter than her own." We also

learn that the young wife and widower had children of their own in this second marriage. These are the children who cling to their mother but not as tightly as the stepchildren, who have lost everything. These very brief words create a powerful image of grief and new responsibilities that readers can easily visualize: the young widow with her own children and her stepchildren; the latter clinging closely to her, since they have now lost both mother and father. But the grave itself does not relate the story of orphaned children completely dependent on their step-mother. Those visitors who come and see the grave do not learn the story of loss and grief and of the responsibilities that the young widow faced when left alone with several children to raise. Instead, all that is visible is a single headstone for a husband and wife.

Lines 9–12

The sonnet's sestet, a six-line stanza, begins with line 9, which completes the phrase begun on line 8. The single stone that rests at the foot of the joint grave contains the words "*Mother and Father*." There is no space on the stone for mention of a second wife or stepmother. The poet's grandmother chose "as though by her own design" to be buried elsewhere. Line 10 relates that she is buried in the corner of the cemetery, in an "outermost plot." Readers also know that she is buried alone, "with no one near." The only connection to her late husband is her "married name" on the stone. In death, there is no place for the second wife. Although she bore him children and raised the children from his first marriage, she remained an outsider, more so even in death than in life. These words echo the fears of any second wife, who, when she marries a widower, wonders if she will ever be more than an inadequate replacement for the first wife.

Lines 13–14

In the final couplet, or the last two lines of the sestet that complete the sonnet, the poet wonders if her grandmother's grave will be mistaken for that of a spinster. Alone in the outermost corner of the cemetery, she has only a last name in common with her husband and his first wife, the "*Mother and Father*," who are buried elsewhere. The commonality of name is all that remains to remind visitors of the connection to her late husband. That shared name, though, could easily be that of a "*Daughter*" or a "pitied *Sister*." The poet is the

TOPICS FOR FURTHER STUDY

- For a research project, visit a cemetery in your area. Select several family groupings of stones, and after you have gathered sufficient information, choose from among the family "histories" that you have amassed and select one of the families for further research. Next, use your community library to search through local newspapers for more information about your chosen family. Look for birth, wedding, and death announcements. Using the information available on the stones and from your newspaper research, create a family tree that traces your chosen family group back several generations. Your family tree should include a short essay explaining what you have learned about both the family you selected and the community in which they lived.

- Select a poem by any nineteenth-century female author and compare it to Emerson's poem in a well-written essay. Compare such elements as content, theme, tone, and word choice. In your evaluation of these two works, consider the different approaches of the two poets. Do you think that Emerson's poem is different in tone and content from the poem by the nineteenth century writer that you chose? How are the two poems similar?

- Take the first line of Emerson's poem and use it as the first line of your own poem. Write a sonnet of fourteen lines by continuing Emerson's line to whatever conclusion fits your own subject or ideas. Try to use the formal English sonnet style, with an octave of eight lines that presents a problem and a six-line sestet that presents a solution.

- Artists are often inspired by poets to create some of the most beautiful art imaginable. For instance, William Blake was inspired by John Milton's poetry to create illustrations of the poet's finest work. Spend some time looking through art books in the library and try to select a picture or illustration that you feel best illustrates Emerson's poem and its images of widowhood, loneliness, and isolation. Then, in a carefully worded essay, compare the art that you have selected to the poetic images that Emerson creates in her poem, noting both the similarities and the differences between them.

- Interview members of your community who have remarried, or who have been a second spouse at some point in their lives. How do the experiences of the people you have interviewed compare with the experiences of the woman in Emerson's poem? Write a report explaining your findings.

---

one who wonders and worries about whether her grandmother's role will be known. It is the poet who leaves her readers wondering if the second wife felt excluded since, as is noted in line 10, she chose to be buried elsewhere "by her own design." There is no evidence in the poem of the grandmother's feelings, but there is ample evidence of the poet's concern. The poem ends with the poet's wondering if her grandmother will be thought of as "one of those who never married." There is a suggestion that to be thought of as a spinster is to be thought of as less than she really was—a wife

and mother. There is a value judgment in the poet's words that once again reflect the author's concern that being the second wife is to be somehow substandard.

THEMES

Acceptance and Belonging

There are connotations to the title "second wife" that suggest images of replacement and a lack of importance. This is particularly true of remarriage when the second wife is replacing a beloved wife who has died. Emerson's choice of words to convey the grandmother's place in this second marriage creates the image of a woman who is only a temporary replacement for the wife who has died. After her husband died, the young widow buried him "close beside" the first wife. The second wife seeks no place for herself next to her husband. The words suggest that she belonged to this marriage only temporarily, since she recognizes that her husband should spend eternity next to his first wife, under one stone that reads "*Mother* and *Father*." The second wife's role as mother to the orphaned children is similarly temporary. At their father's funeral, his sons cling to her "tighter than her own," but when she dies, she is buried "in the corner, outermost plot, / no one near." She is forgotten in death with "her married name the only sign / she belongs." As second wife, her husband was only on loan, a fact she surely knew, since the poet suggests that her grandmother's burial place is "as though by her own design / removed" from her husband's place. In death, it is almost as if the second wife's marriage had never existed. She had never truly belonged.

Life and Death

Emerson's poem makes the transition from life to death with ease. The title of the poem, "My Grandmother's Plot in the Family Cemetery" emphasizes the death and burial. The poet's grandmother is a second wife, having married only because the first wife has died. At the death of her husband, the poem shifts to his grave, where his "sons / clung to her." The grandmother's husband and his first wife are buried together, and their life as husband and wife in death is transformed into a more permanent union than it was in life. The grandmother begins the poem as a young wife, but within fourteen lines, her life ends. Whereas most people see death as a part of life, in this poem it seems as if life is entirely defined by death.

Status

Emerson's poem demonstrates the evolving status of the grandmother, who in the first line is described as "my grandfather's second wife." She is a young woman, who in the space of only a few lines becomes a widow. Only after her widowhood do readers learn that she is also a mother and stepmother. She has been transformed into the sole parent of her late husband's orphaned children. From young woman, to wife, to stepmother, to mother, and to widow, the grandmother moves steadily from one life event to the next, until finally, she also dies and is buried in the same family cemetery as her husband and his first wife. Thus, the status of the speaker's grandmother may rise or change at times, as when her stepchildren cling to her. Nevertheless, the placement of her grave is a final, inalterable comment on her status, and it proves that she will always be second best.

STYLE

End-Stopped Lines

End-stopped lines occur when a phrase or sentence is marked at the end of a line with a mark of punctuation. In a few cases, such as at the end of lines four and eight, Emerson uses a comma to signal a pause for the reader, but except for the few commas that she employs, she rarely employs an end-stop, preferring instead to continue the thought through to the next line.

Enjambment

Enjambment is when the grammatical sense of a line continues beyond the line's end and onto the next line. In Emerson's poem, she uses enjambment to continue the thought through several lines, from the first line to the third, where a period finally creates an end to the opening thought. She does this many times throughout the poem by continuing the narrative to a natural pause, and without creating any artificial pauses at the end of the poem's lines.

Slant Rhyme

Slant rhymes are often called imperfect rhymes or off-rhymes. In slant rhymes there is a close, although not exact, correspondence of sounds. Often the vowels sounds are similar, but the consonant sounds are different. Emily Dickinson was well known for her use of slant rhymes. Emerson uses this technique as well. An example is in the final two lines when she rhymes "pitied" with "married."

Sonnet

The sonnet is a very old form of poetry that was in use in Italy as the Petrarchan sonnet before its adoption in England early in the fifteenth

century. Traditionally the sonnet has been divided into two separate sections. The first eight
lines form one stanza, called the octave.
Technically the octave refers to any eight-line
stanza, but the term is most often applied to
the first part of the sonnet. The final six lines of
the sonnet form the sestet. Traditionally the
octave presents a problem or issue that is then
solved in the sestet. Ever since the sonnet was
adopted by the Elizabethan poets, it has been
undergoing change, both in format and in content. As originally created, sonnets were expressions of love, often containing exaggerated
comparisons of a woman's beauty, her coldness
toward the infatuated lover, or the speaker's
abject voice of rejection. With time, though,
sonnets were used to explore many different subjects and the form was altered to fit the poet's
needs. Here, Emerson also feels free to adapt and
transform the sonnet to fit her needs. Although
she maintains the traditional two-part octave
and sestet, Emerson deviates slightly from traditional sonnet rhyme schemes. The typical rhyming scheme in the octave of an English sonnet is
ababcdcd, which does not work for Emerson's
octave. However, although she abandons convention in the octave, the traditional sestet
rhyme of *efefgg* is maintained by the poet.

HISTORICAL CONTEXT

Widowhood

Given Emerson's age, her grandmother was
probably a young woman during the first decade
of the twentieth century. In 1900, the life expectancy for women in the U.S. was about forty-
seven years, about one year longer than the life
expectancy for men. On average, women married at about twenty-two years of age, and fewer
than 0.5 percent of women were divorced.
Nearly 60 percent of all women chose to marry.
About 10 percent of all women were widowed, a
number that remained consistent throughout the
twentieth century. Most women who married,
had three or four children, but not all women
survived childbirth. In fact, on average, about
sixty women died for every thousand births.
Emerson's poem does not establish a cause of
death for the first wife, but she still had young
children, since readers learn that even years later,
the first wife's sons clung to their stepmother at
their father's funeral. In 1900, the death of a

spouse was the most common cause of remarriage, since divorce was still relatively uncommon. Men often remarried for very practical
reasons. Small children needed a caretaker, and
so serial monogamy was a normal aspect of
marriage, just as it had been for much of early
modern history. Emerson's poem does not suggest whether the second wife is loved. She may
well have been, but for many men, love had little
to do with remarriage after being widowed. A
mother for small children was a more immediate
need. Since the grandmother "as though by her
own design" is buried separately from her husband, perhaps her marriage was based more on
practicality than on romantic love.

The Importance of Family History

Emerson does not establish a determinate time
or place for "My Grandmother's Plot in the
Family Cemetery," but the location is doubtless
intended to be the rural South of her own
upbringing. However, the time and place are
important only to the poet in understanding the
past, which fits well with an important trend of
the late twentieth century—the search for one's
identity—which led to endless searching to complete family genealogies. Initial interest in genealogical research is often traced back to the 1977
miniseries, *Roots*, based on Alex Haley's book
by the same name, which traces Haley's family
history back to a Gambian ancestor who was
brought to America and sold as a slave in 1767.
Although the authenticity of Haley's work as
genealogical research is now in dispute, at the
time of the initial broadcast, television viewers
were enthralled, and many became interested in
tracing their own "roots." By the late 1990s,
genealogical research became available to anyone with a computer and the time to spend
searching family names on the Internet. This
led to an upsurge in the creation of websites
designed to help individuals trace their family
histories back hundreds of years. People who
had not given any thought to great-grandparents
suddenly sought information about their family's origin. Software designed to help amateur
genealogists record and organize information
became readily available, but the real break-
through in easy research was the online release
of government census records that provide information about marriages, deaths, children's names,
and occupations. Immigration and military records
were also made available for online sleuths, who
could now claim distant and virtually unknown

Grave marker in a cemetary *(Jerry Woodhouse | Digital Vision | Getty Images)*

relatives as their own. As people have told their friends and family members of their discoveries, the interest in finding lost family members has continued to grow.

Another aspect contributing to the interest in genealogical research is the availability of data gathered from headstones. Across the country, hundreds of volunteers have spent many hours recording the information found in cemeteries, often locating small family plots like the one Emerson describes in her poem. In another poem from *Pharaoh, Pharaoh*, called "Looking for Grandmother's Grave," Emerson describes her father's search for his mother's grave, which as readers learn from "My Grandmother's Plot in the Family Cemetery," resides "in the corner, outermost plot" of the family cemetery. Emerson's readers can readily understand the importance of the location of her grandmother's grave, especially for those readers who are interested in family histories. The location supplies us with hints about the family, about the grandmother's role in

the family, and about complex family dynamics that would interest any would-be genealogist.

CRITICAL OVERVIEW

The reception for Emerson's 2005 collection of poetry, *Late Wife*, was very positive. The book was awarded the 2006 Pulitzer Prize for Poetry, which created even more interest in Emerson's work. As is often the case with poetry collections, Emerson's book received little interest from critics when first published, but after the Pulitzer Prize was announced, sales of the book increased. This increase in sales is noted by David Gates in a review of Emerson's book printed in *Newsweek*. Gates admits that had Emerson not won the Pulitzer Prize, he would not be writing a review of her book. In spite of the circumstances, Gates comments that *Late Wife* "is such a smart, intense, satisfying and approachable book that readers will return to it

for decades." Later in his review, Gates observes
that Emerson writes poems that are "intellectually and emotionally complicated, but the language is plain and untricky." Because of the
Pulitzer Prize, Gates suggests that "*Late Wife*
will get at least some of the readers it deserves."
Reviewer Janice Harayda would concur with
Gates. In her *One-Minute Book Reviews* article,
Harayda admits that although she does not
always agree with Pulitzer Prize judges, she
does agree with the judges when it comes to
Emerson's book. Harayda describes *Late Wife*
as "the real thing, a haunting collection of 39
poems ... that reflect a deep awareness of both
the fragility and strength of love." According to
Harayda, each of Emerson's poems "stands
gracefully on its own while enriching a larger
story." A slightly more mixed review is offered
by *Philadelphia Inquirer* critic John Freeman,
who labels Emerson "an elegant technician,"
whose poems in the first half of *Late Wife* "are
the most affecting." Freeman claims, though,
that by the time a reader has made it though
the book, it is "hard not to feel trapped, claustrophobic, bullied into a pretzel of sympathy."
Fortunately for Emerson, the Pulitzer Prize
judges did not agree.

CRITICISM

Sheri Metzger Karmiol

*Karmiol has a doctorate in English Renaissance
literature. She teaches literature and drama at the
University of New Mexico, where she is a lecturer
in the university honors program. Karmiol is also a
professional writer and is the author of several
reference texts on poetry and drama. In the following essay, Karmiol examines Emerson's poem
as an epitaph to her grandmother's life.*

Epitaphs, those brief verses or lines used to
commemorate the dead on tombstones, have
much in common with poetry. Although they
may lack the graceful beauty of formal verse,
epitaphs have a lengthy tradition. Reading the
epitaphs engraved in honor of the dead can
reveal much about what a society valued in life.
For instance, Greek epitaphs for women were
often quite lengthy and frequently praised a
woman's faithfulness and obedience to her husband, as well as her ability to weave wool and
keep house. Reportedly, William Shakespeare
was so concerned that his remains would be

WHAT DO I READ NEXT?

- Emerson's second book, *Pinion: An Elegy*
  (2002), is a long poem that uses the two
  voices of a brother and sister to tell the
  story of life on a small southern farm.

- Emerson's first collection of poems, *Pharaoh,
  Pharaoh* (1997), includes poems that focus on
  the role of memory, history, and family as life
  in the southern United States is transformed
  by change.

- The *Longman Anthology of American Poetry*,
  published in 1992, includes poetry from several different time periods. This book provides
  a compilation of poetry that allows students to
  visualize Emerson's poetry within the context
  of other American poetry and helps readers to
  understand how Emerson uses the poetic traditions that influence her work.

- *Otherwise: New and Selected Poems*, by Jane
  Kenyon, was published in 1997 (two years
  after Kenyon's death). Kenyon's poetry
  offers a glimpse at the work of another contemporary woman poet whose poetry also
  focused on life in rural America.

- *Roots*, by Alex Haley, was published in 1976,
  and tells the story of Haley's family history. The
  book sparked a national interest in genealogy.

removed from their burial place at Trinity
Church in Stratford-Upon-Avon, either to be
stored in a charnel house (a communal vault
for human remains) or to be reinterred at
Westminster Abby, that he composed his own
epitaph before his death. His epitaph threatens a
curse to those who would move his body:

> Good friend for Jesus' sake forebeare
> To digg the dust enclosed heare;
> Bleste be the man that spares these stones,
> And curst be he that moves my bones.

Shorter epitaphs are also quite common,
such as Emily Dickinson's stone, with its simple

IT IS EMERSON, WHO IN DISCOVERING THE
GRAVE, GIVES HER GRANDMOTHER THE OPPORTUNITY
TO HAVE HER STORY TOLD."

"Called Back." The occasional wit will engrave, "I told you I was sick," but most epitaphs try to capture something important about the deceased. The boundary between epitaph and poetry is actually quite narrow, as John Dryden demonstrated with some wit in his much quoted "Epitaph Intended for His Wife." Rather than the expected sentimental lament, Dryden wrote: "Here lied my wife: here let her lie! / Now she's at rest—and so am I." Notwithstanding the longevity of early Greek epitaphs, there are practical limitations on the epitaphs engraved on stone. Graveyards disappear, sometimes overtaken by encroaching vegetation, sometimes by encroaching developments. Over time, weather obscures the stones, and in some notable cases, stone rubbings of famous gravestones have worn away the engraving on the stones. But while epitaphs may eventually be lost, poetry lives long after its writer is gone. Dryden's poem is better remembered than the epitaphs engraved on many stones. The transformation from epitaph to poetry is a natural evolution of verse, with poetry providing a more lasting memorial.

Epitaphs have provided a long-standing means of expressing grief or of memorializing the dead, but the study of poetry provides a rich history of accomplishing the same thing through verse. It is poetry that best expresses grief and sorrow and that opens a different way to view death and burial. In his essay "Poets on Poetry: Writing and the Reconstruction of Reality," Robert W. Blake suggests that "poetry is like a lens or prism through which one views the world in a heightened way." For instance, Dickinson's epitaph of "Called Back" tells visitors nothing about the woman and poet who lies buried beneath the stone. It is her poetry that tells her story. In poem number 1147, the poet reminds readers that "After a hundred years / Nobody knows the Place," where a grave might be located, because "Weeds triumphant ranged." Dickinson recognized that stones and cemeteries do not last forever; instead, it is her poetry that continues to be her monument. In "My Grandmother's Plot in the Family Cemetery," Emerson relates the story of her grandmother, the second wife, who buried her much older husband "close beside" his first wife, while she, the second wife, "as though by her own design / removed, is buried in the corner, outermost plot" of the family cemetery. These words create an image of loneliness, leaving readers to wonder if the second wife felt she was an outsider in her own marriage, a sentiment that is symbolized by the location of her grave. Visitors do not learn the second wife's story from the cemetery; they learn it from delving into Emerson's poem. Blake points out that "poetry is for telling people what they hadn't noticed or thought about before."

Poet Robert Frost observed in his poem, "In a Disused Graveyard" that the living often visit cemeteries in search of the dead. Frost described how "The living come with grassy tread / To read the gravestones on the hill." The stones offer only the briefest stories of those who lie buried beneath. The epitaph described in Emerson's poem is a common one that offers too little information. Many graves bear the words, *Mother* and *Father*. In almost all cases, the words tell too little. The people buried there were more than those two words suggest. In Emerson's poem, the "Mother" was a first wife, who died too young, leaving young children to be raised by another woman. The "Father" was a husband to two wives, one of whom is missing from his side, but the stone denies the memory of that second wife. Her history and her very existence are missing from the stone. Because she is not buried nearby, she becomes a greater enigma waiting to be discovered. It is Emerson, who in discovering the grave, gives her grandmother the opportunity to have her story told.

In his Sonnet 55, Shakespeare argues that poetry has the strength to outlast mere stone. Shakespeare writes that "Not marbles, nor the gilded monuments / Of princes, shall outlive this powerful rhyme." He knew that his poetry would live long after he had turned to dust. This is the power that poetry possesses. If not for Emerson's poem, her grandmother's story would remain untold. The gravestone offers no hint of the story of a second wife. The grandmother's burial in a separate section of the family cemetery offers no hint of her life. Because she shares the family name, she could as easily be a "*Daughter* or pitied *Sister*." Edward Byrne, in his article "Everything We Cannot See: Claudia Emerson's *Late Wife*," noted that "the grandmother cedes to the first wife her own right to lie beside her husband." In giving up her burial space, she gives up her identity. Thus, as Byrne commented: "in death the grandmother is relegated to a distant location in the cemetery, almost as if the marriage had been annulled, the relationship to her husband erased, at least in the eyes of those who, like Emerson, might visit her graveside." Emerson returns to the grandmother the history that her burial relinquished. As Shakespeare suggests, poetry has the power to create immortality, when stone has failed: "you shall shine more bright in these contents / Than unswept stone, besmeared with sluttish time." Blake suggests that poetry is for revealing people's lives and for affirming their existence, and that is exactly what Emerson's poem does. Because of "My Grandmother's Plot in the Family Cemetery" Emerson's grandmother will live on long after weeds and weather obscure what little evidence remains of her life and story.

Source: Sheri Metzger Karmiol, Critical Essay on "My Grandmother's Plot in the Family Cemetery," in *Poetry for Students*, Gale, 2008.

Edward Byrne

In the following excerpt from a review of Claudia Emerson's collection Late Wife, *Byrne notes that Emerson's third collection continues and extends the "elevated descriptive language and evocative rendering" of her previous two collections. In addition, however, remarks Byrne, Emerson adds an important autobiographical element. Of the volume's middle section, which includes the poem "My Grandmother's Plot in the Family Cemetery," Byrne states that it "provides an appropriate bridge" between the first and third sections in the volume.*

In her third collection of poetry, *Late Wife*, Claudia Emerson effectively blends the elements of elevated descriptive language and evocative rendering of the past from memory evident in her previous two books. Her poetry continues to comprehensively capture both the physical and the emotional environments, using an exact word choice to examine the distinct characteristics of the external landscape as well as one's internal emotional state. Additionally, Emerson once more brings to this newest collection the

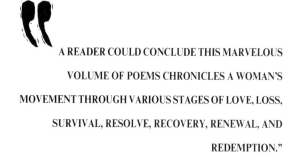

insight and wisdom already discovered by readers of her other works. In *Pharoah, Pharoah* Emerson offered portraits or snapshots of those neighbors and family in the contemporary world around her, and in *Pinion: An Elegy* she immersed her readers in an extended exploration of the inner conflicts afflicting a particular fictional family of another era. However, in *Late Wife* Emerson holds a mirror up to herself for reflection. Now, she brings her acute and estimable poetic talents to the task of meditating upon the importance of one's past and our ingrained, imagined, or invented memories of the objects, events, and individuals involved in influencing the present, assisting in shaping the person one has become.

Emerson remarks upon this in one of the "Late Wife" sonnets addressed to her current husband about the impact the memory of his departed first wife exerts on their lives. In a poem that begins this sequence carrying the same title as the most recent volume, after learning the quilt spread on their bed had been made by her husband's deceased first wife, Emerson states:

> . . . you told me she had
> made it, after we had slept already beneath
>   its loft
> and thinning, raveled pattern, as though
>   beneath
> her shadow, moving with us, that dark, that
>   soft.
> ["Artifact"]

Thus, this quilt handmade by her predecessor remains as a presence in the speaker's marriage, lingering as an ever-present reminder of the love her husband once shared with another, an emotional connection that seems to still linger. Its use on their bed evokes an emotional reaction repeated elsewhere in the sequence of sonnets when the speaker discovers other objects once belonging to the first wife—her driving glove, a daybook chronicling her deteriorating health due to lung cancer, even the x-rays that exposed the woman's terminal illness. The same poem informs the reader of how the speaker's husband had signaled his difficulty in moving beyond his first wife's death:

> For three years you lived in your house
> just as it was before she died: your wedding
> portrait on the mantel, her clothes hanging
> in the closet, her hair still in the brush.

In an Associated Press article soon after the release of *Late Wife*, Emerson recalls how she, coping with a previous unhappy marriage and divorce, and her second husband, a fairly recent widower, both arrived at their relationship from a state of "sadness." Indeed, the poems' speaker in this sequence even realizes moments or locations she had thought the two shared intimately were also overshadowed by the life of the first wife. In "The Hospital" Emerson writes of a "canal path" along which the speaker and her second husband would walk together, "feed the turtles," and witness "the red-winged blackbirds purr and call." Although the speaker believed the canal path was a place possessing private meanings and personal memories reserved for the two of them, she comes to learn otherwise. She finds out the husband and first wife had viewed this scene when she was dying, peering down from a window of the hospital which happens to loom above the canal path:

> ... you have told me how you looked
> down on the narrow pier I thought we had
> discovered, how even in her terror
> she could still see to notice with pleasure
> the bronze of the water, and these alders ...

When the speaker uncovers the first wife's driving glove in a car trunk ("from underneath the shifting junk— / a crippled umbrella, the jack, ragged / maps"), she notices the way the shapes of the woman's fingers remain formed in the glove, and she compares it with her own hand:

> It still remembered
> her hand, the creases where her fingers
> had bent to hold the wheel, the turn
> of her palm, smaller than mine.
> ["Driving Glove"]

Afterwards, the speaker chooses to do nothing but return the glove to the spot where it had been found, to "let it drift, sink, slow as a leaf through water / to rest on the bottom where I have not / forgotten it remains—persistent in its loss."

Emerson preserves this reminder of the deceased woman not only by returning the glove, but also when recording the experience within the lines of this poem. The persistence of memory and the perseverance in the present of those individuals thought lost are among the primary purposes for poetry displayed in much of Claudia Emerson's work.

Just such purposes are evident in "Photograph: Farm Auction," a poem near the beginning of *Late Wife*'s opening section, a series of letters in verse written by a speaker to her former husband, titled "Divorce Epistles." This first section's poems act as an apt counterpart to the sonnets in the "Late Wife" grouping that closes out the volume.

Emerson has explained the construction of the book in the *Blackbird* interview, which appeared in the Fall 2002 issue. At the time Emerson was organizing her new collection, and she described the movement through the book as follows: "the first section is made up of a series of epistles, actually to my ex-husband, and they're all involving Pittsylvania County landscape, and they sound in some ways more like what was in *Pharoah, Pharoah*. But they're linked as well with certain images, certain metaphors that weave their way through. Then the last section of the book I call 'Late Wife,' and it's a sonnet cycle, where I address my new husband, whose first wife died and I felt I had to make peace with that. Then the middle section I call 'Breaking Up the House' right now, and that's about my parents and the homeplace down in Chatham and that kind of thing, and those are— that middle section is a little squirrelly right now, and I don't know exactly what's going on with it. I think I'm almost done with it. In my mind, it's sort of a call-and-response kind of book, where I disappear from my life in some ways to reappear in another life where there has been a disappearance."

In "Photograph: Farm Auction" the couple's marriage has not yet eroded; however, the images lifted by the poet from a photograph her husband (who already had grown distant and less communicative) had taken lend a sense of foreshadowing:

> I have only one of the many
> images I watched you make
> out of your vigilant silence.

I am in it. You were documenting
closure, you would tell me, one
of many—the death of the small farm,
the small town, the way we had
grown up there. In the hothouse
of this frame, I have my back to you.

Easily, readers can draw a parallel between the effect of the poem's main focus, a photograph, and the purpose of the poem itself: each exists to still a moment and to document the details of a memorable event. When the speaker is summoned by her husband to his darkroom, she is reminded of some of the objects she had observed at the auction, although she also is again made aware of the ways art, including photographs or poems, can exaggerate or distort aspects of reality for enhancement of impact and emphasis of importance:

... you called me into the darkroom
to see what I had forgotten. You must
remember how I admired the detail
of a hayfork lying flat in the foreground,
angling toward the camera you had
trained on it so that the many tines
are distorted, longer than they could
have been—like a plate of baleen
from the mouth of a whale, its rich body
harvested for something this small.

The rest of this initial section in *Late Wife* relates the sad disintegration of the speaker's marriage and, as Emerson has noted, represents an autobiographical reflection on her own 19-year first marriage. In fact, the composition of such clearly autobiographical and personal poetry in *Late Wife* apparently caused Claudia Emerson to re-examine the connections to her life behind the poems in her previous two volumes, *Pharoah, Pharoah* and *Pinion: An Elegy*. In an interview on the PBS *News Hour* program, Emerson offered that she had thought it wasn't common for her to draw upon autobiography for source in writing her poetry. However, she now concedes: "I think, sometimes when I look back on the earlier work, my autobiography is in there more than I thought it was at the time, but, no, I had never written anything so close to the personal before this book."

At times, the emotional engagement projected in these poems appears to articulate a degree of disillusionment, perhaps anger. In "Rent" the speaker recalls how the couple once lived in a house being eaten away by termites that had made their way to the couple's bedroom:

"Every spring, the bedroom // filled with termites flying, having come up / from beneath the floor to mate and shed the brief / wings I swept up like confetti ... " She later states even the weakening house had outlasted their marriage, and it is where her husband declared he had found a "finer life": "It stood // those years where it yet stands, where you remained / without me, living you would claim, / another, finer life, nothing the same ... "

Another poem, "Chimney Fire," that recounts the coldness of the couple's bedroom and the developing silence between the two also reports how the speaker dreaded winter in such a cold house. Obviously, the comments on a cold home no longer concern the mere temperature reading on the thermometer ("I began to dread as well / the silence I knew would come yoked // to the cold"), as the poet writes:

... Every night you'd close
the stove down tight before we went
upstairs, and the meager heat
from that slow burn might keep the pipes
from freezing, but it wouldn't reach
the bedroom where we slept beneath
layers leaden as water that would not
float me, dense as mud beneath
that water. In the morning, all
our breathing had turned to ice ...

Similar imagery occurs in "The Last Christmas," in which both members of the marriage are ill: "I had lost my voice; / you were feverish, coughing." The wife must venture out into the freezing winter afternoon to chop firewood since the house is now without power, even the electricity wires are encased in cold: "The lines, still sleeved in ice, / sagged all afternoon above ... " After nearly accidentally cutting her leg with a fall of the axe, the speaker expresses her frustration and maybe a bit of overall despair when she confesses:

... I quit then, certain
I had let it fall where it wanted,
not into seasoned wood but into me.

Surely, the ice would never melt,
the pines would not straighten, I'd never
speak.

Finally, the husband—"pale, glazed from the fever breaking"—tells his wife he thinks he remembers looking down upon her in the winter chill from his bedroom window. The image he believes he'd seen reveals a great deal, as the speaker narrates:

> You said my mouth was open, but I was
> too far away and you could not hear me:
> I was small, mute beneath the window
>   frame,
>
> your breath forming, freezing on the panes
> until you could not see me,
> and there was nothing you could do.

Nevertheless, the sequence of poems in "Divorce Epistles" ends with a wonderful image displaying a slight change of tone upon "reflection" that correctly concludes such an endeavor. In "Frame" Emerson's speaker gives attention to a mirror her husband had once made for her, one of the few household materials from their marriage that he had built ("armless / rocker, blanket chest, lap desk") and she had kept in her new home rather than having given it away to others so as to "not be reminded / of the hours lost ..." The speaker determines the mirror had nearly disappeared, become "invisible, part of the wall, or defined / by reflection—safe—because reflection, / after all, does change." In the closing lines of this fine poem, Emerson's speaker sees the frame outside her changing face, her evolving self-image, in a new way. As she uses the mirror to compose herself and help prepare herself for another day, she notices closely the tone and texture of the wooden frame to this "backward window." Once more, her careful attention to detail is productive and evocative:

> ... I hung it there
> in the front, dark hallway of this house you
>   will
> never see, so that it might magnify
> the meager light, become a lesser, backward
> window. No one pauses long before it.
> This morning, though, as I put on my coat,
> straightened my hair, I saw outside my face
> its frame you made for me, admiring for the
>   first
>
> time the way the cherry you cut and planed
> yourself had darkened just as you said it
>   would.

"Breaking Up the House," the center section of *Late Wife*, provides an appropriate bridge between the two sequences of poems relating to the dissolution of one marriage and the circumstances of the speaker's remarriage. Although Emerson described the early draft of this section as "a little squirrelly" in her *Blackbird* interview,

some of the poetry in this portion of the book seems almost necessary as proof of the transitional phase an individual surely must undergo after enduring the trauma caused by the end of a long marriage and before she can again allow herself the vulnerability and conviction required to step forward toward another marital commitment. The inclusion of all ten poems in this section isn't quite as neatly organized or directly linear as the works in the volume's other two sections appear to be; nevertheless, any reader might view these poems as containing significant background information contributing to the accumulated depth of emotion borne by the entire book.

This middle group of poems in *Late Wife* begins with a piece transparently linked to the themes in the other two parts of the volume. "My Grandmother's Plot in the Family Cemetery" is a sonnet concerning aspects in the life of the speaker's grandmother that correlate to elements in Emerson's own life, particularly being in the difficult position of becoming a second wife. The opening lines read: "She was my grandfather's second wife. Coming late / to him, she was the same age as his first wife / had been when he married her." Despite the love and devotion between her grandmother and grandfather, as well as the grandmother's attachment to her husband's children from his first marriage ("she buried him close beside the one whose sons / clung to her at the funeral tighter than her own / children"), the grandmother cedes to the first wife her own right to lie beside her husband. Consequently, in death the grandmother is relegated to a distant location in the cemetery, almost as if the marriage had been annulled, the relationship to her husband erased, at least in the eyes of those who, like Emerson, might visit her graveside:

> ... My grandmother, as though by her own
>   design
> removed, is buried in the corner, outermost
>   plot,
> with no one near, her married name the only
>   sign
> she belongs. And at that, she could be
>   *Daughter* or pitied
> *Sister*, one of those who never married.

In "House Sitting" Emerson depicts her existence through the transitional period after her first marriage, a time when she found herself alone and without a permanent place to call home: instead, she lives in a house where she is surrounded by bare rooms and emptiness. She portrays her state during this period:

> The first summer I was alone,
> I lived in a borrowed house
> in our hometown. I'd not yet broken
>
> the habit of resorting to that
> place, though my belongings were
> already in another city
>
> and I knew I'd be gone by fall.

Emerson believes the time spent in someone else's mostly empty home rather than a home of her own was worthwhile: "I was relieved there was nothing / there to get used to."

Here, as in other poems of this book, the metaphor of "house" or "home" proves useful. Indeed, the title poem from this section of the collection, "Breaking Up the House," suggests the notion of a home as metaphor for one's personal world, one's life, furnishings gathered like memories of people and events influential in one's past; although, even when those materials are removed and can no longer be seen, their impact remains. Her mother, who has experienced loss and the break up of a house—"a world boxed and sealed"—when she was still a teenager and her parents died, advises the speaker to think about what she "will and will not want." The mother wishes to shield her daughter from the pain of loss that can be felt when removing objects from one's home. Nevertheless, the speaker remarks that the mother "cannot keep me from the house emptied / but for the pale ovals and rectangles // still nailed fast—cleaved to the walls where mirrors, / portraits had hung—persistent, sourceless shadows." Once more, even in the absence of portraits or mirrors from the walls, the pale spaces represent an ongoing presence surrounded by darker markings, and they continue to evoke memories of those whose appearances were once witnessed within their frames.

Throughout this section of the collection, however, Claudia Emerson's speaker can be seen seeking an identity, a firm will, and the strength to endure this test of her survival, so much so that she empathizes with the Civil War wounded she spots in photographs contained in a book at the museum gift shop at Marye's Heights. Her visit to the historic site results in the purchase of a slim, half-priced and remaindered book, *Orthopaedic Injuries of the Civil War*. Browsing through the volume, the speaker notes how "image after image, the book / catalogs particular survivals." The soldiers "had / survived the bullet, the surgeon's knife," and they were often fitted with primitive invented artificial limbs to replace "the anatomic / regions of loss." Finally, the speaker confides: "I bought the book, but not for their / unique disfigurements; it was // their shared expression I wanted—resolve . . ."

A reader could conclude this marvelous volume of poems chronicles a woman's movement through various stages of love, loss, survival, resolve, recovery, renewal, and redemption. The speaker, whose past is documented in the painful language of loss and symbolized by possessions preserved or the absence of ones once owned, learns to possess her present and anticipates a more rewarding future.

In *Late Wife*'s penultimate poem, "Leave No Trace," the speaker and her husband are hiking "into clearing air." This lyrical poem is filled with the typically rich and vivid language one expects to encounter in Emerson's descriptive poetry:

> . . . the falling fog
> had left perfect white stockings on the trees,
>
> an opalescent sheen on every surface.
> Lichen, almost as old as the boulders
> to which it cleaved, glowed gray and green
> without the oppressive sun, and in places
> puddle ice, milky, blind, still reflected
> what the sky had been an hour ago. We cast
> no shadow in that light.

Not only does the couple "cast no shadow," but they also pack all the items brought with them as they leave no trace of their presence there. The two discuss "how everyone fails in some / small way," and the speaker admits she is "relieved in such failure." A sense of acceptance of one's own frailties or faults, as well as acknowledgment of the weaknesses of human nature or errant directions all sometimes follow, appears to remove a burden, perhaps even of guilt or shame, and the subsequent relief permits the couple to at least live together in the present without tugging the shadows of their past with them. Indeed, the poem closes with the couple moving on toward their home and the future, as the speaker follows and focuses on her husband, on the path forward: "my eye / fixed on your back on the trail just ahead."

In the lyrical and lucid lines of the volume's final work, "Buying the Painted Turtle," the couple, again walking in nature, "near / the base of the old dam where the river / became a translucent, hissing wall, fixed / in falling, where, by the size of it, the turtle / had long trusted its defense, the streaming // algae, green, black, red—the garden of its spine—not to fail it." There they observe two boys who have captured the turtle and are mistreating it. The husband and wife buy the turtle from the boys, "to save it, let it go." The couple has purchased life and freedom for the old turtle, providing it another chance, releasing it "into deeper / water, returning to another present, / where the boulders cut the current to cast / safer shadows of motionlessness." Perhaps in a parallel fashion, the couple has now recognized their own second option as well, and they realize the value of time given back, the good fortune of a new opportunity: "We did not talk about what we had bought— / an hour, an afternoon, a later death, / worth whatever we had to give for it."

With this third book of poetry, Claudia Emerson solidifies her standing as an exceptional and attentive poet whose eye for detail and ear for lyricism are once again put to good use. Emerson regards herself as a writer who responds to place, specifically inspired by the rural Virginia countryside where she was raised and its residents she had known growing up. Undoubtedly, she supplies splendid physical descriptions of her Southern surroundings, and her poetry now deserves to be considered alongside other notable contemporary Southern poets. However, the location of most interest and insight in *Late Wife*, as well as her previous two volumes, lies elsewhere. She must be seen as an artist of that inner landscape where a host of emotions reside.

Claudia Emerson's poetry paints this inner landscape just as vividly as she fills the canvas of her page with the Virginia hills and hollers or other touches of Southern terrain. Her words display varying shades of color in the emotional spectrum of the personae in her poems, and the lines of her poetry offer differing angles of light that help illuminate dark parts of her memory, clarifying the complexities of subjects suddenly under view, so that she might feel their influence more fully. Likewise, any reader who assesses Emerson's poems might be guided toward understanding the importance of those subjects

more completely. Consequently, both poet and reader will know now that even those people or objects of our past we no longer can see may continue to impact the present and could be meaningful inspirations in our lives, and we will be reminded that "everything we cannot see is here."

Source: Edward Byrne, "Everything We Cannot See: Claudia Emerson's *Late Wife*," in *Valparaiso Poetry Review*, Vol. 8, No. 1, Fall–Winter 2006–2007, 13 pp.

Susan Settlemyre Williams

In the following interview excerpt, Emerson discusses the genesis and writing of Late Wife. *In addition, she relates her journey from working odd jobs to her decision to attend graduate school and then on to her poetry career.*

SW: *What else are you working on? What do you have coming up now?*

CE: I am finishing what I hope will be the third book, which is really unlike—well, one part of it is similar to my other work. The first section of it—and the working title of the book is *Late Wife*—the first section is made up of a series of epistles, actually to my ex-husband, and they're all involving Pittsylvania County landscape, and they sound in some ways more like what was in *Pharaoh, Pharaoh*. But they're linked as well with certain images, certain metaphors that weave their way through. Then the last section of the book, I call "Late Wife," and it's a sonnet cycle, where I address my new husband, whose first wife died, and I felt I had to make a peace with that. Then the middle section I call "Breaking Up the House" right now, and that's about my parents and the homeplace down in Chatham and that kind of thing, and those are— that middle section is a little squirrelly right now, and I don't know exactly what's going on with it. I think I'm almost done with it. In my mind, it's sort of a call-and-response kind of book, where I disappear from my life in some ways to reappear in another life where there has been a disappearance. So I guess I'm playing with that.

SW: *So there is a sort of narrative but not a strict narrative?*

CE: Not a strict narrative. But some of them are very much linked to others, and I see poems in the first section that are then echoed in the third section and in the middle. So I've had a good time doing it. The work is very different. The sonnet cycle is real different for me, a real break from what I was doing in *Pinion*.

SW: *I wanted to ask you about the sonnet cycle because that seems to be pretty popular right now.*

CE: It is.

SW: *Lots of books have extended ones.*

CE: I think I was most inspired to do it from Ellen [Bryant] Voigt's book *Kyrie*. I really loved that book a lot. I liked hearing the voices in sonnet, I liked what she did with sonnet. Sometimes she's just writing very strict form and other times not, and I enjoyed it a lot. And so I think I had it in the back of my mind that I wanted to try it. And then also, I thought, "If I just write a couple of sonnets, maybe I'll stop doing all this long stuff." And so then I haul off and write fourteen of them, so . . .

SW: *So, what was it like—the sonnet just inherently is going to be shorter and harder to get much of a narrative into. Did you try to make it narrative? I was impressed at how Ellen Voigt did seem to get the . . .*

CE: I think mine is not quite as narrative as what Ellen ended up doing, and I'm relying again on certain key images through that cycle of sonnets—and there aren't that many. I think, of actual, strict sonnets, there are maybe twelve, and then I break from that in the rest of that section.

SW: *So it's something like freeze-frames?*

CE: Yes, it's more like freeze-frames. It picks up throughout, but again, the consistent thing through the whole book is, the first person addresses "you." And that was strictly because I didn't want to assume that I could write anything from my husband's first wife's point of view. I don't know anything about that, so I had to be me in the house with him and write about her. So in every sonnet, I'm juggling three people basically. And it was really hard for me because, all my poetic career, I have insisted to my students that I don't care what really happened, I don't care what really happened, I'm not interested in confession. I've never, ever done that. Now, at the age of forty-five, I suddenly am compelled to write something true, which is very, very dangerous! But I felt I couldn't do it if I had to make things up about that subject, so I've been challenged by it, but I'm really happy with how they've come out.

SW: *Sounds fascinating. Can't wait to see it.*

Just to get a little bit of background too, you're teaching English now at Mary Washington [College], but you didn't really follow what I guess is becoming the conventional academic track for poets, to go from college to MFA to teaching.

CE: No. I did college at the normal age. I graduated in 1979, got married almost immediately, went back home to Pittsylvania County, and then I had a decade where I did a lot of different things. I was a branch manager for a little library for a while in Gretna, Virginia—only a two-room house. I was a substitute teacher. I was a meter reader. I was a part-time rural letter carrier—that was probably the best job that I had. But at the same time, I had a used bookshop in Danville, Virginia. I did a lot of really crazy things, and then I realized I wanted to be serious about writing, and I applied to UNC at Greensboro and was lucky enough to get in, and it changed my life. Made me a better poet; I adored my MFA. But then I had—I don't know how many years—eight years—of working as an adjunct, I guess, between Washington and Lee, as I said, Randolph-Macon Woman's College. I loved every place I taught, but just could never find a tenure-track position, and also my husband at that time didn't want to leave Pittsylvania County, so I was trying to commute, which was real tough. And then I published *Pharaoh, Pharaoh*, and that was the thing that most MFA's need to do tenure-tracking, to get a book out, and I ended up coming to Mary Washington, where I'm real happy.

SW: *In looking back on it, though, are you glad or sorry that you waited so long to get the MFA?*

CE: Both, I think. I felt I was out of practice with being in school, and I was worried about that, but actually I was a wonderful graduate student. I was not a stellar undergraduate, so I was better prepared emotionally, I think, to go to school, but I felt I was late getting started, and I wanted to catch up desperately. I remember having that feeling. So I tell my students I'm not sure it's the best thing to go right from an undergraduate program to a graduate program in creative writing, but I wouldn't wait over five or six years if I had it to do over.

SW: *I guess the other things that I wanted to ask . . . Well, I guess, first of all, obviously you waited a while to go. Were you writing all your life, though?*

CE: No. I always loved to read. I would keep a journal, that kind of thing. I was interested in fiction initially. I wanted to write short fiction. I loved novels, I loved to read novels. I thought maybe I would do that. Poetry sort of chose me. I was writing a lot of poetry when I had the used bookshop and no one came in. I wrote a lot then. But when I applied to Greensboro, I applied with both short fiction and poetry. And Jim Clark, who runs the program, called me up and said, "We'd like to pretend you didn't send the stories." Okay, you want me to be a poet, I'll be a poet. I think it's really funny how I've ended up writing this long poem that insists on a lot of narrative techniques.

SW: There's certainly a strong narrative element in your work, and I guess, actually, that was one of my questions: It's easy to put you in the Southern Narrative Tradition, which all seems to be in capital letters. And I also was thinking about the lineage of Southern women poets, I guess, at least from Eleanor Ross Taylor through Betty Adcock and Ellen Bryant Voigt up to, maybe, Judy Jordan. And I just wondered if you see yourself in those traditions?

CE: I do. I feel a lot of kinship with the other Southern women poets that I've read and admired and met. And really, there aren't that many. I find it fascinating. I mean, if you think about the world of the Southern novel, women just dominate. There are more now—Southern women poets—than there were, but Betty and I have talked about this a lot, and it seems for a long time there weren't that many, at least anthologized or in obvious places where you think you would find Southern women writers.

SW: I know. I've been hunting for them too.

CE: Yeah. That's how I met Betty actually. I was teaching at Washington and Lee, a genre-based course, and my theme was Southern lit, and the anthologies didn't have any women, so I asked Dabney Stuart at W & L if he had any he would recommend, because I knew a few, but I wanted more names. And he had a stack of books, and Betty Adcock was in there, and I read her work and absolutely loved it, and we invited her to come up to Washington and Lee. And we've been friends ever since.

SW: Who else would you consider your influences?

CE: Honestly—and this will sound so provincial of me, and you'll just have to forgive me for it—but my mother gave me Ellen Bryant Voigt's first book when I was sixteen years old. She gave it for Christmas.

SW: You're from the same hometown?

CE: Same hometown, Chatham, Virginia. And I loved it, and I've watched her work ever since, and I've admired it. And she encouraged me early on in my writing, and I've always been very inspired by Ellen and jealous of her. I remember getting one of her books—I've forgotten which one—I had that little, goofy bookshop, and I would open up her book and read a poem and then slam it shut, just in sheer jealousy. Why can't I write this? And I adore her work, and I love Betty, as I've said, so they've been real important to me. But early on, I was influenced, I admit it, by Robert Penn Warren. I loved to read him, and William Faulkner was huge for me just for years and years. He doesn't write poetry, but it doesn't matter. If I'm ever just at a loss, I can read something from Faulkner and feel like writing again.

Source: Susan Settlemyre Williams, "An Interview with Claudia Emerson," in *Blackbird*, Vol. 1, No. 2, Fall 2002, 7 pp.

SOURCES

Blake, Robert W., "Poets on Poetry: Writing and the Reconstruction of Reality," in the *English Journal*, Vol. 79, No. 7, November 1990, pp. 16–21.

Byrne, Edward, "Everything We Cannot See: Claudia Emerson's Late Wife," in the *Valparaiso Poetry Review*, Vol. 8, No. 1, Fall/Winter 2006–2007.

Dickinson, Emily, *The Complete Poems of Emily Dickinson*, edited by Thomas H. Johnson, Little, Brown & Company, 1960, p. 513.

Dryden, John, "Epitaph Intended for His Wife," in *Preface to Poetry*, edited by Charles W. Cooper, Harcourt, Brace & Company, 1946, p. 515.

Emerson, Claudia, "My Grandmother's Plot in the Family Cemetery," in *Late Wife*, Louisiana State University, 2005, p. 25.

Freeman, John, Review of *Late Wife*, in *Philadelphia Inquirer*, April 30, 2006, Sunday Review section.

Frost, Robert, "In a Disused Graveyard," in *The Poetry of Robert Frost*, edited by Edward Connery Lathem, Holt, Rinehart & Winston, 1969, p. 221.

Gates, David, Review of *Late Wife*, in *Newsweek*, June 12, 2006, p. 76.

Harayda, Janice, Review of *Late Wife*, in *One-Minute Book Reviews*, December 3, 2006, http://oneminutebook reviews.wordpress.com/?s=claudia+emerson (accessed May 14, 2007).

Shakespeare, William, "Shakespeare's Epitaph," http://www.poetsgraves.co.uk/shakespeare.htm (accessed March 28, 2007).

———, "Sonnet 55," in *Shakespeare's Sonnets*, edited by Katherine Duncan-Jones, Arden Shakespeare, 2005, p. 221.

FURTHER READING

Behn, Robin, *The Practice of Poetry: Writing Exercises From Poets Who Teach*, Collins, 1992.

> This book is ideal for anyone who wants to learn to write poetry. It consists of a series of exercises designed to help would-be poets begin writing and finding their own poetic voices.

Mullaney, Janet Palmer, ed., *Truthtellers of the Times: Interviews with Contemporary Women Poets*, University of Michigan Press, 1999.

> This collection of fifteen interviews includes a broad spectrum of women's voices, representing a diversity of race, ethnicity, and age. Although Emerson is not included in this collection, these poets speak of the same topics that interest all women poets—women's stories and women's lives as poets.

Pete, Daniel, *Standing at the Crossroads: Southern Life in the Twentieth Century*, Johns Hopkins University Press, 1996.

> This volume provides a survey of southern life and culture, additionally touching on social values pertaining only to women or only to men. An exploration of the differences between rural and urban life in the South is also included.

Stand, Mark, and Eavan Boland, eds., *The Making of a Poem: A Norton Anthology of Poetic Form*, W.W. Norton & Company, 2001.

> This text is an excellent guide to how to read poetry and offers help to the reader who is trying to understand poetic form. This text also includes an anthology of poems that illustrate the various concepts discussed.

Ozymandias

PERCY BYSSHE SHELLEY
1818

Percy Bysshe Shelley wrote "Ozymandias" in 1817, and it was first published in the *Examiner* in 1818. It first appeared in book form in Shelley's *Rosalind and Helen, A Modern Eclogue; with Other Poems* (1819). In the poem, the narrator relates what someone else described to him about pieces of a broken statue lying in a desert. Once a great symbol of power and strength, the statue has become a metaphor for the ultimate powerlessness of man. Time and the elements have reduced the great statue to a pile of rubble. "Ozymandias" describes an unusual subject matter for Shelley, who usually wrote about Romantic subjects such as love, nature, heightened emotion, and hope. But Shelley was also a political writer, and "Ozymandias" provides insight into the poet's views on power, fame, and political legacy. Ultimately, the poem shows that political leadership is fleeting and forgotten, no matter how hard a ruler may try to preserve his own greatness. This poem is widely anthologized, and is featured in the Norton Critical Edition (2nd edition) of Shelley's work titled *Shelley's Poetry and Prose* (2002).

Shelley kept company with an impressive array of writers, poets, and philosophers in his day. Among these was a poet and novelist named Horace Smith, whom Shelley admired for his ability to write and effectively manage his money. It was not uncommon for poets at this time to challenge each other to contests in which the two poets would select a topic or title, write

Percy Bysshe Shelley (*AP Images. Reproduced by permission*)

writing became intertwined in his literary style. His first poetry was published in 1810, as was his first Gothic novel, *Zastrozzi*.

In 1810, Shelley entered University College in Oxford. While studying at Oxford (a one-year stint), Shelley continued to pursue publication. In 1811, the publication of *The Necessity of Atheism* destroyed his family relationships. After expulsion from Oxford, Shelley wrote little and then eloped with sixteen-year-old Harriet Westbrook in August 1811.

Encouraged to pursue writing, Shelley became focused on political and religious subjects. His pamphlets reflect the influence of writers like Jean-Jacques Rousseau and Thomas Paine. Shelley also wrote personal and emotional poems that he kept in a private journal. During 1812 and 1813, Shelley and Harriet visited London, where Shelley connected with friends, publishers, and literary figures. Among these was William Godwin, a radical philosopher Shelley admired. Godwin and his deceased wife (Mary Wollstonecraft) had three daughters, all of whom fell for Shelley; but Shelley fell in love with Mary, the youngest. Outraged and heartbroken, Harriet refused an open marriage and abandoned Shelley. He and Mary ran away together on July 27, 1814, enjoying six weeks in Europe before returning home when they ran out of money. Shunned upon their return, Shelley had to work hard to earn money for himself and Mary. In November, Mary gave birth to a son named Charles. When Shelley's grandfather died in January, Shelley inherited a substantial sum of money. With the couple's financial situation now greatly improved, Shelley was free to focus on his poetry.

In January 1816, Mary gave birth to another son, William. When Mary's sister Claire became Lord George Gordon Byron's mistress, the Shelleys went with her to Lake Geneva to see him. Byron was also a poet, and he and Shelley became fast friends, discussing poetry and philosophy. During this trip, Byron challenged everyone to write a ghost story, and Mary's story became the famed novel *Frankenstein*. Meanwhile, Shelley found the natural surroundings inspiring to his poetic spirit.

The Shelleys' return to England brought the tragic news of the suicides of Mary's other sister and of Harriet. Harriet's death led to lengthy court proceedings concerning their children, who were ultimately placed with a guardian. Shelley married Mary on December 30, 1816.

their individual poems, and submit them to some sort of judging, often publication. Shelley and Smith agreed to write separate poems inspired by a passage they read by the Greek historian Diodorus Siculus. They agreed to write their sonnets about Ozymandias and submit them (with pen names) for publication. Shelley's sonnet was published first, followed by Smith's submission the next month. Today, Shelley's "Ozymandias" is one of his most famous poems.

AUTHOR BIOGRAPHY

Shelley was born on August 4, 1792, to Sir Timothy and Elizabeth Shelley in Sussex, England. He was one of six children, of whom he was the eldest brother. Shelley's halcyon days at the family estate did not prepare him for the bullying by other boys at Syon House Academy, in which he enrolled in 1802. Still, he gained a love for, and education in, sciences such as astronomy and chemistry.

At the age of twelve, Shelley entered Eton College, an elite boys school whose students were drawn from the British aristocracy. During his teenage years, Shelley found that he was very interested in romance. Not surprisingly, love and

They moved to Marlow, where the environment suited Shelley's writing muse, and the couple interacted with such writers as John Keats and Smith. Notably, "Ozymandias" was written during a sonnet contest between Shelley and Smith. Both poets' works were initially accepted for publication by the *Examiner*, although Shelley's appeared first. He wrote the poem in December, 1817, and it was printed in January, 1818. Shelley later included it in *Rosalind and Helen, A Modern Eclogue; with Other Poems*, published in 1819. A family trip to Italy in 1818 further inspired Shelley, and for the rest of his time there, he wrote more poetry and political reform treatises.

During 1822, Mary was dejected and alone. Shelley, on the other hand, was content and carefree, spending the summer sailing and writing. On July 8, however, Shelley's boat encountered a storm that killed both Shelley and his sailing companion. Their bodies were recovered ten days later. Because of Italian law, the bodies had to be cremated, and Shelley's ashes were buried near his friend Keats's remains in the Protestant Cemetery in Rome. Mary and the children returned to England.

POEM TEXT

I met a traveller from an antique land
Who said: Two vast and trunkless legs of stone
Stand in the desert ... Near them, on the sand,
Half sunk, a shattered visage lies, whose frown,
And wrinkled lip, and sneer of cold command,   5
Tell that its sculptor well those passions read
Which yet survive, stamped on these lifeless
        things,
The hand that mocked them, and the heart that
        fed:
And on the pedestal these words appear:
'My name is Ozymandias, king of kings: 10
Look on my works, ye Mighty, and despair!'
Nothing beside remains. Round the decay
Of that colossal wreck, boundless and bare
The lone and level sands stretch far away.

POEM SUMMARY

Lines 1–2

In "Ozymandias," the reader is receiving the information of the poem second-hand. The speaker describes what someone else told him. The speaker

is merely a go-between relating information from the "traveller from an antique land" to the reader. Shelley does this to increase the distance between the mighty figure that once was Ozymandias and the present. Not only does the poem describe the rubble that once was his kingdom, but the speaker is not even looking directly at the rubble. The emotional result is greatly reduced, as when a student reads about an historical event or a piece of art rather than visiting it himself.

The poem begins with the speaker saying that he met a "traveller from an antique land," which brings to mind a country like Greece or Egypt. This traveler told the speaker that, in the middle of a desert, there are pieces of an ancient statue. First, the traveler describes two huge disembodied legs.

Lines 3–5

The legs are said to be standing in the sand of the desert. Near the legs, partially buried in the sand is the statue's broken face. These two body parts—the legs and the face—are at opposite ends of the body, so the resulting image is one that is very chaotic, inhuman, and unintimidating. On the broken face, the traveler could see the expression. It was one with a frown, wrinkled lip, and a "sneer of cold command."

Lines 6–8

The sculptor was very precise in his craftsmanship, creating a very complex and realistic facial expression. The overall effect of these features is harsh. The traveler himself comments that the sculptor clearly understood the driving passion and ambition of his subject. In fact, the traveler suggests that the passions "yet survive, stamped on these lifeless things." Mindful of the lifelessness of the broken pieces of statue, the traveler can still sense the passion that the sculptor strove to preserve in the face. The traveler also notes the "hand that mocked them [the ruler's people], and the heart that fed." This refers to the power of the king's hand to gesture and give commands, all of which reinforced his position of authority over his people. His hand mocked his people; he kept them well below him so that they could not threaten him. Yet at the same time, the ruler was human. He had a heart that made sure his people were fed. Ozymandias used his power to an extent to care for the needs of his people, whether in an attempt to be a good steward of his subjects or to ensure that his rule would continue by maintaining the favor of his people.

Lines 9–11

The last thing the traveler describes about the statue is the pedestal on which it once stood. The pedestal contains the words that Ozymandias wanted to communicate to his own generation and those that would come after him; the words reflect his pride and arrogance. It reads, "My name is Ozymandias, king of kings: / Look on my works, ye Mighty, and despair!"

Lines 12–14

These words are intensely ironic and provide the springboard into most of the thematic material of the poem. After all, as the traveler describes, all around the pedestal is nothingness. A "colossal wreck" of an old statue surrounded by endless sand is all that remains. The landscape is vast and barren.

THEMES

Power

"Ozymandias" is a political poem about the illusion of fame and power. In the poem, Ozymandias was so proud of his own power and so bent on asserting it that he commissioned a great sculpture of himself glorifying his own authority. He must have believed that his political (and, given the time in which the sculpture would have been made) military power was an integral part of his own identity and purpose; after all, the way he chose to be depicted in the sculpture has all the hallmarks of strong rulership. The face is stern and resolute, appearing to be unswayed by anyone with less power than he. The hand keeps his people humble, yet Ozymandias is also the one who ensures that his people are fed. His power is such that his people seemingly would not be able to provide for their own needs without him. In all, the figure of Ozymandias is a commanding and powerful one.

The depiction of power is only part of Shelley's intent in the poem, however, and not even the most important part. More important to Shelley is showing how this great and mighty authority figure is ultimately reduced to rubble. The power he once possessed is long gone by the telling of the poem, and Ozymandias's great monument to his fame as a ruler is eroded by time and the elements. Ozymandias is no longer an intimidating figure at all, and he commands

TOPICS FOR FURTHER STUDY

- Read about the pyramids and the Sphinx in Egypt to learn what their purpose was and why they were built on such an enormous scale. Also, see what you can find out about the adverse effects of the desert climate on these ancient monuments. How are historians and archaeologists taking measures to preserve them? Based on your findings, write a script that could be used by tour guides.

- Choose another of Shelley's famous poems (such as "Hymn on Intellectual Beauty," "Ode to the West Wind," "Mont Blanc," or "To a Skylark") and compare and contrast it to "Ozymandias." Prepare a lesson plan that leads your fellow students through the two poems, suggests conclusions, and prompts the students to make their own observations.

- Using an art form of your choice (painting, sketching, sculpture, digital, etc.), illustrate "Ozymandias." Your depiction should accurately follow the information contained in the poem, although you may take artistic license with additional details or elements.

- What would the adherents of the movement known as literary realism have had to say about this poem? Research the realists' literary point of view, take on the persona of a realistic critic, and write a review of "Ozymandias."

no respect from the "traveller from an antique land," the speaker, or the reader.

Pride

Akin to the theme of power is the theme of pride. Ozymandias was clearly a proud ruler who seems to have been as determined to hold onto power as he was to proclaim it to all generations. There were numerous rulers throughout history who possessed strength, stability, wisdom, and the respect of their people and other nations, and some of them felt compelled to glorify themselves in art and architecture, as did Ozymandias.

While it is possible that the statue described in the poem could have been commissioned by someone other than the king, the traveler indicates that the sculptor knew his subject well. The sculptor was clearly close to Ozymandias, given access to his motives and leadership style in a way that enabled him to carve a realistic face, and to understand the symbolism of the king's hand and heart. These clues lead to the conclusion that Ozymandias oversaw the sculpture, or at the very least, the artist was caught up in the king's pride. Either way, Ozymandias's pride is clearly reflected in the statue.

Ozymandias's pride is also evident in the inscription on the pedestal. It reads, "My name is Ozymanidas, king of kings: Look on my works, ye Mighty, and despair!" This assertive statement to other mighty men is swollen with pride. He calls himself "king of kings," indicating that he sees himself as the greatest of all kings. Then he tells the viewer to observe all he has done and realize that he (the viewer) is tiny in comparison. The viewer's reaction is supposed to be utter despair at his own inferiority. Of course, Ozymandias had this inscription placed on a statue that was intended to last for hundreds of years, reminding future generations of his greatness, power, and accomplishments.

History

"Ozymandias" is a bit of history told by a traveler to the speaker, who then tells it to the reader. It has a strong tie to the oral tradition that has kept literary and historical traditions and lessons alive for hundreds of years. This fact alone prompts the reader to look for an historical lesson in the poem. The lesson reveals itself early; the poem is a cautionary tale about the transitory nature of rulers and their nations. After all, not only is Ozymandias gone, but so is the rest of his particular slice of civilization. The poem is a reminder of the historical reality of cycles of authority and the rise and fall of nations. Because the statue is from an ancient civilization, and others have come and gone between Ozymandias and the speaker's present, the reader can cull a historical lesson. Present-day readers would be wise to learn from Ozymandias and not repeat his mistake of allowing pride to seduce him into believing that his greatness would be admired forever. The poem also demonstrates that tyrannical rulers are nothing new, and that this tendency in man should be watched for among those in power.

STYLE

Sonnet

"Ozymandias" was the result of a sonnet competition with Smith. Shelley succeeded in containing his expression within the confines of the sonnet; the poem is fourteen lines of iambic pentameter, which are very traditional elements. Shelley breaks from tradition in his rhyme scheme, however. Rather than adhere to the English or Petrarchan rhyme schemes, Shelley does something different in "Ozymandias." The rhyme scheme is ABABACDCEDEFEF. What is interesting about this rhyme scheme is that it reinforces the subject and theme of the poem. Many skilled poets create verse that is so well-crafted that every element seems to strengthen the work, and Shelley is no exception. Here, the rhyme scheme actually evolves from start to finish. There is not a rhyme scheme separating an octave and a sestet; there is not a change at the end to finish with a neat couplet. The rhyme scheme of "Ozymandias" gradually changes over time, just as the subject matter (Ozymandias's statue) does. The last two lines have little in common with the first two, just as the rubble of Ozymandias's statue has little in common with the original structure. In both cases, the form is entirely different; only the subject is the same.

Metaphor

"Ozymandias" is at heart a metaphor. The statue represents the kings and kingdoms of the past, subject to the ravages of time, nature, and their own failings. The description of the statue and its inscription reveals tremendous pride and lost power. The statue, once magnificent, lies in ruins in the middle of a desert. It is a metaphor for all kingdoms, which eventually pass out of time to make room for another kingdom, ruler, or ideology. Shelley demonstrates that nothing lasts forever, even a ruler as powerful and fearsome as Ozymandias.

Irony

The inscription and placement of the statue brings a strong sense of irony to the poem. Although in its heyday, the statue's warning to look at Ozymandias's works and despair would have struck fear and reverence into the hearts of onlookers, the setting in the poem is quite different. The inscription reads, "Look on my works, ye Mighty, and despair!" Now, the works are gone and nothing remains but a landscape of endless sand. There are no buildings, monuments, military regiments, or palaces. The "works" seem to be wind and sand—hardly a cause for despair and terror. Ozymandias's pride appears foolish in this setting, and he seems to invite the mocking that he once doled out to his people. It is also ironic that the works that have survived all these years are not Ozymandias's works at all, but the artist's.

HISTORICAL CONTEXT

Romantic Movement

The Romantic Movement in England took place between the publication of William Wordsworth's *Lyrical Ballads* in 1798 and the death of Charles Dickens in 1870. This was during difficult and uncertain times, as the Napoleonic Wars were underway, England faced financial difficulties, the Industrial Revolution brought both hope and despair, and new philosophies such as utilitarianism were finding a voice.

The Romantics elevated the perceived value of the individual, as well as of nature and the wild. Romantic writers tended toward emotional expression that often cycled between ecstasy and despair. The Romantics had an interest in history and mysticism. Symbolism finds its way into much Romantic literature, and writers favored imagination over realism. Although optimism and hope characterized much Romantic literature, cynicism was sometimes expressed in satire. The optimism of the Romantics was not always passive, however, and many who were attracted to the Romantic mindset were more easily swept up in movement for reform and rebellion. Byron, for example, fought for Italy against Austria, and later went to fight against the Turks with Greece for independence. He died in Greece from illness during the war.

Romantic poetry is regarded by many readers as the most accessible and beautiful of the Romantic literature. The dominant Romantic poets were Shelley, Wordsworth, Keats, Byron, Samuel Taylor Coleridge, Robert Browning, Matthew Arnold, and Lord Alfred Tennyson. Of course, the Romantic novelists produced some of the greatest works of fiction; they include Dickens, Jane Austen, Emily and Charlotte Brontë, William Makepeace Thackeray, and George Eliot. The atmosphere of debate, reform, and philosophical inquiry led to an outpouring of criticism and social commentary by writers such as Godwin, John Stuart Mill, and John Ruskin.

Ramses II

Most literary scholars agree that "Ozymandias" is based on the ancient Egyptian ruler Ramses II, or Ramses the Great (1302–1213 B.C.E.). Smith and Shelley had read about him from the work of the Greek historian Diodorus Siculus, who related an inscription describing Ramses as a great king whose works could not be surpassed. As a ruler, Ramses is remembered for his many imposing monuments, as well as for his roles as warrior, king, and peacemaker who made Egypt a world power again. In the years before Ramses's reign, Egypt lacked timber resources and other materials possessed by neighboring lands. Egypt was also politically and militarily weakened, and thus was vulnerable to being invaded and overtaken. Because of these threats to the kingdom, Ramses's father (the pharaoh) had his son trained in battle and military leadership. When he was twenty-five years old, Ramses became pharaoh following his father's death.

In ancient Egypt, the pharaoh held absolute power, although he was expected to rule and treat his people honorably. Ramses was determined to be a monument builder and make a name for himself. He went so far as to remove the names of other pharaohs on existing monuments and replace them with his own name. Ramses's works indicate that he associated himself with the sun god, Ra. The sun imagery compelled the Egyptians to give Ramses greater loyalty. Historians and archaeologists consider the two rock-cut temples at Abu Simbel to be among Ramses's most impressive surviving structures. The temple of Amun-Ra and Ramses features four sixty-seven-foot tall statues of Ramses. In the thirty-first year of his reign, however, an earthquake struck, destroying the top half of one of the statues.

Ramses even sought to construct a new Egyptian capital near his birthplace in the eastern Delta. The city was named "Domain of Ramses Great-of-Victories," but little of the city remains today. Another interesting historical feature of Ramses's construction efforts were battle reliefs. Although Ramses was a skilled and courageous warrior and general who saw many victories, he also suffered military defeats and land losses. But reading the reliefs, an observer

COMPARE
&
CONTRAST

- **1817:** Shelley's "Ozymandias" describes the ruins of a statue of a once-great leader. The expression on the statue's face and the threatening inscription demonstrate the power and harshness of the ruler.

  Today: Saddam Hussein was executed on December 30, 2006, and the war for Iraqi freedom continues after years of struggle. People all over the world still remember the image, in April 2003, of American troops toppling a twenty-foot tall statue of Saddam in Baghdad. Saddam had fled the city, and bringing down the statue represented the destruction of Saddam's reign in Iraq.

- **1817:** The Romantic Period in England is dominated by poets and novelists. Poetry is read widely and appreciated by readers from all segments of society. England takes great pride in its rich poetic heritage, and the Romantic Period became a particularly vibrant movement in this area.

  Today: Readers who choose to read poetry for leisure represent a small percentage of readership. Although students are still exposed to a wide variety of poetry in high school and college, the reading population (which is on the decline) is more interested in fiction and nonfiction than in poetry.

- **1817:** Artifacts from Egypt are just making their way to England in a traveling exhibit. The Romantic Period is characterized by a degree of interest in history, and this atmosphere generates interest in such artifacts. Until now, educated people like Shelley have only read about ancient civilizations in books and learned about them in lectures.

  Today: Archaeologists have made major strides in the last 200 years, and most major cities have Egyptian artifacts in their museums. In the 1990s, there was a major traveling exhibit of artifacts from Ramses II's reign.

would believe that Ramses had handily defeated his enemies in every battle.

Ramses is remembered as a powerful and accomplished king who brought strength and stability to Egypt. He was skilled at international relations, while also reinforcing his status among his own people. He died after sixty-seven years of rule. He was buried in the Valley of the Kings, but robbers stole from, desecrated, and burned the tomb. After being rewrapped and then moved twice, the mummy of Ramses is now in Cairo's Egyptian Museum.

CRITICAL OVERVIEW

Among critics and readers, "Ozymandias" has been a favorite. Critics note that although it is something of a departure from Shelley's poetry, it is in line with his political writings. They also

find the poem accessible and easily understood as the cautionary tale that it is. Critics familiar with Shelley's work as a whole are aware that Shelley's political writings were biting and called for reform. He had no sympathy for injustice or authoritarian rule, so his depiction of Ozymandias's crumbling legacy is certainly expressive of his views of politics. Writing in *ELH*, Christopher R. Miller identifies the deep cynicism of the poem when he writes, "'Ozymandias' might as well be the name for an obsolete god rather than an earthly monarch, and Shelley is really dismissing both: gods bowed to as monarchs, and tyrants worshipped as gods."

While commentators are drawn into Shelley's imagery and layers of meaning, it is the message inadvertently sent through time by Ozymandias that has inspired the most critical commentary. Miller states pointedly that the poem "concerns not only the physical ruins of a statue, but also the historical eclipse of a name." In

Magill Book Reviews, a critic remarks about Ozymandias that "he is to be pitied, if not disdained, rather than held in awe and fear." The critic further observes that Shelley's message is that "the forces of mortality and mutability, described brilliantly in the concluding lines, will erode and destroy all our lives." John Rodenbeck reaches the same conclusion in *Alif: Journal of Comparative Poetics:*

> In Shelley's … view of history, all empires are foredoomed to disappear and for a work of what we call art merely to have outlived one of them hardly signifies anything. If that work is merely a portrait of a tyrant, moreover, the value one places upon it … may well be largely ironical, the irony being present or absent precisely to the degree that the tyranny it was originally supposed to memorialize is in fact remembered at all.

In some ways, the message of "Ozymandias" is to be an encouragement to those who are suffering under an unjust regime, or who are angered by one. Rodenbeck remarks, "What it seeks to remind its readers, instead, is that no tyrannical power lasts forever, no matter how efficient its repressive apparatus or how deep its degree of self-deceit."

CRITICISM

Jennifer Bussey

Bussey holds a master's degree in interdisciplinary studies and a bachelor's degree in English literature. She is an independent writer specializing in literature. In the following essay, she draws parallels and contrasts to the statue described in Shelley's "Ozymandias" and the statue of King Nebuchadnezzar described in the Book of Daniel.

In "Ozymandias," the speaker describes meeting a traveler who tells him about a toppled statue in the desert. The statue was once impressive, large in stature, with a look of stern determination and might. It is a statue of Ozymandias, an ancient king who took pride in his power and authority. Ozymandias attempted to preserve his own legacy of power and fame by building great monuments to himself, but ultimately the statue is a pile of rubble surrounded by endless sand. Building statues to honor themselves was common among ancient rulers, and in the Book of Daniel, King Nebuchadnezzar of Babylon has a dream about a similar statue. The prophet Daniel interprets the dream for him, and the king

WHAT DO I READ NEXT?

- James Bieri's *Percy Bysshe Shelley: A Biography; Youth's Unextinguished Fire, 1792–1816* and *Percy Bysshe Shelley: A Biography; Exile of Unfulfilled Renown, 1816–1822* (both 2005) offer a thorough look at Shelley's life. From birth all the way to death, Bieri relates the influences and events in Shelley's life that formed his poetic voice, relationships, and personality.

- T. G. H. James's *Ramses II* (2002) presents a wealth of historical information about this pharaoh and his rule, alongside photographs of his buildings, pictures of artifacts from his rule, and maps of his kingdom. It is a thorough look at the king, the legacy he hoped to leave, and what is left to understand him.

- *Percy Bysshe Shelley as a Philosopher and Reformer* was released by the Michigan Historical Reprint Series in 2005. It is a digital reproduction of a nineteenth-century document containing a paper about Shelley's political ideas read to the New York Liberal Club in 1875.

- Edited by Donald H. Reiman and Neil Frastat, *Shelley's Poetry and Prose (Norton Critical Edition*, 2003) is a comprehensive collection of Shelley's writings, along with critical input from numerous scholars. Reiman and Frastat provide contextual headnotes, cross-referenced footnotes, and selections from the latest in Shelley scholarship.

- Edited by Lionel Trilling and Harold Bloom, *The Oxford Anthology of English Literature, Volume IV: Romantic Poetry and Prose* (1973) has become a textbook for numerous literature courses for its complete look at Romanticism. The work of Wordsworth, Keats, Shelley, Byron, and Coleridge is featured.

later attempts to build this great statue to himself. What is it about statues that appeals to a king's pride, vanity, and need for immortality? Both Ozymandias and Nebuchadnezzar tried to preserve their greatness through art, but neither ruler's artistic forms lasted forever. Perhaps they hoped that the work of a great artist on something as durable as stone or marble would surely proclaim their glory forever. Perhaps they were essentially insecure and needed to feel that something much larger and longer-lasting would continue their legacies long after their deaths. Rather than pursue accomplishments that have truly meaningful and long-lasting effects, they chose lifeless statues.

In Shelley's poem, the ruler Ozymandias (based on Ramses II, or "Ramses the Great") is remembered only by a crumbling statue in the middle of a desert. The statue was once impressive and certainly must have evoked fear and respect in his people, and maybe even in his enemies. The face is described as having a frown, a sneer, and a wrinkled lip. The expression is so telling about the character of Ozymandias that the traveler describing the statue is sure that the sculptor must have understood the king's passions and nature. What is even more telling is that this description of the face is based on what is left of that part of the statue. Part of the face is broken and shattered. The traveler also describes the hand that mocked his own people, and the heart that fed them. As a leader, Ozymandias was stern and asserted his superiority, but as a human, he made sure his people's needs were met. All of this is preserved in the statue of the king, but the inscription on his pedestal is placed in quotes, indicating that these words typify the king's statements to the world in which he lived. The inscription reads, "My name is Ozymandias, king of kings: Look on my works, ye Mighty, and despair!" It is a daring and threatening statement that in its present context becomes deeply ironic and disturbing. For all his might, wealth, and power, he was ultimately sentenced to the same void that his subjects were.

The poem "Ozymandias" was the product of a friendly sonnet competition with a friend and fellow poet, Smith. Having read about Ramses, Smith and Shelley decided to write about the same topic and submit their poems for publication. Both were published, Smith's one month after Shelley's. What is interesting about Smith's

> WHAT IS IT ABOUT STATUES THAT APPEALS TO A KING'S PRIDE, VANITY, AND NEED FOR IMMORTALITY? BOTH OZYMANDIAS AND NEBUCHADNEZZAR TRIED TO PRESERVE THEIR GREATNESS THROUGH ART, BUT NEITHER RULER'S ARTISTIC FORMS LASTED FOREVER."

version is that it makes a direct reference to Babylon. He writes, "The City's gone, —Nought but the Leg remaining to disclose / The site of this forgotten Babylon." This reference to Babylon calls to mind another statue described in the Bible in the second chapter of the Book of Daniel, a story that takes place in Babylon.

In the Book of Daniel, the prophet Daniel is in captivity in Babylon. He is a servant to King Nebuchadnezzar. When the king has a dream he does not understand, he calls his advisors to first tell him what the dream was (to test their ability to understand things supernaturally) and then to tell him what it meant. They are unable to do so, but after praying, Daniel is able to describe the king's dream about a strange statue, and then interpret it for him. Nebuchadnezzar's dream was about a statue with a head of gold, chest and arms of silver, middle and thighs of bronze, legs of iron, and feet of iron mixed with clay. In the end, the entire statue is destroyed by a stone not cut from human hands. Daniel explains to the king that each metal represents a kingdom. The gold is the Babylonian empire, ruled by Nebuchadnezzar himself. The silver represents the Medo-Persian empire; the bronze represents the Greeks, led by Alexander the Great; the iron and the iron mixed with clay represent a kingdom divided into ten parts. The stone represents the divine kingdom, led by Christ, that ultimately destroys and replaces the earthly kingdoms portrayed in the statue.

Because Nebuchadnezzar was a powerful and wealthy king, he would immediately understand an image of a statue as something created to glorify and memorialize a king or kingdom. That his kingdom was the head of gold spoke to his pride, because the statue's value—and that of the kingdoms it describes—decreases as it moves from the head to the feet. Rather than take the dream interpretation as good counsel and move forward to rule more wisely, Nebuchadnezzar waited about sixteen years and then, with no second (silver) empire overtaking him, decided to build an actual statue. But because his kingdom was the gold, he built the entire statue of gold as a monument to himself and to Babylon. His statue was ninety feet high, and in no way was meant to represent divine wisdom or faith; it was a very tangible reflection of Nebuchadnezzar's pride and arrogance. The same pride and arrogance that is so apparent in the ruins of Ozymandias's statue—a statue that was intended to glorify his power.

In both cases, the statue ultimately does nothing to strengthen the king's rule or preserve his legacy. If anything, Ozymandias's statue only tarnished the memory of his kingdom. And Nebuchadnezzar's statue did not last any more than Babylon did; the Medo-Persian Empire (the silver in the dream statue) took over Babylon in 539 B.C.E. While both Ozymandias and Nebuchadnezzar expected their greatness to be evident in the fact that they could create things of such value and scale, they failed to learn that a lasting legacy does not come from objects. For Ozymandias, his kingdom is gone and all that is left is a statue that he relied on an artist to make. It is actually the artist's work that has staying power and is admired by future generations. The traveler describing the statue remarked not about Ozymandias, but about the sculptor. And in Nebuchadnezzar's case, he would be a footnote in history without Daniel's act of writing the story of his Babylonian captivity. It is the Book of Daniel that is preserved, not anything Nebuchadnezzar created to glorify himself.

The stories of these two statues point to a truth that the power-hungry kings could not see. Statues are mere objects—beautiful and impressive—but objects nonetheless. Because the kings were only interested in the statues as monuments, they saw them as the means to their ends. The statues were to be in service to the king's power and glory. Neither king had any real understanding of what lasts, which are the things of the human spirit. Ozymandias's example illustrates the enduring character of art to capture a historical, emotional, and expressive moment for all time. Ozymandias's legacy is actually not in his hands at all, but solely in the hands of the sculptor. The expression that Ozymandias is remembered

for is the one the sculptor put on his stone face. The inscription is the one the sculptor etched in the pedestal. And the mighty legs and hands are all the work of the sculptor. The sculptor's perception becomes reality, and it becomes history. Nebuchadnezzar's great palaces and his lavish city with all of its prosperity did not last. He felt bullet-proof, so he missed the lesson in the dream; that his kingdom will be replaced by another, which will be replaced by another and so on, until a divine kingdom replaces them all. Cities, laws, buildings, and statues do not last. The will of God has power over all of them, but Nebuchadnezzar did not learn to be faithful until very late in life. Had he and Ozymandias put aside their pride during the zenith of their reigns, there is no telling what kinds of lasting legacies each king might have left.

Source: Jennifer Bussey, Critical Essay on "Ozymandias," in *Poetry for Students*, Gale, 2008.

Christopher R. Miller

In the following excerpt, Miller examines Shelley's attitude toward the concept of heaven, a concept that Shelley initially outlined in his pamphlet Declaration of Rights. *Miller focuses on the manifestations of Shelley's attitude in several of his works, including "Ozymandias." Of this poem, Miller contends that Shelley's treatment of the name of the title character is similar to his treatment of the terms heaven and God.*

. . . As the vehement attack in the *Declaration* suggests, there was a strongly political cast to Shelley's concern with heaven. Conceived as a kingdom, heaven merely replicated earthly notions of monarchy, empire, and class privilege; conceived as a divine reward, it enabled a cynical deferral of earthly justice, an illusory coda to life's struggles. Such a critique is made with pithy force in Blake's "Chimney Sweeper" poem in the *Songs of Experience*, when the young speaker of the title protests that God's priest and king "make up a heaven of our misery." The phrase "make up" subtly implies two acts of creation, one ideological, the other material: the imaginative projection of a heavenly reward out of the wreckage of earthly life, and the construction of a "heaven" of earthly luxuries for the few on the backs of the unfortunate many.

To understand Shelley's poetics of heaven is to see several things about the poet more clearly: his distrust of orthodoxy and superstition, his ideas about language, his poetic geography of time and place, his desire for immortality, and his own deeply self-questioning nature. I begin this essay by describing Shelley's moral, political, and philosophical objections to traditional ideas of heaven, and then consider these objections as they are manifested and complicated in the imaginative work of *Queen Mab* (1813), *Prometheus Unbound* (1820), and a seldom-studied poem called the "Ode to Heaven" (1820). All three works, I argue, are invested in a process of redefining and reimagining heaven. In *Queen Mab* the soul of Ianthe is brought to an otherworldly realm of instruction in which she is given a new rhetoric of heaven and sent back to earth; and in *Prometheus Unbound* the deposition of Jupiter from heaven results in a freshened sense of the promise of the word "heaven." *Queen Mab* might be classified as a didactic poem and *Prometheus Unbound* a lyric drama, but despite their generic differences, they share similar mythopoetic concerns. The latter poem, famously lacking in dramatic action, is better understood as a drama of lexical transformation, which can be signally tracked in varying iterations of "heaven." This strategy of redefinition finds an apt frame in the three-part structure of the "Ode to Heaven," in which three choric participants dramatically differ on their conceptions of the subject of their hymn. Odes traditionally ask how best to praise their subjects; this one is remarkable for its radical uncertainty over what is being praised (or derided)—an uncertainty that reflects Shelley's own.

Scholars of Shelley have long seen the poet as wavering between binary extremes: Lockean empiricism v. Berkeleyan idealism (Earl Wasserman); deconstructive skepticism v. visionary affirmation (Tilottama Rajan); the perceptual v. the sublime (Angela Leighton). In examining Shelley's poetics of heaven, I propose to elaborate these binaries in terms of a productive tension over a problematic word—between naming and refusing to name, visualization and blankness, the visible and the invisible. As an antiauthoritarian thinker, Shelley dismisses the word "Heaven" as a "poisonous name" of orthodox superstition; but as a poet, he mines it for its suggestive possibilities. For Shelley, heaven was at the crossroads between political critique and aesthetic creation, doubt and belief; and in the years after his curtly dismissive attack in the *Declaration of Rights*, he went on to offer more richly imaginative statements of what the word might mean instead.

I. Poisonous Names

The animus toward heaven that Shelley expresses in the *Declaration of Rights* is composed of several motives: youthful rebellion, personal renunciation, moral critique, philosophical speculation, and linguistic reform. Most obviously, as the disparaging reference to priests and grandmothers suggests, Shelley was kicking against the pieties of elders. (In precise familial terms, he was off by a generation, since it was his father Timothy who threatened to disown him for his atheistic provocations.) But he was also disavowing beliefs that he had recently held. As he would later recall in the "Hymn to Intellectual Beauty" (1816), he himself once "called on poisonous names with which our youth is fed" (53), including "Heaven," the verbal residue of unanswered questions about death and mutability:

> No voice from some sublimer world hath ever
> To sage or poet these responses given—
> Therefore the name of God and ghosts and
>   Heaven,
> Remain the records of their vain endeavour.
> (25–28)

To refer to "God" and "Heaven" as "names" was to echo the nominalist skepticism of Locke and Hume—to suggest that "God" and "Heaven" are words rather than essences, and signifiers without perceivable referents. Such words, in Shelley's phrasing, are "records"—memories, in the etymological sense of the word, of past endeavors in faith. A word, then, is a kind of artifact—a point later made in the archeological meditation of "Ozymandias" (1818), which concerns not only the physical ruins of a statue but also the historical eclipse of a name. The verbal inscription on the king's crumbled effigy—"My name is Ozymandias, King of Kings, / Look on my works, ye mighty, and despair!"—could indeed be described as the record of a vain endeavor. Heralded by the Biblical superlative, "King of Kings," "Ozymandias" might as well be the name for an obsolete god rather than an earthly monarch, and Shelley is really dismissing both: gods bowed to as monarchs, and tyrants worshipped as gods.

Shelley's early philosophical struggle with the "name[s]" "God" and "Heaven" is evident in a series of letters he wrote in 1811 to two close confidants, his Oxford classmate (and collaborator on *The Necessity of Atheism*) Thomas Jefferson Hogg and his schoolmaster friend Elizabeth Hitchener. In a strategy of triangulation, Shelley used Hitchener's religious belief and Hogg's vehement atheism as foils to the velleities of his own free-floating speculation; with one, he could be an iconoclast, with the other, he could play the utopian dreamer. Writing to Hitchener, he argues that God is "a name which expresses the unknown cause, the suppositious origin of all existence." The word "God," he concludes, "analogises with the universe, as the soul of man to his body, as the vegetative power to vegetables, the stony power to stones." On the premise that God is fundamentally a name rather than a thing, Shelley aptly demonstrates its superfluity by a linguistic demonstration—the adjectival derivation of "stony power" from stones and "vegetative power" from vegetables. In a letter to Hogg, on the other hand, Shelley was not so quick to demote heaven:

> I love what is superior[,] what is excellent, or what I conceive to be so, & wish, ardently wish to be convinced of the existence of a God that so superior a spirit should derive happiness from my exertions—for Love is Heaven, & Heaven is Love. Oh! that it were. You think so, too,—yet you disbelieve the existence of an eternal omnipresent spirit.

Shelley's reversible equation suggests at least two possibilities: that all we know of love on earth effectively amounts to heaven and that the concept of heaven is informed by the experience of love. Characteristically, Shelley wavers between assertion ("Love is Heaven") and speculation ("Oh! that it were"), and between his own wishes and his friend's interpolated skepticism. The difference between the reductive definition of God and expansive definition of heaven is borne out in the poems that Shelley would later write: whereas he invents alternatives to God ("Power," the "Spirit of the Universe," and so forth), he exploits the versatility and ambiguity of heaven. In this respect, not all words were like material things: while "God," like "Ozymandias," was a verbal ruin, "Heaven" lived on in new forms.

Source: Christopher R. Miller, "Shelley's Uncertain Heaven," in *ELH*, Vol. 72, No. 3, Fall 2005, pp. 577–603.

James A. W. Heffernan

In the following excerpt, Heffernan notes that ekphrasis is the "literary representation of visual art." The critic explores the poetic use of ekphrasis by examining "Ozymandias" as well as John Keats's poem "Ode on a Grecian Urn."

... I chiefly wish to show how graphic art is represented in ekphrastic poetry and how a

> SHELLEY THUS REVEALS THAT IN SPITE OF ITS CLAIMS TO PERMANENCE, BOTH THE MATTER AND THE MEANING OF GRAPHIC ART CAN BE FUNDAMENTALLY CHANGED BY TIME, RECONSTITUTED BY SUCCESSIVE INTERPRETATIONS."

knowledge of ekphrastic traditions can help us understand this kind of representation in specific poems. Traditionally, I have argued, ekphrasis is narrational and prosopopoeial; it releases the narrative impulse that graphic art typically checks, and it enables the silent figures of graphic art to speak. I want to argue now that in "Ode on a Grecian Urn" and "Ozymandias," Keats and Shelley use these ekphrastic traditions to reflect on representation: not just on a particular work of graphic representation, but on the nature of representation itself.

Consider first what Keats does with the ekphrastic tradition of prosopopoeia that flows from the sepulchral epigrams I mentioned earlier. He opens the first stanza of his famous ode by apostrophizing the Grecian urn as a "still unravish'd bride of quietness." Then he himself threatens to ravish the bride by making her speak. "What leaf-fring'd legend," he asks, "haunts about they shape [?]" (l. 5). The quest for legend not only shows the narrative impulse asserting itself from the very beginning of this ekphrastic poem; it also signifies the urge to envoice the urn, for the word *legend* originally meant "to be read," and when a sepulchral inscription was read aloud by a traveler, the inscribed object spoke. But Keats's urn bears no inscription and refuses to answer the kinds of questions normally anticipated and answered by inscribed monuments. "What men or gods are these?" the speaker asks. Instead of saying something like, "I am the tomb of famous Glauca" or "My name is Ozymandias," the urn speaks only silence, voicing neither story nor circumstantial facts, saying nothing at all until it produces a final conundrum that transcends narrative and circumstance alike: "Beauty is truth, truth beauty" (l. 49) ...

Keats's poem makes the act of homage a work of critique, a verbal demonstration of all that must be sacrificed to make the idea of graphic representation at once beautiful and true.

This critical strain underlying the ostensible iconophilia of Keats's ode subtly connects it with another conspicuous example of romantic ekphrasis: Shelley's "Ozymandias." But Shelley's poem is explicitly iconoclastic. While Keats demonstrates that ekphrasis can criticize graphic art in the very act of paying homage to it, Shelley goes one step further, undermining the assumption that graphic art itself can pay lasting and unequivocal homage to what it represents . . .

Shelley's sonnet questions what Keats's ode takes wholly for granted: the imperishability of graphic art. While Keats confidently predicts that the urn will survive the wasting of the present generation as of so many others that came before it, Shelley foresees the ultimate dissolution of the statue. And to signify the imminence of this dissolution, Shelley complicates the opposition between graphic stasis and narrative movement in an extraordinary way: he verbally perpetuates a moment in the history of a statue. Sculpted to represent enduring greatness, it is gradually disintegrating, and Shelley catches it at a pregnant moment of transition between erectness and prostration: the standing legs recall the self-assertive majesty of the original monument while the shattered, half-sunk visage looks ahead to its final oblivion—its ultimate leveling—in "the lone and level sands."

In the sestet of this sonnet, Shelley follows ekphrastic tradition by recording the words on the pedestal and thus envoicing the statue, which resoundingly declares, "Look on my works, ye Mighty, and despair." But these words simply accentuate the transitional status of the monument. The single meaning they originally conveyed has disintegrated into a double meaning that looks backward and forward in time. Like the statue on which they are inscribed, the words at once recall the invincible assurance of Ozymandias and foretell the coming dissolution of his works.

The expression fixed on the shattered, half-sunk face, therefore, cannot serve as the pregnant moment of a narrative to be ekphrastically inferred or furnished about the life of Ozymandias himself. Instead, the fixity of the expression signifies the rigidity of Ozymandias's despotic arrogance, which has petrified his face in a "sneer of cold command" that the sculptor has at once imitated and obeyed, since he undoubtedly worked under orders from the ruler himself. Ozymandias sought to perpetuate his power through the medium of sculpture, through "lifeless things" that would permanently represent his personality. But the sculptor's hand mocks the passions that it represents, and time in turn mocks any aspirations that the sculptor might have had for the immortality of his art. Forever committed to one unchanging expression, neither Ozymandias nor the sculptor can command or control the leveling effects of time, which convert the face of power into an object of ridicule or—as with the grandiloquent inscription—impose upon its twisted features a meaning radically different from the one originally intended, so that what were once the frown and wrinkle and sneer of absolute authority become at last the marks and signs of desperation.

Shelley thus reveals that in spite of its claims to permanence, both the matter and the meaning of graphic art can be fundamentally changed by time, reconstituted by successive interpretations. As William Freedman has recently shown, the whole poem is a study in mediation. After the opening words it is spoken not by the poet himself but by a "traveller" he has met, which is of course Shelley's way of personifying or envoicing a text—his not yet definitely identified literary source. The poet draws the voice of the traveler from the text just as the traveler himself draws the voice of Ozymandias from the inscription on the pedestal. And in each case the relation is mediated. Shelley reads a text in which the traveler reports his reading of an inscription.

Before quoting the inscription and thus envoicing the statue as a whole, however, the traveler reads and envoices the sculpted visage. Its "frown, / And wrinkled lip, and sneer of cold command," he says, "*Tell* that the sculptor well those passions read, / Which yet survive, stamped on these lifeless things, / The hand that mocked them, and the heart that fed." The sculpted face graphically represents the expression of the living ruler, which originally signified passions that the sculptor has inferred or "read" from it. Between the sculpted face and the actual one, therefore, stands the interpretive act of the sculptor, who knows how to read faces well and to represent them in stone so that their expressions can *be* read—can tell us what they signify. Yet the sculpted face tells us as much about the sculptor's ability to read Ozymandias as about Ozymandias himself. As a result, we are led to compare the sculptor's reading of the ruler with the inscription—the ruler's own reading of himself and his works.

To compare the graphic representation and the verbal self-representation is to see that each corroborates the other. Ozymandias's statement can be read as a comment on the statue—clearly one of his most stupendous works—and the statue can be read as a graphic response to the statement, a way of interpreting it in stone. Neither statue nor statement, however, communicates what Ozymandias presumably intended by them both: an immutable assertion of his power. The meaning of both changes radically as the all-too-perishable medium in which they are wrought disintegrates.

The fact that the inscription will disintegrate along with the statue should cause us to question an inference that Shelley's iconoclasm tempts us to draw—which is that language surpasses graphic art in its power and durability. Paraphrasing what Horace said of his odes, Shelley might have said of this sonnet, "Exegi monumentum petra perennius"—I have built a monument more lasting than stone. Raising up his own little tower of words to mark the inexorable leveling of the ancient statue, Shelley makes manifest what virtually all ekphrasis latently reveals: the poet's ambition to make his words outlast their ostensible subject, to displace graphic representation with verbal representation. Yet the fate of everything wrought and inscribed by order of Ozymandias should prompt us to ask how long any work of representation, whether verbal or graphic, can endure. If words cut into stone cannot last, what will happen to words written on paper or even printed in a book? Will Shelley's own poem last as long as the statue of Ramses II, which was already well over a thousand years old when Didorus Siculus described it in the first century B.C.?

Shelley's sonnet leaves us with questions just as disturbing as those raised by Keats's ode. Though Keats is ostensibly iconophilic and Shelley iconoclastic, each in his own way stages a struggle for power between rival modes of representation and makes us see that neither gains absolute victory over the other. Neither verbal narrative nor graphic stasis can fully represent being; neither words nor sculpture can make absolute claims to permanence, stability, or truth. In these two ekphrastic poems, then, Keats and Shelley use the verbal representation of graphic art as a way to reveal the ultimate inadequacy of all representation.

Source: James A. W. Heffernan, "Ekphrasis and Representation," in *New Literary History*, Vol. 22, No. 2, Spring 1991, pp. 297–316.

John R. Greenfield

In the following excerpt, Greenfield gives a critical analysis of Shelley's life and work for the period immediately preceding and following the writing and publication of "Ozymandias."

While at Keswick Shelley conceived a plan to put his radical political ideas into action. He had been working on a pamphlet simply titled *An Address, to the Irish People* (1812), and nothing less would do than publishing it, distributing it, and delivering it in person to its intended audience, the oppressed Irish Catholics. Shelley, Harriet, and Eliza arrived in Dublin in February 1812 and began to distribute the pamphlet, which favored Catholic emancipation but cautioned the Irish to proceed slowly so as not to be drawn into violence. The influence of the philosophes, Jean-Jacques Rousseau, Thomas Paine, Godwin, and Mary Wollstonecraft is evident in the pamphlet, which ranges easily from the specific plight of the Irish to the need for "universal emancipation," clearly echoing Paine's international republicanism in its call for universal brotherhood. Shelley delivered a version of *An Address* to an audience on 28 February and was met with a mixed response, the crowd applauding the sections on Catholic emancipation and hissing some of his antireligious sentiments.

Another "Irish" pamphlet, *Proposals for an Association of those Philanthropists*, followed closely upon the first (March 1812). Despite Godwin's misgivings, expressed strongly to Shelley in letters, lest radical organizations might follow the path of the Jacobinical societies that led to the French Terror, Shelley realized that the Irish would not attain any degree of freedom without unity and organization. The *Proposals* are Shelley's earliest public statement of the way in which love and politics should be inseparable: "Love for humankind" should "place individuals at distance from self," thereby promoting "universal feeling." Shelley felt that he could do no more in Ireland, so the Shelleys and Eliza settled briefly in Cwm Elan, Wales, where Shelley continued to write radical pamphlets. He distilled the arguments in *An Address* and the *Proposals* in *Declaration of Rights*, a broadside which he distributed with the help of his servant Daniel Healey (or Hill), who was arrested, technically for distributing a broadside without a printer's name on it, but really because the material was subversive. This episode incensed Shelley about how little real freedom of the press existed in England; his response was another pamphlet, *A Letter to Lord Ellenborough* (1812), an eloquent argument in favor of freedom of the press and of speech. Rather than pleading his own case, Shelley wisely focuses on the well-publicized trial of Daniel Isaac Eaton, a London bookseller who had been sentenced to prison for publishing part 3 of Paine's *The Age of Reason.*

Amid financial difficulties, local gossip about an immoral household, and fears that Shelley himself might be arrested, the Shelleys and Eliza, now accompanied by Elizabeth Hitchener, who had joined them in Lynmouth, prudently decided to flee and stay for a while near Tremadoc, which attracted Shelley because of an embankment project that would claim land back from the sea. During this early period of his life, Shelley had quietly been composing poems in a notebook, which fell into the hands of the Esdaile family after Shelley's death and which was not published until this century, as *The Esdaile Notebook* (1964). The poems included therein are an interesting mix of very personal poems, treating his feelings for Harriet and some of his moments of despair and isolation, and public, political, and social poems, treating themes of liberty, the Irish cause, the plight of the poor, the futility of war, and his hatred of religious hypocrisy and monarchies. Partaking of the central metaphors of poetic discourse of this time, showing the influence of William Wordsworth, the poems in *The Esdaile Notebook* are written in straightforward language and reiterate the power of nature and the naturalness of poetry. Devoid of mythology, these poems rely upon common personal and political allusions, the eighteenth-century convention of abstractions, contemporary lyric forms and genres, and topical content. Writing these poems was for Shelley a kind of poet's apprenticeship, which he did not feel confident about bringing to the public's eye during his lifetime.

The Shelleys spent periods during 1812 and 1813 in London, where Shelley was able to make new acquaintances among liberal and literary circles and to renew earlier friendships such as those with Hogg and Leigh Hunt, a radical London publisher and writer who was to be a lifelong defender of Shelley. In addition, Shelley became a member of the Boinville circle, an informal literary discussion group, and met Thomas Hookham, a radical bookseller and publisher, and another aspiring writer, Thomas Love Peacock, who became a kind of friendly literary foil for Shelley and later one of his biographers. In October 1812 Shelley finally met his political father, Godwin, who, like Elizabeth Hitchener (expelled from the Shelley circle), failed to live up to Shelley's idealized image of him. Instead of inspiring Shelley with his political wisdom and intellect, Godwin became a nagging financial burden to Shelley for the rest of his life.

Shelley's major literary project at this time was *Queen Mab*, printed by his friend Hookham in May or June of 1813. *Queen Mab* is a political epic in which the fairy queen Mab takes the spirit of Ianthe (the name Percy and Harriet gave their first child, born in June 1813) on a time and space journey to reveal the ideal nature of humanity's potential behind the mistakes of history and the blind acceptance of "outward shows" of power. The poem reiterates many of the themes of Shelley's political pamphlets, attacking the oppressiveness of religious dogma and superstition as well as of customs and institutions such as the monarchy. The poem's perspective is utopian, viewing the pettiness and selfishness of the world from distant, lofty heights and suggesting the great potential of the uncorrupted human soul. The utopian and visionary perspectives of the poem foreshadow the apocalyptic and millennial vision of Shelley's later poetry. That Shelley was using poetry to convey radical political ideas in response to the threats of freedom of the press is clear in his feeling the necessity to assure Hookham that "a poem is safe: the iron-souled attorney general would scarcely dare to attack." Lest his philosophical or political points should get lost in the poetry, Shelley added copious prose notes to the end of the poem, the familiar attacks on religion, monarchy, and wealth, the advocacy of vegetarianism, free love, and free beliefs, and explanatory notes on geology, astronomy, necessity, and the labor theory of value. *Queen Mab* was distributed only privately at the time it was printed, but in 1821 it began to appear in unauthorized, pirated editions, somewhat to Shelley's embarrassment. Interestingly enough, the poem became a kind of radical bible to many in the Chartist movement in the 1830s and 1840s.

Once Shelley became a frequent visitor to the Godwin household, it was inevitable that he would meet the three young women living there: Mary Godwin, Jane (later Claire) Clairmont, and Fanny Imlay. It was equally inevitable that all three women would fall in love with Shelley in varying degrees and that Shelley should fall in love with Mary. As the daughter of Godwin and Mary Wollstonecraft (whose writings Shelley had already read and admired), Mary represented to Shelley an ideal offspring of two great minds. Growing up in the Godwin household had exposed Mary to ideas, and she could read freely in the books in Godwin's library; moreover, she had an independent mind and was willing to argue with Shelley, when they would go to talk by the grave of Mary's mother, rather than be passively molded by him, like Harriet. Perhaps the only real tragedy was that Shelley had not met Mary before he married Harriet. Although Shelley believed he was following Godwin's principles of free love in replacing Harriet with Mary as the object of his highest love and in offering Harriet to live with them as his sister rather than his wife, Godwin bitterly opposed the relationship, and Harriet became estranged and completely shattered. Knowing that Godwin and his wife would do what they could to stop them, Shelley and Mary, accompanied by Jane Clairmont, eloped on the night of 27 July 1814, first to Calais, then to Paris, and on to Switzerland. After a six weeks' stay, the three were forced to return to England because of money problems.

Upon their return to London, the Shelleys were ostracized for their elopement, especially by the Godwins, and Shelley, at least until his grandfather Bysshe died in January 1815, had to spend much of his time trying to raise money from post-obit bonds in order to meet Harriet's needs and satisfy his own many creditors and thus keep out of the hands of the bailiffs. Harriet gave birth to a son, Charles, in November 1814, and in February 1815 Mary gave birth prematurely to a child who died only two weeks later. In his usual pattern Hogg conceived a love for Mary, and Shelley, with Mary's initial consent, agreed to the experiment in free love, but Mary lost interest.

Shelley's only publication in 1814, *A Refutation of Deism: in a Dialogue*, is a two-pronged attack on what he regarded as the crumbling superstructure of the established institutions of religious belief in early-nineteenth-century England. Directed toward intellectuals and Deists, *A Refutation of Deism* employs two interlocutors, Eusebes and Theosophus, to pick apart the arguments supporting both Christianity and Deism, thus leaving atheism as the only rational ground to stand upon.

With improved finances and health in 1815, Shelley not only found the time to write poetry but began to develop a more sophisticated and symbolic style that foreshadows his mature productions. The volume published in 1816, *Alastor; or, The Spirit of Solitude: and Other Poems*, is Shelley's public initiation into the Romantic idiom of poetry pioneered by Wordsworth and perhaps directly inspired by the publication of *The Excursion* in 1814. Shelley had already served his apprenticeship in writing meditative poems in settings of solitude and nature's grandeur while he was in Wales some three or four years earlier.

Alastor, with its use of symbols, visionary elements, and mythic sources (the Narcissus-Echo myth in particular), marks a real advance over Shelley's earlier efforts in writing poetry. Thomas Love Peacock suggested the title to Shelley: Alastor, which refers not to the name of the Poet, but to an evil genius or avenging spirits of solitude. Certainly there are elements of autobiography in the poem, both in the sense that Shelley felt himself to be haunted by real (the bailiffs) or imagined (assailants) spirits at various times in his life and in the sense that in his personal relationships he had made and would again make the same mistake that the Poet makes: of seeking "in vain for a prototype of his conception" of the idealized part of himself. In the preface to the poem Shelley cautions against this solitary quest, warning not only that such pursuits will result in the neglect of one's social duties but that they will lead one to loneliness, alienation, and ultimately death.

Yet what gives *Alastor* vibrancy and tension—life—is that it is not a didactic morality poem; it is a subtle and complex poem in which the two kinds of poetry represented by the Narrator, the Wordsworthian poet of nature, and the visionary Poet of genius are drawn into a kind of complementary conflict. The Narrator relates the story of the Poet's life and quest, interspersing his narration with panegyrics to nature. Like his famous literary counterparts—Werther, St. Preux, the Solitary, Childe Harold—the Poet is alienated early in life, travels, and becomes a wanderer searching for some truth that will give his life meaning. In his travels he develops his sensibilities and imagination by viewing symbolic Shelleyan landscapes (volcanoes, caves, domes, springs), by becoming a vegetarian, and by steeping himself in "the awful ruins of the days of old."

The Poet rejects an Arab maiden in favor of a veiled maid, a vision of his own imagination. Except for her feminine attributes, the veiled maid is his doppelgänger, an "echo" of his own narcissistic desires: [...]. After the Poet imagines that he consummates his physical passion for the veiled maid, the vision of the maid taunts him as he futilely pursues her through a blighted landscape. But he is really pursuing himself, and when he realizes this, he welcomes his early death, the fate of many Romantic poets and heroes. Shelley himself felt the lure of the life of solitude contrasted with the enforced solitude that he had experienced at various periods in his life, including the lack of a receptive audience for his writings. Predictably, with the exception of a favorable article on "Young Poets" in Leigh Hunt's *Examiner* (1 December 1816), *Alastor* was dubbed in the reviews as "obscure" and "morbid."

The year 1816 proved to be exciting for Shelley and Mary and for Claire Clairmont. In January, Mary gave birth to a son, named William after her father, who though he was still cold to Shelley and Mary, continued to be a financial burden on them. In the spring Claire threw herself at Lord Byron, who was recently separated from Lady Byron, and became his mistress. In May she persuaded Shelley and Mary to alter their plans for a trip to Italy and go to Lake Geneva instead, where she knew Byron was headed. The two poets found each other stimulating and spent much time together, sailing on Lake Geneva and discussing poetry and other topics, including ghosts and spirits, into the night. During one of these ghostly "seances," Byron proposed that each person present—himself, Shelley, Mary, Claire, and his physician, Dr. John Polidori—should write a ghost story. Mary's contribution to the contest became the novel *Frankenstein*; published in 1818 with a preface by Shelley, it became one of the most popular works of the whole Romantic period.

For his part Shelley was deeply impressed with the power of the natural scenery, brought on by the combination of the lake and the surrounding mountains, especially Mont Blanc. Both Shelley and Byron were inspired by the associations the area had with Rousseau, whom they regarded as the spiritual leader of romanticism. Shelley was deeply impressed with Rousseau's descriptions of this area in *Julie; ou La Nouvelle Héloïse* (1761). Shelley also "dosed" Byron with Wordsworth's descriptions of nature; this influence is evident in Canto III (1816) of *Childe Harold's Pilgrimage*.

Shelley too did not come out of this Switzerland trip empty-handed. He was stimulated to write two of his finest poems: "Hymn to Intellectual Beauty" and *Mont Blanc*. The "Hymn to Intellectual Beauty" reveals the influence of Wordsworth, of his "Tintern Abbey" and "Ode: Intimations of Immortality" in particular. As Wordsworth does in "Tintern Abbey," Shelley in the "Hymn to Intellectual Beauty" suggests how his imagination and poetic sensitivity were formed by nature, and more significantly, by visitations from the shadowy power of intellectual beauty and how, in turn, he dedicated his poetic powers to intellectual beauty. Much as Wordsworth did in his "Intimations" ode, Shelley laments his feeling that the presence of this power was stronger in his youth.

In *Mont Blanc* Shelley discovers a similar but even more enigmatic power, but the conclusion he reaches is more skeptical, less Wordsworthian. Shelley chose a familiar romantic topic for this poem: Coleridge's "Hymn before Sun-Rise in the Vale of Chamouni," passages from Rousseau's *Julie*, Wordsworth's poetry, and Byron's *Childe Harold* and *Manfred*—all have in common the description of the awesome effect on the observer wrought by Mont Blanc in particular or the Alps in general. Though Shelley much admired the new kind of poetry ushered in by Wordsworth and Coleridge, he was equally convinced by 1815 that both the older poets were political apostates, having sold out to religion and the political status quo in the reaction that followed Napoleon's defeat. Thus the relationship with nature that Shelley explores in *Mont Blanc* is more ridden with skepticism and doubt than the pantheism of Wordsworth or the Christian revelation of Coleridge. The only meaning the poet can draw from the mountain's impenetrable, impassable visage is what his own imagination can supply. To the imaginative observer the mountain provides a parable of creation and destruction in its lower reaches and valleys and of unknowable permanence and power in the majestic solitudes of its uppermost heights. Probably no passage in Shelley's canon has been more widely disputed than the final three lines of *Mont Blanc*: [....]

The enigmatic mountain leaves the speaker with no assurance that the imagination may endow with meaning the awful blankness of nature.

After their return to England, Shelley and Mary were faced with the disasters of two suicides: Fanny Imlay, Mary's half sister and an admirer of Shelley, and Harriet, Shelley's wife. Since both women had been, at least at one time, in love with Shelley, Shelley and Mary must have felt in some measure responsible. Shelley married Mary on 30 December 1816, and became involved in drawn-out court proceedings with the Westbrooks, led by his old adversary Eliza, over the custody of Shelley and Harriet's children, Ianthe and Charles. Some of Shelley's writings, most prominently *Queen Mab*, were cited during the proceedings to show that Shelley held moral and religious opinions that rendered him unfit to assume custody. By the time the case was finally decided in 1818, with Lord Eldon making provisions for the children to be cared for by a guardian, the Shelleys were in Italy with Shelley never to return to England.

In March of 1817 the Shelleys settled in Marlow, an environment that provided the flexibility of moving in literary circles and the tranquillity needed for thinking and writing. Now more friendly with Mary and Shelley, probably because of their marriage, Godwin was a visitor. In addition to regular conversations with Peacock, Shelley became good friends with Leigh Hunt and met some of the young writers in Hunt's circle, including John Keats and Horace Smith. Given the fact that Shelley's liberal friends and acquaintances were politically opposed to the reactionary forces in England after Napoleon's defeat, it is not surprising that Shelley's writings during his Marlow period are politically charged: two pamphlets, *A Proposal for Putting Reform to the Vote Throughout the Kingdom* and *An Address to the People on the Death of the Princess Charlotte*, and one political epic, *The Revolt of Islam*.

Shelley signed both pamphlets "The Hermit of Marlow." The first suggests petitions to increase suffrage, along the lines of what would eventually be put into practice in the 1832 Reform Bill. The second pamphlet (no copies of the first edition are extant) is a rhetorical tour de force in which Shelley chastises even liberals, borrowing a phrase from Thomas Paine's *The Rights of Man*: "We pity the plumage but forget the dying bird." Shelley suggests that in the public outpour of mourning over the untimely death of Princess Charlotte, people, even the friends of liberty and reform, have neglected the executions of three laborers, who in turn become symbols of all the poor and the unjustly treated. Shelley concludes the essay with an allegorical account of the death of Liberty, a valid reason for mourning.

Shelley was again confronted with the problem of censorship with his longest poem in its original version, with its original title: *Laon and Cythna; or, The Revolution of the Golden City: A Vision of the Nineteenth Century*, which was withdrawn after only a few copies were published. Even the comparatively liberal Ollier brothers, Shelley's publishers, objected to the brother-sister incest between the two title characters and to some of the attacks on religion. Shelley took out the incestuous relationship, deleted other objectionable passages, and republished the poem as *The Revolt of Islam; A Poem, in Twelve Cantos*. His description of the poem in the preface suggests some of its structural difficulties: "It is a succession of pictures illustrating the growth and progress of individual mind aspiring to excellence, and devoted to the love of mankind." Dedicated to the idea that "love is celebrated everywhere as the sole law which should govern the moral world," *The Revolt of Islam* provides a poetic forum for Shelley to condemn oppression, religious fraud, war, tyrants, and their consequences [...] and to recommend hope, enlightenment, love, "moral dignity and freedom."

Written in Spenserian stanzas, *The Revolt of Islam* begins with an allegory of the eternal struggle between evil and good[...]. Laon, a Shelleyan hero representing love, begins his narrative in Canto II by relating the natural, loving, and inspiring childhood relationship between himself and Cythna, who appears as a liberated Wollstonecraftian woman. In Cantos III and IV Cythna is captured by soldiers, while Laon is imprisoned and goes mad. A kindly hermit frees him and nourishes him with nature and learning, finally bringing him back to sanity after seven years.

Laon rejoins Cythna as the revolutionary forces of good march into the Golden City. The revolution is kept peaceful as the soldiers throw down their weapons, and, through Laon's intervention, the tyrant Othman is spared the revenge of the people. The forces of reaction overwhelm the patriots, but Cythna saves Laon, and they consummate their love. The king's "Iberian Priest" decides that the only way to stop the famine and pestilence is to burn Laon and Cythna. The burning purifies them, and their spirits travel beyond the mutable world to the Temple of the Spirit, a permanent realm of virtue and happiness. J. G. Lockhart, the reviewer for *Blackwood's* (January 1819), thought the poem obscure and unfinished, and in a way *The Revolt of Islam* was a kind of testing ground for Shelley to work out his system of symbols—caves, rivers, boats, veils—and his political mythology so that he could employ them with greater skill in later works.

Shelley probably wrote *Rosalind and Helen, A Modern Eclogue* before he left England, though the poem was not published by Ollier until 1819. Shelley derives the relationship between Rosalind and Helen from the friendship that had existed between Mary Shelley and Isabel Baxter before her husband, a domestic tyrant like Rosalind's husband, caused the friendship to be broken off. For shock value Shelley introduces the incest theme in the relationship between Rosalind and her brother and the theme of free love in the relationship between Helen and Lionel, whose prototypes are Laon and Cythna. As an aristocrat who writes radical poetry, Lionel appears to be based upon Shelley himself. After both women lose their male lovers, they turn to each other in sisterly love, exchanging tales of woe and social injustice.

For reasons of health and finances, as well as for the obligation to take Allegra, Byron and Claire's child (born in January 1817), to her father, the Shelleys and their children, William and Clara (born in September 1817), together with Claire and Allegra, and the children's nurses set out for Italy in March 1818. For Shelley's development as a poet the change of climate proved fruitful, for he was to write some of his greatest poetry under the clear blue Italian skies. Once in Italy, Shelley found himself in the delicate position of having to mediate between Claire and Byron over Allegra, with the later result of Allegra's being placed in a convent and dying. The expatriates stayed in Pisa and Leghorn before settling for the summer in Bagni di Lucca, in the Apennines. They found congenial company in John and Maria Gisborne and her son, Henry Reveley, an engineer developing a steamboat.

Two poems written at Este, "Lines Written among the Euganean Hills" and *Julian and Maddalo*, grew directly out of Shelley's Italian experiences in the summer and fall of 1818. The immediate source for "Lines" is a day spent in the Euganean Hills overlooking Padua and Venice. The emotional source is Shelley's misery over the death of his child Clara in September 1818 and Mary's subsequent depression and disaffection. The hills are [...] moments of happiness and insight among man's generally dark and miserable existence. That Shelley's recent visit to Byron was very much in his mind is evident in his tribute to him as the poet of Ocean. The imagery of the changing intensity of light during the day reflects the poet's visionary imagination. Shelley concludes this beautiful poem with a wish for domestic tranquillity for himself and those he loves and a hope that the world will recognize its brotherhood and "grow young again."

Julian and Maddalo, not published until its inclusion in *Posthumous Poems* (1824), is Shelley's most direct poetic treatment of his relationship with Lord Byron and reflects conversations during their horseback rides along the Lido while Shelley was visiting Byron at Venice in August 1818. In the poem Julian (Shelley) takes the side of optimism and hope in the face of despondency and evidence of misery, while Maddalo (Byron) takes a pessimistic view, stemming partly from his pride. For the side of hope Julian cites the beauty of Nature in this "Paradise of Exiles, Italy!" and the natural goodness of childhood, describing Shelley's own play with Byron's child Allegra as evidence: [...].

Maddalo accuses Julian of talking "Utopia," citing as evidence for his pessimism a madman who was once as idealistic as Julian. Each thinking he will support his own arguments, they decide to visit the madman, whom commentators have variously identified as Tasso or as Shelley's alter ego. But the madman's soliloquy is inconclusive. He says that part of his suffering is his own doing, but part seems inflicted upon him from some outside power. However, he has retained his ideals and integrity, still believing in the possibility of social reform and eschewing revenge against his lover, who has scorned him for her paramour. He believes that love leads to misery[...]. After hearing the madman's soliloquy, both Julian and Maddalo are subdued and feel pity.[...] Julian returns many years later only to find Maddalo away, the madman and his lover dead, and Maddalo's child a grown woman. He learns from her that the madman's lover returned for a while but deserted him once again.[...] Many of the other poems Shelley wrote during this same period, such as the fine lyric "Stanzas Written in Dejection near Naples," depict Shelley's despair over his estranged relationship with Mary and were also not published until *Posthumous Poems*.

Shelley provided rapturous descriptions of his travels in Italy in his letters to Peacock, expressing his particular delight in Roman ruins. But these delights were balanced, as always seemed to be the case for Shelley and Mary, by yet another tragedy, the death of their son, William, in June 1819. An additional cause for despair was what came to be known as the "Hoppner Scandal," so called because the Shelleys' discharged servant Elise Foggi had related to the Hoppners, Byron's friends in Venice, that unbeknownst to Mary, Claire had born Shelley a child in Naples. Records do support the existence of Shelley's "Neapolitan Charge," Elena Adelaide Shelley, but to this day scholars view the parentage of this child as speculative.

During this 1818-1819 period Shelley wrote what many consider to be his masterpiece, *Prometheus Unbound* (1820), subtitled *A Lyrical Drama*, perhaps to suggest a hybrid genre in the way Wordsworth and Coleridge had signaled their pioneering efforts by titling their first volume of poetry *Lyrical Ballads* (1798). Shelley had been developing the symbolism, imagery, and ideas for the poem for several years. For example, he states in the preface that "the imagery which I have employed will be found ... to have been drawn from the operations of the human mind," a technique he had already used in *Mont Blanc*. Shelley had had a longstanding interest in and familiarity with Aeschylus's *Prometheus Bound*, even translating it for Byron, but he could not accept the idea that Aeschylus had bound the champion of mankind for eternity, or even worse, that Prometheus would have been reconciled with Jupiter in Aeschylus's lost drama, the sequel to *Prometheus Bound*. As Shelley avers in the preface, "I was averse from a catastrophe so feeble as that of reconciling the Champion with the Oppressor of mankind." The choice of Prometheus as his

hero is not surprising, given this mythological character's association with rebellion and isolation from his act of giving fire to man against the gods' wishes and his reputation as a "forethinker" or prophet. For Shelley he came to symbolize the mind or soul of man in its highest potential.

The drama begins with Prometheus bound to a precipice of icy rocks in the Indian Caucasus, the situation of a Romantic outcast. Prometheus has reached the point of desperately needing to reveal his thoughts and so free himself of the self-imprisoning hatred of Jupiter. Many commentators regard line fifty-three [...] as the turning point of the play. Prometheus also "recalls," meaning he both remembers and takes back his curse against Jupiter, thus breaking the wintry deadlock between the two adversaries and initiating a change of consciousness. Believing that Prometheus's recantation of his curse is a sign of submission, Jupiter sends Mercury and the Furies to extract from the Titan the price of his freedom: the secret that contains the key to Jupiter's overthrow. The Furies try to demoralize Prometheus by reciting the great failures of human hope, the co-option of Christianity by reactionary elements and the violence of the Terror in the French Revolution. But the Furies' message of futility is counterbalanced by the Spirits' message of hope and courage.

Asia, the female counterpart of Prometheus and the embodiment of love and nature, opens act 2 in a vale in the Indian Caucasus, waiting for her sister Panthea to come. Asia's and Panthea's lyrics in the following sections image forth a change in nature, signaling the coming of spring, hope, and reawakening that will accompany Asia's reunion with Prometheus. Asia descends into the cave of the enigmatic Demogorgon, who may represent the principle of necessity or of revolution, in order to gain knowledge of how to effect the overthrow of man's oppressor. Demogorgon is terse with Asia, responding to her questions[...]. His terseness stems from his desire to make Asia see the need to change her mental outlook like Prometheus; once this is done, she will understand that the real tyrant exists only in her mind.

Act 3 depicts the fall of Jupiter and thus tyranny from the world. Shelley delighted in making tyrants fall at the moment of their greatest complacency over their omnipotence. Jupiter, thinking that his child Demogorgon will consolidate his power, is shocked to learn that he is a "fatal child," the principle of revolutionary change. Rather than ascend Jupiter's vacant throne, Prometheus retires with Asia and her "sister nymphs," Panthea and Ione, to a cave, forming what one commentator has called "a typically Shelleyan household." Shelley's political point here is that even Prometheus would be corrupted by the structure of power, as were the well-intended French revolutionaries; therefore, the political model is an egalitarian utopia with its roots in the philosophical anarchism of Godwin's *Political Justice* . Since Prometheus and Asia together symbolize the mind of man, the peoples of the earth undergo the same transformation in consciousness: [....]

Act 4, written several months after Shelley had completed the first three in April 1819, is a celestial celebration of the birth of a new age. All of nature joins the Earth and the Moon in celebrating in poetic song the passage into a millennium governed by universal love. Demogorgon's final message to the universe reminds us that maintaining the millennium requires eternal vigilance: [....]

Shelley knew that *Prometheus Unbound* would never be popular, but he thought that it might have a beneficial influence on some already enlightened intellects. In letters to his publisher Ollier, Shelley proclaimed that although this was his "favorite poem," he did not expect it to sell more than twenty copies and instructed Ollier to send copies to Hunt, Peacock, Hogg, Godwin, Keats, Horace Smith, Thomas Moore, and Byron. The reviewers were predictably harsh in their condemnation of the poem's moral and political principles, with the reviewer for the *Literary Gazette and Journal of the Belles Lettres* (9 September 1820) quipping that "no one can ever think [*Prometheus*] worth binding," but there was also praise, with words such as "beauty" and "genius" used in various reviews.

Bound with *Prometheus Unbound* in the volume published in 1820 by Ollier were some of Shelley's finest extended lyrics, including "Ode to the West Wind," "The Cloud," "To a Skylark," and "Ode to Liberty." Written in the autumn of 1819 when the Shelleys were in Florence, "Ode to the West Wind" employs natural imagery and symbolism to foretell not only a change in the physical but in the political climate. Writing in terza rima to suggest the force and pace of the wind, Shelley addresses the wind as

a "Wild Spirit" that is both "Destroyer and Preserver." Shelley asks the wind to drive him forth as it does the leaves, the clouds, and the waves so that his poetic song will have the same irresistible power for change to awaken Earth: [...].

Both "An Ode, Written October 1819, before the Spaniards Had Recovered Their Liberty" and "Ode to Liberty" were written in Shelley's enthusiasm for the recent Spanish revolution. The latter poem recites an idealized history of liberty from its birth in ancient Greece to its most recent appearance in Spain, and its possibilities in England. Recalling Shelley's earlier interests in science, "The Cloud" demonstrates his knowledge of the meteorological cycle of cloud formation. It is perhaps unfortunate for Shelley's reputation that "To a Skylark," a dazzling exercise in metaphor, rather than "Ode to the West Wind," has been his most frequently anthologized poem, for "To a Skylark" suffers by comparison with Keats's "Ode to a Nightingale."

Almost immediately after finishing the first three acts of *Prometheus Unbound*, Shelley began work on another drama, *The Cenci* (1819). This time instead of using mythology and classical literature as his source material, he used the true Renaissance story of the macabre Cenci family, the villainous count and his virtuous daughter, Beatrice, of whom Shelley had a portrait. Shelley believed that this drama, unlike *Prometheus Unbound*, would be both popular and stageable, even suggesting his favorite actress, Miss O'Neill, for the part of Beatrice. The Gothic trappings, the elimination of "mere poetry," and the absence of didactic political instruction were all calculated to make the drama accessible to a wide audience.

Shelley's political disclaimer in the preface is, of course, belied by the fact that Beatrice's rebellion against her tyrannical father is yet another version of Shelley's lifelong struggle against any form of authority, be it kingly, priestly, or fatherly. Count Cenci acts on the assumption that his patriarchal power is absolute, sanctioned as it is by the Pope, the head of Church and State. He knows no checks, first toasting his sons' deaths in a bizarre parody of the communion ceremony, then raping Beatrice, who has been abandoned by all powers—religious, state, personal—who might have helped her. Although the Count raped Beatrice to assert his domination over her and so make his control over his weak family complete, he is not prepared for Beatrice's response of revenge. In Shelley's hands Beatrice's revenge is a revolutionary act against the oppression of patriarchal authority, not a personal vendetta. Though some commentators have found a character flaw in Beatrice because she lacks remorse for her part in the parricide, Shelley's portrayal of her as an ascetic revolutionary personality seems justified.

In his hope that the play would be read widely and staged, Shelley again misjudged the predominance of conservativism in the literary milieu of Regency England. The taboo theme of incest, the horror of parricide, the "blasphemous" treatment of religion, the implicit attack on the family and all patriarchal institutions, and Shelley's own dangerous reputation—all broke the rules of Regency society and ensured *The Cenci* would be condemned by all but a few reviewers and friends, such as Leigh Hunt, to whom the play is dedicated. One reviewer's response is symptomatic: "The ties of father and daughter ... ought not to be profaned as they are in this poem" (*British Review*, June 1821). The play was staged only once in the nineteenth century, by the Shelley Society in 1886.

Shelley's political ire was stirred in 1819 by the shocking events in England that became known as the Manchester Massacre, or "Peterloo." During an assembly in St. Peter's fields, where a crowd was to be addressed by "Orator" Hunt, the local militia charged the crowd, killing at least nine people and wounding many more. Shelley's response was to write several explicitly political poems, including *The Masque of Anarchy* (1832), the sonnet "England in 1819," and "Song to the Men of England," all of which were deemed even by Shelley's friends, such as Leigh Hunt, to whom he sent *The Masque of Anarchy*, to be too dangerous to publish during Shelley's life-time. *The Masque of Anarchy* begins with a dream vision of a procession, or masque, in which Murder, Fraud, and Hypocrisy have masks like Robert Stewart, Viscount Castlereagh; John Scott, Earl of Eldon; and Henry Addington, Viscount Sidmouth—all ministers in the current English government. Anarchy, which Shelley identifies with tyranny and despotism, rides by[...]. Though much of the poem's rhetoric and imagery are violent and revolutionary, Shelley's council to the victims of attacks from oppressors is to respond not with violence in kind, but with passive resistance: [...].

This tactic should shame the soldiers into joining the cause of freedom. Shelley assures the people of their ultimate victory over their oppressors[...]. Shelley must have felt particularly frustrated that all his attempts, both in poetry and prose, to address explicitly the political events of 1819 and 1820 failed to be published during his lifetime.

While Hunt did not deem *The Masque of Anarchy* safe to be published until the more relaxed political climate that accompanied the Reform Bill of 1832, *A Philosophical View of Reform*, written by Shelley during this same period, did not find its way into publication until 1920. Actually, *A Philosophical View of Reform* is a calmer and more carefully reasoned response to Peterloo and the repressive policies of this period than the poems Shelley wrote in response. Shelley's intended audience in the essay is the leaders in the reform movement, and he hoped to consolidate opinion and bring forth action on urgent issues: the need for expanded suffrage, for reforms in the way taxes are levied, and, most important, for greater freedom of speech, press, and assembly.

Lest Shelley should be thought of as only a humorless reformer where politics is concerned and a serious visionary where poetry is concerned, two satires, *Peter Bell the Third* and *Oedipus Tyrannus; or, Swellfoot the Tyrant*, and two light-hearted poems, the "Letter to Maria Gisborne" and *The Witch of Atlas*, suggest the contrary. Perhaps these more playful poems, written in late 1819 and during 1820, were an outlet after his intensive poetic efforts in 1819. Shelley got the idea to write his own *Peter Bell* from reading in the *Examiner* reviews of Wordsworth's *Peter Bell*, published for the first time in 1819, and John Hamilton Reynold's burlesque *Peter Bell: A Lyrical Ballad*, which had actually preceded Wordsworth's poem into print. Though Shelley certainly admired Wordsworth for the advances in poetry that he had helped to initiate, he believed that the elder poet had become a political apostate and that his more recent poetry, such as *Peter Bell*, had become "Dull" [...]. To counteract the pious moralizing in Wordsworth's *Peter Bell*, Shelley portrays his Peter Bell as damned in hell.

Though Shelley never equals the satirical skills of his friend Byron, in *Swellfoot the Tyrant*, written in August 1820, he demonstrates an ability to sustain a satire on political events. Queen Caroline, who was strongly supported by the Whigs, was tried for infidelity, in an effort by George IV and his ministers to prevent her from taking part in the coronation ceremonies—prompting Shelley to write a satirical drama in the manner of Aristophanes, complete with a chorus of pigs, the choice of which was suggested to Shelley by the pigs being brought to market beneath his windows in his summer residence near Pisa. In the drama's climatic scene Iona (Queen Caroline) snatches the green bag full of perjured testimony against her and pours its contents over Swellfoot (George IV) and his ministers, turning them into small predators. Iona mounts the Minotaur (John Bull) and with her loyal pigs gives chase. With all the targets of the satire readily identifiable, it is not surprising that the publisher, J. Johnston, under threat of prosecution, was forced to surrender all remaining copies after only seven were sold.

In the summer of 1820, while staying at the Gisbornes' house in Leghorn while they were away in London, Shelley wrote one of his most informal poems, the "Letter to Maria Gisborne." Written in the style of Coleridge's conversation poems and even recalling the situation of his "This Lime Tree Bower My Prison," Shelley's verse epistle capsulizes his view of himself and his closest friends. Describing himself in the clutter of Henry Reveley's study, Shelley depicts himself first as a spider and a silkworm and then as a scientist and a magician. After recalling the pleasant times he has spent with Maria Gisborne in Italy, Shelley then imagines the Gisbornes in London meeting his friends and briefly characterizes them fondly and playfully: Hunt, Hogg, Peacock, and Smith. The poem concludes with a vision of the future when Shelley will be reunited with all of these friends in a warm and supportive literary community.

Source: John R. Greenfield, "Percy Bysshe Shelley," in *Dictionary of Literary Biography*, Vol. 96, *British Romantic Poets, 1789–1832, Second Series*, edited by John R. Greenfield, Gale Research, 1990, pp. 308–338.

SOURCES

Greenfield, John R., "Percy Bysshe Shelley," in *Dictionary of Literary Biography*, Volume 96, *British Romantic Poets, 1789–1832*, edited by John R. Greenfield, Gale Research, 1990, pp. 308–38.

Harmon, William, and Hugh Holman, "Romantic Period in English Literature," in *A Handbook to Literature*, Prentice Hall, 2003, pp. 448–49.

Miller, Christopher R., "Shelley's Uncertain Heaven," in *ELH*, Vol. 72, No. 3, Fall 2005, p. 577–603.

Review of "Ozymandias," in *Magill Book Reviews*, September 15, 1990.

Rodenbeck, John, "Travelers from an Antique Land: Shelley's Inspiration for 'Ozymandias,'" in *Alif: Journal of Comparative Poetics*, Vol. 24, Annual 2004, pp. 121–50.

Shelley, Percy Bysshe, "Ozymandias," in *Percy Bysshe Shelley: Selected Poems*, edited by Stanley Applebaum, Dover Publications, 1993, p. 5.

FURTHER READING

Bloom, Howard, *Percy Bysshe Shelley*, Chelsea House, 1985.

One of America's preeminent literary scholars walks students through Shelley's works with an eye toward historical and cultural context, literary status, and the Romantic personality. It includes a brief biography and a chronology to aid in research.

Godwin, William, *The Anarchist Writings of William Godwin*, Freedom Press, 1986.

Godwin was a major influence on Shelley's thinking, and he was also his father-in-law. Although Shelley put many of Godwin's ideas into action in his life, Godwin did not always approve. This book explains Godwin's radical ideas and philosophies.

Hogg, Thomas Jefferson, *Life of Percy Bysshe Shelley*, Scholarly Press, 1971.

Hogg and Shelley met at Oxford and were lifetime friends, despite some major challenges along the way. Here, Hogg shares his personal memories and recollections of his friend.

Shelley, Mary Wollstonecraft, *Frankenstein*, W.W. Norton, 1996.

Mary Shelley came up with the idea for the classic novel while in Lake Geneva with her husband, her sister, and Lord Byron. This edition contains the entire novel, along with important explanations, maps, reactions, interpretations, and critical viewpoints.

Requiem

ANNA AKHMATOVA

1963

Anna Akhmatova's most revered poem, "Requiem," found in *The Complete Poems of Anna Akhmatova*, 1992, gives voice to the suffering and punishment of Russian citizens during the years of the Stalin regime. Joseph Stalin, who was the dictator of Communist Russia in all but name, ordered the imprisonment or execution of over one million Russians who were perceived as enemies of the state. The worst of the persecutions took place throughout the 1930s. Indeed, "Requiem" was written over a wide period of time, likely from the 1930s through the 1940s. Little is known about the details of the poem's initial release, but it was first published abroad in Munich, Germany, in 1963. Because the poem portrays the pain that thousands of Russians experienced, the government banned the poem's publication in Russia until 1989.

The poem is told from the perspective of a mother whose son is imprisoned for political resistance against the new Communist regime. The narrator, without resorting to overt sentimentality, shares the emotional trauma of having to wait for extended periods of time to learn of what has happened to her son. In the process of expressing her sorrow and torment, the narrator gives a voice to every Russian who was in a similar situation.

In the beginning of this poem, a stranger asks the narrator if she is able to describe the atrocities that they are experiencing. The narrator

answers: "Yes, I can." This poem is Akhmatova's proof of that statement. Of all the poems that Akhmatova wrote, "Requiem" is the one that is most often quoted from and used to demonstrate the poet's skill. The writing evokes emotion through the simplest of phrases. Lines such as "Husband in the grave, son in prison" demonstrate Akhmatova's minimal use of words to express the greatest of personal tragedies. At the end of the poem, the narrator speaks of creating monuments in order to remember the dead. This poem is itself a monument for Akhmatova and for all who have lost loved ones to political persecution. That is why "Requiem" is not only read as one of Akhmatova's greatest poems, but as one of the greatest poems by any Russian poet, and even as one of the outstanding literary achievements to encompass the tragedies of Communism.

AUTHOR BIOGRAPHY

Akhmatova, whose birth name is Anna Gorenko, was born on June 23, 1889, in Bol'shoi Aontain, the third of six children. She grew up in Tsarskoe Selo, outside of St. Petersburg in northern Russia. Akhmatova is a penname that the poet adopted because her father was afraid that her interest in poetry would mar their upper-class family name. Indeed, Akhmatova tried to begin a more accepted career by entering law school in 1907. However, after one year, she decided to write instead.

When she turned twenty-one, Akhmatova married fellow poet, Nikolay Gumilyov, the creator of a new poetic movement in Russia called the Acmeists. Akhmatova gave birth in 1912, to their son, Lev. That same year, Akhmatova's first poetry collection, *Vecher* ("Evening"), was published in Russia. Her second collection, *Chyotky* ("Rosary"), was published two years later in 1914, solidifying her reputation as a serious poet. Akhmatova's marriage to Gumilyov ended in 1918, the same year Akhmatova married Vladimir Shileiko, a relationship that would end in divorce eight years later. One of the main themes of Akhmatova's poetry at this time reflected her challenges with romantic love.

For the next few years, Akhmatova continued to publish poetry collections, earning high praise from more established poets and acclaim from Russian readers. However, as the Communist government took root, Akhmatova and most poets and artists of the day were persecuted. In 1921, Akhmatova's ex-husband Gumilyov was accused of treason and was subsequently executed. Two years later, Akhmatova's poetry, which was criticized by the government for being too focused on romantic and religious ideas, was completely banned.

Akhmatova married scholar Nikolay Punin and lived with him during the 1920s. This relationship also ended tragically. Punin and Akhmatova's son from her first marriage, Lev, were imprisoned in 1935, as were many of Akhmatova's friends. Akhmatova wrote letters to Stalin, pleading for her husband's and son's release, and she also wrote flattering poems about him. Her requests were eventually granted, but both men would again be arrested. Punin would later die in prison. Akhmatova's son would suffer through a series of releases and re-imprisonments throughout the years but he was released for the final time in 1956. Lev went on to become a cultural geographer, producing questionable theories that nonetheless became very popular, especially after his death in 1992. The imprisonments of her husband, son, and friends inspired Akhmatova's poem "Requiem." The poem was likely written through the 1930s and 1940s, though it was first published in 1963.

Akhmatova struggled with poverty after she could no longer publish her writing, which was her main source of income. Although she continued to write regardless, in order to keep small earnings coming in, she translated famous books into Russian. It was not until after Stalin's death and the subsequent loosening of restrictions on writers that Akhmatova's work became available again to Russian readers. Beginning in 1958 and continuing through the 1960s, Akhmatova's previously written works were once again published in Russia. In 1964, Akhmatova won the Etna-Taormina Prize, an international award for poetry. Two years later, Akhmatova died of a heart attack in Leningrad (St. Petersburg) on March 5, 1966, the same day that Stalin had died in 1953.

POEM SUMMARY

Opening Stanza

Akhmatova opens her poem "Requiem" with a four line stanza that is dated 1961, the latest date attributed to any of the other sections of this poem. This means that she wrote this opening section more than twenty years after the events that inspired the poem—the imprisonment of her son, Lev, in 1935.

In these opening four lines, the narrator makes a statement that connects her personally with the events she is about to describe. The narrator did not seek shelter in a foreign country, she states. She was there with everyone who was, "unfortunately," forced to face the atrocities that are described later in the poem. This poem, in other words, is not based on something the narrator has imagined. The narrator was there, she saw the events described, and she lived through them with others who suffered just as she did.

Because "Requiem" comprises a series of poems, each with their own titles or numbers, the *Poem Summary* of the poem is divided in a way that reflects this. Each section title matches each poem title in "Requiem." The only exception is this section, which appears as untitled in the poem. Also, while some of the sections are dated, others are not, and the overall work does not present events in chronological order.

Instead of a Preface
This second part of the poem is the only section that is written in a prose style. In this section, the narrator mentions the "Yezhov terror," a particularly savage year during the Stalinist regime when the imprisonments of suspected rebels were increased tenfold or more from previous years. Stalin, through one of his officials, Nikolai Yezhov, was intent on ridding the country of everyone who might threaten his power. This is the time when the poet's son and husband were arrested.

Through what appears as a simple description of the narrator standing in a line outside a prison in Leningrad, the narrator turns to a morbid portrayal of what life is like for those who have loved ones on the other side of the fortified prison walls. The narrator then states that she is "recognized." This offers the image of a person standing in a crowd, forgetful of herself as she worries about the people who are inside the prison until she is reminded of herself when she is recognized. She and the woman who has spoken have awoken "from the stupor to which everyone had succumbed." At that moment, the narrator comes back to her own situation and turns to the woman who has recognized her. The woman whispers to her, and the narrator uses the act of

whispering to imply the cautious overtones of the crowd, the paranoia that has swept over the country, and the solemnity of the atmosphere. The woman asks: "Can you describe this?" The narrator responds: "Yes, I can" (indeed, Akhmatova's "Requiem" provides this very description). The woman, with "bluish lips," makes an expression that resembles a smile. In the midst of the suffering, the narrator suggests, this woman is touched by the fact that these events, as horrible as they are, will be recorded and remembered.

Dedication
This section is dated 1940, putting this piece closer to the time when the events that influenced this poem were actually taking place. The section begins with references to nature: mountains and rivers, which react to the grief that the people of Russia are experiencing. The grief is so devastating that the "mountains bow down" and the "Mighty rivers cease to flow." This is an example of pathetic fallacy, where inanimate objects are used to embody a human emotion.

A few lines later in the poem, the narrator will contrast this reaction in nature. In line 6, there is "someone" in the world who is enjoying a "fresh breeze." In line 7, there is someone is enjoying a sunset. These are people who live far away from the terror. But the women who stand outside the prison walls do not notice the wind or the sun. They are focused only on the sounds of the prison, the guards, and the key that keeps their loved ones locked away from them. The waiting women are described like zombies "more lifeless than the dead" who "trudged through the "savaged capital." Nevertheless, the women feel a distant hope. This hope exists because many of the prisoners have not yet been formally tried or sentenced. Thus the women hope, however faintly, that their husbands, fathers, and sons will be pardoned or released.

When a "verdict" is finally decreed, the individual waiting to hear it is "cut off" from the women who still have some hope. The narrator wonders where her "chance friends" (the women who waited with her) are now, and she states that she is "sending my farewell greeting to them." Again, it is reasonable to assume that "Requiem" is the farewell that is being sent.

Prologue
This section in the poem has no date, and the narrator speaks in a general voice, calling upon

"locomotive whistles" that sing "short songs of farewell." There is movement in this section as opposed to the more static previous sections. The prisoners are being taken from inside the penitentiary walls to trains and Black Marias (black police wagons), which will transport them to other prisons or perhaps to be tortured or executed. In the opening lines of this section, the narrator succinctly captures the dismal state of events: "That was when the ones who smiled / Were the dead, glad to be at rest."

I

The section numbered with a Roman numeral I returns with the narrator again using a personal pronoun "I," which was missing in the previous two sections. "I followed you, like a mourner." There are several allusions (references) to death in this stanza. Children are crying, a candle is dying, the prisoner's lips are cold, calling a corpse to mind. Then the narrator says, "I will be like the wives of the Streltsy." This is a reference to a group of special guards called Streltsy, who at one time protected Russia's tsars. However, the Streltsy formed a mutiny against the tsar and were captured and executed. This is why the narrator relates to the tears of their wives.

II

This brief section describes a sick woman who is all alone, presumably the narrator. The power of this stanza is a simple but effective line, one that is often quoted from this poem because it sums up the suffering of the women in general: "Husband in the grave, son in prison." There is not much that needs to be said after that, except that the narrator asks for a prayer to be said for her.

III

In this section, which is also quite brief, the narrator quickly takes on a completely different stance. "No, it is not I, it is somebody else who is suffering." This statement is not actually true, but the narrator is saying that her suffering can no longer be endured.

IV

In part IV, the narrator wishes she had been "shown" what would happen to her and her loved ones. She refers to herself as a "minion," or someone inferior, and also as a "sinner" The reference to Tsarskoye Selo, where the poet was born, brings up memories of her youth. The narrator's depiction of herself as "three-hundredth in line, with a parcel" emphasizes her insignificance. The narrator also notes that she is standing outside Kresty prison. This is the holding prison on the banks of the Neva River, so the narrator is returning to the setting at the beginning of the poem as related in "Instead of a Preface."

V

The next four sections including this section are all dated 1939. At the beginning of this section, however, "seventeen months" have gone by, filled with tears and petitions to the hangman, which well might be a reference to the poems that Akhmatova wrote about Stalin or in his honor, flattering the man, trying to get him to release her son. The narrator still does not know her son's sentence, and she can no longer tell the difference between "a beast" and "a man." She can only see her senses all reflect negativity, such as "dusty flowers," "tracks" that lead to "nowhere," and a "star" that stares relentlessly "straight in the eyes, / And threateing impending death."

VI

The narrator refers to the "light weeks" and "white nights" that "are staring again, / With the burning eyes of a hawk." These images convey a sense of restlessness. The feeling in this part of the poem is that the narrator cannot rid herself of the thought of the possibility of her son's death. It is the first time in this poem that the narrator directly addresses her son. Up until this point, the narrator might have been speaking about any of the prisoners, including her husband and friends. However, in this stanza, she calls out to her son, "dear son," narrowing her focus as well as her suffering to the loss of her child.

VII, The Sentence

Light is still used in this stanza, but not until the last line, where the narrator uses the phrase "Brilliant day." To demonstrate that this phrase should be taken in a negative tone, immediately following this phrase is: "deserted house." The brilliance is to be taken not so much as the warmth of the sun but rather as the stark reality that the narrator must face, that of the "deserted house." The "stone word" in the first line is the reason the house is deserted. It can be presumed from the title of this section and from the preceding phrase that the son has been sentenced.

The narrator then states: "I must turn my soul to stone, / I must learn to live again." In other words, in order for the narrator to survive, she must learn to live without feeling her grief. Notably, at one point in Akhmatova's son's imprisonment, he was sentenced to death, although that sentence was later reversed. Given that this poem is largely autobiographical, at this point in the poem, the reader can assume that the narrator does not yet know that her son's life will be spared, as the next stanzas imply.

VIII, To Death

The narrator addresses death directly and says "I am waiting for you." She invites death to "come in any form," as "a gas shell," (a gas bomb) "Or like a gangster ... with a length of pipe," among other things. It is suggested that death, at least, "dims / the blue luster of beloved eyes," meaning that the narrator's constant pain at the loss of her beloved son will only be lessened by her own death. Here, the narrator also notes that the Yenisey River still swirls and the North Star still shines. Nature continues as if nothing has happened, and this is in direct contrast to the "Dedication" stanza in which the mountains "bow down" and the "rivers cease to flow." This change might suggest that the narrator has lost hope. It might also suggest that the tragedy that has befallen all of the women as a whole (as described in "Dedication") is enough to affect nature, while a single personal tragedy (as it is described here) is not.

IX

While death may end the speaker's anguish, so too will madness, and the narrator has "realized / That I must give in" to insanity. However, in order to escape her grief, the speaker is not allowed to retain her memories; madness "does not allow me to take / Anything of mine with me." Following this statement the speaker lists the things she cannot "take" with her, all of which are her last memories of her son.

X, Crucifixion

In this tenth section, the narrator takes a scene from the Bible, the scene of Christ's crucifixion, to portray her own feelings about her son's death sentence. The narrator mentions Mary Magdalene and Christ's mother, the Virgin Mary. Mary Magdalene is pictured beating her breast and crying. But there is no image, according to the narrator, of Christ's mother. This is because the loss of a son, the narrator suggests, is too powerful an emotion; one so strong that "no one would have dared" to look at the Virgin Mary and witness her grief.

Epilogue I

In the first epilogue, the narrator turns her focus, once again, to the those waiting outside the prison wall. Thus, in this section, the sorrow that is expressed is not the personal sorrow of the narrator but the more universal sorrow embodied by the crowd and expressed in their "eyelids," "cheeks," and "lips." The narrator continues to use the personal pronoun "I," however, describing all that she saw and "learned" while standing in the crowd. The speaker also prays for all who "stood there with me."

Epilogue II

The form of the second epilogue is completely different from any of the other sections in this poem. It is written in couplets, stanzas of two lines each, and the tone of the poem specifically emphasizes those who have died and the speaker's intent to remember and to pray for them. In this way, as mentioned in "Epilogue I," "Epilogue II" reads like a prayer. The narrator is remembering the women who waited with her outside the prison, and, by extension, she is also attempting to honor the dead and the imprisoned. The narrator states that she has "woven a wide mantle for them." The mantle, which is like a shawl or large scarf, could be seen as a symbol for the poem itself, something the narrator has "woven" together to honor the women. The narrator also suggests that a monument might one day be erected in her honor, and she asks for it to be placed where she and the women stood, waiting to see or to hear from their loved ones.

Following this, the speaker indicates that the statue will prevent her from forgetting the horrors she witnessed, even after she has died (a direct contrast from her request to forget everything in "VIII, To Death" and in "IX." Here, the speaker portrays nature as proceeding both with and without regard to the tragedies described in the poem. While the "melting snow" will "stream like tears" from her statue, "the ships of the Neva [will] sail calmly on."

TOPICS FOR FURTHER STUDY

- The suffering in Akhmatova's poem "Requiem" is caused by a ruthless leader attempting to turn his country into a communist state. Other leaders in other countries were also ruthless in their attempts to accomplish the same goal. Research the beginnings of communist China and communist North Korea. What were the effects of early communism on the citizens of these countries? How were they similar in their development to the development of communist Russia? How were they different? How successful were all three governments at achieving their ends? Provide information for your class on your findings.

- Akhmatova uses very simple phrases to achieve an emotional effect in her poetry. Read another poet who speaks of suffering, such as Sylvia Plath in her poem "Daddy." Are the phrases used in Plath's poem as easy to understand as those in "Requiem?" Are they as effective? Do the poems have anything in common other than suffering? What emotions do you feel after reading "Requiem?" What emotions do you feel after reading Plath's poem "Daddy?" Write your own poem to these two poets, expressing your emotional reactions to their works.

- According to the U.S. Department of Justice, in 2005, almost one and a half million people were in prison. Research current statistics about imprisonment in the United States. What are the most common crimes that offenders commit? What are the average terms, or number of years, of their sentence? How do U.S. prison statistics compare to countries in Europe, Asia, or the Middle East? Include statistics on political prisoners. Prepare your statistics and report on them with visual aids such as graphs or slides.

- Research classical composers, listening to recordings of the various requiems they have written. Write a report detailing your findings and your reactions to the music. Next, select your favorite musical piece and prepare a presentation of Akhmatova's poem for your class. First, read the poem aloud without any music. Then read the poem aloud a second time while playing the music in the background. Be prepared to lead a discussion with your class about their different reactions to the poem when it is read with or without the music.

THEMES

Death and Suffering

A requiem is a mass (church service) or song memorializing the dead, thus the title of the poem, which was inspired by the death or imprisonment of Akhmatova's friends and relatives during the communist purges. As the poem progresses, the narrator's depiction of the waiting women leads readers to realize that those who have been left behind (herself, and the women outside of the prison) suffer as much, if not more than, their loved ones. In reality, this poem honors the waiting women. Because of this, the poem is not truly a requiem.

Suffering is often linked with death, as it is in this poem. The prisoners suffer not knowing whether they will live or be executed or if they will ever see their families again. Those who wait for them also suffer, and they stand outside the prison walls waiting and hoping for any news of their loved ones. In some ways death would at least put an end to their uncertainty. Akhmatova's simple images of suffering are emphasized by the plain and yet evocative language that is understated, yet easily understood. Indeed, in "Dedication" simple phrases such as "her tears gush forth," "As if they painfully wrenched life from her heart," and "As if they brutally knocked her flat," are powerful yet straightforward. This allows readers to understand the poetic passages in light of their own experiences of suffering.

Confinement

The most obvious form of confinement, of being held prisoner, is quite literal, but there are also metaphorical images of confinement in this poem. The women outside of the prison whisper to one another, which represents the confinement of conversation (or the lack of free speech). There is also the confinement of emotions, as the women are afraid to express any form of hope or joy. The women are also confined to the wall outside of the prison, as much as their loved ones are confined within it. And then there is the confinement of death, not, according to this poem, for the ones who have died and have thus been liberated, but for the ones who are left behind, permanently confined by their grief and loss.

Loss

Loss abounds through this poem, both literally and figuratively. Due process is lost when citizens are arrested without having committed a crime. There is the loss of freedom of speech as the women whisper because they realize that what they say might be held against them or their loved ones. A loss of identity is insinuated in the poem when the narrator is surprised when someone recognizes her. This might be the loss of public identity but it could also suggest a loss of self-identity, too, as if, in the midst of both a personal and a historical tragedy, the narrator has forgotten who she is. Of course, there is loss of freedom and loss of life, as many are imprisoned or executed. There is also the loss of the ordinary, and even of sanity, as sections of "Requiem" clearly indicate. Most importantly, the poem is a chronicle of lost hope. The narrator first hints that some hope remains and then shows how each woman at the wall loses this hope, the only thing left to them, after hearing a loved one's sentence. The speaker herself also loses hope for the same reason.

Memory

Memory becomes particularly important in the last sections of this poem. When one person dies, their memory is said to live on in their surviving friends and relatives. When one considers such an immense loss of life (as occurred under Stalin) in light of the belief that those who do not remember the past are destined to repeat it. The theme of memory becomes even more

essential to understanding Akhmatova's "Requiem," her mass for the memory of the dead.

Thus, it is important, and maybe even imperative, as this poem suggests, that all those who died in Russia under the Stalinist regime be remembered. A monument, in the least, must be erected to that memory. This poem is such a monument, and the narrator goes even further than this. By hinting that, as a well-known poet, she is likely to be memorialized, the speaker states that she does not want to be remembered as a poet but rather as one of the countless women who stood outside the prison wall. If she is memorialized, she wants to include not just her memories, but the memories of all those prisoners, as well as all those who mourned for those prisoners. The poem itself is famous for these very reasons, not because it memorializes a personal loss or sorrow, but because it memorializes the sorrow of an entire nation.

STYLE

Couplets

All of the stanzas in "Epilogue II," one of the most important sections in the poem, are couplets. Couplets are stanzas that have only two lines, usually ending in rhyme. Couplets are also a form commonly found in some Christian prayers.

Because of the couplet form, when "Epilogue II" is read out loud, it sounds as if the narrator is saying a prayer to the dead. The shortness of the stanzas makes the reader pause and more carefully consider what is being said. This part of the poem also signals a sense of closure not only of the poem (it is the last section, after all), but of the narrator's mourning, which is now transforming from grief into a call for remembrance. This may have been why the poet chose this different format, signaling a final transition of emotions in the whole cycle of this poem.

Elegy

An elegy is, by definition, a song or poem composed to lament someone who has died. Some of the literary elements of an elegy include the loss of a loved one, the universal significance of loss, a progression from grief to consolation or acceptance, and a resolution of mourning. "Requiem" can easily be read as an elegy to the narrator's son. On a more universal level, the poem could be referred to as an elegy for all of the Russian people who suffered under the communist regime. There is no denying, whether this poem is focused on the poet's son or on the country as a whole, that death is a prominent theme in this work. In this, two elements of elegy are fulfilled: the loss of a loved one and the universal significance of loss. Through the cycle of Akhmatova's poem, readers also sense the progression of the narrator's emotions from grief to acceptance, another important element found in elegies. By the end of the poem, the narrator is no longer wishing for death or insanity, but is instead thinking about a monument built to ensure that those who have died will never be forgotten. In these ways, this poem can be, and often is, referred to as an elegy.

Simplicity

The Acmeism movement in Russian poetry, an artistic movement that Akhmatova was a part of, promoted the use of simple, straightforward language, meaning, and allusions. Thus simplicity becomes one of the focal elements of the poem. There are probably no allusions in Akhmatova's poem that Russian-speaking readers would have trouble with. English-speaking readers might have to look up a few details about Russian geography and history, but in spite of this, the emotional impact of Akhmatova's poem is easily translated. Images are kept simple, with a few references to nature, which anyone can appreciate, as well as simplistic descriptions of grief, such as phrases like: "Smiles fade on submissive lips" and "How locks of ashen-blonde or black / Turn silver suddenly" (both in "Epilogue I"); "You are my son and my horror" (in section V); and "Now madness half shadows / My soul with its wing" (in section IX). The poetic images are fresh and emotional but also basic and simple.

Translation

Akhmatova's original poem included end rhymes (words at the ends of the line that rhymed with one another), but in English translation these rhymes do not appear. English-speaking readers are able to gain an understanding and appreciation of the meaning of the poet's work but not an appreciation for all the poetic elements and form that also affect the meaning and interpretation of "Requiem." Unless readers understand both languages, it is difficult to comprehend what, if any, poetic elements in the structure of the poem

have been saved. Therefore the appreciation of the meaning of this poem takes on a greater emphasis than the actual construction of it.

HISTORICAL CONTEXT

Acmeism

The Acmeist movement in poetry was developed in Russia in the early part of the twentieth century by Akhmatova's first husband, the poet Nikolai Gumilyov (1886–1921). Prior to this movement, Russian poets were influenced by symbolism, a writing style that spread from France and throughout Europe to Russia. The symbolists wrote poetry that was metaphysical, or spiritual, in nature, and used romantic and lofty images. In contrast, the Acmeists preferred to have their poetry grounded in ordinary reality; it was an expression of, or reaction to, events in everyday life.

The Acmeist group included Gumilyov, Akhmatova, the poet Sergei Gorodetsky (1884–1967), and the poet Osip Mandelstam (1891–1938), among others. Some of the underlying tenets of this type of poetry were not only to keep language simple, but also to write with a focus on culture. Acmeists practiced the use of restraint in language and imagery and strove to capture an authentic representation of life. The official movement lasted only a couple of years, as Gumilyov, the leader of the group, traveled extensively outside of Russia and therefore was absent much of the time; he later joined the Russian army. The effect of this movement, however, was reflected in later generations of Russian poets. Acmeist poetry reached its peak in the middle of what is often called the Silver Age of Russian poetry, an exceptional period of creativity in poetry, lasting from the end of the nineteenth century until the early twentieth.

Kresty Prison

"Requiem" mentions a prison by the Neva River in St. Petersburg, Russia. This prison is called Kresty Prison, a type of holding station for people who have been arrested but have not yet gone to trial. The word *kresty* means "cross" and refers to the cross-like shape of two of the buildings that make up the prison. There is also the possibility that this might be a reference to the crucifixions that once took place there. The prison was built in 1892. Today, the prison is

COMPARE & CONTRAST

- **1930s:** Writers in Russia are forced to become members of a government controlled union. If their work deviates from the strict union standards, such as including non-socialist beliefs in their writing or criticizing the government, their works are banned from publication. Some defiant writers, such as Osip Mandelstam, are also arrested.

  Today: It is once again becoming more and more dangerous for writers in Russia. Journalists who have criticized the Russian government have been killed, though their murderers have not been brought to justice.

- **1930s:** Joseph Stalin heads the Soviet Union, which is in transition from a system of individual land ownership to a system of collective agriculture. The new communist economy realizes some success, mostly due to progress made in the area of industrialization, where convicted citizens provide free labor.

  Today: Vladimir Putin heads the Russian government as the country continues to transition away from a government controlled economy to a free-market economy. According to a February, 2007, report from the U.S. State Department, however, a shrinking labor force, mostly caused by a birth rate that is lower than the death rate, is likely to contribute to the country's continued economic difficulties.

- **1930s:** The Soviet Union signs an agreement with Nazi Germany to invade Poland. Later, Germany attacks the Russians.

  Today: Russia agrees to work with the United States in the war against terrorism, providing items and services such as hospitals in Afghanistan.

still used as a place of pretrial confinement. As in Akhmatova's poem, the relatives and friends of prisoners still gather at the side of the river, in an attempt to gain a glimpse of the prisoners inside. Messages are often sent back and forth through hand movements that depict various letters, spelling out words.

Yezhov Terror

In the beginning lines of Akhmatova's poem, the narrator mentions the Yezhov terror. Although Stalin's time in power was marked by repression, there was one particular year that was worse than any other. The rise in deaths and mass imprisonments was overseen by the Soviet government (the term Soviet became the name of choice for the Communist regime after the Russian Revolution and referred to the primary unit of government) under the direction of Nikolai Yezhov between 1937 and 1938. During this time, arrests increased tenfold from the previous year (1936); and by then arrests were already estimated to be in the millions. Accurate records were not kept due to the extreme secrecy of the Communist regime. Before Yezhov came to power, people were arrested and not given the benefit of a trial, but this was much more common during the Yezhov Terror. Those who were not immediately executed were sent to labor camps, forced to build roads, canals, and factories. Many later died in the camps or in prison.

In 1936, Yezhov was named the head of the Peoples Commissariat for Internal Affairs. He directed his forces to arrest anyone who was known to be critical of Stalin. Prisoners were tortured and their families threatened until the newly arrested victims signed statements admitting that they were attempting to overthrow the government. Yezhov even became suspicious of the man whom he had replaced and ordered his predecessor's execution. It has been assumed that Yezhov himself was executed as well—supposedly for treason in 1939—two years after he had instigated his year of terror.

German soldiers surrendering to Russian forces (*AP Images*)

Joseph Stalin

Joseph Stalin was born Iosif Vissarionovich Dzhugashvili in 1879, in Georgia, which was then a part of Russia. He was raised in poverty and became interested in socialism as a youth after reading Karl Marx's *The Communist Manifesto* (1848). Stalin promoted socialism in Georgia, working toward the overthrow of the tsarist Russian government. In 1902, he was arrested for leading a workers' strike. He was arrested and exiled several more times throughout the next few years leading up to the Russian Revolution. Stalin's rise to power in Russian politics began when he became friends with Vladimir Lenin (1870–1924), leader of the Russian October Revolution and first head of the Soviet Union. In order to increase his political clout, Stalin was known to eliminate his political rivals either by falsely accusing them of treason and deporting them or by having them executed.

After Lenin was shot in an attempted assassination, Stalin's political power intensified. Although Lenin tried to rid the party of Stalin's aggressive and brutal tactics, Lenin had grown too physically weak on account of his injuries to do so effectively. After Lenin's death in 1924, Stalin assumed total power. Beginning in the 1930s, Stalin eliminated any political person whom he thought was a threat to his power, including those who had helped him to secure his position. This period of time was known as the Great Purge. It has been estimated that more than one million people were arrested and almost half of them eventually died either through torture, execution, or from perishing while in prison or at labor camps. Another 14 million people may have died due to Stalin's collectivization reform in agriculture, which forced many farmers to give up their farms and move to more barren land. On the positive side, many historians credit Stalin for creating a vital industrial economy during his reign, but this was due in large part to having significantly lowered the wages of workers and also stemmed from the use of prison labor. Another of Stalin's purges involved the military. Stalin had many military leaders killed, and this made the Soviet Union particularly vulnerable to Germany's invasion in 1941. Stalin managed to be victorious in these battles but at an enormous cost, as an estimated 27 million Russians died during World War II.

Stalin died of a stroke in 1953. Three years later, Nikita Khrushchev, then Soviet leader, denounced Stalin in a famous speech before the twentieth Communist Party Congress. Following this, political prisoners were released and authors who had once been unable to publish their work were once again allowed to do so, telling of their horrifying experiences under Stalin's reign. Thereafter, in effect, the Soviet Union attempted to purge Stalin from its history. In 1961, Stalin's remains were removed from their honorary position in a tomb next to Lenin.

CRITICAL OVERVIEW

Praised and loved by Russians as well as readers around the world, Akhmatova's "Requiem" has been referred to by many critics as the best of all of her poems. Although known for her eloquence in writing about emotions, this particular poem demonstrates this skill to a far greater degree than many of her other works.

Writing for the *Seattle Times*, Douglas Smith (in his review of Elaine Feinstein's biography, *Anna of All the Russias: A Life of Anna Akhmatova*), states that Akhmatova is "one of the most revered poets in Russia." Smith adds: "yet she is regrettably little known, and much less read, in the West." Smith explains that Akhmatova wrote "her epic poetic cycle 'Requiem,' as a testament to the horrors of Stalin's Great Terror that for years she kept in her head, too fearful to set it down on paper." Smith adds that "Requiem" marks "Akhmatova's transformation from a poet of intimate personal emotions to 'the voice of a whole people's suffering.'"

In "Bearing the Burden of Witness: *Requiem*," Nancy K. Anderson states that Akhmatova was not only able to write about the devastation that she experienced, but she was also able to convey what almost every Russian citizen was experiencing at that time. Anderson explains that because of this, the poem is both lyric and epic. "As befits a lyric poem," Anderson writes, "it is a first-person work, arising from an individual's experiences and perceptions." Anderson continued: "Yet there is always a recognition, stated or unstated, that while the narrator's sufferings are individual, they are anything but unique: as

befits an epic poet, she speaks of the experience of a nation." It is this universal statement of suffering that makes this poem so appealing. Anderson then continues, stating that the appeal of Akhmatova's poem is also due to the poet's ability "to express intense and almost overwhelming emotion within a precisely designed artistic structure, giving her words the force that confinement within a narrow channel gives to flood waters." Anderson further attempts to explain why Akhmatova's poem is so universal in its appeal. She writes: "Paradoxically, it is precisely Akhmatova's consciousness that she is just another woman in the line [outside the prison] that makes her more than just another woman in the line, that gives her the unique power of being able to speak not just for herself, but for them all." Another aspect of this poem that Anderson praises is the narrator's victory over oppression. "When the suffering woman overcomes the first and most natural impulse of fleeing from pain and is able to perform the great spiritual feat of choosing to stand and endure, she can no longer be crushed," Anderson states. "She has gained the stature necessary for the role of witness." And for this reason, "'Requiem,' the monument that she [Akhmatova] built, will stand throughout the ages, watching over the dead with grief and faithfulness and love."

David N. Wells, writing in *Anna Akhmatova: Her Poetry*, points out that this poem, although it looks, at first sight, like a simple poem, is deceptively complex and carefully formatted to convey deep emotions in relatively few words. "The superficial clarity and simplicity" of the poem "belie a considerable underlying complexity of imagery, allusion and compositional technique." The ten sections of this poem are "situated within a symmetrical framework of two introductory and two concluding poems which emphasise the courage and persistence of Russian women outside the prisons of the 1930s and lay great weight on the power of poetry to record their sufferings and to transcend them."

Finally, Ervin C. Brody, writing for the *Literary Review*, describes the poet in this way: "A chronicler of the isolated and intimate psychological events of a woman's emotional and intellectual life as well as the political events in the Soviet Union, Anna Akhmatova is one of Russia's greatest poets and perhaps the greatest woman poet in the history of Western culture." Brody then praises "Requiem" by stating that it is "majestic, bitter, lamenting." Brody went on to note that "the poems are written in classical form with ... customary simplicity and intensity. There is no better or more sensitive account of those dramatic historical days." Brody finds that Akhmatova's poem "cuts an iconoclastic swath through Soviet literature, stirs the heart, and opens the mind in its interaction between this woman-poet and her society. Rarely have the impoverished and powerless had such an eloquent advocate."

CRITICISM

Joyce M. Hart

Hart has degrees in English and creative writing and is a freelance writer and published author. In the following essay, she examines Akhmatova's poem for the five stages of dealing with death as proposed by the psychologist Elisabeth Kübler-Ross.

In 1969, shortly after Akhmatova died, Elisabeth Kübler-Ross wrote *On Death and Dying*. The book is famous for defining the psychological process (the five stages of grief) that people go through when faced with death, either news of their own impending death, or the death of a loved one. Although Akhmatova obviously did not read the book, her poem "Requiem" displays this very process. Kübler-Ross defined the psychological stages of grief as progressing through denial or isolation, then onto anger, which is followed by bargaining, then depression or despair, and, finally, acceptance. Although the five stages are expressed in Akhmatova's poem, they are not presented in the same order as Kübler-Ross has suggested. This discrepancy can be attributed to the lack of chronology in the dating of the various sections of Akhmatova's poem. Readers do not know for certain when Akhmatova wrote these sections or in what order, and they do not appear to progress in strict chronological order.

The first stage of grief in Kübler-Ross's list is that of denial or isolation. In the poem's section called "Instead of a Preface," the narrator refers to a woman who wakes up from a "stupor to which everyone had succumbed." This image implies a self-imposed isolation on the part of everyone standing at the wall (or even everyone in Russia). This state of mind causes each person to withdraw into him- or herself, thus avoiding any further pain. In essence, this is the definition

WHAT DO I READ NEXT?

- *Poems of Anna Akhmatova* (1997), translated by Stanley Kunitz and Max Hayward, is presented both in Russian and in English. This collection offers poems written over Akhmatova's lifetime, from those written in her early years to those written just before her death, and "Requiem" is included. This collection provides an excellent introduction to Akhmatova's body of work.

- Emma Gerstein knew Akhmatova during the Yezhov Terror and the years surrounding it. In the book *Moscow Memoirs: Memories of Anna Akhmatova, Osip Mandelstam, and Literary Russia under Stalin* (2004), Gerstein recounts those times. Gerstein was included in the same circle of poets as Akhmatova and kept journals of the time she shared with these now famous writers.

- Marina Tsvetaeva was a contemporary of Akhmatova. Some literary critics claim she was even more powerful as a Russian poet than Akhmatova, who is better known to English-speaking audiences. The poems in Tsvetaeva's *Selected Poems*, republished in 1999 (5th edition), recounts Tsvetaeva's journey from teenage poetess to political exile.

- Together with Akhmatova and Tsvetaeva, Bella Akhmadulina is also considered one of the most important Russian female poets. Akhmadulina's poetry can be found in the 1993 publication *The Poetic Craft of Bella Akhmadulina*. Akhmadulina is a more modern poet, first published in 1955, and is not known for writing about politics. Rather, her work explores love and relationships.

of being in a state of shock, and certainly shock would be a reasonable reaction to the emotional terror of having to face so many deaths during the days of Stalin's reign, and of grappling with the uncertainty of the fates of friends and loved ones.

> BARGAINING IS THE THIRD STAGE OF GRIEF AS
> DEFINED BY KÜBLER-ROSS. IN 'REQUIEM,' THE BAR-
> GAINING ASPECT PRESENTS ITSELF IN A LINE FROM
> SECTION V, IN WHICH THE NARRATOR MENTIONS THAT
> SHE HAS BEGGED THE HANGMAN FOR HER SON'S
> RELEASE ('I FLUNG MYSELF AT THE HANGMAN'S FEET')."

Denial, still part of Kübler-Ross's first stage of dealing with death, appears in the poem's section simply titled "III." This stanza begins with "No, it is not I, it is somebody else who is suffering." At this point, the narrator denies a connection with her own feelings. There is no way, the narrator states, that she could have possibly withstood so much suffering. The narrator has instead submerged herself into darkness, or as she says it, the "Night." She does not want to see what is happening around her: "Let them shroud it in black, / And let them carry off the lanterns." The narrator does not want to face the pain that she will feel upon looking at the dead, and so she denies that pain by denying death, hiding it from the light ("let them carry off the lanterns"). In the darkness, or in her state of denial, she can pretend that the murders are no longer real, thus alleviating her pain.

Kübler-Ross's second stage in the process of accepting death is anger, and in "Requiem," anger is expressed in section IV. In this part of the poem, the narrator berates herself. She yells at herself, "you mocker, / Minion of all your friends." This suggests that the narrator thinks of herself as a fraud or as less worthy than her friends. In this section, the narrator is critical of her past behavior, and she rebukes herself for being young and naive and unaware of the terrible tragedies that would occur in the future. Indeed, she even calls herself a "Gay little sinner." In section V of the poem, there are also hints of anger. Here the narrator's anger is more connected to her son and his impending death, as if the narrator does not know where else to aim her feelings. She tells him how she has been struggling, and the narrator even appears to blame the son for her distress: "For seventeen months I've been crying out, / Calling you home." When the narrator states that "Everything is confused forever," this is a reference to her conflicting feelings ("You are my son and my horror"). The speaker's confusion is also caused by her inability to tell the difference between a "beast" and a "man." The narrator's anger is a way of lashing out at death, of attempting to assert some force or control over a situation in which that narrator feels, and is, totally powerless—a phenomenon that Kübler-Ross also discusses.

Bargaining is the third stage of grief as defined by Kübler-Ross. In "Requiem," the bargaining aspect presents itself in a line from section V, in which the narrator mentions that she has begged the hangman for her son's release ("I flung myself at the hangman's feet"). In actuality, Akhmatova wrote flattering passages dedicated to Stalin, the man who was responsible for imprisoning her son. She did so in the hopes that Stalin would commute her son's sentence, which Stalin eventually did. The reference to the hangman, in this poem, most likely alludes to Stalin, and further confirms the bargaining element. It could also be said that the speaker's attempts to achieve oblivion from her grief by seeking insanity in section IX is also a form of bargaining. More explicitly, going mad will cause the speaker to lose her memories of her son (madness "does not allow me to take / Anything of mine with me"), and the speaker attempts to bargain with this requirement to no avail: "No matter how I plead with it, / No matter how I supplicate."

Section IX of the poem begins with the lines, "Now madness half shadows / My soul with its wing," and this could signal the onset of the fourth stage of grief, that of depression or despair. The narrator's depression is so strong that she contemplates either succumbing entirely to insanity or to death. Indeed, the speaker clearly indicates that she wants to die in "VIII, To Death." The depression (or madness) "beckons toward the black ravine." In the second stanza of section IX, several of Kübler-Ross's stages are apparent. Here the narrator is "Raving as if it were somebody else," and this line implies denial—a denial of selfhood and a denial of the pain and depression she is experiencing.

"Epilogue I" also carries heavy overtones of depression and despair. In this section, the narrator recounts all that she has seen and "learned"; she has learned what despair looks like. The narrator uses phrases such as "faces fall," and "terror darts from under eyelids." She also mentions "How suffering traces lines / Of stiff cuneiform on cheeks." This section continues with descriptions of hair that turns grey overnight ("suddenly"), and "Smiles [that] fade on submissive lips." Then the narrator changes her focus and prays for herself and for all those who have suffered what she has suffered. While a prayer can take the form of bargaining, this prayer signals instead the final stage of grief: acceptance. This is because the speaker widens her focus from her own pain to the pain of those around her. Furthermore, the section that follows, "Epilogue II," attempts to channel this pain into a monument of remembrance. Thus, the narrator accepts her grief because she is no longer fighting against it; instead, she embraces it by using it to honor the dead.

There is also a hint of acceptance in section VII of this poem. Her son's sentence has been decreed, and in some way the narrator feels relief for having finally found out what the sentence will be. "Never mind, I was ready. / I will manage somehow," the first stanza reads. In what could also be perceived as a further gesture of acceptance, the speaker admits: "I must learn to live again." Still, it is at the poem's end, in "Epilogue II," where true acceptance occurs. When the section opens, it is clear that some time has passed ("Once more the day of remembrance draws near"). The tone of the narrator's voice is more tempered and reflective. The anger and depression are missing in the lines of this last section of the poem. Here, the narrator simply states without emotion: "I see, I hear, I feel you," and she recounts her past pain in a neutral manner. The narrator no longer beseeches death or insanity, and she no longer attempts to make sense of the situation by determining who is a man and who is a monster. The sense of immediate anguish has passed, and the tone of this section is exceedingly calm. The narrator also mentions that she wants to name all those who have died (and all those who waited at the wall with her) so that they will always be remembered. And, even without the list, "I will remember them always," she states. The narrator will remember by writing about them, and by talking about them with "my exhausted mouth / Through which a hundred million scream." Even the last two lines of the poem embody acceptance or peace, as "a prison dove coo[s] in the distance, / And the ships of the Neva sail calmly on."

Source: Joyce M. Hart, Critical Essay on "Requiem," in *Poetry for Students*, Gale, 2008.

Sharon M. Bailey

In the following excerpt, Bailey explores the ways in which "Requiem" serves as an elegy to the entire country of Russia. Bailey focuses on a concept that she calls the "pathetic fallacy," which "springs from the rupture—caused by death—of the human's perception of his relationship to nature."

... In "Requiem," it is apparent perhaps to a greater degree than in the traditional elegy, that the subject is not so much the son as the mother. In fact, the framing poems make no mention of the son, and barely discuss the prisoners at all. The epigraph, which answers the question "Where did this happen?," answers without alluding to the arrests, and defines, for the remainder of the cycle, the subject as "I"—Akhmatova herself. Dan Latimer also emphasizes the survivor over the deceased in his definition of the elegy. The most essential theme, he writes, is the disruption of the survivor's sense of justice in the universe:

> The first [essential theme of any elegy] is the expression of disbelief that death would come to one so beautiful, so vital (Adonis), so gifted (Bion, Keats), so noble (Caesar, Lincoln), so earnest and dedicated (Eduard King). This question involves what Rilke calls "des Unrechts Anschein," the appearance of injustice.
>
> (25–26)

A slight reformulation of this idea would be that the events have disrupted the survivor's sense of a rational and predictable order in his or her own life. At the same time as Akhmatova is grieving the loss of her son in "Requiem," she is also grieving, for example, the lack of continuity between her own happy youth in Tsarskoye Selo in poem "IV" or her childhood by the sea in "Epilogue II" and her present misery. The arrest of her son initiates a breakdown of the poet's perception of an understandable reality.

The loss in "Requiem," however, is more than nostalgia for lost youth. At this point "Requiem" exhibits a complexity that goes beyond that of a traditional elegy. In the traditional elegy, much of the suffering of the survivor stems from a consciousness that he/she is not immune from the fate of the deceased. In "Requiem," the suffering of the survivor is real and not just the result of an awareness of potentialities. The same political machinery which is responsible for the arrests and executions of the sons also sentences the wives and mothers to a different type of suffering. The uncertainty, helplessness and injustice that accompany arrest of a family member is a fate that makes life outside the prison no more desirable than arrest itself, and in this sense, "Requiem" is an elegy written on the occasion of the arrest of the son and the subsequent "living death" of the mother. This living death is reflected in the depictions of the women, which show them lacking social qualities, such as speech and identity, and physical qualities, such as warmth and breath.

Analogous to the isolation imposed on the prisoners, the wives and mothers are shown to be essentially deprived of speech—a deprivation which prevents them from joining into a healthy community. On the one hand, this speechlessness is a consequence of the physical suffering. Even to produce her whispered question, one of only two examples of spoken communication in the cycle, the woman of "Instead of a Preface" had to rouse herself from a stupor into which everyone had fallen. On the other hand, there is a disconcerting absence of anyone to whom the women could speak. The arresting soldier is represented only by a blue-topped cap ("To Death"), the executioner by feet ("V"), and guard and warden by bolted doors ("Epilogue II") or the rasping key ("Dedication"). Denied articulate, human speech, the women wail like the wives of the Streltsy ("I"), cry like the mother pleading for her son or Mary Magdalene ("V" and "Crucifixion"), howl like the woman against whom the door is slammed ("Epilogue II"), or fall silent like John and the Mother ("Crucifixion"). Speech is above all a social act, but the arrest of their sons and husbands have left the women isolated, not only from the one arrested, but even from each other. Even though the women stand in line together, they are unable to form a community. In this respect, their experience is much like the isolation imposed on the prisoners within the prison . . .

It has been shown that "Requiem" achieves universal significance by appealing to a broad audience and, more importantly, by emphasizing the magnitude of the atrocity—repeatedly focusing first on the victims as individuals and then on the victims as part of a countless mass. Sacks also stresses the importance of generic convention to the universal appeal of an effective elegy. He argues throughout his book that the conventions are not artificial literary devices, but

are reflections of natural human impulses. Due to space limitations it is not possible to list all of the conventions and their examples in "Requiem." I will therefore limit my discussion to the one convention which, in my opinion, is used most effectively in the cycle. The pathetic fallacy, according to Lambert, is one of the most universal conventions of the elegy and basic to grief itself:

> In funeral laments from all cultures and from all stages of civilization we see a desire on the part of the mourner (expressed either as wish or as fact) to involve the whole world in his own particular sorrows. Nature is made culpable, is made to suffer, is made to sympathize.
>
> (xxvi)

A predictable, perhaps even cliché, example of this can be found in the first lines of the "Dedication": "Pered etim gorem gnutsia gory, / Ne techet velikaia reka" ("Mountains bow down to this grief, / Mighty rivers cease to flow"). In other instances, the moon visits the grieving woman of "II," and the White Nights keep watch over the son and speak of his suffering. However, it is not only nature that participates in the grief, but also the man-made environment of Leningrad, and even Russia as a symbolic cultural and ethnic entity.

The pathetic fallacy springs from the rupture—caused by death—of the human's perception of his relationship to nature. For the conscious and self-contemplating human, the natural cycle of death and rebirth creates a dilemma . . . In short, the death of an individual tears apart the mourner's perception of unity between nature, death and humanity—death comes out of season, spring branches wither and freeze, and the eternal cycle is broken. Thus the pathetic fallacy has its root in the human need to recreate an order in which man, rather than nature, is supreme. Sacks, who like Smith essentially subordinates all other elegiac conventions to the pastoral, writes that the pathetic fallacy allows the elegist to create a fiction whereby the mutability of nature is not the cause of his suffering, but rather changes in nature appear to depend on him (20) . . .

The sense of injustice in a traditional elegy lay not in the fact that death strikes, but in that death struck this once, in an untimely manner, an individual whom we wish would have stayed with us longer. Death is cruel, it is arbitrary, it is indifferent to the accomplishments or promise of its victims, but for all this, it is not without rationale (Smith 8). An atrocity such as the Holocaust or the Terror, on the other hand, defies comprehension. What words can describe a situation that has no meaning? However, this leads to the moral problem of acknowledging the events; if there are no words with which to speak of the atrocity, how will it be remembered? Thus Brodsky writes, "At certain periods of history it is only poetry that is capable of dealing with reality by condensing it into something graspable, something that otherwise could not be retained by the mind" (52). Theodor Adorno, who is famous for his proclamation that it is "barbaric to continue to write poetry after Auschwitz" (87), also admits that poetry is indispensable: "Suffering—what Hegel called the awareness of affliction—also demands the continued existence of the very art it forbids; hardly anywhere else does suffering still find its own voice, a consolation that does not immediately betray it" (88). The successful poem portrays the events without rationalization, preserving the memory of those who suffered, while at the same time preserving the sense of overwhelming chaos. The elegy for such an atrocity must find consolation through memory that does not impose reason.

This complicated task is achieved even within the ten central poems of "Requiem." In addition to expressing her grief with nearly textbook accuracy, Akhmatova conveys historical information about what happened, and more importantly its toll on the men who were arrested and the women who were left behind. Many of the images used to describe the poet's state of mind are images of arrest and death and serve the dual function of describing what happened to the son and what the mother felt as a result. For example, in "To Death" the poet wishes desperately to be in her son's place: to be arrested, dead or in Siberia, and in "IX" she recreates the experience of half-death, "Uzhe bezumnie krylom / Dushi zakrylo polovinu" ("Now madness half shadows / My soul with its wing") . . .

However, it is a final, moral aspect that sets "Requiem" apart from the traditional elegy and forces us to look for a new definition of consolation. The vicarious arrest and imprisonment of the mother conveys the memory of the suffering felt both by the arrested men within the prison and the women waiting outside. "Requiem" aspires not only to immortalize the son or even the mother's love for her son, but to acknowledge the reality of the Terror in such a way that will not allow history to forget. The poetic

consolation, which Adorno writes does not immediately betray the suffering it portrays, is the memorialization of the events as they truly happened. Akhmatova's overarching goal in the ten central poems is to immortalize an entire nation victimized by the Terror. . . .

The grief expressed in the central ten poems is raw, internal, not inherently within the realm of language, and expressed without a strong sense of an implied reader. This is not the case in the framing poems. These poems, as already pointed out above, seem to address the reader directly. The "Dedication," for example, prepares the reader with an outline of the sequence of events to be portrayed in the cycle: the arrest and imprisonment, the waiting in line, and the sentencing and isolation (Amert 45–46). The "Prologue" and "Epilogue I" summarize the Terror from the perspective of the arrested and the women left behind, respectively. These three poems demonstrate the successful resolution of the poet's work of mourning, insofar as they state with relative directness what the poet only intimates in the central poems. However, it is in "Epilogue II" and "Instead of a Foreword" that Akhmatova most clearly articulates her strategies to overcome the suffering of the Terror.

Whereas the ten central poems are by their very existence a memorial to the victims of the Terror, "Epilogue II" lays emphasis on the act of articulating memory as a defense against the continued suffering. In this poem, Akhmatova purposefully invokes language itself as a weapon. Throughout the cycle the poet, as well as all of the women, are shown bewildered, speechless and defeated. In "Epilogue II," Akhmatova overcomes this. Geographic locations distinguish themselves from each other and remain fixed to their proper historical significance. The women with whom Akhmatova stood in line begin to stand out from the mass as individuals, for as Amert writes,

> In contrast to the collective portrait evoked in the first part of the "Epilogue," the poet conjures up brief yet individualized portraits of three of her addressees and then articulates her unrealizable wish to call all of the women by name, thereby commemorating them individually—the antithesis of their depersonalization during the Ezhov Terror.

(52)

Akhmatova even restores to the women the power of speech. Aside from the whispered question in "Instead of a Preface," the only moment of articulate speech is by the beautiful woman in the "Epilogue": "Siuda prikhozhu, kak domoi!" ("Coming here's like coming home").

On a more fundamental level, however, "Epilogue II" makes clear that Akhmatova intends for the cycle to itself supply the words to name the atrocities which could only be met with silence at the time. Sacks writes that the poetic form of the elegy is a verbal "presence" which fills the "absence" caused by death (xi–xiii). The need to create a "presence" through language is only that much more acute when the elegy is for victims of an atrocity, since, as we have seen, Terror deprives the victims of the means of articulating their pain and, by isolating the women at the time and then finally scattering them, eliminates the potential audience. Akhmatova uses the image of weaving a cloth of words as a means of creating a tangible "presence" to displace the "absence" created by the Terror. Sacks writes that it is

> worth noting the significant frequency with which the elegy has employed crucial images of weaving, of creating a fabric in the place of a void. . . . To speak of weaving a consolation recalls the actual weaving of burial clothes and shroud and this emphasizes how mourning is an action, a process of work.

(18–19)

Akhmatova uses exactly the image of weaving a cloth of words. Unable to name each woman and not knowing what has become of them, she nevertheless seeks to fill the void of their silence with a veil of their own words: "Dlia nikh sotkala ia shirokii pokrov / Iz bednykh, u nikh zhe podslushannykh slov" ("I have woven a wide mantle for them / From their meager, overheard words"). On the one hand, this cloth she weaves may be seen as a burial shroud, with which, perhaps, she offers a token rite to those who had been executed in secret and buried without a memorial service or grave marker. Perhaps also it is a shroud with which Akhmatova puts to rest her grief of the ten central poems. But more than just covering and concealing what has happened, this cloth also makes it visible. The women have been scattered without any record of their having been there. Akhmatova's veil of words solidifies them into a group, protects them from obscurity, and replaces their physical absence with a verbal presence.

Source: Sharon M. Bailey, "An Elegy for Russia: Anna Akhmatova's 'Requiem,'" in *Slavic and East European Journal*, Vol. 43, No. 2, Summer 1999, pp. 324–46.

David N. Wells

In the following excerpt, Wells discusses the emotional states found in the various poem segments in "Requiem." The critic argues that these various emotional themes are given coherence by the two introductory segments, "Dedication" and "Introduction."

. . . Although "Requiem" has no plot in any conventional sense, the ten numbered poems which form its centre do represent a process of emotional change. They do this through a lyrical examination of a series of emotional states presented in a chronological sequence which is rendered coherent by the two unnumbered introductory poems entitled 'Posvyashchenie' ('Dedication') and 'Vstuplenie' ('Introduction'). 'Dedication' in particular not only makes it clear that the poems which follow are written in the name of a large and anonymous group of women, but also specifies the time frame of the cycle:

Gde teper' nevol'nye podrugi
Dvukh moikh osatanelykh let?

Where now are the chance friends
Of those two demoniacal years?

'Introduction', on the other hand, focuses rather on place:

I nenuzhnym priveskom boltalsya
Vozle tyurem svoikh Leningrad.

And Leningrad dangled around its prisons
Like a useless appendage.

By later referring more broadly to the sufferings of 'Rus', it affirms that the description of Leningrad is meant to stand also for the entire country.

The central section of the poem begins with an arrest, laconically described in the first line of poem No. 1: 'They took you away at dawn.' The scene is likened to a funeral, but a note of defiance is implied by the heroine's comparison of herself to the wives of the Strel'tsy in the last two lines:

Budu ya, kak streletskie zhenki,
Pod kremlevskimi bashnyami vyt'.

Like the wives of the Strel'tsy
I shall howl under the Kremlin towers.

In the poems which follow, however, this defiance gives way to passivity and to a gradual breakdown of personality. In the second poem the speaker sees herself partly as someone else:

Eta zhenshchina bol'na,
Eta zhenshchina odna,

Muzh v mogile, syn v tyur'me,
Pomolites' obo mne.

This woman is ill,
This woman is alone,
Son in prison, husband in the grave,
Pray for me.

And in the third poem the gap between mental processes that predate the arrest and the current reality is rendered explicit. The speaker is unable to believe that it is indeed her own actions that she is watching:

Net, eto ne ya, eto kto-to drugoi stradaet.
Ya by tak ne mogla

No, it is not I, it is somebody else who is suffering
I should not have been able to bear it.

The fourth poem marks a particular stage in the history of individual prisoners—their mothers and wives queuing outside the Kresty prison in Leningrad in order to hand over parcels, and shows the speaker, more resignedly now, contrasting her present fate with her life in earlier years. The fifth, explicitly situated seventeen months after the arrest, shows increasing disorientation:

Vse pereputalos' navek,
I mne ne razobrat'
Teper', kto zver', kto chelovek

Everything has been muddled for ever,
And now I cannot work out
Who is a beast and who is a human being.

This is also reflected in the sixth poem. The seventh, entitled 'Prigovor' ('Sentence'), initiates a further new stage. Notification that her son has been sentenced—presumably to death—throws the speaker back into despair:

I upalo kamennoe slovo
Na moyu eshche zhivuyu grud'.

And the word fell like a stone
On my still living breast.

She is led into another round of denial and suppression of her emotions:

U menya segodnya mnogo dela:
Nado pamyat' do kontsa ubit',
Nado, chtob dusha okamenela,
Nado snova nauchit'sya zhit'

Today I have many things to do:
I must kill my memory off completely,
My heart must turn to stone,
I must relearn how to live.

The next two poems deal with different and more extreme manifestations of despair: in the first (No. 8) the speaker invites death to come to her to release her from her torments; in the second (No. 9) it is insanity which is seen as the only possible form of consolation even though it will remove all memories of the past, the welcome as well as the terrible.

Up to this point the numbered poems of the narrative sequence had been written almost entirely in the first person. (The exceptions are No. 2, which is written partly in the third person, and No. 4, which is written as a second-person address by the speaker to herself.) The tenth and final poem of the inner narrative, which represents the carrying out of the sentence passed in the seventh poem, that is the execution of the heroine's son, switches to the third person, discursively reflecting her inability to speak after this latest shock. In order to describe this culmination of the narrative, Akhmatova has recourse to Biblical history and finds a model in the crucifixion of Jesus, and particularly in the responses of female figures—Mary Magdalene and Mary the Mother of Jesus—to the crucifixion:

Magdalina bilas' i rydala,
Uchenik lyubimyi kamenel,
A tuda, gde molcha Mat' stoyala,
Tak nikto vzglyanut' i ne posmel.

Mary Magdelene beat her breast and sobbed,
The beloved disciple turned to stone,
But no one even dared to look
At where the Mother stood in silence.

Haight has suggested that the three figures here represent three different stages of suffering: Mary Magdalene the defiance of poem No. 1, John the beloved disciple the paralysis of, for example, No. 7, and Mary the Mother a deep understanding arrived at by passing through all stages. The silence of Mary the Mother at the moment of the crucifixion, however, may represent not so much wisdom as a state of catatonia induced in her, as in the first-person heroine of the narrative, by the finality of her son's death.

However, invoking the crucifixion is not merely a method for projecting the sufferings of women in Russia in the late 1930s on to a universal plane. In theological terms the crucifixion implies the resurrection, and the memorialising function of the "Requiem" cycle foreshadowed in 'Dedication' (and affirmed in the introductory prose passage added in 1957) is rendered explicit in the two poems which form its 'Epilogue'.

Having passed through the Terror documented in the ten poems of the narrative, the speaker finds she has survived and is able to record the experience of her sisters:

> I ya molyus' ne o sebe odnoi,
> A obo vsekh, kto tam stoyal so mnoyu,
> I v lyutyi kholod, i v iyul'skii znoi,
> Pod krasnoyu oslepsheyu stenoyu.

> And I pray not for myself alone,
> But for all those who stood there with me
> In the bitter cold and in the heat of July
> Under that blind red wall.

The final poem contains an affirmation of the power of words to recall the female, indirect victims of Stalinism and also an assertion that the act of recalling has its own therapeutic and protective effect:

> Dlya nikh sotkala ya shirokii pokrov
> Iz bednykh, u nikh zhe podslushannykh slov.

> For them I have woven a broad shroud
> From poor words, overheard from them.

Having established the power of such a monument, Akhmatova then, secure in the knowledge of its durability, turns to the question of a sculptural monument to herself as the author of "Requiem". In considering where such a monument should be placed, Akhmatova rejects locations that have associations with her life and poetry before "Requiem"—the Black Sea coast and the park at Tsarskoe Selo—and insists that it should be outside the prison walls in Leningrad, so that even in death she should not forget the events of the 1930s. This choice too marks a partial rejection of the poetry of Akhmatova's youth now that her pen has found its vocation as public chronicler of the Terror.

Source: David N. Wells, "Stalinism and War: Works of the 1930s and 1940s," in *Anna Akhmatova: Her Poetry*, Berg, 1996, pp. 64–95.

SOURCES

Akhmatova, Anna, "Requiem," in *The Complete Poems of Anna Akhmatova*, Zephyr Press, 1992, pp. 384–94.

Anderson, Nancy K., "Bearing the Burden of Witness: *Requiem*," in *The Word that Causes Death's Defeat: Poems of Memory*, Yale University Press, 2004, pp.181–93.

Bailey, Sharon M., "An Elegy for Russia: Anna Akhmatova's *Requiem*," in *Slavic and East European Journal*, Vol. 43, No. 2, Summer 1999, pp. 324–46.

Binyon, T. J., *Pushkin: A Biography*, HarperCollins, 2003.

Brody, Ervin C., "The Poet in the Trenches: *The Complete Poems of Anna Akhmatova*," in *Literary Review*, Vol. 37, No. 4, Summer 1994, pp. 689–704.

Carlisle, Olga Andreyev, *Poets on Street Corners, Portraits of Fifteen Russian Poets*, Random House, 1968.

Figes, Orlando, *A People's Tragedy: The Russian Revolution*, Pimlico, 1997.

Kübler-Ross, Elisabeth, *On Death and Dying*, reprint edition, Scribner, 1997.

Romano, Carlin, "Russian Literature in the Age of Putin," in *Chronicle of Higher Education*, March 2, 2007.

Smith, Douglas, "The Voice of Russian People's Suffering," in the *Seattle Times*, April 2, 2006.

U.S. Department of Justice, Office of Justice Programs, Bureau of Justice Statistics, *Corrections Statistics*, http://www.ojp.usdoj.gov/bjs/correct.htm (accessed February 28, 2007).

Wells, David N., "Stalinism and War: Works of the 1930s and 1940s," in *Anna Akhmatova: Her Poetry*, Berg, 1996, pp. 64–77.

FURTHER READING

Brown, Clarence, *The Portable Twentieth-Century Russian Reader*, Penguin Classics, 2003.
> Brown has brought together an extensive look at the last century's most prominent figures in Russian literature, with works by Akhmatova and her contemporaries Alexander Blok and Olsip Mandelstam. For a broader view of authors, Brown also provides prose works by Leo Tolstoy, Anton Chekhov, Alexander Solzhenitsyn, and Boris Pasternak, to name a few. This collection provides a great introduction to the masters of Russian literature.

Dalos, Gyorgy, *The Guest from the Future: Anna Akhmatova and Isaiah Berlin*, Farrar, Straus and Giroux, 2000.
> In 1945, Akhmatova met Isaiah Berlin, a Russian-born scholar and diplomat who was living in England. Berlin told Akhmatova stories of living in a free society, something she had not experienced firsthand. Berlin inspired Akhmatova, and she wrote one of her famous poems, "Poem without a Hero," with Berlin as the central figure. In his book, Dalos presents historic details woven together with correspondence between Berlin and Akhmatova.

Mawdsley, Evan, *The Stalin Years: The Soviet Union, 1929–53*, 2nd edition, Manchester University Press, 2003.
> A professor of international history at Glasgow University, Mawdsley discusses the effect of Stalin's politics on the culture and economics

of the country, and on Russia's foreign relationships with other countries. Stalin's ideology and its effects are pieced together from historic accounts as well as official documents that have only recently been made public.

Reeder, Roberta, *Anna Akhmatova: Poet and Prophet*, Picador USA, 1995.

Reeder's biography of Akhmatova has gained much praise over the years. She not only writes about the poet's life, but also includes critical analyses of Akhmatova's work. Reeder also offers glimpses of the poets that influenced Akhmatova, presenting a comprehensive understanding of the poet's life and work.

A Satirical Elegy on the Death of a Late Famous General

JONATHAN SWIFT

1765

Jonathan Swift's "A Satirical Elegy on the Death of a Late Famous General" was written in 1722 upon the death of the English general John Churchill, the Duke of Marlborough. The poem was first published formally in 1765, when it appeared in *Jonathan Swift, Works*, edited by John Hawkesworth. Churchill, the duke disparaged in the poem, had a checkered diplomatic and military career. Thus, he became the object of an unsympathetic satirical elegy by Swift, who was one of his leading political enemies.

Swift is known as a great prose satirist rather than as a poet, although he wrote a voluminous amount of poetry, and "A Satirical Elegy on the Death of a Late Famous General" certainly falls well within his favored mode of expression. Swift is universally known for his novel *Gulliver's Travels*, a sharp, bitter, and angry satire on everything from the nature of the English government to human nature itself. He is also author of prose satires such as *A Tale of a Tub*, a commentary on the corruptions of the Christian religion; *The Battle of the Books*, his entrance into an ongoing learned argument over the superiority of ancient or modern writers; and *A Modest Proposal*, a tract in which he suggests selling Irish babies of under a year old to rich Englishmen for food as a way to deal with the problem of Irish poverty.

The text of Swift's "A Satirical Elegy on the Death of a Late Famous General" can be found

Jonathan Swift (*The Library of Congress*)

in *The Wadsworth Anthology of Poetry*, edited by Jay Parini and published by Thomson Wadsworth in 2006.

AUTHOR BIOGRAPHY

Swift was born in Ireland to English parents on November 30, 1667. His father, also called Jonathan Swift, a solicitor, died several months before his birth. His mother, Abigail Errick, left Swift in Ireland with his nurse and went to live in England. Until Swift entered the Kilkenny School, some sixty miles from Dublin, he was shuttled back and forth between Ireland and England, sent to stay with his mother, his nurse, or his father's family. At age fourteen, Swift entered Trinity College, Dublin. He was awarded a B.A. in 1686 and began work on a master's degree. In early winter, 1688, William of Orange, a Protestant, overthrew King James II, the Catholic king of England. In Catholic Ireland, Trinity College was thrown into chaos and its classes suspended. As a result of the political turmoil, Swift left Ireland and Trinity College for England in 1689 without getting the master's degree that he had been working towards at the time.

Against this background, Swift came of age intellectually and politically. Within the context of shifting powers and fierce political and religious enmities, Swift had to make his career. In England, Swift became a part of the household of Sir William Temple, statesman and diplomat, whom he served as secretary. At Moor Park, Temple's residence, Swift met Esther Johnson. She was eight years old at the time, her father was dead, and she was the daughter of one of Temple's servants. Swift became her tutor and developed a lifelong relationship with her, which perhaps extended even to matrimony, but that is not clear. He wrote about her, assigning her literary manifestation the name Stella.

Swift was plagued with fits of dizziness, and he left Moor Park for Ireland in 1690 for his health, but soon returned to England. In 1692, Swift earned an M.A. from Hertford College, Oxford University. Afterwards, he again left Moor Park for Ireland, where he was ordained as a priest in the Church of Ireland and became the administrator of a church in Kilroot. Unhappy with his assignment there and perhaps disappointed in love, rejected by Jane Waring, to whom he had proposed marriage, Swift returned to Moor Park again in 1696. He stayed there until Temple's death in 1699, helping him ready his memoirs and letters for publication. At this time, Swift wrote *The Battle of the Books*. After Temple's death, Swift accepted an offer to work as secretary and chaplain to the Lord Justice Charles Berkeley in Ireland. The job, however, Swift learned upon his arrival, had been given to someone else. He managed to secure several other positions in St. Patrick's Cathedral, Dublin, instead. In 1702, in Dublin, Swift obtained a Doctor of Divinity degree from Trinity College. In the spring of 1702, Swift returned to England in order to bring Esther Johnson back to Ireland with him. Historical speculation estimates that they may have married fourteen years later, but no authoritative evidence of their marriage exists.

During the first decade of the eighteenth century, Swift published *A Tale of a Tub* and *The Battle of the Books*, and he began to gain recognition for his writing. He became friendly with the poet Alexander Pope, the playwright John Gay, and the satirist John Arbuthnot (who was also a physician). In 1713, the group formed the Scriblerus Club.

After 1707, Swift became active in English and Irish secular and ecclesiastical politics. In

1710, Swift became editor of the Tory paper *Examiner*. He wrote strenuously against continuing England's continental war and pointedly against the Duke of Marlborough's role in the war. Indeed, after Marlborough's death, Swift disparaged him in his poem "A Satirical Elegy on the Death of a Late Famous General," which was written in 1722, and posthumously published in a collection of Swift's works in 1765.

By this time, Swift had become a close advisor to the Tory government. In 1714, when Queen Anne died and the Tories were displaced by the Whigs, who came to power with the ascendancy of George I to the throne, Swift returned to Ireland as Dean of St. Patrick's Cathedral in Dublin. In Ireland, Swift continued to write political pamphlets urging justice for Ireland. Swift also began writing *Gulliver's Travels*, which was published in 1726 and enjoyed enormous success, multiple printings, and immediate translation into French, German, and Dutch.

Swift died in 1745, a hero to the Irish, after a prolonged and debilitating illness that began in 1738. He was buried beside Esther Johnson, who had died in 1728. He bequeathed most of his fortune to the establishment of a hospital for the mentally ill.

POEM TEXT

His Grace! impossible! what dead!
Of old age too, and in his bed!
And could that mighty warrior fall?
And so inglorious, after all!
Well, since he's gone, no matter how,   5
The last loud trump must wake him now:
And, trust me, as the noise grows stronger,
He'd wish to sleep a little longer.
And could he be indeed so old
As by the newspapers we're told?   10
Threescore, I think, is pretty high;
'Twas time in conscience he should die.
This world he cumbered long enough;
He burnt his candle to the snuff;
And that's the reason, some folks think,   15
He left behind so great a s—k.
Behold his funeral appears,
Nor widow's sighs, nor orphan's tears,
Wont at such times each heart to pierce,
Attend the progress of his hearse.   20
But what of that, his friends may say,
He had those honors in his day.
True to his profit and his pride,
He made them weep before he died.
Come hither, all ye empty things,   25

Ye bubbles raised by breath of kings;
Who float upon the tide of state,
Come hither, and behold your fate.
Let pride be taught by this rebuke,
How very mean a thing's a Duke;   30
From all his ill-got honors flung,
Turned to that dirt from whence he sprung.

POEM SUMMARY

Stanza 1

Swift's "A Satirical Elegy on the Death of a Late Famous General" is divided into two parts. The first twenty-four lines are the words of a talkative man on a London street speaking to an acquaintance who never gets the chance to say anything. The speaker seems to have run into his silent friend and been told of the death of the Duke of Marlborough, and of the approach of his funeral procession. The poem begins with an expression of his surprise, but, clearly, not of his grief. "His Grace!" he says. "Impossible! what, dead!" This might be read as solemn shock, and yet the tone is more like unbelief, and the tone of the lines following does not suggest sadness. There are three exclamations, as if the speaker were repeating unbelievable but actually rather satisfying news. The three lines following show the pedestrian nature of the great warrior's death: "Of old age too, and in his bed! / And could that mighty warrior fall, / And so inglorious, after all?" If there is any doubt that the tone of the poem is not solemn, it is resolved by the fifth line, which gives the duke an easy dismissal: "Well, since he's gone, no matter how." The words "no matter how" allude derisively to the place of the duke's death, his bed, not the field of honor. He died in comfort, not in sacrifice. The following line then slides into an apparently inoffensive observation regarding the Christian belief that before the last judgment, when souls will be confined to Hell or sent to Heaven, a trumpet will awake the sleeping dead: "The last loud trump must wake him now." This line also indicates that the soldier's trumpet has been replaced by an otherworldly trumpet. The next two lines assure the duke his place in Hell. "And, trust me, as the noise" of the trumpet of the last judgment "grows stronger," the speaker assures us, the duke will "wish to sleep a little longer" because the sound signals his damnation.

The tone and the poem itself are disrespectful to a dead man, a man who, the poem will argue, has earned this particular disrespect despite the usual injunction against speaking badly of the departed. The next four lines continue to show the speaker's scorn: "And could he be indeed so old / As by the newspapers we're told? / Three-score, I think, is pretty high; / 'Twas time in conscience he should die!" The attitude of "Good riddance to the Duke," is expressed quite directly. The next line begins to suggest why it was "time in conscience he should die." The now dead General "cumbered," or burdened, "the world" with his presence. The second section of the speaker's vilification ends with another commonplace, now about burning a candle "to the snuff," till the bad-smelling, charred end of it. With another deft turn, the speaker moves from the image of the candle burning to the end and thus producing a bad smell to the duke's burned out life. The metaphorically burned candle accounts for the "great ... s——k" (stink) that the duke has "left behind." Notably, readers are left to conclude for themselves what "s——k" might stand for, but this is an easy task given the rhyming couplets. Indeed, the preceding line in the poem ends with the word "think."

Evidence of the stink left by the memory of Churchill's life comes in the nature of his funeral procession, which is announced with enough pomp to allow the announcement a full line, begun by an introductory "Behold." Following this, the speaker suggests the things that would customarily accompany a funeral procession, but that are lacking in this case. "Nor widows' sighs, nor orphans' tears ... Attend the progress of his hearse." Here is a man whose passing rouses no grief. "But what of that?," the speaker interrupts himself lest his description should be deemed to discredit the duke. The duke does not need such honor now, the speaker adds, not because he is dead but because "He had" honor "in his day." Then the speaker turns the knife once more and recasts this praise as a final condemnation. The quality of being "true" becomes a vice. "True to his profit and his pride," that is, loyal to accumulating wealth and titles, gifts and honors for himself through war and corruption. "He made them weep before he died." People do not weep for him now, the speaker reflects, since they have wept because of him already. The militarism he represented and the warfare he practiced were the agents of many deaths and attendant grief.

Stanza 2

The second part of the poem, the last eight lines, shifts away from a particular focus on the duke and even away from scorn for him. Now he is to be used as an exemplum: "Come hither, / all ye empty things" the speaker says, addressing powerful men, who in actuality are no more than "bubbles raised raised by the breath of kings / Who float upon the tide of state." Here, the speaker is disparaging earthly vanity, particularly the kind derived from titles, decorations, and military and political might. Men are compared to bubbles blown up by the breaths of monarchs, but bubbles burst, and men die. Rather than being independent creatures, such men are bound to circumstances and caprice. They are driven by the tides of political power. This is the lesson of the poem, which the speaker reiterates. "Come hither," he repeats, and now offers a direct warning: "and behold your fate!" It is not only the Duke of Marlborough to whom the poet is pointing when he speaks of human vanity. It is to an implicit "you," to the "you" suggested by "all ye empty things," and to the "you" addressed in "behold your fate!" The warnings are meant for anyone reading the poem who cannot sense their own insignificance and mortality. There is a lesson in the duke's death. Death itself is as much a rebuke as the dearth of mourning at the duke's funeral: "Let pride be taught by this rebuke, / How very mean a thing's a duke." The word "mean" indicates pettiness and insignificance. A duke is but a man. Thus, a man is an insignificant thing. He dies and returns to the earth: "From all his ill-got honors flung, / Turned to that dirt from whence he sprung." In these final lines, the poem returns its focus to the duke himself. The speaker refers to Marlborough's "ill-got honors" and suggests that in death Marlborough has undergone a metamorphosis. The word "turned" suggests that the duke is not only returned to the earth but that he has been turned into dirt, his own, true essence. For the duke came from dirt, meaning not just from the earth, but that he gained his power from his association with unclean things such as war, embezzlement, and a corrupt political party.

THEMES

Death and Mutability

Implicitly and explicitly, Swift's elegy presents the idea that it is human folly to believe in permanence. Mutability, or change, is inevitable. Fortune changes during life's course, as, in fact, the duke's fortune did several times. He enjoyed

TOPICS FOR FURTHER STUDY

- Imagine the death of a prominent national political figure, or choose one who has recently died and write a satirical elegy on his or her death.

- From among films and television programs, choose two satires and write an essay comparing the subjects they satirize, the goals of the programs or films, and the ways in which they accomplish what they set out to do. Be specific in your comparisons.

- With several of your classmates, write a skit satirizing some aspect of school life and present it in front of the class. In a set of production notes accompanying your presentation, discuss the issues you confronted in creating your skit, focusing particular attention on the limits you decided could not, or should not, be overstepped and why.

- Read Alexander Pope's mock epic poem *The Rape of the Lock* or Samuel Johnson's satiric novel *Rasselas* and prepare a lesson in which you introduce either work to your class and explain the satirical themes and the satirical context of either work.

- Research the War of the Spanish Succession and Marlborough's role in it and prepare a brief for or against Marlborough's conduct during the war.

- After doing research on the rise of the Whigs and the Tories, compare the political battles the two parties fought with each other at the beginning of the eighteenth century to the political campaigns the Republicans and Democrats have waged against each other at the beginning of the twenty-first century. Present your findings to the class.

military victories and suffered military defeats. He was both rewarded and snubbed by people in powerful places throughout his career. Swift does not focus, however, on this kind of change in his elegy. In the poem, death is presented as the greatest agent of change, and the guarantor of impermanence. Although the duke had been a powerful man in his lifetime, he succumbed to death, as every man does. Thus his glory, and the glory of all men, proves transient. In "A Satirical Elegy on the Death of a Late Famous General," the "General" is shown as a man who lived life without any awareness of death and who sought glory and treasure for himself as if he might always possess them. Those who viewed the duke as if he was a great power were also deluded, as is indicated by the opening exclamations. Indeed, those who might once have spoken of the duke with awe, speak of him instead with disdain and contempt upon his death. In the closing stanza, the poet himself speaks in his own voice, not through a persona, or character whom he pretends to be. Swift compares all who enjoy glory to "bubbles." Bubbles, of course, can and do burst, and their form is fleeting, as is the life of a man.

Reputation

If everything is subject to change, as the poem asserts, and if death indicates a final and inglorious reversal of fortune, consequently mocking the concept of pride, is there anything that can defeat mutability? If anything can, it is reputation. One's good name can outlive one's deeds, just as the history of one's virtues and accomplishments can outlive those virtues and accomplishments in their concrete forms. The victory, then, that the poet achieves over the duke is his ability to disparage Churchill's life and career. Towards the conclusion of the opening stanza, Swift defines the duke's reputation when he speaks of the misery he has caused others in the course of his career. The disrespect the poet shows threatens to undermine the final possibility remaining to the duke, that of achieving a glorious historical legacy. The poet speaks of the duke not as of a man worthy of honor but as a worthless man who will leave nothing for those who survive him to esteem.

Vanity

The Duke of Marlborough, the general, is the focus of Swift's satire, but he is also used as an example of pride, an example that can be used to teach a larger lesson or to draw a universal conclusion. What makes the general such fitting material for satire is the magnitude of the self-importance, vanity, and pride that he demonstrated during his lifetime. The duke's pride and vanity can be measured by what Swift saw as greed for recognition and reward, and by the pain the duke caused others in pursuit of his own best interests. Swift is explicit about the general's greed in the final lines of the opening stanza, using the very words "profit" and "pride" in line 23. A model of proud vanity, the general is hardly the only practitioner of this vice. Swift begins the closing stanza with a call for "all ye empty things," which means everyone, for everyone is plagued to some degree by vanity. Through the life of the duke, the poem attempts, as it says in line 29, to teach the reader that "by this rebuke / How very mean a thing's a Duke." If a titled duke is a mean thing (and here the term is used to indicate insignificance), how much more unimportant are all those who cannot even boast such rank? Human beings come from the dirt and return to the dirt, and many live their lives in the midst of dirt. That this recognition ought to cure people of vanity is the moral theme of the poem.

STYLE

Elegy

Originally, the elegy was a Latin poem characterized by rhymed couplets with each of the lines composed in a specific meter. The first line introduced a subject and the second line completed it. Usually love or death was the subject of an elegy, as opposed to the heroic acts and tragic events of warfare. Swift uses the form, but subverts it by introducing a tone of mockery and depreciation in order to provide the duke with a final, parting insult.

Mockery

From the very title onwards, the duke is being mocked. Rather than being named in the title, he is called "a Late Famous General." There is a hint of disdain there, suggesting the emptiness of fame and rank. The tone of mockery continues in the first lines. The duke becomes the object of a cheap, tabloid sort of gossip. "His grace! Impossible! What dead!" The mockery continues throughout the poem and, in fact, is amplified as the poem progresses. Not only does the speaker mock the duke, so do circumstances. No mourners grace his funeral procession. Despite all his earthly accomplishments, his body turns to dirt and his soul, at the trumpet's sound, will supposedly enter hell.

Rhymed Couplets

Swift's "A Satirical Elegy on the Death of a Late Famous General," like much of eighteenth-century verse, is written in rhymed couplets, pairs of lines that rhyme. While such a rhyme scheme can serve forms of verse other than satire, it is particularly suited for satire because each second line gives the poet the opportunity to conclude an observation with a rhyme that accomplishes a sense of wit and finality. This is especially true because the first line of the couplet imitates a rising tone of voice and the second a falling, as in the seventh and eighth lines: "And, trust me, as the noise grows stronger / He'd wish to sleep a little longer." The satisfying resolution achieved through rhyme illustrates the poet's command of his subject and focuses attention on his skill and, consequently, his superiority to his subject. In Swift's poem, the arch, wry, and detached effect of an *a,a; b,b* rhyme scheme is evident. The duke is "dead" in his "bed," and some folks "think" he left behind a stink.

Satire

Satire is an early poetic form once practiced by Greek and Roman poets, who used it to ridicule and reform human and social evils. The Greek playwright, Aristophanes, c. 448–380 B.C.E. satirized everything from philosophy to warfare. The Roman satirist Petronius, c. 27–66 C.E. satirized Roman decadence and new wealth. Since then, satire has been used to edify as it entertains, as it is most commonly used to promote societal change through the use of humor. Although "A Satirical Elegy on the Death of a Late Famous General" ridicules Swift's political enemy, it also discusses loftier ideas regarding vanity, morality, and mortality.

HISTORICAL CONTEXT

The Instability of the English Monarchy

By the 1700s, the English monarchy had been unstable for centuries. Henry VIII contributed greatly to its instability when he broke with the pope, in 1534, and separated English Christianity from Roman Catholicism. Not only did Henry form the Anglican Church with the Archbishop of Canterbury as its head, he also, by this very break, fostered a rivalry between Catholics and Protestants in England, a rivalry that became political as well as religious. Subsequently, the

COMPARE
&
CONTRAST

- **Early 1700s:** England is divided about the War of Spanish Succession, with the Whigs endorsing the war against France and the Tories opposing it.

  Today: England is the primary partner of the United States in the Iraq War. The ruling Labor government supports the war, but the majority of English citizens oppose it.

- **Early 1700s:** Writing in the *Examiner*, Swift attacks men like Marlborough who continue the continental war and profit from it.

Today: Journalists like Robert Fisk, writing in the London *Independent*, write critically about the war in Iraq and uncover the corruption involved in pursuing it.

- **Early 1700s:** Swift presents the news of the Duke of Marlborough's death from the point of view of a common gossip.

  Today: Papers like the *Daily Mail* in England and the *New York Post* in the United States present news in terms of gossip about well-known personalities.

monarchs of England were either Protestant, like Elizabeth I, or Catholic, like her successor, James I. In 1642, the Protestant Puritans began an attack on the English monarchy. The nine-year struggle ultimately led to the defeat of the forces of King Charles I in 1649, and the establishment of the English commonwealth. The commonwealth was defeated in 1660 and Charles's son, King Charles II, returned from exile in France to rule in England. Catholicism, as well as the monarchy, was restored to England. But when Charles's successor, James II, was overthrown in 1688 by the Protestant William of Orange, England again became Protestant and remained Protestant thereafter.

Religion was not the only issue causing the instability of the English throne. The power of the king was also an issue, as was the struggle to limit the power of the English monarch. As early as 1215, a group of English barons forced King John to sign the Magna Carta, a document curtailing his authority and increasing their rights. By Swift's time, the English monarchy had evolved from an absolute monarch ruling by divine right, that is, with God's approbation, into a constitutionally limited monarchy functioning alongside a parliament controlled by political parties. Such a development made it possible for the satirical form that Swift favored

to develop and survive the wrath of the very powers it mocked and rebuked.

The War of the Spanish Succession

When Charles II, king of Spain, died childless in 1700, he named Philip, Duke of Anjou, the grandson of Louis XIV, king of France, as his heir. This provided Louis with the opportunity to unite Spain and France into one kingdom and into a mighty European power under his control. The Dutch, the Austrians, and the English declared war on Louis in 1702 in order to thwart his designs and protect their own interests. The war lasted until 1713, when the Treaty of Utrecht was signed. By the terms of the Treaty of Utrecht, Philip remained king of Spain, but the Spanish monarchy was kept separate from the French monarchy. Marlborough was undoubtedly a hero of the war. But military ventures, no matter what their outcome, were abhorred by Swift, whose political beliefs were second to or determined by his hatred of war. Marlborough, moreover, despite his victories, appeared to win them at the expense of, rather than for, his countrymen. His military campaigns in the service of English royal power, caused death and grief to the English, but served as opportunities for Marlborough to advance himself and profit financially from war.

Engraving of English general John Churchill, first Duke of Marlborough (Hulton Archive / Getty Images)

The Whigs and the Tories

Under William and Mary, political parties based on conflicting interests began to have significant power. The Whigs favored the power of Parliament over the King and Court. They favored Protestantism over Catholicism, and in the early eighteenth century, Whigs supported the English continental war against France. The Tories represented the court party, supported the Anglican Church, and were eager to end the War of the Spanish Succession. The Tories were interested in making England a sea-power dominant in trade, which it became. Marlborough was a Whig. Swift, by the early 1700s had become a Tory, impelled greatly by his deep opposition to war and to the Whig support of the continental war.

CRITICAL OVERVIEW

Much has been written about Swift and his prose works, but much less has been written on his poetry and on "A Satirical Elegy on the Death of a Late Famous General." The first disadvantage Swift encounters as a poet is the age in which he lived. The tastemakers of the nineteenth century simply did not respect the verse of the eighteenth century as real poetry. J. A. Downie, in

Jonathan Swift: Political Writer cites late nineteenth-century critic and Swift biographer, Henry Craik, who asserted in 1882, "We cannot claim for any of [Swift's] verses the qualities of real poetry. ... We find in them no flights of imagination: no grandeur either of emotion or of form: and even the deftness of his rhythmical skill never attains to the harmony of poetic utterance."

Regarding his verse, however, Swift is his own first and most uncompromising critic. "I have," David Ward quotes Swift as saying, in *Jonathan Swift: An Introductory Essay*, "been only a man of rhymes, and that upon trifles, never having written serious couplets in my life." Indeed, there is evidence of this sentiment in Swift's "Verses on the Death of Dr. Swift." In an excerpt of the poem provided by Downie, Swift even rhymed his discontent with himself as a poet; he considered the work of his friend, Alexander Pope, to be superior:

> In Pope, I cannot read a Line
> But with a Sigh, I wish it mine:
> When he can in one Couplet fix
> More Sense than I can do in Six:
> It gives me such a jealous Fit,
> I cry, Pox take him, and his Wit.

Indeed, Swift's universal renown is for a great *prose* satire, for *Gulliver's Travels*, and for several other highly esteemed if somewhat less well-known satirical prose works like *A Modest Proposal, The Battle of the Books*, and *A Tale of a Tub*, which Harold Bloom, in an introductory essay to a volume of *Modern Critical Views: Jonathan Swift*, has called "the most powerful prose work in the language." Regarding Swift's poetry, Ward takes issue with the author's humility, asserting that "there is enough really impressive work to justify the claim that Swift is among the best minor poets in the English language." It is moreover doubtful that Swift believed the content of "A Satirical Elegy on the Death of a Late Famous General" was trivial, especially because the poem deliberately trifles with the reputation of a famous man regarded by some as great. In that poem, as in all of Swift's satire, Edward W. Rosenheim, Jr., argues in *Swift and the Satirist's Art* that Swift's strategy was to show that "Man's myopic complacency can be fought only by devastating attacks on the very foundations of his self-esteem." Swift believed, Rosenheim argues, that "without the benefit of reasoned argument, without nuances, [Man] must be shown raw fact about his origins and endowments. From his fraudulent pinnacle of

WHAT DO I READ NEXT?

- W. H. Auden's, "The Unknown Citizen" was written in 1939 and was first published in 1940. Auden's poem is a satire on war, patriotism, and the docility of citizens to the government's demands.

- e. e. cumming's, "next to of course god" (1926), is a satirical sonnet cast in the form of an American politician's jargon-filled Fourth of July oration.

- Winston Churchill's *Marlborough: His Life and Times* was published in 1968. This book, written about Churchill's ancestor, presents the story of the Duke of Marlborough's life and career. Here, the duke is portrayed as a good man and even as a hero.

- Charles Dickens's *Hard Times* was first published in serial installments in Dickens's magazine *Household Words* between April 1 and August 12, 1854. As in many of Dickens's longer novels, there are a number of plot strands that fan out and rejoin each other. Of particular interest is the strand concerning Mr. Gradgrind, the satiric object of Dickens's contempt for the followers of the Utilitarian philosopher, Jeremy Bentham, whom Dickens saw as promoting materialism and denying the importance of the human spirit.

- Henry Fielding's *Tom Jones* (1729) is an epic novel that not only carries a complicated and moral plot but is also a comic novel that satirizes several literary forms as well as many human follies.

- Dwight MacDonald's *Parodies: An Anthology from Chaucer to Beerbohm and After* was printed in 1960. MacDonald has assembled an anthology of literary parodies and satires of famous works as well as of particular persons and issues.

- William Morris's *News from Nowhere* appeared in print in 1890. Morris's utopian novel, by imagining a future world that is the opposite of the world as it was in England at the end of the nineteenth century, satirizes late nineteenth-century England by exposing its barbarities and cruelties.

- Alexander Pope's *The Dunciad*, first published in 1728 and again in a revised version in 1743, is a long poem in rhymed couplets in which Pope directs scorn at his literary inferiors.

- *Gulliver's Travels* (1726) is Swift's best-known novel. The narrator, Captain Gulliver, in four journeys, explores the depths of mankind's follies and the extent of his own capacity to accept humanity.

---

self-admiration, he must, in truth, be 'turned to that dirt from whence he sprung.'" Thus, Swift's power as a satirist is not in argument, but in subversion of the esteem usually conferred upon his target through rhetorical ridicule.

Writing about satire in general, Northrop Frye explains in *Anatomy of Criticism*, that "two things ... are essential" to a successful piece of satire. "One is wit or humor founded on fantasy or a sense of the grotesque or absurd, the other is an object of attack." Certainly, both are present in "A Satirical Elegy on the Death of a Late Famous General." The object of attack, Marlborough, is unambiguously present. The satire on his death,

which imagines his death as provoking neither mourning nor ceremony, ought to be grotesque, as it ought to be absurd, since it is contrary to accepted practice and sentiment.

CRITICISM

Neil Heims

Heims is a writer and teacher living in Paris. In the following essay, Heims argues that Swift not only satirizes Marlborough in "A Satirical Elegy on the Death of a Late Famous General," but also satirizes the elegiac form in general. Heims also

> THE PURPOSE OF THE POEM IS LESS TO RECOG-
> NIZE THE DUKE, EVEN IN HIS DIABOLICAL ASPECT, THAN
> TO USE HIM AS AN EXAMPLE AGAINST VANITY AND
> PRETENSION."

*compares the poem to an earlier prose satire about
the duke that Swift wrote several years before
Churchill's death.*

Swift's last literary encounter with his old
enemy, John Churchill, First Duke of Marlborough, was his "A Satirical Elegy on the Death of
a Late Famous General." The poem was the last
slight he could bestow on a man whom he held in
contempt and whom he had already savaged
twelve years before, in 1710. Then, in a broad-
sheet called the *Examiner*, a Tory journal that
Swift edited, Swift accused the duke of lining his
own pockets at the expense of the English people. Simply by calling his poem on Churchill's
death "A Satirical Elegy on the Death of a Late
Famous General," Swift shows his contempt by
refusing to directly name the duke.

If the poem is a satire, as the title indicates,
what or who is it satirizing or ridiculing? The
answer seems reasonably to be the "Late Famous
General." But that is not entirely clear. The elegy
is written, according to its title, not on him but
on his "Death." Therefore the satire is not satirizing the general. The elegy itself, as a literary
form, is being satirized. An elegy, properly,
offers praise for its subject, laments the deceased,
and offers consolation to those grieving for him.
Swift's "A Satirical Elegy on the Death of a Late
Famous General" does not do that. Churchill's
death is the vehicle Swift uses in order to subvert
the elegiac form. Instead of offering a tribute to
Churchill, the verses condemn him to Hell, and,
they assert, deservedly so. To use an elegy in this
way satirizes the elegy, even does violence to it,
by setting it to perform a task directly opposed
to its intended purpose.

Why would Swift take this approach?
Because, in Swift's view, the duke had polluted
and violated each of the revered institutions he
entered. Thus, his death is used here to do the
same. Churchill was corrupt as a general and

corrupt as a member of the queen's governing
party. Alive, he had corrupted his offices. Now
dead, he corrupts a poetic form just by being its
subject. The condemnation and diminution of
Churchill are woven into the poem, but complete
damnation is left for the last line: "Turned to
that dirt from whence he sprung." Swift uses
the word "dirt," not the more common terms
"dust," "earth," or "soil." This enforces the idea
of the duke's inherent filthiness.

Damning is precisely what Swift intended to
do regarding Churchill. The general was an
enemy of formidable proportions, a man firmly
connected to the Whig establishment. His victories over the French armies in the War of the
Spanish Succession, while not yet, in 1710, conclusive, made him seem indispensable to the
nation, especially in his own eyes. Once the
Tories, who were eager to end the war and sign
a peace treaty with France, had, in 1710, defeated
the Whigs at the polls, they began to consider
how to lessen Churchill's political power without
injuring their plans for peace. The Tory plan was
to expose the duke's faults and topple him
through dishonor and shame rather than by strip-
ping him of his powers directly. Swift's power of
satirical invective was the means they chose to
further the duke's undoing.

In the *Examiner* of November 23, 1710, Swift
took on the duke's power and popularity by using a
satirical strategy of reversal. He began by arguing
that opposition to "the late removals at Court,"
that is, the recent changes in ministers and the
Whigs's loss of power at court, was caused by
"the Fear of giving Uneasiness to a General who
hath been long successful abroad: And accordingly, the common Clamor of Tongues and Pens
for some Months past, hath run against the Base-
ness, the Inconstancy and Ingratitude of the whole
Kingdom to the Duke of Marlborough." Swift,
thus, begins by establishing as his major premise
and by seeming to accept its veracity, that England
has been ungrateful to Churchill. Swift continues,
as if he were making a serious argument, to show
the terrible extent of that ingratitude. Swift
presents a straight-faced table, titled "Bill of BRIT-
ISH Ingratitude," comparing the way England has
rewarded the duke with "A Bill of ROMAN Gratitude," which lists the rewards received by Roman
heroes of the ancient Republic. Comparing the two
columns, as if he were making entries in a ledger,
Swift shows that Roman heroes were rewarded by
their countryman to the tune of 994 pounds, 11

shillings, tenpence. The duke, columns beside the Roman entries show, in a national display of ingratitude, has been given, altogether, 540,000 pounds. Rather than arguing against the duke's arrogance and corruption, Swift seems to side with the duke's advocates, focusing on the accounts, leaving it for his readers to conclude indignantly that those of the duke's party who proclaim "British Ingratitude" toward the duke are absurd. Only at the conclusion of his satire does Swift quietly make his point unambiguous. "We find many ungrateful Persons in the world," Swift writes, "but we *make* more, by setting too high a Rate upon our Pretensions, and undervaluing the Rewards we receive." That is the moral lesson of Swift's satire. His indictment is the indictment of unchecked power.

However, in "A Satirical Elegy on the Death of a Late Famous General," Swift does not need to focus on the details of political or economic issues. The Duke of Marlborough is dead, and what is death if not the ultimate check on power? Now, Swift's attack need not be on the duke or his deeds and misdeeds, but it must be on the underlying vice or vices that caused them. It must be on the demeaning effect of corruption on a corrupt man, and it must demonstrate the folly of human vanity, from which most corruption springs. Swift takes aim at Churchill's vanity from the first words and insists on humbling the duke by withholding any expression of grief at his passing or of awe at his accomplishment. Swift achieves Churchill's deflation by making the poem's speaker slightly detached: a gossip who enjoys talking about the great and powerful with an undeserved familiarity. The duke is not regarded by the speaker as a person but as a celebrity, and as a celebrity, he is subject to public opinion. Swift shows the effects of corruption when he writes of the "great" stink that remains in Churchill's wake. By this stink, the duke is compared to the Devil himself, the incarnation of evil, who is notorious for leaving the unpleasant smell of sulfurous brimstone behind him.

The purpose of the poem is less to recognize the duke, even in his diabolical aspect, than to use him as an example against vanity and pretension. "Let pride be taught by this rebuke, / How very mean a thing's a Duke," Swift writes in the poem's concluding lines. He is no longer using the voice of the street persona who spoke the first twenty-four lines. This is not a flighty statement. The "rebuke" spoken of is death itself. The duke's greatness at last, through the agency of the poem, has achieved a certain useful virtue as it becomes an edifying example of the vanity of human covetousness. Even the degree of fame and power that the duke had achieved is reduced to nothing by the greater power of death.

Source: Neil Heims, Critical Essay on "A Satirical Essay on the Death of a Late Great General," in *Poetry for Students*, Gale, 2008.

Hermann J. Real

In the following essay, Real examines what motivations Swift may have had for his negative portrayal of the Duke of Marlborough in the poem. The critic finds answers to Swift's attitude in another of his works, Journal to Stella.

Swift's "Satirical Elegy" has been variously labeled "unchivalrous," "ungenerous," even "as vicious as it was unnecessary." Undoubtedly, value judgments like this are not only motivated by a conviction, frequent in theories of satire, that the satirist should attack only what is corrigible, but even more by a maxim which has been a guideline of tact ever since Solon: *De mortuis nil nisi bene.* One might well ask why, for Swift, this rule did not apply to Marlborough. The answer, I think, lies in the *Journal to Stella*, where Swift characterized Marlborough as "covetous as Hell, and ambitious as the Prince of it." Thus for Swift, Marlborough obviously did not, as all satiric victims do, merely exhibit some moral deficit, but a moral deficit of diabolical proportions. In other words, Marlborough was the incarnation of the devil. This becomes evident in vv. 13–6 of the poem:

> This world he cumber'd long enough;
> He burnt his candle to the snuff;
> And that's the reason, some folks think,
> He left behind *so great a s—k.*

The satiric implications of these lines are lost if the candle image is interpreted merely as a symbol of the "passage of time and the ephemerality of life." Nor is it simply an ironic inversion of the interpretation associated with the candle in emblematic literature, *aliis in serviendo consumor.* More to the point is an idea which seems to have been widely spread in superstition and folklore: "The devil leaves a stink behind." As Samuel Butler put it in "Upon Modern Critics":

> And as the *Devil*, that has no Shape of's own,
> Affects to put the ugliest on,
> And leaves a Stink behind him, when he's
>   gone..

IN ONE WAY OR ANOTHER, THEN, THE CLEVER JEST, THE BITTER INDICTMENT, AND THE PESSIMISTIC IDEA THAT THE EVILS UNDER ATTACK ARE SOMEHOW IN THE NATURE OF THINGS ARE THE COMPONENTS OF SWIFT'S PORTRAIT SATIRE."

If the interpretation is correct, evaluations like "unchivalrous," "ungenerous" or "vicious" are no longer legitimate, for what good could Swift, or anybody for that matter, have said about the Devil? *De mortuis nil nisi vere.*

Source: Hermann J. Real, "Swift's 'A Satirical Elegy on the Death of a Late Famous General,'" in *Explicator*, Vol. 36, No. 2, Winter 1978, pp. 26–27.

Alan S. Fisher

In the following essay, Fisher discusses several of Swift's biographical "portraits" in the following excerpt, including "A Satirical Elegy on the Death of a Late Famous General." Of this poem, Fisher notes that it begins "with lamentation," as most elegies do, before turning into a mocking, devastating portrait of the Duke of Marlborough.

Critics long have recognized that portraits are a major source of insight in the satirical verse of Dryden and Pope. Portraits are largely ignored in Swift, however, probably because verse is not Swift's most important medium, and because he uses portraits in his verse rather sparsely. Nevertheless, I believe they are worth studying, for they will provide the same critical focal point for Swift as they do for the study of his contemporaries.

Portraits have this importance because they are a specially rich kind of metaphor. On the surface, they do not seem metaphoric at all, they seem biographical—statements based on a set of facts about a man. (Such "facts" may actually be legends, half-truths, or outright lies, but whether they are true or false, all portraits rely upon the reader's willingness not to challenge them.) Metaphors, on the other hand, deal in analogies, not in facts: the biographical character sketch becomes a portrait, in the sense I use the term, only when its details become analogical—that is, when they fall into a pattern, or concept, or essence, some entity which exists in the imagination, largely free from the pressure of objective factuality. To study portraits, therefore, is to study the way an author transforms the facts of the world he inhabits into the patterns of his imagination—in short, it is to study how his mind works. . . .

I

Swift was aware that a portrait is a metaphor and not a biography. One of his earliest portraits, "The Description of a Salamander" (1705), begins with lines that exactly define the portraitist's creed:

> . . . men have got from Bird and Brute
> Names that would best their Natures suit:
> The *Lyon, Eagle, Fox* and *Bear*
> Were Hero's Titles heretofore,
> Bestow'd as Hi'roglyphicks fit
> T' express their Valor, Strength or Wit.
> For, what is understood by *Fame*
> Beside the getting of a Name? (7–14)

The portraitist is a giver of names, and a "name," as we see, is an analogy—the precise one that distills a man's character and deeds into a meaningful essence.

In the piece at hand, however, it soon develops that Swift is not conferring a name, but is ironically defending one already given. John, Lord Cutts, the poem's victim, was a soldier who had earned the nickname, "salamander." Salamanders, according to *OED*, were "supposed to live in, or be able to endure fire"; to call a soldier one was to pay tribute to his bravery. Swift defends the relevance of the name from Pliny's *Natural History*, a source which includes much more about salamanders than their ability to endure fire:

> . . . our Author has defin'd
> This Reptil, of the Serpent kind,
> With gawdy Coat, and shining Train,
> But loathsom Spots his Body stain:
> Out from some Hole obscure he flies
> When Rains descend, and Tempests rise,
> Till the Sun clears the Air; and then
> Crawls back neglected to his Den. (29–36)

Swift now fits this analogically to a whole class of men:

> SO when the War has rais'd a Storm
> I've seen a *Snake* in human Form,
> All stain'd with Infamy and Vice,
> Leap from the Dunghill in a trice,

Burnish and make a gaudy show,
Become a General, Peer and Beau,
Till Peace hath made the Sky serene,
Then shrink into it's Hole again. (37–44)

And with the analogy thus established, Cutts must stand upon his name: "*All this we grant— why, then look yonder | Sure that must be a* Salamander!" (45–46).

This piece works differently from the usual portrait because it is little concerned with essences. We do not understand the significance of Cutts by understanding the class of men to which he belongs; what we understand is a typical process which Cutts represents—the way in which it always happens, during wars, that "reptiles" become the leaders of men. Consequently, the poem does not so much deal with a finished concept, like Salamanderism, as with putting that concept through a process of redefining, and what is left after reading the poem is not a sense that now we understand the concept better, but a sense that before we understood it very falsely. The poem's interest in concepts is to destroy the false, but not necessarily to build up true ones in their place.

In other words, the focus of the poem is devaluative. So also is most satire: what sets this poem apart is the emphasis it gives to devaluation. Most satirists try to avoid making devaluation seem their principal point of interest. They treat evil as a coating of rust upon the good, and their devaluating is therefore a kind of scouring, the ultimate purpose of which is to uncover an ideal truth that everyone knows is under the rust. The only ideal Swift seems to offer, however, is Salamanderism. In the common understanding, this is a cliché, hapless before Swift's derision, and in the poem's revised understanding, it is no ideal at all, but a paradigm of rottenness. There being no ideal of truth, what becomes "truth" in this poem is the process of devaluation itself, and what becomes ideal in it is the vigor and gusto with which the devaluation is carried out. This vigor makes us aware of sensing somewhere in our experience of the poem a critical, detached, free-standing intellect. The poem offers nothing to believe in, save this intellect: if processes only, not concepts, are truth, then surely the process closest to an ideal is the critical one, which subjects concepts— especially such egregiously empty ones—to destruction.

Swift's portrait satire adopts this pattern: the world is understood in terms of process, not essence; devaluation is truth; and the closest approach to a true ideal is the irreverent, critical intellect which sees through false ideals. Such ultimate skepticism is not complete until skepticism itself is treated skeptically; this happens in another early piece, "V[an]'s House" (1708). "Van" is John Vanbrugh, the playwright who also was an architect, and who built a house for himself upon the ruins of a wing of Whitehall Palace which had burned down in 1703. Being both poet and builder, Vanbrugh calls to mind the mythical archetype of Amphion, whose power of singing was such that the very stones obeyed his will. Swift's first concern is to deal with the myth, bypassing its idealistic side and forcing it into a context of literalism and process:

IN Times of *Old*, when Time was *Young*,
And Poets their own Verses Sung,
A Verse could draw a Stone or Beam
That now would overload a Team;
Lead 'em a Dance of many a Mile,
Then rear 'em to a goodly Pile.
Each Number had it's diff'rent Pow'r;
Heroick Strains could build a Tow'r;
Sonnets, or Elogies to *Chloris*
Might raise a House about two Stories;
A Lyric Ode would Slate; a Catch
Would Tile; an Epigram would Thatch. (1–12)

This destroys the myth, of course, but it does one other thing as well: it connects that destruction with modernism. The attitude of these lines is a matter of the present debunking the past, and although Swift truly intends the debunking—Amphionism being an impossible concept— we also see this process as a paradigm of the way the present recasts the world of the past in its own paltry mold. Modern thinking is insolently literalistic; the insolence can be amusing, but the literalism cheapens. Turning from this passage to his attack on Vanbrugh, Swift turns the paradigm of modern devaluation upon the modern devaluators themselves. Vanbrugh, the modern Amphion, takes his place within a myth turned into farce by the very habits of thinking he represents.

Granted a reinstatement of the Amphionic power, Vanbrugh falls to scribbling a play, which, in modern style, he plagiarizes. His matching power to build, therefore, extends only to second-hand bricks (Whitehall's ruins). As the play is written, the house arises: two acts are the cellar (because "the plot as yet lay deep"); two acts are two rooms above; the fifth act is the roof; the epilogue is the outhouse. When completed, poets throng to it as the shrine of their ancient power restored, and a fitting shrine it is, for it is so tiny that they have difficulty finding it among the other ruins on the site. At this point, the symbolism of the poem comes fully into focus: the smallness of the house is correlative to the paltry talent of its builder and to the spirit of modernism itself, which not only is paltry, but is corrupting:

> Born like a *Phoenix* from the Flame,
> But neither *Bulk*, nor *Shape* the same:
> As Animals of largest Size
> Corrupt to Maggots, Worms and Flyes.
> A Type of *Modern* Wit and Style,
> *The Rubbish of an Antient Pile*. (121–126)

This poem has the familiar elements: the incessant transforming of a concept (the power of Amphion) into processes, the equating of devaluation with truth, the free, critical spirit one senses behind it all. But it adds something very important to this formula: the ambiguity it casts upon the process of devaluation. For devaluation can be used both by true men of taste and by pretenders to taste, and though devaluation is truth in all cases, the truth it yields in the hands of a pretender is perfunctory or simply worthless. Debunking itself is not valuable, Swift says, what matters is the mind we sense behind it.

Twenty years later, Swift's procedure has not changed. Here are some lines on George II, addressed to anyone who would praise him:

> ... your Encomiums, to be strong,
> Must be apply'd directly wrong:
> A Tyrant for his Mercy praise,
> And crown a Royal Dunce with Bays:
> A squinting Monkey load with charms;
> And paint a Coward fierce in arms.
> Is he to Avarice inclin'd?
> Extol him for his generous mind ... (117–124)

Tyrant, dunce, monkey, coward, avaricious man—all are concepts, and all come together in some grand concept: George is the worst of all possible kings. This, however, is not an interesting thing to call him; the interest one has in these lines is not the concept they present, but the process they embody. What this process is appears a few lines earlier, where Swift confesses that satirists are "blackeners":

> 'Tis not deny'd that when we write,
> Our Ink is black, our Paper white;

> And when we scrawl our Paper o'r'e,
> We blacken what was white before.
> I think this Practice only fit
> For dealers in Satyrick Wit ... (107–112)

—and anyone who praises the king must undertake a process precisely the reverse. Swift addresses his hypothetical panegyrist:

> ... you some white-lead ink must get,
> And write on paper black as Jet:
> Your Int'rest lyes to learn the knack
> Of whitening what before was black. (113–116)

These lines go beyond their attack on supine panegyrics and take on a metaphorical significance. It is natural and true that paper should be white and ink, black: to reverse them is unnatural and false. But if the satirist is natural and true, so also is the "blackening" he admits to: for good or for ill, devaluation is truth.

Swift's most celebrated portrait satire is his "Satirical Elegy" on Marlborough. Again a concept (Marlborough's reputation) is broken down into processes and devaluated. The piece begins, as elegies should, with lamentation, but this one becomes a mockery, the casual banality of typical town conversation:

> And could he be indeed so old
> As by the news-papers we're told?
> Threescore, I think, is pretty high;
> 'Twas time in conscience he should die.
> This world he cumber'd long enough;
> He burnt his candle to the snuff;
> And that's the reason, some folks think,
> He left behind *so great a s—k*. (9–16)

One critic asserts that this is not the voice of Swift speaking, but the voice of the Town itself. Seen this way, the passage becomes meaningful in two respects: in the first place, the Town giveth and taketh away such greatness as Marlborough had—"Marlborough's reputation will quickly be destroyed by the very men who praised him while he was alive and powerful"; secondly, the passage is an example of devaluative criticism in hands unworthy of it—true though it may be, we need not admire it. There is an ironic poetic justice in all this: Marlborough exposed in his true paltriness by minds whose own paltriness once made him great.

The critical intellect behind the poem does not appear until its last eight lines, in which the voice changes sharply:

> Come hither, all ye empty things,
> Ye bubbles rais'd by breath of Kings;

Who float upon the tide of state,
Come hither, and behold your fate.
Let pride be taught by this rebuke,
How very mean a thing's a Duke;
From all his ill-got honours flung,
Turn'd to that dirt from whence he sprung.
(25–32)

"Dirt" expresses Swift's personal disgust, but it contains a broader meaning in its allusion to "dust." Dust is the end of all things mortal; to mention it here is to remind the reader that the very processes of living are enemies of human constructs, concepts, and essences. The principles of devaluation and decay are laws of the universe. Again, when the poem insists that we must recognize the truth of such processes, it does not insist that we admire them. The somber power of these lines—and that of Swift's critical intelligence—derives from this ability to recognize the true power of decay, without admiring it.

II

"Dirt," in the Marlborough elegy, provides a convenient paradigm of Swift's satirical method. Three things can be said about the word: (i) it is a stroke of wit that springs a joke: we expect one monosyllable that begins and ends with "d" and "t," but we get another and strangely more appropriate one; (ii) it delivers a severe indictment, for "dirt" is synonymous to filth and excrement; (iii) it alludes, as I have said, to the process of decay built into the fabric of the world we must live in, a process about which we can do little or nothing. The compression of these effects and ideas into a single word is unusual in Swift's verse, but the mixture itself, in varying proportions, occurs in all of the portrait satires.

They all entertain the reader with a jest, usually accepting a standard formula and extracting from it unexpected consequences. In the examples at hand, Cutts is a salamander not because he is brave, but because he is a reptile; Vanbrugh is an Amphion not in the ancient, but in the modern construing of the myth; George II is the perfect panegyric hero, not by the conventional, but by the "true" standards of panegyric. Nearly every portrait that appears in Swift is based on a reversal, a redefinition, or an unexpected jolt. Jests notwithstanding, Swift's portraits always bring strong indictments upon their subjects. Reptilian ugliness represents the moral ugliness Swift finds in Cutts; Vanbrugh building or writing is compared to maggots devouring a carcass; the true George II is a "squinting monkey"; and Marlborough is reduced to a stinking vapor.

The jesting and the damning are obvious enough. The pessimism, though not always blatant, is also basic. In the Marlborough piece, decay is poetic justice for a wicked man. But although its justice may be some consolation, the portrait also reminds us that decay works upon all men, good and evil alike. In the other pieces the pessimism is less general, but equally important. With Cutts, Swift restricts himself to the consequences of war, but one of those consequences is a natural process by which salamanders in all their ugliness *always* emerge from their holes. The Vanbrugh piece is not heavily pessimistic, but there is an undertone: nobody would *want* these modern forms and processes, yet there seems to be no way anyone can avoid them. In the portrait of George II, the pessimism is political: "this monkey tyrant is our king," Swift seems to say; "we cannot get rid of him, but we do not have to worship him."

In one way or another, then, the clever jest, the bitter indictment, and the pessimistic idea that the evils under attack are somehow in the nature of things are the components of Swift's portrait satire. This combination causes a complicated reaction. We laugh at evil as something paltry, for Swift shows it in poses of utter absurdity; yet we must hate as well as laugh, because whatever the pose, evil is extremely ugly—Swift's terms for it usually are physically shocking; and further, we recognize that neither laughing nor getting sick is likely to change what exists. No one accepts something so ridiculous and so ugly with philosophic detachment, yet Swift allows no illusions about doing away with it. It is there, and all we can say is that we are not obliged to like it.

Source: Alan S. Fisher, "Swift's Verse Portraits: A Study of His Originality as an Augustan Satirist," in *Studies in English Literature, 1500–1900*, Vol. 14, No. 3, Summer 1974, pp. 343–56.

Robert W. Uphaus

In the following excerpt, Uphaus argues that while Swift does indeed reshape traditional poetic conventions in much of his work, he still works within those traditions. The critic notes that Swift subverts the "conventional three-part structure of the elegy—praise, lamentation, consolation"—in

"THE COMMONNESS OF MARLBOROUGH'S

DEATH SUGGESTS, ONCE AGAIN, THAT SWIFT IS SUSPI-

CIOUS OF PUBLIC GREATNESS BECAUSE IT LEADS MEN

TO OVERESTIMATE THEIR INHERENT WORTH."

"Satirical Elegy," but Uphaus contends that the work is still recognizable as an elegy.

A number of Swift's poems have often been used as evidence of his opposition to poetry—his "anti-poetic" it is most often called. Such assertions, regrettably, have tended to assume that Swift's poems "demonstrate all the limits, and none of the uses, of conventional literary categories." By measuring a selection of Swift's poems against this assumption, I intend to show how Swift makes poetry by projecting his own vision of reality—a simultaneous opposition to the visionary imagination and a firm commitment to the material world as the primary source of human knowledge—within certain traditional literary conventions. That Swift alters or reshapes poetic conventions should not be surprising, for this is the traditional prerogative and responsibility of poets. Indeed, this is how good poets make meaning. ...

Now it is not my intention to philosophize about the profundity or the inherent poetic magic of obscenity, but since Swift's obscenity is often used as evidence of his "anti-poetic" attitude, I would like to suggest that the obscenity in "The Description of a Salamander" is both conventional (that is, it has poetic precedents) and thematically necessary. As much as I may agree with Sir Harold Williams that this poem about Lord John Cutts is a "scurrilous invective against a brave man," I do not find the poem "inexcusable," because, given the conventions of invective, the one thing I do *not* expect is fairness and impartiality.

The creation of this poem appears to have occurred this way. Swift, capitalizing on the nickname "Salamander" which Cutts had won at the siege of Namur and remembering Pliny's description of a salamander in his *Natural History*, seized the opportunity to exploit the

parallels between a mythical salamander, alleged to have the power to endure fire, and Lord Cutts, who is also said to have endured fire—gunfire. From this parallel, as the following lines show, Swift quickly points to the dislocation between the titles of classical heroes and the ironic appropriateness, in his view, of calling a "modern" hero a salamander:

> So men have got from Bird and Brute
> Names that would best their Natures suit:
> The *Lyon, Eagle, Fox* and *Boar*
> Were Hero's Titles heretofore,
> Bestow'd as Hi'roglyphicks fit
> To shew their Valor, Strength or Wit.
> For, what is understood by *Fame*
> Besides the getting of a Name?
> But e're since Men invented Guns,
> A different way their Fancy runs;
> To paint a Hero, we enquire
> For something that will conquer fire. (ll.7–18)

Two lines later he writes a couplet whose rhyme words "grander" and "Salamander" effectively disclose the poem's ironic version of Cutts's heroism. By invoking what Irvin Ehrenpreis has called "parallel history," Swift uses Cutts as an example of his culture's trivialization of genuine heroism; among other things, the poem suggests that any warfare which uses guns is distinctly unheroic. But there are two other characteristics of a salamander which Swift applies to Cutts— its gaudy skin and serpentine shape, and its resistance to heat.

In the first instance, the parallel is both general and obvious:

> So when the War has rais'd a Storm
> I've seen a *Snake* in human Form,
> All stain'd with Infamy and Vice,
> Leap from the Dunghill in a trice,
> Burnish and make a gaudy show,
> Become a General, Peer and Beau,
> Till Peace hath made the Sky serene,
> Then shrink into it's Hole again. (ll.37–44)

But for the second characteristic, the salamander's coolness, Swift may well have had in mind the opening lines of John Cleveland's "The Antiplatonic," which employs a popular seventeenth-century literary figure for a lover's coolness to passion. I quote some lines from Cleveland's poem:

> For shame, thou everlasting Woer,
> Still saying Grace and ne're fall to her!
> Love that's in Contemplation plac't,
> Is *Venus* drawn but to the Wast.

Unlesse your Flame confesse its Gender,
And your Parley cause surrender,
Y'are Salamanders of a cold desire,
That live untouch't amid the hottest fire.

Cleveland's military metaphor (parley, surrender, fire) is, of course, appropriate to Swift's subject. But Swift goes several steps beyond the genial wit of Cleveland's poem. Here is *his* obscene version of Cutts's alleged coolness amid love's "hottest fire":

SO have I seen a batter'd Beau
By Age and Claps grown cold as Snow,
Whose Breath or Touch, where e'er he came,
Blew out Love's Torch or chill'd the Flame:
  (ll.57–60)

And Swift continues in a more explicitly syphilitic vein for a few more lines. What seems to me decidedly worth noticing, in light of the assumptions about Swift's alleged "anti-poetry," is that this poem is firmly rooted in the conventions of invective; as nasty as the poem may be, its meaning emerges and is shaped by recognizable literary precedents. Swift certainly has worked at collapsing Cutts's grandeur, but he has not "engineered" the collapse of poetic language.

It would appear, at first reading, that "A Satirical Elegy on the Death of a late Famous General" (namely, Marlborough) is nothing more than a repetition of "The Description of a Salamander." Such, however, is not the case. This poem is much more than an invective; it is an inverted elegy in which Swift contrasts Marlborough's military greatness (a fact Swift seems willing to concede) with the mundane circumstances of Marlborough's unheroic death. If Swift had stopped at this point, the poem would certainly have resembled an invective. But the fact is, he uses Marlborough's pride to reinforce the lesson of Ecclesiastes: "Vanity of vanities; all is vanity. What profit hath a man of all his labour which he taketh under the sun?"

To begin my discussion of this poem, I would like to contrast the opening of Swift's "Satirical Elegy" with Henry King's elegy, "The Anniversarie." Both poems are based on similar literary conventions (down to almost the last image), although their thematic intent clearly differs. I may be laboring the obvious, but it seems to me that the difference between the two poems does not necessitate our calling one poem poetry and the other "anti-poetry." Rather, the two poems are an effective object lesson of the expansiveness of the language and conventions

of poetry. Here are the opening lines of King's elegy:

So soone grow'n old? Hast thou bin six
  yeares dead?
Poore Earth, once by my Love inhabited!
And must I live to calculate the time
To which thy blooming Youth could never
  climbe,
But fell in the ascent? Yet have not I
Study'd enough Thy Losse's History?
How happy were mankind, if Death's strict
  Lawes
Consum'd our Lamentations like the Cause!
Or that our grief, turning to dust, might end
With the dissolved body of a friend!

And here are the first sixteen lines of Swift's elegy:

His grace! impossible! what dead!
Of old age too, and in his bed!
And could that Mighty Warrior fall?
And so inglorious, after all!
Well, since he's gone, no matter how,
The last loud trump must wake him now:
And, trust me, as the noise grows stronger,
He'd wish to sleep a little longer.
And could he be indeed so old
As by the news-papers we're told?
Threescore, I think, is pretty high;
'Twas time in conscience he should die.
This world he cumber'd long enough;
He burnt his candle to the snuff;
And that's the reason, some folks think,
He left behind *so great a stink*.

The conventional three-part structure of the elegy—praise, lament, consolation—has dropped out of sight, but not out of mind. Swift knows what the usual procedures of elegy require, but he plays the reader's expectations against the obvious informality of the poem. The commonness of Marlborough's death suggests, once again, that Swift is suspicious of public greatness because it leads men to overestimate their inherent worth. In this regard, Swift is actually writing in the main line of Augustan poetry; one recalls, for example, Dr. Johnson's harsh lines in *The Vanity of Human Wishes* about the distinctly unheroic last days of Swift and Marlborough: "From Marlb'rough's eyes the streams of dotage flow / And Swift expires a driv'ler and a show" (ll. 317–18). Moreover, the final lines of "A Satirical Elegy" use Marlborough in much the same way that Dr. Johnson uses Charles XII of Sweden: "He left the name, at which the world grew pale,

/ To point a moral, or adorn a tale" (ll.221–22). One need only compare these lines with the conclusion of Swift's elegy:

> Come hither, all ye empty things,
> Ye bubbles rais'd by breath of Kings;
> Who float upon the tide of state,
> Come hither, and behold your fate.
> Let pride be taught by this rebuke,
> How very mean a thing's a Duke;
> From all his ill-got honours flung,
> Turn'd to that dirt from whence he sprung.

The images of dirt and water, coupled with the verb "sprung," precisely locate the incongruity between man's common origin and his grand aspirations. This is a poem written with Old Testament fervor and poetic tact: that Swift turns the dust of King's elegy into dirt, that he reduces the conventional restorative waters of weeping to the airy bubbles of the vanity of human wishes, in no way compels us to conclude that he was writing anything other than effective poetry. ...

Let me quote from Swift's address to a young beginner in "On Poetry":

> How shall a new Attempter learn
> Of diff'rent Spirits to discern,
> And how distinguish, which is which,
> The Poet's Vein, or scribling Itch? (ll.71–74)

Again, I think it's instructive to realize the literary precedents from which Swift inherits this distinction between the "Poet's Vein" and "scribling Itch," for his attack on bad poetry could mistakenly be called "anti-poetry." (Herbert Davis, for example, has said that "Swift is of course not concerned in this poem with any poetic ideal.") The Latin origin of "scribling Itch" ("scribendi cacoethes") occurs in Juvenal's *Seventh Satire* (1.52). The exact phrase also occurs in Oldham's imitation of Boileau's *Eighth Satire*, and other variations of this phrase are in Rochester's "An Allusion to Horace," Dryden's translation of Boileau's *Art of Poetry*, and Roscommon's "Essay on Translated Verse." Looking beyond Swift's poem, the phrase "Poetick Itch" appears in Pope's "Epistle to Augustus." I mention these occurrences only as evidence of Swift's intent, which is not to collapse poetry, but to align himself with poets and poems written in defense of poetry.

The terrible distortion of the "anti-poetry" thesis, then, is this: the charge has been brought against a poet who is himself attempting to preserve the distinction between genuine poetry and derivative scribbling. Swift attacks those men whose lack of talent subverts the dignity of poetry, and yet in doing so he has been mistakenly called an "anti-poet." But even a cursory look at "On Poetry: A Rapsody," I hope, has demonstrated that Swift's attack on *bad* poetry ought not to be taken as an attempt to collapse the resources of poetic language. It would require a "Perverseness in the Mind" to misconstrue the intent of the following passages from "On Poetry":

> *Hobbes* clearly proves that ev'ry Creature
> Lives in a State of War by Nature.
> The Greater for the Smaller watch,
> But meddle seldom with their Match.
> (ll.319–22)

. . .

> But search among the rhiming Race,
> The Brave are worried by the Base.
> If, on *Parnassus*' Top you sit,
> You rarely bite, are always bit: (ll.327–30).

. . .

> Thus ev'ry Poet in his Kind,
> Is bit by him that comes behind;
> Who, tho' too little to be seen,
> Can teaze, and gall, and give the Spleen;
> Call Dunces, Fools, and Sons of Whores,
> Lay *Grubstreet* at each others Doors;
> Extol the *Greek* and *Roman* Masters,
> And curse our modern Poetasters.
> Complain, as many an ancient Bard did,
> How Genius is no more rewarded;
> How wrong a Taste prevails among us;
> How much our Ancestors out-sung us;
> Can personate an awkward Scorn
> For those who are not Poets born:
> And all their Brother Dunces lash,
> Who crowd the Press with hourly Trash.
> (ll.341–56)

There is another way that we can look at "On Poetry: A Rapsody," one that best summarizes all that I have been trying to say in this paper. This poem does not simply depict the presence of good and bad poetry; it suggests, as well, that only through the careful preservation of the distinction between the "Poet's Vein" and "scribling Itch" will truthful language remain invulnerable to barbarism and decadence. This poem, together with the others I have examined, deals ultimately with one basic conflict—that between mankind's susceptibility to the language of pride and flattery and the poet's obligation to uphold the language of virtue and truth. In an age darkened by uncreating words (to use Pope's phrase), the best a sensitive poet could do was either to retreat into a highly private kind of poetry and defend his own integrity (which Pope was tempted to do) or else aggressively seek out the causes of such decadence and publicly expose them as Pope did in *The Dunciad*. I think in his late career the choice for Swift was even narrower than this: it was either silence or satire, complete abdication or militant attack. That Swift chose to attack the scribblers who were progressively corrupting the resources of poetry is wholly consistent with the responsibilities of the poet. That he aligned his verse with, rather than against, the traditional uses of poetry is ample evidence of his faith in poetry as a vehicle for truth.

Source: Robert W. Uphaus, "Swift's Poetry: The Making of Meaning," in *Eighteenth-Century Studies*, Vol. 5, No. 4, Summer 1972, pp. 569–86.

SOURCES

Bloom, Harold, "Introduction," in *Modern Critical Views: Jonathan Swift*, edited by Harold Bloom, Chelsea House Publishers, 1986, p. IX.

Cody, David, "Jonathan Swift: A Brief Biography," http://www.victorianweb.org/previctorian/swift/bio.html (accessed March 30, 2007).

Downie, J. A., *Jonathan Swift: Political Writer*, Routledge & Kegan Paul, 1984, p. 305.

Foot, Michael, *The Pen and The Sword*, MacGibbon & Kee, 1958, pp. 36–72, 133–54.

Frye, Northrop, *Anatomy of Criticism*, Princeton University Press, 1957, p. 224.

Rosenheim, Edward W., Jr., *Swift and the Satirist's Art*, University of Chicago Press, 1963, p. 229.

Swift, Jonathan, "A Satirical Elegy on the Death of a Late Famous General," in *The Wadsworth Anthology of Poetry*, edited by Jay Parini, Thompson Wadsworth, 2006, pp. 151–2.

Ward, David, *Jonathan Swift: An Introductory Essay*, Methuen & Co. Ltd., 1973, p. 184.

FURTHER READING

Berwick, Donald, *The Reputation of Jonathan Swift, 1781–1882*, 1941; reprinted by Haskell, 1965.

This is a compendium of essays and biographies about Swift written during these years.

Bredvold, Louis I., "The Gloom of the Tory Satirists," in *Eighteenth-Century English Literature: Modern Essays in Criticism*, edited by James L. Clifford, Oxford University Press, 1959.

Bredvold defines and explores what he calls "gloom," which he argues characterizes the writings of both Swift and his contemporary, Alexander Pope. Bredvold also argues that there is a moral purpose for these writers' satires.

Ehrenpreis, Irvin, *Swift: The Man, His Works, and the Age*, in three volumes, Methuen, 1962–1983.

This is a highly regarded biography of Swift, focusing on the man himself and on his role in his times.

Ellis, Frank H., *Swift vs. Mainwaring: The Examiner and the Medley*, Clarendon Press, 1985.

Ellis compiles satiric, political pieces Swift wrote and the response made to them by Arthur Mainwaring, a Whig opponent.

Jack, Ian, *Augustan Satire: Intention and Idiom in English Poetry, 1660–1750*, Clarendon Press, 1952.

This study primarily explores the kind of satiric poetry Pope and John Dryden wrote and what their purposes were in writing it.

Lord, George deForest. et al., eds., *Poems on Affairs of State: Augustan Satirical Verse, 1660–1714* in seven volumes, Yale University Press, 1963–1975.

A collection of hundreds of satirical poems, written between 1660 and 1714, the book reflects the political and cultural issues of the times. There are copious notes for clarification and orientation, and the poems are arranged chronologically and thematically.

September 1, 1939

W. H. AUDEN

1939

W. H. Auden's "September 1, 1939" is a poem about war and the futility of war. The title refers to the date that Germany crossed the border to invade Poland, an act of aggression that escalated in the following days to draw many countries allied with one side or the other into the fighting, quickly leading to the start of the Second World War.

The poem was first published on October 18, 1939, in the *New Republic*. It was then included in Auden's 1940 collection, *Another Time*. Soon after that, though, Auden disavowed it. The uplifting tone that dominates the last two stanzas seemed to him too trite and self-congratulatory for the serious issues raised earlier.

Despite Auden's later regret, however, this poem has struck a chord of admiration with generations of readers. It was particularly influential in the days after the terrorist attacks of September 11, 2001, when it was circulated on the internet and read aloud in public. The poem's views of violence and reprisal seemed to apply accurately to the attacks sixty years later, especially since the poem takes place in New York City and focuses on the modern obsession with tall buildings. In truth, as the poem itself points out, the urges for attack, revenge, and complacency have been woven into the fabric of Western society since ancient times.

Because of Auden's personal dislike for this poem, it was not included in his *Collected Poems*, and was still left out of the 2007 edition of that

W. H. Auden (*The Library of Congress*)

book. It can be found in the 1990 volume *W. H. Auden: Selected Poems*, which was revised and expanded in 2007 for the 100th anniversary of Auden's birth.

AUTHOR BIOGRAPHY

Wystan Hugh Auden was born on February 21, 1907, in the industrial town of York, England, where he grew up. His father was a physician and his mother was a nurse, and from them he received an interest in engineering and science that, with his natural intelligence, enabled him to go to Oxford University on a scholarship. While there, though, he started writing poetry, which quickly became his major occupation. He became associated with other poets, called "the Auden Group," that included writers who were to also go on to literary fame, such as Stephen Spender, C. Day Lewis, and Louis MacNeice. His first major dramatic work, "Paid on Both Sides: A Charade," was accepted for publication by T. S. Eliot in *Criterion* while Auden was still at Oxford. It was published in 1930. Eliot's influence also led to a book-length collection of Auden's poetry later that year.

Auden went to Berlin for eighteen months after graduating from Oxford, and then he settled in to teaching in England for the next five years. In 1935, he married Erika Mann, the daughter of the German writer Thomas Mann. Auden was homosexual, and this marriage was one of convenience, to enable Erika Mann to obtain an English passport and flee the rising turmoil in Germany.

Auden traveled extensively from 1936 to 1939, serving as an ambulance driver in the Spanish Civil War and covering the Communist revolution in China for newspapers, all the while recording his impressions of war in his poetry. As the Nazi war machine expanded Germany's power, Auden decided to leave the continent, and in 1939 he moved from England to America with the poet Christopher Isherwood, who had been a friend and collaborator since grammar school. Later that year, Auden first heard of the German invasion of Poland that occurred on the first of September via news reports while living in America. He wrote "September 1, 1939" soon after, and it was first published in the *New Republic* on October 18, 1939. The poem was also included in Auden's 1940 collection, *Another Time*. Auden became a U.S. citizen in 1946, though he did travel in Italy and Austria after the war. He returned to Oxford as a Professor of Poetry from 1956 to 1961, although he had been a poor student there. From 1954 to his death in 1973, he maintained residences in New York City and Kirchstetten, Austria, and was a chancellor of the Academy of American Poets. In his later years, his writing became increasingly oriented toward problems of Christianity.

When Auden died in Vienna on September 29, 1973, he was one of the world's best-known and most revered poets.

POEM TEXT

I sit in one of the dives
On Fifty-second Street
Uncertain and afraid
As the clever hopes expire
Of a low dishonest decade: 5
Waves of anger and fear
Circulate over the bright
And darkened lands of the earth,
Obsessing our private lives;
The unmentionable odour of death   10
Offends the September night.

Accurate scholarship can
Unearth the whole offence
From Luther until now
That has driven a culture mad,   15

Find what occurred at Linz,
What huge imago made
A psychopathic god:
I and the public know
What all schoolchildren learn,   20
Those to whom evil is done
Do evil in return.

Exiled Thucydides knew
All that a speech can say
About Democracy,   25
And what dictators do,
The elderly rubbish they talk
To an apathetic grave;
Analysed all in his book,
The enlightenment driven away,   30
The habit-forming pain,
Mismanagement and grief:
We must suffer them all again.

Into this neutral air
Where blind skyscrapers use   35
Their full height to proclaim
The strength of Collective Man,
Each language pours its vain
Competitive excuse:
But who can live for long   40
In an euphoric dream;
Out of the mirror they stare,
Imperialism's face
And the international wrong.

Faces along the bar   45
Cling to their average day:
The lights must never go out,
The music must always play,
All the conventions conspire
To make this fort assume   50
The furniture of home;
Lest we should see where we are,
Lost in a haunted wood,
Children afraid of the night
Who have never been happy or good.   55

The windiest militant trash
Important Persons shout
Is not so crude as our wish:
What mad Nijinsky wrote
About Diaghilev   60
Is true of the normal heart;
For the error bred in the bone
Of each woman and each man
Craves what it cannot have,
Not universal love   65
But to be loved alone.

From the conservative dark
Into the ethical life
The dense commuters come,
Repeating their morning vow;   70
"I will be true to the wife,
I'll concentrate more on my work,"
And helpless governors wake
To resume their compulsory game:
Who can release them now,   75

Who can reach the deaf,
Who can speak for the dumb?

All I have is a voice
To undo the folded lie,
The romantic lie in the brain   80
Of the sensual man-in-the-street
And the lie of Authority
Whose buildings grope the sky:
There is no such thing as the State
And no one exists alone;   85
Hunger allows no choice
To the citizen or the police;
We must love one another or die.

Defenceless under the night
Our world in stupor lies;   90
Yet, dotted everywhere,
Ironic points of light
Flash out wherever the Just
Exchange their messages:
May I, composed like them   95
Of Eros and of dust,
Beleaguered by the same
Negation and despair,
Show an affirming flame.

POEM SUMMARY

Stanza 1

The opening lines of "September 1, 1939" place the poem's speaker in a bar in New York City. Auden, who had recently immigrated to the United States after living in Europe all his life, wrote this poem to record his response to the news that on the date mentioned in the title, the German army had invaded Poland, an act of aggression that was to grow, in a matter of days, into the Second World War. In line 5, "a low dishonest decade" refers to the slow buildup to this event, which was precluded by negotiations and treaties meant to prevent just such an attack, which seemed, in retrospect, inevitable. The reference to "Waves of anger and fear" that "Circulate over the bright / And darkened lands" is an acknowledgement that this invasion was happening in a new age of mass media, when radio could relay news across the globe more instantaneously than had ever been possible before.

Stanza 2

Line 14 mentions Martin Luther, a 16th century German monk and theologian who is widely considered one of the most important thinkers in history. Luther's writings, coming just as the

MEDIA ADAPTATIONS

- Though Auden's dislike of this poem meant that he was not recorded reading it, the poet Dylan Thomas included Auden's poem on an album from the Caedmon label titled *Dylan Thomas Reads the Poetry of William Butler Yeats and Others*, released in 1971. This recording was rereleased on compact disk by Caedmon Records/HarperCollins Publishers in 2002.

printing press made it possible to reproduce and distribute written materials, challenged basic tenants of Christianity, leading to the Protestant Reformation: nearly four hundred million Protestant Christians follow some form of religious practice that is directly related to Luther's theories. This poem indicates that Luther was the start of an "offence," one which "has driven a culture mad" because of the anti-Semitism that Luther came to espouse later in life. Luther's idea that the Jewish faith could be obliterated by converting all Jews to Christianity later turned angry and dark, as he advocated violence against Jews and the destruction or confiscation of their property. His ideas were adapted by the Nazi party in the twentieth century as intellectual support for their own virulent anti-Semitism.

Linz, mentioned in line 16, is the area in Austria where Adolf Hitler, the Chancellor who drove the Germans to war on September 1, was born. He considered it his home town, and wanted it to be a major cultural center of the Third Reich. Hitler traveled to Linz to make the formal announcement of his plans to annex Austria into the German empire on March 13, 1938. One of the Nazis' major concentration camps, Mauthausen, was built just fifteen miles from Linz in August of 1938. It began as a place to incarcerate thieves and prostitutes, but starting in May of 1939, it began taking in political prisoners almost exclusively.

"Imago," used in line 17, is a term from biology, referring to the final stage of development for an insect, its adult form. In psychology, the word is used to describe an image developed in childhood of an idealized person; that image, carried over into adulthood, causes conflicts when it bumps up against reality. Auden uses "imago" to imply that humans' need to worship someone or something has created an image that allows, or even encourages, the type of violence that will only stir up more violence in retaliation.

Stanza 3

Thucydides was a general of ancient Athens who was sent into exile after a military defeat in 411 BCE. In the book that he wrote in exile, *History of the Peloponnesian War*, Thucydides reproduces several famous speeches, including Pericles's funeral oration, which praises democracy and the people who have died in the defense of it. In this stanza, Auden faults centuries of humanity for not seeing beyond the "rubbish" of Thucydides's noble words, continuing to make the same mistakes as people made back then because pain and grief are "habit-forming."

Stanza 4

Starting around the turn of the century, buildings began to reach new heights, using steel beams to hold them together instead of just concrete walls. The word "skyscraper" was coined in the late nineteenth century, but over the decades newer construction designs allowed for taller and taller buildings: New York City's Empire State Building, built in 1931, held the record as the world's tallest building for 40 years. Manhattan is an island, with limited space to expand except up, and has therefore always attracted skyscraper development. In this poem, Auden inverts the conventional view of skyscrapers, seeing them, not as achievements, but as signs of failure, an "excuse." To him, they represent the drive of imperialism, a policy of powerful countries exerting control over smaller ones. As he wrote in New York City, he drew comparisons between the conspicuous signs of capitalism around him and the military aggression of Germany.

Stanza 5

The poem returns to the setting established in the first stanza, describing the people sitting at the bar. In this stanza, Auden examines the reaction of ordinary Americans to the world-changing events in Europe on that day. He records their apathy and their desperation that things must continue as they always have, that "The music must always play." The bar that he is in, described as a "dive" in the poem's first line, is referred to here as a "fort" because of the common person's desperation to hold out uncomfortable news. In the second half of the stanza he refers to people living in the delusion of comfort as children, living in fear and deluded into thinking that they are shielded from harm because they have been happy and good, when in fact the opposite is true: this truth is hidden by tradition, custom, and "conventions."

Stanza 6

In this stanza, Auden compares the rants of "windiest" militants and famous politicians to the deepest desires of the common people. What they have in common is that the desire for love is not a wish for everyone to love everyone else, but for oneself to be loved by everyone.

Vaslav Nijinsky (1890–1950) was a famous Russian ballet dancer, considered by many to be one of the greatest dancers of all time. At the height of his career, in 1909, he became romantically involved with Russian businessman and philanthropist Serge Diaghilev, whose financial support helped make the *Ballets Russes* one of the most important and successful companies of its time. In 1919, Nijinsky suffered a nervous breakdown, and spent the rest of his life in a series of mental institutions. According to Sam Diener in an annotated commentary of "September 1, 1939" in *Educators for Social Responsibility*, Nijinsky wrote in his diary that "Some politicians are hypocrites like Diaghilev, who does not want universal love, but to be loved alone." Auden uses some of these same words, and certainly the same sentiment, in this stanza of the poem.

The phrase "bred in the bone," in line 62, is a shortened version of the proverb "What's bred in the bone will come out in the flesh," which means that habits that are rooted deep within the essence of human beings will always show themselves in human behavior.

Stanza 7

The common people are held up to comparison with their political rulers in this stanza. In the first few lines, members of the working class are characterized as "commuters" who travel to work in the city. Their journey from the darkness to "the ethical life" indicates an attempt to become morally better than they are, but their morals are characterized by hollow platitudes that only serve to support the traditional understanding of social order. The politicians, who might be thought of as being in charge, are in fact "helpless." Their actions are not the exertion of their will, but some sort of "compulsory game" from which they cannot gain "release." Citizens and politicians alike are presented in the last lines of the stanza as being deaf and mute (dumb).

Stanza 8

After a long stretch of observation, the poet returns to self-reflection, thinking about where his own role is in this complex social order. As in previous stanzas, he recognizes the social order, that is followed by both citizens and political rulers alike, to be a lie that is balanced on the competing ideas that "there is no such thing as the State" but that "no one exists alone." The poem recognizes the fact that there needs to be social order, but that the prevailing social order is one of mutual agreement and is not necessarily the way that things have to be. He does not blame either side of the political equation, recognizing that both citizens and those who hold political power are driven by the basic concern for their own survival, but still, he knows that the answer to life's mystery is not one of fighting against one another in fear of going hungry, but to love one another. In line 88, Auden presents love for each other as being unequivocally necessary for life.

Stanza 9

The poem's final stanza restates its claims of fear and helplessness. After talking about the world in general, though, it starts to recognize the exceptions to the rule, the individuals who can see through the mistaken assumptions that lead the rest of the population toward hate and apathy. There are people, characterized here as "points of light," who recognize the human situation but are still willing to be positive. Auden acknowledges his own connection to them, stating that, like them, he is made "Of Eros and of dust": "Eros" is a god of the ancient Greeks who is associated with love and sexuality, which are usually considered basic ingredients of human personality, while "dust" is a reference to the fact that humans are connected to the physical world as mortal objects.

The "affirming flame" of the poem's last line is an echo of the author's claim, in line 78, that "All I have is a voice." In both cases, there is no specific course of action offered to combat the situation described here. The poem does not advocate any one political stance, but instead presents speaking out against fear and complacency as the best that one can do in the modern world.

THEMES

Power

One of Auden's central concerns in this poem is the way that power has traditionally been exerted over masses of people. One clear manifestation of that is when governments use force against each other with no better justification than that they have the power to do it, as was the case with Hitler's invasion of Poland. The shocking thing about that move was that it was morally condemned by so much of the world, which subsequently entered into the fight against Hitler's Axis powers in order to stop what was viewed as unjustified aggression. The treaties and social conventions that could have kept Germany at bay did little to stop Germany from annexing Poland: what mattered was that Germany had the power to do so.

The poem goes on to bring up Martin Luther's assertions that force should be used to convert Jewish people to Christianity. The idea of using power to compel religious thought seems self-contradictory, but Auden presents it as a theme that remained constant from the sixteenth century to the twentieth. Though he shows that there have always been backlashes and repercussions, just as there was inevitable opposition to the annexation of Poland, his point is that those in power continue to disregard the inevitable results and to assert their power.

The brazen use of power is shown in this poem to exist across the centuries, across all types of governments. Stanza 3 openly draws an historical link between democracy and dictatorship in the ways that governments take advantage of people's pain and grief to secure their loyalty. In stanza 4, the poem uses skyscrapers, which are symbolic of the power of technology and capitalism, to be signs of imperialism, which is the spread of government by force over

TOPICS FOR FURTHER STUDY

- Auden refers to the 1930s as "a low, dishonest decade." Choose two adjectives that you think best describe the past ten years, and write a three-paragraph essay explaining your choices.

- Every year, a list of the world's worst dictators is published by *Parade* magazine. Find the most recent list and focus on one of the dictators, reading some biographical information about that person. Write that dictator's response to this poem, explaining why he or she thinks social repression is justified.

- In the 1930s, skyscrapers were often used as symbols of humankind's potential for technological achievement. Find pictures representing some accomplishment you think Auden would use to represent society if he were writing this poem today, and present it to your class with an explanation of why you think it is a potent symbol.

- Most Americans paid little notice to the events in Europe on September 1, 1939. There was not widespread support for U.S. involvement in the war until two years later, when Pearl Harbor was bombed by the Japanese. Conduct a series of interviews and write a chart showing different attitudes toward involvement in conflicts in other countries in the twenty-first century.

unwilling populations. Throughout the poem, Auden gives one example after another of ways in which those who have power force their will on those who are weaker.

Fear

According to this poem, the fact that governments and other social institutions are able to impose their power over ordinary people is less serious than the fact that many people give up their own judgment and allow themselves to be ruled by fear. The poem mentions fear early, in line 3, and the concept expands from there throughout the rest of its length. Stanzas 5 through 7, in particular, focus on ways that average citizens give in to their own fears of what unknown, unforeseeable things would happen to them if they tried to stand up against familiar traditions. Line 50, for example, refers to a bar as a "fort" and presents New York City, and cities like it, as "a haunted wood." Even though cities are usually considered the opposite of unpopulated wooded areas, Auden makes the connection by implying that both are ruled by unseen forces that people cannot understand, and so they become fearful.

In stanza 7, Auden quotes the common citizens as they try to make bargains to protect themselves from the things that they fear. Their words are phrased as vows that they will do things they assume will please those who hold power over them, even though there is no real evidence that the ones they fear actually have control over them or care what they do. In the following stanza, Auden refers to the thing they fear as, respectively, "the folded lie," "The romantic lie," and "the lie of Authority."

Hope

Much of this poem is dedicated to documenting the frightening state of the modern world. In the end, though, the poem comes around to examining what can be done to oppose the dark forces that make life so frightening. Stanza 8 starts with the poet affirming that his one weapon against all that is wrong is his "voice," implying that speaking out against injustice is a step that may be small but is still significant. Auden advises his reader that the power of the government is just an illusion with the claim that "there is no such thing as the State." He goes on to note that the people in charge of the government are really just people, and not that different than ordinary citizens, when he points out that hunger affects all the same way. By breaking down the overwhelming power of government and tradition like this, he makes the task of opposing it seem at least approachable.

In the last stanza, the poem even recognizes a certain category of good people, identified as "the Just," with a capital "J." These are people who exchange messages of hope with each other, who tend to hope in the same way that one would tend "an affirming flame" against the negative forces that are trying to extinguish it.

STYLE

First Person

"September 1, 1939" starts as a first person account, with the poet appearing within the poem, addressing himself as "I." The setting given in this first stanza is a bar in New York City, where the speaker of the poem says that he is at the time of the invasion of Poland. After that powerful start, however, the first person form of address disappears for most of the poem. Situations are described objectively, not from the limited, subjective perspective of one individual. Facts are given, but little is said about the point of view of the writer.

The author brings himself into the poem in just a few places. In line 19, for example, he prefaces a claim as something that "I and the public know," a phrase that makes the thought so universal that the poet does not see it as something just for the general public, joining them in seeing things this way. In the fifth stanza, he describes what the people in the bar are thinking, but he describes them as an observer, distancing himself from their thoughts. Later in that stanza, and in other places throughout the poem, he includes himself in the human situation by using the word "we," but that word is used so generally that it tells nothing about him or his situation.

In the last two stanzas, the poet discusses himself as a writer. In stanza 8, he refers to the "voice" he has, which gives him a tool to stand against authority, while in stanza 9 he prays for the courage to forget his human fears and limitations. The poem is framed, in the beginning and the end, as if it is a personal statement, though the intervening stanzas ignore the role of the observer and try to relay reality as all people can experience it.

Allusion

An allusion is an indirect reference to some previous event. Because it is not explained in the context of the artistic work, the artist using this technique must trust audiences to either have enough background knowledge to understand what is being alluded to or to do the research to look up allusions that are unfamiliar.

"September 1, 1939" is rife with allusions, starting with the title: although Auden's original audience for this poem, published in October 1939, would certainly have known the significance of

COMPARE
&
CONTRAST

- **1939:** Americans hear vague news about the invasion of Poland through a few news agencies.

  Today: Thanks to advances in travel and communications, an event that occurs anywhere in the world can be recorded by citizens and broadcast to other citizens all over the world within minutes.

- **1939:** Poland is invaded and its territory divided by Germany and the Soviet Union, losing its political independence.

  Today: Since the fall of the Soviet Union in 1991, Poland has rebounded as an economically vibrant, culturally rich, independent country.

- **1939:** Hitler ignores treaties and social conventions to launch an attack against a neighboring country that is the beginning of a massive plan to overtake the countries of Europe.

  Today: To combat terrorism, the United States government has adapted a policy of

preemptive attack. The overthrow of Iraq in 2003 was not followed by any subsequent expansion.

- **1939:** The League of Nations, an international governing body established in 1919, lacks the strength to stop Germany from attacking another country.

  Today: Multinational squads of peacekeepers are routinely sent by the United Nations to ensure that those who have signed peace treaties live up to their bargain.

- **1939:** The United States has been mired in the Great Depression for the past decade. Citizens feel that they have enough problems in their own country and cannot afford to meddle in the situation in Europe.

  Today: The United States has been one of the world's wealthiest countries since World War II. Moral and strategic considerations are more important than economic considerations when deciding possible military action.

---

that date, he had to trust that the event would have the lasting implications to make that title relevant to future readers. Allusions to Fifty-Second Street, and to Luther and Linz and Thucydides and Nijinsky and Diaghilev, could serve to distance some readers from the poem's core meaning, but those who understand the allusions will be able to feel a greater appreciation of Auden's view of the world.

HISTORICAL CONTEXT

The Invasion of Poland
The events that occurred on September 1, 1939, were long in coming. They had their roots in the world order established by the Treaty of Versailles at the end of World War I. Maps

were reconfigured at that time to allow Poland access to the Baltic Sea, so that it could be economically independent from Germany. For years, the German people resented the fact that a "Polish Corridor" had been designed, dividing Germany from East Prussia, and the fact that the port city of Danzig, which had a predominantly German population, had been ceded to Poland.

When Adolf Hitler rose to power in Germany in 1933, he actively pursued German claims to the disputed territories. With the German-Polish Non-Aggression Treaty, signed on January 26, 1934, both sides agreed to keep the current borders intact for ten years. In 1938, however, Hitler's Nazi Party pursued a policy of expansion, and claims for the territory that had been given up after World War I intensified. Poland rejected plans that would run a road

German invasion of Poland, September 1, 1939 *(Hulton Archive / Getty Images)*

through the Polish Corridor, connecting Germany with East Prussia, because the plans seemed designed to divide and weaken Poland. Germany withdrew from the 1934 treaty, but signed new agreements with Poland and other European countries to avoid war.

At the same time that it was promising to avoid war, Germany was meeting with Russia to form an alliance. The Molotov-Ribbentrop Pact, signed on August 23, 1939, contained provisions for a realignment of Europe that were not made public until after the war. The basic division of the continent would give Germany control over the western third of the continent and Russia control over the eastern two thirds. With Soviet cooperation assured, Germany invaded Poland a week after the pact was signed. On September 17th, Russia invaded Poland from the east.

The Resulting World War

Two days after the invasion began, before Auden actually wrote this poem, the United Kingdom, New Zealand, and Australia declared war on Germany, in accordance with mutual defense pacts that they had signed with Poland. Within hours, France had declared war too. South Africa joined the fight on September 6th, and Canada joined on September 10th. The fact that the invasion had escalated quickly into a

global conflict did little to help Poland, though. Poland was defeated on October 6th and entirely occupied by Germany and the Soviet Union.

After that, Germany expanded across Europe, defeating Norway, the Netherlands, Belgium, and France in 1940. In June of 1941, Germany turned against the Soviet Union, which, along with Italy and Japan, was a member of the Axis Powers after signing a treaty of alliance the previous year. Despite the spread of war, American citizens chose to stay uninvolved: the country provided weapons and money to the United Kingdom and France, but diplomatically, the United States remained neutral. Indeed, the United States did not commit to fighting until Japan attacked the naval base at Pearl Harbor, Hawaii, on December 7, 1941, in an attempt to cripple American military capacity in the Pacific. Because Japan was allied with Germany, the U.S. declaration of war against Japan drew America into the European arm of the war as well.

CRITICAL OVERVIEW

Critics usually divide Auden's career into two phases, with "September 1, 1939" set at the beginning of the second. The first phase, when the poet was a young man in England, was characterized by his fascination with language: as Bruce Guernsey noted in *Library Journal* when reviewing a collection of Auden's writings from that time, "Above all, what we see implied here is a belief in the word as a tool of understanding both self and society." By the time Auden moved to America, shortly before this poem was written, his mastery of the poetic form was widely recognized. In his essay "W. H. Auden in America," critic Edmund Wilson pointed out that the move to the United States did not seem to have changed his "essential nature. Auden's genius is basically English—though in ways which, in the literary world, seem at present [1956] rather out of fashion." He went on to say that for Auden, America had "given him a point of view that is inter- or supernational." Auden had soured on politics as a result of his travels around the world and experiences with Communist regimes that once offered him hope, and he gradually lost his interest in psychology, as most of the intellectual world did, as its newness wore off. His poetry took on more and more historical illusions and became increasingly intellectual and less emotional.

Readers generally found the later Auden to be less artistically satisfying, although he continued to be recognized as a master of his craft. Still, he won the Pulitzer Prize in 1948 for his collection *The Age of Anxiety* and a National Medal for Literature in 1967. In the last three decades of his life, Auden became less interested in poetry and more interested in other intellectual pursuits: though generally considered to still be one of the greatest of living poets, he was also much less read or talked about than he was as an up-and-coming young man in the 1920s and 1930s. A 1972 *Listener* review by critic Frank Kermode of Auden's newest book began by noting that "Auden's new collection will hardly vex or bother anybody: it will give pleasure to all who have learned to take pleasure from his games, and bore or disappoint those who either haven't, or who gave him up when he grew quieter, more explicit, more conversational."

"September 1, 1939" has always been a popular favorite of Auden's mature works, even though the poet himself dismissed it as rubbish and openly explained that he wished he had never written it. After the terrorist bombings on September 11, 2001, the poem took on a phenomenal new life. The poem was read on National Public Radio and quoted extensively in print, in the *New Yorker*, and in other publications.

CRITICISM

David Kelly

Kelly is an instructor of literature and creative writing in Illinois. In this essay, he considers whether Auden's eventual dislike for this poem was justified.

"September 1, 1939" is one of those rare works of art that finds more acceptance and admiration from the reading public than it did from the man who wrote it. All too often, things go the other way around, with authors too full of pride in their creations to notice when a poem fails to connect with the people who are supposed to be at the receiving end of the communication process. In this case, though, the author was the one who had to insist on the poem's flaws, even though the public's admiration for the work never really diminished. Auden tried altering it, and, unsatisfied, ended up scrapping the whole thing, removing it from publication while it was still one of his most popular works. People remembered it, though, and it has continually popped up in poetry anthologies since its first publication. Then, after the terrorist attacks of September 11, 2001, the audience for this particular poem blossomed. Readers locked on to the similarities between "September 1, 1939" and the events of the day forty-two years later. It was difficult to avoid the geographical connection, with Auden's opening lines placing the poem in New York City, the site of the most conspicuous carnage of that day. It was difficult to avoid associating Auden's use of tall buildings as symbols of modern society gone haywire with the fact that the attackers also saw the towering World Trade Centers as symbols of decadence. There was no way to miss the fact that the poem was about an evil aggressor's attack on a complacent, unsuspecting public. In the end, what the public wanted most from the poem was what Auden most regretted about writing it: the uplifting suggestion that civilization can, without much effort, protect itself from the hostility that lurks beneath the surface of the civilized soul.

The question that is raised by the way that Auden turned against this poem is not, of course, whether or not it is possible for a poem to be a failure even if millions of readers find it touching: greeting card shops are filled with the works of poetasters who churn out works that are almost always touching, even though no one would mistake them for art. Leaving aside the question of

WHAT DO I READ NEXT?

- Edward Mendelson was Auden's literary executer and editor of recent editions of his works. Mendelson's biography, *Early Auden*, published in 1981, covers Auden's life up to 1942 and includes the story of how the poet wrote his poem and later came to denounce it.

- Auden formatted this poem to be close in style to William Butler Yeats's famous work "Easter 1916," written to mark the event of the famed Easter Uprising in Ireland. Yeats's poem, originally published in his collection *Michael Robartes and the Dancer*, can be found in *The Collected Poems of W. B. Yeats*, published by Scribner in 1996.

- Auden's poetry was rich with classical allusions, a method that took on a life of its own in his collection *The Shield of Achilles*. This book was published in 1951, as Auden was progressing in the philosophical phase that started when he moved to America in 1939. It contains 28 poems centering on the Trojan war. This book won a National Book Award in 1952.

- Samuel Hynes's collective biography *The Auden Generation: Literature and Politics in England in the 1930s* (1976) shows the lives and emerging attitudes of Auden and his contemporaries, such as C. Day Lewis, Stephen Spender, Christopher Isherwood, and George Orwell as the signs of the coming war became clearer.

the subject, because there are millions of cases where artists have had only a general idea of the full range of implications of their work: imagine, for instance, how surprised Shakespeare would be to hear the ideas brought forth by centuries of scholarly analysis on his work. But Auden was one of the most brilliant literary critics of the twentieth century. His view of any poem, even his own, deserves attention. In this case, however, it could well be that Auden's perspective is flawed. There is always the likelihood that he, nor any other poet for that matter, could ever gain enough distance from his work to make an objective judgment call.

The story has been told and retold. Edward Callan reports, in his essay "Disenchantment with Yeats: From Singing-Master to Ogre," that as Auden put it himself in his foreword to *W. H. Auden: A Bibliography, 1924–1968*:

> "Rereading a poem of mine, '1st September, 1939,' after it had been published, I came to the line 'We must love one another or die,' and said to myself: 'That's a damned lie! We must die anyway.' So, in the next edition, I altered it to 'We must love one another and die.' This didn't seem to do either, so I cut the stanza. Still no good. The whole poem, I realized, was infected with an incurable dishonesty and must be scrapped."

This explanation implies that, even as Auden tried to contain the "lie" with successive amputations, like a surgeon going after a virulent, malignant form of cancer, it kept spreading until the whole poem was contaminated with dishonesty from top to bottom. As admirable that it might seem that Auden would want to save his poem's purity, is "We must love one another or die" really such a "damned lie"? Of course, love is not medicine, an elixir for eternal life, but Auden certainly must have known that he was not the only one to realize that fact. For

whether a work is popular or not, the even more significant question to be asked is whether the masses might be right in this case, and "September 1, 1939" is actually a better poem than Auden thought.

It would be entirely too presumptuous to second-guess Auden on this matter. That is not to say that a poem's author has insight into the work that should be considered the last word on most readers, the "death" that the poem refers to would be taken as a symbolic, spiritual death: the numbing of the soul, the loss of emotions, that could be expected to follow naturally as a result of an inability to love.

Assuming, then, that Auden, whatever else he may have thought of them, did not think his readers were gullible enough to think that love could actually stave off death, then his objection to the line must have been based on its symbolic meaning. It is a poet's right to want to take back what he has said, but the vehemence with which Auden went after this thought—trying to alter it, then to suppress the line, the stanza, then the whole poem—is not proportional to the damage that could be done, either to the reader's mind or the author's reputation, if people went on thinking that love could be seen as a defense against symbolic death.

There is a broader explanation that has been given for Auden's dislike of "September 1, 1939," having to do with his embarrassment about being the person who committed to print the poem's loftier sentiments. The adjustment from "love each other or die" to "love each other and die" reflects his desire to retain the poem's dark tone: removing the causal link between love and death, the poem admits a resignation to whatever fate might send. In addition to his second thoughts over this line, it has been said that Auden also regretted the shift in tone in the poem's two final stanzas, starting with "All I have is a voice / To undo the folded lie" and ending with "May I ... Show an affirming flame." Surely, this area of the poem, where Auden suggests that something can actually be done to counter the centuries of hatred and ignorance that he outlines throughout most of its length, is key to the poem's enduring popularity. But, as an artist, the inconsistency was too gross for him to live with.

This brings back a question at the base of all poetry, about the balance between art and the popular imagination. In general, the majority of people have always been inclined to feel more kindly toward works that comfort them, telling them that things are getting better or at least that they can, without much effort. Artistic vision, on the other hand, quite often compels poets to pursue thoughts that the majority will try to avoid. This schism between the popular and the artistic is exacerbated in "September 1, 1939" by the fact that the popular part of the

work really does not fit in with the rest of the poem's darker tone. Auden was right to recognize that the final two stanzas stand out, but he was also right that the rest of the work does not stand up without them: the poem is harsh in its assessment of the human condition and human potential, and leaving it without indicating some way to move things in the right direction makes it feel empty and short-sighted, as if only one side of the story is being told. A third way, one that might have caused the author less embarrassment, would have been to offer a ray of hope at the end without claiming that the hope will come from the author himself.

Over the years, there have been other reasons given for why Auden might have soured on this poem after its initial publication, including his judgment that it represented a flawed attempt at writing in the style that William Butler Yeats used in his famous piece "Easter, 1916." Regardless, each explanation pits the public's fondness for "September 1, 1939" against Auden's artistic vision. Neither is absolutely right: though Auden was often right about matters of artistry, in this case it seems that he was too easily embarrassed, too willing to throw out the good with the bad. And though the mass populace's taste in poetry is often suspect, there is still something to be said for a poem that has such a powerful and enduring effect.

Source: David Kelly, Critical Essay on "September 1, 1939," in *Poetry for Students*, Gale, 2008.

James Miller

In the following essay, Miller takes an in-depth look at the poem's allusion to Vaslav Nijinsky (1890–1950), a famous Russian ballet dancer, and his lover, the Russian businessman and philanthropist Serge Diaghilev. Miller claims that because Auden was a homosexual, his reference to the relationship between Nijinsky and Diaghilev is significant. Miller also posits that the turbulent relationship that existed between Nijinsky (the artist) and Diaghilev (the businessman) further reflects and reinforces the overall theme of "September 1, 1939."

Although scholarship exists that deals with the homoerotic encoding in some of Auden's poems, a large section of criticism regarding "September 1, 1939" has been of a formalistic bent. One of the main themes in the poem is fascism. Although touched upon briefly, Auden's allusion to the relationship between Nijinsky and Diaghilev manages nonetheless to both encode and explore the theme of homoeroticism. The way the allusion is encrypted allows one to understand the wily movements of the poem as a means of critiquing the power of art in an authoritarian and homophobic society.

During the thirties formalist criticism prevailed, a practice that eschewed the external circumstances as influential during a work's conception. I will argue that Auden's situation and the external circumstances of 1939 pressured him to a degree that may have been overlooked by formalist criticism. A current 2003 reading is able to trace dualistic aspects of Auden's personal life, which may have been highly influential in such poems as "September 1, 1939." Auden's dualism can be defined as the adversarial clash of reigning as the unofficial poet laureate, a position entailing public scrutiny and surveillance and also being homosexual, a position that in the thirties could not bear an ounce of public scrutiny without reprimand. As the unofficial poet laureate, Auden was equivalent to a politician addressing the entire American constituency. Such a position requires extreme caution about how one is received. Prudence was even more necessary because Auden had emigrated to the United States from England and enjoyed American citizenship. His position as an esteemed professional poet and professor could also include the duty of giving the political forecast for the United States. Such a position entails a great deal of external pressure. This dualism could in turn pressure the poet to encrypt his personal concerns.

To see encoding in the poem, one can divide it into a macro and micro reading and observe how the two interweave and often create two separate subjects. On the macro scale, the dawn of World War II, Nazi Germany, and an erudite damning of the historicity of the world are present: "Mismanagement and grief: We must suffer them all again." Using a micro scale paints a different picture, arguably a self-portrait: "I sit in one of those dives / On Fifty-second Street / Uncertain and afraid / [...] / Faces along the bar." One sees the poet hiding in a shabby bar, on account of his sexual orientation. The micro aspect of the poem may be coded, cloaked under the pretext of a war, but the fact that Auden, a member of the rentier class, is carousing among the poor, is peculiar and warrants investigation.

The poet presents similarly blurred macro/ micro pictures in his allusion to Nijinsky. His choice of a homosexual couple is not conspicuous because he transfers the situation rapidly to a larger sphere, man's Ur-fallacy or "error bred in the bone." He moves swiftly from the dancer's plight of unrequited love into a singular trenchant comment on man's Ur-fallacy, a tendency towards selfish love. Yet his mention of Diaghilev and Nijinksy is a kind of personalized reference, considering it was a homosexual affair. The nature of the ballet dancer's madness is also fitting for both a global and personalized reading.

Nijinsky was diagnosed early with a persecution mania and then later confirmed as a schizophrenic (Buckle 410). Persecution mania is a fitting aspect of paranoia for certain minorities of the 1930s in postindustrial countries: Jews, who represented a large section of Eastern Europe, for example, and homosexuals, who made up a hefty cross section of New York City. Nijinsky, despite feelings of persecution, was nevertheless a world famous Russian ballet dancer, described by A. L. Rowse as "probably the greatest dancer the world has seen" (qtd. in Buckle 142). The striking similarities between the poet and his subject become obvious, seeing that Nijinsky was extremely subject to the public eye, much like Auden, and that they both were homosexuals in countries lacking tolerance for different sexual orientations. Auden's probable identification with Nijinsky and his mention of the ballet dancer in "September 1, 1939" display perhaps even a postmodernist tendency of constructing works to communicate with marginalized individuals. Nijinsky is the Amnesty International poster child for the "international wrong," the "wrong" the poet could not explain without implicating the United States, a country whose citizenship he enjoyed. This stanza, although often overlooked by critics, is the instance in which Auden exposes the current perhaps milder fascism, a force that did not reside entirely in Nazi Germany.

Aside from Auden's probable identification with Nijinsky, aspects of Diagilev also lend more coherence to the pair as possibly being the sliding signifiers for the poem. Some speculate that Nijinsky's madness was brought on by Diagilev's impossible demands of him as a dancer, as an artist. Diagilev was described as:

> proud of his resemblance to Peter the Great, he was always a dictator. [...] Both ruthless and tender hearted, but the ruthlessness was that of the artist: when each [dancer] had nothing new to offer, Diagilev passed on to the next who

had. This led to some heartaches and in the case of Nijinsky—tragedy" (Rowse, qtd. in Buckle 140–41).

In this light, art or the relentless pursuit of art, is easier to understand as a form of fascism. The theme of dictatorship, weaved throughout the poem, is also strengthened with the example of Diagilev, an auteur, whose instruments or works were human beings. Auden's choice of this particular dancer and his patron also show a kind of self-reflexivity in the poem. Auden, as an artist, a transmitter of culture, might fear becoming too prescriptive in "September 1, 1939." Mentioning Nijinsky and Diagilev could be an acknowledgement of the dangerous consequences of art's power to prescribe, its inherent danger of becoming a kind of master narrative. Art, viewed as a master narrative, is the quest for the perfect form, the mastering of a medium with the aim of expression.

Diagilev's "ruthless" search for the aesthetic ideal ignored human, physiological barriers or limits, and in doing so was progressive yet dehumanizing. On the one hand, Diagilev's artistic vision in ballet was innovative and constructive, committing Nijinsky's name to fame. Conversely it was just as destructive because the pursuit of perfection led Nijinsky to madness; he eventually committed himself to a mental asylum for the last thirty-five years of his life. Nijinsky's madness could be pivotal in Auden's understanding of the dangerous and pernicious nature of any aesthetic pushed too far. Auden, perhaps because he was an artist, recognized the danger of tyrannizing ideologies more poignantly in the tragedy of an artist than in the case of Hitler's fascism.

Recognizing the thematic significance of Auden's allusion is key because it establishes a unity in the poem, emphasizing the overarching theme of dictatorial elements lurking and manifesting themselves everywhere, from the aims of artists or their patrons to the extreme case of Hitler. As sliding signifiers, Nijinsky and Diagilev indicate that even the pursuit of art, despite its potential for subversion or transcendence, can appropriate forms of tyranny. Moreover, Auden's allusion, because it is dodgy, tacitly comments on the homophobic and tyrannizing tendencies authoritarian systems espouse.

Source: James Miller, "Auden's 'September 1, 1939,'" in *Explicator*, Vol. 62, No. 2, Winter 2004, pp. 115–19.

Nicholas Jenkins

In the following excerpt, Jenkins places "September 1, 1939" in both a literary and biographical context. Jenkins notes that the poem's opening lines were influenced by the poetry of Ogden Nash, and adds that Auden, a recent emigrant from England, had been studying American styles of poetry when he wrote "September 1, 1939." Jenkins also describes the poem as "a piece of emotional reportage," calling it "one of the century's key lyrics."

. . . Sitting in a railway carriage in the middle of Kansas at the end of August, Auden wrote to a friend, "There is a radio in this coach so that every hour or so, one has a violent pain in one's stomach as the news comes on." He arrived in New York just in time for Europe's descent into the maelstrom. Hitler invaded Poland on September 1, 1939, and that night Auden went, apparently alone, to a place called the Dizzy Club, on West Fifty-Second Street. It was probably there, in the noisy bar—"packed to the rafters with college boys and working-class youths" is how Norse described it—that Auden began one of his most famous poems, "September 1, 1939." It was another elegy, this time a farewell to his generation's "clever hopes," aspirations that he had in part been responsible for molding. The thirties had been called "the Age of Auden"; now Auden himself wrote off the entire "low dishonest decade." Yet, oddly, given that this is one of Auden's most sombre poems, the opening cadence is borrowed from one of America's great comic poets, Ogden Nash. Auden, in his early months in the States, had self-consciously searched for American local styles, and had written to a friend about his discovery of Nash's idiom, misquoting from the poem "Spring Comes to Murray Hill": "As I sit in my office / On 23rd Street and Madison Avenue." Auden's new poem begins, "I sit in one of the dives / On Fifty-Second Street."

But Nash's equable comic accent is drowned out by a more strident rhetoric as the American bar scene gives way to the supercharged power of global indictment:

> Into this neutral air
> Where blind skyscrapers use
> Their full height to proclaim
> The strength of Collective Man,
> Each language pours its vain
> Competitive excuse:
> But who can live for long

In an euphoric dream;
Out of the mirror they stare,
Imperialism's face
And the international wrong.

Auden wrote the poem over a weekend, but he would spend a good part of the rest of his life regretting it. He soon came to loathe what he felt was its sanctimoniousness and (as he saw it) the frivolity of its famous assertion that "we must love one another or die." In a letter to a friend who had admitted that she found it memorable, he fumed, "The reason (artistic) I left England and went to the U.S. was precisely to *stop* me writing poems like 'Sept 1st 1939' the most dishonest poem I have ever written. A hang-over from the U.K. It takes time to cure oneself."

But poems, like children, defy their creators. Auden later made dogged attempts to extirpate "September 1, 1939" from his canon, but it has become one of his most quoted works. You can see why Auden was dissatisfied. After presenting a despairing picture of individual isolation, Auden asks portentously:

Who can release them now,
Who can reach the deaf,
Who can speak for the dumb?

There is no explicit answer, but the implication is that it is the poet who can restore contact and community to the lonely and the self-immured. Yet, in spite of this remorseless self-elevation, "September 1, 1939" continues to be an important poem. Not since Andrew Marvell's "Horatian Ode" had a poet made equivocation and doubt in the face of a major political event seem so representative a condition. As a piece of emotional reportage, Auden's threnody is a perfect register of the strangely muted onset of the century's worst event, and as long as we read poems for what they describe as well as for what they diagnose, it will remain one of the century's key lyrics. ...

Source: Nicholas Jenkins, "Goodbye, 1939," in *New Yorker*, April 1, 1996, pp. 88, 90–94, 96–97.

Samuel Hynes

In the following excerpt, Hynes provides varied critical insight on "September 1, 1939," including a brief explication of noteworthy aspects of the poem, and discussion of Auden's numerous literary influences. While Hynes does shed further light on Auden as an emigrant, the critic predominantly focuses on Auden's main artistic concerns, most of which can be seen in "September 1, 1939."

> 'SEPTEMBER 1, 1939' IS AN UNSUCCESSFUL POEM, BUT IT IS A USEFUL ONE TO BEGIN WITH, BECAUSE IN IT AUDEN MADE A FIRST ATTEMPT TO DEAL WITH THE MAJOR PROBLEMS THAT CONCERNED HIM IN THESE CRUCIAL YEARS: HOW TO THINK HISTORICALLY ABOUT PRESENT DISASTER; HOW TO BE AN ARTIST IN A BAD TIME; AND HOW, AND WHAT, TO AFFIRM."

Hynes identifies these themes as: "History, Art, and Necessity."

... By 1939, it seemed clear to him, as it did to many other Europeans, that the crisis they were facing was not simply another war but the failure of an ideology. *If* fascism existed, and dominated Europe, *if* another world war was coming, then the liberal western conception of man must be wrong in fundamental ways—more than wrong, *dead.* By leaving England when he did, Auden was freeing himself from that dead liberal ideology. Man's condition would have to be understood differently from now on: as existentially alone, cut off from the old roots, the old comforts and securities. And if that was true, then England was the wrong place for an English poet. When an old friend opposed Auden's move, on the grounds that it was dangerous for a writer to sever his native roots, Auden replied that the concept of roots was obsolete: "What I am trying to do," he explained to E. R. Dodds, "is to live deliberately *without* roots."

It was an extraordinary decision to make—to go in quest of a life that would be a parable of the condition of Modern Man, as though one could become a Kafka character, or the Wandering Jew, by an act of will. Even the word *quest* itself seems a bit literary and elevated for what was, after all, just another Atlantic crossing. I use it nonetheless, because it was a word—and a concept—that Auden was using a lot then, most notably in his other major poem of these years, the sonnet sequence called "The Quest." Questing was on his mind, because that's what he saw himself as doing: journeying to meet the future.

For a European writer who aspired to rootlessness, America was the obvious place to go. "The attractiveness of America to a writer," Auden told an interviewer for the *Saturday Review* in 1940, "is its openness and lack of tradition. In a way it's frightening. You are forced to live here as everyone will be forced to live. There is no past. No tradition. No roots— that is in the European sense." In this rootless society a European could escape the past, and become what Auden desired to be: the entirely Modern Man. And then, presumably, he could write Modern Poems.

What such poems would be like we may infer from the poems that Auden wrote during his first year in America—for example "September 1, 1939," a poem that commemorates the day on which the Germans invaded Poland, and liberalism and the thirties died. In the poem a rootless man sits in a rootless place—what could be better for that than a New York bar?—and meditates on what has ended—and why. Around him are rootless, undifferentiated human beings—the faces at the bar, the dense commuters—none having any relation to the speaker, or to each other, none an agent in its own life. The forces that operate in the world of the poem are blank abstractions: Collective Man, Important Persons, Authority, the State. Even the skyscrapers are blind.

Nothing happens in the poem; nothing changes; nothing connects. Yet it ends with two stanzas of affirmation:

> All I have is a voice
> To undo the folded lie . . .
>
> Yet, dotted everywhere,
> Ironic points of light
> Flash out wherever the Just
> Exchange their messages . . .

The manuscript (in the Berg collection) shows that this floating affirmation was originally even stronger. Auden must have been thinking of two canceled stanzas when he said that the poem was "infected with an incurable dishonesty," and excluded it from later collections of his poems. For sentimentality is a form of dishonesty, and "September 1, 1939" is certainly sentimental: it sentimentalizes loneliness, it sentimentalizes the role of the artist (what good will his voice do in a world war?), and it sentimentalizes the idea of affirmation itself in that final image of the points of light that flash messages without content. (It is worth noting

that Auden got that image from E. M. Forster, who had written, just the year before in *I Believe:* "It's a humiliating outlook—though the greater the darkness, the brighter shine the little lights, reassuring one another, signalling, 'Well, at all events I'm still here. I don't like it very much, but how are you?'" In the manuscript Auden first used Forster's word *little*, before he hit on *ironic*. Perhaps part of Auden's dissatisfaction with the poem was his recognition that he had not yet cast off Forsterian liberalism: he had brought some of his roots with him.)

"September 1, 1939" is an unsuccessful poem, but it is a useful one to begin with, because in it Auden made a first attempt to deal with the major problems that concerned him in these crucial years: how to think historically about present disaster; how to be an artist in a bad time; and how, and what, to affirm. The poem is therefore a sort of first draft of "New Year Letter." Thinking historically may be the most difficult task that a modern writer can assume, especially in a time of war. In the twentieth century it has been impossible to think about any war in historical terms while it was going on: war-writing, and war-thinking, is always apocalyptic. Auden tried in "September 1, 1939" to see the war, as it began, as an historical consequence: he mentions Protestantism and imperialism, and invokes Thucydides; but there is really no argument offered, only sketchy materials for one. One way to look at the work that followed is to regard it as a series of expansions and revisions of this first wartime view of Modern Man, in the mess of history that he had made.

The years 1939–1940 were productive ones for Auden. In those two years he published two books and wrote another, published more than fifty poems and many reviews, all this while lecturing and teaching, and even for a time running a Brooklyn boardinghouse. And he read: "I have never written nor read so much," he wrote to a friend in late 1939. What he was reading was not primarily literature but science, philosophy, and religion: the sorts of books that a man might turn to who was trying to construct for himself a new understanding of man-in-history. You can get some sense of what this reading was, if you look through Auden's notes to "New Year Letter": Hans Spemann's *Embryonic Development and Induction*, Margaret Meade's *Growing up in New Guinea*, the journals of Kierkegaard, Werner Jaeger's *Paideia*, Nietzsche's *Postscript to the*

Case of Wagner, Charles Williams's *Descent of the Dove*, Collingwood's *Metaphysics*, Köhler's *The Place of Value in a World of Facts.*

If you read through the whole body of Auden's prose for these years, you will find that quotations from these writers keep turning up, often in quite unlikely places, sometimes more than once. And you will find other repetitions— certain definitions and analyses and formulations. You *could* argue from this evidence that he had simply overextended himself, and was meeting his journalistic deadlines by cannibalizing his own writings. But that doesn't seem an adequate explanation, given the extraordinary fertility of his mind; I think it would be more accurate to say that at this time Auden had certain preoccupations, and that his repetitions express the power of those preoccupations to force their way into everything he wrote. This is true of even his most casual book reviews, in which he would habitually swerve from his ostensible subject—a life of Voltaire or an anthology by de la Mare—to write about his real concerns.

You can group those concerns under three general headings: History, Art, and Necessity; *everything* that he wrote during these years had to do with one or more of these subjects. And you might go on to say that in fact these are all aspects of one master question. Auden put that question in a review he wrote of Harold Laski's *Where Do We Go from Here?* Laski's title, he said, posed an unreal question: "The only real question, and this itself becomes unreal unless it is asked all the time, is *where are we now?*" Everything that Auden wrote—every review, every lecture, every poem—was a draft of an answer to that question. ...

Source: Samuel Hynes, "The Voice of Exile: Auden in 1940," in *Sewanee Review*, Vol. 90, No. 1, Winter 1982, pp. 31–52.

SOURCES

Auden, W. H., "September 1, 1939," in *W. H. Auden: Selected Poems*, edited by Edward Mendelson, Vintage Books, 1979, pp. 86–9.

Callan, Edward, "Disenchantment With Yeats: From Singing-Master to Ogre," in *W. H. Auden*, edited by Harold Bloom, Chelsea House, 1986, pp. 170–71.

Diener, Sam, Annotations and Commentary on "September 1, 1939," in *Educators for Social Responsibllilty*, http://
www.esrnational.org/september1_1939annotated.htm (accessed May 8, 2007).

Guernsey, Bruce, Review of *The English Auden: Poems, Essays and Dramatic Writings, 1927–1939*, in *Library Journal*, Vol. 103, No. 10, May 15, 1978, p. 1062.

Jenkins, Nicholas, "Either Or or And: An Enigmatic Moment in the History of 'September 1, 1939,'" in *Yale Review*, Vol. 90, No. 3, July 2002, pp. 22–39.

Kermode, Frank, "Faithing and Blithing," in the *Listener*, October 26, 1972, pp. 551–52, reprinted in *W. H. Auden: The Critical Heritage*, edited by John Haffenden, Routledge, 1997, p. 470.

Miller, James, "Auden's 'September 1, 1939,'" in the *Explicator*, Vol. 62, No. 2, Winter 2004, pp. 113–18.

Wilson, Edmund, "W. H. Auden in America," in *The New Statesman and the Nation, LI*, June 9, 1956, pp. 658–59, reprinted in *Auden: A Collection of Critical Essays*, edited by Monroe K. Spears, Prentice-Hall, Inc., 1964, p. 54.

Yezzi, David, "What Auden Believed," in the *New Criterion*, Vol. 24, March 2006, p. 9.

FURTHER READING

Hecht, Anthony, "Poetry Makes Nothing Happen: *Another Time*," in *The Hidden Law*, Harvard University Press, 1993, pp. 81–180.

> Hecht, a noted literary critic, devotes a long section of this essay about Auden's 1940 poetry collection to an analysis of "September 1, 1939."

Jarrell, Randall, *Randall Jarrell on W. H. Auden*, edited by Stephen Burt and Hannah Brooks-Motl, Columbia University Press, 2005.

> In this series of six lectures that Jarrell, one of the twentieth century's greatest American poets and critics, delivered at Princeton in 1952, Auden's career is treated with the kind of tough skepticism that could only come from a peer.

Jung, Carl Gustav, "Psychology and Literature," in *The Spirit in Man, Art, and Literature*, Princeton University Press, 1971, pp. 84–108.

> When Auden uses the phrase "Collective Man" in the poem, he is referring directly to a concept that is proposed by Jung in this essay. Much of the poem is patterned on Auden's understandings of Jung's theories.

Pierre, Walter, "Auden's Political Vision," in *W. H. Auden: The Far Interior*, edited by Alan Bold, Visions Press International, 1985, pp. 47–72.

> Readers hoping to make sense of this poem should understand the poet's political view, which is explained here in one relatively brief essay.

Telephone Conversation

WOLE SOYINKA

1963

Wole Soyinka's poetry has often been described as a powerful and serious agent to social change. His themes are primarily concerned with the promotion of human rights and African politics. At the same time, such poems as "Telephone Conversation" reveal a lyrical understanding of the rhythms and resonances of language balanced with humor and a deeply felt compassion for the human condition. Appearing initially in the collection *Modern Poetry from Africa* (1963), the poem is a provocative interrogation of racial prejudice, misguided civility, and the power of language to create ghettos of race and of spirit. Negotiating elegantly between the subtleties of irony and the social criticism of sarcasm, "Telephone Conversation" always maintains a thoughtful distance from the emotional minefields of its subject matter, transforming itself into a poem that sets aside anger and frustration in favor of humor as a means to achieve a deeper understanding and spirit of integration and harmony.

Out of Soyinka's large body of work, "Telephone Conversation" is one of his most well-known and most often anthologized poems. It may be found in *Perrine's Literature: Structure, Sound, and Sense*, edited by Thomas Arp and Greg Johnson, published by Thomson in 2006.

AUTHOR BIOGRAPHY

Akinwande Oluwole Soyinka was born in Isara, Nigeria on July 13, 1934 (Wole is the shortened

Wole Soyinka *(Hulton Archive / Getty Images. Reproduced by*
permission)

form of Oluwole). A member of the Yoruba tribe, he was well schooled as a child in the stories of tribal gods and folklore, mostly because of his grandfather, who was a respected tribal elder. Soyinka's parents represented another powerful influence in the young boy's life. His mother was a convert to Christianity and his father was headmaster at the local British-model school. Not surprisingly, Soyinka as a youngster was very familiar with the tensions that defined colonial Africa in the early decades of the twentieth century, as tribal culture collided, sometimes violently, with the imperatives of British colonizers.

Soyinka took up writing very early in his life, publishing poems and short stories in the Nigerian literary magazine *Black Orpheus* before leaving his homeland to attend the University of Leeds in England. He returned to Nigeria in 1960, the same year that the country declared its independence from colonial rule. A prolific writer, Soyinka gained prominence initially for his work as a playwright of such politically motivated works as *The Swamp Dwellers* (1958), *The Lion and the Jewel* (1959), and *A Dance of the Forests* (1960).

It was during this same prolific period that Soyinka's "Telephone Conversation" appeared in the 1963 collection *Modern Poetry from Africa*. Two years later, he was arrested for allegedly forcing a radio announcer to report incorrect election results. Soyinka was released three months later, after the international writers group PEN made public the knowledge that no evidence had ever been produced in support of the arrest. He was arrested again two years later for his vocal opposition to the civil war that was threatening to split the country along longstanding tribal lines. Accused of helping Biafran fighters buy military jets, Soyinka spent two years in prison, despite the fact that he was never formally charged with any crime.

During his imprisonment, much of it spent in solitary confinement, Soyinka kept a prison diary, which was published in 1972 as *The Man Died: Prison Notes of Wole Soyinka*. He also wrote a trilogy of nonfiction books that trace the trajectory of his life and family: *Aké: The Years of Childhood* (1980), *Isara: A Voyage Around Essay* (1989), and *Ibadan: The Penkelemes Years: A Memoir, 1946–1965* (1994).

Following a period of self-imposed exile, Soyinka was among a group of pro-democracy activists charged with treason for his criticism of the military regime of General Sani Abacha. Facing a death sentence in Nigeria, he spent many years lecturing throughout Europe and the United States, including stays at Yale and Cornell University, where he served as the Goldwin Smith professor for African Studies and Theatre Arts from 1988 to 1991. It was during these expatriate years that Soyinka wrote *Art, Dialogue and Outrage: Essays on Literature and Culture* and *The Open Sore of a Continent: A Personal Narrative of the Nigerian Crisis* (1996). In 1999, he turned his attention to the role of the South African Truth and Reconciliation Commission in *The Burden of Memory, the Muse of Forgiveness*.

A poet as well as a dramatist and essayist, Soyinka has published several collections, including *Idanre and Other Poems* (1967), *Ogun Abibiman* (1976), *Mandela's Earth and Other Poems* (1988), and *Samarkand and Other Markets I Have Known* (2002).

Internationally recognized for both his writing and his advocacy of democracy and civil rights, Soyinka has collected an impressive catalogue of rewards and honors, including the John

Whiting Drama Prize (1966), the Nobel Prize for Literature (1986), and the Enrico Mattei Award for Humanities (1986). Soyinka continues to travel the world speaking on the behalf of the oppressed and the marginalized.

POEM SUMMARY

Lines 1–10

"Telephone Conversation" is exactly what its title promises: an imagined conversation between a African man and a presumably white landlady with accommodations to rent. Some of the idioms in the poem mark the general geography of the poem as England, most likely London. The city saw a substantial influx of African immigrants throughout the post-war decades, a period that also saw a rise of racial tensions in the country, so such conversations would not have been unfamiliar.

The poem opens with the African speaker clarifying the essential information about the location, the cost, and similar business details. The landlady is initially described as being of "good-breeding," a standing that makes her questions about the color of the speaker's skin seem suddenly and dramatically out of place. Specifically, she wants to know if he is light or very dark skinned, a distinction that seems to carry particular weight within the racial atmosphere of the day.

Lines 11–18

From this pointed and clearly prejudicial question, the poem moves smoothly between the thoughts of the speaker as he considers the question as a political statement and the landlady's insistent repetition of the same questions or variations thereof. As the conversation unfolds, it becomes a painful accumulation of ironic miscommunication and blatant racism. The more the speaker tries to answer the questions, the deeper the exchange slips into irony as the speaker answers the woman with cool logic that clouds rather than clarifies the situation. At first comparing himself to chocolate, for instance, the speaker settles on describing himself as "West African sepia," a term he knows will further confuse his listener.

Lines 19–35

As the speaker's ironic tone takes hold of the conversation, he begins to describe various body parts, from his hair to the soles of his feet, in an effort to explain to her that he is, like all people, several different colors. The final lines of the poem carry a double-edged message. The first is clear: making a judgment about a person's character based solely on the color of their skin is the key absurdity of racial prejudice. The second layer of the closing lines underscore the meeting of absurdity with additional absurdity, an approach Soyinka often brings to his explorations of such situations, as the speaker invites the woman to "see" for herself all of the varied colors of the body parts he catalogues.

THEMES

Racial Conflict

"Telephone Conversation" is a dramatic dialogue in which a person of color responds to the racial prejudices of a woman with whom he is trying to negotiate rental accommodations. As the poem begins, the speaker's well-educated and polished voice, as heard on the telephone, make him acceptable to the landlady, but when he turns to the crucial moment of "self-confession," the truth of racial conflict comes to the foreground. The landlady clearly does not want a tenant of color, yet at the same time is trapped by the code of civil conduct that will not allow her to acknowledge what might be considered an uncivilized racial prejudice. The cluster of assumptions articulated by the well-bred landlady gather into an almost textbook definition of racism. She is xenophobic (exhibiting an irrational fear of foreigners, such as the African caller). She engages a vocabulary of racial stereotypes (making hasty generalizations based on skin color or ethnic background), and her unwillingness to rent to a man of color reinforces a policy of racial segregation or what has been called ghettoization (the practice of restricting members of a racial or ethnic group to certain neighborhoods or areas of a city).

But even as she weaves her way through a series of deeply prejudicial questions, ranging from "HOW DARK?" to "THAT'S DARK, ISN'T IT?" the woman reveals the confused underside of racial attitudes. At no point in the poem does the speaker internalize the sense of

TOPICS FOR FURTHER STUDY

- Given that the tensions explored in Soyinka's poem stem in large part from the collision of British (colonial) and African (colonized) cultures, research the history of the colonization of an African country of your choice. Construct a timeline that traces the major shifts in colonial presences, the key dates and events that led to the various shifts, the shifts in both geographic (borders) and cultural (language, religion) makeup, as well as any other aspect of the history that you feel is significant.

- "Telephone Conversation" is a poem that is full of colors, not only of skin but of voices and buses, for instance. Write an essay in which you discuss the meanings of each of the colors mentioned, and the importance of what or whom they are attached to.

- Write a poem or series of poems that attempt to capture the subtleties and complexities of some of the political or social issues that dominate your community or your country.

- Set up a formal debate in your classroom that takes this proposition as its starting point: "Poetry is an effective medium for making people aware of racial prejudice and social injustice."

---

inferiority that is being projected upon him, nor does he react in anger to her narrow-mindedness. Instead, he engages language in a calm and highly sophisticated manner, elevating the poem from diatribe or attack to a much more effective end of allowing readers to see the world through the absurd lens of racial prejudice.

Poetry and Politics

Although the school of New Criticism struggled to keep the worlds of politics and poetry at arm's length, a poem such as "Telephone Conversation" is a reminder that poets in some parts of the world,

or of certain ethnic or racial backgrounds, do not get to choose one side of that divide or the other. Their very existence is politically charged. For a speaker like the one in Soyinka's poem, the politics lingering behind such seemingly benign words as "dark" and "light," for instance, are partly the pressures that threaten to fragment a community and that resist a spirit or imagination that might want to promote a sense of wholeness or integration. Words, especially when used as labels, divide the world of Soyinka's poem in the same insidious and powerful ways as any political agenda might.

It is this potential for divisiveness that the poem's speaker attempts to undercut in the closing lines of the poem, when he effectively breaks down the landlady's powerful (but unstated) fixation with the word "dark" through his own list of the various shadings that might clarify for her the abstraction of darkness. As the speaker notes, he is simultaneously a man who is "brunette," "raven black," and, in a wonderful twist, "peroxide blonde" on the palms of his hands and soles of his feet.

STYLE

Satire

Satire is a technique that uses humor and irony to undercut misguided behaviors or to censure social and political attitudes. From its origins in the writing and culture of the ancient Greeks, satire has remained a powerful tool of moral judgment. The tone of satiric literature ranges from the detached irony of Soyinka's "Telephone Conversation" to fully expressed anger and vehement contempt. Given that most satire relies heavily on balancing humor and word play with criticism, it is appropriate that irony is one of its chief tools.

The satiric voice in Soyinka's poem is put in place through a series of linguistic and thematic juxtapositions. While the speaker notes that the landlady to whom he speaks is of "good-breeding" with a voice that is "lipstick-coated, long gold-rolled," he is also quick to attach a series of words to her that carry an overabundance of negative connotations. She is described as "clinical" and as having a "light impersonality" to her demeanor. Elsewhere in the poem readers are told that her accent "clang[s]" and that her silences are "ill-mannered." All of this takes place in a setting that is itself a circumstance that contributes to the satire, being described variously as "rancid" and as appealing as the sound and feel of "squelching tar."

At its best, satire reveals a sophisticated versatility of speech, a strong moral center through which one might speak to social and cultural improprieties. Put simply, satire is defined, in large part, by many of the same traits that readers can attribute to "Telephone Conversation."

Ironic Detachment

The figure of the speaker in "Telephone Conversation" is clearly positioned as an observer of his own situation. He is not a victim nor is he angry, despite the blatant racial prejudice that he is forced to negotiate throughout his telephone exchange with the landlady. Oscillating between humor and irony, the speaker deploys his words with a cool and logical double edge. More specifically, the speaker brings literal and intended meanings into opposition during the course of the conversation, as when he attempts to clarify the situation by comparing himself to chocolate or, in the closing lines, when he asks the woman "wouldn't you rather / See for yourself?" It is in the opposition of these meanings (the man certainly does *not* want himself likened to a food, for instance) that Soyinka unleashes the criticism of the poem. Standing back from the immediate emotions of the moment, the speaker effectively illuminates the woman's racial assumptions, hidden usually behind what Tanure Ojaide, in his book *The Poetry of Wole Soyinka*, catalogues as "her sophistication, affectation, and artificiality." Indeed, it is the cool logic of the speaker's response that at once establishes the woman's social status and gives readers an insight into the confused politics and insensitivity of the landlady.

HISTORICAL CONTEXT

Colonialism in Africa

The history of European dominance of Africa through military and economic strategies is a long and often bloody one. The 1880s marked the intensification of conflicts between European countries for control of the regions of Africa. Especially prominent countries in the imperial project for the last part of the nineteenth and early twentieth century were France (especially in West Africa), Great Britain (East and South Africa, the Gold Coast), Belgium (the Congo), Spain (the Western Sahara), Italy

(North Africa), and Germany (East Africa). The struggle for control of African territories was driven in part by the rich natural resources of the various regions of the continent as well as by a desire to control crucial routes for overseas trade. The political and economic tensions that circulated just below the surface of the struggle for Africa informed many of the international crises that led to World War I. The rush to colonize the Congo, the rebellions that threatened the building of the Suez Canal, and the seemingly perpetual battles over control of the Nile headwaters are three examples of many crises provoking incidents that are usually recognized as precipitating the political tensions that erupted into war in 1914.

Furthermore, the cultural impact of Colonialism was immense. The varied cultures of each African locality were subsumed by the culture of the country occupying that locality. In short, native Africans were treated as second-class citizens by the ruling class of European colonists. Thus, it is important to note that though Soyinka's poem explores the speaker's experiences of racism and displacement in a foreign country, that speaker would likely be subject to similar experiences in his own birthplace as well.

Immigration to Britain

In Britain, prior to the 1900s, there was often tension arising over governmental and cultural attitudes towards immigration. Originally these tensions grew from hostility towards peoples of a different culture and appearance, most notably towards members of the growing Jewish community and later towards immigrants from Russia and Eastern Europe. Due to the tensions and concerns created by immigration, the British parliament decided to restrict immigration in 1905, a decision that has repercussions even today as the country continues to maintain very strong legislative control of immigration levels.

Following World War II, Britain suffered through a slow and often debilitating return from the economic hardships of the previous decades. The economy was able to rebuild, albeit slowly, and the signs of recovery proved a beacon to immigrants who were seeking refuge or a better lifestyle in the United Kingdom. Under the British Nationality Act of 1948, the British Government decided to embark on a major change in the law of nationality throughout the

COMPARE & CONTRAST

- **1960s:** When the speaker mentions pushing "Button B, Button A" he is referring to the fact that in old style British public payphones a caller had to press a series of buttons once coins were deposited in order to maintain a connection with the person on the other end of the phone.

  Today: Public payphones in Britain allow callers a number of options (standard, text, and email) as well as accepting a full range of payment methods, including credit and debit cards.

- **1960s:** The speaker refers to himself as "African," which is a reductive and overly simplistic term that underscores the nature of the racial stereotypes that saw the whole of the African continent as an undifferentiated continent lacking any form of ethnic, social, or cultural distinctions.

  Today: Although such racial stereotyping still occurs in Britain and elsewhere, the language has changed slightly to reflect national or regional distinctions. The term African would be replaced, for instance, by a more regional (South African) or national (Nigerian) reference.

- **1960s:** African immigrants in Europe and African-Americans in the United States mostly live and work in segregation.

  Today: While racial segregation is not as explicit as it once was, it still exists to some degree on account of economic inequality.

Commonwealth. All other Commonwealth countries, with the exception of Ireland, had their own British subject nationality status. Since the middle of the twentieth century, racial tensions have ebbed and flowed in Britain, driven in part by the economic climate of the day and by the realization that the large populations of different nationalities, notably South Asians, Africans, East Asians, and Eastern Europeans, have reconfigured Britain into a country populated predominantly by people with a foreign heritage.

Racism in Britain

Throughout the eighteenth and nineteenth centuries, racial policies and trade practices were a central mechanism for controlling a disenfranchised work force comprised largely of Scottish and Irish workers. As immigrant populations expanded through the early twentieth century, so did the discriminatory conduct, which had to take into account the presence of an increasing number of workers of Jewish heritage as well as immigrants from Russia and Eastern Europe.

Britain was also amongst other early capitalist societies to utilize the slave trade, which positioned itself neatly to benefit economically from the dramatic African migration that came to define the 1950s. African immigrants provided a cheap labor force that could support the post-war recovery. Despite these obvious and far-reaching economic benefits, African communities within the larger metropolitan areas were subordinated and often reviled, their members treated as second class citizens. Racial tensions, fueled by a growing sense of powerlessness, increasingly public and vocal discrimination, and a sputtering economy, reached a flash point in the 1980s, a decade marked by rioting in various parts of the country. It was reported by the "Joint Campaign Against Racism" that there were more than 20,000 attacks on non-indigenous peoples living in Britain in 1985 alone. More recently, racism continues in forms of public displays of racial intolerance, a rise in racially motivated crime, and increasing tensions between immigrant populations and local law enforcement agencies.

CRITICAL OVERVIEW

In his retrospective study of *The Poetry of Wole Soyinka*, Tanure Ojaide notes that as one of Soyinka's earliest poems, "Telephone Conversation" differs substantively from his later poems. "In the early poems," Ojaide argues, Soyinka "is interested in individuals in society, and there is a psychological and social bias" that is clearly articulated. Additionally, he "presents the characters and their mental attitudes for ridicule, sympathy, and amusement. The voice" of these early poems "is critical," the language "simple, and the major poetic devices" brought into play include "sarcasm, irony, hyperbole, and repetition."

Significantly, Ojaide goes on to state, this is a poem in which "the voice of the poet is distinct. There is no bitterness in the voice, no sense of urgency in the light criticism, no vision of inhumanity as in the later poems." This is a poem that focuses on the absurdity of an individual who behaves badly and whose own ignorance of the racial diversity in which she lives leaves her out of touch with society.

It is the reconnection to the realities of a world divided on political and racial lines that many other critics comment on when considering Soyinka's poetry. In his article "Poetry as Revelation: Wole Soyinka," critic D. I. Nwoga, for instance, celebrates Soyinka's poetry for its power to establish for readers "a new reality," providing "a new background to [an individual's] understanding and judgement of particular things, actions and situations." Moreover, Nwoga continues, these are poems that redirect "our wills and planning for the future." Writing for *Transition*, Stanley Macebuh bends this critical emphasis in a slightly different direction, arguing in his article, "Poetics and the Mythic Imagination," that Soyinka's "abiding concern" in his poetry has always "been with myth" rather than with history or politics, and more specifically with developing a kind of mythic "significance for contemporary life in Africa." Soyinka is, as Alan Jacobs asserts in "Wole Soyinka's Outrage: The Divided Soul of Nigeria's Nobel Laureate," "a writer of spectacular literary gifts" who has made his mark on contemporary literature in part due to his profundity as "an acclaimed lyric and satirical poet."

CRITICISM

Klay Dyer

Dyer holds a Ph.D. in English literature and has published extensively on fiction, poetry, film, and television. He is also a freelance university teacher, writer, and educational consultant. In this essay, he discusses Soyinka as a poetic historian whose "Telephone Conversation" can be read as an unambiguous attempt to trace the roots of racial prejudice through the exploration of language as a cultural and political tool.

To many critics and scholars, Soyinka is the preeminent African activist-writer of the twentieth century, and, when turning to his poetry, a writer who clearly favors the dramatic over the experimental or the lyric. While these labels do celebrate Soyinka's skill and passion as a writer, they do, ironically, shortchange one aspect of his writing: his skill as a kind of poetic historian inspired and challenged into unambiguous attempts to trace the roots of racial prejudice in the textures and meaning of language itself. His often anthologized poem "Telephone Conversation" is not so much a record of yet another instance of misguided prejudice as it is a demonstration of the manner in which such attitudes are deployed and sustained within a culture. Prejudice, in this sense, can be reimagined as both a pattern of social attitudes as well as a product of language itself.

To recognize Soyinka's preoccupation with the racial overtones of language itself is to discover one of the sources of his creative energy. At times, Soyinka's poetry is defined by a dignified simplicity that appeals to ease of access and the immediate recognition of readers. Read from this angle, Soyinka's language is almost casually serene, a marker of "good-breeding" and "lipstick-coated." In the opening lines of "Telephone Conversation," Soyinka's speaker sees the cost of his own subservience to the "pressurized" constrictions of language as "reasonable," and his own expectations when entering into the negotiations are "indifferent." As the poem opens, readers experience an African man willing to accept the language of "good-breeding" and the veneer of attitudes and politics that can be best described as "gold-rolled." There is a political and spiritual complacency to these opening lines, an unwillingness to upset the cultural expectations that lead to this exchange. Language is not *expected* to be

WHAT DO I READ NEXT?

- Soyinka's *Climate of Fear: The Quest for Dignity in a Dehumanized World* (2004) explores the political and human rights implications in what he calls the current climate of fear. In a book that has been called a defining work of our age, he discusses the international conflict between power and freedom, the motives behind unthinkable acts of violence, and the meaning of human dignity.

- Equally valuable is Soyinka's *The Burden of Memory, the Muse of Forgiveness* (1999), a series of three lectures delivered at the De Bois Institute of Harvard University. Intensely political and powerfully lyrical, these pieces are a seminal exploration of the role of South Africa's Truth and Reconciliation Commission.

- Racial conflict and the complex issues surrounding the politics of color are central to M. G. Vassanji's *The Book of Secrets* (1994), an outstanding historical novel set in East Africa. The best of M. G. Vassanji's early novels, it transforms the history of South Asians in Kenya and Tanzania from 1913 to 1988 into an absorbing narrative that is part love story, part war story, part mystery, part national history, and part journey of self-discovery.

- Chinua Achebe's *Collected Poems* (2004) is a powerful collection from the writer often considered one of the founding fathers of African literature in English. Drawing on three books of poetry, and including seven previously unpublished poems, this collection, like the poetry of Soyinka, explores an intimate poetic engagement with politics, war, and culture. Writing in tones that are at once ironic, generous, and tender, Achebe draws deeply on mythic traditions and promised futures by way of confronting the contemporary world's harsh reality of violence and exploitation.

> '*TELEPHONE CONVERSATION*' ENGAGES IN A MORAL INDICTMENT OF LANGUAGE ITSELF, AND MORE PARTICULARLY IN THE SURREPTITIOUS SLIPPAGE BETWEEN MEANING AND PREJUDICE."

problematic in the opening stages of this conversation, and, for a few lines at least, it remains comfortably polite.

Despite the apparent complacency of these opening lines, Soyinka is pointing to the link between the assumptions of language and the conceptual framework from which prejudice receives its power. The once-colonized African speaker is, despite his civility, acutely aware of his unwillingness in the moment to deploy language back against itself and, in turn, back against these assumptions. Put in other words, the speaker plays the language game with confidence and with a learned (or is it instinctive?) understanding of the powers of silence. When faced with a breach in protocol, as in the moment of his "self-confession," the speaker expects and receives a moment of silence.

Moving through this silence, Soyinka's speaker begins to delve deeper into the language of the moment, and to illuminate its power to function as a tool of both the civilized veneer and the apparatus of prejudicial politics. In the moments following the silence, the language of the poem becomes less serene, less able to conceal the frustrations building within the speaker and the landlady. This point is amply illustrated by the sudden shift from the world of the civil and the polite to a world defined by the "stench / Of rancid breath" and the cacophony of "squelching tar." Even silence has been reconfigured in this new world, pushed to the limits of the "ill-mannered" and the incomprehensibility of the "dumbfounded." Language, only moments earlier the marker of civil discourse, becomes an invitation to what the speaker calls "revelation" in an instant of silence.

Failing to grapple with the political and racial realities that overwhelm the conversation, the landlady struggles to find her own linguistic bearings. Her voice, once "lipstick-coated" and "cigarette-holder tipped" veers suddenly toward the "clinical" tinged with a "light / Impersonality." If simplicity and accessibility were the defining characteristics of the poem's opening lines, the middle portion of the poem leads the speaker to opt for confusing ideas rather than support an ease of understanding. Describing himself as "West African sepia," the poet sends his listener spiraling into a new type of silence, one that stands in, confusedly, "for [a] spectroscopic / Flight of fancy." Reader and landlady alike are left scrambling to decode the metaphor and to unravel the now confused meanings of the speaker's language.

Significantly, it is in this moment of confusion that truth "clang[s]" hard against the faux civility of the landlady's earlier words. And it is in this collision that language itself cracks open, revealing its deeper political and cultural implications. Once confident in her control of words, the landlady finds herself suddenly rewritten into a position of weakness, forced to "conced[e]" that she does not understand this new and poetic turn of phrase. "DON'T KNOW WHAT THAT IS" she responds curtly. Coincidentally, in this moment of realignment, grammar itself is revisited. First-person pronouns slide into silence, and the contracted form of "do not" pushes the exchange toward the colloquial and even the vulgar. To make this point doubly clear, Soyinka has her repeat both idea and syntax in her next line: "THAT'S DARK, ISN'T IT?"

With this combination of concession and question, the landlady exposes the prejudicial underbelly of language itself. The political impact of race and discrimination is let loose in the poem, shredding the veneer of civility that had once contained the misconceptions of the woman's worldview. From this point onwards, the friction of the poem increases, as the speaker, a man of eloquence and calm, dismantles both the word darkness (dismembering it into various shadings) and the landlady's prejudice (dragging it into the full light of articulation).

And with this friction, the poem shifts dramatically from being an exchange that foregrounds the sense of hearing (and listening) to a foregrounding of the sense of sight. "You should see / The rest of me" the speaker tells the landlady, offering to provide her with the optic proof of his race and of her intolerance. Forced to see for herself the collapse of her language, her

civility, and her control, the woman moves to the fourth level of silence explored in the poem: she moves to terminate the conversation by hanging up. The speaker, in his last and most ironic challenge to her former reliance on the shadowy language of racial prejudice, offers to breach the distance separating them as conversationalists and as people. "Wouldn't you rather / See for yourself," he pleads. The verb "see" resonates through the poem, meaning both see the speaker for herself (and study his various shades of darkness) *and* see for herself the error of her misguided prejudice.

"Telephone Conversation" engages in a moral indictment of language itself, and more particularly in the surreptitious slippage between meaning and prejudice. This is not a poem that seeks serenity in language but demands transformation, change, and most of all awareness.

Source: Klay Dyer, Critical Essay on "Telephone Conversation," in *Poetry for Students*, Gale, 2008.

Thomson Gale

In the following essay, the critic gives a critical analysis of Soyinka's work.

Many critics consider Wole Soyinka Africa's finest writer. The Nigerian playwright's unique style blends traditional Yoruban folk-drama with European dramatic form to provide both spectacle and penetrating satire. Soyinka told *New York Times Magazine* writer Jason Berry that in the African cultural tradition, the artist "has always functioned as the record of the mores and experience of his society." His plays, novels, and poetry all reflect that philosophy, serving as a record of twentieth-century Africa's political turmoil and its struggle to reconcile tradition with modernization. As a young child, Soyinka was comfortable with the conflicting cultures in his world, but as he grew older, he became increasingly aware of the pull between African tradition and Western modernization. Eldred Jones stated in his book *Wole Soyinka* that the author's work touches on universal themes as well as addressing specifically African concerns: "The essential ideas which emerge from a reading of Soyinka's work are not specially African ideas, although his characters and their mannerisms are African. His concern is with man on earth. Man is dressed for the nonce in African dress and lives in the sun and tropical forest, but he represents the whole race."

> EACH POEM OR FRAGMENT OF JOURNAL HE MANAGED TO SMUGGLE TO THE OUTSIDE WORLD BECAME A LITERARY EVENT AND A REASSURANCE TO HIS SUPPORTERS THAT HE STILL LIVED, DESPITE RUMORS TO THE CONTRARY."

Ake, Soyinka's village, was mainly populated with people from the Yoruba tribe and was presided over by the *ogboni*, or tribal elders. Soyinka's grandfather introduced him to the pantheon of Yoruba gods and to other tribal folklore. His parents were key representatives of colonial influences, however: his mother was a devout Christian convert and his father acted as headmaster for the village school established by the British. When Soyinka's father began urging Wole to leave Ake to attend the government school in Ibadan, the boy was spirited away by his grandfather, who administered a scarification rite of manhood. Soyinka was also consecrated to the god Ogun, ruler of metal, roads, and both the creative and destructive essence. Ogun is a recurring figure in Soyinka's work and has been named by the author as his muse.

Ake: The Years of Childhood, Soyinka's account of his first ten years, stands as "a classic of childhood memoirs wherever and whenever produced," stated *New York Times Book Review* contributor James Olney. Numerous critics have singled out Soyinka's ability to recapture the changing perspective of a child as the book's outstanding feature; it begins in a light tone but grows increasingly serious as the boy matures and becomes aware of the problems faced by the adults around him. The book concludes with an account of a tax revolt organized by Soyinka's mother and the beginnings of Nigerian independence. "Most of 'Ake' charms; that was Mr. Soyinka's intention," wrote John Leonard of the *New York Times*. "The last fifty pages, however, inspire and confound; they are transcendent." Olney was of a similar opinion, writing that "the lyricism, grace, humor and charm of 'Ake' ... are in the service of a profoundly serious viewpoint .... Mr. Soyinka, however, does this dramatically, not discursively. Through recollection, restoration and re-creation, he conveys a personal vision that was formed by the childhood world that he now returns to evoke and exalt in his autobiography. This is the ideal circle of autobiography at its best. It is what makes 'Ake' in addition to its other great virtues, the best introduction available to the work of one of the liveliest, most exciting writers in the world today."

Soyinka published some poems and short stories in *Black Orpheus*, a highly regarded Nigerian literary magazine, before leaving Africa to attend the University of Leeds in England. There his first play was produced. *The Invention* is a comic satire based on a sudden loss of pigment by South Africa's black population. Unable to distinguish blacks from whites and thus enforce its apartheid policies, the government is thrown into chaos. "The play is Soyinka's sole direct treatment of the political situation in Africa," noted Thomas Hayes in the *Dictionary of Literary Biography Yearbook: 1986*.

Soyinka returned to Nigeria in 1960 shortly after the country's independence from colonial rule had been declared. He began to research Yoruba folklore and drama in depth and incorporated elements of both into his play *A Dance of the Forests*, which was commissioned as part of Nigeria's independence celebrations. In his play, Soyinka warned the newly independent Nigerians that the end of colonial rule did not mean an end to their country's problems. It shows a bickering group of mortals who summon up the *egungun* (spirits of the dead, revered by the Yoruba people) for a festival. They have presumed the *egungun* to be noble and wise, but they discover that their ancestors are as petty and spiteful as any living people. "The whole concept ridicules the African viewpoint that glorifies the past at the expense of the present," suggested John F. Povey in *Tri-Quarterly*. "The sentimentalized glamour of the past is exposed so that the same absurdities may not be reenacted in the future. This constitutes a bold assertion to an audience awaiting an easy appeal to racial heroics." Povey also praised Soyinka's skill in using dancing, drumming, and singing to reinforce his theme: "The dramatic power of the surging forest dance [in the play] carries its own visual conviction. It is this that shows Soyinka to be a man of the theatre, not simply a writer."

After warning against living in nostalgia for Africa's past in *A Dance of the Forests*, Soyinka lampooned the indiscriminate embrace of

Western modernization in *The Lion and the Jewel*. A *Times Literary Supplement* reviewer called this play a "richly ribald comedy," which combines poetry and prose "with a marvellous lightness in the treatment of both." The plot revolves around Sidi, the village beauty, and the rivalry between her two suitors. Baroka is the village chief, an old man with many wives; Lakunle is the enthusiastically Westernized schoolteacher who dreams of molding Sidi into a "civilized" woman.

In *Introduction to Nigerian Literature*, Eldred Jones commented that *The Lion and the Jewel* represents "a clash between the genuine and the false; between the well-done and the half-baked. Lakunle the school teacher would have been a poor symbol of any desirable kind of progress ... . He is a man of totally confused values. [Baroka's worth lies in] the traditional values of which he is so confident and in which he so completely outmaneouvres Lakunle who really has no values at all." Bruce King, editor of *Introduction to Nigerian Literature*, named *The Lion and the Jewel* "the best literary work to come out of Africa."

Soyinka was well established as Nigeria's premier playwright when, in 1965, he published his first novel, *The Interpreters*. The novel allowed him to expand on themes already expressed in his stage dramas and to present a sweeping view of Nigerian life in the years immediately following independence. Essentially plotless, *The Interpreters* is loosely structured around informal discussions among five young Nigerian intellectuals. Each one has been educated in a foreign country and returned, hoping to shape Nigeria's destiny. They are hampered by their own confused values, however, as well as the corruption they encounter everywhere. Some reviewers likened Soyinka's writing style in *The Interpreters* to that of James Joyce and William Faulkner. Others took exception to the formless quality of the novel, but Eustace Palmer asserted in *The Growth of the African Novel:* "If there are reservations about the novel's structure, there can be none about the thoroughness of the satire at society's expense. Soyinka's wide-ranging wit takes in all sections of a corrupt society .... . He is careful to expose [the interpreters'] selfishness, egoism, cynicism and aimlessness. Indeed the conduct of the intellectuals both in and out of the university is a major preoccupation of Soyinka's in this novel. The aimlessness and superficiality of the lives of most of the interpreters is patent."

Neil McEwan pointed out in *Africa and the Novel* that for all its seriousness, *The Interpreters* is also "among the liveliest of recent novels in English. It is bright satire full of good sense and good humour which are African and contemporary: the highest spirits of its author's early work. ... Behind the jokes of his novel is a theme that he has developed angrily elsewhere: that whatever progress may mean for Africa it is not a lesson to be learned from outside, however much of 'modernity' Africans may share with others." McEwan further observed that although *The Interpreters* does not have a rigidly structured plot, "there is unity in the warmth and sharpness of its comic vision. There are moments which sadden or anger; but they do not diminish the fun." Palmer noted that *The Interpreters* notably influenced the African fiction that followed it, shifting the focus "from historical, cultural and sociological analysis to penetrating social comment and social satire."

The year *The Interpreters* was published, 1965, also marked Soyinka's first arrest by the Nigerian police. He was accused of using a gun to force a radio announcer to broadcast incorrect election results. No evidence was ever produced, however, and the PEN writers' organization launched a protest campaign, headed by William Styron and Norman Mailer. Soyinka was released after three months. He was next arrested two years later, during Nigeria's civil war. Soyinka was completely opposed to the conflict and especially to the Nigerian government's brutal policies toward the Ibo people who were attempting to form their own country, Biafra. He traveled to Biafra to establish a peace commission composed of leading intellectuals from both sides; when he returned, the Nigerian police accused him of helping the Biafrans to buy jet fighters. Once again he was imprisoned, this time held for more than two years although never formally charged with any crime. Most of that time, he was kept in solitary confinement. When all of his fellow prisoners were vaccinated against meningitis, Soyinka was passed by; when he developed serious vision problems, they were ignored by his jailers. He was denied reading and writing materials, but he manufactured his own ink and began to keep a prison diary, written on toilet paper, cigarette packages and in between the lines of the few books he secretly obtained. Each poem or fragment of journal he managed to smuggle to the outside world became a literary event and a reassurance to his supporters that he still lived, despite rumors to the contrary. He was released in 1969 and left Nigeria soon after, not returning until a change of power took place in 1975.

Published as *The Man Died: Prison Notes of Wole Soyinka*, the author's diary constitutes "the most important work ever written about the Biafran war," believed Charles R. Larson, contributor to *Nation*. "'The Man Died' is not so much the story of Wole Soyinka's own temporary death during the Nigerian Civil War but a personified account of Nigeria's fall from sanity documented by one of the country's leading intellectuals." Gerald Weales's *New York Times Book Review* article suggested that the political content of *The Man Died* is less fascinating than "the notes that deal with prison life, the observation of everything from a warder's catarrh to the predatory life of insects after a rain. Of course, these are not simply reportorial. They are vehicles to carry the author's shifting states of mind, to convey the real subject matter of the book; the author's attempt to survive as a man, and as a mind. The notes are both a means to that survival and a record to it." Larson underlined the book's political impact, however, noting that ironically, "while other Nigerian writers were emotionally castrated by the war, Soyinka, who was placed in solitary confinement so that he wouldn't embarrass the government, was writing work after work, books that will no doubt embarrass the Nigerian Government more than anything the Ibo writers may ever publish." A *Times Literary Supplement* reviewer expressed similar sentiment, characterizing *The Man Died* as "a damning indictment of what Mr. Soyinka sees as the iniquities of wartime Nigeria and the criminal tyranny of its administration in peacetime." Many literary commentators felt that Soyinka's work changed profoundly after his prison term, darkening in tone and focusing on the war and its aftermath.

In the *Dictionary of Literary Biography Yearbook: 1986*, Hayes quoted Soyinka on his concerns after the war: "I have one abiding religion—human liberty . . . . conditioned to the truth that life is meaningless, insulting, without this fullest liberty, and in spite of the despairing knowledge that words alone seem unable to guarantee its possession, my writing grows more and more preoccupied with the theme of the oppressive boot, the irrelevance of the color of the foot that wears it and the struggle for

individuality." In spite of its satire, most critics found *The Interpreters* to be ultimately an optimistic book. In contrast, Soyinka's second novel *Season of Anomy*, expresses almost no hope for Africa's future, wrote John Mellors in *London Magazine*, commenting that the author seemed to write the book "in a blazing fury, angry beyond complete control of words at the abuses of power and the outbreaks of both considered and spontaneous violence . . . . The plot charges along, dragging the reader (not because he doesn't want to go, but because he finds it hard to keep up) through forest, mortuary and prison camp in nightmare visions of tyranny, torture, slaughter and putrefaction . . . . [M]urder and mutilation, while sickeningly explicit, are justified by . . . the author's anger and compassion and insistence that bad will not become better by our refusal to examine it."

Like *Season of Anomy*, Soyinka's postwar plays are considered more brooding than his earlier work. *Madmen and Specialists* was described as "grim" by Martin Banham and Clive Wake in *African Theatre Today*. In the play, a doctor returns from the war trained as a specialist in torture and uses his new skills on his father. The play's major themes are "the loss of faith and rituals" and "the break-up of the family unit which traditionally in Africa has been the foundation of society," according to Charles Larson in the *New York Times Book Review*. Names and events in the play are fictionalized to avoid censorship, but Soyinka has clearly "leveled a wholesale criticism of life in Nigeria since the Civil War: a police state in which only madmen and spies can survive, in which the losers are mad and the winners are paranoid about the possibility of another rebellion. The prewar corruption and crime have returned, supported by the more sophisticated acts of terrorism and espionage introduced during the war." Larson believed that, in large part, the play was a product of the time Soyinka spent in prison as a political prisoner. "It is, not surprisingly, the most brutal piece of social criticism he has published," Larson commented.

In a similar tone, *A Play of Giants* presents four African leaders—thinly disguised versions of Jean Bedel Bokassa, Sese Seko Mobutu, Macias Ngeuma, and Idi Amin—meeting at the United Nations building, where "their conversation reflects the corruption and cruelty of their regimes and the casual, brutal flavor of their rule," commented Hayes, in whose opinion the play demonstrates that, "as Soyinka has matured he has hardened his criticism of all that restricts the individual's ability to choose, think, and act free from external oppression ... . [It is] his harshest attack against modern Africa, a blunt, venomous assault on ... African leaders and the powers who support them."

In *Isara: A Voyage around "Essay,"* Soyinka provides a portrait of his father, Akinyode Soditan, as well as "vivid sketches of characters and culturally intriguing events that cover a period of fifteen years," Charles Johnson related in the *Washington Post*. The narrative follows S.A., or "Essay," and his classmates through his years at St. Simeon's Teacher Training Seminary in Ilesa. Aided by documents left to him in a tin box, Soyinka dramatizes the changes that profoundly affected his father's life. The Great Depression that brought the Western world to its knees during the early 1930s was a time of economic opportunity for Africans. The quest for financial gain transformed African culture, as did Mussolini's invasion of Ethiopia and the onset of World War II. More threatening was the violent civil war for the throne following the death of their king. An aged peacemaker named Agunrin resolved the conflict by an appeal to the people's common past. "As each side presents its case, Agunrin, half listening, sinks into memories that unfold his people's collective history, and finally he speaks, finding his voice in a scene so masterfully rendered it alone is worth the price of the book," Johnson claimed. The book is neither a strict biography nor a straight historical account. However, "in his effort to expose Western readers to a unique, African perspective on the war years, Soyinka succeeds brilliantly," Johnson commented. *New York Times* reviewer Michiko Kakutani wrote that, in addition, "Essay emerges as a high-minded teacher, a mentor and companion, blessed with dignity and strong ideals, a father who inspired his son to achievement."

In his 1996 work, *The Open Sore of a Continent: A Personal Narrative of the Nigerian Crisis*, Soyinka takes an expansive and unrestrained look at Nigeria's dictatorship. A collection of essays originally delivered as lectures at Harvard, *The Open Sore* questions the corrupt government, the ideas of nationalism, and international intervention. The book begins with the execution of Ken Saro-Wiwa. For Soyinka, his

death, along with the annulment of the elections in 1993, signaled the disintegration of the state. According to Robert D. Kaplan in the *New York Times Book Review*, Soyinka "uses these harsh facts to dissect, then reinvent not just Nigeria but the concept of nationhood itself."

In 1998 Soyinka ended a self-imposed exile from Nigeria that began in 1993 when a democratically elected government was to have assumed power. Instead, General Ibrahim Babangida, who had ruled the nation for eight years, prohibited the publication of the voting results and installed his deputy, General Sani Abacha, as head of the Nigerian state. Soyinka, along with other pro-democracy activists, was charged with treason for his criticism of the military regime. Faced with a death sentence, Soyinka went into exile in 1994, during which time he traveled and lectured in Europe and the United States. Following the death of Abacha, who held control for five years, the new government, led by General Abdulsalem Abubakar, released numerous political prisoners and promised to hold civilian elections. Soyinka's return to his homeland renewed hope for a democratic Nigerian state. When confronted following a series of lectures at Emory University in early 2004 with questions about why he continues to struggle against almost overwhelming political odds, Soyinka was quoted by Richard Halicks in the *Atlanta Journal-Constitution* as commenting: "My conviction simply is that power must always be defeated, that the struggle must always continue to defeat power. I don't go looking for fights. People don't believe this, I'm really a very lazy person. I enjoy my peace and quiet. There's nothing I love better than just to sit quietly somewhere, you know, have a glass of wine, read a book, listen to music, that really is my ideal existence." However, just months after that comment, Soyinka was tear gassed and again arrested, albeit briefly, while protesting the government of President Olusegun Obasanjo for what he and other human rights activists called, according to Andrew Meldrum of the *Guardian*, "a civilian dictatorship." Following his release, the almost-seventy-year-old Soyinka vowed to launch new antigovernment protests, which simply confirmed a statement he made several months before the arrest, quoted by Halicks, that seems to sum up his undaunted commitment to human liberty: "In prison I had lots of time to ponder, 'Why do I do things that get me into trouble?' I didn't find an answer. I also, to my surprise, didn't incur any internal suggestion that, when I get out of this one, I will stop. It has never occurred to me to stop."

Soyinka's work is frequently described as demanding but rewarding reading. Although his plays are widely praised, they are seldom performed, especially outside Africa. The dancing and choric speech often found in them are unfamiliar and difficult for non-African actors to master, a problem Holly Hill noted in her London *Times* review of the Lincoln Center Theatre production of *Death and the King's Horseman*. She awarded high praise to the play, however, saying it "has the stateliness and mystery of Greek tragedy." When the Swedish Academy awarded Soyinka the Nobel Prize in Literature in 1986, its members singled out *Death and the King's Horseman* and *A Dance of the Forests* as "evidence that Soyinka is 'one of the finest poetical playwrights that have written in English,'" reported Stanley Meisler of the *Los Angeles Times*.

In 2005 Soyinka published *Climate of Fear: The Quest for Dignity in a Dehumanized World*, a series of lectures that were initially presented at London's Royal Institution. The lectures discuss all of the current political and environmental forces that create a 'climate of fear' and posit that the true function of fear is to rob of dignity, and that the function of robbing of dignity is to dehumanize. Although Derek Hook, writing in *Theoria*, called the lectures "important critical contributions," he also noted that they are "frequently offset by an unfortunate mode of psychologism." Hook was perhaps more laudatory when he stated "insofar as Soyinka's discussion retains a balance . . . it holds something of promise." A *Kirkus Reviews* critic was more positive, commenting that the "gracefully stated" volume "wanders the boundary between memoir and political essay." Interestingly, Soyinka's *You Must Set Forth at Dawn: A Memoir*, was released shortly after the publication of *Climate of Fear*.

Soyinka has continued to publish valuable work throughout his forty-year career. Hayes, in a summary of Soyinka's literary importance, once stated: "His drama and fiction have challenged the West to broaden its aesthetic and accept African standards of art and literature. His personal and political life have challenged Africa to embrace the truly democratic values of the African tribe and reject the tyranny of power practiced on the continent by its colonizers and by many of its modern rulers."

> THE DRAMATIC EXCHANGE RELIES ON WIT, HUMOUR, IRONY, HYPERBOLE, COMPOUND WORDS, SCIENTIFIC VOCABULARY, CLOSELY-KNIT EXPRESSION, SUGGESTIVENESS, AND DIALOGUE INTERSPERSED WITH NARRATION AND COMMENTS."

Source: Thomson Gale, "Wole Soyinka," in *Contemporary Authors Online*, Thomson Gale, 2006.

Tanure Ojaide

In the following essay, Ojaide explores the early poems of Soyinka, of which "Telephone Conversation" is one. The critic notes that the voice in these early poems is lighter, more playful, and less bitter than that of Soyinka's later poems, plays, and novels.

"The Immigrant," "And the Other Immigrant," "My Next Door Neighbour," and "Telephone Conversation" are among Soyinka's early poems. Though the first three appeared in *Black Orpheus* in 1959 and the fourth in *Modern Poetry from Africa* in 1963, these poems, from evidence of subject-matter, style, and social orientation in an alien environment, seem to have been written between 1954 and 1959. This was the period Soyinka studied at the University of Leeds and worked in England. I use *early* to refer to these poems written in England as distinct from the very early college poems written in Nigeria, which I have chosen not to include in this study.

These early poems are different from the later poems, *Idanre and Other Poems* and *A Shuttle in the Crypt*, written in Nigeria, and obviously based on the poet's experience of his own culture and the nation's turbulent sociopolitical happenings. In the early poems, the poet is interested in individuals in society, and there is a psychological and social bias. He presents the characters and their mental attitudes for ridicule, sympathy, and amusement. The voice is critical, but playful—light, ironic, refined, and cool. The language is simple, and the major poetic devices are metaphor, sarcasm, irony, hyperbole, and repetition. These poems in their humorous portrayal of characters and the witty use of language apparently belong to the same early period in which Soyinka wrote such light satirical plays as *The Trials of Brother Jero* and *Before the Blackout.*

In these early poems the voice of the poet is distinct. There is no bitterness in the voice, no sense of urgency in the light criticism, no vision of inhumanity as in the later poems; what is present, rather, is a characterization of individuals who behave strangely and foolishly in society. The poet is an observer, not the victim he is later to become. Unlike the satirical voice of the prison poems, which is maudlin and pathetic, the voice of the early poems is playful if satirical, exuberant, and not infrequently humorous as the poet sympathizes with some of those he satirizes—such as the immigrants—and is amused by others, for example, his next-door neighbour.

The speaker of "The Immigrant" describes a black man in London, who is refused a dance by a white girl and, feeling that she has snubbed him only because he is black, goes into the street to seek a white prostitute on whom he plans to carry out his revenge. The speaker distances himself from the subject of the poem, describing the immigrant in sarcastic terms. The immigrant knows

> That this equation must be sought
> Not in any woman's arms
> But in the cream-laid
> De-Odo-ro-noed limbs
> Of the native girl herself.

The "equation," reinforced by "paired" and "reciprocal," suggests the immigrant's desire for equal relationship, though he possesses neither integrity nor confidence in himself. The poet satirizes him with comments such as "Though he will deny it" and "scans the gaudy bulbs / (For the fiftieth time)." Besides, "his swagger belies" his desperation. The immigrant only draws from the girl he asks for a dance a "bored appraisal," and she refuses him the dance without the "usual palliative / False-bottom smile."

The speaker finds the black immigrant and the white girl equally matched. She is fashionably dressed but her body is "foolish"; in other words, she is ugly and foolish. As for the immigrant, he wears a "flashy incredible tie." They are so well-matched that:

> Her face exchanges
> Vulgarity
> For his uncouthness.
> And the plumb of their twin minds
> Reads Nil.

The parallel syntactical and verbal expressions, "vulgarity" and "uncouthness," describe their identical appearance; they are twins. The girl's "barbed" dismissal hurts the black man like a wound which has grown "septic." It is the immigrant who interprets the girl's eyes as saying: "You? Not for any price!" The man's psychological hurt is represented physically to show its painful effect on him. He has the urge to knife her so that she will feel the same wound on a physical dimension; but he has become nervous and disarmed:

> The blade remained
> In the sweat-filled pocket.

The immigrant is so obsessed with what he regards as an insult that he feels the other people are aware of his disgrace, and they seem to "jeer at his defeat." Because the girl is white and the couples he sees are white, he projects his humiliation as coming from them:

> He knew now the fatality
> Of his black, flattened nose.

Wanting revenge in one form or another, the immigrant checks his pocket for money and goes into the street for a white prostitute to have

> Quick revenge
> Lusts for the act
> Of degradation of her sex and race.

The repeated "seeks" emphasizes his desperation and continued nervousness, for he "makes his choice at random / Haggles somewhat at the price" and goes with her to pass the night "In reciprocal humiliation." The immigrant is further humiliated because he is unable to find a native girl of mutual equality, but pays to be paired. The street girl is humiliated because she accepts him for the money he will pay her and not for love. So there is similarity between the immigrant and this prostitute in their shared humiliation. He is as much like the girl who rejects him as the one who accepts him.

The speaker's voice is casual, but satiric. The poet uses simple and effective words; for instance, the immigrant has a "little brain," which explains his distorted reasoning. The speaker interjects sarcastic and belittling comments to portray the immigrant in a negative light. The poet's techniques involve subtle use of words, compound words, metaphor, hyperbole, British idiom ("He ran a gauntlet . . ."), repetition, and subtle sound patterns. The poem is a social and psychological exegesis. The poet sees the black immigrant as tending to see personal humiliation as racially motivated, and in an attempt to respond to discrimination, driving himself into a deeper psychological mess. The immigrant is not right in judging the girl who refused him a dance as a white person rather than as an individual. The poet's viewpoint seems to be that people should be judged individually and not on race lines.

Because the poet is more interested in describing a scene in "The Immigrant," he is reportorial and less intense than in "And the Other Immigrant," in which he wears a mask and speaks in the first person. The speaker of "And the Other Immigrant" personally reveals his self-conceit. The language is mainly sarcastic and ironic and undercuts his claims to dignity. The poet is amused by this other immigrant whom he satirizes.

The other immigrant finds his dignity sewn "Into the lining of a three-piece suit." His Van Heusen collar is crisp, stiff, and "Out-Europes Europe" in its whiteness. "Stiff" is negative in spite of the speaker's feeling that he is well-dressed. The poet is being sarcastic and hyperbolic in making the immigrant admit that the whiteness of his dress "Out-Europes Europe." The poet makes him repeat "three piece suit" and "dignity" to draw attention to his narcissistic personality. Because he feels he is well-dressed, he considers many workers "riff-raff," who will "wilt at the touch of ice;" that is, his so-called social inferiors fear him, and his cold contempt hurts them. This immigrant is so arrogant that he thinks he can "do without them," a claim to self-sufficiency which is false because he buys things on hire-purchase.

He keeps to his "kind," presumably his fellow members of the black elite:

> For I condemn
> All whiteness in a face.

He is a racist. He identifies himself with African nationalism, and authoritatively asserts:

> But only fools can doubt
> The Solve-All
> Philosopher's stone attributes
> Of Up-Nasser-Freedom-for-Africa.

Ironically, it is only fools who believe there is a "Solve-All / Philosopher's stone" in any movement. The philosopher's stone, the key to turning base metals to gold and a panacea that will ensure longevity (and even physical immortality), was satirized by Chaucer and Ben Jonson as an illusion. Soyinka also uses it satirically in

this context to show that the immigrant is deceiving himself. It is ironic that the immigrant who disdains white faces employs western philosophical concepts to express himself The poet is satirical of nationalist claims that all African problems will be solved at independence.

The date of this poem's publication, 1959, is significant. By 1959 a few African countries had become independent. The following year Nigeria and some dozen other countries became independent. It was a time of nationalism in Africa. Nasser, who seized power from King Farouk, was the symbol of African nationalism after the Suez Crisis. The immigrant is trying to boost his ego by associating himself with a heroic African; he is a pseudo-nationalist. The poet is sceptical of the immigrant's claim to nationalism.

The immigrant's slogan is "Négritude," a movement Soyinka has consistently castigated as unnecessary. Soyinka must be throwing jibes at Negritude intellectuals, who proclaim "blackness" and African authenticity but wear three-piece suits and embrace many western social and cultural ways. If the immigrant is a genuine nationalist and negritudinist, he ought not to gloat over his suit but dress in a traditional African way. His claims to nationalism and black cultural pride would be more in tune with a *sokoto* or an *agbada*, traditional African outfit, than a three-piece suit. There is a tension in him between public assertion of blackness and a private admiration of himself as acceptable to the upper class in a white society. This conflict reinforces his hypocrisy and debunks his claims to negritude. He sees himself as living well in the foreign society, but buys his three-piece suit, the source of his dignity, on hire-purchase. He lives a thrifty life to survive. His expectation of material advantages when he goes to his home country reveals his selfishness and the hollowness of his nationalism. Ironically, at home he will be the "one-eyed man" who is "king."

The technique of the poet is to make this immigrant ludicrous in dress, behaviour, and speech so that he can be perceived as the opposite of a dignified personality. To the poet, it is not what you claim you are that matters, but the impression you leave with society from your views, behaviour, and action. The poet puts into his mouth words which in their dissonance refute his claims. All along, the poet deflates him as a black prig in an English society who is arrogant and vain, hypocritical, snobbish, and undignified. Like the earlier immigrant discussed, he has a psychological problem. While this immigrant feels he is hurting others, the earlier one feels hurt by a white girl. While this immigrant feels superior; the first one feels treated like an inferior. One rejects, the other is rejected. Soyinka uses similar techniques of irony and sarcasm, exaggeration, indirection, and repetition to portray them in their antithetical but similar psychological problems. . . .

The race problem which has been treated with levity in the immigrant poems is treated from the poet's personal experience in "Telephone Conversation."

"Telephone Conversation" involves an exchange between the black speaker and a white landlady. This poem more than any other is enriched by Soyinka's experience of drama. It appears that the speaker is so fluent in the landlady's language that she is unable to make out that he is black and a foreigner. But he, knowing the society for its racial prejudice, deems it necessary to declare his racial identity rather than be rejected later when she discovers that he is black. When he tells her that he is African, she seems stunned and there is "Silenced transmission of / Pressurized good-breeding." When she speaks, her voice is

> Lipstick coated, long gold-rolled
> Cigarette-holder tipped.

These details are evidence of her sophistication, affectation, and artificiality. The poet establishes the lady's social status so as to make her mental attitudes ironic.

The lady asks the speaker, "HOW DARK?" which he is at first too confused to answer: "Surrender pushed dumbfoundment to simplification." He suspects that she is trying to humiliate him because "Her accent was clinical, crushing in its light / Impersonality." The alliterative verse musically represents the sense of crushing. The man prepares himself for a verbal confrontation and replies, "West African sepia." The landlady seems confused over this shade of darkness and becomes silent, an interval described as "Silence for spectroscopic flight of fancy"; and admits "DON'T KNOW WHAT THAT IS." He explains, "Like brunette," which the lady conceives as dark, but for the speaker, "Not altogether." The poem ends as the speaker elaborates on the diverse colours that make up his body, a display which apparently exasperates the lady and makes her drop the receiver. She is made to feel narrow-minded and simplistic, and she loses the verbal battle in her own language to an outsider.

The satiric voice is established through many devices. The poet uses words with negative connotations to portray the lady. She "swore," and her accent is "light," insensitive. There is a pun on "light" because she has preference for "light" people, and her voice is light. There is an abundance of descriptive epithets ranging from "indifferent," "silenced," through "pressurized," "lipstick coated," "long goldrolled / Cigarette-holder tipped" to "rancid," "clinical," "light," and "peroxide." The speaker's own bottom is "raven black." The dramatic exchange relies on wit, humour, irony, hyperbole, compound words, scientific vocabulary, closely-knit expression, suggestiveness, and dialogue interspersed with narration and comments. The speaker is highly versatile in his expression. The poet successfully debunks colour discrimination in society and, indirectly through the speaker's performance in the exchanges, extols the individuality of human beings in spite of colour differences.

The voice and viewpoint are influenced by the environment, poetic aims, and techniques of the poet. The voice in Soyinka's early poems is satirical, but light and playful, quite distinct from the voice in the later poems informed by harsh personal experiences and a national crisis.

Source: Tanure Ojaide, "Early Poems," in *The Poetry of Wole Soyinka*, Malthouse Press, 1994, pp. 15–22.

SOURCES

Amuta, Chidi, "The Ideological Content of Soyinka's War Writings," in *African Studies Review*, Vol. 29, No. 3, September 1986, pp. 43–54.

Boyle, Elizabeth Heger, "Gesture without Motion? Poetry and Politics in Africa," in *Human Rights Review*, Vol. 2, No. 1, October-December 2000, pp. 134–39.

George, Olakunie, *Relocating Agency: Modernity and African Letters*, State University of New York Press, 2003.

Jacobs, Alan, "Wole Soyinka's Outrage: The Divided Soul of Nigeria's Nobel Laureate," in *Books & Culture*, Vol. 7, No. 6, November-December 2001, pp. 28–31.

Jeyifo, Biodun, *Wole Soyinka: Politics, Poetics, Postcolonialism*, Cambridge University Press, 2004.

Macebuh, Stanley, "Poetics and the Mythic Imagination," in *Transition*, Vol. 50, October 1975–March 1976, pp. 79–84.

Nwoga, D. I., "Poetry as Revelation: Wole Soyinka," in *Critical Perspectives on Wole Soyinka*, edited by James Gibbs, Three Continents Press,1980, p. 173.

Ojaide, Tanure, *The Poetry of Wole Soyinka*, Malthouse Press, 1994, pp.15, 21.

Soyinka, Wole, "Telephone Conversation," in *Perrine's Literature: Structure, Sound, and Sense*, edited by Thomas R. Arp, Greg Johnson, and Laurence Perrine, Thomson, 2006, pp. 1006–07.

Wright, Derek, *Wole Soyinka: Life, Work, and Criticism*, York Press, 1996.

FURTHER READING

Egar, Emmanuel, *The Poetics of Rage: Wole Soyinka, Jean Toomer, and Claude McKay*, University Press of America, 2005.

An exploration of the role of the poet in times of political unrest and social uncertainty, Egar's book takes three poets from two countries as representatives of the power of poetry to resist oppressive politics.

Fraser, Robert, *West African Poetry: A Critical History*, Cambridge University Press, 1986.

While many studies of African poetry tend to concentrate either on its political content or on its relationship to various European schools, Fraser's book explores West African poetry as a unique literary form with roots set deep in oral poetry in the vernacular.

Jeyifo, Biodun, *Wole Soyinka: Politics, Poetics, and Post-colonialism*, Cambridge University Press, 2004.

Jeyifo explores Soyinka's works with regard to the author's sensibilities to the representational ambiguity and linguistic exuberance found in Yoruba culture. More significantly, the analyses of this study emphasize the context of Soyinka's sustained engagement with the violence of collective experience in post-independence, postcolonial Africa and the developing world.

Ojaide, Tanure, "Two Worlds: Influences on the Poetry of Wole Soyinka," in *Black American Literature Forum*, Vol. 22, No.4, Winter 1988, pp.767–76.

A detailed discussion of the influences that have shaped Soyinka's poetry, with particular attention to the marriage of tribal and modern qualities in the poems.

Waterfalls in a Bank

A. K. RAMANUJAN

1986

"Waterfalls in a Bank" is a poem by A. K. Ramanujan, a twentieth-century Indian poet who lived in the United States for most of his adult life. The poem was first published in Ramanujan's collection of poems *Second Sight* (1986), which is currently out of print. It is also available in *The Oxford India Ramanujan* and *The Collected Poems of A. K. Ramanujan*. The poem is set in a bank in Chicago, where the poet's attention is caught by a man-made waterfall. As he gazes at the waterfall, it stimulates his memory, and much of the poem consists of a stream of varied imagery, including some scenes from his past in India. "Waterfalls in a Bank" is typical of Ramanujan's work in the sense that as an Indian immigrant living in Chicago, Illinois, he lived in two cultural worlds, East and West, which for him also represented the past and the present, respectively. His poetry considers the tensions involved in this situation, and as such, his work is part of the contribution made to American literature over the last twenty years or so by immigrants from South Asia who have endeavored in their writing to come to terms with their experience in the United States.

AUTHOR BIOGRAPHY

Indian poet, translator and philologist, A(ttipat) K(rishnaswami) Ramanujan was born March 16, 1929, in Mysore, India, the son of Attipat Asuri

(a professor of mathematics) and Seshamal Krishnaswami. Ramanujan's mother instilled in him at an early age a love of literature and mythology. Ramanujan started writing poetry in his native language, Kannada, when he was fifteen or sixteen. He attained a B.A. degree, with honors, from Mysore University in 1949, and the following year was awarded an M.A. in English from the same university.

During the 1950s, Ramanujan was a lecturer at various colleges in India, and he also earned graduate diplomas in Dravidian linguistics from Deccan College, Poona, in 1958 and 1959. He then received a Fulbright travel fellowship and a Smith-Mundt fellowship that enabled him to come to the United States and study at Indiana University in Bloomington for his Ph.D. in linguistics, which he was awarded in 1963. In the early 1960s, Ramanujan moved to Chicago, Illinois, where he lived for the remainder of his life. From 1962 to 1965, he was assistant professor of linguistics (Tamil and Dravidian languages) at the University of Chicago, then associate professor from 1966 to 1968, and finally professor of linguistics and Dravidian studies, from 1968 until his death in 1993. He was also professor on the committee on social thought, 1972–1993, and the chair of the department of South Asian languages and civilizations from 1980 to 1985. During the 1960s and 1970s, he was a visiting professor at other universities, including the University of California at Berkeley, the University of Wisconsin, Madison, and Carleton College in Minnesota.

In addition to his academic work, which ranged across four Indian languages, Tamil, Kannada, Telugu and Sanskrit, Ramanujan published several volumes of poetry in English, including translations and original work. *Fifteen Poems from a Classical Tamil Anthology* (1965) was a translation from classical Tamil literature. This was followed a year later by his first collection of original poetry, *The Striders* (Oxford University Press, Delhi, 1966), in which he recalls the India of his childhood. *Speaking of Siva* (1973), Ramanujan's translation of ancient Indian devotional poems, received a National Book Award nomination in 1974. His second volume of original poetry, *Relations*, was published in 1971; *Second Sight* followed in 1986. This volume included the poem, "Waterfalls in a Bank." In August of 1983, Ramanujan was awarded a MacArthur Fellowship Grant.

Ramanujan married Molly Daniels, a Syrian Christian from India, in 1962. Daniels was a journalist and novelist. They had a daughter and a son; they also married and divorced twice. The second divorce took place a few years before Ramanujan's death of a heart attack on July 13, 1993, in Chicago at the age of sixty-four.

After his death, another collection of Ramanujan's poetry, *The Black Hen*, was published with *The Collected Poems of A. K. Ramanujan* (1995). The volume won the Sahitya Akademi Award for Best Poems in English; a further volume, *Uncollected Poems and Prose*, was published in 2001.

POEM SUMMARY

Stanzas 1–5

"Waterfalls in a Bank" is set in a bank in Hyde Park in Chicago, Illinois. The poet has been in the bank a while before the poem begins, and the first line, "And then one sometimes sees waterfalls," suggests that his glance has just fallen on some kind of decorative waterfall that has been installed in the lobby. As he looks at the waterfall, he starts to see it metaphorically, influenced by his knowledge of Tamil poetry (Tamil is an ancient language in India), as "wavering snakeskins" and "cascades of muslin." Muslin is a fine, thin cotton cloth, also called India muslin. For centuries, muslin was made by hand in India, but during British colonial rule, the muslin industry was deliberately destroyed by the British in order to supplant it with imported British goods. In other words, the poet is here allowing images from the culture of his native India to flood into his mind as he observes the waterfall. This creates an immediate contrast, not only between present and past but also between cultures, East and West.

More images follow as the poet continues to gaze at the waterfall. Perhaps produced by the downward flow of the water, the images that come into his mind now are of "living and dying children" who "tumble towards old age." Then, further, the waterfall creates contradictory impressions in his mind of love ("lovesongs") and war ("Biafra"). Biafra is a region in southeast Nigeria, in Africa, that was the scene of war and famine in the 1960s. In 1967, Biafra declared itself an independent state, and a three-year civil war followed. Up to a million people, including many children, died as a result of famine.

These two words, "lovesongs" and "Biafra," with their opposite connotations, seem to combine to produce the image that immediately follows, which unifies music and war: "orchestras in bombsites." It appears that the poet's mind, stimulated by the sight of the waterfall, is now engaged in a kind of free association of images. The next image is of "hunger's saints in the glass-house alley," which could suggest both the sadhu, the begging saint in Indian tradition, seeking alms from passers-by, perhaps the Biafran children who starved during the civil war, and perhaps also, the homeless people in Chicago, begging in the "glasshouse alley" of Chicago's massive skyscrapers.

After the image of the children reappears, it is followed by a more extensive image, taking up six lines, which will conclude the first section of the poem. The image appears to go back to the poet's native India, perhaps to his own family. It is of an old woman ("grandmother") acting as midwife as her daughter—perhaps the poet's mother—who is in childbirth. The scene appears to be a home rather than a hospital, perhaps in a village rather than a city, where old folk beliefs still linger, as evidenced by the four lemons that are placed there to provide "good omens"; in other words, to produce good luck at a birth.

Stanzas 6–10

The stream of images stimulated by the waterfall now ended, the poet reflects, using images that suggest the financial institution in which he finds himself. Using the language of commerce, he speaks of himself "transact[ing] with the past," and he is aware of the wide gap, both in time and culture, between the present and the past. The past is like "another / country with its own customs, currency, / stock exchange." Continuing the financial metaphor, he states that he is always "at a loss when I count my change." At a loss can mean that he does not understand what is happening; it can also mean that in the transaction between past and present, which includes an interchange between two extremely different cultures, he has come off the loser in the deal. Perhaps change in this instance is a pun, referring to both coin and the cultural changes wrought over time to the poet's country. Perhaps he means that what he possesses in the present is less than he had in the past, or that the attempt to bridge two cultures is in some sense unsatisfactory or confusing.

The poet then returns to more images from the past, including one that had earlier been stimulated by the waterfall ("dying children") and two new ones: "Assam politics" (Assam is a northeastern state of India, south of the eastern Himalayas), and "downtown Nairobi." Since Nairobi is the capital of Nigeria, this reference recalls the mention of Biafra in the previous section.

These images "fall through" the poet as he "rise[s]" among them, and they leave him with "mud on my nose," an earthy image that seems to summon in the poet's mind a flurry of apparently unrelated images of earth, growth, regeneration, and death in plant, animal and human kingdoms:

> a rhododendron rising from a compost
> of rhododendrons, chicken bones,
> silk of girlish hair,
> and the nitrogen of earthworms.

The final image in these lines is a reference to the fact that the secretions of earthworms contain nitrogen, a nutrient essential for plant growth.

Stanzas 11–16

The poet returns once again to the waterfall, this time hearing rather than seeing the water fall. He also hears the "papers rustle"—perhaps some activity going on near him in the bank—and then he is transported once again by the waterfall, this time back to an incident he remembers from his childhood in India. An old, almost paralytic "sadhu" (a wandering ascetic holy man), is hobbling along the pebbled sidestreet near the poet's childhood home. Then with one finger he lifts his loincloth and urinates, aiming the stream of urine at two red flowers on an oleander bush. At that moment, a car turns the corner, and caught in the beam of the headlights, the arc of the urine stream appears, in three successive metaphors, transformed into "yellow diamonds," "instant rainbows" (which for some reason are "scared") and "spurts of crystal." This effect is produced, paradoxically, by the "commonplace cruelty of headlights," which illuminate in a stark but transformative way an act which should be private.

Stanzas 17–20

The final section of the poem moves further afield in its setting. Instead of a waterfall inside a Chicago bank, it considers Chicago itself. Whereas much of the poem up to this point has been looking backwards, to the past in a different culture, this section takes place in the present. There has been a "seven-day snowfall" in Chicago, which has produced chaos, clogging traffic and grounding planes as well as sundry other effects; it "muffles screams, garbage cans, pianos." This is a reference to the blizzard that hit Chicago in January 1979. The storm did not actually last seven days. It started on Friday night, January 12, and lasted until 2 a.m. Sunday January 14. On top of 7–10 inches of snow that remained on the ground following a New Year's Eve blizzard, 20.3 inches of new snow fell. This set a record in Chicago for total snow on the ground. It did indeed cause the chaos the poem describes. Transportation, including buses, trains, and cars, came to a halt for several days. Garbage piled up in the streets.

The poet states that the storm "topples a mayor and elects another / who promises clearance / of debts and snowfalls." This is a reference to the dissatisfaction among Chicago residents about the perceived slowness of Mayor Anthony Bilandic and the city in dealing with the blizzard. This dissatisfaction played a large role in the defeat of the mayor in the mayoral election on February 27, 1979. The victorious candidate, Jane Byrne, who previously had been given little chance of winning, made up much ground by exploiting the perceived ineffectiveness of Bilandic.

The reference to recent events in Chicago is followed by two images suggestive of the "silent / white effects" of falling snow: "tickertape on astronauts" (a reference to the practice in the United States during the 1960s and 1970s of giving tickertape parades for returning astronauts) and "white flower on black thorn."

The last line of the poem, "And my watchers watch, from their nowhere perches," is enigmatic and perhaps can be explained only with reference to other poems by Ramanujan. It suggests that, in spite of all the activity of his mind that he has recorded in the poem, another part of himself (his "watchers")—perhaps a deeper level of his own mind that is not so localized in time and space ("nowhere perches")—simply observes the scene, undisturbed by the musings that have both stimulated and troubled him.

TOPICS FOR FURTHER STUDY

- Write a poem in the style of "Waterfalls in a Bank," beginning with some object you see that stimulates images or memories of the past. At some point in the poem, evaluate whether what you have gained in life is equal to what has been lost to the past.

- Research the history of immigration to the United States from India and other South Asian countries over the last twenty years. Write an essay in which you discuss what the experience of Indian Americans has been. Are they generally a prosperous or an impoverished group? Are they concentrated in specific geographical areas? What problems have they faced in adapting to life in the United States? How do they compare to other immigrant groups?

- Make a class presentation in which you discuss at least three important differences between American culture and Indian culture. You could choose to discuss religion, family, sports, movies, the arts, government, health care, or any other aspect of the two cultures. What kind of cultural misunderstandings might arise when Americans visit India?

- Locate and interview several immigrants in your school or community. Talk to them about why they came to the United States and how they have adjusted to life in America. What have been their challenges? How have they coped with language and other cultural differences? Record the interview, then write an article about the people you interviewed that could be sent to your local newspaper.

THEMES

Contrast of Opposites

"Waterfalls in a Bank" achieves its effects by contrasting several sets of opposites: inner and outer, past and present, West and East. The poem takes place in a quintessential Western setting, inside a bank in Chicago. The setting suggests modernity, commerce, the objective world of business. But the poet, as he observes the waterfall that has been constructed in the bank, is taken back in time, through a stream of mental images, to India, his country of origin. This occurs particularly in sections 1 and 3, with its respective images of the woman in childbirth being assisted by her own mother, and the aged, crippled holy man in a street that the poet remembers from his childhood home. The poet comments cryptically about this interaction between past and present, which also involves a contrast between the Western culture in which he now lives and the Eastern culture in which he grew up, in the words:

> As I transact with the past as with another country with its own customs, currency, stock exchange, always
>
> at a loss when I count my change ...

This suggests a certain regret on the part of the poet at what he has lost in leaving his own country to come and live in the United States, with its completely different ways.

East and West, as well as past and present, are starkly juxtaposed at the end of section 3. The old sadhu, a representative of an ancient, spiritual culture, is starkly illuminated, in his act of urination, in the headlights of an oncoming car, the product of the industrial civilization of the West.

Following this excursion into an Indian past, the poem returns to the firm reality of the present and the outer world of day-to-day life rather than the inner world of memory. January in Chicago, with its snowstorms, snarled traffic, and failing city services, presents another sharp contrast with the "dark sidestreet" of the poet's childhood home in India.

Transformation of the Ordinary

Much of the poem consists of a stream of images stimulated by the poet's contemplation of the waterfall in the bank. The images may at first seem somewhat random, but they do lead to a climactic moment in section 3, in which the ordinary is transformed into the extraordinary. This is hinted at in the first lines of the poem, which suggest the possibility of transformation. The poet sees the waterfalls "as the ancient Tamils saw them, / wavering snakeskins, / cascades of muslin." This suggests not simply poetic metaphor, but a different way of seeing ordinary phenomena. The suggestion that mundane, everyday perception might be transcended is taken up again and made more dramatic and explicit in

the vignette about the sadhu who urinates on the street and whose act is suddenly illuminated in the headlights of the car. The excretion of a waste product from the body, an act common to all humans and almost always performed in private, is here transformed into something precious. The stream of urine is seen as "a trajectory of yellow diamonds, / scared instant rainbows, ejecting spurts / of crystal." Infusing this most basic of bodily functions with imagery of precious stones, crystals and a beautiful natural phenomenon like the rainbow, is indeed an unexpected illumination, ironically produced by "the commonplace cruelty" of the glare of the headlights. It suggests that beauty, if it can be found in the stream of an old man's urine, might be found anywhere in creation.

STYLE

Free Verse

The poem is written in free verse. Unlike traditional verse, free verse does not employ poetic techniques such as regular meter and rhyme, and line lengths may be variable. Free verse also employs a much looser structure than traditional poetry. However, "Waterfalls in a Bank" does follow a clear structure, although the poet invents it for himself rather than following any traditional form. The poem is divided into four unnumbered sections, each consisting of between three and five verses. Each unrhymed verse consists of two and a half lines. After sections 2, 3, and 4, an extra line is added, standing alone. The first two of these extra lines are grammatically linked to the previous verse; the final extra line, "And my watchers watch, from their nowhere perches," is independent, grammatically and thematically, from what has preceded it, and acts as a kind of coda to the poem. (Coda is a term used in music to describe a few measures added to the end of a piece.)

Unifying Images

Although many of the images seem random (as might be expected since they are part of the stream of the poet's memory), there are some unifying elements. The reference to children who "tumble towards old age" foreshadows the images of the "bentover grandmother" and the old sadhu later in the poem; the image of "living and dying children" may suggest the childbirth scene which

COMPARE
&
CONTRAST

- **1980s:** In the late 1980s, postcolonial criticism begins to emerge as a distinct category in literary criticism. Postcolonial critics question long-held assumptions made by liberal humanist critics about the universality of Western literature, arguing that such "universalist" views undervalue the literature of other cultures and regions.

  Today: Postcolonial criticism is a well established and burgeoning field of critical inquiry. Postcolonial critics show the limitations of the Western literary canon partly because of its failure to empathize with other cultures and ethnicities. Postcolonialism examines cultural differences and how they are represented in literary texts; it seeks to reevaluate aspects of other cultures that have been marginalized and devalued by Western writers.

- **1980s:** In 1983, Harold Washington becomes Chicago's first African-American Mayor. A popular mayor, he is known for his efforts to build coalitions between neighborhood groups, community development, the creation of the Ethics Commission and the creating of more minority business contracts.

  Mayor Washington wins reelection in 1987, but dies in office later that year.

  Today: Chicago Mayor Richard M. Daley has been in office since 1989. He is the first Chicago mayor to be elected for five consecutive terms. Under his tenure, Chicago sees a growth in tourism, the modernization of the Chicago Transit Authority, the building of Millennium Park and the development of Chicago's North Side.

- **1980s:** Beginning with Salman Rushdie's *Midnight's Children*, the 1980s witness a rapid increase in Indian literature written in English. Writers such as Anita Desai and Bharati Mukherjee achieve popular success through mainstream publishers.

  Today: Indian authors writing in English continue to attain critical and commercial success, winning national and international literary awards and attracting the attention of the mass media. In 2002, Arundhati Roy publishes a collection of essays, *The Algebra of Infinite Justice* (2002); in 2005, Salman Rushdie publishes the novel, *Shalimar the Clown*, set in a fictional small town in Kashmir.

concludes the first section. The main unifying image in the poem, however, is that of falling water, in its different forms. The waterfall in the bank, the primary image that in a sense produces all the others, is related both to the stream of urine emitted by the sadhu, and the falling snow in Chicago (snow being water in another form).

HISTORICAL CONTEXT

Postcolonial Literature
Ramanujan's work is generally classified as postcolonial literature. The term refers to the literature produced in nations, mostly African and Asian, that were formerly under European colonial rule, in most cases until after World War II. Postcolonial literature also includes work by citizens of formerly colonized countries, such as Ramanujan, who live and work in the West. Since India was under British rule until 1947, the literature of that country since its independence is considered to be postcolonial.

Postcolonial writing considers the interactions between the indigenous culture and the colonizing power. It is a reaction against negative stereotyping of non-European cultures by the colonizing West. This topic was first examined in depth by Edward Said in his

Women pick tea at a plantation in 1993 in Munnar, India (*Robert Nickelsberg | Getty Images*)

book *Orientalism* (1978), in which he showed how the West had constructed an image of non-Western cultures (the Orient or the East) that took for granted the superiority of the West. This viewpoint defined the colonialized culture only through Western eyes and was completely unable to understand and evaluate it from a morally and culturally neutral perspective.

Postcolonial writers examine how the subjugated society has been affected by colonial rule, and they find themselves occupying two cultural worlds. The legacy of the colonizing power, with its influence on such things as language, culture, ways of knowing, and self-identity, coexists with the need to rediscover an authentic form of expression, free of that dominating Euro-centered perspective. Postcolonial literature therefore subverts the European, outsider view and replaces it with narratives that assert the value of indigenous culture. An example of this is contained in *Things Fall Apart* (1958), a novel by the Nigerian writer, Chinua Achebe. Nigeria, like India, is a former

British colony. Achebe's novel is about a late nineteenth-century community leader who opposes colonialism. Achebe employs traditional proverbs and other stylistic devices to present the indigenous Igbo culture (that predates the Western-created nation of Nigeria), in a positive light, reclaiming it from the negative portrayals of Africa that had dominated European writing.

Other well-known postcolonial writers include the Nigerian, Buchi Emecheta, whose work, notably *In the Ditch* (1972), deals with the role of women in African societies; Frantz Fanon, who was born in the French colony of Martinique and examined the effects of racism and colonization in *Black Skin, White Masks* (1952) and *The Wretched of the Earth* (1961); and Jamaica Kincaid, born on the island of Antigua when it was still under British rule (Antigua became self-governing in 1967 but did not gain full independence until 1981). Kincaid's novel *A Small Place* (1988) expresses anger at the effects of colonization, which attempted to turn Antigua into a small version of England, without regard to its native culture.

Indian Literature in English

Indian literature in English is considered as a subgenre of postcolonial literature, since English was the language used by the colonizing power in India. It has a relatively short history. The first literature in English by an Indian was a travel narrative by Sake Dean Mahomet, *The Travels of Dean Mahomet*, published in England in 1793. During the early part of the twentieth century, the best known Indian writers in English were probably Rabindranath Tagore (1861–1941), who wrote poetry in Bengali as well as English, and R. K. Narayan (1906–2001), whose novels were set in the fictional south Indian town of Malgudi.

More recently, an increasing number of Indian writers, including those who live in English-speaking countries, have chosen to write in English rather than any of the many languages of their native India. The advantage of this to the writer is that he or she can potentially reach a much larger audience, but some critics have questioned whether postcolonial literature written in the language of the colonizer is the most relevant or best choice for the culture of the former colony.

Ramanujan, whose native tongues were the Indian languages Tamil and Kannada, but who wrote his poetry in English, noted some of the problems that a writer faces in using a second language, one not usually learned in childhood. In an interview with Chiranton Kulshrestha, published in *The Oxford India Ramanujan*, Ramanujan stated, "A great deal of Indian writing is upstairs English, platform English, idiom-book English, newspaper English. With no slang available, they are stuck in a 'register', a formality, a learned posture." He comments further that Indian poetry written in English is bound to be limited. Commenting on those Indians who, like himself, write in English, he said, "[we] have probably written ourselves into the margin, because of such splits in our persons and our language. ... [we] also get separated from the great community of people in India."

Be that as it may, the amount of literature written by Indians in English continues to grow rapidly. The most famous such writer is Salman Rushdie, who was born in India but now lives in the United States. His most acclaimed novel is *Midnight's Children* (1981). Other prominent works written in English by Indians include *Jasmine* (1988) by Bharati Mukherjee, who like Rushdie lives in the United States; *A Suitable Boy* (1994) by Vikram Seth; *The Great Indian Novel* (1989) by Shashi Tharoor; *A Clear Light of Day* (1980), by Anita Desai; *The God of Small Things* (1997) by Arundhati Roy; and *Such a Long Journey* (1991) by Rohinton Mistry.

Among Indian poets writing in English, the most prominent in the second part of the twentieth century were Dom Moraes (1938–2004), who lived much of his life in Mumbai, India, and Nissam Ezekiel, who came from India's Jewish community.

CRITICAL OVERVIEW

Over the years, Ramanujan's poetry has won considerable praise from critics. Writing in *Contemporary Literature*, Jahan Ramazani notes that as early as the 1960s, Indian contemporaries have hailed Ramanujan as the best Indian English poet. R. Parthasarathy, a fellow Indian poet, declares, in a comment that might well apply to "Waterfalls in a Bank": "What sets Ramanujan apart from other poets is his unique tone of voice, a feature that accounts for the characteristic style of his poetry" (quoted by Sukhbir Singh in *Dictionary of Literary Biography*). "Waterfalls in a Bank" has attracted specific attention from Bruce King in *Three Indian Poets*. King writes that the poem "really does seem to get everything past and present into an amazing tumble of images." He argues that the poem is about "living in a world of confusion" but the final line reveals that "inside us there is another, calm self, unrooted in a particular environment, unaffected by the flux of reality, which watches, calmly, knowingly, and judges simply by being uncommitted, objective." Ramazani discusses the "climactic scene" of the poem, featuring the old sadhu, as a coming together of East and West which characterizes Ramanujan's poetry as a whole:

> A humble world lit up by poetic form, an ancient sensibility startled by its encounter with modernity, a traditional Brahman past metamorphosed by the onset of the Western present—in short, a metaphor-making poesis that hybridizes and transfigures its cultural sources.

WHAT DO I READ NEXT?

- *Speaking of Siva* (1973) is a collection of translations by Ramanujan of short free verse lyrics written to the Hindu god Siva by four wandering Indian saints who lived from the ninth to the twelfth centuries C.E.

- *Selected Poems by Rabindranath Tagore* (2004) brings together new translations of nearly 150 poems by Tagore, many of which have been translated into English for the first time. They provide a representative range of Tagore's poetry. There is also an introduction, by Sankha Ghose, and detailed notes.

- *Collected Poems: 1954–2004* (2004), by Dom Moraes, contains the work of one of the greatest of India's poets who write in English. Moraes published ten volumes of poetry during his long career, and readers have always responded to the beauty and technical skill of his verse as well as its wide-ranging themes.

- *The Oxford Anthology of Modern Indian Poetry* (1998), edited by Vinay Dharwadker, contains the work of 125 poets in English and English translation from fourteen Indian languages. It gives an overview of the major poets and movements in Indian poetry in the last one hundred years. Poets represented include Tagore, Subramania Bharati, Nirala, G. Shankara Kurup, Kaifi

Azmi, Anuradha Mahapatra, Saleem Peeradina, and Vikram Seth.

- *Early Indian Poetry in English: An Anthology: 1829–1947*, edited by Eunice de Souza (2005), is a selection of Indian poetry written in English in the nineteenth and early twentieth centuries. Poets represented include Manmohan Ghose, Kasiprsad Ghose, Joseph Furtado, Henry Derozio, Toru Dutt and her father Govin Chunder Dutt, Annaji, B. M. Malabari, Sarojini Naidu, Beram Saklatvala, Samuel Solomon, and Raman Vakil. In her introduction, de Souza argues that previous anthologists have underplayed the large role played by Indian writers in English in shaping nineteenth century Indian literature.

- In *Modern Indian Poetry in English*, revised edition (2004), Bruce King brings his classic work up to date. King examines changes in direction in Indian poetry, adding five chapters to the original edition which discuss the work of newer poets such as Menka Shivdasani, Tara Patel, Imtiaz Dharker, Charmayne D'Souza, Mukta Sambrani, Meena Alexander, Sujata Bhatt, Chitra Banerjee Divakurni, Ranjit Hoskote, Jeet Thayil, C. P. Surendran, Vijay Nambisan, R. Raj Rao, Bibhu Padhi, Tabish Khair, and G. J. V. Prasad.

CRITICISM

Bryan Aubrey

Aubrey holds a Ph.D. in English. In this essay, he analyzes how Ramanujan's experience of living in two distinct cultural worlds is reflected in "Waterfalls in a Bank" and other poems from Ramanujan's collection Second Sight.

As a poet of the Indian diaspora, one of Ramanujan's concerns in "Waterfalls in a Bank"

and in other poems he published in the collection *Second Sight* is to evaluate his experience as an Indian living in the United States. Like many immigrants, he lives in two distinct cultural and linguistic worlds, and as he remembers his homeland he must also learn how to respond authentically to the very different culture in which he has chosen to live. This is not an easy thing to do, and much in the poet's work suggests an unresolved tension between his Indian heritage and the day-to-day reality of living in Chicago, a large city so

THIS NON-ACTIVE PART OF THE POET'S SELF IS NOT LOCATED WITHIN THE BOUNDARIES OF TIME AND SPACE THAT NORMALLY DEFINE A PERSON'S SENSE OF IDENTITY, WHICH IS WHY THE 'WATCHERS' OCCUPY 'NOWHERE PERCHES'; THEY ARE NOT CONFINED WITHIN A BODY, OR A MIND, OR A PERSONALITY; THEY STAND APART."

utterly unlike the environment in which he spent his childhood, youth, and early manhood.

"Waterfalls in a Bank" presents a picture of the poet arrested in a moment of contemplation of a waterfall that has been set up in a Chicago bank. The setting represents the epitome of Western financial power, prestige and materialism—the objective world of economics and business. But the sight of the waterfall is the stimulus that takes the poet to an inner world far removed from the bank in which he stands. A flurry of images and metaphors arise in his mind, some of which go back to his memories of his childhood in India. The key image in this respect is of the crippled old sadhu, the wandering ascetic, who embodies a nonmaterial, impoverished but spiritual way of being in the world that is the opposite of everything implied by the prosperous bank in Chicago's Hyde Park.

There would seem to be little doubt, on the evidence of this poem, that in the "transaction" between two cultures that the poet enacts in his life, he believes that the loss is greater than the gain. Using the language of financial exchange, he is, he says, "always / at a loss when I count my change." And as if to verify that statement, in contrast to the rich, variegated stream of images in which he recalls India, the last section of the poem registers only the coldness and the chaos of Chicago during a winter snowstorm.

This dual perspective, in which the present-day West interacts in the poet's mind with his past in the East, is apparent in a number of poems in Ramanujan's collection *Second Sight*. The title itself suggests the double perspective of a man living in two cultures, present and past, West

and East, and bridging the gap between them as best he can. For example, in the poem "Extended Family," the poet describes bathing before dawn in his home:

> the dry chlorine water
> my only Ganges
>
> the naked Chicago bulb
> a cousin of the Vedic sun

The chlorinated water is what comes through the faucets in a modern American city, whereas the Ganges is the holy river in India to which pilgrims travel many miles in order to bathe in it to purify their souls. Likewise, the harsh light emitted by an electric bulb—a product of human ingenuity and technology—is a far cry (the word "cousin" in the poem is to be read ironically) from the fiery god that was the Vedic sun. The Vedas are ancient religious texts from India, dating back, in all probability, to the second millennium B.C.E.. The sun was associated with Agni, the god of fire, who was greeted in poetic fashion by the ancient seers who wrote the Rig Veda: "The great fire at the beginning of the dawn has sprung aloft, and issuing forth from the darkness has come with radiance. AGNI, the bright-bodied, as soon as born, fills all dwellings with shining light."

In "Chicago Zen," the poet expresses a similar kind of double vision. Like "Waterfalls in a Bank," this poem is set in Chicago, and also like the other poem, it has verses in which the immediate city scene is dissolved in the poet's mind in favor of a rich vein of images drawn from an exotic culture:

> The traffic light turns orange
> on 57th and Dorchester, and you stumble,
>
> you fall into a vision of forest fires,
> enter a frothing Himalayan river

Thus, "Chicago Zen" gives expression to the kind of disorientation experienced by the immigrant in the big American city. The new environment is, it would seem, the "country [that] cannot be reached" except by religiously following all its small rules, and even then, for the immigrant, there is always something that does not feel quite right. To use the image with which the poem ends, it is like descending a flight of stairs with a sense of unease, waiting "for the last / step that's never there." This is the frequent experience of the immigrant, never to feel entirely at home, however hard he or she tries to adjust to the alien land. It applies particularly to first-generation immigrants who make the transition, as Ramanujan did, as adults. Nothing can ever really replace the culture in which they grew up and which shaped their outlook on the world.

Indeed, it is Ramanujan's Indian spiritual and philosophical heritage that provides a clue to that final enigmatic line in "Waterfalls in a Bank": "And my watchers watch, from their nowhere perches." After all the kinetic imagery in the poem that tumbles out from the poet's memory comes this final cryptic, stationary image of mysterious "watchers" on their "nowhere perches." What does the poet mean by this unusual image, which seems unrelated to the rest of the poem?

Interestingly, a reading of the other poems in *Second Sight* provides a number of examples of these "watchers." "Looking for the Centre" is yet another poem set in Chicago. Playing on the idea of searching in the city for a Center for Missing Children that has recently changed location, the poem becomes something of a metaphysical quest, through Ramanujan's characteristically exotic imagery, for the elusive center of the poet's being. The poem ends:

> And my watchers
> watch, cool as fires
> in a mirror.

As in "Waterfalls in a Bank," the watchers observe but do not act. The fires of desire do not move them. The same is true in the poem "The Watchers," which is devoted entirely to this notion of silent, detached observers who watch over events and happenings in the life of the poet without making any judgment: "They impose nothing, take no positions."

It would seem that the poet is referring not to some entity outside himself, but to a deeper aspect of his own being, a part of himself that remains calm, undisturbed, and uninvolved even as the active part of his being thinks and acts and goes about his day-to-day business. This non-active part of the poet's self is not located within the boundaries of time and space that normally define a person's sense of identity, which is why the "watchers" occupy "nowhere perches"; they are not confined within a body, or a mind, or a personality; they stand apart.

Ramanujan is clearly fascinated by this notion of some larger aspect of the self that stands apart from the constant busyness of the mind. He puzzles over the nature of the watchers in his poem "Questions," wondering if they were present at the moment of his birth, when his "head's soft crown bathed in mother's blood." In other words, are the watchers part of some eternal continuum of life that predates his personal existence?

As an epigraph to this poem he quotes a passage from the *Mundaka Upanishad*, an ancient Indian religious text:

> Two birds on the selfsame tree:
> one of them eats the fruit of the tree,
> the other watches without eating.

This is a reference to the notion, fundamental to ancient Indian spirituality, that there are two aspects of the human self. The first bird represents the individual self, that involves itself in the experience of the world of the senses; the second bird is the universal Self (the word is usually capitalized when used in this sense) that is the silent witness to everything, an eternal, omnipresent reality that is the individual's higher, unchanging self, identical with Brahman, the universal divine consciousness.

Drawn to this idea, Ramanujan translates it into the image of the silent, nonjudgmental watchers on their "nowhere perches" (the image is suggestive of the birds in that passage from the *Mundaka Upanishad*) but as the poem "Questions," which ends with an unanswered question, suggests, he is not prepared to embrace it without reservations. Ramanujan is no orthodox Hindu; on the contrary, he identifies himself as something of a skeptic. In his poem "Middle Age" he confesses his "belief in unbelief"; he is "wedded to doubt." This suggests yet another pull of opposites within the mind of the poet, between Western rationalism—which he claims consciously to embrace—and the Eastern spirituality of his heritage, which is also deeply embedded within him and is what allows "Waterfalls in a Bank," a poem made up of a series of helter-skelter, tumbling images, to end on a note of quiet, detached contemplation. As this immigrant poet, caught uncomfortably between two worlds, scurries around the streets of Chicago, busy as all Westerners are and doing what Westerners do, his Eastern roots pull at him still from their nowhere perches and will not quite let him go.

Source: Bryan Aubrey, Critical Essay on "Waterfalls in a Bank," in *Poetry for Students*, Gale, 2008.

Sukhbir Singh

In the following essay, Singh gives a critical analysis of Ramanujan's work.

A. K. Ramanujan started writing poetry in his mother tongue, Kannada, at the early age of fifteen or sixteen. He later became a trilingual Anglophile writer who wrote poetry, fiction, and prose in Kannada, Tamil, and English. His poetry and fiction are deeply rooted in Indian culture, and his subjects are widely spread over the Indian social landscape. He believed throughout his artistic career that "creativity does not come from cosmopolitanism. Creativity comes out of sustained attention to one's own experience, one's own landscape," as he told Rama Jha in the January-June 1981 issue of *Humanities Review*. He therefore portrayed in his poems a realistic picture of Indian society in a variety of aspects—sometimes sacred, sometimes sunny, and sometimes somber. His work offers an elaborate collage of everyday Indian life, reflecting the emotional ups and downs experienced by the people because of prevalent social contradictions and persistent cultural compulsions in Indian society. As a poet, Ramanujan highlighted the existing hypocrisies of Indian society—especially in such key areas as religious taboos, marital relations, cultural conventions, family ties, and caste consciousness. In his poetry he treated many of these issues with mild sarcasm, because most Indian social institutions depend on conventional beliefs that often prove detrimental to the natural growth of one's body, mind, and soul. In satirizing some of these beliefs, Ramanujan operated out of the rationalist and reformist convictions of an artist. As he put it in conversation with A. L. Becker and Keith Taylor, included in *Uncollected Poems and Prose* (2001), "And, of course, I had the notion that only a kind of modern rationalism was the answer to all the problems that we had: the caste system, the problems of a hierarchy by birth. It seemed to me then, it still does, as unfair. That's true of many modern Indians." His avowed aim was to diversify the notions of Indian civilization, since he considered the Brahminical view of Hindu upper-class society as a hierarchical one.

Attipat Krishnaswami Ramanujan was born on 16 March 1929 in Mysore, India, to Attipat Asuri and Seshamal Krishnaswami. His father was a professor of mathematics who fostered in him a rationalistic bent of mind and fired his imagination with creative zeal. His mother was a housewife who induced in him a taste for culture, literature, mythology, and folklore.

IN RAMANUJAN'S LATER YEARS HE PUBLISHED *SECOND SIGHT* (1986). . . . THIS PERIOD CLIMAXES HIS CREATIVE LIFE IN TERMS OF AESTHETIC ASSESSMENT AND ACCEPTANCE OF CERTAIN EARLIER IDEAS AND ISSUES. HIS PERCEPTIONS, PREFERENCES, AND PROJECTIONS OF THE TWO SOCIETIES HE HAD LIVED IN AND THEIR SOCIAL DICHOTOMIES ARE NOW PRESENTED FAR MORE COHERENTLY AND CONVINCINGLY THAN EARLIER."

Tales in south India are not bedtime stories but food-time tales. And the local folks taught him native wisdom and turned him to native literature in Kannada. Hence, some of his poetic concerns characterizing his ironic view of Indian society reflect certain early influences on him of classical Kannada and Tamil literature and the life of people in the state of Karnataka. To attack the oppressive conventions of conservative Indian society, Ramanujan makes use of the native myths, legends, folklore, and folktales in his poetry. In his talk with Becker and Taylor, Ramanujan affirmed: "My interest has always been in the mother tongues ... because I have always felt that mother tongues represent a democratic, anti-hierarchic, from-the-ground-up view of India. And my interest in folklore has also been shaped by that. I see in these counter-systems, anti-structures, a protest against official systems."

Ramanujan obtained his B.A. (Honors) degree in 1949 and an M.A. in English in 1950 from the University of Mysore, and he earned graduate diplomas in Dravidian linguistics from Deccan College, Poona, in 1958 and 1959. Following the completion of his master's degree, Ramanujan worked as a lecturer in different colleges in India from 1950 until 1957 and at the University of Baroda in 1957-1958. He then went to the United States in 1959, having received a Smith-Mundt Fellowship that enabled him to work for his Ph.D. in linguistics from Indiana University in Bloomington, which he received in 1963. While in the United States, he married

Molly Daniels, a Syrian Christian from India, in 1962. Daniels-Ramanujan did her Ph.D. on Saul Bellow with Bellow himself and later became a journalist and a writer of fiction. Her novel *The Salt Doll* (1978) was given the Illinois Arts Council Award for fiction. Ramanujan and Daniels-Ramanujan were married and divorced twice in their long life together.

Despite the many years he spent in the United States, his interest in the native languages and the people of his native land never diminished. As a nonresident Indian in the United States, Ramanujan refused to see himself as an exile or an expatriate. In his opinion, a writer who is forced like Aleksandr Solzhenitsyn to live in another country may be an exile or an expatriate, but he denied that someone like Bharati Mukherjee can consider herself to be so since she had willingly chosen to live abroad. He said in conversation with Jha, "I think it's sentimental to call oneself an exile because this is voluntary and one is fulfilling oneself in various ways by living in this country. So to sentimentalize it and say that oh I am an expatriate, I am an exile . . . these are words which I would not use about myself." With his easy sense of settlement to the nonnative environment, Ramanujan shows even in his poetry how a poet can adapt the English language for the expression of a native Indian sensibility. He imbues his English prosody with his native spirit and exploits his knowledge of Kannada poetics to enhance the sonority of the English verse. "My knowledge of English has been deeply affected by my knowledge of Indian literature and poetics," he told Jha. "If English cuts us from our culture it won't get us very far. . . . Indian English when it is good, does get its nourishment . . . from each individual's knowledge of Indian culture and Indian languages. It certainly does for me. That is what binds us back to our childhood and early years."

Because he supplemented his English verse with the knowledge of his mother tongue and its poetics, Ramanujan avoided the common predicament of most Indo-Anglian poets who invariably feel divided because they have to express a native sensibility in an alien dialect. He negotiates this schism between his Indian sensibility and English idiom by artistically synchronizing the "inner" form of his thought with the "outer" form of the English language. As R. Parthasarathy quotes Ramanujan, "English

and my disciplines (linguistics, anthropology) . . . give me my 'outer' forms—linguistic, metrical, logical and other such ways of shaping experience: and my first thirty years in India, my frequent visits and field trips, my personal and professional preoccupations with Kannada, Tamil, the classics and folklore give me my substance, my 'inner' forms, images and symbols. They are continuous with each other, and I can no longer tell what comes from where." Ramanujan thus formulates an artistically viable idiom to synchronize freely his experiences, beliefs, social issues, and cultural diversity with his poetry.

With his belief in cultural plurality, Ramanujan used his work to address certain fundamental cultural, social, and religious issues that he encountered in both India and the United States. These issues appeared to him appropriate for the language he chose for them. To him a poem comes in a language suitable to the idea it expresses. As he told Jha, "You cannot choose the language. I don't think there is a choice. If there is a choice, it is not a poem. I would even define the poem as that where the line between language and thought is not there, or between form and content, which is what the etymology of the Sanskrit word *sahitya* implies." He wrote in whichever language the poem came to him spontaneously—Kannada, Tamil, or English. If he chose any one of these languages for his verse, his expression was enriched by his knowledge of the other two. As he told Becker and Taylor, "In the three languages I know well, whichever one I am working in, the other two are present. I am not a *tabula rasa*. I always think of my languages as certain kinds of musical instruments. If you pluck one string there are other strings that resonate. Like the Indian sitar, there are strings that the musician never touches. They are resonating strings. It is like that for all of us. Everything we know is resonating with what we talk about in the foreground." The creative path he pursued was also part of his efforts at advancing multiculturalism in the world, for he did so by writing in two native languages and one international language. His poetry and translations acquainted people in the East and the West with what they did not know about the Indian culture.

While completing his doctorate, Ramanujan worked with the University of Chicago as a research associate in 1961 and thereafter as an assistant professor of linguistics, specializing in

Tamil and Dravidian languages, until 1965. During this period, in 1963, he received the American Institute of Indian Studies and the Indian School of Letters Fellowship. He also translated poems from classical Tamil literature and published them as his first collection, *Fifteen Poems from a Classical Tamil Anthology* (1965). The collection includes translations of love poems from the earliest of the eight anthologies of classical Tamil. These poems are in the form of dramatic monologues of the lover or the beloved in a figurative language. They evoke a vast panorama of picturesque landscapes before the eyes of the reader. In an interview with Chirantan Kulshrestha, republished in *Uncollected Poems and Prose*, he recalled that "These classical Tamil poems attracted me by their attitude to experience, to human passion, and to the external world; their trust in the bareness, the lean line with no need to jazz it up or ornament it. They seemed to me Classical, anti-Romantic, using the words loosely as we know them in European literature." Ramanujan's promotion as associate professor at the University of Chicago in 1966 coincided with the publication of *The Striders*, his first collection of original poetry, which clearly evidences in themes, techniques, and symbolism the impact of classical Tamil poetry on his sensibility. The themes in *The Striders* are connected to his native place and the people with whom he interacted in early life. His subjects include family members, local festivals, ceremonies, rituals, forests, birds, beasts, rivers, and reptiles. As he affirms, "I have tried [in *The Striders*] to keep the human scene central. ... The more I pay attention to the human world, for me the line between the poem and the novel, the lyric and the story, begins to blur; and anyway in Indian poetry there's never been a clear line. Any single poem implies a persona, a voice, and a specific scene, a whole dramatic situation." For that reason, in these poems the personal emotions dominate over technical concerns.

Ramanujan simultaneously worked on his next volume of translations, *The Interior Landscape: Love Poems from a Classical Tamil Anthology*, which he published a year later, in 1967. Under the influence of the classical Tamil poetry included in *The Interior Landscape*, Ramanujan reveals in *The Striders* a nostalgia for landscapes of places he had visited in early life. His love of the landscape frequently surfaces in the images of moonlit and starlit nights, noontime sun, evenings, lakes, flowers, marketplaces, birds, and beautiful women. He perceives in them the primal energy that propels humans through life. In "I Could Have Rested," Ramanujan measures the motion of time and the movement of life in terms of nesting birds: [...]. In "On a Delhi Sundial," he astutely mingles the temporal and the transcendental: [...]. In this context, Vinay Dharwadker observes that "the clock that clicks inside the natural mechanism of any living body is also the clock ticking away in the natural world outside, and it is the nature of this universal clock to tick inexorably towards the terminal irony of death."

Ramanujan worked as professor of Dravidian studies and linguistics at the University of Chicago from 1968 until 1972. He also lectured as guest faculty at the University of California, Berkeley, in 1968 and the University of Wisconsin, Madison, in 1971. By now he was an established translator and was given the Tamil Writers' Association Award in 1969. With respect to his own poetry, he attained considerable technical and thematic maturity with his second collection, *Relations* (1971), which is written in the classical Tamil and medieval style of *bhakti* poetry. In this collection Ramanujan depicts human bondage through family affiliations that deny freedom. Such social trappings create disharmonies at different levels of life. In his opinion, the social network of relationships is a necessity as well as a snare. [...]. After he divorced Daniels-Ramanujan the first time, he wrote a poem titled "Love Poem for a Wife, 1." The poem reveals how the unshared past before marriage with the wife becomes a source of agony and estrangement: [...].

In these poems, the nostalgia of *The Striders* volume for homeland is replaced by an objective assessment of the past. This detachment is amply evident from the ironic humor ingrained in his projections of family members such as his parents, aunts, wife, and father-in-law. He achieves such objectivity after a long stay in the United States, where his engagement with an alien culture led him to look at people and places from his early life more dispassionately. Treating humorously his parents and other relatives helps him overcome his earlier absorption in his childhood and attachment to his people. In "Small-Scale Reflections on a Great House," Ramanujan portrays an ironic picture of his childhood home, saying that nothing that comes into this house goes out: [...]. Similarly, in "Obituary," his reaction to the death of his father verges on cynicism:

[...]. In "Love Poem for a Wife, 2," he pacifies himself after undergoing the agony of his remarriage with Molly through the poetic description of a dream: [...].

With his dispassion, Ramanujan even looks mockingly at Hinduism and Indian history. Some aspects of Hindu culture and Indian history have become remote for him. He declares that he was "anti-hierarchic"—that is to say, against the Hindu caste system—right from his youth. He therefore makes use of the ancient Tamil and Kannada myths, legends, and folktales in his poetry because they are more secular, democratic, and egalitarian. They give due recognition to women and the downtrodden of Indian hierarchical society.

Between 1971 and 1986, Ramanujan did not publish any collection of poetry. From 1972 he was associated with the Committee on Social Thought at the University of Chicago and lectured as visiting professor at the University of California, Berkeley, in 1973 and Carleton College in Northfield, Minnesota, in 1978. During this period Ramanujan did a good amount of translation work from the ancient Tamil and Kannada into English; he translated *Speaking of Siva* (1973), U. R. Anantha Murthy's *Samskara: A Rite for a Dead Man* (1976), Nammalvar's *Hymns for the Drowning: Poems for Visnu* (1981), and *Poems of Love and War: From the Eight Anthologies and the Ten Long Poems of Classical Tamil* (1985). These translations project a rare poetic achievement of the Dravidian culture in the south of India, and they portray a complete picture of the ancient Indian civilization in the subcontinent. Taken together, they show how the poetry and culture complemented and supplemented each other in ancient India. Ramanujan always supplied his translations with prefaces, notes, afterwords, and commentaries to offer models of genuine translations. It helped him produce a coherent theory of translation from Indian languages into English. For him the art of translation is immensely useful but never original and perfect. It involves merely turning one language into another for the convenience of a target audience. A work in translation never carries the full fragrance and absolute originality of the actual text, since the author never wrote his work for translation into another language. He was catering precisely to a particular group of people at a certain time. So the time, people, and place are extremely important in the life of a text. As Ramanujan told Becker and Taylor, "Literatures are so deeply grounded in their cultures and in the cultures they carry. . . . To cross from one language to another—which is, after all, what translation means—is a very imperfect business. And there is much damage in translating. But there it has to be pointed to [as notes], and in pointing itself some of the damage is undone. In showing what can be done, the reader can make the leaps that are necessary." Ramanujan turned the ideas of Walter Benjamin and Jacques Derrida about translation to his own favor, and his skills as a translator exceeded those of many established translators in the subcontinent. In Ramanujan's view, the translator cannot escape the shadow of the original, and his task is to develop a relevant supplement. How well the text can be translated does not depend upon the inherent treasure in the poem but on certain crucial outside factors. With the efforts of the translator the text is reborn.

In Ramanujan's later years he published *Second Sight* (1986), *Another Harmony: New Essays on the Folklore of India* (1986), which he coedited with Stuart Blackburn, and *Folktales from India: A Selection of Oral Tales from Twenty-Two Languages* (1991). This period climaxes his creative life in terms of aesthetic assessment and acceptance of certain earlier ideas and issues. His perceptions, preferences, and projections of the two societies he had lived in and their social dichotomies are now presented far more coherently and convincingly than earlier. His preoccupation with the mysteries of life evidences an acceptance of change over fixed specificity. Also, in this collection he reveals a more complex understanding of Indian myths, legends, history, rituals, customs, and conventions. A. N. Dwivedi observes that "taken together, these poems tend to reinforce the thought that the poet is heavily inclined towards all that is India, including his Indian associations and Hindu gods and goddesses." This propensity intensified in him as a result of his translations from the classical Kannada and Tamil literatures and his continued contact with India over the years. He visited India regularly and collected new materials, met old friends, delivered lectures, and read from his latest poems to poetry lovers.

In this phase, Ramanujan frequently entertains the thoughts of birth and death in his poems. His references to fire, water, darkness, and death in many poems point to a subliminal awareness of the approaching end of his life. "Fire," "Birthdays," "Shadows," "One More on a Deathless Theme," "Elegy," "Death and the Good Citizen," and "Death in Search of a Comfortable Metaphor" are some examples of poems in which he displays his apprehension of death. Images of death and ruin, the passing of time, and darkness point to his reconcilement to the idea of the transience of life and the temporariness of the world. This mood further results in a transcendence of earthly bonds and boundaries. Many poems in *Second Sight* reflect his penchant for meditation and philosophy, and, in Dharwadker's opinion, these preoccupations appear "interspersed with passages reflecting on certain 'epiphanic' moments in his life."

Ramanujan's death anxiety in *Second Sight* could as well be a part of his increasing age and the maturing influence of the modernist British and American writers on him. This influence is evident from his poems, which are concrete embodiments of his ideas. He synchronizes his technique of writing poetry with his experience, education, erudition, and vision of life. His language is simple, his rhythms musical, and his imagery suggestive. In "Snakes," one of his more popular poems, the poet uses the language of daily conversation to articulate his childhood apprehensions. His choice of words, however, their placement in a rhythmical pattern, and the play of sounds and colors bring the picture alive with relevant suggestions and sensations. Similarly, in another short but suggestive poem, "Still Life," Ramanujan conveys his response to a woman who has left him feeling like a half-eaten salami sandwich. The half-eaten sandwich [...] offers a visually comic image of incompleteness and disconnection, simultaneously evoking a picture of the woman as a biting animal.

Like the modernists to European culture, Ramanujan's attitude to Indian culture in some of his poems can often be satirical. His satire tended to be mild, however. For instance, in "The Last of the Princes" he gently mocks the poor financial condition of the erstwhile rulers of India: [...]. Similarly, in "History" he makes fun of greedy relatives: [...]. A few poems even verge on being caricatures. In "At Forty," he mimics Jatti, the gym teacher, [...]. In "Pleasure," he lampoons a Jain monk craving the female body after a long spell of celibacy: [...].

As a Hindu Brahmin living in Chicago from the early 1960s, Ramanujan at times resorts to a jocular style to overcome his nostalgia for the world he left behind, as in "Conventions of Despair": [...]. Withdrawal into his Hindu mind brings him equanimity and enables him to have an objective and detached view of a mundane world. Ramanujan's grandmother, parents, wife, aunts, and their children surface frequently in his poetry. They inhabit his poetic world as living entities and impart an autobiographical hue to his art, as in "Love Poem for a Wife, 2": [...]. They all inspire his imagination and ignite the creative spark in him. At the thought of his family members and other acquaintances Ramanujan plunges into a world of odds and oddities, fun and frivolities, and greed and grief. His relatives acquire symbolic forms, and they quite often appear as the embodiments of abstract ideas in his poetry: [...].

Ramanujan also makes abundant use of figures, images, and symbols to convey his poetic thoughts in a distinctive manner. His study of anthropology, William Butler Yeats, Ezra Pound, T. S. Eliot, Wallace Stevens, William Carlos Williams, Sanskrit poetics, and haiku poetry of Japan had given him a figurative and symbolic bent of mind. From the French symbolists he had learned to concretize the delicate nuances of his deep emotions and observations. Because of his mathematician father, he also made frequent use of Euclidian figures that were familiar from childhood—geometrical and astronomical shapes such as lines, circles, squares, rectangles, triangles, quadrangles, oblongs, and parabolas.[...] Because of Ramanujan's geometric perfection and figurative delineation, Nissim Ezekiel, a fellow poet, remarked in the 18 June 1972 issue of the *Illustrated Weekly of India* that "A. K. Ramanujan is the precision instrument of Indian English poetry."

Similarly, Ramanujan employs trees, flowers, fruits, and leaves as symbols of unity, beauty, and fertility in his poems.[...] In "Birthdays," the poet subtly brings out the oneness of nature with humans both dead and alive: [...]. In "The Day Went Dark," he combines the colors of flowers and leaves to infuse erotic energy into the patterns of his newly acquired carpet:[...]

Allusions also play a significant role in Ramanujan's poetry. He alludes to ancient myths, stories, legends, literary figures, folklore, artists, scientists, and gods and goddesses of several countries and cultures. These allusions broaden the horizons of his thoughts and themes;

they often give his poetry a universal dimension. Weaving together the folk with the canonical, the mythical with the mundane, and the national with the international, Ramanujan uses the technique of allusion to ballast his poetry with humanist values. The poet was not sure whether this aspect of his creativity was something his readers were aware of, however. He told Becker and Taylor, "I actually put in quotes. Very few people have noticed those quotes. But that's part of my expressive means. I've read Pound, and I've read Indian things. I think with them. Why shouldn't I use what I have?" Thus, in "The Opposable Thumb," Ramanujan identifies three types of hands to show the importance of the thumb by obliquely alluding to Swami Vivekananda's description of the Purusha[...]. In "Love Poem for a Wife, 2," the "half-woman half- / man" [...] alludes to the Hindu god Shiva and goddess Shakti—together in one form as *ardhanareshwar* (half-man and half-woman). Similarly, in "Entries for a Catalogue of Fears," the poet evokes William Shakespeare's *Hamlet* (circa 1600-1601) [...] or John Keats's *Ode to a Nightingale* (1819)[....] Ramanujan's allusions to sources past and present often juxtapose antiquity and modernity, thereby making both European and Indian traditions relevant to the contemporary Indian poet writing in English.

Ramanujan died suddenly of a heart attack on 13 July 1993 in Chicago at the age of sixty-four. He was survived by a daughter, Krittika, and a son, Krishnaswami, and left behind a substantial body of unpublished poetry, essays, and translations. At the time of his death he did not enjoy good relations with his former wife, Daniels-Ramanujan; they were divorced a few years earlier. Writing in the *Times of India* on 25 July 1993, Ramanujan's colleagues and friends of old standing, Susanne and Lloyd Rudolph, paid him a rich tribute: "Raman's distinguishing characteristics were his humanity and modesty. He spoke softly but deftly. He picked friendships, not fights. … He preferred irony and humor to scoring points. A polymath; a demanding scholar with demanding standards; a teller of tales." Much of the material Ramanujan left behind has been published posthumously by Daniels-Ramanujan, Krittika Ramanujan, and Ramanujan's friend Dharwadker. Volumes they have published include *When God Is a Customer: Telugu Courtesan Songs by Ksetrayya and Others* (1994); which Ramanujan had compiled with Velcheru Narayana Rao and David Shulman; *The Collected Essays of A. K. Ramanujan* (1994);

The Collected Poems of A. K. Ramanujan (1995); *A Flowering Tree and Other Oral Tales from India* (1997), and *Uncollected Poems and Prose*. One therefore does not find a note of finality in his poetic career, unlike in the cases of his literary gurus such as Yeats, Pound, and Eliot. As one moves from the earlier poems in *The Striders* to the later pieces in *The Black Hen* (2000), however, it becomes evident that Ramanujan was moving toward a more conclusive and concrete phase. His early poems are more personal—they speak about the poet's youthful anger, anxiety, anguish, and apathy toward social, cultural, and religious anomalies around him. In them he derides the inhuman and the unjust and chides the guilty vociferously. In *Relations* and *Second Sight*, he seems to have come out of the early phase of excitement and experimentation. In those collections the poet exhibits more clarity of thought and better control over his language. As Bruce King observes, "*Relations* is somewhat different from the earlier book in that the style is less imagistic, the movement of lines more supple, the narrator more present as speaker. There is intelligence and personality. The poetry is more discursive, more conversational as well as more reflective. There is less flatness of tone, more humor, wit, irony, comedy." In *Second Sight*, Ramanujan further improves his control over his subject matter and speaks more freely about personal, spiritual, and sexual matters.

In *The Black Hen*, Ramanujan establishes himself among the well-known Indian poets writing in English because of his mature vision, variety of themes, felicity of expression, and metaphysical subtlety. The titles of the poems in *The Striders* ("The Striders," "Self-Portrait," "Sometimes," "Conventions of Despair," "Anxiety," "Images," and "The Fall"), compared to the poems in *The Black Hen* ("Shadows," "Fire," "Fog," "Fizzle," "Difficulty," "Elegy," "Pain," and "Fear No Fall"), testify to his range of movement and mature preoccupations in this phase. In Krittika Ramanujan's assessment, the poems in this posthumous collection are "in some ways different from their predecessors. At first reading, they seem light, easy, some almost like exercises. After a few readings, a complete reversal takes place. When the poems are read in sequence, they seem entirely different. The ear begins to hear the voice as full, rhythmic, passionate, complex, changeable, and in variety of voices, styles and forms." The poems in the early collections are replete with details and documentation. In contrast, the later volumes are characterized by precision and cohcrence and aimed at the evocation of the spiritual. For instance, in "The Fall," the falling man fears he is "a mere body" [...]. In "Fear No Fall," the fallen man does not fear as he hears a spiritual calling from both within and without: [...].

Critics have, on the whole, received Ramanujan's work favorably. In "How It Strikes a Contemporary: The Poetry of A. K. Ramanujan" (1976), an appreciation written for the *Literary Criterion*, R. Parthasarathy, a fellow poet, declares: "What sets Ramanujan apart from other poets is his unique tone of voice, a feature that accounts for the characteristic style of his poetry." In "The Self in A. K. Ramanujan's Poetry," an essay included in *Contemporary Indian Verse in English: An Evaluation* (1980), Kulshrestha praises Ramanujan for making unconventional use of the English language. He believes that for Ramanujan "the cultivation and enrichment of a unique personal idiom is not a process that takes place in a vacuum, but is symptomatic of a poet's active concern with the dynamics of his sensibility, the precious tones, movements, and distinctions of his own being as an individual and artist." G. N. Devy, in "Alienation as a Means of Self-Exploration: A Study of A. K. Ramanujan's Poetry" (*Chandrabhaga*, Winter 1981), observes that the sense of alienation implicit in some of Ramanujan's significant poems "seems to be the inevitable outcome of the nature of his life-pattern—an Indian Brahmin married to a Syrian Christian, living in Chicago, teaching Dravidian languages and linguistics, twice removed from his natural linguistic context, first from Tamil to Kannada and then from Kannada to English."

S. G. Jainapur, in the chapter on Ramanujan for his book *Poetry, Culture, and Language: Indo-Anglian Poets from Karnataka* (1987), hails him as "a distinguished poet, with an individual voice of his own, both in English and Kannada" and highlights such distinct qualities of his poetry as "nostalgia and memory, family relationships, self-search as a Hindu, and love." Emmanuel Narendra Lall, in an essay about Ramanujan for his 1983 book *The Poetry of Encounter: Three Indo-Anglian Poets, Dom Moraes, A. K. Ramanujan, and Nissim Ezekiel* (1983), praises the poet for his deft use of irony, images, control over language, and the synthesis of the Eastern and Western traditions in his poetry: "His poems take their origin in a mind that is simultaneously Indian and Western; therefore they succeed in opening more passages to India."

S. K. Desai, in an essay for the 1984 collection *Perspectives on Indian Poetry in English*, compares Ramanujan with Eliot and Pound in terms of prosody and expatriate sensibility: "For Ramanujan, memories, which are perceptions that live through time, are a means to explore the nature of Time. Through memories he is not seeking his roots in the area of darkness, nor is he exploring the wounded or healthy Hindu civilization. He is using them simply to explore the existential problems of time and what it does to life." P. K. J. Kurup, in a chapter on the poet for the anthology *Contemporary Indian Poetry in English* (1991), commends him for having "cultivated and enriched a unique personal idiom, that shows the poet's concern with the dynamics of his sensibility in terms of concrete images." King, in his *Three Indian Poets: Nissim Ezekiel, A. K. Ramanujan, Dom Moraes* (1991), admires Ramanujan's erudition, which is reflected in his poems in the variety of his allusions and range of his references, from Sigmund Freud to the Upanishads.

Longer studies of Ramanujan's poetry are equally appreciative of his poetic art and liberal humanism. S. N. Pandey, in "Feminist Concerns in Ramanujan's Poetry" (1998), applauds the poet for supporting the cause of women in his poetry: "Ramanujan strives to express his solidarity with women's cause whatever be the genre, poetry or folktales." Among full-length studies of Ramanujan's poetry, Dwivedi's *A. K. Ramanujan and His Poetry* (1983) focuses on the Indian themes, and his *The Poetic Art of A. K. Ramanujan* (1995) notes gratifyingly that Ramanujan "has not naturalized the Western themes and traditions so much as the Indian ones, and that he has stood his ground and proved his mettle, without shifting his allegiance."

Ramanujan steadily achieved ripeness by evolving an idiom well suited to deeper explorations of the innermost areas of his poetic psyche. According to Jainapur, "There are very few poets in the Indo-Anglian milieu today who equal him." He lived a life of diverse experiences that lent variety, richness, and depth to his poetry. There is hardly any aspect of life, whether sacred or profane, material or spiritual, that he has left untouched in his poems. As an Indian he found his culture and religion full of possibilities for poetic treatment; as a resident of the United States he informed Indian people about the need to review some of their traditions in the wake of Western ideas of progress; and as a humanist he stressed the need for social equality and universal peace. The publication of his uncollected poems posthumously has allowed readers to view the extent of his achievement even more readily.

Source: Sukhbir Singh, "A. K. Ramanujan," in *Dictionary of Literary Biography*, Vol. 323, *South Asian Writers in English*, edited by Fakrul Alam, Thomson Gale, 2006, pp. 285–95.

Jahan Ramazani

In the following excerpt, Ramazani examines the metaphors present in Ramanujan's poetry and in his translation work. Of "Waterfalls in a Bank," Ramazani argues that it reflects the poet's "understanding of the parallels between metaphor, intercultural translation, and intertemporal connection." The critic also contends that in this poem Ramanujan "metaphorically bridges the distances between past and present, East and West."

. . . Long underestimated and therefore perhaps still in need of introduction, Ramanujan's poetry now seems poised on the brink of worldwide recognition. In 1995 Oxford University Press published *The Collected Poems of A. K. Ramanujan*, gathering together *The Striders* (1966), *Relations* (1971), and *Second Sight* (1986), as well as material for an incomplete fourth volume, *The Black Hen*. Since the sixties, Indian contemporaries like Nissim Ezekiel and R. Parthasarathy have hailed Ramanujan as the best Indian English poet. If Ramanujan's earlier poetry is sometimes overwhelmed by the satiric ferocities of Pound and Eliot, Anglomodernist influences nevertheless helped Ramanujan to fend off the sentimentality and abstraction that often clouded Indian English verse after independence. His later volumes, above all *Second Sight*, ever more successfully absorb and remake the forms, tonalities, and tropes inherited from English-language poets like William Carlos Williams, Wallace Stevens, and William Butler Yeats, brilliantly fusing them with the traditions of ancient and medieval Dravidian poetry. A MacArthur Award-winning professor of linguistics at the University of Chicago, Ramanujan translated and studied South Indian literatures, garnering Western and Eastern recognition for these and other neglected, non-Sanskrit traditions of India. Resisting the "monism" and even "cultural imperialism" of proponents of a single "pan-Indian Sanskritic Great Tradition," Ramanujan reaffirmed that "cultural traditions in India are indissolubly plural and often conflicting"

> RAMANUJAN DECOMMODIFIES AND INDIANIZES THE CONFINED WATERFALL IN AN AMERICAN BANK, PUTTING METAPHOR TO WORK IN A KIND OF REVERSE COLONIZATION."

("Where Mirrors Are Windows" 188–89). "India does not have one past," he emphasized, "but many pasts" ("Classics" 135). Best known in the West for his crystalline translations of classical and medieval Tamil and Kannada verse, Ramanujan draws on many features of these older literatures in his own Anglophone poetry: the strikingly vivid and structural use of metaphor, the intensification of one image by another, "montage" and "dissolve" effects, streams of association, flowing syntax, spare diction, avoidance of heavily stressed rhythms, delight in irony and paradox, precise observation of both interior (*puram*) and exterior (*akam*) worlds, and reliance not on metaphysical abstraction but physical detail for complex thinking (Afterword 246, 287).

As translator of classical Dravidian poetry, Ramanujan renders its forceful metaphors into contemporary English, using them in turn as models for his own Anglophone poetics. His indigenous models complement Anglomodernist principles of concision, economy, and nondecorative use of metaphor, as seen in an example of ancient Tamil poetry that almost seems proto-imagist:

> The bare root of the bean is pink
> like the leg of a jungle hen,
> and herds of deer attack its overripe pods.

In Ramanujan's translation, the metaphor of the exposed root—emphatically visible and vulnerable—superimposes hen leg on bean root, hybridizing vegetable and animal, color and taste, autochthony and mobility. Considering the broad contours of Ramanujan's career, one might speculate that this Tamil metaphor of a root that mutates into a mode of transportation may have held his interest for other reasons as well. Though rooted in South Indian Brahman culture since his birth in Mysore in 1929, Ramanujan lived from 1959 in the United States, wrote primarily in English, drew on modern Anglo-American poetry, and criticized Sanskrit-based Indology, Hindu zealotry, and Indian revivalism. Conversely, though an English-language poet in the United States, he devoted his life to South Asian studies, wrote primarily about India, drew inspiration from Dravidian literatures, and often seemed clinically detached from the English language he worked in. On this last point, R. Parthasarathy notes that Ramanujan's use of English "has a cold, glass-like quality," as if "to turn language into an artifact" ("How It Strikes" 196). Ramanujan writes from within English yet as if outside it—a recognizably postcolonial practice that Gilles Deleuze and Felix Guattari have famously if unfortunately labeled "minor literature." Ramanujan even describes himself as split between his "'outer' forms"—"English and my disciplines (linguistics, anthropology)"—and his "'inner' forms"—his lived Indian experience and lifelong study of its cultures (qtd. in Parthasarathy, "How It Strikes" 197). Poet and translator, Ramanujan relies on both metaphor and translation to interweave his outer and inner worlds while exploring the gaps between them. Describing the translator's "several double allegiances," Ramanujan suggests that metaphor and translation function for him as closely related forms of mediation between languages, cultures, perhaps even halves of the brain (Afterword 297).

"The word *translate*, as you know," Ramanujan once commented, "is only Latin for the Greek word *metaphor*. Both mean 'carry across'" ("Classics" 136–37). As translator and scholar, Ramanujan labored to carry poetry across differences of language, time, and culture, all the while reflecting in his own English-language poetry on what is lost in translation. At the heart of Ramanujan's poetry are ironic, if plangent, meditations on transfer and loss between East and West, on survivals and disappearances between past and present. As a switchboard through which spatiotemporal differences migrate and meet, metaphor discursively locates and animates this in-betweenness. Close analysis of passages from Ramanujan's finest lyrics may help to probe in detail these and other connections between metaphor and the postcolonial. Specifically, I tease out of Ramanujan's poetry the many forms that metaphor takes in mediating postcoloniality: as contact point between one culture and another; as connective tissue of postcolonial memory; as agent of cultural reproduction; as

conduit between the postcolonial subject and its origins or endings; and as discursive incarnation of resemblances between the postcolonial self and its private, national, or transnational family.

The opening of "Waterfalls in a Bank" in *Second Sight* reflects Ramanujan's immersion in the work of translation and, more broadly, his understanding of the parallels between metaphor, intercultural translation, and intertemporal connection:

> And then one sometimes sees waterfalls
> as the ancient Tamils saw them,
> wavering snakeskins,
>
> cascades of muslin.

From Tamil into English, from ancient to contemporary, Ramanujan translates metaphors of snakeskins and muslin, which in turn "translate" waterfalls. His eye a "rainbow bubble," Ramanujan would, as he rhymes in a later poem, "see all things double"—or perhaps even quadruple, as with this waterfall ("Mythologies 2," *Collected Poems* 226). Beholding stereoscopically a man-made waterfall in a Chicago bank, Ramanujan's vision is split metaphorically between waterfall and snakeskin/muslin. This metaphorical juncture straddles, in turn, the "postcolonial" junctures of India and the United States, old Tamil texts and his own emergent writing. To see through the prism of postcoloniality, with its fusion of alien perspectives, is already to possess something akin to the double vision of metaphor. Ramanujan decommodifies and Indianizes the confined waterfall in an American bank, putting metaphor to work in a kind of reverse colonization. The ancient Indian vehicles of snakeskin and muslin paradoxically enliven with danger and wonder an image hackneyed in Western poetry.

Summoning the multiple relations of resemblance in nature (American and Tamil waterfalls), culture (the U.S. and India), and time (ancient and contemporary), Ramanujan compares such metaphorical "transactions between contexts" to money exchanged in a bank:

> As I transact with the past as with another
> country with its own customs, currency,
> stock exchange, always
>
> at a loss when I count my change . . .

In exchanges between past and present as well as one culture and another, one is transformed by the transaction; here, the poet is punningly "at a loss" to understand his profound "change," both impoverished and enriched by his submission to an alien economy. In a later essay, Ramanujan again compares the mutually transformative experience of cross-temporal encounter with the anthropological experience of cross-cultural encounter: "The past is another country, as the saying goes. With the past, too, one adds oneself to it as one studies it. One is changed by it and the past itself is changed by one's study of it" ("Classics" 132). Postcolonial quester after origins, Ramanujan nevertheless represents the cultural past as irrecuperable and unknowable in and of itself, unlike the static past of the revivalist. In "Waterfalls in a Bank," as in other poems by Ramanujan and indeed other postcolonial writers, metaphor is a primary conceptual and linguistic site of both intercultural and intertemporal exchange. As in Ramanujan's not-just-financial bank, it is a place where diverse perspectives, cultures, and temporalities come together to be transacted, transposed, compared, and defamiliarized.

In the climactic scene of "Waterfalls in a Bank," Ramanujan again metaphorically bridges the distances between past and present, East and West. Standing in a Western financial institution, the Brahman poet remembers from his childhood the mirror image of what he might have become—a Brahman mendicant ascetic. Rheumatoid, diseased, spasmodic, the sadhu lifts his loincloth with one finger and "pisses" on two flowers beside the street. The modern West commingles with the ancient East in the metaphorical blending of the bank's waterfall with the sadhu's "stream" of urine. But the most remarkable transfusion of cultural opposites occurs when "a car turns the corner," illuminating the sadhu's urination:

> Headlights make his arc
>
> a trajectory of yellow diamonds,
> scared instant rainbows, ejecting spurts
> of crystal, shocked
>
> by the commonplace cruelty of headlights.

This startling confluence of Western modernity and an ancient Eastern way of life produces an epiphanic moment, when—to speak a little grandly of an old man's urination—both liquid and light seem transfigured into something beyond themselves, beyond either East or West, precolonial or postcolonial. A luminous "exchange of contexts," this climactic image figures in part Ramanujan's own poetry: a humble world lit up by poetic form, an ancient sensibility startled by its encounter with

modernity, a traditional Brahman past metamorphosed by the onset of the Western present—in short, a metaphor-making poesis that hybridizes and transfigures its cultural sources. Having begun in metaphoric transactions between old Tamil metaphors and a waterfall in a Chicago bank, Ramanujan's poem culminates in the creation of a new metaphor for the postcolonial experience of living in twin temporalities, seemingly unrelated, surely unintegrated, yet suddenly bridged, breached, and transfused by unpredictable moments of resemblance . . .

The imaginative relations between oneself and one's ending, oneself and one's beginning are, as we have seen in Ramanujan's poetry, crucially dependent on metaphor—on linguistic bridges that both traverse and mark the gaps between past, present, and future. As indicated by Ramanujan's metaphoric crossings between different tenses of his existence, the dislocation and relationality that metaphor metaphorizes as spatial are also temporal. The lyric subject constructs itself partly out of the resemblances between itself and the otherness of its bodily, psychic, and cultural pasts, partly out of the resemblances between itself and the otherness of its possible destinies—its imaginary afterlives in the bodies, works, and minds of the future. Crossings between now and then, here and there, one body and another are in turn isomorphic, as Ramanujan's poetic metaphors have shown, with passages between one's own culture and others . . .

Thus his use of metaphor benefits from being understood within the context of the doubleness and displacement, the hybridity and interstitiality usually associated with postcoloniality. So too, his postcoloniality is best explored through the prism of metaphor, the complex rhetorical site of resemblance and "double vision" in his poetry. While vigorously practicing a metaphoric poetics, Ramanujan also shines a light throughout his poetry on what metaphor leaps across—gaps in time and place, differences of culture and history. The postcolonial experience helps to explain not only Ramanujan's exuberant use of metaphor but also his ironic awareness of the edges and differences crossed by metaphor, as we have seen in his poignant fingering of the fissures that separate him from his origins and endings—from other times, other places, other traditions, even other members of his extended family. Ramanujan's agility in fusing passionate attachment to metaphor with trenchant skepticism, rainbow-eyed postcolonialism with postcolonial irony, positions him to be read in coming decades as one of the leading poets of the postcolonial world. As the field of postcolonial studies attends to the significant interrelations between metaphor and postcoloniality, perhaps it will begin to grant Ramanujan and other Anglophone poets like Goodison, p'Bitek, and Brathwaite, Wole Soyinka and Agha Shahid Ali the close literary analysis that their work richly rewards.

Source: Jahan Ramazani, "Metaphor and Postcoloniality: The Poetry of A. K. Ramanujan," in *Contemporary Literature*, Vol. 39, No. 1, Spring 1998, pp. 27–53.

SOURCES

King, Bruce, *Three Indian Poets: Nissim Ezekiel, A. K. Ramanujan, Dom Moraes*, Oxford University Press, 1991, pp. 101–02.

Kulshrestha, Chirantan, "Interview," in *The Oxford India Ramanujan*, edited by Molly Daniels-Ramanujan, Oxford University Press, 2004, unpaginated.

Ramanujan, A. K., "Waterfalls in a Bank," in *The Oxford India Ramanujan*, edited by Molly Daniels-Ramanujan, Oxford University Press, 2004, pp. 189–91.

Ramazani, Jahan, "Metaphor and Postcoloniality: The Poetry of A. K. Ramanujan," in *Contemporary Literature*, Vol. 39, No. 1, Spring 1998, p. 36.

Singh, Sukhbir, "A. K. Ramanujan," in *Dictionary of Literary Biography*, Vol. 323, *South Asian Writers in English*, edited by Fakrul Alam, Thomson Gale, 2006. pp. 285–95.

Webster, W. F., ed., *Rig-Veda Sanhita: A Collection of Hindu Hymns of the Rig-Veda*, Vol. VII, translated from the original Sanskrit by H.H. Wilson, Cosmo Publications, 1977, p. 1.

FURTHER READING

Dwivedi, A. N., *A. K. Ramanujan and His Poetry*, Doaba House, 1983.

Dwivedi analyzes Ramanujan's poetry in terms of theme, form, imagery, versification, the Indian-ness of his work, his modernity, and his place in contemporary Indo-English poetry. This book was published before the appearance of "Waterfalls in a Bank."

Kurup, P. K. J., *Contemporary Indian Poetry in English: With Special Reference to the Poetry of Nissim Ezekiel, Kamala Das, A. K. Ramanujan, and R. Parthasarathy*, Atlantic, 1991.

In his chapter on Ramanujan, Kurup praises the poet for having cultivated a unique personal idiom.

Mehrotra, Arvind Krishna, *A History of Indian Literature in English*, Columbia University Press, 2003.

This is essential reading for anyone who requires a comprehensive history of Indian writing in English. Covering a period from 1800 to the present, this collection of essays examines the work of the canonical Indian poets, novelists, and dramatists writing in English—such as Rudyard Kipling, Rabindranath Tagore, R. K. Narayan, and Salman Rushdie—as well as lesser-known literary figures who have made significant contributions to the evolution of Indian literature in English. One essay is devoted to the work of Ramanujan. The book includes 150 rare photographs and sketches of writers and their contexts.

Pandey, Birendram, ed., *Indian Poetry in English*, Atlantic, 2001.

This book contains twenty essays on the most significant works of the leading contemporary Indian poets writing in English. The poets discussed include Ramanujan, Daruwalla, K. R. S. Iyengar, Niranjan Mohanty, S. N. Tripathi, P. Raja, Vikram Seth, R. N. Sinha, D. H. Kabadi, Aurobindo, T. Basudeo Reddy and O. P. Bhatnagar.

Ramazani, Jahan, *The Hybrid Muse: Postcolonial Poetry in English*, University of Chicago Press, 2001.

Ramazani argues that postcolonial poets from Africa, India and the Caribbean have expanded the range of literature in English, infusing modern and contemporary poetry with indigenous metaphors. He also considers postcolonial poets of Ireland. Ramanujan is among the poets discussed, as well as W. B. Yeats, Derek Walcott, Louise Bennett, and Okot p'Bitek.

Yet we insist that life is full of happy chance

LYN HEJINIAN

1980

In the early 2000s, Lyn Hejinian's "Yet we insist that life is full of happy chance" appeared destined to remain a work in progress. The original version of the poem (and the one reprinted here) was first included in Hejinian's collection *My Life* (1980), which was composed of thirty-seven sections, each comprised of thirty- seven sentences. When she first wrote it in 1978, Hejinian planned to write an autobiographical poem in a form that corresponded to her age (thirty-seven). But as time passes, the numerical markers of a person's age increase, and in 1987, Hejinian released a revised edition of the original poems, expanded to reflect the fact that she was then eight years older. Just as Hejinian's life had lengthened to included forty-five years, so, too, did the collection, now expanded to forty-five sections, containing the original poems, each with eight new lines. Later, Hejinian published a number of independent sections that suggest a continuation of *My Life* to include memories of the 1990s.

Taken together the verse paragraphs arrange Lyn Hejinian's memories of childhood and growing up along a series of contextual threads. The first thread attempts (sometimes successfully, sometimes futilely) to relate each intimate memory to the next, providing the poem with a sense of cohesion that the poem resists in many other ways through its fragmented and discontinuous structure. The second contextual thread brings in the political and cultural background of these

personal memories, addressing the events and ideas that defined the times during which Hejinian matured as a person and a poet. The third, more theoretical thread intersects with the previous two, locating both memory and cultural ideas in relation to the philosophical issues involved in writing autobiography and the struggle to bring forward a story of a self-conscious life. "Yet we insist that life is full of happy chance" is section twenty-nine of the first edition of *My Life*.

AUTHOR BIOGRAPHY

Lyn Hejinian was born on May 17, 1941, in San Francisco, California, to Chaffee Earl Hall Jr., a high school teacher, and Carolyn Frances Erskine. She left the West Coast to earn a B.A. from Harvard University in 1963 then returned to the Bay Area at the age of twenty-seven and immediately became involved in the arts, specifically poetry. Her first prose pamphlet, *A Thought Is the Bride of What Thinking*, was published in 1976. This work reveals a poet's determination to challenge word usage and reorder syntax. The writing urges readers past the familiar into questions about the nature of art and language. The prolific Hejinian is best known for her book-length prose poem, *My Life* (1980, 1987), in which "Yet we insist that life is fully of happy chance" appears.

A distinguished editor and translator as well as poet, Hejinian was involved in a number of important publishing projects, including Tuumba Press, Atelos, and the influential *Poetics Journal*, all based in Berkeley. Her work in these areas received recognition: she received grants from the National Endowment of the Arts for editorial projects (1978, 1979, and 1986) and for her work as a translator (1988). She was also awarded three editor grants from the California Arts Council.

Hejinian's teaching career was extensive and diverse, including positions at the California College of Arts and Crafts (Oakland), in the poetics program at the New College of California (San Francisco), and as an adjunct faculty member at the University of California at Berkeley. She also served as a visiting or guest lecturer at such prestigious writing programs as the Naropa Institute in Boulder, Colorado and the Iowa Writers' Workshop.

In August 1989, Hejinian, along with Language poets Michael Davidson, Ron Silliman, and Barrett Watten, traveled to the then Soviet city of Leningrad at the invitation of Poetic Function, a collective of experimental Russian poets. The gathering took place at a particularly important moment in world history, between the Tiananmen Square protests that ended in tragedy in June and the fall of the Berlin Wall in November of that same year. This meeting came to be seen in many ways as the perfect example of the Language movement, merging poetry, poetics, and politics in a global context previously unrealized. As a result of the meeting, the four American poets published a long collaborative poem called *Leningrad: American Writers in the Soviet Union* (1991).

Hejinian's first marriage, to John Hejinian, ended in a 1972 divorce. She married composer and musician Larry Ochs in 1977, and as of 2007, the couple continued to live and teach in Berkeley, California.

POEM TEXT

The windows were open and the morning air was, by the smell of lilac and some darker flowering shrub, filled with the brown and chirping trills of birds. As they are if you could have nothing but quiet and shouting. Arts, also, are links. I picture an idea at the moment I come to it, our collision. Once, for a time, anyone might have been luck's child. Even rain didn't spoil the barbecue, in the backyard behind a polished traffic, through a landscape, along a shore. Freedom then, liberation later. She came to babysit for us in those troubled years directly from the riots, and she said that she dreamed of the day when she would gun down everyone in the financial district. That single telephone is only one hair on the brontosaurus. The coffee drinkers answered ecstatically. If your dog stays out of the room, you get the fleas. In the lull, activity drops. I'm seldom in my dreams without my children. In the distance, down the street, the practicing soprano belts the breeze. As for we who "love to be astonished," money makes money, luck makes luck. Moves forward, drives on. It was the present time for a little while, and not so new as we thought then, the present always after war. Ever since it has been hard for me to share my time. The yellow of that sad room was again the yellow of naps, where she waited, restless, faithless, for more day. Reason looks for two, then arranges it from there. But can one imagine a madman in love. Goodbye; enough that was good. There was a pause, a rose, something on paper. Because desire is always embarrassing. At the beach, with a fresh flush. The child looks out. At a distance, the sun *is* small. There was no proper Christmas after he died. That triumphant blizzard had brought the city to its knees. I am a stranger to the little girl I was, and more—more strange. One sits in a cloven space. Patterns promote an outward likeness, between little white silences. The big trees catch all the moisture from what seems like a dry night. Reflections don't make shade, but shadows are, and do. In order to understand the nature of the collision, one must know something of the nature of the motions involved—that is, a history. He looked at me and smiled and did not look away, and thus a friendship became erotic. Luck was rid of its clover.

POEM SUMMARY

The first two sentences of "Yet we insist that life is full of happy chance" describe open windows, an image of separation and contact. Closed windows symbolize distance and the division between inner and outer worlds. Thrown open, as they are in this poem, windows are thresholds that invite crossing over from one side to the other. These sentences describe the air, scent, and sound that come in through the windows.

The third and fourth sentences of the poem point to other moments of merging, or what Hejinian calls "collisions." "Arts," including writing or reading poetry, create mental thresholds. The act of thinking brings a picture to mind, a "collision" of the image as it forms in thought.

From this point forward, the poem weaves together images that draw from private memories, which give abbreviated glimpses into the past or into fragments about the past. One memory is of a babysitter whose views on recent riots are anything but reassuring, of the absence of "a proper Christmas" after a loved one has died, and the shift when a friendship becomes erotic. These memories create the fragments of the story of a life.

Other sentences seem to refer to the political context, as in "Freedom then, liberation later" and "Reason looks for two, then arranges it from there." These sentences are disconnected from and influence the shape of memories that weave through the paragraph. As a person reads the poem, the political backdrop blends almost like the immediate lilac scent.

The third, more complex thread that runs through the poem pertains to Hejinian's interrogation of the structures of language and the capacity of language to capture the complexities of an individual life. The sentence, "That single telephone is only one hair on the brontosaurus," for instance, conjoins two objects, the telephone and the hair, which are completely unrelated. The effect is surreal and nonsensical. The expectation of order and sense in syntax is totally frustrated.

But Hejinian explains there is a method to the apparent randomness: "In order to understand the nature of the collision," the speaker proposes, "one must know something of the nature of the motions involved—that is, a history." Considering the poem in the light of this assertion allows the reader to recognize how "Yet we insist that life is full of happy chance" treats collisions as symbols that refuse to be organized by usual logic and grammatical structure. The history of this life includes randomness and incongruities. These unlinked parts collide with a tradition of poetry and autobiography that favors organized patterns and linear progressions over randomness.

THEMES

Expectations in Reading Poetry

Hejinian does not write in the way readers of poetry may expect. She does not use conventional syntax and grammar. She uses fragments and jumps around. Moreover the text looks and reads more like prose than poetry. The poem is surprisingly complex in form and content, quite unlike conventional lyric poetry, which has familiar images, themes, and form. The readers' task is to sense meaning in the illogic of the poem and to make meaning out of what seems illogical, even meaningless. Hejinian's use of head notes is an example of this illogic.

The head notes are dividers between poems and sections of *My Life*, but they also illustrate how the work does not comply with convention. What the head note means is unclear. It is italicized and located near the left margin. The way it is printed is confusing: it may be a summary, a quotation from the body of the text, or a marginal remark on the text.

Another complication lies in the fact that the titles of almost all of the thirty-seven (or

TOPICS FOR FURTHER STUDY

- Write a prose poem diary covering a week in your life. Include fragments and various seemingly unrelated topics, which when taken together present a collage of the seven days.

- Study the subject of memory. Write an essay in which you describe a time when the immediate circumstances caused you to remember something you had not thought about for a long time. Reflect on whether your memory has remained the same through time or is different now than it was in the past.

- Make a poster on which you arrange as a broken narrative or story various words and images cut from magazines that were intended to be taken as a whole. Present your poster to your class and have students analyze it and offer different readings of it.

- In a small group, select four subjects that are loosely related and have individuals write ten sentence fragments on slips of paper that pertain to these subjects in some way. Put the slips of paper all together. Then as a group, decide how to use these fragments to write a prose poem in the manner of the Language poets.

---

forty-five) prose segments reappear as a sentence or part of a sentence in another prose poem in the collection. The words, "Yet we insist that life is full of happy chance," for example, appear in section thirty-four ("One begins as a student but becomes a friend of clouds") with some variation: "Yet he insisted that his life had been full of happy chance, that he was luck's child." For readers approaching the expanded version of the poem, the complication is more daunting. In the later version, for instance, the head note to poem sixteen appears in various reformations in five later sections. As Paul Naylor points out in his *Poetic Investigations: Singing the Holes of History* (1999), by the time

attentive readers conclude the expanded version of *My Life*, they may see that, "in fact, eight of the forty-five sentences in section 16 appear [in earlier poems] as epigraphs."

On the one hand, Hejinian's head notes reassure readers entering her collection that they are in well marked surroundings. The notes serve as textual signposts, guiding readers through the maze of seemingly disjoined and disconnected sections of the poem. In this sense, the head notes take on the traditional position of authoritative guide to the poem, marking "Yet we insist that life is full of happy chance" as a poem that explores both the fullness (often to overflowing) of life as well as the often serendipitous brilliance of the seemingly ordered existence of the life each individual inhabits. On the other hand, Hejinian's head notes transform into content in other poems, blurring the distinction between title and text and suggesting in this way another form of interlaced connection.

The Nature of Memory

In *My Life* in total and in "Yet we insist that life is full of happy chance" as a representative part, Hejinian intends to show both visually and linguistically how language constructs memory. The thoughts become mental images which then are transformed into words. The language that holds the image packages the past as memory. Spoken or unspoken, written down or not, the language forms an individual's sense of the autobiographical past.

To understand a life requires understanding both the process of building memories and the limits in that process. The poems in *My Life* are devoted to demystifying the sanctity of memory by exposing the constructed nature of memory. Through repetition, through using words ambiguously and with multiple meanings, and leaving the text (and the life) open-ended or fragmented, Hejinian prevents any single idea or single remembered moment from serving as a focal point. Memories of adolescent moments juxtapose with incongruous moments from later life or early childhood, fact blends with fiction, and fragment brushes elegantly with fragment, allowing memory to emerge as a montage rather than an unbroken line.

Attempting to fix a memory on a page (through text or a photograph, for instance) is an inevitably frustrating exercise. Then, too, as "Yet we insist that life is full of happy chance" suggests, readers and writers negotiate gaps in their own memory, engaging in a selective process that mixes up bits of truth and fiction. It is a "happy chance" but a rare one, the poem suggests, when a past event is retrieved and shaped through various times of remembering and retelling.

STYLE

Prose

My Life is an extended prose poem, which means that it is written and printed as prose rather than as poetry, with a standard right margin, familiar sentence form, and customary patterns of punctuation and syntax. It is actually a hybrid of forms (poetry combined with prose), which often leaves booksellers and librarians unsure about how to catalogue it; *My Life* may be found filed as a novel, as short fiction, as poetry (with no indication of its unique form), or as autobiography. Clearly, *My Life* is a work that resists classification.

Written in a prose that has the usual attributes of poetry, including careful attention to sound (rhyme and rhythm), imagery, and figurative language (similes and metaphors), *My Life* creates tension between poetic strategies and prose structures. Dating as far back as the book of Psalms and renovated most influentially in the writing of the expatriate American writer Gertrude Stein (1874–1946), prose poems blend the power of clarity commonly associated with prose and the complexity of language and emotion commonly associated with lyric poetry.

The prose frame makes such a poem as "Yet we insist that life is full of happy chance" a relatively accessible example of experimental poetry. Taken individually, many of the sentences deliver clear, albeit sometimes surprising or disturbing messages. For example, the sentence, "She came to babysit for us in those troubled years directly from the riots, and she said that she dreamed of the day when she would gun down everyone in the financial district," has a familiar sentence structure. The meaning of the sentence is clear as is its familiar grammar and syntax.

But closer examination of this sentence uncovers some incongruities. There is, for instance, the disorienting juxtaposition of the familiar and domestic act of babysitting (with its connotations of security and calm) with the

violence and chaos of "riots" as well as the implications of a babysitter who dreams of "gun[ning] down" innocent people. Domesticity and revolution collide in this sentence. The word "from" in this sentence seems at once in place and out of place. One might expect a word indicating time (before or after the riots), but Hejinian slips in this preposition that suggests a source or a cause. The "troubled years" are no longer separated syntactically from the implications of "the riots" but are instead connected to them. No longer isolated in time as an aberration in an otherwise peaceful culture, the riots are positioned as the source or the beginning of a series of years that are now seen as "troubled." The tone and meaning of this sentence is suddenly dislocated from the familiarity of its own syntax just as the image of the babysitter is dramatically relocated to a world of riots and violent dreams.

"Yet we insist that life is full of happy chance" stretches and fragments syntax and even sentence form itself (the basic unit of prose). The often repeated sentence, "There was a pause, a rose, something on paper" is metaphoric while such a fragment as "Moves forward, drives on" fractures the logic found in a complete sentence. Facing the fragments of the poem, readers sense that these poems create a kind of linguistic friction: fragments of prose rub and bump against each other in order to create a prose that is not prose but poetry, in which meaning comes through gaps as well as through the images.

Repetition

In the opening poem of *My Life*, Hejinian states that "repetitions, [are] free from all ambition," an idea that serves as a mantra for the poem as it unfolds. *My Life* privileges the creative energies of repetition, especially because it is antithetical to the linear trajectory of a traditional autobiography. Certain key phrases, like the frequent line, "There was a pause, a rose, something on paper," appear throughout the sections of the book. But whereas in conventional poetry these repetitions would be given metaphoric or symbolic significance, Hejinian seems to insert them randomly, in unexpected and, at times, incongruous ways. Key words, most noticeably "history," also recur in numerous sections. At other times, words are used as both nouns and verbs within the same section.

Repetition serves a number of purposes within each poem and throughout the collection.

Thematically, repetition underscores both the individuality of each occurrence of a word or phrase (defined by its context) and the connection of each occurrence to the broader pattern of the poem.

With key words, phrases, and images repeating in the new context of subsequent sections, Hejinian shows how the meanings of words are not fixed and how words acquire meaning from their context and the position they have in the grammar of that context. Thus the relationship between a word and its context shapes the word's meaning. The shifting terrain of a given word or phrase reminds the reader of the multiple possibilities of meaning and the impossibility of settling one word into a single fixed slot within the text.

HISTORICAL CONTEXT

L = A = N = G = U = A = G = E Poetry

L = A = N = G = U = A = G = E poetry, sometimes printed in this way after the style of the journal that took this word as its title, is the name given to the poetry written by a loosely organized group of avant-garde poets that emerged in New York and San Francisco in the early 1970s. Prominent members of the group include Hejinian, Charles Bernstein, Bruce Andrews, Ron Silliman, and Steve McCaffery. The group published their poetry most often in the pages of the journal L = A = N = G = U = A = G = E, which appeared in the late seventies. The goal of the journal was to raise questions about the relationship between language, reality, and culture.

The Language poets, as they also came to be known, made broad claims about what their experimental poetry could accomplish. Their works inquired into the relationship between poetry and political activism and social justice. Language poetry, as they understood it, was a social enterprise that made demands on readers to think about what they read and how they read. Indeed, Language poetry made reading itself a political activity that could either support or challenge the policies and practices of governments and other powerful organizations.

To the Language poets, the personal writing that had come to define the lyric poetry of the 1950s and 1960s was naïve. Lyric poetry, they argued, failed to acknowledge the power of language to shape the way that individuals express private thoughts as well as the way that readers understand text. Language poets set out to make language strange and incomprehensible to draw attention to the assumptions readers have about words, poetry, and the world itself. The poem becomes an unstable and shifting ground of word play, diverse styles, and a mix of familiar and strange sentences and ideas that force the reader to make sense of what defies logic.

Each poem becomes a new opportunity to try out words and to put words in new combinations, some of which might be rhythmic and beautiful, and others that might be less so. But what the poem sounds like, looks like, or means is not the main focus of the Language poet. The aim is to create a dissonance in language that disrupts reliance on conventions of about writing and causes ideas to be seen in a new way.

The 1970s

In North America, the arrival of the 1970s signaled a number of important shifts in attitudes and politics that helped energize Lyn Hejinian's poetry. The decade marked a shift away from the social activism and protests that defined the 1960s, with the exception of environmental concerns which actually rose in public attention through the seventies. Replacing social activism as the 1970s unfolded was an emphasis on gathering experiences for pleasure and personal gain. It was this shift from the social to the personal that the Language poets reacted against as they worked to make social justice and broad social issues a focal point of their poetry. Hejinian, for instance, blends references to riots and violence in the financial district into a poem that is ostensibly the story of a woman's life.

In emphasizing the social consciousness of poetry, the Language poets echoed a trend that was to define another medium that continued to rise to prominence during the seventies: television. The seventies saw Norman Lear's groundbreaking weekly show *All in the Family*, which brought socially relevant issues to a diverse, mainstream audience. When the series premiered in 1971, American audiences heard words that had never been heard on television before, especially words relating to sexuality, race, class, and political attitudes. In the same ways that the Language poets set out to make familiar language strange, *All in the Family* made popular assumptions about society openly strange and in some instances uncomfortably so.

Another issue that defined the 1970s was the oppressive economic recession that took hold of North America. The decade saw a potent combination of low output, rising unemployment, and dramatic increases in consumer products that came to be known as *stagflation*, a compound word that joined the terms *stagnation* and *inflation*. As Hejinian makes clear in "Yet we insist that life is full of happy chance," the seventies was a decade that placed a keen emphasis on the workings of the financial district. It was, as she suggests, an era in which the saying "money makes money" became the mantra of a generation.

CRITICAL OVERVIEW

My Life is often praised by reviewers as an exciting experiment in both poetry and autobiography. As Nancy R. Ives wrote in the *Library Journal*, *My Life* is a collection of poems that "captures experience in discrete, brilliant bits of imagery and sound." "The result," Ives concludes, "is an intriguing journey that both illuminates and perplexes, teases and challenges, as it reveals an innovative artist at work." Giving readers permission to glance into "the lives of women who write," *My Life* is especially appealing "to those interested in the avant-garde and the unusual."

Looking at Hejinian's *Happily* but in the process describing Hejinian's work as a whole, Danielle Dutton notes how Hejinian explores such themes as "happiness, time, fate, logic, birth ... in run-on lines and paragraphs ... that often seem only peripherally related to one another." Informing Hejinian's explorations, Dutton explains, is a sensitivity that allows her to write "from a specific domestic spot and with a keen awareness" of what Dutton describes as "the activeness of things." Hejinian uses her poetry to show that "everything is dynamic and exists in relation to everything else." Dutton also applauds Hejinian's commitment to a poetic structure that it is at once intimate and public, creative and theoretical. Hejinian's collections create "an act of reading for the reader, a rhythmic temporal experience, like the duration of a day, film, or piece of music, all of which begin and end while maintaining the inherent possibility/assurance of beginning again."

A reviewer for *Publishers Weekly* suggests that *My Life* has definitely had an impact on American poetry. Described as "an urtext of language poetry," it has "found its way onto countless contemporary poetry and women's studies syllabi, as well as the bookshelves of poets and other readers, for the complex transparency of its thought and the beauty of its language." This reviewer's forecast is equally positive: Any reader or bookseller "with limited poetry sections" must recognize *My Life* as an "essential" inclusion on the shelves.

CRITICISM

Klay Dyer

Dyer holds a Ph.D. in English literature and has published extensively on fiction, poetry, film, and television. He is also a freelance university teacher, writer, and educational consultant. In this essay, he discusses Hejinian's "Yet we insist that life is full of happy chance" as part of a broader project to reenergize the autobiographical tradition in contemporary culture.

Lyn Hejinian's *My Life* is, as its title promises, a collection that takes as its focus the story of a life, or in this case an autobiography in which a speaker recounts her memories of her own past. A compound word, autobiography brings together three Greek words: *auton* (self), *bios* (life), and *graphein* (write). It is important to distinguish, as Hejinian does, autobiography from the closely related but distinct term: memoir. Traditionally, an autobiography focuses on the details of a life as they come to relate to the context of the living of that life. It is, in other words, a recounting of the life *and* the times of the person writing the autobiography. Henry David Thoreau's *Walden* (1854), Harriet Jacobs's *Incidents in the Life of a Slave Girl* (1861), and Malcolm X's *The Autobiography of Malcolm X* are important examples of North American autobiographies. A memoir is written differently; it may include content fitted to a certain theme or subject without accounting for the whole life from birth on, or it may be an account of witnessing an historic event, omitting autobiographical parts not relevant to the chosen historic subject. Memoir may focus more on the emotions invested in certain memories than on the facts that define those events.

With the classical understanding of the term autobiography in mind, two more criteria are important for readers to remember. The first is

WHAT DO I READ NEXT?

- Interested readers may enjoy Hejinian's 1978 work, *Writing Is an Aid to Memory*. In this book, Hejinian sees memory as a way of understanding the past and creating the future.

- Robert Kroetsch's 2001 fictional work, *The Hornbooks of Rita K*, tells the story of the life and disappearance of the fictional poet Rita Kleinhart, who at age fifty-five was last seen in the Museum of Modern Art in Frankfurt on June 26, 1992. All that remains of Rita are mounds of poems: finished, unfinished, and unfinishable. As her intimate friend Raymond sorts through the papers in her abandoned ranch house, the fragments gather together into a mystery, a romance, and a primer on the wonders of language.

- Bruce Andrews and Charles Bernstein edited *The L=A=N=G=U=A=G=E Book: Poetics of the New* in 1984, an essential guide to the politics and practices of this experimental group of poets.

- Readers more interested in a scholarly analysis of how long poems make their meaning will find Brian McHale's *The Obligation toward the Difficult Whole: Postmodernist Long Poems* (2004) a valuable resource.

---

that autobiography is generally assumed to be nonfiction, a type of writing in which actual events are presented in logical arrangement. In autobiography, this shape usually follows a chronology that begins in childhood, continues through adolescence, and concludes somewhere in adulthood. This logical structure is matched in autobiography by a text that respects the facts and is accurate in its representation of characters. While an autobiography is not a work of fiction, it does allow some leeway when dealing with people's memories, recalled dreams, or

> THESE POEMS FOCUS ON THE PROCESS OF A LIFE UNFOLDING RATHER THAN ON THE PRODUCT THAT A LIFE BECOMES."

---

fears. The second criterion added to the basic definition of autobiography is one that is often left unspoken or implied in the writing of the life story. Autobiography assumes that the life story being told has some significant social message or moral lesson to bring to the reader. In some autobiographical writing, such as *The Diary of Anne Frank* (1947), the power of the message becomes the defining characteristic of the writing.

Of course, keeping autobiography and memoir apart is difficult exercise, and one that often fails when put to a formal test. William Wordsworth's famous poem *The Prelude or, Growth of a Poet's Mind* (published in 1850), for instance, is an important autobiographical poem, but there are many passages in the work that incorporate the emotional intimacy of memoir. Hejinian picks up on this tradition of fusing autobiography and memoir in *My Life*, grounding her poetry in a kind of mistrust of the tools available to a traditional autobiographical writer. Determined to tell her life story, Hejinian explores the form and structure of autobiography as well as the language that is traditionally used in the telling of the life story. A challenge to the conventions and structures of autobiographical writing, *My Life* is a collection of prose poems that resist the impulse to give a cohesive shape to a life that might be used to entertain and educate a reader. In fact, the poems that constitute *My Life* attempt to show readers new ways to approach life stories as they unfold across the page.

In *My Life*, Hejinian challenges the traditional structure of the autobiographical story. Rather than a unified, chronological prose narrative, she develops a kind of hybrid, or mixing, of prose *and* poetry as her form of choice. It is a rewarding mixture. On the one hand, the prose aspects of *My Life* provide readers with a sense of familiarity when approaching this book. The opening sentence of "Yet we insist that life is full of happy chance," for instance, works neatly to establish a scene or a setting that most readers can imagine: "The windows were open and the morning air was, by the smell of lilac and some darker flowering shrub, filled with the brown and chirping trills of birds." This is not a world totally unfamiliar to the reader, who can recall with some clarity of their own the feeling of a spring morning air and perhaps even the morning sounds of birds outside the window.

My Life also delivers a familiar blend of life *and* times. The poems situate memories in relation to "those troubled years directly from the riots" and in terms of many of the persistent concerns of contemporary culture: "freedom," art, money, friendship, and sex. There is also a glimpse at the darker side of this culture within which a life has been lived. "Yet we insist that life is full of happy chance" bristles with the possibilities of violence, war, the discomfort of "white silences," and madness. This is not an autobiography that hides the dark side of either the life itself or the times in which that life continues to unfold.

But at the same time, Hejinian's life story is unfamiliar territory for readers expecting a traditional autobiographical structure. The more emotional aspects of the story are handled more poetically. Hejinian introduces emotion into the life story with sentences or phrases of poetry that are so concise and imaginative that they are difficult to understand. Such lines as "That single telephone is only one hair on the brontosaurus" or "There was a pause, a rose, something on paper" mystify the reader. Equally unclear is how each emotional bit of poetry relates to the more familiar prose sentences. In one sense, this is a poem in which the expected clarity and order of ideas are pushed aside to make way for word play and illogical juxtapositions. But the questions still remain. How does the brontosaurus relate to the morning air of the opening line, for instance? What does the love of a madman have to do with a childhood memory of a backyard barbecue? Readers expect connections but do not find them.

So what is the social message or moral lesson of Hejinian's autobiographical *My Life*? This life story teaches readers that the telling of a life story, like the living of a life, is complicated. This autobiography shows the life to be a porous and multifaceted accumulation of ideas, memories, and emotions. Life in this poem is a place in which the unexpected and the unfamiliar mingle

with the known and the familiar. Blending personal memories with a kind of cultural history as well as prose with poetry, *My Life* blurs the boundaries of genres, autobiography and memoir, prose and poetry, fiction and nonfiction, and events experienced and the emotions that such experiences generate.

The story of a life, as Hejinian argues, is also a story that resists definition by one term (prose or autobiography) or another (poetry or memoir). A life is a story that resists the traditional pressures of chronology in favor of an organization that is more organic, more fragmented, and in an odd way more natural than a unified story with a beginning (childhood), a middle (adolescence), and an end (adulthood leading to death). "Yet we insist that life is full of happy chance" joins with the other poems of Hejinian's *My Life* to challenge the idea of a life *line* as an ordered and logical way to understand a life story. Instead these poems offer through metaphor a fluid movement across time (past to present) and space (place to place). These poems embrace the multiplicities and chances that might be seen elsewhere as hindering an organized life lived with a purpose. These poems focus on the process of a life unfolding rather than on the product that a life becomes.

This is not to suggest that "Yet we insist that life is full of happy chance" is void of the relevant facts and personal intimacies that distinguish an autobiographical text. The recognitions that "I am a stranger to the little girl I was" or that "I'm seldom in my dreams without my children" provide intimate glimpses into a woman's life. At the same time, this poem reaches into the life of every reader, inviting each reader to think about such big ideas as "arts, also, are links" and "reflections don't make shade, but shadows are, and do." These poems ask the reader to think about how these ideas might apply to one's own life and one's own stories. Art and emotion, shadow and light, private and public all come together in this poem to represent to the reader the densities of a life lived fully.

Source: Klay Dyer, Critical Essay on "Yet we insist that life is full of happy chance," in *Poetry for Students*, Gale, 2008.

Lyn Hejinian

In the following essay, Hejinian articulates her sense of what poetry does and how poetry relates to the social and subjective context in which it

THE CONTEXT, IN OTHER WORDS, IS THE MEDIUM OF OUR ENCOUNTER, THE GROUND OF OUR BECOMING (I.E., HAPPENING TO BE) PRESENT AT THE SAME PLACE AT THE SAME TIME."

occurs. She argues that nothing happens out of context, and only by exploring the context of any event does one uncover its meaning.

1.

Poetics is not personal. A poetics gets formed in and as a relationship with the word.

Poetics is where poetry's engagement with meaning as meaningfulness gets elaborated—poetics is the site of poetry's reason—where the plurality of its logics and the viability of its contexts are tested and articulated.

A poetics considers how and what a specific poem means within itself and its own terms and how and why it means (and is meaningful) within a community that congregates around it—around it as writing in general and around certain specific writings and writing practices in particular.

I espouse a poetics of affirmation. I also espouse a poetics of uncertainty, of doubt, difficulty, and strangeness. Such a poetics is inevitably contradictory, dispersive, and incoherent while sustaining an ethos of linkage. It exhibits disconnection while hoping to accomplish reconnection.

2.

Aesthetic discovery can be congruent with social discovery. Aesthetic discovery occurs through encounters, at points of contact, and so too does political and ethical discovery.

These points of contact or linkages are the manifestation of our logics; they give evidence of our reasoning and they also serve as the sites for our reasons—our reasons to do what we do.

3.

At points of linkage, the possibility of a figure of contradiction arises: a figure we might call by a Greek name, *xenos*. *Xenos* means "stranger" or "foreigner," but more importantly, from *xenos*

two English words with what seem like opposite meanings are derived: they are *guest* and *host*.

A guest/host relationship comes into existence solely in and as an occurrence, that of their meeting, an encounter, a mutual and reciprocal contextualization. The host is no host until she has met her guest, the guest is no guest until she meets her host. In Russian the word for "occurrence" captures the dynamic character of this encounter. The word for event in Russian is *sobytie; so* (with or co-) and *bytie* (being), "being with" or "with-being" or "co-existence." Every encounter produces, even if for only the flash of an instant, a xenia—the occurrence of coexistence which is also an event of strangeness or foreignness. A strange occurrence that, nonetheless, happens constantly—we have no other experience of living than encounters. We have no other use for language than to have them.

Foreignness is different from alienation; the two notions are differently nuanced. Alienation connotes separation, detachment. Foreignness, of course, may suggest that too, in that a feeling of foreignness is a feeling of being where one doesn't belong—but where alienation involves a step back from a situation, foreignness involves a step into it. The alienated withdraws, the foreigner proceeds and becomes a guest.

4.

The guest/host encounter creates "a space of appearance"—which in classical Greek thought constitutes the polis, the place, as Hannah Arendt puts it, for "the sharing of words and deeds." Arendt continues: "The polis ... is the organization of the people as it arises out of acting and speaking together, and its true space lies between people living together for this purpose, no matter where they happen to be."

She goes on to make a further and very important point: "To be deprived of it means to be deprived of reality, which, humanly and politically speaking, is the same as appearance. To men the reality of the world is guaranteed by the presence of others, by its appearing to all; 'for what appears to all' [says Aristotle in the *Nichomachean Ethics*], 'what appears to all, this we call Being.'"

An apparent opposition arises here, between the ancient Greek political notion that reality exists in and as commonality, which in turn establishes communality versus the contemporary (though century-old) aesthetic notion that the commonplace and the habituation that occurs within it produce a dulling of reality, which it is the business of art to revitalize or revivify.

But it is a false opposition, one that is resolved within the treasuring of living, that is valued as the dearest thing in life by both ancients and moderns. We have always wanted things to be real, and we have always wanted to experience their reality since it is one with our own.

The notion that the world is common to us all is vital. We need the world—which is to say all things need all other things; we all need each other—if we are to exist as realities. As George Oppen puts it in his poem "A Narrative": "things explain each other, Not themselves."

Reality consists of all that is the world that is common to us all; and it is inextricably related to the space of appearance, the polis.

A valuable contribution to this notion of the polls is contained in Charles Altieri's character-ization of the creative ground and its citizen, the creative self: the creative ground is "a source of energy and value in the objective order that oth-erwise mocks subjective consciousness" ; the cre-ative self is one "whose activity discloses or produces aspects of that ground which have potential communal significance. Art becomes a social and cultural force and not some form of individual therapy or self-regarding indul-gence in the resources of the individual's imagination."

5.

Along comes something—launched in context.

That something is occurring means it is tak-ing place, or taking a place, in the space of appearance.

It is almost automatic to us to assume that this *something* (on the one hand) and *we* (on the other) exist independently—that *something* was independently elsewhere (out of sight and mind) prior to coming into the zone in which *we* per-ceive it and which we, at the moment of this perceptual encounter, designate as context. Furthermore, it is at the moment that we per-ceive this something that we ourselves come into that context—into our coinciding (by chance?) with something . . . The context, in other words, is the medium of our encounter, the ground of our becoming (i.e., happening to be) present at the same place at the same time. By this

reasoning, one would also have to say that con-text too is launched—or at least that it comes into existence *quâ* context when something is launched—in such a way as to become percep-tible to us and thereby to involve us—whomever we are—strangers (even if, perhaps, only momentarily strangers) to each other previously and now inseparable components of the experience.

As strangers (foreigners), it is hard for us to find the "right words" (themselves simultane-ously demanding context and serving as it) for what we experience in that perception and involvement.

Usually comparisons are the first things for-eigners make. "The dark castle on the hill is like a cormorant on a rock stretching its crooked wings in the sun" or "The pink wet light in Saint Petersburg on a winter day is like a summer San Francisco fog," etc. Such comparisons, reaching out of the present situation to another, previously experienced, recollected one, may appear to constitute the "making of a context" for the current context, but a context made in such a way is a transported one, acquired by way of metaphor. And such metaphors, cast in the form of similes and intended to smooth over differences, deny incipience, and to the degree that they succeed, they thereby forestall the acquisition of history.

But the phrase or sentence "Along comes something—launched in context" announces a moment of incipience; one could even say that it is itself, as a phrase or utterance, a moment of incipience. Something that wasn't here before is here now; it appears and it appeared to us, and it is acknowledge by the sensation *this is happening*.

6.

I would like now to introduce a notion that Heidegger (in "On the Way to Language") terms "propriation." "Language lets people and things be there for us," he says, meaning lan-guage's proper effect, the effect of propriation.

Language grants (acknowledges, affirms) and shows (or brings into the space of appear-ance) what it grants: each utterance is a saying of the phrase "this is happening."

As Goethe says (in lines quoted by Heideg-ger): "Only when it owns itself to thanking / Is life held in esteem." "To own" here is used in the sense also of "to own up," which is to give oneself over, to experience hospitality, *xenia,* the guest/

host relationship. And to enter the relationship of xenia is to accept its obligations. "Every thinking that is on the trail of something is a poetizing, and all poetry a thinking," says Heidegger. "Each coheres with the other on the basis of the saying that has already pledged itself . . . , the saying whose thinking is a thanking."

To propriate, then, is to grant, to acknowledge, to own up, to love, to thank, to make a hospitality bond with.

This is intimately connected to poetic uses of language. In Greek culture, as you know, the *symbolon* or symbol was a token representing xenia—a token broken in half and divided between guest and host to be carried as proof of identity that could be verified by comparing its other half—a token by which a stranger becomes a guest.

The word as symbol establishes a guest/host relationship between speaker and things of the world. We are strangers to the things of which we speak until we speak and become instead their guests or they become ours. This transformation of the relation in which two beings are strangers to each other into a relation in which they are guest-host to each other is propriation.

"Propriation is telling"—a speaking that matters. We tell in order to become guests and hosts to each other and to things—or to become guests and hosts to life.

7.

I want to bring forward another Greek term, *thaumzein*: *thaumzein* names our great wonder that there is *something* rather than *nothing*, our "shocked wonder" (to quote Hannah Arendt) "at the miracle of Being."

This is an incipient experience for philosophy as for poetry, both of which are excited into activity by *thaumzein* and the perplexity that comes with it.

Hannah Arendt locates it in what she calls natality—beginning, the highly improbable but regularly happening coming into existence of someone or something. Here, in a unique and singular happening, commonality too comes into existence. One thing that is common to us all is that we are born; another is that we are different from each other. Singularity and commonality are the same occurrence, and this condition of natality remains with us. Human lives, as Arendt says, are "rooted in natality in so far as

they have the task to provide and preserve the world for, to foresee and reckon with the constant influx of newcomers who are born into the world as strangers."

To be rooted in natality means that humans are born, and to be born is to become the beginning of somebody, "who is a beginner him [or her]self."

"[M]en [and women], though they must die, are not born in order to die but in order to begin."

To begin has two senses: one gets begun and one causes beginnings. "The new beginning inherent in birth can make itself felt in the world only because the newcomer possesses the capacity of beginning something anew, that is, of acting."

8.

To value the new was, of course, a widely held and explicit tenant of modernist aesthetics, as in Pound's often cited commandment, "Make it new." Viktor Shklovsky's more thoughtful, more self-reflexive, and better analyzed aphorism—"In order to restore to us the perception of life, to make a stone stony, there exists that which we call art"—takes the behest further, making newness not an end in itself but a strategy employed for the sake of enhancement of experience, and as an affirmation of life. "Only the creation of new forms of art can restore to man sensation of the world, can resurrect things and kill pessimism." Shklovsky goes on, of course, to elaborate a now familiar set of devices intended to restore palpability to things—retardation, roughening, etc.—that are major elements (and, in ways that can be taken as troubling, even the stock in trade) of so-called innovative poetry to this day (eighty-three years later). Contemporary poets—myself among them—have embraced this project. Comments variously repeating or attempting to extend Shklovsky's proposition appear throughout my teaching notebooks:

> Language is one of the principal forms our
> curiosity takes.
> The language of poetry is a language of
> inquiry.
> Poetry takes as its premise that language (all
> language) is a medium for
> experiencing experience. It provides us with
> the consciousness of consciousness.
> To experience is to go through or over the
> limit (the word comes from

the Greek *peras*—term, limit); or, to experience is to go beyond where
one is, which is to say to be beyond where
one was (the prepositional
form *peran*, beyond).
Imagine saying that at one stage of life, one's
artistic goal is to provide
experience (new or revivified, restored to
palpability) and at another
(later) it is to provide the joy of that
experience.
After how much experience can one feel free
of the fear that one hasn't
lived (the fear of an unlived life)?

It is the task of poetry to produce the phrase *this is happening* and thereby to provoke the sensation that corresponds to it—a sensation of newness, yes, and of renewedness—an experience of the revitalization of things in the world, an acknowledgment of the liveliness of the world, the restoration of the *experience* of our experience—a sense of living our life. But I do not want to imply that to produce such a sensation is necessarily to produce knowledge nor even a unit of cognition; rather, its purpose is to discover context and, therein, reason.

Admittedly, several obvious (and boringly persistent) problems arise when *experience* is assigned primacy of place in an aesthetics and its accompanying discourse of value—when it is given the status of final cause and taken as an undisputed good. First, giving preeminence to experience would seem to demand what is termed "authenticity."

Happily, one can debunk this on the same basis that one can debunk a second problem, which I could describe as anti-intellectual and ultimately philistine. In assuming a positive value to experience for its own sake, and in advocating thereby an art that heightens perceptibility, one risks appearing to privilege sensation over cogitation, to promote immediacy and disdain critique. There is a danger of implying that the questioning of experience may serve to distance and thereby diminish at least aspects of it, and that this is antithetical to "real" artistic practice. This is the basis of art's supposed hostility to criticism, theory (thought), and occasional hostility even to examination of its own history. Or, to put it another way, on these grounds, the philistine romantic attempts to ground his or her rejection of context.

And here is the basis for a dismissal of these two related problems. One cannot meaningfully say "This is happening" *out* of context. At the very moment of uttering the phrase, "natality" occurs. And from that moment of incipience, which occurs with the recognition of the experience of and presented by the phrase *along comes something—launched in context* through the phrase *this is happening*, we are *in* context, which is to say, in thought (in theory and with critique) and in history.

There is no context without thought and history. They exist through reciprocation of their reason. Otherwise, there is no sensation, no experience, no consciousness of living. And, to quote Tolstoi just as Shklovsky does: "If the complex life of many people takes place entirely on the level of the unconscious, then it's as if this life had never been."

9.

And here I'll introduce one last Greek term: *eudaimonia*, which is often translated as happiness, but more accurately it means "a flourishing." Eudaimonia is what the Greeks called the sheer bliss of simply being alive. Eudaimonia is the joy one experiences in the mattering of life—in the sufficiency of its matter. It is pleasure in the fact that it matters.

It is matter with history, not so much because it has a past as because it cares about the future.

What "matters" must be concerned with what will come to matter: the future. We care about the idea of what's going to happen to humanity. If we didn't, life would be meaningless. If we knew the world was going to end, we wouldn't be willing to continue. To flourish in the present requires requiring, which is to say, the future. Eudaimonia literally means to be "with a demon"—eu-daimonia—one "who accompanies each man [and woman] throughout … life, who is his [or her] distinct identity, but appears and is visible only to others." This daimon is the future.

As writers we care for and about the future; we make it matter. I can only agree with Viktor Shklovsky when he says that "the creation … of art can restore to [us] sensation of the world, [it] can resurrect things and kill pessimism."

Source: Lyn Hejinian, "Poetic Statement: Some Notes toward a Poetics," in *American Women Poets in the 21st Century: Where Lyric Meets Language*, edited by Claudia

Rankine and Juliana Spahr, Wesleyan University Press, 2002, pp. 235–41.

Juliana Spahr

In the following essay, Spahr gives a critical analysis of Hejinian's work.

An unusual lyricism and descriptive engagement with the everyday world crucially establish Lyn Hejinian as a forceful contemporary poet. Hejinian is a founding figure of the language writing movement of the 1970s, and her work, like most language writing, enacts a poetics that is theoretically sophisticated, one that comments on and discusses such philosophical ideas as poststructuralist and deconstructive theory as it refigures the poem as information system or argument. While language writing is stylistically diverse and, as a movement, difficult to reduce to a particular style, most writers in this group are concerned with writing in nonstandardized, often nonnarrative, forms. Language writing is community-centered and often takes as its subject progressive politics and social theory. Hejinian's work, for example, is resolutely committed to exploring the political ramifications of the ways that language is typically used. But her work differs importantly from the traditional, identity-affirming political poem of most left-wing writers. It is easier to trace the influence of language philosopher Ludwig Wittgenstein's aphoristic statement that "the limits of my language mean the limits of my world," or to apply Viktor Shklovsky's theory of "making strange" to Hejinian's work than it is to relate her work to the contemporary poetry usually anthologized in the Norton or Heath anthologies of American literature.

But while language writing tends to be anticonfessional and antirealist, Hejinian's work does not reject these forms. Rather, it insists that alternative means of expression are necessary to truly represent the confessional or the real. Her work, repeatedly concerned with biography or autobiography, explores the relationship between alternative writing practices and the subjectivity that the normal practices of biography and autobiography often obscure. The alternative form that Hejinian uses most frequently is what has come to be called the "new sentence." Hejinian has said that her "major goal has been to escape *within* the sentence, to make an enormous sentence—not necessarily long ones, but capacious ones."

> WHILE THE RHETORIC AROUND HEJINIAN'S 'OPEN TEXT' IS COMMON TO THE LANGUAGE POETRY MOVEMENT, HER APPLICATION OF THIS RHETORIC TO THE GENRE OF AUTOBIOGRAPHY, AS IN *MY LIFE* (1980), USEFULLY COMPLICATES MODELS OF SUBJECTIVITY AND THE ROLE LANGUAGE HAS IN SHAPING SUBJECTIVITY."

Hejinian was born in 1941 to Chaffee Earl Hall Jr. and Carolyn Frances Erskine in Alameda, California, and grew up in an academic family. Her father was a high school teacher and aspiring novelist who served in World War II and later became an academic administrator at the University of California and at Harvard University. He died in 1968. Erskine remarried and is a homemaker.

Hejinian attended Harvard University and graduated with a B.A. in 1968. In 1961 she married John P. Hejinian and had two children - Paull, born in 1964, and Anna, born in 1966. In 1968 Hejinian moved back to the West Coast, settling in the San Francisco Bay area. She was divorced in 1972. In 1973 she returned to rural California and began writing poetry seriously. In July 1977 Hejinian returned to the San Francisco Bay area. This same year she married Larry Ochs, a well-known composer and jazz musician. It was in San Francisco that Hejinian met Rae Armantrout, Steve Benson, Carla Harryman, Tom Mandel, Bob Perelman, Kit Robinson, Ron Silliman, and Barrett Watten. This loosely formed community began at that time to formulate the aesthetic and theoretical discourses of language writing through various journals, such as *This, Miam, Tottel, Ou,* and presses, such as Tuumba Press, which Hejinian founded in 1976.

From 1976 to 1984 Hejinian was the editor of Tuumba Press, producing fifty books. Tuumba Press was responsible for establishing and disseminating the early works of a large number of San Francisco Bay language writers. Beginning in the 1970s, as major houses published less and less poetry, small presses proliferated, and the innovative editing of these presses caused the current renaissance of experimental writing. Tuumba Press, run solely by Hejinian, provides an excellent example of the innovative possibilities of small press publishing. Through Tuumba Hejinian involved herself in a means of literary distribution that was mainly outside the limitations of the economic marketplace and controlled by a member of the community the literature helped define. Hejinian's work with Tuumba Press was, as she remarks in an interview with Manuel Brito, "simply an extension of my writing, of my being a poet. Small presses, magazines, poetry readings are the constructs of our literary life and provide conditions for writing's meanings." Hejinian is currently on the faculty of the graduate Poetics Program at the New College of California and works part-time as an assistant to a private investigator for capital crime defense and death row appeals.

Crucial to understanding Hejinian's work is the realization that it cultivates, even requires, an act of resistant reading. Her work is deliberately unsettling in its unpredictability, its diversions from conventions, the ways it is out of control. In her essay "The Rejection of Closure" (1985), she develops a theory of an "open text" that defines both her earlier and her current work. An "open text," she writes, "is open to the world and particularly to the reader.... [It] invites participation, rejects the authority of the writer over the reader and thus, by analogy, the authority implicit in other (social, economic, cultural) hierarchies."

For the open text to reject the authority of the writer over the reader, it engages in a series of disruptive techniques that expose the reader to the possibilities of meaning that he or she brings to the text. In Hejinian's work the disruptive technique most often used is what fellow poet Ron Silliman has called the "new sentence." The new sentence is a form of prose poem, composed mainly of sentences that have no clear and definite transitions. When reading the new sentence, Hejinian writes, "the reader (and I can say also the writer) must overleap the end stop, the period, and cover the distance to the next sentence.... Meanwhile, what stays in the gaps, so to speak, remains crucial and informative. Part of the reading occurs in the recovery of that information (looking behind) and the discovery of newly structured ideas."

The gap created by a text that moves from subject to subject invites the reader to participate, to bring his or her own reading to the text. Hejinian guides her readers to moments where they are required to recognize and use their own interpretive powers in the reading act, but, at that point, the work is neither passive nor full of signifiers that the reader can merely fill as he or she wants. Hejinian's work does not resist the fact that reading carries with it the tendency to appropriate from the written words of the text but, indeed, capitalizes on that tendency.

In 1972 Hejinian self-published her first work, *a gRReat adventure*, a mixed-genre collage that includes drawings, poems, and a collaboration with Doug Hall, who was then working as a performance artist. Few copies of this work exist because Hejinian destroyed most of them. The pursuit of an "open text" informs Hejinian's early chapbooks: *A Thought Is the Bride of What Thinking* (1976), a collection of three essays on narrative, knowledge, and communication; *A mask of Motion* (1977), a chapbook-length poem on the breakdown of subjectivity and history; and *Gesualdo* (1978), a chapbook-length annotated prose poem. It is *Gesualdo*, which, by using the biography of the composer Don Carlo Gesualdo (1560-1613) as a context for an exploration of literary and sexual passion, perhaps best prefigures the attention to forms of life writing that define Hejinian's later work. In this poem the life of Gesualdo weaves through first-person observations about the nature of subjectivity and the relationship between the narrator and Gesualdo.

Hejinian's first book-length collection, *Writing Is an Aid to Memory* (1978), continues her wrestlings with the confessional systems of memory and the difficulties of portraying these systems without smoothing over the questions they raise. As she writes in the preface, "memory cannot, though the future return, and proffer raw confusions." Instead, in this poem about memory Hejinian presents an excess of information. The poem is composed of forty-two sections of loosely gathered phrases. These phrases, usually five to eight words, are spread out over the page. In the diverse content of these poems, memories, details from everyday life, and scientific information are combined and connected by a narrative voice that self-reflexively questions the poem's construction and its narrator's role. *Writing Is an Aid to Memory* intends, as Hejinian writes, to portray the way that, "though we keep company with cats and dogs, all thoughtful people are impatient, with a restlessness made inevitable by language." The portrayal of such a restlessness, a primary condition of our postmodern world that is defined more and more by the remote-induced, constantly changing images of mass media, is a central concern throughout Hejinian's work.

While the rhetoric around Hejinian's "open text" is common to the language poetry movement, her application of this rhetoric to the genre of autobiography, as in *My Life* (1980), usefully complicates models of subjectivity and the role language has in shaping subjectivity. A good example of just how "open" Hejinian intends her open text to be is evident in the fact that there are two editions of *My Life* (and there is a rumor that Hejinian continues to add to this poem). *My Life* was published in 1980, and then a revised expanded edition was published in 1987. The 1980 edition sold out quickly and the 1987 edition is in its third printing. *My Life* is currently the most important of Hejinian's work and has attracted much scholarly attention. The first edition, written in 1978 when Hejinian was thirty-seven, has thirty-seven sections, each with thirty-seven sentences. In the second edition, eight new sentences were interpolated into each of the previous thirty-seven sections, and eight new sections, each with forty-five sentences, were added.

The form of *My Life* is that of the prose poem. In it the full sentence has replaced the phrasal unit of *Writing Is an Aid to Memory*. Each section begins with a sentence or phrase that is later repeated at some time in the book (although at times the phrase or sentence is slightly altered). The autobiography, with its two editions, is a work characterized by its multiplicity; it is written as a mix of autobiographical confession and language-centered aphorism, of poetry and prose. Its content moves through reminiscence and observation, moves nonsynchronically through the past and the present.

While *My Life* is undeniably autobiographical, Hejinian crucially refuses to adopt a stable-subject position and to indulge in a rhetoric of self-propaganda or self-restoration. This work, through its attention to alternative and multiple ways of telling, refuses to invoke the transparent language conventions that often compose autobiography. It does not allow its readers to ask and then decide who Lyn Hejinian is, but rather,

it places them squarely within a representational crisis that forces them to attend to and interrogate their customary ways of interpreting and reading themselves. Hejinian's emphasis is more on the roles the self of *My Life* wants to play than it is on an absolutely gendered, or otherwise subjected, narrative. As she writes, referencing the title, "My life is a permeable constructedness." An example of the subject's "permeable constructedness" can be seen in Hejinian's frequent repetition of the phrase "I wanted to be ..." This phrase takes many forms in the "early years" of her book: "In any case, I wanted to be both the farmer and his horse when I was a child, and I tossed my head and stamped with one foot as if I were pawing the ground before a long gallop." Or, "I wanted to be a brave child, a girl with guts." Or "If I couldn't be a cowboy, then I wanted to be a sailor." Or, "she pretends she is a blacksmith.... Now she's a violinist." Gradually the declaration of "I wanted to be..." changes into a new form, into the "I am...." But Hejinian's "I am..." differs radically from the repetitive tautology of "I am I," a statement that speaks to a grammatical connection between the subject and the object of identity. Instead, Hejinian writes, "I am a shard, signifying isolation - here I am thinking aloud of my affinity for the separate fragment taken under scrutiny."

My Life pushes the reader into an act of choosing among multiplicities. In *My Life* a resignified, fluctuating subjectivity is accompanied, ideally, by the resistance of the reader. Hejinian's model of subjectivity denies essentialist notions of the subject at the same time that it cultivates the powers of the reader by opening an anarchic space for reader response. By writing an autobiography, a genre that in its most clichéd form claims a representative relationship between author and narrator, as an open text, Hejinian directs attention to the role language has in shaping subjectivity. *My Life* provokes useful and important questions: for example, how might the very linear structure of narrative, which in autobiography centers most detail around the subject, further perpetuate essentialist notions of the subject? How might the grammatical structures of our language, in which being is continually bestowed on the subject by its primacy in the hierarchy of the sentence, do the same? While *My Life* does not directly answer these questions, it usefully complicates any answers that we might have.

In 1983 Hejinian traveled to Leningrad and Moscow with Ochs, her husband, who was on tour with the Rova Saxophone Quartet. In these cities she met some contemporary, samizdat Russian poets such as Vladimir Aristov, Arkadii Dragomoshchenko, Aleksei Parshchikov, Ilya Kutik, Nadezhda Kondakova, Viktor Krivalin, Olga Sedakova, Marianne Zoschenko, and Ivan Zhdanov. She also began a friendship with Leningrad poet Dragomoshchenko that continues to influence her work. From Dragomoshchenko she learned Russian and began, with Elena Balashova, to translate his and other Russian poets' works. She returned to Russia again in 1989 with the American poets Michael Davidson, Ron Silliman, and Barrett Watten. Together they wrote *Leningrad: American Writers in the Soviet Union* (1991), a book that is part travel narrative, part political commentary, part cultural studies.

Leningrad is very much a text of the language movement. The collaborative nature of the piece is common to language writers, many of whom enact their theoretical concerns with questions of community through communal writing practices. Further, its theoretically astute discourse reflects the current philosophical trends that encourage a fragmented subjectivity, especially in relation to East European nationalism and racism. The four poets in this collection alternate voices and discuss various ways post-Glasnost society forces them to confront their own politics of encounter. The possibilities and manifestations of community play a major role in this book. Hejinian, for instance, describes her interest in things Russian as an "exterior passion, or desire" that is "stirred by an insatiable identity. Being there is to be in a state of incommensurability and hence of inseparability, as if that were the status or 'human' nature of Not-me." But while Russia is often posed as the space of the "Not-me," Hejinian's work transcends this dichotomy. Her statement on Russia as the place of identity-centered difference concludes with her losing herself "in the crowds flowing on the Nevsky."

The dissolution of national boundaries also defines Hejinian's next works, *Oxota: A Short Russian Novel* (1991), a revised version of a novel originally titled *The Hunt*, and *The Cell* (1992). *Oxota*, *The Cell*, and *Leningrad* are in many ways an interconnected trilogy, and often a story will appear in more than one book, although always in a different form. *Oxota* was

written by Hejinian during her many visits to Russia, and *The Cell* was written concurrently from October 1986 to November 1988. Both works are sentence-based.

Oxota is to some extent novelistic, composed of short chapters that often read as if they were an independent scene or comment. Each chapter is composed of a very free adaptation of the fourteen-line stanza form used by Aleksandr Pushkin in *Eugene Onegin*. While *Oxota* is in many ways an autobiography in which fragments of conversation overlie a narrative continuum involving the author, Dragomoshchenko, his wife, Zina, and other friends of the author's, *Oxota* extends the work Hejinian began in *My Life*. *My Life* is more an internal text than an external. In contrast, the concerns of *Oxota* spill outward toward the global, as is evident in its attention to things like nationalism, art, and identity in Russia and the United States.

Oxota opens with the statement "This time we are both," indicating just how all persuasive both the tensions of an "insatiable identity" and Hejinian's friendship with Dragomoshchenko are. While a linguistic division separates the United States and Russia, and Hejinian and Dragomoshchenko, as well, this division in *Oxota* is "not a displacement but relocation" of the difficult permeabilities of identity. Hejinian, for example, reverses the cliché "lines of state" in the sentence "Our language was divided into states of line" to speak to the various possible states of the poetic or grammatical line. *Oxota* then plots, as Hejinian writes, the way that "Our experiences achieve pathos when they force us to acknowledge that the significances and meanings of things - things we've known, it would seem, forever, and certainly since early childhood - have changed - or rather, when we are forced to absorb the memory of being utterly unable to catch or trace or name the moment of transition when one meaning changed to another - the moment of interruption in the course of our knowing such things."

In *The Cell*, a book-length collection of poems with their dates of composition, the line is shorter—most often five words—than in Hejinian's previous work, giving the poems a sort of formal hesitancy. The writing here is involved with the daily, the everyday encounter, but, at the same time, continues to examine *Oxota's* global concerns with nation and identity. Hejinian's interest in biographical questions continues in the poem "The Cell" in its examination of subjectivities. But here the biographical figure has been replaced by the biological cell, which highlights the inability to isolate the smallest part of anything from its context. As Hejinian writes, "there are no / single notes, no unique gender," and further, "the question 'who?' disappears." Processes of identification instead are skewed in this collection, crossing even human/animal boundaries: "Feeling female in identification with / a male animal."

The most recent book in Hejinian's varied, developing career is *The Cold of Poetry* (1994), a collection of previously published and now out-of-print shorter works. The movement from the internal to the external that occurs between *My Life* and *Oxota* suggests a trend in Hejinian's poetry toward a re-thinking of the language writing movement's emphasis on the form as being the primary location of the politics of the piece. Her work seems to be moving toward a merging of the formal concerns of language poetry with the social concerns of cultural studies. In Hejinian's work, then, social reformation interacts with global transformation. She is currently writing several collaborative works - one with Dragomoshchenko and another with Carla Harryman, a long, picaresque book on eros and sex; she is also writing a feature-length film with the American cinematographer Jackie Ochs.

Source: Juliana Spahr, "Lyn Hejinian," in *Dictionary of Literary Biography*, Vol. 165, *American Poets Since World War II, Fourth Series*, edited by Joseph Conte, Gale Research, 1996, pp. 102–107.

Marnie Parsons

In the following essay, Parsons situates Hejinian's My Life *project within the context of the* L=A=N=G=U=A=G=E *movement within which she explores the function of language and meaning as a marker of an individual's life. Rather than closing off life through language, the poetic sections of* My Life *are shown here as opening outward into the ebbs and flows of intuition, memory, and the expansive fluidity of language. The emphasis in this poem is placed on process rather than on stability, and on a reader's engagement rather than on a traditional critical explication.*

Lyn Hejinian's *My Life* meanders lovingly over its own minutiae. Or perhaps leaps is a better word for the vigorous shifts and the continual non sequiturs that mark this 'autobiography,' with its probing and passionate language

> HEJINIAN ADDS HER ELOQUENT 'VOICE' TO THE MANY OTHERS INSISTING THAT THE WORLD AND THE SELF ARE COMPOSED OF LANGUAGE."

ebbing and flowing over a lifetime. In both the first and the second editions Hejinian withholds the stable reassurances of genre and form. Rather than titled or numbered chapters, there are long paragraphs—thirty-seven in the first edition, forty-five in the second. Each paragraph begins with an italicized phrase, seemingly unrelated to what follows, and each, Hejinian suggests, is 'a time and place, not a syntactical unit' (1987). Gone are clear divisions between poetry and prose, lyric and narrative. Gone is any clear association of history with memory.

Hejinian belongs to the 'L=A=N=G=U=A=G=E' poetry movement, so it's no surprise that her autobiography challenges the function of verbal expression and the nature of meaning, as well as genre, by overlaying itself with a musical arrangement of language, an emphasizing of the material aspects of words. Meaning is everywhere in this text—and yet nowhere for one unwilling to listen closely. For Hejinian's meaning is neither traditionally conceived nor stable. Her 'life' is a clustering of phrases and fragments, where sequences of more than three clearly and semantically linked sentences are quite rare; it is a dramatic working through of Ron Silliman's theory of the 'new sentence.' The reader must sift and reshape the text. No easy way through or out of the book is offered; nor should it be, because *My Life* is the articulation not just of Hejinian's own life, but of a reader's as well.

> 'What follows a strict chronology has no memory' (Hejinian 1987, 13).

Charles Olson talks of 'selection' in his essay, 'Human Universe'; writing and even living, he says, are a whittling down of 'that lovely riding thing, chaos' (1966). Each involves the organization of a universe, of poem or person, through selection from an incomprehensibly rich mass of stimulae and sensations, bits and pieces. 'For any of us, at any instant,' he claims, 'are juxtaposed to any experience, even an overwhelming single one, on several more planes than the arbitrary and discursive which we inherit can declare' (1966). Selecting inevitably betrays the flow between these planes, creates a flaw in one's perception of a universe that does not revolve around humanity's limited means of expressing itself.

Since writing and living are a betrayal of one's 'lived' experience, what is memory? Born in. Lived at. Schooled at. Married him. Bore her. Stories of such turning-points or times of shift, even when thick with description, thin one out. Where are: the postcard of Emily Brontë's dog; the red and white package of Hungarian Mammoth Squash seeds (world record—451 lbs! Absolutely the largest squash you can grow!); the blue plastic E with feet; cobalt therapy, a flying squirrel: postage stamps on a 'S.A.S.E.'; a stamped thin tin bird with fuchsia wings; ants crawling out of peonies my mother cut for my sixth grade teacher; dandelions, from this window, from this angle: blossoms on the maple tree. Where is the language for the plenitude of which such details are only crude indicators?

Lyn Hejinian offers a selection. But what she selects, how she reorganizes her life, produces not a chronology of significant events, but a sonal and visual dramatization of how language constructs one's 'reality' and one's memories. She presents an intuition of the 'pure duration,' the ongoingness, the presentness of time, and simultaneously the wonderful plasticity, the expansive, procreative embrace of both memory and language.

> 'Thinking about the time in the book, it is really the time of your life' (Hejinian 1987, 55).

Not only is the book the lived time it recounts; it is the time spent writing the book, and reading it. Beyond this, Hejinian's language—her fragments, her repetitions, her memories and echoes—assault the notion of a language whose logic flows with time, that can be read or experienced only in a forward-moving or progressive time frame. By constantly and variously reworking words and phrases so they reappear nonsequentially and seem almost unmotivated, Hejinian tries to break out of narrative and linguistic chronology.

Which is not to suggest that *My Life* has no narrative progression. The subtle movement of language from a distilled child's voice (more recalled than reenacted) to the more 'mature'

sensibility of a crafter of words, together with the increase of 'theoretical' asides, produces an understated portrait of the artist. But Hejinian is more immediately concerned with linguistic and temporal 'transgression,' with resisting traditional and staid notions of the time of language, by revealing its spatial nature, rendering it an object to be not remembered so much as *renewed* ('I heard it anew not again' she writes [1987]). Memory is a useful means for renewing language and experience both; it musses up chronology, adjusts or shifts 'reality,' dragging history into (making history into) the present.

> 'Is that a basis for descriptive sincerity. I am a shard, signifying isolation—here I am thinking aloud of my affinity for the separate fragment taken under scrutiny' (Hejinian 1987, 52).

Hejinian's minutiae: '*A pause, a rose, something on paper*' (7); 'Foxtails, the juice of a peach, have fallen on the flesh of this book' (39); 'What I felt was that figs resemble kidneys' (55); 'Those hard white grains of sand are flea eggs' (62); 'The calves of the cowboy's legs are rubbed shiny, left with no hairs. Pelicans hatch naked from the egg' (86).

Here is an exquisiteness of detail so lyrically precise, so supple, that Hejinian's is not the only life reclaimed. Just saying the title includes the reader. Each time I read this book, I feel the weight and wonder of my own childhood slinking up the skin on my arms, smell the summers of too-many-barbecues and ketchup-cooking-at-the factory; I find another moment of my life waiting to be rediscovered. Things once extraneous are loved into an intensity that selection had denied them. And more important, words are given an intensity, a thisness, of their own; they begin to exist *as* words, rather than as linguistic referrals to a greater and other 'Outside.'

What helps excavate these 'extraneous' elements and moments in life is the seeming *lack* of selection, the apparent randomness with which fragments seemingly peripheral to the major events of a life are thrown together. For instance, Hejinian doesn't describe giving birth, but remarks instead, 'When the baby was born I lost considerable importance, surrendered it to him, since now he was the last of his kind' (1987, 64). The observation is, as usual, a non sequitur: 'Yet I admit I'm still afraid of something when I refuse to rise for the playing of the national anthem. The sailor on the flood, ten times the morning sun, made of wooden goldfish. When the baby was born I lost considerable importance, surrendered it to him, since now he was the last of his kind. "Fundamental dispersion," he said, and then, "no nozzle." The coffee drinkers answered ecstatically, pounding their cups on the table' (1987, 64). This type of dislocation requires that one read not for a definitive meaning, but rather to engage the process of the making of meaning and to discover the web of potential relations that resonates between sentences. Their connection is one of interwoven tissue, the texture of muscle rather than the firm definition of bone.

> 'Only fragments are accurate. Break it up into single words, charge them to combination' (Hejinian 1987, 55).

If this text charts a lifeline, it traces it from one striking detail to another, from incarnation to new incarnation of individual words, from point to point. 'A point, in motion, is a line' (1987) for Hejinian, and the points that constitute her life *are* in constant motion. 'Strange,' Rilke writes, in the first *Duino Elegy*,

> to see meanings that clung together once, floating away
> in every direction. And being dead is hard work
> and full of retrieval before one can gradually feel
> a trace of eternity.—Though the living are wrong to believe
> in the too-sharp distinctions which they themselves have created
> (1984, 155).

With each recurrence in *My Life* of a phrase, of an image, eventually of a word, meaning does not merely gather; 'language [becomes] restless' (Hejinian 1987, 17) and 'meanings ... [float] away / in every direction' (Rilke 1984, 155)—lodging temporarily with an old friend, a new companion, until the individuality, the creases and crevices of each word-image-phrase are momentarily enlivened. 'But a word is a bottomless pit' (Hejinian 1987, 8). There is always more to retrieve and imagine. Hejinian's act of retrieval, while it still involves a degree of selection, undercuts those 'too-sharp' distinctions of the resolutely or obsessively 'selective,' those living who are so busy hewing out their own world they neither revel in chaotic source, nor acknowledge that they have indeed selected, shaped, their world.

> 'Language which is like a fruitskin around fruit' (Hejinian 1987, 43).

Life as language: 'The dictionary presents a world view ... The bilingual dictionary doubles that, presents two' (Hejinian 1987, 79). Hejinian adds her eloquent 'voice' to the many others insisting that the world and the self are composed of language. Her version is partly comprised of theoretical statements. Single sentences (for instance, 'To some extent, each sentence has to be the whole story' [1987, 67]) give outright and as completely as possible her belief that life is built with and upon language. But these sentences are rarely presented as something beyond the thoughts of a particular moment. They are organic with the process of observation from which such asides grow. And while theoretical statements are signposts, they are not maps. No one can claim authority on how to interpret the signs Hejinian leaves. Each reader finds her own paths through this labyrinthine text.

In *The dance of the intellect,* Marjorie Perloff talks of Hejinian's creation of 'a language field that could be anybody's autobiography, a kind of collective unconscious whose language we all recognize' (1985, 225). Hejinian mentions 'a portrait bowl' (1987, 25); I think of a linguistic 'play box,' a first-cousin-once-removed to the one James Reaney creates in *Colours in the Dark*, and comments upon in his preface to it: 'The theatrical experience in front of you now is designed to give you that mosaic-all-things-happening-at-the-same-time-galaxy-higgledy-piggledy feeling that rummaging through a play box can give you' (1969, v). But *My Life* doesn't have the 'ancestral coffin plates' and 'school relics' (or the eventually cohering world vision) that are in Reaney's play box (1969, v). Hejinian's toys and eccentric ephemera are words; her game is language.

> 'Mischief logic; Miss Chief' (Hejinian 1987, 29).

Hejinian handles words. She picks them up, turns them over, looks at their underbellies. Some she turns over and over—each use a different game, a new possibility; some she discards as broken; some she breaks. This handling allows sound and matter to assert themselves almost continually throughout this text, requiring that its reader at the very least register linguistic disturbance, but more usually revel in such disruption.

Juxtaposition is also part of the game. Her juxtapositions sit a serious meditation next to a commonplace assertion to see what friction comes of such elbow rubbing: 'If I was left unmarried after college, I would be single all my life and lonely in old age. In such a situation it is necessary to make a choice between contempt and an attempt at understanding, and yet it is difficult to know which is the form of retreat. We will only understand what we have already understood. The turkey is a stupid bird. And it is scanty praise to be so-called well-meaning' (1987, 53). The wit here is more subtle than that in Hejinian's conflation of Stein and William—'No ideas but in potatoes' (1987, 70). But the subtlety is invigorating; the reader is called to play along. Rejoice in displacement, illogic; recognize the suppleness, the plasticity, of language and of meaning not firmly bound by conventional expression. 'Collaborate with the occasion' (1987, 29).

Aphorisms abound: 'Pretty is as pretty does … See lightning, wait for thunder' (1987, 7). As Perloff points out, these aphorisms are 'just slightly out of sync,' a result of 'the language of adults [impinging] on the child's world with all its prescriptions, admonitions, and "wisdoms,"' (1985, 224) and of the often witty juxtaposition of sentences throughout the book. Clichés are questioned too, or at least called to a reader's attention, though not with the unremitting thoroughness of Christopher Dewdney's *The Dialectical Criminal: Hand in Glove with an Old Hat* (1983, 168–9): 'You cannot linger "on the lamb" ' (Hejinian 1987, 11); 'We "took" a trip as if that were part of the baggage we carried. In other words, we "took our time" ' (1987, 47). Grammatical rules are rephrased: 'Pronouns skirt the subject' (1987, 77). Some are 'contradicted': 'After C, I before, E except' (1987, 68). Hejinian toys with wandering letters, as in 'I've heard that it once was a napron' (1987, 77) or in the frequently repeated phrase 'a name trimmed with colored ribbons' (ibid., 14, passim), which finds its 'source' in 'a pony perhaps, his mane trimmed with colored ribbons' (1987, 15). In all these instances, she calls attention to how language changes, how literalism tampers with meaning and with the world constructed out of language.

She exults in the phonic play of words, the rhyming slip of letters, the compelling nature of rhythm: 'Between plow and prow' (1987, 65); 'Raisins, cheese, the Japanese' (1987, 64). Such phonic play illuminates the limitations of 'sense.' A reader soon finds herself lingering not over meanings, but over the tumble of the words, themselves—'The grass in my glass' (1987, 68); 'I was not afraid in the dark, hearing the low owl,

in the light, the bird knocking in the sun. I heard it anew not again' (1987, 82).

'If words matched their things we'd be imprisoned within walls of symmetry' (Hejinian 1987, 70).

Because the narrow language of the symbolic, in its transparency, cannot contain and express the many planes on which any thing exists, such language 'stops' that thing, moves away from its fluctuating reality. Hejinian remarks on this in her essay 'The Rejection of Closure': 'Children objectify language when they render it their plaything, in jokes, puns, and riddles, or in glossolaliac chants and rhymes. They discover that words are not equal to the world, that a shift, analogous to parallax in photography, occurs between thing (events, ideas, objects) and the words for them—a displacement that leaves a gap' (1984b, 138).

This gap shows in *My Life*: 'I insert a description: of agonizing spring morning freshness, when through the open window a smell of cold dust and buds of broken early grass, of schoolbooks and rotting apples, trails the sound of an airplane and a flock of crows' (1987, 48). Self-consciously she names this 'a description'— she is not offering a landscape, a setting. She is giving words instead.

Yet her continual repetition of words in a changing context lets them shimmer with varying resonances and dramatizes how the longing for a union between word and thing can be superseded by the pure power of a word that means itself, fully, intensely. For Hejinian the union between word and object can be had only by making the word itself an object, not by joining it to the object to which it refers. By saying things intensely, she marks the movement away from referential fusion of word and world, and further still, marks the deflection of a potentially stable meaning. The randomness of repetition and reorientation suggests that, despite Hejinian's careful joinings and juxtapositions, meaning travels of its own accord. Words become glorious in their new oldness. They stand intensely as themselves.

'We had been in France where every word really was a bird, a thing singing' (Hejinian 1987, 85).

'One of my favourite words was birds and will be. If they are but flights to a conclusion, I will wait patiently to look at them' (Hejinian 1987, 89).

Stein claims that language can exist 'as birds as well as words' (1935c, 30), and that words are a part of the strangeness of the world. Certainly, the insistent rise and fall of words is a source of strangeness in *My Life*; the continual repetition (or 'insistence' as Stein suggests—in 'Portraits and Repetitions' [1935b, 166–7]—it might more properly be termed) of the commonplace speech that marks life. Michel Foucault has commented that 'we live in a world completely marked by, all laced with, discourse, that is to say, utterances which have been spoken, of things said, of affirmations, interrogations, of discourses which have already occurred' (Ruas 1986, 177). This is very much Hejinian's world. Her writing of it is an intense listening.

> 'The obvious analogy is with music, which extends beyond the space the figure occupies' (Hejinian 1987, 57).

> 'When you speak you play a language. The obvious analogy is with music' (Hejinian 1987, 82).

It would be a poor listener who did not pick up on Hejinian's 'obvious analogy' with music since it is an important theme (and a theme more musical than literary) throughout *My Life*. Not only because it self-reflexively accounts for the repetitions ('The new cannot be melodic, for melody requires repetition' [1987, 62]), but also because it suggests something important about meaning in this book. Because most statements are decontextualized, and because the reader must 'make' her own sense, meaning is clearly an issue here. Hejinian raises the question of meaning in many of her theoretical musings: '*What is the meaning hung from that depend*' (1987, 16). How much does one need to mean, to be intelligible, and why? What sort of assumptions about language hang on a desire to mean? 'What is one doing to, or with, the statement (the language) or the stated (the object or the idea) when one *means* it' (1987, 42).

Or, *how* does one mean? Ultimately the *how* overrides the what. How Hejinian means is musically—not merely with correspondence between word and thing; not purely referentially. She is not striving for a referential meaning. Sentences, like *A pause, a rose, something on paper* (1987, 7), are themes (in the musical definition of the word); they are repeated in ever changing configurations, and even as they accrue associative and contextual meaning, they develop a potent sound value. Their continual echoes stand as musical ideas, aural images that vary and combine to create an 'intuitive' lyric that speaks intimately, trustingly.

'Sensual,' reverberating sense challenges logical, cerebral sense; dislocating, subverting orders challenge more evident, predictable orders. Despite the rigour, the concentration, the extreme exertion that goes into creating them, music and the musical language of *My Life* move beyond the cerebral. '[But] though I could say the music brought these places "home" to me,' Hejinian writes, 'the composition itself grew increasingly strange as I listened again, less recognizable, in the dark, as when one repeats a word or phrase over and over in order to disintegrate its associations, to defamiliarize it' (1987, 113). A work of this intensity that tries so hard to construct one grammar out of another, to defamiliarize the very substance of one's world and 'self,' is an act of incredible control and precision. What makes Hejinian so successful is her 'lack of clarity,' her leap beyond pure idea to emotion, spirit rhapsody.

> 'Through the window of Chartres, with no view, the light transmits the color as a scene. What then is a window' (Hejinian 1987, 65).

A window: transparent. Clear-cut reference. Hejinian offers another take on this metaphor; a 'window-language' that is not transparent, that lets both window and language exist as, and for, themselves, to demonstrate their own beauty. If language must be a window, why not one like the stained glass of Chartres, why not one of colour and texture, a composition that is its own landscape, that adds tincture to the world outside and noticeably alters what little 'reality' one perceives through it?

Source: Marnie Parsons, "What Then Is a Window,'" in *Touch Monkeys: Nonsense Strategies for Reading Twentieth-Century Poetry*, University of Toronto Press, 1994, pp. 206–14.

Marjorie Perloff

In the following excerpt, Perloff explains the concept that shapes Hejinian's ongoing My Life *project, with particular emphasis on section 29 ("Yet we insist that life is full of happy chance") as representative of the poetic vision. Showing how Hejinian revised the section to reflect her own aging process, Perloff explores how the collection as a whole challenges the conventional sequence of an autobiography through its overlapping images,*

MY LIFE THUS BECOMES, ODDLY, *MY ART* OR *MY WRITING*, THE NATURAL GIVING WAY TO THE ARTIFICIAL, THE INDIVIDUAL SELF TO THE BODY OF WORDS."

ideas, and other details, both within and across sections.

A related process characterizes Lyn Hejinian's remarkable *My Life*. When this "autobiography" was first written in 1978, it had 37 sections, one for each of Hejinian's then 37 years, and each section had 37 sentences. The (unnamed) number assigned to each section governs that section's content: thus 1 has its base in infant sensations, in 9 the references are to a gawky child, in 18 someone is "hopelessly in love," in 22 there are allusions to college reading, in the form of Nietzsche, Darwin, Freud, and Marx. It is not that these sections are "about" the year in question, for each is a collage made up of numerous interpolations—memories and meditations, axioms and aphorisms. Nevertheless, in the course of the narrative, the references gradually shift from childhood to adolescence to adult thought and behavior.

The writing of a life, Hejinian believes, has no beginning, middle, or end: it goes on as long as the author lives. Accordingly, in 1986 when she turned 45, Hejinian revised *My Life*, adding eight sections to the narrative as well as adding eight new sentences to each section, these eight spliced into the text at irregular intervals. Here, for example, is 29, with the eight new sentences distinguished from the rest for convenience:

Yet we insist
that life is full
of happy chance

The windows were open and the morning air was, by the smell of lilac and some darker flowering shrub, filled with the brown and chirping trills of birds. As they are if you could have nothing but quiet and shouting. Arts, also, are links. I picture an idea at the moment I come to it, our collision. Once, for a time, anyone might have been luck's child. Even rain didn't spoil the barbecue, in the backyard behind a polished traffic, through a

landscape, along a shore. Freedom then, liberation later. She came to babysit for us in those troubled years directly from the riots, and she said that she dreamed of the day when she would gun down everyone in the financial district. That single telephone is only one hair on the brontosaurus. The coffee drinkers answered ecstatically. If your dog stays out of the room, you get the fleas. In the lull, activity drops. I'm seldom in my dreams without my children. MY DAUGHTER TOLD ME THAT AT SOME TIME IN SCHOOL SHE HAD LEARNED TO THINK OF A POET AS A PERSON SEATED ON AN ICEBERG AND MELTING THROUGH IT. IT IS A POETRY OF CERTAINTY. In the distance, down the street, the practicing soprano belts the breeze. As for we who "love to be astonished," money makes money, luck makes luck. Moves forward, drives on. CLASS BACKGROUND IS NOT LANDSCAPE—STILL HERE AND THERE IN 1969 I COULD FEEL THE SCOPE OF COLLECTIVITY. It was the present time for a little while, and not so new as we thought then, the present always after war. Ever since it has been hard for me to share my time. The yellow of that sad room was again the yellow of naps, where she waited, restless, faithless, for more days. THEY SAY THAT THE ALTERNATIVE FOR THE BOURGEOISIE WAS GULLIBILITY. CALL IT WATER AND DOGS. Reason looks for two, then arranges it from there. But can one imagine a madman in love. Goodbye; enough that was good. There was a pause, a rose, something on paper. I MAY BALK BUT I WON'T RECEDE. Because desire is always embarrassing. At the beach, with a fresh flush. The child looks out. THE BERRIES ARE KEPT IN THE BRAMBLES, ON WIRES ON RESERVE FOR THE BIRDS. At a distance, the sun *is* small. There was no proper Christmas after he died. That triumphant blizzard had brought the city to its knees. I am a stranger to the little girl I was, and more—more strange. BUT MANY FACTS ABOUT A LIFE SHOULD BE LEFT OUT, THEY ARE EASILY REPLACED. One sits in a cloven space. Patterns promote an outward likeness, between little white silences. The big trees catch all the moisture from what seems like a dry night. Reflections don't make shade, but shadows are, and do. In order to understand the nature of the collision, one must know something of the nature of the motions involved—that is, a history. He looked at me and smiled and did not look away, and thus a friendship became erotic. Luck was rid of its clover.

This particular section has as its epigraph or leitmotif one of the optimistic clichés we associate with Hejinian's mother: "Yet we insist that life is full of happy chance." It begins, like many of the childhood sections, with a pleasant nature image: windows open, morning air, smell of lilac, chirping birds. But the mood is meditative, the time evidently "those troubled years" when babysitters came "directly from the riots." Indeed, further down the page we learn that it is 1969, when "I could feel the scope of collectivity." The text presents us with small children, including a daughter who "had learned to think of a poet as a person seated on an iceberg and melting through it." Yet, from another angle, the narrator thinks of hers as a "poetry of certainty." Being a poet, in any case, takes place against the "yellow of naps," and against what seems to be a new love relationship, a "friendship [that] became erotic."

In this context, the eight new sentences play a curious part. Not only don't they stand out; once inserted into the text, they are wholly absorbed into its momentum so that it is impossible to tell where the seams are. Some of the phrases provide new information (like the date 1969), some carry on the image patterning, like "The berries are kept in the brambles, on wires on reserve for the birds." The point, I think, is that, as Hejinian puts it in the eighth new sentence, "many facts about a life should be left out, they are easily replaced." This is precisely what her own text does: a given "fact of life" will be "replaced" or at least recontextualized so as to take on somewhat different meanings by being inserted between a new X and Y. And yet, as in a jigsaw puzzle or mosaic, the replacement strategies don't alter the fact that the "pieces" are very similar—cut, as it were, from the same cloth.

At one level, then, *My Life* is an elaborate, one might say Oulipean, number game, with its 37×37 (or 45×45) square, each number having the appropriate tempo and mood assigned to it. And furthermore, the formal patterning is heightened by the repetition of the short italicized phrases placed in the white square that begins each section, phrases that are then permutated throughout the text, appearing and reappearing in different contexts. In 29, for example, we find the leitmotif of 1 ("A pause, a rose, something on paper") and 2 ("As for we who 'love to be astonished'"), embedded in the text, as indeed they are throughout *My Life*.

Why such formal artifice in what is usually taken to be a genre as "natural" as autobiography? I shall come back to this question but first I want to look at the text at the level of microstructure and see how the individual units themselves are structured and how they function in the larger picture.

The images invoked in this passage are largely the sort every little girl would notice and later remember: the wallpaper with its "pattern of small roses," "the white gauze curtains which were never loosened," the ominous "shadow of the redwood trees" outside the window and the sunset reflected in it, the "little puddle" that is sometimes "overcast," indicating cloudy weather, the uncle with the wart on his nose and his "jokes at our expense" and the deaf aunt who is "nodding agreeably." And further: there are the proverbs that adults recount to children: "Pretty is as pretty does," or such lessons in necessity as "See lightning, wait for thunder." Even the "moment yellow," which later turns "purple" is the staple of "girls' books" and *Seventeen* magazine: what could be more banal, more everyday than such references to childhood?

But of course there is something else going on here. As against the conventional autiobiography, Hejinian's everywhere undermines sequence: *b* does not follow *a*, and the connectives are often missing. And further, this is an autobiography that provides almost no direct references to the basic facts—what city the poet lives in, where her father works, where she goes to school, whom she marries, how old her children are, and so on. True, we can surmise that the story opened some time in the early forties, since the narrator's father is returning from the war. Or again, in 29, the assumption is that father has died—"There was no proper Christmas after he died"—especially since 28 contains the sentence "I wanted to carry my father up all those stairs." But even these central "events" remain shadowy, peripheral—events that take place, so to speak, at the outer edges of the screen whose real focus is on something else.

That something else may be defined as the creation of a language field in which "identity" is less a property of a given character than a fluid state that takes on varying shapes and that hence engages the reader to participate in its formation and deformation. The scene is set by the first italicized phrase, *A pause, a rose, something on paper.* Are the "pause" and the "rose" nouns in apposition or do they refer to the same thing? The consonantal endings (*z*) link the two mono-syllabic words, but even then, we can't specify their meaning or relate them with certainty to the "something on paper." When the phrase recurs in the third section, it is embedded in images of plant, animal, and insect life:

> As if sky plus sun *must* make leaves. A snap-dragon volunteering in the garden among the cineraria gapes its maw between the fingers, and we pinched the buds of the fuschia to make them pop. Is that willful. Inclines. They have big calves because of those hills. Flip over small stones, dried mud. We thought that the mica might be gold. A pause, a rose, something on paper, in a nature scrapbook. What follows a strict chronology has no memory. (ML 13)

Here the phrase makes sense as referring to something seen on the page of a scrapbook, something one pauses over. But the next appearance of the phrase comes in a comic account of Mother's way of eating pudding, "carving a rim around the circumference of the pudding, working her way inward toward the center, scooping with the spoon, to see how far she could separate the pudding from the edge of the bowl before the center collapsed, spreading the pudding out again, lower, back to the edge of the bowl." "You could tell," adds the narrator, "that it was improvisational because at that point they closed their eyes." That what was improvisational? The pudding-eating ritual just described or something quite different? And why would improvisation make one want to close one's eyes? Because one has seen it all before and it's boring? Because the improvisation is frightening? There is no way to tell and, in any case, the scene now "cuts" to the familiar "*A pause, a rose, something on paper.*"

The recurrence of these leitmotifs (e.g., *What is the meaning hung from that depend? The obvious analogy is with music*, or *Like plump birds along the shore*) has an oddly reassuring effect. It is the poet herself who is pausing to put "something on paper," something that is her written offering, her "rose." In the course of *My Life* these phrases become markers, signposts around which much that is confusing in one's life can coalesce. "What is the meaning hung from that depend?" can be taken as an epigraph for the whole text even as "the obvious analogy is with music" fits any number of "analogies" that come up in the narrative, and there are dozens of

bodily forms that emerge "Like plump birds along the shore."

Indeed, throughout *My Life* the italicized *phrase-making* serves to remind us that, as Hejinian put it in the title of an early book of poems, "Writing [is] an aid to memory." It is the act of writing itself that transforms *Everygirl* into the author of the autobiography. Let us go back to the opening page for a moment and see how this process works. *My Life* opens with a classic Hollywood shot: the "purple moment" when the baby girl at the top of the stairs sees the front door open on Father, returning from the war, evidently (for this is what adults tell the child later) "younger, thinner than when he had left"—all this against the background of rose-patterned wallpaper and white gauze curtains. But the Hollywood shot would not include the sentence, "In certain families, the meaning of necessity is at one with the sentiment of pre-necessity." The remark is gently satiric, pointing to the family's need to predict what will happen, to control future events, to plan the transformation of "pre-necessity" into "necessity." And this sentence is, in its turn, followed by the terse, "The better things were gathered in a pen"—a sentence open for a wide range of interpretations, for example:

> The better toys were gathered in the playpen.
> The better dishes (the good china) were kept in a special closet.
> The better *objets d'art* were kept in a cor-doned-off area, as untouched as
> the windows behind the white gauze curtains.

And so on. However we read "better things" and "pen," what emerges is that this is a family that makes discriminations between "better" and "worse" things, that is concerned with hierarchy, propriety, and orders—the "rigidity which never intrudes," as we read a few lines further down—and that the narrator recalls registering a certain puzzlement about these things.

But these implications are never pressed or even clarified. Rather, new sentences are introduced that are as equivocal semantically as they are normal grammatically. "The plush must be worn away": there's a sentence anyone can construe. But what plush? From a stuffed animal? A sofa? And who is saying or thinking these things? Is the "she" who "stepped into people's gardens to pinch off cuttings from their geraniums and succulents" the girl herself or her mother or someone else? Here the *cause* is cited—the stepping into other people's gardens *so as* to pinch off cuttings—but note that the cause is separated both from the agent and from the result. For we never know whether the neighbors catch "her" taking their cuttings or even who "she" is. We only know that in this "Wool station" (elderly aunts knitting and "nodding, agreeably"), "the afternoon happens, crowded and therefore endless." Crowded with what? Well, as the preceding sentence tells us, "Long time lines trail behind every idea, object, person, pet, vehicle, event." Everything finally *matters* but how and to whom? "If only you could touch," says the narrator, "or, even, catch those gray great creatures"—a reference, perhaps, to the clouds above reflected in those puddles but also, quite possibly, to imaginary creatures read about in children's books or emerging from the narrator's "radio days."

Throughout *My Life*, secrets seem about to be revealed, enigmas about to be clarified, but the moment of revelation never comes. In the final sections of the expanded *My Life*, the familiar leitmotifs—"What is the meaning hung from that depend," "The obvious analogy is with music"—recur and almost cushion the reader's recognition that nothing has been or is going to be resolved. "I confess candidly," says the narrator, "that I was adequately happy until I was asked if I was," the question, evidently, having been put to her on a trip to the Soviet Union. But then, "happiness is worthless, my grandfather assured me when he was very old, he had never sought it for himself or for my father, it had nothing to do with whether or not a life is good. The fear of death is residue, its infinity overness, equivalence—an absolute." (ML 115). And the final sentence of the book is "Reluctance such that it can't be filled."

This reluctance, this deferral of meaning and denial of plenitude, is central to Hejinian's conception of writing. "Where once one sought a vocabulary for ideas," Hejinian remarked in an early essay, "now one seeks ideas for vocabularies." *My morphemes mourned events* is one of the text's leitmotifs, and indeed Hejinian really does filter "events" through the morphemes of their articulation. Hers is autobiography that not only calls attention to the impossibility of charting the evolution of a coherent "self," the psychological motivation for continued action, but one that playfully deconstructs the packaged model crowding the bookstore shelves today—the autobiography,

say, of Nancy Reagan or Shelley Winters, of Lee Iacocca or the Kennedys' chauffeur. In the popular imagination, after all, autobiography is the form in which you explain how you got where you are now. Ancestry and childhood invariably play a role as do, in most cases, schooling and the friction with one's childhood and teenage peers. In popular autobiography, these tentative forays toward separation invariably lead, sooner or later, to the Big Break followed by the Big Gamble and often by the Big Mistake(s).

Again, in popular or what we might call "informational" autobiography, language is largely and intentionally transparent, a vehicle used to convey facts, detail events, and produce, here and there, rhetorical flourishes that demand our attention. The emphasis remains on event and character—the shaping of a life according to social and cultural norms and constraints. It is this mode that *My Life* calls into question, refusing, as it does, to go for the Big Break, the Big Defeat, not even displaying the climactic moment of sex, of motherhood, of vocation. "Memory," says the narrator at one point, "is the money of my class." Which is to say, beware of the self-indulgence that "memory" brings, the endless dwelling on what happened or might have happened. The construction of "my life," for that matter, must compete with the constructions of others: "There were more storytellers than there were stories, so that everyone in the family had a version of history and it was impossible to get close to the original, or to know 'what really happened'" (ML 21).

No "characters," no "events," and finally, no "self," at least not in the usual sense of that word. It is difficult, reading *My Life*, to define the "I" of Lyn Hejinian, the particular person that she is, although of course the narrator's verbal habits and references do convey an identifiable voice and style. But compared to, say, Yeats's autobiography or Henry Adams's or even William Carlos Williams's, Hejinian's displays a studied refusal to engage in introspection, a steady suspicion of Romantic self-consciousness. As the narrator remarks wittily in 12, "Now that I was 'old enough to make my own decisions,' I dressed like everyone else" (ML 36).

What remains individual, however, is the construction of the artwork that "my life," any life, can prompt. For after all, even a phoneme can make a difference as when we come across such phrases as "seeming is believing" or "x plus you." Accordingly, the permutated phrases, many of them with quotes inside the quotes so as to signal the endless clichéing of language—*As for we "who love to be astonished," When one travels one might "hit" a storm, What memory is not a "gripping" thought*—work to create an intricate network, a highly wrought textuality that is enhanced by the strictness of the autobiograhy's number system: 45 × 45, each unit having its square white box containing the key phrase. *My Life* thus becomes, oddly, *My Art* or *My Writing*, the natural giving way to the artificial, the individual self to the body of words.

The pleasure of Hejinian's text—and here we come back to the larger issue of the rule-generated text in late twentieth-century writing—has less to do with what happens to her protagonist in the course of the "story" than with the reader's discovery that, however random and disjunctive the book's events, conversations, aphorisms, and commentaries seem to be at the level of microstructure, each unlisted number, when extracted, gives us a key to the behavior of "Lyn" at age *x* or *y*. Or does it? As in the case of Perec's *Life: A User's Manual*, *My Life* introduces a certain "bend" or clinamen into the carefully articulated mathematical structure. In 29, for example, the opening sentence with its reference to "brown and chirping trills of birds" could just as well be the opening sentence of number 3 or 4, and many other sentences and phrases—"The berries are kept in the brambles, on wires on reserve for birds," "The big trees catch all the moisture from what seems like a dry night"—defy the text's larger number system so that the "saturated structure" of *My Life* cannot be replicated.

The goal of such procedural writing may well be, as Michel Butor has put it, "to escape the poem that sticks to the poet like a suit of clothing (even if it is a 'splendid' one), so as to try to find, in a structure that is very confining and yet very rich in formal relations, a more profound poetic grammar." "Mathematics," according to this way of thinking (see OU 93), "repairs the ruin of rules." It also repairs, we might add, the "ruin" of a "free verse" determined primarily by speech rhythm and "natural" pause—a speech rhythm used brilliantly by the Modernist poets and their heirs of the fifties and sixties but now increasingly problematic as "authentic voice" models and

"natural speech" paradigms show increasing signs of strain. *A pause, a rose, something on paper:* something, perhaps, that takes us from the impasse of "free speech" rhythms to the "rhythm of cognition" (ML 92).

Source: Marjorie Perloff, "The Return of the (Numerical) Repressed: From Free Verse to Procedural Play," in *Radical Artifice: Writing Poetry in the Age of Media*, University of Chicago, 1991, pp. 162–70.

SOURCES

Dutton, Danielle, Review of *Happily*, in *Review of Contemporary Fiction*, Vol. 23 No. 2, Summer 2003, pp. 128–29.

Hejinian, Lyn, *My Life*, Burning Deck, 1980, pp. 5, 7, 81–82.

———, "Yet we insist that life is full of happy chance," in *My Life*, Burning Deck, 1980, pp. 71–73.

Ives, Nancy R., Review of *My Life*, in *Library Journal*, December 1987, pp. 104–05.

Naylor, Paul, *Poetic Investigations: Singing in the Holes of History*, Northwestern University Press, 1999, p. 119.

Review of *The Language of Inquiry*, in *Publishers Weekly*, Vol. 247, No. 49, December 4, 2000, p. 68.

FURTHER READING

Delville, Michel, *The American Prose Poem: Poetic Form and the Boundaries of Genre*, University of Florida Press, 1998.

> This study provides an engaging discussion of the form from its origins through more contemporary renderings, with a particular focus on contemporary American prose poets.

Jarraway, David R., "*My Life* through the Eighties: The Exemplary L = A = N = G = U = A = G = E of Lyn Hejinian," in *Contemporary Literature*, Vol. 33, No. 2, Summer 1992, pp. 319–36.

> This essay summarizes the ideas of the L = A = N = G = U = A = G = E poets and analyzes Hejinian's *My Life* as a key example of such experimental poetry. Jarraway focuses on Hejinian's mechanics and politics and how these affect the meaning

Peters, Robert, *Where the Bee Sucks: Workers, Drones, and Queens of Contemporary American Poetry*, Asylum Arts, 1994.

> This book is a compilation of poems and prose pieces (usually about poetry and poetics) written by various American poets of the late

twentieth century. The collection closes with an essay on Language poetry.

Simpson, Megan, *Poetic Epistemologies: Gender and Knowing in Women's Language-Oriented Writing*, State University Press of New York, 2000.

Simpson's book covers twentieth-century poetry. It provides critical introductions to a full range of works by a dozen women writers. The long chapter on Hejinian includes a discussion of *My Life*.

Glossary of Literary Terms

A

Abstract: Used as a noun, the term refers to a short summary or outline of a longer work. As an adjective applied to writing or literary works, abstract refers to words or phrases that name things not knowable through the five senses.

Accent: The emphasis or stress placed on a syllable in poetry. Traditional poetry commonly uses patterns of accented and unaccented syllables (known as feet) that create distinct rhythms. Much modern poetry uses less formal arrangements that create a sense of freedom and spontaneity.

Aestheticism: A literary and artistic movement of the nineteenth century. Followers of the movement believed that art should not be mixed with social, political, or moral teaching. The statement "art for art's sake" is a good summary of aestheticism. The movement had its roots in France, but it gained widespread importance in England in the last half of the nineteenth century, where it helped change the Victorian practice of including moral lessons in literature.

Affective Fallacy: An error in judging the merits or faults of a work of literature. The "error" results from stressing the importance of the work's effect upon the reader—that is, how it makes a reader "feel" emotionally, what it does as a literary work—instead of stressing its inner qualities as a created object, or what it "is."

Age of Johnson: The period in English literature between 1750 and 1798, named after the most prominent literary figure of the age, Samuel Johnson. Works written during this time are noted for their emphasis on "sensibility," or emotional quality. These works formed a transition between the rational works of the Age of Reason, or Neoclassical period, and the emphasis on individual feelings and responses of the Romantic period.

Age of Reason: See *Neoclassicism*

Age of Sensibility: See *Age of Johnson*

Agrarians: A group of Southern American writers of the 1930s and 1940s who fostered an economic and cultural program for the South based on agriculture, in opposition to the industrial society of the North. The term can refer to any group that promotes the value of farm life and agricultural society.

Alexandrine Meter: See *Meter*

Allegory: A narrative technique in which characters representing things or abstract ideas are used to convey a message or teach a lesson. Allegory is typically used to teach moral, ethical, or religious lessons but is sometimes used for satiric or political purposes.

Alliteration: A poetic device where the first consonant sounds or any vowel sounds in words or syllables are repeated.

Allusion: A reference to a familiar literary or historical person or event, used to make an idea more easily understood.

Amerind Literature: The writing and oral traditions of Native Americans. Native American literature was originally passed on by word of mouth, so it consisted largely of stories and events that were easily memorized. Amerind prose is often rhythmic like poetry because it was recited to the beat of a ceremonial drum.

Analogy: A comparison of two things made to explain something unfamiliar through its similarities to something familiar, or to prove one point based on the acceptedness of another. Similes and metaphors are types of analogies.

Anapest: See *Foot*

Angry Young Men: A group of British writers of the 1950s whose work expressed bitterness and disillusionment with society. Common to their work is an anti-hero who rebels against a corrupt social order and strives for personal integrity.

Anthropomorphism: The presentation of animals or objects in human shape or with human characteristics. The term is derived from the Greek word for "human form."

Antimasque: See *Masque*

Antithesis: The antithesis of something is its direct opposite. In literature, the use of antithesis as a figure of speech results in two statements that show a contrast through the balancing of two opposite ideas. Technically, it is the second portion of the statement that is defined as the "antithesis"; the first portion is the "thesis."

Apocrypha: Writings tentatively attributed to an author but not proven or universally accepted to be their works. The term was originally applied to certain books of the Bible that were not considered inspired and so were not included in the "sacred canon."

Apollonian and Dionysian: The two impulses believed to guide authors of dramatic tragedy. The Apollonian impulse is named after Apollo, the Greek god of light and beauty and the symbol of intellectual order. The Dionysian impulse is named after Dionysus, the Greek god of wine and the symbol of the unrestrained forces of nature. The Apollonian impulse is to create a rational, harmonious world, while the Dionysian is to express the irrational forces of personality.

Apostrophe: A statement, question, or request addressed to an inanimate object or concept or to a nonexistent or absent person.

Archetype: The word archetype is commonly used to describe an original pattern or model from which all other things of the same kind are made. This term was introduced to literary criticism from the psychology of Carl Jung. It expresses Jung's theory that behind every person's "unconscious," or repressed memories of the past, lies the "collective unconscious" of the human race: memories of the countless typical experiences of our ancestors. These memories are said to prompt illogical associations that trigger powerful emotions in the reader. Often, the emotional process is primitive, even primordial. Archetypes are the literary images that grow out of the "collective unconscious." They appear in literature as incidents and plots that repeat basic patterns of life. They may also appear as stereotyped characters.

Argument: The argument of a work is the author's subject matter or principal idea.

Art for Art's Sake: See *Aestheticism*

Assonance: The repetition of similar vowel sounds in poetry.

Audience: The people for whom a piece of literature is written. Authors usually write with a certain audience in mind, for example, children, members of a religious or ethnic group, or colleagues in a professional field. The term "audience" also applies to the people who gather to see or hear any performance, including plays, poetry readings, speeches, and concerts.

Automatic Writing: Writing carried out without a preconceived plan in an effort to capture every random thought. Authors who engage in automatic writing typically do not revise their work, preferring instead to preserve the revealed truth and beauty of spontaneous expression.

Avant-garde: A French term meaning "vanguard." It is used in literary criticism to describe new writing that rejects traditional approaches to literature in favor of innovations in style or content.

B

Ballad: A short poem that tells a simple story and has a repeated refrain. Ballads were originally intended to be sung. Early ballads, known as folk ballads, were passed down through generations, so their authors are often unknown. Later ballads composed by known authors are called literary ballads.

Baroque: A term used in literary criticism to describe literature that is complex or ornate in style or diction. Baroque works typically express tension, anxiety, and violent emotion. The term "Baroque Age" designates a period in Western European literature beginning in the late sixteenth century and ending about one hundred years later. Works of this period often mirror the qualities of works more generally associated with the label "baroque" and sometimes feature elaborate conceits.

Baroque Age: See *Baroque*

Baroque Period: See *Baroque*

Beat Generation: See *Beat Movement*

Beat Movement: A period featuring a group of American poets and novelists of the 1950s and 1960s—including Jack Kerouac, Allen Ginsberg, Gregory Corso, William S. Burroughs, and Lawrence Ferlinghetti—who rejected established social and literary values. Using such techniques as stream of consciousness writing and jazz-influenced free verse and focusing on unusual or abnormal states of mind—generated by religious ecstasy or the use of drugs—the Beat writers aimed to create works that were unconventional in both form and subject matter.

Beat Poets: See *Beat Movement*

Beats, The: See *Beat Movement*

Belles- lettres: A French term meaning "fine letters" or "beautiful writing." It is often used as a synonym for literature, typically referring to imaginative and artistic rather than scientific or expository writing. Current usage sometimes restricts the meaning to light or humorous writing and appreciative essays about literature.

Black Aesthetic Movement: A period of artistic and literary development among African Americans in the 1960s and early 1970s. This was the first major African-American artistic movement since the Harlem Renaissance and was closely paralleled by the civil rights and black power movements. The black aesthetic writers attempted to produce works of art that would be meaningful to the black masses. Key figures in black aesthetics included one of its founders, poet and playwright Amiri Baraka, formerly known as LeRoi Jones; poet and essayist Haki R. Madhubuti, formerly Don L. Lee; poet and playwright Sonia Sanchez; and dramatist Ed Bullins.

Black Arts Movement: See *Black Aesthetic Movement*

Black Comedy: See *Black Humor*

Black Humor: Writing that places grotesque elements side by side with humorous ones in an attempt to shock the reader, forcing him or her to laugh at the horrifying reality of a disordered world.

Black Mountain School: Black Mountain College and three of its instructors—Robert Creeley, Robert Duncan, and Charles Olson—were all influential in projective verse, so poets working in projective verse are now referred as members of the Black Mountain school.

Blank Verse: Loosely, any unrhymed poetry, but more generally, unrhymed iambic pentameter verse (composed of lines of five two-syllable feet with the first syllable accented, the second unaccented). Blank verse has been used by poets since the Renaissance for its flexibility and its graceful, dignified tone.

Bloomsbury Group: A group of English writers, artists, and intellectuals who held informal artistic and philosophical discussions in Bloomsbury, a district of London, from around 1907 to the early 1930s. The Bloomsbury Group held no uniform philosophical beliefs but did commonly express an aversion to moral prudery and a desire for greater social tolerance.

Bon Mot: A French term meaning "good word." A *bon mot* is a witty remark or clever observation.

Breath Verse: See *Projective Verse*

Burlesque: Any literary work that uses exaggeration to make its subject appear ridiculous, either by treating a trivial subject with profound seriousness or by treating a dignified subject frivolously. The word "burlesque" may also be used as an adjective, as in "burlesque show," to mean "striptease act."

C

Cadence: The natural rhythm of language caused by the alternation of accented and unaccented syllables. Much modern poetry—notably free verse—deliberately manipulates cadence to create complex rhythmic effects.

Caesura: A pause in a line of poetry, usually occurring near the middle. It typically corresponds to a break in the natural rhythm or sense of the line but is sometimes shifted to create special meanings or rhythmic effects.

Canzone: A short Italian or Provencal lyric poem, commonly about love and often set to music. The *canzone* has no set form but typically contains five or six stanzas made up of seven to twenty lines of eleven syllables each. A shorter, five- to ten-line "envoy," or concluding stanza, completes the poem.

Carpe Diem: A Latin term meaning "seize the day." This is a traditional theme of poetry, especially lyrics. A *carpe diem* poem advises the reader or the person it addresses to live for today and enjoy the pleasures of the moment.

Catharsis: The release or purging of unwanted emotions—specifically fear and pity—brought about by exposure to art. The term was first used by the Greek philosopher Aristotle in his *Poetics* to refer to the desired effect of tragedy on spectators.

Celtic Renaissance: A period of Irish literary and cultural history at the end of the nineteenth century. Followers of the movement aimed to create a romantic vision of Celtic myth and legend. The most significant works of the Celtic Renaissance typically present a dreamy, unreal world, usually in reaction against the reality of contemporary problems.

Celtic Twilight: See *Celtic Renaissance*

Character: Broadly speaking, a person in a literary work. The actions of characters are what constitute the plot of a story, novel, or poem. There are numerous types of characters, ranging from simple, stereotypical figures to intricate, multifaceted ones. In the techniques of anthropomorphism and personification, animals—and even places or things—can assume aspects of character. "Characterization" is the process by which an author creates vivid, believable characters in a work of art. This may be done in a variety of ways, including (1) direct description of the character by the narrator; (2) the direct presentation of the speech, thoughts, or actions of the character; and (3) the responses of other characters to the character. The term "character" also refers to a form originated by the ancient Greek writer Theophrastus that later became popular in the seventeenth and eighteenth centuries. It is a short essay or sketch of a person who prominently displays a specific attribute or quality, such as miserliness or ambition.

Characterization: See *Character*

Classical: In its strictest definition in literary criticism, classicism refers to works of ancient Greek or Roman literature. The term may also be used to describe a literary work of recognized importance (a "classic") from any time period or literature that exhibits the traits of classicism.

Classicism: A term used in literary criticism to describe critical doctrines that have their roots in ancient Greek and Roman literature, philosophy, and art. Works associated with classicism typically exhibit restraint on the part of the author, unity of design and purpose, clarity, simplicity, logical organization, and respect for tradition.

Colloquialism: A word, phrase, or form of pronunciation that is acceptable in casual conversation but not in formal, written communication. It is considered more acceptable than slang.

Complaint: A lyric poem, popular in the Renaissance, in which the speaker expresses sorrow about his or her condition. Typically, the speaker's sadness is caused by an unresponsive lover, but some complaints cite other sources of unhappiness, such as poverty or fate.

Conceit: A clever and fanciful metaphor, usually expressed through elaborate and extended comparison, that presents a striking parallel between two seemingly dissimilar things—for example, elaborately comparing a beautiful woman to an object like a garden or the sun. The conceit was a popular device throughout the Elizabethan Age and Baroque Age and was the principal technique of the seventeenth-century English metaphysical poets. This usage of the word conceit is unrelated to the best-known definition of conceit as an arrogant attitude or behavior.

Concrete: Concrete is the opposite of abstract, and refers to a thing that actually exists or a description that allows the reader to experience an object or concept with the senses.

Concrete Poetry: Poetry in which visual elements play a large part in the poetic effect. Punctuation marks, letters, or words are arranged on a page to form a visual design: a cross, for example, or a bumblebee.

Confessional Poetry: A form of poetry in which the poet reveals very personal, intimate, sometimes shocking information about himself or herself.

Connotation: The impression that a word gives beyond its defined meaning. Connotations may be universally understood or may be significant only to a certain group.

Consonance: Consonance occurs in poetry when words appearing at the ends of two or more verses have similar final consonant sounds but have final vowel sounds that differ, as with "stuff" and "off."

Convention: Any widely accepted literary device, style, or form.

Corrido: A Mexican ballad.

Couplet: Two lines of poetry with the same rhyme and meter, often expressing a complete and self-contained thought.

Criticism: The systematic study and evaluation of literary works, usually based on a specific method or set of principles. An important part of literary studies since ancient times, the practice of criticism has given rise to numerous theories, methods, and "schools," sometimes producing conflicting, even contradictory, interpretations of literature in general as well as of individual works. Even such basic issues as what constitutes a poem or a novel have been the subject of much criticism over the centuries.

D

Dactyl: See *Foot*

Dadaism: A protest movement in art and literature founded by Tristan Tzara in 1916. Followers of the movement expressed their outrage at the destruction brought about by World War I by revolting against numerous forms of social convention. The Dadaists presented works marked by calculated madness and flamboyant nonsense. They stressed total freedom of expression, commonly through primitive displays of emotion and illogical, often senseless, poetry. The movement ended shortly after the war, when it was replaced by surrealism.

Decadent: See *Decadents*

Decadents: The followers of a nineteenth-century literary movement that had its beginnings in French aestheticism. Decadent literature displays a fascination with perverse and morbid states; a search for novelty and sensation—the "new thrill"; a preoccupation with mysticism; and a belief in the senselessness of human existence. The movement is closely associated with the doctrine Art for Art's Sake. The term "decadence" is sometimes used to denote a decline in the quality of art or literature following a period of greatness.

Deconstruction: A method of literary criticism developed by Jacques Derrida and characterized by multiple conflicting interpretations of a given work. Deconstructionists consider the impact of the language of a work and suggest that the true meaning of the work is not necessarily the meaning that the author intended.

Deduction: The process of reaching a conclusion through reasoning from general premises to a specific premise.

Denotation: The definition of a word, apart from the impressions or feelings it creates in the reader.

Diction: The selection and arrangement of words in a literary work. Either or both may vary depending on the desired effect. There are four general types of diction: "formal," used in scholarly or lofty writing; "informal," used in relaxed but educated conversation; "colloquial," used in everyday speech; and "slang," containing newly coined words and other terms not accepted in formal usage.

Didactic: A term used to describe works of literature that aim to teach some moral, religious, political, or practical lesson. Although didactic elements are often found in artistically pleasing works, the term "didactic" usually refers to literature in which the message is more important than the form. The term may also be used to criticize a work that the critic finds "overly didactic," that is, heavy-handed in its delivery of a lesson.

Dimeter: See *Meter*

Dionysian: See *Apollonian and Dionysian*

Discordia concours: A Latin phrase meaning "discord in harmony." The term was coined by the eighteenth-century English writer Samuel Johnson to describe "a combination of dissimilar images or discovery of occult resemblances in things apparently unlike." Johnson created the expression by reversing a phrase by the Latin poet Horace.

Dissonance: A combination of harsh or jarring sounds, especially in poetry. Although such combinations may be accidental, poets sometimes intentionally make them to achieve particular effects. Dissonance is also sometimes used to refer to close but not identical rhymes. When this is the case, the word functions as a synonym for consonance.

Double Entendre: A corruption of a French phrase meaning "double meaning." The term is used to indicate a word or phrase that is deliberately ambiguous, especially when one of the meanings is risque or improper.

Draft: Any preliminary version of a written work. An author may write dozens of drafts which are revised to form the final work, or he or she may write only one, with few or no revisions.

Dramatic Monologue: See *Monologue*

Dramatic Poetry: Any lyric work that employs elements of drama such as dialogue, conflict, or characterization, but excluding works that are intended for stage presentation.

Dream Allegory: See *Dream Vision*

Dream Vision: A literary convention, chiefly of the Middle Ages. In a dream vision a story is presented as a literal dream of the narrator. This device was commonly used to teach moral and religious lessons.

E

Eclogue: In classical literature, a poem featuring rural themes and structured as a dialogue among shepherds. Eclogues often took specific poetic forms, such as elegies or love poems. Some were written as the soliloquy of a shepherd. In later centuries, "eclogue" came to refer to any poem that was in the pastoral tradition or that had a dialogue or monologue structure.

Edwardian: Describes cultural conventions identified with the period of the reign of Edward VII of England (1901-1910). Writers of the Edwardian Age typically displayed a strong reaction against the propriety and conservatism of the Victorian Age. Their work often exhibits distrust of authority in religion, politics, and art and expresses strong doubts about the soundness of conventional values.

Edwardian Age: See *Edwardian*

Electra Complex: A daughter's amorous obsession with her father.

Elegy: A lyric poem that laments the death of a person or the eventual death of all people. In a conventional elegy, set in a classical world, the poet and subject are spoken of as shepherds. In modern criticism, the word elegy is often used to refer to a poem that is melancholy or mournfully contemplative.

Elizabethan Age: A period of great economic growth, religious controversy, and nationalism closely associated with the reign of Elizabeth I of England (1558-1603). The Elizabethan Age is considered a part of the general renaissance—that is, the flowering of arts and literature—that took place in Europe during the fourteenth through sixteenth centuries. The era is considered the golden age of English literature. The most important dramas in English and a great deal of lyric poetry were produced during this period, and modern English criticism began around this time.

Empathy: A sense of shared experience, including emotional and physical feelings, with someone or something other than oneself. Empathy is often used to describe the response of a reader to a literary character.

English Sonnet: See *Sonnet*

Enjambment: The running over of the sense and structure of a line of verse or a couplet into the following verse or couplet.

Enlightenment, The: An eighteenth-century philosophical movement. It began in France but had a wide impact throughout Europe and America. Thinkers of the Enlightenment valued reason and believed that both the individual and society could achieve a state of perfection. Corresponding to this essentially humanist vision was a resistance to religious authority.

Epic: A long narrative poem about the adventures of a hero of great historic or legendary importance. The setting is vast and the action is often given cosmic significance through the intervention of supernatural forces such as gods, angels, or demons. Epics are typically written in a classical style of grand simplicity with elaborate metaphors and allusions that enhance the symbolic importance of a hero's adventures.

Epic Simile: See *Homeric Simile*

Epigram: A saying that makes the speaker's point quickly and concisely.

Epilogue: A concluding statement or section of a literary work. In dramas, particularly those of the seventeenth and eighteenth centuries, the epilogue is a closing speech, often in verse, delivered by an actor at the end of a play and spoken directly to the audience.

Epiphany: A sudden revelation of truth inspired by a seemingly trivial incident.

Epitaph: An inscription on a tomb or tombstone, or a verse written on the occasion of a person's death. Epitaphs may be serious or humorous.

Epithalamion: A song or poem written to honor and commemorate a marriage ceremony.

Epithalamium: See *Epithalamion*

Epithet: A word or phrase, often disparaging or abusive, that expresses a character trait of someone or something.

Erziehungsroman: See *Bildungsroman*

Essay: A prose composition with a focused subject of discussion. The term was coined by Michel de Montaigne to describe his 1580 collection of brief, informal reflections on himself and on various topics relating to human nature. An essay can also be a long, systematic discourse.

Existentialism: A predominantly twentieth-century philosophy concerned with the nature and perception of human existence. There are two major strains of existentialist thought: atheistic and Christian. Followers of atheistic existentialism believe that the individual is alone in a godless universe and that the basic human condition is one of suffering and loneliness. Nevertheless, because there are no fixed values, individuals can create their own characters—indeed, they can shape themselves—through the exercise of free will. The atheistic strain culminates in and is popularly associated with the works of Jean-Paul Sartre. The Christian existentialists, on the other hand, believe that only in God may people find freedom from life's anguish. The two strains hold certain beliefs in common: that existence cannot be fully understood or described through empirical effort; that anguish is a universal element of life; that individuals must bear responsibility for their actions; and that there is no common standard of behavior or perception for religious and ethical matters.

Expatriates: See *Expatriatism*

Expatriatism: The practice of leaving one's country to live for an extended period in another country.

Exposition: Writing intended to explain the nature of an idea, thing, or theme. Expository writing is often combined with description, narration, or argument. In dramatic writing, the exposition is the introductory material which presents the characters, setting, and tone of the play.

Expressionism: An indistinct literary term, originally used to describe an early twentieth-century school of German painting. The term applies to almost any mode of unconventional, highly subjective writing that distorts reality in some way.

Extended Monologue: See *Monologue*

F

Feet: See *Foot*

Feminine Rhyme: See *Rhyme*

Fiction: Any story that is the product of imagination rather than a documentation of fact. Characters and events in such narratives may be based in real life but their ultimate form and configuration is a creation of the author.

Figurative Language: A technique in writing in which the author temporarily interrupts the order, construction, or meaning of the writing for a particular effect. This interruption takes the form of one or more figures of speech such as hyperbole, irony, or simile. Figurative language is the opposite of literal language, in which every word is truthful, accurate, and free of exaggeration or embellishment.

Figures of Speech: Writing that differs from customary conventions for construction, meaning, order, or significance for the purpose of a special meaning or effect. There are two major types of figures of speech: rhetorical figures, which do not make changes in the meaning of the words, and tropes, which do.

Fin de siecle: A French term meaning "end of the century." The term is used to denote the last decade of the nineteenth century, a transition period when writers and other artists abandoned old conventions and looked for new techniques and objectives.

First Person: See *Point of View*

Folk Ballad: See *Ballad*

Folklore: Traditions and myths preserved in a culture or group of people. Typically, these are passed on by word of mouth in various forms—such as legends, songs, and proverbs—or preserved in customs and ceremonies. This term was first used by W. J. Thoms in 1846.

Folktale: A story originating in oral tradition. Folktales fall into a variety of categories, including legends, ghost stories, fairy tales, fables, and anecdotes based on historical figures and events.

Foot: The smallest unit of rhythm in a line of poetry. In English-language poetry, a foot is typically one accented syllable combined with one or two unaccented syllables.

Form: The pattern or construction of a work which identifies its genre and distinguishes it from other genres.

Formalism: In literary criticism, the belief that literature should follow prescribed rules of construction, such as those that govern the sonnet form.

Fourteener Meter: See *Meter*

Free Verse: Poetry that lacks regular metrical and rhyme patterns but that tries to capture the cadences of everyday speech. The form allows a poet to exploit a variety of rhythmical effects within a single poem.

Futurism: A flamboyant literary and artistic movement that developed in France, Italy, and Russia from 1908 through the 1920s. Futurist theater and poetry abandoned traditional literary forms. In their place, followers of the movement attempted to achieve total freedom of expression through bizarre imagery and deformed or newly invented words. The Futurists were self-consciously modern artists who attempted to incorporate the appearances and sounds of modern life into their work.

G

Genre: A category of literary work. In critical theory, genre may refer to both the content of a given work—tragedy, comedy, pastoral—and to its form, such as poetry, novel, or drama.

Genteel Tradition: A term coined by critic George Santayana to describe the literary practice of certain late nineteenth- century American writers, especially New Englanders. Followers of the Genteel Tradition emphasized conventionality in social, religious, moral, and literary standards.

Georgian Age: See *Georgian Poets*

Georgian Period: See *Georgian Poets*

Georgian Poets: A loose grouping of English poets during the years 1912-1922. The Georgians reacted against certain literary schools and practices, especially Victorian wordiness, turn-of-the-century aestheticism, and contemporary urban realism. In their place, the Georgians embraced the nineteenth-century poetic practices of William Wordsworth and the other Lake Poets.

Georgic: A poem about farming and the farmer's way of life, named from Virgil's *Georgics*.

Gilded Age: A period in American history during the 1870s characterized by political corruption and materialism. A number of important novels of social and political criticism were written during this time.

Gothic: See *Gothicism*

Gothicism: In literary criticism, works characterized by a taste for the medieval or morbidly attractive. A gothic novel prominently features elements of horror, the supernatural, gloom, and violence: clanking chains, terror, charnel houses, ghosts, medieval castles, and mysteriously slamming doors. The term "gothic novel" is also applied to novels that lack elements of the traditional Gothic setting but that create a similar atmosphere of terror or dread.

Graveyard School: A group of eighteenth-century English poets who wrote long, picturesque meditations on death. Their works were designed to cause the reader to ponder immortality.

Great Chain of Being: The belief that all things and creatures in nature are organized in a hierarchy from inanimate objects at the bottom to God at the top. This system of belief was popular in the seventeenth and eighteenth centuries.

Grotesque: In literary criticism, the subject matter of a work or a style of expression characterized by exaggeration, deformity, freakishness, and disorder. The grotesque often includes an element of comic absurdity.

H

Haiku: The shortest form of Japanese poetry, constructed in three lines of five, seven, and five syllables respectively. The message of a *haiku* poem usually centers on some aspect of spirituality and provokes an emotional response in the reader.

Half Rhyme: See *Consonance*

Harlem Renaissance: The Harlem Renaissance of the 1920s is generally considered the first significant movement of black writers and artists in the United States. During this period, new and established black writers published more fiction and poetry than ever before, the first influential black literary journals were established, and black authors and artists received their first widespread recognition and serious critical appraisal. Among the major writers associated with this period are Claude McKay, Jean Toomer, Countee Cullen, Langston Hughes, Arna Bontemps, Nella Larsen, and Zora Neale Hurston.

Hellenism: Imitation of ancient Greek thought or styles. Also, an approach to life that focuses on the growth and development of the intellect. "Hellenism" is sometimes used to refer to the belief that reason can be applied to examine all human experience.

Heptameter: See *Meter*

Hero/Heroine: The principal sympathetic character (male or female) in a literary work. Heroes and heroines typically exhibit admirable traits: idealism, courage, and integrity, for example.

Heroic Couplet: A rhyming couplet written in iambic pentameter (a verse with five iambic feet).

Heroic Line: The meter and length of a line of verse in epic or heroic poetry. This varies by language and time period.

Heroine: See *Hero/Heroine*

Hexameter: See *Meter*

Historical Criticism: The study of a work based on its impact on the world of the time period in which it was written.

Hokku: See *Haiku*

Holocaust: See *Holocaust Literature*

Holocaust Literature: Literature influenced by or written about the Holocaust of World War II. Such literature includes true stories of survival in concentration camps, escape, and life after the war, as well as fictional works and poetry.

Homeric Simile: An elaborate, detailed comparison written as a simile many lines in length.

Horatian Satire: See *Satire*

Humanism: A philosophy that places faith in the dignity of humankind and rejects the medieval perception of the individual as a weak, fallen creature. "Humanists" typically believe in the perfectibility of human nature and view reason and education as the means to that end.

Humors: Mentions of the humors refer to the ancient Greek theory that a person's health and personality were determined by the balance of four basic fluids in the body: blood, phlegm, yellow bile, and black bile. A dominance of any fluid would cause extremes in behavior. An excess of blood created a sanguine person who was joyful, aggressive, and passionate; a phlegmatic person was shy, fearful, and sluggish; too much yellow bile led to a choleric temperament characterized by impatience, anger, bitterness, and stubbornness; and excessive black bile created melancholy, a state of laziness, gluttony, and lack of motivation.

Humours: See *Humors*

Hyperbole: In literary criticism, deliberate exaggeration used to achieve an effect.

I

Iamb: See *Foot*

Idiom: A word construction or verbal expression closely associated with a given language.

Image: A concrete representation of an object or sensory experience. Typically, such a representation helps evoke the feelings associated with the object or experience itself. Images are either "literal" or "figurative." Literal images are especially concrete and involve little or no extension of the obvious meaning of the words used to express them. Figurative images do not follow the literal meaning of the words exactly. Images in literature are usually visual, but the term "image" can also refer to the representation of any sensory experience.

Imagery: The array of images in a literary work. Also, figurative language.

Imagism: An English and American poetry movement that flourished between 1908 and 1917. The Imagists used precise, clearly presented images in their works. They also used common, everyday speech and aimed for conciseness, concrete imagery, and the creation of new rhythms.

In medias res: A Latin term meaning "in the middle of things." It refers to the technique of beginning a story at its midpoint and then using various flashback devices to reveal previous action.

Induction: The process of reaching a conclusion by reasoning from specific premises to form a general premise. Also, an introductory portion of a work of literature, especially a play.

Intentional Fallacy: The belief that judgments of a literary work based solely on an author's stated or implied intentions are false and misleading. Critics who believe in the concept of the intentional fallacy typically argue that the work itself is sufficient matter for interpretation, even though they may concede that an author's statement of purpose can be useful.

Interior Monologue: A narrative technique in which characters' thoughts are revealed in a way that appears to be uncontrolled by the author. The interior monologue typically aims to reveal the inner self of a character. It portrays emotional experiences as they occur at both a conscious and unconscious level. Images are often used to represent sensations or emotions.

Internal Rhyme: Rhyme that occurs within a single line of verse.

Irish Literary Renaissance: A late nineteenth- and early twentieth-century movement in Irish literature. Members of the movement aimed to reduce the influence of British culture in Ireland and create an Irish national literature.

Irony: In literary criticism, the effect of language in which the intended meaning is the opposite of what is stated.

Italian Sonnet: See *Sonnet*

J

Jacobean Age: The period of the reign of James I of England (1603-1625). The early literature of this period reflected the worldview of the Elizabethan Age, but a darker, more cynical attitude steadily grew in the art and literature of the Jacobean Age. This was an important time for English drama and poetry.

Jargon: Language that is used or understood only by a select group of people. Jargon may refer to terminology used in a certain profession, such as computer jargon, or it may refer to any nonsensical language that is not understood by most people.

Journalism: Writing intended for publication in a newspaper or magazine, or for broadcast on a radio or television program featuring news, sports, entertainment, or other timely material.

K

Knickerbocker Group: A somewhat indistinct group of New York writers of the first half of the nineteenth century. Members of the group were linked only by location and a common theme: New York life.

Kunstlerroman: See *Bildungsroman*

L

Lais: See *Lay*

Lake Poets: See *Lake School*

Lake School: These poets all lived in the Lake District of England at the turn of the nineteenth century. As a group, they followed no single "school" of thought or literary practice, although their works were uniformly disparaged by the *Edinburgh Review*.

Lay: A song or simple narrative poem. The form originated in medieval France. Early French *lais* were often based on the Celtic legends and other tales sung by Breton minstrels—thus the name of the "Breton lay." In fourteenth-century England, the term "lay" was used to describe short narratives written in imitation of the Breton lays.

Leitmotiv: See *Motif*

Literal Language: An author uses literal language when he or she writes without exaggerating or embellishing the subject matter and without any tools of figurative language.

Literary Ballad: See *Ballad*

Literature: Literature is broadly defined as any written or spoken material, but the term most often refers to creative works.

Lost Generation: A term first used by Gertrude Stein to describe the post-World War I generation of American writers: men and women haunted by a sense of betrayal and emptiness brought about by the destructiveness of the war.

Lyric Poetry: A poem expressing the subjective feelings and personal emotions of the poet. Such poetry is melodic, since it was originally accompanied by a lyre in recitals. Most Western poetry in the twentieth century may be classified as lyrical.

M

Mannerism: Exaggerated, artificial adherence to a literary manner or style. Also, a popular style of the visual arts of late sixteenth-century Europe that was marked by elongation of the human form and by intentional spatial distortion. Literary works that are self-consciously high-toned and artistic are often said to be "mannered."

Masculine Rhyme: See *Rhyme*

Measure: The foot, verse, or time sequence used in a literary work, especially a poem. Measure is often used somewhat incorrectly as a synonym for meter.

Metaphor: A figure of speech that expresses an idea through the image of another object. Metaphors suggest the essence of the first object by identifying it with certain qualities of the second object.

Metaphysical Conceit: See *Conceit*

Metaphysical Poetry: The body of poetry produced by a group of seventeenth-century English writers called the "Metaphysical Poets." The group includes John Donne and Andrew Marvell. The Metaphysical Poets made use of everyday speech, intellectual analysis, and unique imagery. They aimed to portray the ordinary conflicts and contradictions of life. Their poems often took the form of an argument, and many of them emphasize physical and religious love as well as the fleeting nature of life. Elaborate conceits are typical in metaphysical poetry.

Metaphysical Poets: See *Metaphysical Poetry*

Meter: In literary criticism, the repetition of sound patterns that creates a rhythm in poetry. The patterns are based on the number of syllables and the presence and absence of accents. The unit of rhythm in a line is called a foot. Types of meter are classified according to the number of feet in a line. These are the standard English lines: Monometer, one foot; Dimeter, two feet; Trimeter, three feet; Tetrameter, four feet; Pentameter, five feet; Hexameter, six feet (also called the Alexandrine); Heptameter, seven feet (also called the "Fourteener" when the feet are iambic).

Modernism: Modern literary practices. Also, the principles of a literary school that lasted from roughly the beginning of the twentieth century until the end of World War II. Modernism is defined by its rejection of the literary conventions of the nineteenth century and by its opposition to conventional morality, taste, traditions, and economic values.

Monologue: A composition, written or oral, by a single individual. More specifically, a speech given by a single individual in a drama or other public entertainment. It has no set length, although it is usually several or more lines long.

Monometer: See *Meter*

Mood: The prevailing emotions of a work or of the author in his or her creation of the work. The mood of a work is not always what might be expected based on its subject matter.

Motif: A theme, character type, image, metaphor, or other verbal element that recurs throughout a single work of literature or occurs in a number of different works over a period of time.

Motiv: See *Motif*

Muckrakers: An early twentieth-century group of American writers. Typically, their works exposed the wrongdoings of big business and government in the United States.

Muses: Nine Greek mythological goddesses, the daughters of Zeus and Mnemosyne (Memory). Each muse patronized a specific area of the liberal arts and sciences. Calliope presided over epic poetry, Clio over history, Erato over love poetry, Euterpe over music or lyric poetry, Melpomene over tragedy, Polyhymnia over hymns to the gods, Terpsichore over dance, Thalia over comedy, and Urania over astronomy. Poets and writers traditionally made appeals to the Muses for inspiration in their work.

Myth: An anonymous tale emerging from the traditional beliefs of a culture or social unit. Myths use supernatural explanations for natural phenomena. They may also explain cosmic issues like creation and death. Collections of myths, known as mythologies, are common to all cultures and nations, but the best-known myths belong to the Norse, Roman, and Greek mythologies.

N

Narration: The telling of a series of events, real or invented. A narration may be either a simple narrative, in which the events are recounted chronologically, or a narrative with a plot, in which the account is given in a style reflecting the author's artistic concept of the story. Narration is sometimes used as a synonym for "storyline."

Narrative: A verse or prose accounting of an event or sequence of events, real or invented. The term is also used as an adjective in the sense "method of narration." For example, in literary criticism, the expression "narrative technique" usually refers to the way the author structures and presents his or her story.

Narrative Poetry: A nondramatic poem in which the author tells a story. Such poems may be of any length or level of complexity.

Narrator: The teller of a story. The narrator may be the author or a character in the story through whom the author speaks.

Naturalism: A literary movement of the late nineteenth and early twentieth centuries. The movement's major theorist, French novelist Emile Zola, envisioned a type of fiction that would examine human life with the objectivity of scientific inquiry. The Naturalists typically viewed human beings as either the products of "biological determinism," ruled by hereditary instincts and engaged in an endless struggle for survival, or as the products of "socioeconomic determinism," ruled by social and economic forces beyond their control. In their works, the Naturalists generally ignored the highest levels of society and focused on degradation: poverty, alcoholism, prostitution, insanity, and disease.

Negritude: A literary movement based on the concept of a shared cultural bond on the part of black Africans, wherever they may be in the world. It traces its origins to the former French colonies of Africa and the Caribbean. Negritude poets, novelists, and essayists generally stress four points in their writings: One, black alienation from traditional African culture can lead to feelings of inferiority. Two, European colonialism and Western education should be resisted. Three, black Africans should seek to affirm and define their own identity. Four, African culture can and should be reclaimed. Many Negritude writers also claim that blacks can make unique contributions to the world, based on a heightened appreciation of nature, rhythm, and human emotions—aspects of life they say are not so highly valued in the materialistic and rationalistic West.

Negro Renaissance: See *Harlem Renaissance*

Neoclassical Period: See *Neoclassicism*

Neoclassicism: In literary criticism, this term refers to the revival of the attitudes and styles of expression of classical literature. It is generally used to describe a period in European history beginning in the late seventeenth century and lasting until about 1800. In its purest form, Neoclassicism marked a return to order, proportion, restraint, logic, accuracy, and decorum. In England, where Neoclassicism perhaps was most popular, it reflected the influence of seventeenth- century French writers, especially dramatists. Neoclassical writers typically reacted against the intensity and enthusiasm of the Renaissance period. They wrote works that appealed to the intellect, using elevated language and classical literary forms such as satire and the ode. Neoclassical works were often governed by the classical goal of instruction.

Neoclassicists: See *Neoclassicism*

New Criticism: A movement in literary criticism, dating from the late 1920s, that stressed close textual analysis in the interpretation of works of literature. The New Critics saw little merit in historical and biographical analysis. Rather, they aimed to examine the text alone, free from the question of how external events—biographical or otherwise—may have helped shape it.

New Journalism: A type of writing in which the journalist presents factual information in a form usually used in fiction. New journalism emphasizes description, narration, and character development to bring readers closer to the human element of the story, and is often used in personality profiles and in-depth feature articles. It is not compatible with "straight" or "hard" newswriting, which is generally composed in a brief, fact-based style.

New Journalists: See *New Journalism*

New Negro Movement: See *Harlem Renaissance*

Noble Savage: The idea that primitive man is noble and good but becomes evil and corrupted as he becomes civilized. The concept of the noble savage originated in the Renaissance period but is more closely identified with such later writers as Jean-Jacques Rousseau and Aphra Behn.

O

Objective Correlative: An outward set of objects, a situation, or a chain of events corresponding to an inward experience and evoking this experience in the reader. The term frequently appears in modern criticism in discussions of authors' intended effects on the emotional responses of readers.

Objectivity: A quality in writing characterized by the absence of the author's opinion or feeling about the subject matter. Objectivity is an important factor in criticism.

Occasional Verse: poetry written on the occasion of a significant historical or personal event. *Vers de societe* is sometimes called occasional verse although it is of a less serious nature.

Octave: A poem or stanza composed of eight lines. The term octave most often represents the first eight lines of a Petrarchan sonnet.

Ode: Name given to an extended lyric poem characterized by exalted emotion and dignified style. An ode usually concerns a single, serious theme. Most odes, but not all, are addressed to an object or individual. Odes

are distinguished from other lyric poetic forms by their complex rhythmic and stanzaic patterns.

Oedipus Complex: A son's amorous obsession with his mother. The phrase is derived from the story of the ancient Theban hero Oedipus, who unknowingly killed his father and married his mother.

Omniscience: See *Point of View*

Onomatopoeia: The use of words whose sounds express or suggest their meaning. In its simplest sense, onomatopoeia may be represented by words that mimic the sounds they denote such as "hiss" or "meow." At a more subtle level, the pattern and rhythm of sounds and rhymes of a line or poem may be onomatopoeic.

Oral Tradition: See *Oral Transmission*

Oral Transmission: A process by which songs, ballads, folklore, and other material are transmitted by word of mouth. The tradition of oral transmission predates the written record systems of literate society. Oral transmission preserves material sometimes over generations, although often with variations. Memory plays a large part in the recitation and preservation of orally transmitted material.

Ottava Rima: An eight-line stanza of poetry composed in iambic pentameter (a five-foot line in which each foot consists of an unaccented syllable followed by an accented syllable), following the abababcc rhyme scheme.

Oxymoron: A phrase combining two contradictory terms. Oxymorons may be intentional or unintentional.

P

Pantheism: The idea that all things are both a manifestation or revelation of God and a part of God at the same time. Pantheism was a common attitude in the early societies of Egypt, India, and Greece—the term derives from the Greek *pan* meaning "all" and *theos* meaning "deity." It later became a significant part of the Christian faith.

Parable: A story intended to teach a moral lesson or answer an ethical question.

Paradox: A statement that appears illogical or contradictory at first, but may actually point to an underlying truth.

Parallelism: A method of comparison of two ideas in which each is developed in the same grammatical structure.

Parnassianism: A mid nineteenth-century movement in French literature. Followers of the movement stressed adherence to well-defined artistic forms as a reaction against the often chaotic expression of the artist's ego that dominated the work of the Romantics. The Parnassians also rejected the moral, ethical, and social themes exhibited in the works of French Romantics such as Victor Hugo. The aesthetic doctrines of the Parnassians strongly influenced the later symbolist and decadent movements.

Parody: In literary criticism, this term refers to an imitation of a serious literary work or the signature style of a particular author in a ridiculous manner. A typical parody adopts the style of the original and applies it to an inappropriate subject for humorous effect. Parody is a form of satire and could be considered the literary equivalent of a caricature or cartoon.

Pastoral: A term derived from the Latin word "pastor," meaning shepherd. A pastoral is a literary composition on a rural theme. The conventions of the pastoral were originated by the third-century Greek poet Theocritus, who wrote about the experiences, love affairs, and pastimes of Sicilian shepherds. In a pastoral, characters and language of a courtly nature are often placed in a simple setting. The term pastoral is also used to classify dramas, elegies, and lyrics that exhibit the use of country settings and shepherd characters.

Pathetic Fallacy: A term coined by English critic John Ruskin to identify writing that falsely endows nonhuman things with human intentions and feelings, such as "angry clouds" and "sad trees."

Pen Name: See *Pseudonym*

Pentameter: See *Meter*

Persona: A Latin term meaning "mask." *Personae* are the characters in a fictional work of literature. The *persona* generally functions as a mask through which the author tells a story in a voice other than his or her own. A *persona* is usually either a character in a story who acts as a narrator or an "implied author," a voice created by the author to act as the narrator for himself or herself.

Personae: See *Persona*

Personal Point of View: See *Point of View*

Personification: A figure of speech that gives human qualities to abstract ideas, animals, and inanimate objects.

Petrarchan Sonnet: See *Sonnet*

Phenomenology: A method of literary criticism based on the belief that things have no existence outside of human consciousness or awareness. Proponents of this theory believe that art is a process that takes place in the mind of the observer as he or she contemplates an object rather than a quality of the object itself.

Plagiarism: Claiming another person's written material as one's own. Plagiarism can take the form of direct, word-for- word copying or the theft of the substance or idea of the work.

Platonic Criticism: A form of criticism that stresses an artistic work's usefulness as an agent of social engineering rather than any quality or value of the work itself.

Platonism: The embracing of the doctrines of the philosopher Plato, popular among the poets of the Renaissance and the Romantic period. Platonism is more flexible than Aristotelian Criticism and places more emphasis on the supernatural and unknown aspects of life.

Plot: In literary criticism, this term refers to the pattern of events in a narrative or drama. In its simplest sense, the plot guides the author in composing the work and helps the reader follow the work. Typically, plots exhibit causality and unity and have a beginning, a middle, and an end. Sometimes, however, a plot may consist of a series of disconnected events, in which case it is known as an "episodic plot."

Poem: In its broadest sense, a composition utilizing rhyme, meter, concrete detail, and expressive language to create a literary experience with emotional and aesthetic appeal.

Poet: An author who writes poetry or verse. The term is also used to refer to an artist or writer who has an exceptional gift for expression, imagination, and energy in the making of art in any form.

Poete maudit: A term derived from Paul Verlaine's *Les poetes maudits* (*The Accursed Poets*), a collection of essays on the French symbolist writers Stephane Mallarme, Arthur Rimbaud, and Tristan Corbiere. In the sense intended by Verlaine, the poet is "accursed" for choosing to explore extremes of human experience outside of middle-class society.

Poetic Fallacy: See *Pathetic Fallacy*

Poetic Justice: An outcome in a literary work, not necessarily a poem, in which the good are rewarded and the evil are punished, especially in ways that particularly fit their virtues or crimes.

Poetic License: Distortions of fact and literary convention made by a writer—not always a poet—for the sake of the effect gained. Poetic license is closely related to the concept of "artistic freedom."

Poetics: This term has two closely related meanings. It denotes (1) an aesthetic theory in literary criticism about the essence of poetry or (2) rules prescribing the proper methods, content, style, or diction of poetry. The term poetics may also refer to theories about literature in general, not just poetry.

Poetry: In its broadest sense, writing that aims to present ideas and evoke an emotional experience in the reader through the use of meter, imagery, connotative and concrete words, and a carefully constructed structure based on rhythmic patterns. Poetry typically relies on words and expressions that have several layers of meaning. It also makes use of the effects of regular rhythm on the ear and may make a strong appeal to the senses through the use of imagery.

Point of View: The narrative perspective from which a literary work is presented to the reader. There are four traditional points of view. The "third person omniscient" gives the reader a "godlike" perspective, unrestricted by time or place, from which to see actions and look into the minds of characters. This allows the author to comment openly on characters and events in the work. The "third person" point of view presents the events of the story from outside of any single character's perception, much like the omniscient point of view, but the reader must understand the action as it takes place and without any special insight into characters' minds or motivations. The "first person" or "personal" point of view relates events as they are perceived by a single character. The main character "tells" the story and may offer opinions about the action and characters which differ from those of the author. Much less common than omniscient, third person, and first person is the "second person" point of view, wherein the author tells the story as if it is happening to the reader.

Polemic: A work in which the author takes a stand on a controversial subject, such as abortion or religion. Such works are often extremely argumentative or provocative.

Pornography: Writing intended to provoke feelings of lust in the reader. Such works are often condemned by critics and teachers, but those which can be shown to have literary value are viewed less harshly.

Post-Aesthetic Movement: An artistic response made by African Americans to the black aesthetic movement of the 1960s and early '70s. Writers since that time have adopted a somewhat different tone in their work, with less emphasis placed on the disparity between black and white in the United States. In the words of post-aesthetic authors such as Toni Morrison, John Edgar Wideman, and Kristin Hunter, African Americans are portrayed as looking inward for answers to their own questions, rather than always looking to the outside world.

Postmodernism: Writing from the 1960s forward characterized by experimentation and continuing to apply some of the fundamentals of modernism, which included existentialism and alienation. Postmodernists have gone a step further in the rejection of tradition begun with the modernists by also rejecting traditional forms, preferring the anti-novel over the novel and the anti-hero over the hero.

Pre-Raphaelites: A circle of writers and artists in mid nineteenth-century England. Valuing the pre-Renaissance artistic qualities of religious symbolism, lavish pictorialism, and natural sensuousness, the Pre-Raphaelites cultivated a sense of mystery and melancholy that influenced later writers associated with the Symbolist and Decadent movements.

Primitivism: The belief that primitive peoples were nobler and less flawed than civilized peoples because they had not been subjected to the tainting influence of society.

Projective Verse: A form of free verse in which the poet's breathing pattern determines the lines of the poem. Poets who advocate projective verse are against all formal structures in writing, including meter and form.

Prologue: An introductory section of a literary work. It often contains information establishing the situation of the characters or presents information about the setting, time period, or action. In drama, the prologue is spoken by a chorus or by one of the principal characters.

Prose: A literary medium that attempts to mirror the language of everyday speech. It is distinguished from poetry by its use of unmetered, unrhymed language consisting of logically related sentences. Prose is usually grouped into paragraphs that form a cohesive whole such as an essay or a novel.

Prosopopoeia: See *Personification*

Protagonist: The central character of a story who serves as a focus for its themes and incidents and as the principal rationale for its development. The protagonist is sometimes referred to in discussions of modern literature as the hero or anti-hero.

Proverb: A brief, sage saying that expresses a truth about life in a striking manner.

Pseudonym: A name assumed by a writer, most often intended to prevent his or her identification as the author of a work. Two or more authors may work together under one pseudonym, or an author may use a different name for each genre he or she publishes in. Some publishing companies maintain "house pseudonyms," under which any number of authors may write installations in a series. Some authors also choose a pseudonym over their real names the way an actor may use a stage name.

Pun: A play on words that have similar sounds but different meanings.

Pure Poetry: poetry written without instructional intent or moral purpose that aims only to please a reader by its imagery or musical flow. The term pure poetry is used as the antonym of the term "didacticism."

Q

Quatrain: A four-line stanza of a poem or an entire poem consisting of four lines.

R

Realism: A nineteenth-century European literary movement that sought to portray familiar characters, situations, and settings in a realistic manner. This was done primarily by using an objective narrative point of view and through the buildup of accurate detail. The standard for success of any realistic work depends on how faithfully it transfers common experience into fictional forms. The realistic method may be altered or extended, as in stream of consciousness writing, to record highly subjective experience.

Refrain: A phrase repeated at intervals throughout a poem. A refrain may appear at the end of each stanza or at less regular intervals. It may be altered slightly at each appearance.

Renaissance: The period in European history that marked the end of the Middle Ages. It began in Italy in the late fourteenth century. In broad terms, it is usually seen as spanning the fourteenth, fifteenth, and sixteenth centuries, although it did not reach Great Britain, for example, until the 1480s or so. The Renaissance saw an awakening in almost every sphere of human activity, especially science, philosophy, and the arts. The period is best defined by the emergence of a general philosophy that emphasized the importance of the intellect, the individual, and world affairs. It contrasts strongly with the medieval worldview, characterized by the dominant concerns of faith, the social collective, and spiritual salvation.

Repartee: Conversation featuring snappy retorts and witticisms.

Restoration: See *Restoration Age*

Restoration Age: A period in English literature beginning with the crowning of Charles II in 1660 and running to about 1700. The era, which was characterized by a reaction against Puritanism, was the first great age of the comedy of manners. The finest literature of the era is typically witty and urbane, and often lewd.

Rhetoric: In literary criticism, this term denotes the art of ethical persuasion. In its strictest sense, rhetoric adheres to various principles developed since classical times for arranging facts and ideas in a clear, persuasive, appealing manner. The term is also used to refer to effective prose in general and theories of or methods for composing effective prose.

Rhetorical Question: A question intended to provoke thought, but not an expressed answer, in the reader. It is most commonly used in oratory and other persuasive genres.

Rhyme: When used as a noun in literary criticism, this term generally refers to a poem in which words sound identical or very similar and appear in parallel positions in two or more lines. Rhymes are classified into different types according to where they fall in a line or stanza or according to the degree of similarity they exhibit in their spellings and sounds. Some major types of rhyme are "masculine" rhyme, "feminine" rhyme, and "triple" rhyme. In a masculine rhyme, the rhyming sound falls in a single accented syllable, as with "heat" and "eat." Feminine rhyme is a rhyme of two syllables, one stressed and one unstressed, as with "merry" and "tarry." Triple rhyme matches the sound of the accented syllable and the two unaccented syllables that follow: "narrative" and "declarative."

Rhyme Royal: A stanza of seven lines composed in iambic pentameter and rhymed *ababbcc*. The name is said to be a tribute to King James I of Scotland, who made much use of the form in his poetry.

Rhyme Scheme: See *Rhyme*

Rhythm: A regular pattern of sound, time intervals, or events occurring in writing, most often and most discernably in poetry. Regular, reliable rhythm is known to be soothing to humans, while interrupted, unpredictable, or rapidly changing rhythm is disturbing. These effects are known to authors, who use them to produce a desired reaction in the reader.

Rococo: A style of European architecture that flourished in the eighteenth century, especially in France. The most notable features of *rococo* are its extensive use of ornamentation and its themes of lightness, gaiety, and intimacy. In literary criticism, the term is often used disparagingly to refer to a decadent or over-ornamental style.

Romance: A broad term, usually denoting a narrative with exotic, exaggerated, often idealized characters, scenes, and themes.

Romantic Age: See *Romanticism*

Romanticism: This term has two widely accepted meanings. In historical criticism, it refers to a European intellectual and artistic movement of the late eighteenth and early nineteenth centuries that sought greater freedom of personal expression than that allowed by the strict rules of literary form and logic of the eighteenth-century neoclassicists. The Romantics preferred emotional and imaginative expression to rational analysis. They considered the individual to be at the center of all experience and so placed him or her at the center of their art. The Romantics believed that the creative imagination reveals nobler truths—unique feelings and attitudes—than those that could be discovered by logic or by scientific examination. Both the natural world and the state of childhood were important sources for revelations of "eternal truths." "Romanticism" is also used as a general term to refer to a type of sensibility found in all periods of literary history and usually considered to be in opposition to the principles of classicism. In this sense, Romanticism signifies any work or philosophy in which the exotic or dreamlike figure strongly, or that is devoted to individualistic expression, self-analysis, or a pursuit of a higher realm of knowledge than can be discovered by human reason.

Romantics: See *Romanticism*

Russian Symbolism: A Russian poetic movement, derived from French symbolism, that flourished between 1894 and 1910. While some Russian Symbolists continued in the French tradition, stressing aestheticism and the importance of suggestion above didactic intent, others saw their craft as a form of mystical worship, and themselves as mediators between the supernatural and the mundane.

S

Satire: A work that uses ridicule, humor, and wit to criticize and provoke change in human nature and institutions. There are two major types of satire: "formal" or "direct" satire speaks directly to the reader or to a character in the work; "indirect" satire relies upon the ridiculous behavior of its characters to make its point. Formal satire is further divided into two manners: the "Horatian," which ridicules gently, and the "Juvenalian," which derides its subjects harshly and bitterly.

Scansion: The analysis or "scanning" of a poem to determine its meter and often its rhyme scheme. The most common system of scansion uses accents (slanted lines drawn above syllables) to show stressed syllables, breves (curved lines drawn above syllables) to show unstressed syllables, and vertical lines to separate each foot.

Second Person: See *Point of View*

Semiotics: The study of how literary forms and conventions affect the meaning of language.

Sestet: Any six-line poem or stanza.

Setting: The time, place, and culture in which the action of a narrative takes place. The elements of setting may include geographic location, characters' physical and mental environments, prevailing cultural attitudes, or the historical time in which the action takes place.

Shakespearean Sonnet: See *Sonnet*

Signifying Monkey: A popular trickster figure in black folklore, with hundreds of tales about this character documented since the 19th century.

Simile: A comparison, usually using "like" or "as", of two essentially dissimilar things, as in "coffee as cold as ice" or "He sounded like a broken record."

Slang: A type of informal verbal communication that is generally unacceptable for formal writing. Slang words and phrases are often colorful exaggerations used to emphasize the speaker's point; they may also be shortened versions of an often-used word or phrase.

Slant Rhyme: See *Consonance*

Slave Narrative: Autobiographical accounts of American slave life as told by escaped slaves. These works first appeared during the abolition movement of the 1830s through the 1850s.

Social Realism: See *Socialist Realism*

Socialist Realism: The Socialist Realism school of literary theory was proposed by Maxim Gorky and established as a dogma by the first Soviet Congress of Writers. It demanded adherence to a communist worldview in works of literature. Its doctrines required an objective viewpoint comprehensible to the working classes and themes of social struggle featuring strong proletarian heroes.

Soliloquy: A monologue in a drama used to give the audience information and to develop the speaker's character. It is typically a projection of the speaker's innermost thoughts. Usually delivered while the speaker is alone on stage, a soliloquy is intended to present an illusion of unspoken reflection.

Sonnet: A fourteen-line poem, usually composed in iambic pentameter, employing one of several rhyme schemes. There are three major types of sonnets, upon which all other variations of the form are based: the "Petrarchan" or "Italian" sonnet, the "Shakespearean" or "English" sonnet, and the "Spenserian" sonnet. A Petrarchan sonnet consists of an octave rhymed *abbaabba* and a "sestet" rhymed either *cdecde, cdccdc,* or *cdedce.* The octave poses a question or problem, relates a narrative, or puts forth a proposition; the sestet presents a solution to the problem, comments upon the narrative, or applies the proposition put forth in the octave. The Shakespearean sonnet is divided into three quatrains and a couplet rhymed *abab cdcd efef gg.* The couplet provides an epigrammatic comment on the narrative or problem put forth in the quatrains. The Spenserian sonnet uses three quatrains and a couplet like the Shakespearean, but links their three rhyme schemes in this way: *abab bcbc cdcd ee.* The Spenserian sonnet develops its theme in two parts like the Petrarchan, its final six lines resolving a problem, analyzing a narrative, or applying a proposition put forth in its first eight lines.

Spenserian Sonnet: See *Sonnet*

Spenserian Stanza: A nine-line stanza having eight verses in iambic pentameter, its ninth verse in iambic hexameter, and the rhyme scheme ababbcbcc.

Spondee: In poetry meter, a foot consisting of two long or stressed syllables occurring together. This form is quite rare in English verse, and is usually composed of two monosyllabic words.

Sprung Rhythm: Versification using a specific number of accented syllables per line but disregarding the number of unaccented syllables that fall in each line, producing an irregular rhythm in the poem.

Stanza: A subdivision of a poem consisting of lines grouped together, often in recurring patterns of rhyme, line length, and meter. Stanzas may also serve as units of thought in a poem much like paragraphs in prose.

Stereotype: A stereotype was originally the name for a duplication made during the printing process; this led to its modern definition as a person or thing that is (or is assumed to be) the same as all others of its type.

Stream of Consciousness: A narrative technique for rendering the inward experience of a character. This technique is designed to give the impression of an ever-changing series of thoughts, emotions, images, and memories in the spontaneous and seemingly illogical order that they occur in life.

Structuralism: A twentieth-century movement in literary criticism that examines how literary texts arrive at their meanings, rather than the meanings themselves. There are two major types of structuralist analysis: one examines the way patterns of linguistic structures unify a specific text and emphasize certain elements of that text, and the other interprets the way literary forms and conventions affect the meaning of language itself.

Structure: The form taken by a piece of literature. The structure may be made obvious for ease of understanding, as in nonfiction works, or may obscured for artistic purposes, as in some poetry or seemingly "unstructured" prose.

Sturm und Drang: A German term meaning "storm and stress." It refers to a German literary movement of the 1770s and 1780s that reacted against the order and rationalism of the enlightenment, focusing instead on the intense experience of extraordinary individuals.

Style: A writer's distinctive manner of arranging words to suit his or her ideas and purpose in writing. The unique imprint of the author's personality upon his or her writing, style is the product of an author's way of arranging ideas and his or her use of diction, different sentence structures, rhythm, figures of speech, rhetorical principles, and other elements of composition.

Subject: The person, event, or theme at the center of a work of literature. A work may have one or more subjects of each type, with shorter works tending to have fewer and longer works tending to have more.

Subjectivity: Writing that expresses the author's personal feelings about his subject, and which may or may not include factual information about the subject.

Surrealism: A term introduced to criticism by Guillaume Apollinaire and later adopted by Andre Breton. It refers to a French literary and artistic movement founded in the 1920s. The Surrealists sought to express unconscious thoughts and feelings in their works. The best-known technique used for achieving this aim was automatic writing—transcriptions of spontaneous outpourings from the unconscious. The Surrealists proposed to unify the contrary levels of conscious and unconscious, dream and reality, objectivity and subjectivity into a new level of "super-realism."

Suspense: A literary device in which the author maintains the audience's attention through the buildup of events, the outcome of which will soon be revealed.

Syllogism: A method of presenting a logical argument. In its most basic form, the syllogism consists of a major premise, a minor premise, and a conclusion.

Symbol: Something that suggests or stands for something else without losing its original identity. In literature, symbols combine their literal meaning with the suggestion of an abstract concept. Literary symbols are of two types: those that carry complex associations of meaning no matter what their contexts, and those that derive their suggestive meaning from their functions in specific literary works.

Symbolism: This term has two widely accepted meanings. In historical criticism, it denotes an early modernist literary movement initiated in France during the nineteenth century that reacted against the prevailing standards of realism. Writers in this movement aimed to evoke, indirectly and symbolically, an order of being beyond the material world of the five senses. Poetic expression of personal emotion figured strongly in the movement, typically by means of a private set of symbols uniquely identifiable with the individual poet. The principal aim of the Symbolists was to express in words the highly complex feelings that grew out of everyday contact with the world. In a broader sense, the term "symbolism" refers to the use of one object to represent another.

Symbolist: See *Symbolism*

Symbolist Movement: See *Symbolism*

Sympathetic Fallacy: See *Affective Fallacy*

T

Tanka: A form of Japanese poetry similar to *haiku*. A *tanka* is five lines long, with the lines containing five, seven, five, seven, and seven syllables respectively.

Terza Rima: A three-line stanza form in poetry in which the rhymes are made on the last word of each line in the following manner: the first and third lines of the first stanza, then the second line of the first stanza and the first and third lines of the second stanza, and so on with the middle line of any stanza rhyming with the first and third lines of the following stanza.

Tetrameter: See *Meter*

Textual Criticism: A branch of literary criticism that seeks to establish the authoritative text of a literary work. Textual critics typically compare all known manuscripts or printings of a single work in order to assess the meanings of differences and revisions. This procedure allows them to arrive at a definitive version that (supposedly) corresponds to the author's original intention.

Theme: The main point of a work of literature. The term is used interchangeably with thesis.

Thesis: A thesis is both an essay and the point argued in the essay. Thesis novels and thesis plays share the quality of containing a thesis which is supported through the action of the story.

Third Person: See *Point of View*

Tone: The author's attitude toward his or her audience may be deduced from the tone of the work. A formal tone may create distance or convey politeness, while an informal tone may encourage a friendly, intimate, or intrusive feeling in the reader. The author's attitude toward his or her subject matter may

also be deduced from the tone of the words he or she uses in discussing it.

Tragedy: A drama in prose or poetry about a noble, courageous hero of excellent character who, because of some tragic character flaw or *hamartia*, brings ruin upon him- or herself. Tragedy treats its subjects in a dignified and serious manner, using poetic language to help evoke pity and fear and bring about catharsis, a purging of these emotions. The tragic form was practiced extensively by the ancient Greeks. In the Middle Ages, when classical works were virtually unknown, tragedy came to denote any works about the fall of persons from exalted to low conditions due to any reason: fate, vice, weakness, etc. According to the classical definition of tragedy, such works present the "pathetic"—that which evokes pity—rather than the tragic. The classical form of tragedy was revived in the sixteenth century; it flourished especially on the Elizabethan stage. In modern times, dramatists have attempted to adapt the form to the needs of modern society by drawing their heroes from the ranks of ordinary men and women and defining the nobility of these heroes in terms of spirit rather than exalted social standing.

Tragic Flaw: In a tragedy, the quality within the hero or heroine which leads to his or her downfall.

Transcendentalism: An American philosophical and religious movement, based in New England from around 1835 until the Civil War. Transcendentalism was a form of American romanticism that had its roots abroad in the works of Thomas Carlyle, Samuel Coleridge, and Johann Wolfgang von Goethe. The Transcendentalists stressed the importance of intuition and subjective experience in communication with God. They rejected religious dogma and texts in favor of mysticism and scientific naturalism. They pursued truths that lie beyond the "colorless" realms perceived by reason and the senses and were active social reformers in public education, women's rights, and the abolition of slavery.

Trickster: A character or figure common in Native American and African literature who uses his ingenuity to defeat enemies and escape difficult situations. Tricksters are most often animals, such as the spider, hare, or coyote, although they may take the form of humans as well.

Trimeter: See *Meter*

Triple Rhyme: See *Rhyme*

Trochee: See *Foot*

U

Understatement: See *Irony*

Unities: Strict rules of dramatic structure, formulated by Italian and French critics of the Renaissance and based loosely on the principles of drama discussed by Aristotle in his *Poetics*. Foremost among these rules were the three unities of action, time, and place that compelled a dramatist to: (1) construct a single plot with a beginning, middle, and end that details the causal relationships of action and character; (2) restrict the action to the events of a single day; and (3) limit the scene to a single place or city. The unities were observed faithfully by continental European writers until the Romantic Age, but they were never regularly observed in English drama. Modern dramatists are typically more concerned with a unity of impression or emotional effect than with any of the classical unities.

Urban Realism: A branch of realist writing that attempts to accurately reflect the often harsh facts of modern urban existence.

Utopia: A fictional perfect place, such as "paradise" or "heaven."

Utopian: See *Utopia*

Utopianism: See *Utopia*

V

Verisimilitude: Literally, the appearance of truth. In literary criticism, the term refers to aspects of a work of literature that seem true to the reader.

Vers de societe: See *Occasional Verse*

Vers libre: See *Free Verse*

Verse: A line of metered language, a line of a poem, or any work written in verse.

Versification: The writing of verse. Versification may also refer to the meter, rhyme, and other mechanical components of a poem.

Victorian: Refers broadly to the reign of Queen Victoria of England (1837-1901) and to anything with qualities typical of that era. For example, the qualities of smug narrowmindedness, bourgeois materialism, faith in social progress, and priggish morality are often considered Victorian. This stereotype is contradicted by such dramatic intellectual developments as the theories of Charles Darwin, Karl Marx, and Sigmund Freud (which stirred strong debates in England) and the critical attitudes of serious Victorian writers like Charles Dickens and George Eliot. In literature, the Victorian Period was the great age of the English novel, and the latter part of the era saw the rise of movements such as decadence and symbolism.

Victorian Age: See *Victorian*

Victorian Period: See *Victorian*

W

Weltanschauung: A German term referring to a person's worldview or philosophy.

Weltschmerz: A German term meaning "world pain." It describes a sense of anguish about the nature of existence, usually associated with a melancholy, pessimistic attitude.

Z

Zarzuela: A type of Spanish operetta.

Zeitgeist: A German term meaning "spirit of the time." It refers to the moral and intellectual trends of a given era.

Cumulative Author/Title Index

Cumulative Nationality/ Ethnicity Index

Subject/Theme Index

Honor
    Goblin Market: 102, 108
    Ozymandias: 178, 189
    Requiem: 197-198, 207
    *A Satirical Elegy on the Death of a
        Late Famous General:* 216-218,
        232

Hope
    September 1, 1939: 239
Hope
    Conversation with a Stone: 44, 54, 60
    Dream Song 29: 69, 71, 73, 75-76,
        79, 88
    Goblin Market: 94, 98, 101, 104,
        109
    The Man-Moth: 141, 146-147, 151
    Ozymandias: 171, 176, 178-179,
        188-190, 192
    Requiem: 196, 198-200, 206
    September 1, 1939: 234, 239, 242,
        244, 246, 249
    Telephone Conversation: 260-262,
        265
Human Condition
    Conversation with a Stone: 57
Humanism
    Conversation with a Stone: 47, 55,
        58, 60
    Waterfalls in a Bank: 273, 284-286
Humiliation and Degradation
    Telephone Conversation: 261,
        264-266
Humor
    Borges and I: 25, 29-30, 36
    Conversation with a Stone: 52,
        59-60
    Dream Song 29: 72, 78-79, 88
    The Man-Moth: 136, 147-148
    *A Satirical Elegy on the Death of a
        Late Famous General:* 219, 222,
        225, 228
    Telephone Conversation: 250,
        253-254, 259-260, 263-264, 266
    Waterfalls in a Bank: 270, 281,
        283-284
    *Yet we insist that life is full of
        happy chance:* 310, 313-314

I

Identity
    Borges and I: 19-20
Ignorance
    Conversation with a Stone: 41, 44,
        52, 55, 57
    Dream Song 29: 64
    September 1, 1939: 239, 244
Imagery and Symbolism
    Archaic Torso of Apollo: 5-6, 9, 12
    Borges and I: 21, 26, 34-35
    Conversation with a Stone: 42,
        49-50, 52, 54, 61

Dream Song 29: 71, 85-87
Goblin Market: 90, 100-102,
    104-105, 107, 110, 112-113
Iola, Kansas: 115, 122, 125,
    129-130
The Man-Moth: 136-141, 143-144,
    146-149, 152
*My Grandmother's Plot in the
    Family Cemetery:* 161, 163-164,
    166-167
Ozymandias: 171, 175-177,
    185-187, 189-192
Requiem: 200-201, 204, 208
*A Satirical Elegy on the Death of a
    Late Famous General:* 225, 227,
    230
September 1, 1939: 238, 244
Telephone Conversation: 258,
    263-264
Waterfalls in a Bank: 268, 270,
    272, 275, 277-278, 283, 286-289
*Yet we insist that life is full of
    happy chance:* 292, 294, 296,
    298, 300, 310-311
Imagination
    Conversation with a Stone: 41, 44,
        48-49, 51-52, 58-60
    Dream Song 29: 65-66, 71-73, 82,
        86-87
    The Man-Moth: 141, 150
    Ozymandias: 176, 187-189
    *A Satirical Elegy on the Death of a
        Late Famous General:* 218,
        221-222, 225, 227, 229
    Waterfalls in a Bank: 279, 283
    *Yet we insist that life is full of
        happy chance:* 300, 305, 315
Immigrants and Immigration
    Telephone Conversation: 252,
        254-255, 263-266
    Waterfalls in a Bank: 268, 276-278
Impatience
    Borges and I: 22, 29-30
    Dream Song 29: 63, 66, 72, 75-76,
        81, 84
    *Yet we insist that life is full of
        happy chance:* 291, 305, 309, 312
Imperialism
    September 1, 1939: 235-236, 238,
        247-248
Individual and Society, The
    Conversation with a Stone: 47
Ingratitude
    *A Satirical Elegy on the Death of a
        Late Famous General:* 223-224
Insanity
    Dream Song 29: 65, 67, 80, 83, 88
    Ozymandias: 189-190
    Requiem: 198, 201, 206-207, 209,
        211
    September 1, 1939: 245-246
    *Yet we insist that life is full of
        happy chance:* 291, 298, 312, 316

Irony
    Borges and I: 20-21, 24, 26-27,
        29-30, 33-34, 36
    Conversation with a Stone: 39, 43,
        50-52, 57-59, 61
    Dream Song 29: 65, 72, 74-75,
        79-82
    Ozymandias: 174-176, 178-179
    *A Satirical Elegy on the Death of a
        Late Famous General:* 224, 227,
        229
    Telephone Conversation: 250,
        252-254, 256-258, 263, 265-266
    Waterfalls in a Bank: 279, 281,
        284-289
Islamism
    Ozymandias: 188-189

K

Killers and Killing
    Borges and I: 22, 31
    Conversation with a Stone: 44, 55, 59
    Dream Song 29: 65, 69, 71, 75-76,
        82, 87
    Requiem: 202-203, 211
Kindness
    Archaic Torso of Apollo: 4, 8-9, 11
Knowledge
    Archaic Torso of Apollo: 6
Knowledge
    Archaic Torso of Apollo: 3, 6-10, 12
    Borges and I: 18, 21, 25-26, 28, 30,
        34-35
    Conversation with a Stone: 40-43,
        45, 47-50, 53, 55, 57
    Iola, Kansas: 116, 120, 122, 125
    Ozymandias: 182, 190-191
    September 1, 1939: 234, 239, 244
    Waterfalls in a Bank: 269, 280,
        283, 285
    *Yet we insist that life is full of
        happy chance:* 292, 294-296,
        302, 304, 308-309, 317

L

Landscape
    Conversation with a Stone: 46, 53,
        56-60
    Dream Song 29: 67, 70-71, 73-74,
        88
    Goblin Market: 94-97, 110, 114
    Iola, Kansas: 116-117, 119, 121,
        124-132
    *My Grandmother's Plot in the
        Family Cemetery:* 162-163, 167
    Ozymandias: 171-175, 177-179,
        185, 187-190, 192-193
    Requiem: 196-198, 201-202,
        206-208, 212
    Telephone Conversation: 251,
        258-259, 261, 263

Subject/Theme Index

Dream Song 29: 62-73, 75-89

Goblin Market: 91, 93, 98, 108, 112-113

Iola, Kansas: 117, 119, 122, 125, 128, 130

Ozymandias: 180-181, 187, 191-192

Requiem: 197, 199-200

September 1, 1939: 233, 235, 237, 243, 246, 249

Waterfalls in a Bank: 270-272, 280-284, 289

Yet we insist that life is full of happy chance: 291, 293, 296, 303-308, 310-312, 314-316

Mystery and Intrigue

Borges and I: 16, 21, 25, 31-32, 34-36

Dream Song 29: 66-67, 71, 76, 79, 82

Myths and Legends

Archaic Torso of Apollo: 1-3, 5-14

Borges and I: 28, 31, 34-36

Goblin Market: 90-95, 97-114

Ozymandias: 180-182, 185-186, 189-193

A Satirical Elegy on the Death of a Late Famous General: 224-229

Telephone Conversation: 251, 256-257, 259, 261, 263, 267

Waterfalls in a Bank: 269, 279, 282-284, 287

N

Naive Question, The

Conversation with a Stone: 42

Naivete

Conversation with a Stone: 42-43, 47, 53, 55

Narration

Borges and I: 18-21, 26-34

Dream Song 29: 72, 79-80, 87-88

Iola, Kansas: 124, 127

The Man-Moth: 136-141, 144, 146, 150

My Grandmother's Plot in the Family Cemetery: 155, 157, 167-169

Ozymandias: 171, 182-184, 186, 188

Requiem: 194-202, 204-207, 211-212

Telephone Conversation: 251, 257, 262-263, 266

Waterfalls in a Bank: 274-275, 284

Yet we insist that life is full of happy chance: 297, 300, 304-308, 312-315

Nationalism and Patriotism

Telephone Conversation: 262, 265

Naturalism

Conversation with a Stone: 47, 55, 60

Nature

Archaic Torso of Apollo: 9, 13

Conversation with a Stone: 42, 44, 48-50, 52-55, 59-61

Dream Song 29: 63, 65-66, 75-76, 80, 85

Goblin Market: 91, 99-102, 104, 107-109, 111, 113

Iola, Kansas: 132

The Man-Moth: 141, 150

My Grandmother's Plot in the Family Cemetery: 167

Ozymandias: 171, 175-176, 179, 181-182, 185-191

Requiem: 196, 198, 201, 207-208

A Satirical Elegy on the Death of a Late Famous General: 214, 216-217, 225, 228, 231

Telephone Conversation: 255

Waterfalls in a Bank: 278, 281, 283, 285, 287

Yet we insist that life is full of happy chance: 291-293, 304, 306-308, 310, 312-314

Nature of Memory, The

Yet we insist that life is full of happy chance: 293-294

Nomadic Life

Iola, Kansas: 126, 132

North America

Borges and I: 22, 24, 26, 29

The Man-Moth: 134

September 1, 1939: 235, 240-242, 245

Waterfalls in a Bank: 268-269, 271-272, 274-276, 279-281, 285-287

O

Obsession

Dream Song 29: 65-67, 73

Ode

Ozymandias: 181-184, 187, 191

Old Age

Waterfalls in a Bank: 269-270, 272, 288

Order and Disorder

Iola, Kansas: 120

Other, The

Conversation with a Stone: 41-42

P

Painting

Archaic Torso of Apollo: 1-2, 7-9, 11, 14

Conversation with a Stone: 40, 54, 56-57

The Man-Moth: 152

Parody

Borges and I: 25, 29

Passivity

Goblin Market: 99-100, 110

Patience

The Man-Moth: 148-150

Perception

Archaic Torso of Apollo: 4-9, 11, 14

Conversation with a Stone: 45, 52-54, 57, 60

Dream Song 29: 65, 67, 69-70, 72, 75, 79-80, 89

Goblin Market: 90, 94, 104, 107-110, 114

Iola, Kansas: 118-119, 122-123, 127, 130, 132

Requiem: 194, 207-209

Telephone Conversation: 254, 257-259, 264-265

Waterfalls in a Bank: 270-272, 281, 283-284, 288

Yet we insist that life is full of happy chance: 296, 300-301, 306, 308, 311

Permanence

Conversation with a Stone: 52-53, 59-60

Dream Song 29: 62, 65-66, 70, 72, 86, 88

My Grandmother's Plot in the Family Cemetery: 157, 165

Ozymandias: 174, 177, 180, 182-184, 187, 189

Persecution

Dream Song 29: 65, 72, 82-83, 85, 87

Goblin Market: 100, 109, 112

Requiem: 194-195, 202, 208-210, 212

September 1, 1939: 245

Perseverance

The Man-Moth: 133-134, 138, 146-147

My Grandmother's Plot in the Family Cemetery: 163, 166

Personal Identity

Archaic Torso of Apollo: 8, 12

Borges and I: 17, 19-21, 31-34

Yet we insist that life is full of happy chance: 301-303, 305-306, 313

Personification

Archaic Torso of Apollo: 5, 9, 11

Goblin Market: 98-99, 103, 106, 108, 113

Requiem: 196, 198, 207

Waterfalls in a Bank: 277, 283

Philosophical Ideas

Borges and I: 19, 22, 24-25, 31, 36

Conversation with a Stone: 39, 50, 52, 54, 56-58, 60-61

Dream Song 29: 63, 69, 72, 74-75, 79-80

T

Time and Change
  Archaic Torso of Apollo: 11-15
  Conversation with a Stone: 42-43,
    51, 54, 61
  Dream Song 29: 68, 77, 86, 89
  Goblin Market: 94, 101
  *My Grandmother's Plot in the
    Family Cemetery:* 157, 161, 163,
    165
  Ozymandias: 173, 178, 181, 189,
    191
  *A Satirical Elegy on the Death of a
    Late Famous General:* 217-218,
    220, 227-228
  Telephone Conversation: 250, 258,
    260
  Waterfalls in a Bank: 272-273,
    275, 285, 288-289
  *Yet we insist that life is full of
    happy chance:* 301, 307, 314-315
Tone
  Archaic Torso of Apollo: 4, 6
  Conversation with a Stone: 43-44,
    54-56, 60-61
  Dream Song 29: 75-76, 80, 88
  Goblin Market: 99, 112-113
  *My Grandmother's Plot in the
    Family Cemetery:* 156, 165
  Requiem: 197-198, 207
  *A Satirical Elegy on the Death
    of a Late Famous General:*
    216, 219
  September 1, 1939: 233, 243-244
  Telephone Conversation: 252-253,
    259, 261
  Waterfalls in a Bank: 275,
    284-285
Totalitarianism
  Conversation with a Stone: 42
Transformation of the Ordinary
  Waterfalls in a Bank: 272
Trust
  Iola, Kansas: 119, 128
  *A Satirical Elegy on the Death of a
    Late Famous General:* 216, 219,
    230

U

Ugliness
  *A Satirical Elegy on the Death of a
    Late Famous General:* 224, 228
Uncertainty
  Borges and I: 16, 20, 24, 29, 32-34
  Conversation with a Stone: 47, 51,
    53, 55, 57, 61
  Dream Song 29: 71, 75, 78-79,
    81-82, 84, 87
Understanding
  Archaic Torso of Apollo: 5, 7, 11
  Borges and I: 24, 31
  Conversation with a Stone: 42,
    44-45, 48-52, 54-55, 59
  Dream Song 29: 64
  Goblin Market: 111
  Iola, Kansas: 120, 122
  The Man-Moth: 137, 150, 152
  Ozymandias: 180, 182, 184, 186
  Requiem: 200-201, 209, 211
  September 1, 1939: 237, 242, 246,
    248
  Telephone Conversation: 250,
    256-258, 266
  Waterfalls in a Bank: 282, 286-287
  *Yet we insist that life is full of
    happy chance:* 293, 296-297,
    304, 307, 310
Utopianism
  Conversation with a Stone: 48, 55,
    57, 59
  Ozymandias: 182, 185, 189, 191

V

Vanity
  *A Satirical Elegy on the Death of a
    Late Famous General:* 218-219

W

War, The Military, and Soldier Life
  Archaic Torso of Apollo: 2-3, 14
  Borges and I: 17, 22-23, 26, 28,
    30, 34
  Conversation with a Stone:
    44-45, 58

  Ozymandias: 174, 176, 185, 188,
    192
  Requiem: 202-204, 208, 212
  *A Satirical Elegy on the Death of a
    Late Famous General:* 214,
    216-223, 225-226, 228-231
  September 1, 1939: 233-234, 236,
    238, 240-241, 243, 245, 247-248
  Telephone Conversation: 251-252,
    254-255, 257, 260-262, 266
  Waterfalls in a Bank: 269-270,
    273, 282
  *Yet we insist that life is full of
    happy chance:* 291, 298, 303,
    307, 312-314
Wildlife
  Archaic Torso of Apollo: 1, 4, 6, 11,
    13-14
  Conversation with a Stone: 55,
    58-60
  Goblin Market: 92-94, 96-97,
    100-101, 105, 112
  Iola, Kansas: 125-127, 129-130,
    132
  *A Satirical Elegy on the Death of a
    Late Famous General:* 225-229
  Waterfalls in a Bank: 270, 278,
    281, 283, 286
  *Yet we insist that life is full of
    happy chance:* 291, 298, 307-
    308, 310-314, 316
Wisdom
  Ozymandias: 174-175, 180-181,
    185
World War Ii
  Borges and I: 22-23, 29
  Conversation with a Stone: 39, 44,
    46
  Dream Song 29: 70, 72, 74-75, 82
  September 1, 1939: 233, 235-236,
    238, 240-241, 245-246

Y

Yearning
  Goblin Market: 93-94, 97-98, 101,
    109

Cumulative Index of First Lines

I

I am not a painter, I am a poet (Why I Am Not a Painter) V8:258

I am silver and exact. I have no preconceptions (Mirror) V1:116

I am the Smoke King (The Song of the Smoke) V13:196

I am trying to pry open your casket (Dear Reader) V10:85

I became a creature of light (The Mystery) V15:137

I cannot love the Brothers Wright (Reactionary Essay on Applied Science) V9:199

I don't mean to make you cry. (Monologue for an Onion) V24:120–121

I felt a Funeral, in my Brain, (I felt a Funeral in my Brain) V13:137

I gave birth to life. (Maternity) V21:142–143

I have just come down from my father (The Hospital Window) V11:58

I have met them at close of day (Easter 1916) V5:91

I haven't the heart to say (To an Unknown Poet) V18:221

I hear America singing, the varied carols I hear (I Hear America Singing) V3:152

I heard a Fly buzz—when I died— (I Heard a Fly Buzz— When I Died—) V5:140

I know that I shall meet my fate (An Irish Airman Foresees His Death) V1:76

I leant upon a coppice gate (The Darkling Thrush) V18:74

I lie down on my side in the moist grass (Omen) v22:107

I looked in my heart while the wild swans went over. (Wild Swans) V17:221

I met a traveller from an antique land (Ozymandias) V27:173

I prove a theorem and the house expands: (Geometry) V15:68

I saw that a star had broken its rope (Witness) V26:285

I see them standing at the formal gates of their colleges, (I go Back to May 1937) V17:112

I shook your hand before I went. (Mastectomy) V26:122

I sit in one of the dives (September 1, 1939) V27:234

I sit in the top of the wood, my eyes closed (Hawk Roosting) V4:55

I thought wearing an evergreen dress (Pine) V23:223–224

I was angry with my friend; (A Poison Tree) V24:195–196

I was born too late and I am much too old, (Death Sentences) V22:23

I was born under the mudbank (Seeing You) V24:244–245

I was sitting in mcsorley's. outside it was New York and beautifully snowing. (i was sitting in mcsorley's) V13:151

I will arise and go now, and go to Innisfree, (The Lake Isle of Innisfree) V15:121

If all the world and love were young, (The Nymph's Reply to the Shepard) V14:241

If ever two were one, then surely we (To My Dear and Loving Husband) V6:228

If every time their minds drifted, (What the Poets Could Have Been) V26:261

If I should die, think only this of me (The Soldier) V7:218

If you can keep your head when all about you (If) V22:54–55

If you want my apartment, sleep in it (Rent) V25:164

I'm delighted to see you (The Constellation Orion) V8:53

"Imagine being the first to say: *surveillance*," (Inventors) V7:97

Impatient for home, (Portrait of a Couple at Century's End) V24:214–215

In 1790 a woman could die by falling (The Art of the Novel) V23:29

In 1936, a child (Blood Oranges) V13:34

In a while they rose and went out aimlessly riding, (Merlin Enthralled) V16:72

In China (Lost Sister) V5:216

In ethics class so many years ago (Ethics) V8:88

In Flanders fields the poppies blow (In Flanders Fields) V5:155

In India in their lives they happen (Ways to Live) V16:228

In May, when sea-winds pierced our solitudes, (The Rhodora) V17:191

In the bottom drawer of my desk . . . (Answers to Letters) V21:30–31

In the evening (Another Night in the Ruins) V26:12

In the groves of Africa from their natural wonder (An African Elegy) V13:3

In the Shreve High football stadium (Autumn Begins in Martins Ferry, Ohio) V8:17

In the sixty-eight years (Accounting) V21:2–3

In Xanadu did Kubla Khan (Kubla Khan) V5:172

Ink runs from the corners of my mouth (Eating Poetry) V9:60

Is it the boy in me who's looking out (The Boy) V19:14

It is a cold and snowy night. The main street is deserted. (Driving to Town Late to Mail a Letter) V17:63

It is an ancient Mariner (The Rime of the Ancient Mariner) V4:127

It is in the small things we see it. (Courage) V14:125

It is said, the past (Russian Letter) V26:181

It little profits that an idle king (Ulysses) V2:278

It looked extremely rocky for the Mudville nine that day (Casey at the Bat) V5:57

It must be troubling for the god who loves you (The God Who Loves You) V20:88

It seems vainglorious and proud (The Conquerors) V13:67

It starts with a low rumbling, white static, (Rapture) V21:181

It was in and about the Martinmas time (Barbara Allan) V7:10

It was many and many a year ago (Annabel Lee) V9:14

Its quick soft silver bell beating, beating (Auto Wreck) V3:31

I've known rivers; (The Negro Speaks of Rivers) V10:197

J

Januaries, Nature greets our eyes (Brazil, January 1, 1502) V6:15

Just off the highway to Rochester, Minnesota (A Blessing) V7:24

just once (For the White poets who would be Indian) V13:112

L

l(a (l(a) V1:85

Let me not to the marriage of true minds (Sonnet 116) V3:288

Let us console you. (Allegory) V23:2–3

Listen, my children, and you shall hear (Paul Revere's Ride) V2:178

Little Lamb, who made thee? (The Lamb) V12:134

Long long ago when the world was a wild place (Bedtime Story) V8:32

M

Made of the first gray light (One of the Smallest) V26:141

maggie and milly and molly and may (maggie & milly & molly & may) V12:149

Mary sat musing on the lamp-flame at the table (The Death of the Hired Man) V4:42

May breath for a dead moment cease as jerking your (Curse) V26:75

Men with picked voices chant the names (Overture to a Dance of Locomotives) V11:143

Morning and evening (Goblin Market) V27:92

"Mother dear, may I go downtown (Ballad of Birmingham) V5:17

Much Madness is divinest Sense— (Much Madness is Divinest Sense) V16:86

My black face fades (Facing It) V5:109

My father stands in the warm evening (Starlight) V8:213

My heart aches, and a drowsy numbness pains (Ode to a Nightingale) V3:228

My heart is like a singing bird (A Birthday) V10:33

My life closed twice before its close— (My Life Closed Twice Before Its Close) V8:127

My mistress' eyes are nothing like the sun (Sonnet 130) V1:247

My uncle in East Germany (The Exhibit) V9:107

N

Nature's first green is gold (Nothing Gold Can Stay) V3:203

No easy thing to bear, the weight of sweetness (The Weight of Sweetness) V11:230

Nobody heard him, the dead man (Not Waving but Drowning) V3:216

Not like a cypress, (Not like a Cypress) V24:135

Not marble nor the gilded monuments (Sonnet 55) V5:246

Not the memorized phone numbers. (What Belongs to Us) V15:196

Now as I was young and easy under the apple boughs (Fern Hill) V3:92

Now as I watch the progress of the plague (The Missing) V9:158

Now I rest my head on the satyr's carved chest, (The Satyr's Heart) V22:187

Now one might catch it see it (Fading Light) V21:49

O

O Captain! my Captain, our fearful trip is done (O Captain! My Captain!) V2:146

O Lord our Lord, how excellent is thy name in all the earth! who hast set thy glory above the heavens (Psalm 8) V9:182

O my Luve's like a red, red rose (A Red, Red Rose) V8:152

O what can ail thee, knight-at-arms, (La Belle Dame sans Merci) V17:18

"O where ha' you been, Lord Randal, my son? (Lord Randal) V6:105

O wild West Wind, thou breath of Autumn's being (Ode to the West Wind) V2:163

Oh, but it is dirty! (Filling Station) V12:57

old age sticks (old age sticks) V3:246

On either side the river lie (The Lady of Shalott) V15:95

On the seashore of endless worlds children meet. The infinite (60) V18:3

Once some people were visiting Chekhov (Chocolates) V11:17

Once upon a midnight dreary, while I pondered, weak and weary (The Raven) V1:200

One day I'll lift the telephone (Elegy for My Father, Who Is Not Dead) V14:154

One foot down, then hop! It's hot (Harlem Hopscotch) V2:93

one shoe on the roadway presents (A Pied) V3:16

Our vision is our voice (An Anthem) V26:34

Out of the hills of Habersham, (Song of the Chattahoochee) V14:283

Out walking in the frozen swamp one gray day (The Wood-Pile) V6:251

Oysters we ate (Oysters) V4:91

P

Pentagon code (Smart and Final Iris) V15:183

Poised between going on and back, pulled (The Base Stealer) V12:30

Q

Quinquireme of Nineveh from distant Ophir (Cargoes) V5:44

Quite difficult, belief. (Chorale) V25:51

R

Recognition in the body (In Particular) V20:125

Red men embraced my body's whiteness (Birch Canoe) V5:31

Remember me when I am gone away (Remember) V14:255

S

Shall I compare thee to a Summer's day? (Sonnet 18) V2:222

She came every morning to draw water (A Drink of Water) V8:66

She sang beyond the genius of the sea. (The Idea of Order at Key West) V13:164

She walks in beauty, like the night (She Walks in Beauty) V14:268

She was my grandfather's second wife. Coming late (My Grandmother's Plot in the Family Cemetery) V27:154

Side by side, their faces blurred, (An Arundel Tomb) V12:17

Since the professional wars— (Midnight) V2:130

Since then, I work at night. (Ten Years after Your Deliberate Drowning) V21:240

S'io credesse che mia risposta fosse (The Love Song of J. Alfred Prufrock) V1:97

Sky black (Duration) V18:93

Sleepless as Prospero back in his bedroom (Darwin in 1881) V13:83

so much depends (The Red Wheelbarrow) V1:219

So the man spread his blanket on the field (A Tall Man Executes a Jig) V12:228

So the sky wounded you, jagged at the heart, (Daylights) V13:101

Softly, in the dark, a woman is singing to me (Piano) V6:145

Some say it's in the reptilian dance (The Greatest Grandeur) V18:119

Some say the world will end in fire (Fire and Ice) V7:57

Something there is that doesn't love a wall (Mending Wall) V5:231

Sometimes walking late at night (Butcher Shop) V7:43

Cumulative
Index of Last Lines

Is Come, my love is come to me. (A Birthday) V10:34

is love—that's all. (Two Poems for T.) V20:218

is safe is what you said. (Practice) V23:240

is still warm (Lament for the Dorsets) V5:191

It asked a crumb—of Me (Hope Is the Thing with Feathers) V3:123

It had no mirrors. I no longer needed mirrors. (I, I, I) V26:97

It is our god. (Fiddler Crab) V23:111–112

it is the bell to awaken God that we've heard ringing. (The Garden Shukkei-en) V18:107

it over my face and mouth. (An Anthem) V26:34

It rains as I write this. Mad heart, be brave. (The Country Without a Post Office) V18:64

It was your resting place." (Ah, Are You Digging on My Grave?) V4:2

it's always ourselves we find in the sea (maggie & milly & molly & may) V12:150

its bright, unequivocal eye. (Having it Out with Melancholy) V17:99

It's the fall through wind lifting white leaves. (Rapture) V21:181

its youth. The sea grows old in it. (The Fish) V14:172

J

Judge tenderly—of Me (This Is My Letter to the World) V4:233

Just imagine it (Inventors) V7:97

L

Laughing the stormy, husky, brawling laughter of Youth, half-naked, sweating, proud to be Hog Butcher, Tool Maker, Stacker of Wheat, Player with Railroads and Freight Handler to the Nation (Chicago) V3:61

Learn to labor and to wait (A Psalm of Life) V7:165

Leashed in my throat (Midnight) V2:131

Leaving thine outgrown shell by life's un-resting sea (The Chambered Nautilus) V24:52–53

Let my people go (Go Down, Moses) V11:43

life, our life and its forgetting. (For a New Citizen of These United States) V15:55

Life to Victory (Always) V24:15

like a shadow or a friend. *Colombia.* (Kindness) V24:84–85

Like Stone— (The Soul Selects Her Own Society) V1:259

Little Lamb, God bless thee. (The Lamb) V12:135

Look'd up in perfect silence at the stars. (When I Heard the Learn'd Astronomer) V22:244

love (The Toni Morrison Dreams) V22:202–203

Luck was rid of its clover. (Yet we insist that life is full of happy chance) V27:292

M

'Make a wish, Tom, make a wish.' (Drifters) V10: 98

make it seem to change (The Moon Glows the Same) V7:152

midnight-oiled in the metric laws? (A Farewell to English) V10:126

Monkey business (Business) V16:2

More dear, both for themselves and for thy sake! (Tintern Abbey) V2:250

My foe outstretchd beneath the tree. (A Poison Tree) V24:195–196

My love shall in my verse ever live young (Sonnet 19) V9:211

My soul has grown deep like the rivers. (The Negro Speaks of Rivers) V10:198

N

never to waken in that world again (Starlight) V8:213

newness comes into the world (Daughter-Mother-Maya-Seeta) V25:83

Nirvana is here, nine times out of ten. (Spring-Watching Pavilion) V18:198

No, she's brushing a boy's hair (Facing It) V5:110

no—tell them *no*— (The Hiding Place) V10:153

Noble six hundred! (The Charge of the Light Brigade) V1:3

nobody,not even the rain,has such small hands (somewhere i have never travelled,gladly beyond) V19:265

Not a roof but a field of stars. (Rent) V25:164

not be seeing you, for you have no insurance. (The River Mumma Wants Out) V25:191

Not even the blisters. Look. (What Belongs to Us) V15:196

Not of itself, but thee. (Song: To Celia) V23:270–271

Nothing, and is nowhere, and is endless (High Windows) V3:108

Nothing gold can stay (Nothing Gold Can Stay) V3:203

Now! (Alabama Centennial) V10:2

nursing the tough skin of figs (This Life) V1:293

O

O Death in Life, the days that are no more! (Tears, Idle Tears) V4:220

O Lord our Lord, how excellent is thy name in all the earth! (Psalm 8) V9:182

O Roger, Mackerel, Riley, Ned, Nellie, Chester, Lady Ghost (Names of Horses) V8:142

o, walk your body down, don't let it go it alone. (Walk Your Body Down) V26:219

Of all our joys, this must be the deepest. (Drinking Alone Beneath the Moon) V20:59–60

of blood and ignorance. (Art Thou the Thing I Wanted) V25:2–3

of gentleness (To a Sad Daughter) V8:231

of love's austere and lonely offices? (Those Winter Sundays) V1:300

of peaches (The Weight of Sweetness) V11:230

Of the camellia (Falling Upon Earth) V2:64

Of the Creator. And he waits for the world to begin (Leviathan) V5:204

Of what is past, or passing, or to come (Sailing to Byzantium) V2:207

Oh that was the garden of abundance, seeing you. (Seeing You) V24:244–245

Old Ryan, not yours (The Constellation Orion) V8:53

On the dark distant flurry (Angle of Geese) V2:2

on the frosty autumn air. (The Cossacks) V25:70

On the look of Death— (There's a Certain Slant of Light) V6:212

On your head like a crown (Any Human to Another) V3:2

One could do worse that be a swinger of birches. (Birches) V13:15

Or does it explode? (Harlem) V1:63

Or help to half-a-crown." (The Man He Killed) V3:167

or last time, we look. (In Particular) V20:125

Or might not have lain dormant forever. (Mastectomy) V26:123

or nothing (Queen-Ann's-Lace) V6:179

or the one red leaf the snow releases in March. (ThreeTimes My Life Has Opened) V16:213

ORANGE forever. (Ballad of Orange and Grape) V10:18

our every corpuscle become an elf. (Moreover, the Moon) V20:153

outside. (it was New York and beautifully, snowing . . . (i was sitting in mcsorley's) V13:152

owing old (old age sticks) V3:246

P

patient in mind remembers the time. (Fading Light) V21:49

Perhaps he will fall. (Wilderness Gothic) V12:242

Petals on a wet, black bough (In a Station of the Metro) V2:116

Plaiting a dark red love-knot into her long black hair (The Highwayman) V4:68

Powerless, I drown. (Maternity) V21:142–143

Práise him. (Pied Beauty) V26:161

Pro patria mori. (Dulce et Decorum Est) V10:110

R

Rage, rage against the dying of the light (Do Not Go Gentle into that Good Night) V1:51

Raise it again, man. We still believe what we hear. (The Singer's House) V17:206

Remember the Giver fading off the lip (A Drink of Water) V8:66

Ride me. (Witness) V26:285

rise & walk away like a panther. (Ode to a Drum) V20:172–173

Rises toward her day after day, like a terrible fish (Mirror) V1:116

S

Shall be lifted—nevermore! (The Raven) V1:202

Shantih shantih shantih (The Waste Land) V20:248–252

share my shivering bed. (Chorale) V25:51

Show an affirming flame. (September 1, 1939) V27:235

Shuddering with rain, coming down around me. (Omen) V22:107

Simply melted into the perfect light. (Perfect Light) V19:187

Singing of him what they could understand (Beowulf) V11:3

Singing with open mouths their strong melodious songs (I Hear America Singing) V3:152

Sister, one of those who never married. (My Grandmother's Plot in the Family Cemetery) V27:155

slides by on grease (For the Union Dead) V7:67

Slouches towards Bethlehem to be born? (The Second Coming) V7:179

So long lives this, and this gives life to thee (Sonnet 18) V2:222

So prick my skin. (Pine) V23:223–224

Somebody loves us all. (Filling Station) V12:57

spill darker kissmarks on that dark. (Ten Years after Your Deliberate Drowning) V21:240

Stand still, yet we will make him run (To His Coy Mistress) V5:277

startled into eternity (Four Mountain Wolves) V9:132

Still clinging to your shirt (My Papa's Waltz) V3:192

Stood up, coiled above his head, transforming all. (A Tall Man Executes a Jig) V12:229

strangers ask. *Originally?* And I hesitate. (Originally) V25:146–147

Surely goodness and mercy shall follow me all the days of my life: and I will dwell in the house of the Lord for ever (Psalm 23) V4:103

syllables of an old order. (A Grafted Tongue) V12:93

T

Take any streetful of people buying clothes and groceries, cheering a hero or throwing confetti and blowing tin horns . . . tell me if the lovers are losers . . . tell me if any get more than the lovers . . .

in the dust . . . in the cool tombs (Cool Tombs) V6:46

Than from everything else life promised that you could do? (Paradiso) V20:190–191

Than that you should remember and be sad. (Remember) V14:255

that does not see you. You must change your life. (Archaic Torso of Apollo) V27:3

That then I scorn to change my state with Kings (Sonnet 29) V8:198

that there is more to know, that one day you will know it. (Knowledge) V25:113

That when we live no more, we may live ever (To My Dear and Loving Husband) V6:228

That's the word. (Black Zodiac) V10:47

the bigger it gets. (Smart and Final Iris) V15:183

The bosom of his Father and his God (Elegy Written in a Country Churchyard) V9:74

the bow toward torrents of *veyz mir.* (Three To's and an Oi) V24:264

The crime was in Granada, his Granada. (The Crime Was in Granada) V23:55–56

The dance is sure (Overture to a Dance of Locomotives) V11:143

The eyes turn topaz. (Hugh Selwyn Mauberley) V16:30

the flames? (Another Night in the Ruins) V26:13

The garland briefer than a girl's (To an Athlete Dying Young) V7:230

The guidon flags flutter gayly in the wind. (Cavalry Crossing a Ford) V13:50

The hands gripped hard on the desert (At the Bomb Testing Site) V8:3

The holy melodies of love arise. (The Arsenal at Springfield) V17:3

the knife at the throat, the death in the metronome (Music Lessons) V8:117

The Lady of Shalott." (The Lady of Shalott) V15:97

The lightning and the gale! (Old Ironsides) V9:172

The lone and level sands stretch far away. (Ozymandias) V27:173

the long, perfect loveliness of sow (Saint Francis and the Sow) V9:222

The Lord survives the rainbow of His will (The Quaker Graveyard in Nantucket) V6:159

You live in this, and dwell in lovers'
    eyes (Sonnet 55) V5:246
You may for ever tarry. (To the
    Virgins, to Make Much of
    Time) V13:226

you who raised me? (The Gold Lily)
    V5:127
you'll have understood by then what
    these Ithakas mean. (Ithaka)
    V19:114